SCHOOL FINANCE

ACHIEVING HIGH STANDARDS WITH EQUITY AND EFFICIENCY

THIRD EDITION

RICHARD A. KING
University of Northern Colorado

AUSTIN D. SWANSON
State University of New York at Buffalo

SCOTT R. SWEETLAND
The Ohio State University

BOSTON   NEW YORK   SAN FRANCISCO
MEXICO CITY   MONTREAL   TORONTO   LONDON   MADRID   MUNICH   PARIS
HONG KONG   SINGAPORE   TOKYO   CAPE TOWN   SYDNEY

Vice President and Editor-in-Chief, Education: Paul A. Smith
Series Editor: Arnis E. Burvikovs
Editorial Assistant: Christine Lyons
Marketing Manager: Tara Whorf
Editorial-Production Administrator: Susan Brown
Editorial-Production Service: Matrix Productions Inc.
Composition and Prepress Buyer: Linda Cox
Manufacturing Buyer: JoAnne Sweeney
Cover Coordinator: Kristina Mose-Lisbon
Electronic Composition: Publishers' Design and Production Services, Inc.

Library of Congress Cataloging-in-Publication Data
King, Richard A. (Richard Auld),
 School finance: achieving high standards with equity and efficiency / by
Richard A. King, Austin D. Swanson, Scott R. Sweetland—3rd ed.
  p. cm.
 Includes bibliographical references and index.
 ISBN 0-205-35498-X
 1. Public Schools—United States—Finance. 2. Government aid to education—United States   3. Federal aid to education—United States. 4. Education—Aims and objectives—United States.
I. Swanson, Austin D. II. Sweetland, Scott R. III. Title.
LB2825 .S739   2003
379.1′22′0973—dc21   2002066483

Printed in the United States of America
10   9   8   7   6   5   4   3   2   08   07   06   05   04   03

CONTENTS

PREFACE

When we began forming ideas for this continuing exploration of school finance, there was a noticeable shift in the focus of educational policies. For many years, school finance analysts and policy makers discussed the nature of inputs that local, state, and national governments made available to fuel the educational enterprise. What had been primarily a concern about the degree of *horizontal equity* of revenue sources in policy debates and in judicial reviews of state finance structures became a concern about the *sufficiency* of resources to enable students to reach high standards and performance expectations. Guthrie and Rothstein (2001) succinctly characterized the shifting policy context: "Old school finance concepts evaluate education in terms of revenue. New finance concepts of adequacy evaluate revenue in terms of education" (p. 99).

Readers of the first two editions of *School Finance: Its Economics and Politics* by Austin Swanson and Richard King will note many changes in this third edition. We welcome Scott Sweetland, who created the computer simulations for the second edition, as a co-author. In addition, the title itself foreshadows a new theme throughout the text—achieving high standards with equity and efficiency—that reflects the shift in policy direction cited above. We devote substantial attention to evolving concerns about the adequacy of resources to enable all students to reach performance expectations and to the links between resource allocation and the realization of district and school goals. Equity and adequacy are necessary but not sufficient conditions. No amount of resources will close the achievement gaps among groups in the United States unless they are used in a cost-effective manner. Therefore, much attention is also given to the condition of efficiency.

Although there are substantial changes in the content of this edition, the strong points of the prior editions have been preserved. This third edition continues to convey the importance of understanding contemporary issues in terms of concepts derived from traditional economic and political frameworks and models. Like its predecessors, this text also explores school finance policies and practices in their current social, political, and economic contexts.

THE CHANGING CONTEXT OF SCHOOL FINANCE

The release of the first edition in 1991 occurred near the end of what has become known as the first wave of the current educational reform movement. In the United States, the publication of *A Nation At Risk: The Imperative for Educational Reform* by the National Commission on Excellence in Education (1983) urged a series of reforms in national and state policies. This report characterized excellence in several ways, emphasizing the importance of setting high expectations and goals for all learners—and then providing assistance in every way possible to help students reach them. The touchstone of the excellence movement was improving student achievement by such actions as strengthening graduation requirements, lengthening the school day and year, and improving teacher qualifications.

v

Learning from the lack of success of the first-wave initiatives and from experiences of the United Kingdom, Australia, New Zealand, and other nations (Beare & Boyd, 1993), the second wave of reform efforts underwent a shift in focus. In what has become known as the restructuring movement, policy makers in the early 1990s proposed a variety of structural reforms to strengthen teaching and learning. States became more aggressive in developing standards, curricular frameworks, and statewide achievement testing. Others challenged these "top-down" reforms and advocated such "bottom-up" reforms as school restructuring, school-based management, teacher empowerment, and parental choice of schools. The second edition of this text was released during this restructuring movement (1997).

Policy makers in many nations now recognize that there is no single reform that will fully meet the challenges of school improvement. The third (and current) wave of reform is a broader *systemic reform* effort than were the prior movements. Although the seeds of this movement were sown early in the 1990s (Smith & O'Day, 1991), the policy changes followed and blended with those of the prior excellence and restructuring movements. In this emerging systemic reform movement, a coordinated set of policy initiatives include *centralized* goal setting and accountability via standards, curricula, and testing programs; *decentralized* reforms via school-site decision making involving teachers, administrators, staff, parents, and community members; and *family choice* of schooling within the public sector through charter schools and across public and private sectors through vouchers for low-income families. The direction of this systemic reform movement is clearly focused on improving school and student performance through standards-based curricula and assessments. However, the means of implementing and financing these systemic reforms in all schools and states remain to be determined.

Just prior to the dawn of the new millennium, a report by the Committee on Education Finance of the National Research Council (1999) presented a new context within which school finance would be developed and critiqued in this third wave of reform. The committee discussed the challenge before policy makers:

> A new emphasis on raising achievement for all students poses an important but daunting challenge for policy makers: how to harness the education finance system to this objective. This challenge is important because it aims to link finance directly to the purposes of education. It is daunting because making money matter in this way means that school finance decisions must become intertwined with an unprecedented ambition for the nation's schools: never before has the nation set for itself the goal of educating children to high standards. (p. 1)

This systemic reform movement, with its emphasis on the adequacy of revenue to enable all students to meet high standards and on efficiency in linking allocations to performance expectations and outcomes, provides the context for this third edition.

It is within this ever-changing policy context that we embark on this third edition's exploration of *School Finance: Achieving High Standards with Equity and Efficiency*. Of particular concern are several major school finance issues that we explore in this edition:

- Balancing deeply rooted differences in values about education (such as, equity, liberty, and efficiency) in making resource allocation decisions.
- Improving the effectiveness of resource use in large, urban districts whose students have the greatest difficulty in meeting high academic standards.
- Using resources allocated to education effectively and efficiently in relation to state standards and district and school goals.
- Identifying new sources of funds to supplement traditional revenue from local, state, and federal governments.

- Expanding state finance structures to include funding for preschools.
- Understanding judicial reviews of states' responsibilities to fund school operations and facilities equitably and adequately.
- Determining the adequacy of resources provided by society in terms of desired educational outcomes in addition to exploring the more traditional concern over funding equity.
- Examining efficiency and the links between resources and the realization of district and school goals.
- Reorganizing the use of existing resources in schools to improve student achievement.
- Providing performance-based allocations of state money to schools and performance- and skills-based pay for teachers as incentives for school improvement.
- Empowering schools and parents to make decisions about priorities in the uses of public monies and the procedures they might follow.

STRATEGY OF THE TEXT AND COMPUTER SIMULATIONS

This third edition, like the previous two editions, takes a balanced approach to understanding school finance issues by using paradigms of both the economist and the political scientist. The strategy of the book is to respect the importance of economic theory in analyzing the impact of existing and alternative policies. At the same time, we recognize that such theories do little to help students and policy makers understand the forces shaping school finance legislation and the process through which financial policy is implemented. Thus, in order to help readers fully understand what has happened, and what is likely to happen, in the development of school finance policy, this edition continues to emphasize concepts drawn from the field of political science along with economic concepts.

The book is intended to be a primary resource for graduate courses in school finance and the economics of education. The prior editions have also been adopted successfully as primary reading for courses on educational politics and policy analysis. In addition to these academic uses as a textbook, this book has served as a general reference for analysts of education policy at the state and national levels. School district administrators, including superintendents and school business officials, who deliberate finance issues with constituents and oversee allocations of funds to schools, have benefited from the discussions of equity and efficiency. School principals, who are becoming more involved in financial decisions as they acquire and monitor the use of school-level resources, need to become more familiar with the concepts and models that underlie finance policies and budgeting practices. The discussion of school finance systems in the context of reform in the prior editions also found an audience in international markets, particularly in Australia, Canada, and the United Kingdom.

Other important features of the book are the activities and computer simulations included with many of the chapters to help readers apply and extend the concepts we discuss in the text. The range of suggested activities, including computational problems and activities such as interviewing administrators and policy makers, enables instructors and students to choose among various strategies to reinforce the chapter content. These diverse activities satisfy the curiosity of advanced users of the text without frustrating those who are new to the study of school finance.

Our goal in including computer simulations in the second and third editions has been to help readers experiment with data in order to understand concepts and policy options more fully. The level of difficulty of these simulations increases throughout the book in what we have referred to as a "developmental approach" to teaching and applying spreadsheets. In Chapter 2, beginning users of spreadsheets are encouraged to learn the basic commands of spreadsheets by inserting data, adding columns, and developing simple formulas. Advanced users can bypass these initial problems and begin with the more challenging simulations of Chapter 3 and beyond. All users should conduct additional "what if" analyses after completing the planned simulations. The suggested further activities that accompany the simulations also encourage students to relate the simulations to concepts introduced in the chapters or to apply their spreadsheet skills to analyze administrative or policy dilemmas that they have encountered.

Rather than including instructions for these computer simulations in the text as in the prior edition, Allyn & Bacon is maintaining a companion website. We introduce simulations at the ends of chapters, but the complete instructions and solutions are available at **www.ablongman.com/edleadership**

ORGANIZATION OF THE BOOK

Drawing on political and economic models, Part I begins with a discussion of the educational decision-making process in a political–economic system that is divided between public and private sectors. We emphasize five values—equality, liberty, fraternity, efficiency, and economic growth—in talking about the impact of public and private values on decisions made about education. We demonstrate how changes in the priorities assigned to these values lead to corresponding changes in public policy. The shift in public priorities from equity and fraternity during the 1960s and 1970s to those related to efficiency, economic growth, and liberty in the 1980s and 1990s serves as a case in point. The concern for efficiency continues to be expressed, early in the new millennium, in state and federal policies that hold school personnel accountable for ensuring that all students can meet higher expectations for learning. Yet, as we emphasize

in this edition, the adequacy of resources is critical in reaching equity and efficiency goals. Liberty is valued as facilitating the realization of efficiency as parental choice among public schools, charter schools, and vouchers becomes more widely available.

Expanding the resource base for schools is critical in helping all students achieve at high levels. In Part II we examine the sources of money that society devotes to support public education. We begin with an overview of the federated tax structure in the United States and discuss criteria that can be used for evaluating taxation policies. After exploring primary state and federal revenue sources for education, we devote much attention to the property tax. This local revenue source has historically been important in financing educational programs and facilities in the United States and continues to provide over 40 percent of the resources consumed by public schools. Part II concludes with a discussion of nontax revenue sources for education. These include borrowing, investments, foundations, partnerships with other organizations, volunteerism, and user fees.

State and national governments expand the capabilities of local communities to provide educational programs. Their efforts make possible a more equitable and adequate educational system, while also raising expectations for school outcomes. The focus of Part III is the merits and structure of general and categorical aid programs at state and federal levels in the United States. We present a number of models that states adapt in making allocations of general aid to school systems. The most common approach has become the foundation program, in which state revenue equalizes local district taxes in (ideally) ensuring an adequate level of funds for schools. We describe many adjustments in these basic formula structures that allocate additional funds in recognition of the costs of special programs and the priorities expressed by legislators. We also discuss several constructs for measuring educational need, wealth or revenue-generating ability, and the fiscal effort that districts make in relation to state policy. This part concludes with an examination of the federal government's role in financing education. We develop several themes that have provided a historical rationale for this level of involvement, highlight provisions of the recently enacted No Child Left Behind Act of 2001, and discuss trends that have been evident in allocations among federal programs.

In Part IV, we examine the potential of school finance policies to achieve high standards. We discuss the evolution of concepts of equity, efficiency, and adequacy through the decisions that federal and state courts have made when they address whether disparities in revenue among districts violate constitutional provisions. We then turn to the definition and measurement of equity and adequacy. This latter term is defined as providing sufficient resources to enable all students to achieve high performance levels—the ideal state of vertical equity. We examine evidence concerning the efficiency of public schools provided by studies of how schools use resources, effective schools, program evaluations, and economies of scale.

In Part V, we examine how changing the incentives provided by financial rewards in state policies and by teacher compensation within districts might improve school and student performance. We then look at the potential for improving student performance and consumer satisfaction by injecting marketlike forces into the structure for delivering educational services. The reforms examined include various models of school-based management and budgeting, as well as vehicles for giving families the opportunity to choose what schools their children attend.

In Part VI, we conclude the text with a discussion of some implications of the systemic reform movement that was described in the opening chapter on the changing policy context. We return to the political–economic model developed in Chapter 1 as a framework for analyzing the themes of systemic reform. We discuss policies related to setting goals and objectives, identifying recipients of services, determining levels of investment, producing and distributing services, and allocating resources.

ACKNOWLEDGMENTS

Many people have helped shape the ideas presented in this and the two previous editions of this book. Our teachers, colleagues, and students have been—and in many cases continue to be—a part of our developing an understanding of school finance concepts. Just as the political and economic climate changes over time, we as researchers and teachers within the field continually reflect on and alter our thinking about finance policies and practices.

We listened to suggestions and critiques of manuscripts by many individuals representing a variety of perspectives on the issues addressed. However, as authors we assume full responsibility for the ideas presented. Among the individuals we have to thank for encouraging and assisting us in the three editions are Robert Arnold, Illinois State University; Daniel Brown, University of British Columbia; Brian Caldwell, University of Melbourne, Australia; Timothy Cybulski, Ohio State University; Frank Engert, University of Maine at Farmington; Patrick Galvin, University of Utah; Corrie Giles, State University of New York at Buffalo; Vivian Hajnal, University of Saskatchewan; Richard Hatley, University of Missouri-Columbia; Mary Hughes, University of Arkansas; Thomas Jones, University of Connecticut; Theodore Kowalski, University of Dayton; Barbara LaCost, University of Nebraska; John MacMahon, University of British Columbia; Bettye MacPhail-Wilcox, North Carolina State University; Betty Malen, University of Maryland; Judith Mathers, Oklahoma State University; Kenneth Matthews, University of Georgia; Richard Maxwell,

Ashland University; Eugene McLoone, University of Maryland; Paul Montello, Georgia State University; David Nyberg, State University of New York at Buffalo; Fergus O'Sullivan, University of Lincoln, United Kingdom; William Poston, Jr., Iowa State University; Lawrence F. Rossow, University of Oklahoma; Nancy Schilling, Northern Arizona University; Catherine Sielke, University of Georgia; William Sparkman, University of Nevada at Reno; Thomas Surratt, University of South Carolina; Tyra Turner, Arkansas State University; Thomas Valesky, Florida Gulf Coast University; Deborah Verstegen, University of Virginia; J. D. Willardson, Brigham Young University; and Edward Willet, Houghton College. We also greatly appreciate the assistance of Deborah Bennett-Woods, Darren O'Hern, Mei-Chih Lu, and Liang Zhoa in locating resources and refining databases for this edition.

Finally, we acknowledge the support of our families and the encouragement of our students as we prepared the three editions of this text. Former students are making use of finance knowledge and skills in their professional lives; many are now teaching and researching school finance issues. Their experiences in studying and applying the traditional and evolving concepts vital to this field have made a difference in the ways in which we help future students explore school finance policy and practice. Past and future students provide the inspiration to write a textbook to guide others' understanding of the economics and politics of education.

REFERENCES

Beare, H., & Boyd, W. L. (Eds.). (1993). *Restructuring schools: An international perspective on the movement to transform the control and performance of schools*. London: Falmer.

Guthrie, J. W., & Rothstein, R. (2001). A new millennium and a likely new era of education finance. In S. Chaikind & W. J. Fowler, Jr. (Eds.), *Education finance in the new millennium* (pp. 99–119). Larchmont, NY: Eye on Education.

National Commission on Excellence in Education. (1983). *A nation at risk: The imperative for educational reform*. Washington, DC: U.S. Government Printing Office.

National Research Council. (1999). *Making money matter: Financing America's schools*. A report by the Committee on Education Finance, ed. H. F. Ladd & J. S. Hansen. Commission on Behavioral and Social Sciences and Education. Washington, DC: National Academy Press.

Smith, M. S., & O'Day, J. (1991). Systemic school reform. In S. H. Fuhrman and B. Malen (Eds.), *The politics of curriculum and testing* (pp. 233–267). Bristol, PA: Falmer.

part I

Establishing a Context for Understanding School Finance Policy

For the past two decades, the American people have focused their collective attention on improving the effectiveness and equity of the public schools of the nation. The National Commission on Excellence in Education (1983) report entitled *A Nation at Risk* articulated the crisis, and confronting it remains prominent on the national agenda. The challenge we face is not so much a function of the deterioration of the quality of public education in its traditional format as it is the result of global social and economic changes that are rendering irrelevant much of what the system was designed to do in and for another era. The solution requires realignment or redesign of the system in order to enable educators to prepare graduates to live and work successfully and happily under new conditions.

Through twenty years of rigorous debate and experimentation, a consensus appears to be building on what to do and by what means to do it. The approach that has evolved calls for establishing and monitoring content and performance standards by central authorities and designing and implementing instructional delivery systems by school authorities. For the first time in the history of this nation, schools are being called on to bring *all* students to high levels of academic performance. In a world of scarce resources, this means school finance decisions must be closely intertwined with the curricular intent of the schools.

Although there is much agreement on the general pattern of reform, there is little agreement on the details of implementation. Achieving agreement is a political process that unfolds in school districts, state legislatures, Congress, and state and federal courts. Among the important details to be worked out is the accompanying financial structure. In this book, we explore the implications of these revolutionary structural and philosophical changes for school finance policy and examine the merits of possible policy options. In this first section, we build a contextual basis for understanding the interplay of the forces that will shape future fiscal strategies and policies.

Education deals with matters related to the heart and soul of the individual citizen and, at the same time, is critical to the political and economic welfare of the nation and to its security. To ensure that both individual and societal demands for schooling are met, decisions about the provision of education are made in both the public and the private sector. Decisions are made in the public sector through political processes by governments, whereas decisions are made in the private sector by individuals through markets. Politics—the process by which values are allocated within society—differs from economics—the study of the allocation of scarce resources within society. Economics is concerned with the production, distribution, and consumption of commodities. Achieving efficiency in the use of resources is the objective of economics, where efficiency is defined as securing the highest level of societal satisfaction at the least cost of scarce resources.

Obviously, one's value priorities strongly influence one's judgment about what is an efficient allocation of material resources. Thus there is a continuing interaction between economics and politics. Public finance of education is one point of interaction. Decisions about the public finance of education will be made in political arenas, but the decisions made in those arenas will have strong economic implications for individuals and businesses, as well as for communities, states, and the nation. Individuals and businesses will respond independently to political decisions by deciding whether to participate in government programs or to supplement or substitute for government programs by purchasing services provided through the private sector.

In this first part of the text, we set the stage for studying school finance issues by examining the nature of the educational problems confronting us, the individual and societal values that influence the decisions we will make, and the workings of the political and economic systems within which solutions will be crafted.

chapter **1**

FINANCING SCHOOLS TO ACHIEVE HIGH STANDARDS FOR ALL

A Global Shift In Priorities

Issues and Questions

- *Achieving High Standards with Equity and Efficiency*: What is the context within which the United States and other nations are examining the goals of education and the structure to achieve these goals?
- *Social and Economic Influences on Education*: How have macro societal forces worked to change the mission of public schooling?
- *Core Values and School Finance Policy:* What are the traditional core values that have influenced school finance policy?
- *Policy Implications of Shifts in Priorities Given to Core Values*: How have shifts in priorities among core values affected the governance of education and the structures for delivering educational services?
- *International Comparisons*: How do recent movements to transform control over education and its resources compare among the United States, England, Australia, and New Zealand?
- *Implications for Assessing and Developing Educational Policies*: What propositions flow from the comparative analysis of education reform that might guide the development of school finance policy?

For two decades, the American people have focused their collective attention on improving the effectiveness of the public schools of the nation. The crisis was well articulated in *A Nation at Risk* (National Commission on Excellence in Education) in 1983, and confronting it remains a crucial issue on the national agenda. Through twenty years of rigorous debate and experimentation, a consensus appears to be building on what to do and by what means to do it. The patterns that are emerging are remarkably similar to those evolving in other Western democracies that face similar challenges.

The initial response to improving student achievement in the mid-1980s followed a conventional top-down approach. States raised expectations for students and teachers through increased high school graduation and teacher certification requirements during this first wave of reform. Policy makers and state education departments also initiated longer school days and years, competency tests, standardized curricula, and promotion criteria for students. These policies did little to alter the prevailing ideas about teaching and learning and did not involve teachers directly in the reform process (Smith & O'Day, 1991). The deficiencies of this approach were quickly apparent.

A second wave of reform that began in the late 1980s called for a fundamental rethinking and restructuring of the schooling process. This wave viewed schools as the basic unit of educational productivity and made them the focus for improvement. Change efforts at the school level emphasized capacity building, especially through the professional development of teachers, and governance changes that brought teachers, parents, and other members of the immediate community into the decision process (Ladd & Hansen, 1999). Decentralized decision making did bring new ideas and energy to schools. However, many of the issues addressed at the school level, including higher expectations for student performance, were universal in nature and could be addressed more effectively and efficiently at state and national levels. Addressing universal issues at the school level did not provide sufficient coherence for a highly complex system to function well in a multifaceted society.

The third wave of reform, which has been dominant now for a decade, appears to be the consensus that we have noted. This movement calls for the establishment and monitoring of standards by central authorities and for the design and implementation of instructional delivery systems by school authorities.

> This systemic strategy operates alongside the second wave of school reform; it emphasizes state (and to a lesser degree federal) actions to complement school and district restructuring by creating a more coherent environment within which successful schools can thrive and by creating external pressure for change when it does not emerge spontaneously. The linchpin in the system is the development of content standards expressing shared understandings about what students need to know and be able to do, with which other elements of the educational system (school curricula, assessments, teacher education and professional development, and accountability) can be aligned. (Ladd & Hansen, 1999, p. 156)

Although there is much agreement on the general pattern of reform, there is little agreement on the details of implementation. Achieving agreement is a political process that unfolds in school districts, state legislatures, Congress, and state and federal courts. Among the details to be worked out is the accompanying financial structure. In this book, we explore the implications of these revolutionary structural and philosophical changes for school finance policy and examine the merits of possible policy options.

The crisis is not so much a function of the deterioration of the quality of public education in its traditional format as it is the result of global social and economic changes making much of what the system was designed to do in and for another era irrelevant. The solution requires realignment or redesign of the system in order to enable educators to prepare graduates to live and work successfully and happily under the new conditions. To this end, we take a broad view in defining school finance to include the governance (decision-making structure) of education as well as its more traditional aspects, revenue-generating and resource allocation policies.

In this chapter, we examine the social and economic roots of the current crisis in education. We show how changes in technology and demographics have worked together to change national core values, social structures, and the mission of public schooling. We conclude by presenting a generic political–economic model of the process for making education policy. This model will serve as a principle of organization for the book and for the discussion and analysis of issues. A comparative analysis uses the model to explore school reform initiatives of the United States, England, Australia, and New Zealand. We then draw from the analysis a series of propositions that can serve as a guide to the development of school finance policy.

SOCIAL AND ECONOMIC PRESSURES ON PUBLIC POLICY

Massive technical and demographic changes have affected the way we work, communicate, and relate to each other; indeed, the way we perceive our world has been altered. In this section, we look at how world views have been transformed. We show how the system of schooling must respond if we are to avoid undesirable demographic consequences that could shake the very foundation of our social and political democracy.

Shifting Paradigms

This is the first time in our history that the quality of the education of citizens has been recognized politically as being strategically important to national success and survival. The forces leading to educational reform are not unique to American education, however, because they reflect worldwide changes in social, economic, political, and technological relationships. Toffler (1980, 1990) dubbed these forces "the third wave" and, subsequently, "the Powershift Era." Naisbitt (1982; Naisbitt & Aburdene, 1990) identified them as "megatrends." Drucker (1989) referred to their amalgam as "the post industrial society," "the post business society," and "the information age." Whatever it is called, the age we have entered is quite different from that which preceded it. The magnitude of the shift has been likened to the shift from feudalism to capitalism and to that from an agriculturally based economy to industrialization. All social institutions must make appropriate adjustments to survive. Educational institutions are no exception.

As a result, our guiding paradigms are shifting (Kuhn, 1970) along with changes in social and economic structures. The power of nations to control and/or regulate their own economies has been seriously weakened by economic globalization. Many of the world's totalitarian governments have fallen, largely because of their inability to control the information their citizens receive in the wake of the astonishing technological advances in electronic communications and in data processing, storage, and retrieval. In several instances, these totalitarian governments have been replaced with more democratic institutions. There has also been a decline in overt hostility among the most powerful nations of the world. Yet growing conflict among ethnic groups and violent regional rivalries have expanded, reaching even the shores of the United States. As national borders become invisible to technological and economic forces, individuals cling to their ethnic heritages, seeking to maintain their personal identities and a sense of belonging in their struggles against anomie.

There is both optimism and concern as the new millennium begins. Naisbitt and Aburdene (1990), optimists building on Naisbitt's (1982) successful predictions of a decade earlier, see the triumph of the individual and the demise of the collective. With newfound freedom, they predict a global economic boom, a renaissance in the arts, and a growing interest in things spiritual. According to them, a new free-market socialism will become the dominant socio-economic structure, and the welfare state will be privatized. Women increasingly will assume leadership roles, and global lifestyles and cultural nationalism will emerge. Biology will dominate the sciences, and Pacific rim nations will dominate economic relationships.

Not everyone is as optimistic about the future as Naisbitt and Aburdene. Galbraith (1992), for example, sees a growing disparity between the haves and the have nots in the United States and predicts that eventually the have nots will rise in rebellion. According to Galbraith, the disparity is growing because for the first time in American history, "the contented" constitute the majority of the population and are in complete control of government. This contented majority does not support social legislation that redistributes wealth by levying higher taxes on the rich and providing greater services for the poor. Galbraith argues that it was the social legislation engineered by Lloyd George in the early twentieth century that saved British capitalism during the years between the two world wars. Likewise, it was the social legislation of Franklin Roosevelt that saved capitalism in the United States during the Great Depression. In each instance, the legislation was opposed by the contented, who lost in the political arena, but now that the contented are firmly in the majority, there is little hope of government enacting legislation to bridge the gap between the haves and the have nots. Galbraith predicts that social breakdown will result, and we may already be seeing its vanguard in the slum ghettos of our major cities.

Galbraith's concerns are backed by an analysis of the wage structure in the United States by Pierce and Welch (1996). They found that the returns that accrue to white males from school-ing and labor market experience in the United States over the past twenty-five years have risen along with wage inequality. They also found that, increasingly, secondary-level schooling results in higher earnings only as it prepares students for college.

Census data reveal the close link between income and education (U.S. Bureau of the Census, 2000a). A male high school dropout in 1970 earned on average $29,377 in constant 1999 dollars, 83 percent of the earnings of an average male high school graduate, $35,553; by 1998 the average dropout's earnings had fallen to $17, 876, or 70 percent of the average high school graduate's earnings, $25,864. Over the same period, the high school graduate was losing ground to the college graduate. In 1970 the average male college graduate earned $44,031, or 24 percent more than the average male high school graduate; by 1998 the advantage of the college graduate had grown to 56 percent, with an average annual salary of $40,363. These patterns are illustrated in Figure 1.1. It is important to note that for all education categories for males, purchasing power in constant 1999 dollars declined over the period 1970 to 1998: 39 percent for the high school dropout, 27 percent for the high school graduate, 22 percent for the male with some college, and 8 percent for the male holding a bachelor's degree or higher. In other words, the purchasing power of the high school dropout in 1970 actually exceeded that of the high school graduate in 1998. The purchasing power of the male with some college in 1998 was only slightly (about $800) higher than that of a high school dropout in 1970. The decline for the male with at least one college degree was marginal in comparison with the other categories.

Comparing the male trend lines with those of females in Figure 1.1 shows the generally lower earnings of females. However, females are closing the gap, and unlike those of the males, their trend lines are rising modestly for all education categories. Further, females who

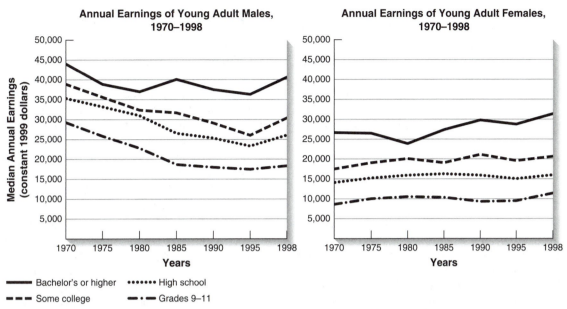

FIGURE 1.1. Trends in Median Annual Earnings (in constant 1999 dollars) of All Wage and Salary Workers Ages 25–34, by Gender and Educational Attainment, 1970–1998

SOURCE: U.S. Bureau of the Census (2000b).

hold at least a bachelor's degree are increasing their earnings advantage over females in the other education categories. In 1970 the average female college graduate earned $26,772, or 82 percent more than the average female high school graduate, $14,681; by 1998 the earnings of the average female college graduate, $30,774, had increased to 100 percent over the earnings of the average high school graduate, $15,356.

A study of economic returns from education in Canada (Paquette, 1991) concluded that it is a perfectly reasonable decision for persons to drop out of high school if they have no intention of completing four years of college. Technology has deskilled most work to the point where there is little employment income advantage associated with the lower levels of educational attainment. Really significant differentials in earning power occur only for those holding baccalaureate and advanced degrees. Paquette (1991, p. 475) concluded that "The reallocation of economic benefits from education reflects inescapably a massive deskilling of

work and rapidly increasing reliance in all sectors on 'costlessly replaceable' part-time and temporary help that can be hired, fired and scheduled, as well as paid, according to computer—the 'just-in-time' workers of the post-industrial age." The circumstances are quite different for most degree holders; the tradiional benefits from further education accrue only for them. A high school diploma, or even an associate degree, holds little more economic significance today than completion of primary school did fifty years ago. Cohn (1997) challenged Paquette's findings with respect to the lack of economic value of a secondary diploma; he did agree, however, that the economic benefit of "some university" or a junior college was low compared to that of completing a four-year degree. Cohn suggests that one policy implication is that an effort should be made to reduce the dropout rates of colleges and universities.

The failure of many American students to complete high school, and the linkage between dropping out and later unemployment and crime are other concerns of policy analysts. For the first time since such statistics have been collected, the United States has fallen behind most other industrialized nations in the rate at which students complete secondary school (Langemann, 1999). There is also a racial/ethnic bias on this statistic; nearly 92 percent of white 19-year-olds have completed high school, compared with 87 percent of African American students and 75 percent of Hispanic students (National Center for Education Statistics, 1999, Table 105). Some 82 percent of persons in prisons are high school dropouts, and they cost about $24,000 per person per year in public support (Hodgkinson, 1993). Only about one-quarter of minority high school dropouts find employment shortly after leaving school. This compares with one-half of white dropouts. Even the minority high school graduate has difficulty finding employment; 75 percent of majority students are successful in finding employment shortly after graduation, compared with barely half of minority students.

Muscle power has been replaced by brain power. Even through the middle of the twentieth century, people with little formal education could find well-paying manual jobs with which to support themselves and others. As a consequence of technological advances, this type of employment no longer exists to any great extent. The machines that have replaced manual laborers require better-educated operators, and the inventors and designers of those machines and accompanying systems require high levels of formal education. Thus the extent of one's formal education is now closely linked to one's economic well-being. In the past, formal education was an option; today education is the passport to full participation in the social, political, and economic aspects of our society. Those without that passport are unable to participate fully in our society and face the prospect of becoming members of a permanent underclass, as we shall see in the next section.

The Making of an Underclass

The United States faces the real possibility of developing a structural underclass, and many believe that the nature of the public school system is both a primary cause of this problem and a potential instrument for solving it. Although the economic boom of the 1990s reduced the percentage of persons living in poverty by 0.5 percent, at the end of that decade 31.1 million persons, or 11.3 percent of the U.S. population, were still in this category. The burden of poverty was not shared equally among ethnic groups, however; 22.1 percent of blacks were living in poverty, along with 21.2 percent of Hispanics and 10.8 percent of Asian. This compares with 7.5 percent of the white population living in poverty. Nearly 18 percent of all school-age children (between the ages of 5 and 17) living in poverty in 1998. The share of aggregate household income controlled by the lowest fifth of income earners has decreased from 4.1 percent in 1969 to 3.6 percent in 1997, while the share of the highest fifth increased from 43.0 percent to 49.4 percent. Most notably, the share of income controlled by the top 5 percent of households increased from 16.6 percent to 21.7 percent (U.S. Bureau of the Census, 2000a).

The problems created by the increasing numbers of children coming from the ranks of poverty is compounded by changes in family structures. The characteristics of American families have changed markedly since 1970. By 1998, 27 percent of families with children under 18 were headed by a single parent, compared with 11 percent in 1970 (see Table 1.1). Single females headed 22 percent of such households, single males the remaining 5 percent. The lack of dual income makes it more difficult to escape poverty, especially for female-led single-parent households. In 2000, nearly 25 percent of households headed by a female with "no husband present" lived in poverty compared with less than 5 percent of married-couple households. For households headed by

TABLE 1.1.

Status of Families with Own Children under 18, 1970–1998

	1970	*1980*	*1990*	*1998*
Number (thousands)				
Married couples	25,532	24,961	24,537	25,269
Families headed by a single female	2,858	5,445	6,599	7,693
Families headed by a single male	341	616	1,153	1,798
Percent				
Married couples	88.7	80.5	76.0	73.0
Families headed by a single female	10.0	17.5	20.4	22.0
Families headed by a single male	1.3	2.0	3.6	5.0

Source: NCES, 2001. U. S. Department of Commerce, Bureau of the Census, *Current Population Reports*, Series P-20, "Household and Family Characteristics," various years, unpublished data.

a black or Hispanic female, over 34 percent lived in poverty.

The proportion of public school enrollment represented by minority groups (those most likely to be ravaged by poverty) has increased steadily during the past thirty years. In 1999 minority groups represented nearly 39 percent of the total enrollment in public elementary and secondary schools, an increase of almost 16 percent since 1972. This increase was due largely to growth of the Hispanic population. In 1999 black and Hispanic students accounted for 16.5 and 16.2 percent of public school enrollment, respectively, up 2 percent for blacks and 10 percent for Hispanics (National Center for Education Statistics, 2001). The growth in numbers and proportions of the minority population is due in part to their higher fertility rates as compared with the majority. Another important factor is an upsurge in immigration, especially of persons from Asia and Latin America. The trend is expected to continue as the proportion of the populations from minority groups grow to exceed fifty percent in many states, large cities, and school districts.

In addition to being 3 times as likely to be impoverished, minority children are more likely to encounter other "risk factors" such as coming from a single-parent household, having limited English proficiency, and having a parent or sibling (or both) who has dropped out of school. Minority children are 3.5 times as likely to have two or more of these risk factors as are white children. The effect is also intergenerational; 62 percent of children under age six who are below the poverty level have parents who did not complete high school. The rate drops to 26 percent, if one parent completed high school and to 7 percent if one parent had some schooling beyond high school ("Poverty and Education," 1992).

These demographic changes contribute to a rapidly growing underclass in the United States. As the gap widens between the haves and the have nots, schools face challenges in helping a more diverse and less privileged student body achieve high academic expectations.

CHANGES IN PRIORITIES GIVEN TO CORE VALUES

In Western societies, public policy for schools has been designed around five core values: liberty or freedom, equality or equity, fraternity or citizenship, efficiency, and economic growth. The first three are ethical values derived from the doctrine of natural rights expressed as early as 1690 by the English philosopher John Locke (1956) in his *Second Treatise of Government*. Leaders of both the

American and French revolutions in the late eighteenth and early nineteenth centuries used Locke's arguments to justify those revolutions and in constructing their governments following victory. Efficiency and economic growth are practical or derived values that enhance the realization of the three ethical values. Efficiency and economic growth became primary objectives of public policy only during the twentieth century.

Private schooling had long been available to the privileged and to the religious. Public schools and universal primary schooling were originally established by fledgling democracies in the nineteenth century to weaken the inherited social class structure and to facilitate the development of a citizenry capable of wisely exercising newly won rights of suffrage, serving on juries, and discharging other responsibilities thrust upon them by their new democratic form of government. In the case of the United States, public schools also served an important function of establishing a national identity apart from that of its English heritage and, later, to "Americanize" the hoards of immigrants seeking asylum and new opportunities. Thus the motivations for establishing public schools were purely political in the nineteenth century.

Initially, the public schools served only the primary grades, and their demand on the public purse was modest. In an economy dominated by subsistence farming, there wasn't a strong link among education, production, and wealth. With industrialization and urbanization, the relationship between education and economic welfare strengthened. As technology became highly sophisticated and we entered into the information age, having a well-educated citizenry took on added significance as an economic and national survival tactic. Providing higher levels of education to all people has become increasingly expensive and, correspondingly, has elevated the practical values of efficiency and economic growth to at least parity with the ethical values of liberty,

equality, and fraternity. Thus, at the beginning of the twenty-first century, education is seen as making critical political and economic contributions to the general welfare as well as to personal well-being.

Values Defined

Practically all of our activities occur within the contexts of attitudes about good and bad, right and wrong, or better and worse. Behavior, therefore, is a constant reflection of beliefs about how the world is structured, and actions taken are based—implicitly or explicitly—on those philosophical considerations (Foster, 1986).

Values are conceptions of the desirable (Parsons, 1951; Hodgkinson, 1983; Hoy and Miskel, 1991). A value is an enduring belief that a specific mode of conduct or state of existence is personally or socially preferable to an opposite or converse mode. Values are consciously or unconsciously held priorities that are expressed in all human activity. A value system is an enduring organization of values along a continuum of relative importance (Rokeach, 1973).

If values were completely stable, individual and social change would be impossible. If values were completely unstable, continuity of human personality and society would be impossible. The hierarchical conception of values enables us to define change as a reordering of priorities and, simultaneously, to see the total value system as relatively stable over time.

Metavalues

Hodgkinson (1983, p. 43) defined *metavalue* as "a concept of the desirable so vested and entrenched that it seems to be beyond dispute or contention—one that usually enters the ordinary value calculus of individual and collective life in the form of an unexpressed or unexamined assumption." He identified the dominant metavalues in administration and organizational life as efficiency and effectiveness.

Nyberg (1993, p. 196) contended that "The moral universe is the same for everyone in that it is based on concern for human dignity, decency, voluntary relations that are not oppressive, and some kind of spiritual fulfillment." The specifics differ from person to person, group to group, place to place, and time to time, but the basis of concern remains consistent—a foundation on which metavalues are built. We are all similar, but each person is unique.

In making practical application of his theory about value structures, Rokeach (1973) sought to identify ideals or values that are singled out for special consideration by all political ideologies. He hypothesized that the major variations in political ideology are fundamentally reducible to opposing value orientations concerning the political desirability or undesirability of freedom and equality in all their ramifications. Getzels (1957, 1978) characterized the national core values as "sacred." He identified four sacred values as being at the core of the American ethos: democracy, individualism, equality, and human perfectibility.

The literature on educational policy makes frequent explicit or implicit reference to these or similar values. Boyd (1984) and Koppich and Guthrie (1993) referred to equality, efficiency, and liberty as competing values of particular societal concern in making education policy in Western democracies. Wirt (1987) noted a general agreement among nations that the major values in education are quality (excellence or human perfectibility), equity, efficiency, and choice (liberty or freedom). Kahne (1994) referred to equity, efficiency, and excellence as the central concern of education policy analysts but criticized them for not giving equal attention to the formation of democratic communities—that is, to fraternity.

Throughout this book, we focus on five metavalues or objects of policy that are particularly relevant to making decisions about the provision and consumption of educational services: liberty, equality/equity, fraternity, efficiency, and economic growth. With changing social circumstances, each has experienced advances and declines in priority in the formulation of public policy, but none has ever lost its relevance entirely. A fundamental shift appears to be taking place today in the relative priorities assigned to these five values.

Liberty is the right to act in the manner of one's own choosing, not subject to undue restriction or control, whereas *equality* refers to the state, ideal, or quality of being equal, as in the state of enjoying equal social, political, and economic rights. In this policy context, equality is construed in terms of civil rights, not in terms of personal characteristics and abilities.

Nyberg (1981, pt. II) cautioned that "freedom" (or liberty) derives its meaning at least in part from the times in which it was used. He pointed out that between 1787 and 1947, a transformation took place in the United States from "freedom as natural rights (rights *against* the government, rights of independence), to civil rights (rights to *participate* in civil government), to human freedoms (rights to the *help* of government in achieving protection from fear and want)" (pp. 97–98).

Parallel transformations have taken place in the meaning of equality. Initially, equality was viewed in terms of rights only and not of conditions; people were to be treated the same by law, custom, and tradition. When considered as such, equality was the instrument for guaranteeing liberty as originally defined. In recent times, the operational definitions of equality have expanded to include factors of condition also. It has become accepted that some persons are handicapped in enjoying liberty because of circumstances beyond their control, such as minority status, gender, poverty, and physical and psychological impairments. Within the current sociopolitical context, emphasis is placed on the *appropriateness* of treatment. Thus equality has taken on connotations of equity, "the state, ideal, or quality of being just, impartial and fair" (Morris, 1969, p. 443). Education has become a principal instrument of social policy for removing or reducing the liabilities of these conditions (for example, special education and compensatory education programs). With a broadened definition of equality, equity comes into direct conflict with the value of liberty as originally defined, because the policies of remediation involve not only the disadvantaged person but all others as well. Liberty requires an opportunity for expression through individual freedom (for example, educational vouchers and family choice of schooling), whereas equity requires some curbing of individual freedom (for example, school desegregation, mainstreaming, and expenditure caps).

In his international analyses, Caldwell (1993) observed a blending of the values of equity and excellence:

> The emerging view of equity and excellence suggests an emphasis on ensuring that each individual student has access to the particular mix of resources in order to best meet the needs and interests of that student . . . . Expressed another way, the merging of equity and excellence may involve, among other things, a shift from uniformity in resource allocation, with all decisions at the center, to different patterns of resource allocation according to the particular mix of student needs at the school level, with more decisions at the school level in determining these patterns. (p. 163)

Clune (1993) observed such a trend in the United States. He saw equity being defined in terms of a high minimum level of achievement for all pupils as the common goal for educational adequacy *and* sufficient resources to meet that goal. In other words, the equity of resource allocation is beginning to be judged on the basis of its ability to support equitable student outcomes, not necessarily on the basis of the evenness of distribution of inputs, as has been the practice in the past. Thus *adequacy* and *capacity* are terms that have entered the modern lexicon of education finance, modifying definitions of *equality* and *equity*.

Adequacy focuses on outputs and outcomes, requiring the setting of absolute rather than relative standards. Looking at equity through the lens of adequacy forces the linking of school finance issues with fundamental issues of education reform and student achievement. Defining adequacy in an operational sense (i.e., providing sufficient resources to build the capacity of schools) will be difficult and will be addressed later, especially in Chapters 10 and 11. Adequacy has both qualitative and quantitative aspects. Its qualitative aspects involve matters of curriculum—identifying and defining those educational experiences that are essential for all children. Quantitative aspects require specifying satisfactory levels of achievement. Thus, defining equity in terms of adequacy

> holds promise of overcoming two serious theoretical weaknesses with the more common concept of equality of opportunity. First, equality of opportunity—the idea that all children should have an equal chance to succeed and that education is one of the most efficient tools for ensuring this—is insufficiently attentive to *which* educational outcomes matter most in the sense of making an important contribution to the life prospects of individuals. Second, equal education opportunity requires no particular level of achievement, nor does it forbid significant inequalities in achievement between high-achieving and low-achieving individuals so long as variations in achievement are not associated with "morally irrelevant" characteristics. (Ladd & Hansen, 1999, pp. 105–106)

The value of *fraternity* refers to a common bond producing a sense of unity, community, and nationhood. Building a sense of national identity is today a primary mission of schools in developing countries. This was a mission of schooling in the United States after it broke its colonial ties to England and emerged from the Revolutionary War as thirteen independent states. Later, the school became an important instrument of the "melting pot" strategists during the nineteenth century (Ravitch, 1985, chap. 14; Tyack, 1974). There is still a need for the schools to be a force welding together the nation as immigration continues to enlarge ethnic diversity and as disparities in family income continue to grow.

Like equity, fraternity imposes constraints upon liberty. Cremin (1976) noted an inescapable and obvious relationship between the concepts of education and community (that is, fraternity). Referring to Dewey's (1916) *Democracy and Education*, Cremin wrote, "[T]here must be ample room in a democratic society for a healthy individualism and a healthy pluralism, but that individualism and that pluralism must also partake of a continuing quest for community" (p. 72). Nyberg (1977, p. 217) characterized the historical and social functions of a school as "a method by which individuals become communities, and through which these communities describe themselves."

Efficiency, the ratio of outputs to inputs, is of more recent concern in education. Efficiency is increased by improving the probability of realizing targeted outcomes from available resources or by maintaining a given level of outcomes using fewer resources. As institutions that function largely in the public sector, schools do not face the stringent discipline for efficient operations (internal efficiency) imposed by the market on institutions that operate in the private sector (Benson, 1978; Guthrie, Garms, and Pierce, 1988). Governments in capitalistic countries tend to deal with issues where economic concerns are not overriding. In the educational lexicon, efficiency concerns are expressed in terms of "accountability" and reaching high "standards" with available resources.

Increasing the aggregate national production of goods and services through *economic growth* involves the development of skills needed in the workforce to support the economy so that it will expand at a desired pace, thereby enhancing the general welfare. Economic growth is closely tied to human capital development, as is discussed in Chapter 2. The objective of promoting economic growth, like that of efficiency, is of relatively recent interest. When public education was developing in the nine-

teenth century, the general skill requirements of the workforce were minimal, and where special skills were required, they were usually developed through apprenticeship programs in the private sector. As the entry-level skills required by business, industry, and the professions became more sophisticated, public schools increasingly took on vocational responsibilities. Concern over economic growth will continue to gain in importance as a criterion for evaluating educational policy as international competition and the level of skills demanded in the labor market increase further.

Policy making in education is particularly difficult because it is deeply enmeshed in these and other competing public and private values. During the last two decades, concern over the lack, among recent school graduates, of the skills necessary to perpetuate national economic growth at a competitive pace led policy makers to examine more closely the efficiency of the schooling system. As a consequence, policy makers set high standards for student achievement, established mechanisms to monitor progress toward those standards, and created incentives to motivate teaching professionals to work toward those ends. In building incentives for excellence into the system, policy makers looked to the private sector and, in some instances, experimented with creating quasi-market conditions by increasing competition among schools and accountability of professional employees. Competition has resulted in more liberty for the school clients involved, because it provides more school choice options. Where funding of schools has been linked to the movement of children, a subtle form of accountability has been placed on professional educators. The liberty of professionals has been enhanced through innovations such as site-based management and charter schools that, at the same time, offer clients greater options in exercising choice among schools. Some argue that under these new circumstances, efficiency and liberty alone will not result in excellence for all children in the absence of adequate school capacity. These critics urge an expanded understanding of equity.

As desirable as each of the five values may be, because of the conceptual inconsistencies among them, it is not possible to emphasize all at the same time in public policy—or in individual lives. Priorities must be established among them by individuals and by society. This is a dynamic process in that individuals' priorities change with circumstances, and when there has been a sufficient shift among individuals, shifts in public priorities follow (Ravitch, 1985, chap. 5). We are currently in a particularly active period of weighing value priorities with respect to education. The nation has never before set for itself the goal of educating *all* children to high standards. This new emphasis poses an extremely difficult problem for policy makers: how to link financial resources directly to instructional procedures that will facilitate the realization of the ultimate objective.

A GENERIC POLITICAL–ECONOMIC MODEL OF THE EDUCATION POLICY-MAKING PROCESS

The massive social and economic changes that have confronted society, resulting in a reevaluation of core value priorities, has produced a political climate wherein fundamental policy changes are not only possible but also likely. This means that modifying the existing structure is only one of many policy options under consideration. To provide a framework for evaluating alternative policy options, we present here a generic model of the policy-making process as it pertains to education in particular.

Our model is an elaboration of Easton's (1965) simplified model of a political system. (See Figure 1.2.) A political system is considered to be an *open* system—that is, one that draws resources from its environment, processes them in some fashion, and returns the processed resources to the environment. All systems tend toward *entropy*, or disorganization, and they must consciously combat this tendency in order to maintain equilibrium. A key function for combating entropy is *feedback*, the continual monitoring of a system's internal operations and relationship with its environment. Accurate feedback is particularly critical to a system's health in that the system depends on the environment for resources without which the system would shrink and die. Equilibrium is maintained by modifying or adapting system structures and processes on the basis of the analysis of feedback (cybernetics). Maintaining equilibrium is a dynamic process leading to growth and evolution of the system in harmony with its environment.

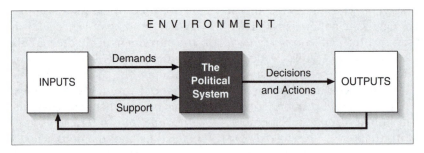

FIGURE 1.2. A Simplified Model of a Political System

Source: D. Easton. (1965). *A Systems Analysis of Political Life*. Chicago: University of Chicago Press, p. 32. Copyright 1965 by University of Chicago Press. Reprinted by permission.

Easton's model conceptualizes public policy as a response by a political system to forces from the environment. Environmental pressures or inputs come in the forms of (1) demands for public action through interest groups and (2) support of government by individuals and groups through obeying laws, paying taxes, and accepting outcomes of elections. The inputs are processed through the political system and transformed into policy outputs. Political systems consist of sets of identifiable and interrelated institutions and activities at all levels of government, such as those associated with the U.S. Congress, state and county legislatures, common councils, town councils, village boards, school boards, commissions, authorities, and courts. Feedback in a political system is both formal and informal. Formal feedback is provided through elections, referenda, hearings, and policy analysis. Informal feedback occurs through personal interactions of officials with constituents and others.

Figure 1.3 portrays our adaptation of Easton's (1965) model to education policy making. Social values and goals (of multiple interest groups) are treated as "demand" inputs to the policy-making process in the new model. Other demand inputs include existing knowledge (e.g., the professional expertise of teachers and administrators) and requirements for a qualified workforce. The latter requirement is, at the same time, a "support" input in that trained personnel (teachers and administrators) are needed to implement any educational policies that are made, and indeed, the qualifications of available labor will strongly influence which

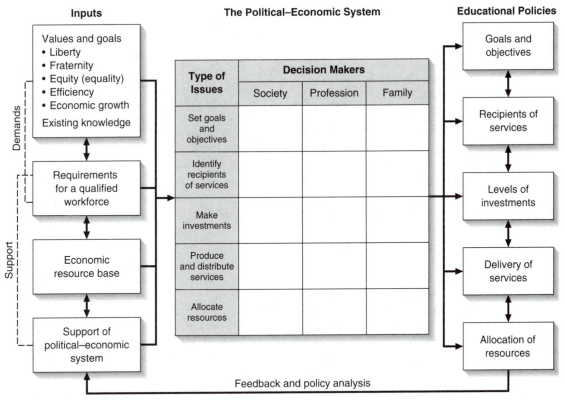

FIGURE 1.3. A Generic Model of the Political–Economic System of Education Policy Development

education policy alternatives are feasible and which are not. Other support inputs include the economic base from which resources must be drawn to finance implementation and the behavior of citizens in general that sustain the political–economic system.

Easton's political system is represented by the grid in the center of Figure 1.3 that is labeled "The Political–Economic System." The vertical dimension of the grid represents the issues that need to be decided; its horizontal dimension represents the interests and expertise of potential decision makers—that is, individuals (or families), the teaching profession, and society. Regardless of who makes the decisions, there are five broad areas in which education policy must be formulated (Benson, 1978). These are

- Setting goals and objectives for the educational enterprise.
- Determining for whom educational services are to be provided.
- Determining the level of investment in population quality (e.g., education) to promote economic growth and the general welfare.
- Determining the means by which educational services are to be provided.
- Allocating resources to and among educational services.

The potential concern of each group of decision makers extends to each of the issues, although the actual level of interest and expertise of a given group varies from issue to issue. Societal concerns expressed by individuals and interest groups are moderated through the political process of government, including school boards, and through the formation of coalitions, such as those now negotiating national curricula and standards and procedures for the national certification of teachers and administrators. Societal concerns take precedence over family and professional concerns for those issues in education where there is significant spillover of benefits ("collective" or "public" goods defined in Chapter 2) and where there

are redistributive considerations (shifting of wealth and benefits from one group to another).

The teaching profession (including administrators and other certified personnel) holds the technical expertise about schooling. As employees of educational system(s), these professionals also have a vested interest in the conditions of employment. Teachers, along with other members of the polity, participate in general elections and referenda and the political activities accompanying them. Professional educators also have a very strong impact on public policy through the lobbying activities of their unions and professional associations. Lobbyists for the National Education Association (NEA) and the American Federation of Teachers (AFT) are particularly effective at the state and national levels. At the local level, in addition to serving on various school district advisory committees, teachers and administrators greatly influence education policy through the collective bargaining process (Bacharach & Shedd, 1989: Mitchell, 1989).

Parents are the guardians of the interests and needs of individual children. The family usually has the most intimate knowledge about and caring concern for the child. It is usually through the family that the child's voice is heard (Bridge, 1976; Coons & Sugarman, 1978; Clune, 1995). In addition to participating in school board elections and referenda, individual parents may approach school board members, school administrators, or teachers directly to express their concerns. They may also align themselves with other parents who have similar concerns, forming such associations as the National Congress of Parents and Teachers (PTA) and the Council for Basic Education (CBE) that direct their activities largely at influencing state and federal policy. Other parent groups focus on the needs of children with special conditions such as being emotionally disturbed, physically disabled, or intellectually gifted.

Organizations such as the League of Women Voters and the American Association of University Women embrace education issues as a continuing secondary concern. Other organizations attempt to influence education policy as a means of accomplishing ends that transcend the school. These might include taxpayer groups or groups with a specific political agenda, such as civil rights, affirmative action, pro-choice or anti-abortion advocacy, environmental protection, the promotion of patriotism, and religious fundamentalism.

Easton's outputs of decisions and actions are represented by the rectangle at the right of Figure 1.3. The outcomes of the process are educational policies and practices, categorized in the figure according to the five types of issues that were addressed through the political–economic system. The policies and practices are a composite of decisions made formally and informally by society, the profession, and the family. A feedback loop is indicated from the educational policies representation to the input representation. Feedback is provided by elections, hearings, surveys, and policy analysis and through a variety of informal channels. Information passing through the feedback loop will influence future decisions and behaviors.

Allocation of Power and Authority Over Education in the United States

Determining a satisfactory pattern for the distribution of power and authority is a continuing problem in making public policy for education. The generic model of the political–economic system of education policy development (see Figure 1.3) contains a decision matrix called the political–economic system that arrays issues that need to be determined against potential decision makers. We now use that matrix to describe the evolution of the allocation of authority over the making of decisions about education in the United States. In the next section, we use the matrix to compare current allocation patterns in England, Aus-

tralia, and New Zealand. This is followed by a cross-national analysis, placing the four countries in juxtaposition. In the final section of this chapter, we develop guidelines for school finance policy based on the comparative analysis.

The allocation of power and authority among interested parties influences the nature of the decisions made and the effectiveness with which they are implemented. Several of the school reform initiatives under serious consideration in many places, and already initiated in some, reallocate power and authority in significant ways—for example, via achievement standards and accountability procedures, parental choice of schools, and site-based management. Elmore (1993) and Weiler (1993) suggested that the education reform debates raging throughout the world have little to do about improving the quality of teaching and learning in schools. In the final analysis, it is about power and the distribution of power (see also Archer, 1984; Slater, 1993).

Elmore (1993) has been critical of the tendency of analysts to treat reforms that centralize power and reforms that decentralize power as absolutes. Rather, he suggested that the underlying issues be addressed in terms of what should be loosely governed (decentralized) and what should be tightly governed (centralized):

> Implicit in this question is the assumption that multiple levels of government, as well as their constituencies, all have an interest in the governance of the schools, but that if they all attempt to assert equal influence over all matters of schooling, the system will collapse of its own organizational complexity. Thus the issue is not *whether* one level of government or another should influence education but rather *how much* influence of *what kind* any level of government should exert over *what factors*. (p. 51)

McGinn and Street (1986) characterize centralization and decentralization as a dyad:

> Decentralization is not primarily an issue of control by government of individual citizens. Instead it is a question of the distribution of power among

various groups in society. A highly participatory society—one in which all citizens actually do participate—is likely to require a competent and powerful state that actively and continuously seeks to redistribute power among groups and individuals in the society. The location of authority in local government does not protect the local citizen from tyranny, and the redistribution of power through the market mechanism in a society that currently is highly inequitable is a guarantee that inequities will persist and worsen. On the other hand, competition and markets can contribute to social justice in circumstances where there is a relatively equitable balance of powers among the participants in the competition or market. . . . A strong state must first achieve some minimal degree of social equity so that decentralization can lead to genuine participation. (pp. 489–490)

The common school concept emerged early in the nineteenth century when agriculture dominated the U.S. economy and most people lived in rural areas. The common school was "public," but the formal governance structure was similar to the town meeting, and the communities served were typically very small. Even in the few cities of that period, which were small by today's standards and were without suburbs, school governance was at the ward level. School consolidation started in cities with the establishment of city school districts; from there, school districts grew along with their cities and the bureaucracies that managed them. Centralization of rural schools began after the turn of the twentieth century. Tyack (1974) reported it this way:

> This movement to take control of the rural common school away from the local community and to turn it over to the professionals was part of a more general organizational revolution in American education in which laymen lost much of their direct control over the schools. In the cities schoolmen pioneered new bureaucratic patterns of educational organization. They sought to "free education from politics. . . ." (p. 25)

Returning to Figure 1.3 as a point of reference, control over education was largely in the hands of families through a town meeting format at the origin of public education in the United States. The teaching profession was weak, and the larger society as represented by the state was relatively inactive other than to provide enabling legislation. The principles of liberty and equality of educational opportunity (among socioeconomic classes but not among races) were dominant within communities that were largely heterogeneous with respect to social class. Government was small, as was its demand for economic resources. Efficiency was not yet a concern of government in general or of the schools.

Despite the dispersion of control, there was a remarkable uniformity among the schools. There was a general Protestant–Republican ideology that was shared among school crusaders such as Horace Mann and Henry Barnard. The purpose of public education was assumed to be training upright citizens by inculcating a common denominator of nonsectarian morality and nonpartisan civic instruction. The school itself was to be free, open to all children, and public in support and control (Tyack, 1993). The key to this uniformity was not central government control but the force of common cultural beliefs in shaping institutions—what Tyack calls "the invisible hand of ideology" (p. 5).

With the growing sophistication of the teaching profession, especially its administrators, professional control and bureaucratization grew substantially during the first half of the twentieth century—representing a shift of authority to the left in Figure 1.3 (Callahan, 1962; Tyack, 1993). States became more involved by enacting compulsory attendance laws, setting certain basic standards for teacher certification, consolidating rural schools, and providing some financing, including minimal equalization aid. The federal government entered the scene by providing aid for vocational education. Liberty was less a concern than before; efficiency considerations came into play for the first time; and equity concerns began to take on a statewide dimension.

Following World War II, there was a rapid expansion of suburbs and suburban school districts. Municipalities and school districts became quite homogeneous in socioeconomic status and ethnicity, the white middle class being concentrated in the suburbs (Banfield, 1970, 1974). Deprived of the leadership of a vibrant middle class, urban centers suffered a decline in the quality of educational services. During the 1950s and through the 1970s, civil rights suits were successfully pursued in federal courts to correct the inequities that resulted (Levin, 1987). Litigation was followed by state and federal legislation, which had the effect of making specific court decisions universal. Local decisions about the nature and distribution of educational services were constrained by national and state guidelines and mandates concerning pupil assignment and discipline, teacher employment, and curriculum.

Also in the 1970s, society's influence was enlarged with respect to the allocation of resources, again through litigation followed by legislation (Berne & Stiefel, 1983; Guthrie, Garms & Pierce, 1988, chap. 8). States increased their participation in financing school operations, school buildings, and transportation. The federal role in school finance became a significant factor for the first time in the 1960s and 1970s, coming in the form of categorical aid grants that were focused on poor and disabled children within urban centers. State education departments and the United States Department of Education grew in size and influence. There was a perceived decline in student achievement and, along with it, in the credibility of the teaching profession. The principle of equity was the dominant concern during this period and was defined in racial and ethnic as well as socioeconomic terms. Liberty and efficiency suffered as the constraints placed on local school districts by state and federal governments grew. The dominant decision makers had become the state and federal governments, representing society in Figure 1.3.

Perceived deterioration in the quality of student achievement during the 1970s became a national concern early in the 1980s with the publication of numerous reports on the state of education. The current educational reform movement followed. To arrest the decline in standards, most states intervened with mandated curricula, competency examinations for both students and teachers, and stiffer requirements for teacher certification and student diplomas. This initial phase of the reform movement further constrained what remained of the discretionary authority of educational officials at the school district level. As a consequence, there was a substantial mismatch between aspirations for schools and the reality of those schools for many individuals and communities. The locus of authority had completed its movement from the family and the profession to society at large.

But legislating higher standards did not necessarily produce higher standards (Iannaccone, 1985), and state governors, among others, were quick to notice. From the mid-1960s through the early 1980s, efficiency and equity had been pursued through centralized authority. Policy implementation studies of that period (Chubb & Moe, 1985, 1990; Coleman & Hoffer, 1987; Coons & Sugarman, 1978; Elmore & McLaughlin, 1988; Farrar, DeSanctis, & Cohen, 1980; McNeil, 1986; Wise, 1979, 1988) showed that federal and state governments are particularly effective in dealing with issues of equity and access. However, such governments appear to be less effective in dealing with matters of efficiency and "production"—that is, how schools are organized and operated. We have learned from experience. There is a renewed appreciation of the concept of liberty in the United States and a tendency to pursue efficiency through decentralized authority and equity through centralized authority. This division has been referred to as systemic reform.

Liberty and efficiency are back as policy concerns (Iannaccone, 1988). School-based decision making and family choice of schooling represent important tactics in an overall strategy of decentralization. These tactics return some decision-making authority to parents and teachers in order to introduce market-like forces into the public school sector for the purpose of increasing the efficiency of that sector and better aligning parental expectations and educational services provided. A strong desire to retain equity as a guiding principle has led to its reconceptualization in terms of adequacy and building school capacity to ensure resources sufficient to enable all children to achieve high standards.

International Comparisons

There are a number of striking similarities in the movements to transform the control and performance of schools that are under way in the United States, England, Australia, Canada, and Japan (Beare & Boyd, 1993). A common political concern motivating reform is to obtain or to maintain international economic competitiveness. This concern is so great that national governments are taking leading roles in educational reform initiatives, even in countries such as the United States and Australia where there is no constitutional authority for such intervention. There is also a similarity in the nature of the reforms. Greater managerial authority is devolving to schools, and parents are being allowed more discretion in selecting the state-supported schools their children attend. Countering these decentralizing forces are centralizing forces. Most countries are developing, or have already established, national/state standards, national/state curricula, and national/state assessments (Caldwell & Spinks, 1998).

Having reviewed the evolution of structural reform in the United States using the matrix in Figure 1.3, we now look at the cases of England, Australia, and New Zealand. These nations share a common language and a similar cultural–political heritage with the United States. Canada is not included in the review be-cause reforming education has not received the national and provincial attention given to it by the countries being considered. While its English-speaking allies were focusing on school reform, bilingual Canada was preoccupied with its constitutional crisis and was giving preservation of the union top priority (Lawton, 1993). Some districts in Canada, however, have adopted innovative restructuring, such as the school site management scheme in Edmonton, Alberta, featured in Chapter 14.

England

During World War II, a coalition government restructured England's school system through the Education Act of 1944. During those periods when the Labour party was in control of the national government after World War II, it gradually made the system less selective via the steady reduction in the number of grammar schools for the academically proficient and the introduction of comprehensive secondary schools to serve children of all academic abilities. When the Conservative party came to power in 1979 under the leadership of Margaret Thatcher, it stayed the demise of the remaining grammar schools and initiated a process of reform that eventually led to the fundamental changes embodied in the Education Reform Act of 1988. The Conservative party remained in power for 18 years until 1997, when, under the leadership of Tony Blair, a "new" Labour party took the reigns of power with a decisive majority. Having divested itself of its left-wing socialist arm, Labour was a more centrist party than the one that had ruled following World War II. In the election of 1997, Labour captured the political middle ground, which the Conservatives had begun to abandon because of the growing influence of their right-wing neo-liberals and traditionalists (Levacic, 1999). Labour chose to leave most of the reforms initiated by the Conservatives in place, modifying them only at the margin.

Until the Education Reform Act of 1988, the English educational system was characterized as "a national system locally administered" (Department of Education and Science, 1978). Between 75 percent and 80 percent of the system's financing was provided by the national government. Administration was left to divisions of local government called Local Education Authorities (LEAs) and to school heads (principals). The LEAs were responsible for rationalizing the education system, making sure that there was provision for all children, establishing criteria for the assignment of children to schools, and supplementing national funding. The 1944 Act had encouraged the satisfaction of parental preferences in school assignment when possible, and parents had the right of appeal to the secretary of state for education if they disagreed with their LEA on a particular pupil placement.

Local Authorities (of which LEAs are a part) established the education budget under the 1944 Act. However, they were severely constrained by decisions made at the national level through negotiations between representatives of local authorities and the national government. Teachers' salary levels were also established at the national level through negotiations between the national government and representatives of local authorities on the one side of the bargaining table and representatives of teachers unions on the other. As a result, the slight variations in expenditure level per pupil among LEAs were modest compared with those experienced in the United States.

School heads were given a rather free hand in organizing their schools and in designing the curriculum under the 1944 Act. National examinations provided for some curricular uniformity at the upper secondary level. Curricular variety was matched with organizational variety. Following the 1988 reforms and subsequent amendments, a national curriculum largely eliminated curricular innovation at the school level, but organizational variety was enhanced. As before the reforms, there are selective and comprehensive schools, single-sex and mixed schools, and schools sponsored by religious and other organizations. The 16–19 age cohort continues to be accommodated in "sixth forms" attached to secondary schools (providing, primarily, an academic curriculum) and in sixth-form colleges (academic), technical colleges, and tertiary colleges (providing both technical and academic curricula). Also, there continue to be independent schools for those who desire an elitist education and who can afford the tuition. Most church schools continue to be maintained by the state sector, and all state-maintained schools must include religious education in their curricula and conduct assemblies of Christian worship. Independent schools have never received direct state support.

The Education Reform Act of 1988 gave the secretary of state for education 415 new specific powers, and subsequent legislation has added further to the secretary's authority. The Act "shifted power away from LEAs to the central authority, contrary to the established tradition of avoiding too much central control" (Lawton, 1992, p. 47). Expenditure levels are now virtually set by the national government, and the share of primary- and secondary-school expenditures paid by the national government has grown to 80–85 percent. Variation in expenditure per pupil among LEAs is even less now than it was before. A national curriculum accompanied by national assessment procedures ensures a high degree of national uniformity in instruction at the school site. Each of the nation's 26,000 schools is inspected once every four years in a procedure supervised by Her Majesty's Chief Inspector through the Office for Standards in Education (OFSTED). The results of school inspections and assessments are published for the information of parents and other interested parties. Each year, schools must report to parents on their children's progress with respect to national curriculum standards.

Countering the centralization actions are some actions that clearly decentralize authority. Government financial support is distributed through the LEAs. The LEAs pass these grants, plus the local supplements, on to the schools, withholding only an amount sufficient to provide for strategic management, ensuring that sufficient school places are available, school improvement, and special education. The amount withheld by the LEAs is less than 10 percent of the total allocation. The grants to schools provide for their operating expenses, including all staff salaries. They are paid to each school's governing body by its LEA largely on the basis of enrollment and age of pupils. Schools can determine their own staffing patterns, make their own personnel decisions (including administrators' pay within national guidelines), and contract for support services such as building maintenance, accounting, purchasing, payroll, insurance, and auditing.

Schools are divided into three governance categories: community, voluntary, and foundation. Voluntary and foundation schools differ from community schools in that they are affiliated with a body of persons other than an LEA that holds assets in trust for the purposes of the school such as land, buildings, and endowments. Schools with religious affiliations make up the voluntary category. Assets for community schools are held by LEAs. The LEA is the employer of staff for community schools and for some voluntary schools, but the governing body determines staff establishment, appointments, disciplinary actions, and dismissals. Governing bodies of foundation schools and of some voluntary schools are the employers of staff and exercise the same control over staff as in community schools.

The authority previously held by LEAs to control pupil intake of schools has been severely curtailed. Parents have gained additional representation on governing bodies and have considerable influence on the placement of their children in schools. LEAs are the admissions authority for community schools and for some voluntary schools. Foundation schools and the remaining voluntary schools act as their own admissions authorities. Each area has

a local forum made up of stakeholder representatives that coordinates admission arrangements. These forums are encouraged to provide parents with all information about area schools in one booklet and to coordinate school admissions procedures so that parents need make only one application. School admissions criteria must be clear, fair, and objective and, except for grammar schools, cannot include ability, although some specialized schools are allowed to consider "aptitude." Schools with religious affiliations can give preference to students of the same faith. A formal appeals process is available to parents dissatisfied with the placement of their children (Levacic, 1999).

In terms of the framework provided by Figure 1.3, society in England is strengthening its control over the setting of goals and objectives for education through mandating a core curriculum, national student assessment, national evaluation of schools, and the allocation of resources in terms of expenditure per pupil. On the other hand, the family voice in decisions about the distribution of services (the selection of schools) is enhanced. Parental choice indirectly strengthens the family's influence on all other decisions, although it appears that oversubscribed schools are selecting parents. Despite the removing of much professional discretionary power over curriculum, the teaching profession still maintains strong influence over the implementation of the curriculum. In other respects, the influence of professionals is strengthened by shifting to the school level decisions about the allocation of resources to the instructional process.

Australia

Traditionally, Australian schools have operated as highly centralized state systems (Butts, 1955; Hancock, Kirst, & Grossmam, 1983; Partridge, 1968). There are no local education authorities (i.e., school districts). Teachers and administrators are selected, employed, and assigned by the respective state bureaucracies, although some states, notably Victoria, have begun to allow school input into the process. Each state has developed a curriculum and standards framework in eight key learning areas specified in national goals: the arts, English, health and physical education, languages other than English, mathematics, science, studies of society and the environment, and technology. Each state has also developed its own scheme for assessing student achievement in some of the learning areas, most commonly literacy and mathematics. Schools are informed of the levels of performance of their students and are provided with normative statistics from schools with similar characteristics for purposes of comparison. Individual school performance is not published by the state, although state average performance is.

Similar to the situation in the United States, the Australian commonwealth government has no constitutional authority to intervene in educational matters. The national government provides directly less than 10 percent of the funding of government schools, most of which is categorical in nature. However, the commonwealth government has been the prime leader of school reform initiatives for the last two decades (Louden & Browne, 1993). Initial commonwealth ventures into education were coordinated through the Australian Schools Commission, the Curriculum Development Centre, and the Commonwealth Department of Education. Commonwealth intervention in education over the past twenty years has been motivated largely by grave concern over Australia's economic competitiveness internationally and by the belief that its future prosperity is associated with the development of a highly educated and skilled workforce. This was clearly manifested in 1987 when federal education affairs were placed under a superministry called the Department of Employment, Education, Training and Youth Affairs. National education policy is also guided by the Ministerial Council on Education, Employment, Training and Youth Affairs (MCEETYA), which is composed of state, territory, com-

monwealth, and Australian ministers with responsibility for the portfolios of related areas. MCEETYA was the instrument through which the *National Goals for Schooling* (which are also known as *The Adelaide Declaration*) were developed in 1999. These goals provided the framework within which state curricula and standards were produced. Specific grants tied to commonwealth intentions encourage compliance. For example, grants for the improvement of literacy carry with them a condition that the recipient state participate in a national system of benchmark tests.

The commonwealth government's influence is further enhanced by the fact that Australian states depend directly on it for significant amounts of their revenue. Unlike state governments in the United States and provinces in Canada, state governments in Australia do not levy direct income taxes (although they have the power to do so). Income tax collection is coordinated through the federal government, a portion of which is returned to the states through the Grants Commission. The power of the commonwealth government to vary grants to the states and to make special grants gives it very significant policy-making power beyond that specified in its constitution (Louden and Browne, 1993). The principles of efficiency, pluralism, and liberty direct the current federal political agenda for funding schools in Australia. In contrast, equity has dropped to a lower priority from the dominating position it held in previous decades.

In the 1960s, public funding was extended to private schools, first by the federal government and subsequently by state governments. The change was made primarily to save the Roman Catholic schools from collapse at a time when public schools were finding it difficult to accommodate their own burgeoning enrollments. The intent was equalitarian—to upgrade the quality of education in the underfinanced Catholic sector (Hogan, 1984)—because for the most part, Roman Catholic parochial schools serve a nonelitist working-class constituency.

Elitist, high-expenditure Protestant and independent schools that cater to business and professional classes also benefited from the aid, although not so much as less affluent schools. Today, the publicly subsidized private schools offer a low-cost alternative to the public schools. Overall, 30 percent of school-age children attend private schools. Nearly two-thirds of these children are enrolled in Catholic schools, although the non-Catholic component of the private sector is the most rapidly growing. The proportion of enrollment in private senior secondary schools is 36.7 percent (MCEETYA, 1998, cited by Caldwell, 2001). Private schools, regardless of affiliation, set the standard of excellence in Australia (Boyd, 1987; Anderson, 1993).

In essence, Australia has two publicly financed systems of education—one highly centralized and the other highly decentralized. Ironically, nongovernment schools (the decentralized system) have come to serve as models for the reform of government schools (the centralized system). Government schools have been perceived as being impersonal, uncaring, and institutional in character (Anderson, 1993). Teachers and principals in government schools have tended to identify with the Teaching Service (the state bureau for employing teachers) rather than with the schools and communities in which they serve. Historically, personnel transfers have been frequent, and assignments have been made by formula and longevity, not in view of local conditions or merit. Anderson (1993, p. 195) concluded that the value contrasts between the two sectors are fairly clear: "choice versus equity, pluralism versus social cohesion, individual responsibility versus collective responsibility through the state. The private sector is regulated by the market, the public by bureaucratic and political accountability."

The necessity to improve the efficiency of the public sector has led to similar changes in all states. Central bureaucracies have been reduced; significant authority has devolved to schools; public involvement at the school level has been enhanced through the creation of policy formulation boards; parental choice of schools has been enhanced; and greater accountability requirements have been put into place at both school and system (state) levels (Caldwell, 2001).

In terms of the framework provided by Figure 1.3, state and commonwealth governments (society) in Australia continue to make decisions for public schools concerning the setting of goals and objectives, the monitoring of accountability, and the allocation of resources. These functions are being centralized even further, as the foundation has been laid for a national curriculum framework and testing program (Caldwell, 1993). Decisions about the production of services have been shifted to the school level in some states, especially Victoria, to be made by policy boards that include representatives of the teaching profession, parents, and the community served.

For private schools (except for elite private schools), state governments strongly influence the amount spent per pupil. But the way the money is spent is determined by school trustees in consultation with their professional employees. Decisions about production of services are left largely to the discretion of private school employees within the constraints of state curriculum and standards frameworks and within the unique goals and objectives set by the school trustees and the school budget. The family can choose a public school (increasingly, *among* public schools) and among many private schools, most of which charge tuition low enough to make them affordable to most families.

Through all these policy changes, Louden and Browne (1993) viewed the school as escaping relatively unscathed in Australia. They noted both centralization and decentralization in anticipating

a trend to new centralism, greater devolution of management responsibility to schools accompanied by strengthened centralizing of policy generation, goal setting, and performance monitoring. There will be continuing tension between federal and state authorities in formulating education policies with the former being interested in central planning with the nation's economic well-being the central concern, and the latter emphasizing devolution and grass-roots considerations. (p. 133)

Anderson (1993) was pessimistic about ever again restoring the quality of Australian public schools to the point where they can successfully compete with the publicly subsidized private schools. He projected two alternative futures: either the public schools would become residual institutions for special education students and children of parents on welfare, or public and private schools would be reconfigured into some form of integrated system. McGaw (1994) lamented that the dominant goals of Australian education are no longer equity and effectiveness; he argued that the goal is now to strengthen the national economy with a strong presumption that cheaper will be more efficient. McGaw contended that the Australian public would prefer defection from the public schools and a reduced call upon public provision in order that discretionary private resources might be increased, reducing the need for tax support.

In a study of administrative and regulatory mechanisms affecting school autonomy in Australia prepared for the Department of Employment, Education, Training and Youth Affairs, Caldwell (1998) identified twenty forces impinging on efforts to provide greater autonomy for schools in the public sector; eight of these are driving forces and twelve are constraining forces. He concluded that further changes in current patterns of authority, responsibility, and accountability are unlikely unless state governments have the will and parliamentary mandate to take action to add to the driving forces or to mitigate the constraining forces. He referred to the reforms in the State of Victoria initiated in 1993 as "the high water mark in school autonomy for the fore-

seeable future" (p. 2). The Victorian reforms will be described in some detail in Chapter 14, which focuses on issues surrounding site-based management and decision making.

New Zealand

In their history of New Zealand education reforms between 1984 and 1996, Graham and Susan Butterworth (1998) quote from the speech that Charles Bowen, architect of the New Zealand state school system, delivered in 1877 when introducing into the House of Representatives the education bill that would ultimately be passed and would establish the system:

> The Bill we plan to submit to this House provides for local administration, subject to ultimate central control in certain particulars, especially in matters of expenditure. . . . Government is perfectly satisfied that the general administration of the schools must be left in the hands of Local Boards: for without such local administration it would be impossible to keep up the public interest which is necessary in an educational system. (Cited by Butterworth and Butterworth, 1998, p. 9)

But as early as the turn of the twentieth century, local autonomy had seriously eroded and the center was in firm control of the education system. Toward the end of the twentieth century, the system had become viewed as being overly centralized and as having too many decision points. To redress the balance of authority, a Task Force to Review Education Administration was appointed in 1987 under the leadership of Brian Picot, a successful and respected businessman with an impressive record of public service. The report of this task force provided the blueprint for structural (or governance) reform, not to be confused with curricular reform, which came later and had a different history. Although many have portrayed the reforms that followed as radical (Macpherson, 1993) and as urged on by free-market ideologues, Butterworth and Butterworth (1998) characterized them as conservative in philosophy in that they were built on the founding traditions of public education in New Zealand. According to these analysts, the reforms represented more a revolution from within than an overthrow of the establishment by outsiders.

New Zealand embarked on its program of reform in October 1989. Although New Zealanders traditionally have cherished popular sovereignty and have preferred local government over central government, the education system had a strong centrist orientation, being controlled and administered through the national Department of Education, three regional offices, and ten education boards. Secondary schools had boards of governors, and primary schools had school committees, all acting within policy established at the center.

A bipartisan parliamentary committee concluded in 1986 that the quality of teaching in public schools was being undermined by three conditions: provider capture (control of the education service by professional educators, as was also the case with the Thatcher government when it enacted the 1988 reforms in England and with the Liberal government when it enacted the 1991 reforms in Victoria, Australia); grossly elaborated structures of educational administration, with ineffective lines of accountability and communication; and obsolete administrative attitudes and practices (Macpherson, 1993). Education became a major issue in the national elections of 1987; subsequently, more direct action was taken with the appointment of the Picot task force.

The Picot (1988) task force found an urgent need for greater responsiveness in public education. It reported that the administrative capacities of the system were inadequate to deal with the combined effects of new technology, changing and plural values, new cultural sensitivity, and the intensifying demands on educational services. The system was found to be overcentralized with high vulnerability to pressure groups, excessive ministerial intervention,

and a culture of centralism and dependence. The devolution to school-level boards of trustees of decision-making authority to administer school operations and to implement a national curriculum framework, with accountability audited by an independent Education Review Office, was seen as an effective means to alter the balance of power between the education establishment and the clients of the system. The government enacted most of the task force's recommendations in 1989.

The 1989 reforms centered on the school as the unit that sustains the relationship between learner and teacher. Prior to the effective date of the reforms, each school community elected a board of trustees (with parents in the majority) that was responsible for developing a charter of organization that presented the philosophy and goals of the school, its instructional program, and its plan for using resources. The intent of the Picot task force was that each charter reflect local needs and conditions within guidelines established by the national government; in practice, the national guidelines became so prescriptive that there was little leeway to accommodate local differences (Butterworth & Butterworth, 1998; Fiske and Ladd, 2000). Each charter is approved by the Ministry of Education and serves as the basis of accountability as monitored by the newly created Education Review Office. Boards of trustees of schools are also responsible for the appointment of principals, who in turn recommend the appointment of staff. Teachers continue to be employed by and paid by the Department of Education. Schools receive a block grant for operations, which represents about 30 percent of all resources consumed. The task force had recommended that the block grant to schools also include teachers salaries, but this was dropped from the final legislation because of strong opposition by the teachers unions. The auditor general conducts financial audits.

The reforms abolished the ten regional education boards that had overseen primary education. The Department of Education was greatly reduced in size and limited in its responsibilities, now serving in an advisory role, managing property, distributing funds, and developing national guidelines for personnel, administration, governance, and curriculum. The State Services Commission negotiates terms of service for administrators and teachers with their respective unions.

The Picot task force also had recommended, and the 1989 law provided, that parents be free to enroll their children in schools outside their residential attendance zones. However, children residing within a school's attendance zone would be given preference, and admission of others would be at the discretion of the principal on a space availability basis. A new government changed this practice in 1991, and the elimination of school attendance zones permitted unobstructed parental choice. By 1997 over half of the schools in major cities were oversubscribed, placing these schools in a position where they could select their students (Fiske & Ladd, 2000). In 1999 Parliament required school enrollment schemes to be approved by the secretary of education. Only a few schools have been closed as a result of parental choice of schools, but several that serve children of low socioeconomic families are experiencing serious difficulties and have required further intervention by the national government. The scheme appears to be working well for the great majority of schools, however (Butterworth & Butterworth, 1998; Fiske & Ladd, 2000).

With respect to the decision matrix in Figure 1.3, after the establishment of public schools in 1877, New Zealand experienced a rapid shift in control from families to society. After the reforms beginning in 1989, power was more widely dispersed. Government retained control over the level of financing, but considerable discretion was given to school trustees with respect to the allocation of operating expenditures and the selection of personnel. School assessment was entrusted to an independent body at the national level—a move that centralized authority outside the profession. The Department of Education retained some influence over curriculum. The principal's role was strengthened at the school level but at the price of job security. The issue of job security for principals was placed in the hands of boards of trustees. Parental influence was strengthened politically through their roles in selecting and serving as school trustees and through choice of schools for their children.

Juxtaposition

The framework presented in Figure 1.3 for allocating authority in a system of schools provides a useful lens through which to observe and evaluate these events within a society over time and across societies at a given time. In this section, the experiences of the United States, England, Australia, and New Zealand are discussed in terms of the elements and relationships suggested by the model. In the next section, twelve propositions are derived from the analysis based on this juxtaposition. They may be useful as guides in developing school finance and other education policy.

Policy makers are embarking on similar educational reform strategies regardless of their political orientations. England's reform was initiated by a Conservative government but was retained with only minor changes when a Labour government gained power in 1997. In New Zealand, the initiator was a Labour government; but the reforms were retained, largely unaltered, by a Conservative government. In Australia, the Labour party and various conservative parties at the state level initiated the reforms. At the national level in the United States, a Republican president in cooperation with the National Governors' Association initially led the reform effort, but a capture of the White House by the Democrats in 1992 led to little change in policy. At the state level, both Republican and Democratic administrations have brought about similar reforms. Drucker

(1980), in speaking generally about the paradigm shifts we are experiencing universally, wrote,

> The new realities fit neither the assumptions of the Left or of the Right. They do not mesh with "what everybody knows." They differ even from what everybody, regardless of political persuasion, still believes reality to be. "What is" differs totally from what both Right and Left believe "ought to be." (p. 10)

In the preface to his book analyzing the direction of education reform in England, Lawton (1992) made a similar observation:

> During the course of 1989 and 1990, I also had the opportunity of visiting a number of other countries and talking to visitors from a wide variety of education systems. It was remarkable that so many of these countries, whatever the political complexion of the government in power, were undertaking "reforms" which in England were described as "Thatcherite." Clearly something was happening politically and educationally on more than a national scale. (p. ix)

Whitty, Power, and Halpin (1998) noted that, "The almost simultaneous emergence of similar reforms across continents has led some to suggest that the current restructuring of education needs to be understood as a global phenomenon" (p. 31). We share the opinion that the current educational reform movement is a worldwide event; further, we believe that it is a response to universal forces, not just to parochial ones.

The United States developed a highly decentralized system of public schooling a century and a half ago to further the objectives of equality in a sparsely populated, agrarian society. As the nation grew in population and became more industrialized and urbanized, a relatively equitable rural system evolved into a highly inequitable and divisive urban/suburban system. Efforts to restore equity brought oppressiveness, impersonality, and inefficiency to the bureaucratically managed system. England had a nationally coordinated system with extraordinary powers delegated to schools, especially over matters of curriculum. The *laissez faire* approach to curriculum was seen as an impediment to national economic survival in a global economy. As a result, the curriculum was nationalized, standards were set, and a national evaluation scheme was put into place. In other respects, schools were given much greater discretion over staff and organizational decisions at the expense of LEAs, and parents were granted greater influence over school policy through membership on school councils and more options in choosing schools for their children.

In search of equity and efficiency, Australia and New Zealand developed highly centralized systems of public schooling. Also in the name of equity, Australia extended considerable financial assistance to mostly underfinanced private schools, a move that had the unintended consequence of enhancing aspects of liberty. Whereas the government and nonelite private schools now operate at about the same expenditure levels per pupil in Australia (McGaw, 1994), the nongovernment schools are setting the standards of excellence and efficiency. In seeking to bring efficiency to government schools, all Australian states have moved to trim the central educational bureaucracies and to vest authority in schools. At the same time, control over curriculum and assessment are not being delegated. To restore some of the social control over equity that was lost in the public financing of private schools, there is a movement toward greater public regulation of private schools. Public schools are becoming more like private schools, and private schools are becoming more like public schools.

The patterns in England and New Zealand are the clearest, perhaps, because they are rooted in unitary national systems. The reallocation of power is apparent; as McGinn and Street (1986) suggested in a quotation cited earlier, it is not government versus citizens but a restoring of the balance of power among government and citizens to improve efficiency and liberty. In many respects, the United States and England on the one hand, and Australia and New Zealand on the other, are moving in opposite directions (Murphy, 1983). However, having started at opposite ends of the spectrum, they appear to be moving toward each other (Hughes, 1987). The patterns struck by the education reform acts of England and New Zealand could well be prototypes of the educational structures that states[1] in Australia and the United States are seeking.

In comparing the four countries, we see similar policies being used concurrently for similar and different ends. Local management of schools and family choice are being used in all countries to bring about greater efficiency in the system by inducing market-like forces. In the United States, largely because of constitutional protections, efficiency must be achieved while a degree of equity is retained. Thus, in the United States, efficiency is being pursued through school site management and family choice within a general policy of comprehensive schools. The situation is not so clear in Australia and New Zealand. There is considerable concern among some analysts that Australia's policy of supporting private schools is leading toward a selective system (Potts, 1999) in the absence of such protections as are provided in the U. S. Constitution. There is also some evidence that the schools of New Zealand are becoming more homogeneous in socioeconomic characteristics (Fiske & Ladd, 2000).

Whitty, Power, and Halpin (1998), in a comparative study of the four countries we have examined, along with Sweden, expressed strong concern over the apparent injection of greater inequity into reformed systems of education. They concluded, however, that

We have identified a number of developments that might help to provide a context in which to construct a truly public education system. Bearing in mind the negative effects of the reforms we have described in this book, we believe that a genuinely revitalized civil society has some potential to counter-balance the state and prevent it dominating and atomizing the rest of society. This could provide the conditions for . . .an articulation between the particular and the universal, a forum, if you like, for creating unity without denying specificity. (p. 141)

The education systems of the United States and England were among the most decentralized in the world. Thus, it may come as no surprise to observers of the international scene that the two countries are centralizing some functions that have been traditionally left to the periphery. The fact that they are also decentralizing to schools and parents some functions that had been the province of school districts and local education authorities may, on the surface, appear to be inconsistent with their centralizing initiatives. This is not necessarily the case, however. Cummings and Riddell (1994) warned against confusing the requirements for macro and micro levels of education policy. England and the United States appear to be centralizing macro policy (setting a national curriculum and standards) and decentralizing micro policy (the organization and management of schools and the placement of pupils therein).

Australia and New Zealand had highly centralized school systems—Australia at the state level and New Zealand at the national level. In Australia, further centralization is taking place in the development of curriculum frameworks and in assessment, the federal level having been assigned some new responsibility for these functions, which had previously been solely the province of the states. At the same time, Australian states (some more rapidly than others) are shifting significant authority and responsibility to the school level and have increased parental and community participation in decision making at that level. New Zealand has kept much of the responsibility for

---

[1]The State of Virginia did embrace in 1992 a package of reforms similar to those in place in England, and the State of South Australia appears to be on the verge of doing likewise.

curriculum development and assessment at the national level, although the role of professional educators in these functions has been reduced. Authority removed from the center in New Zealand has been placed directly with school trustees and school principals. Parental and community influence has been strengthened through empowering parents and citizens to elect school trustees, to serve as trustees, and to choose schools for their children to attend. Like England and the United States, Australia and New Zealand are maintaining control of macro policy at the center and delegating responsibility for micro policy.

After two decades of reform efforts, and with only modest progress to show for it, American observers may be amazed, and perhaps a bit envious, at the speed and relative ease with which the other three countries adopted their reform programs, which have now been in operation for a full decade or more. Only the State of Kentucky has come close to matching their record in the United States, and its quick action was spurred by judicial intervention. Differences in size and complexity may be part of the explanation, but probably even more important are the differences in the structures of government, to be discussed further in Chapter 2. Unlike the United States, the other three countries have parliamentary forms of government and adhere much more closely to the tenets of political party discipline. The political party in the majority in the three countries selects the executive—that is, the prime minister—and sets the policy agenda. With division of powers, as in the United States, different political parties frequently hold the executive and legislative branches, and the two legislative houses themselves may likewise be divided. Because our political parties are more coalitions of interest groups than ideologically driven, party discipline is weaker, allowing for crossover voting on almost any issue. The parliamentary form of government allows for greater speed in making decisions and produces policy that is more pure from an ideological

perspective, but it may also sacrifice full consultation and overlook minority opinion. For example, in England and New Zealand and in the State of Victoria in Australia, teachers and teachers unions were left out of the deliberation process on education reforms, and there has been concern, backed by some evidence, that the reforms adopted may be contributing to greater social inequalities (Whitty, Power, & Halpin, 1998). Because of the broad consensus required to get legislation passed, coupled with protections offered by the Bill of Rights and an active judiciary monitoring them, such results are less likely in the United States (OECD, 1994), but the process of consultation requires much time. Nevertheless, given the many cultural similarities among the four nations, the reform accomplishments of England, New Zealand, and Australia (and those of other countries not considered) provide policy makers in the United States with invaluable empirical evidence on the possible impact of a variety of policy strategies under consideration here.

GUIDES FOR SCHOOL FINANCE POLICY

In analyzing the situations in England, Australia, New Zealand, and the United States with the aid of the framework presented in Figure 1.3, we offer a number of propositions as guides to formulating education policy in general and school finance policy in particular.

Proposition 1. The optimal provision of educational services for a society requires the *distribution* of authority among government, the teaching profession, and families.

Proposition 2. Consensus on what is the optimal provision of educational services is dynamic, shifting over time in response to changes in social, economic, political, technological, and ideological contexts.

Proposition 3. The family generally has the most intimate knowledge about, and caring concern, for the child and is accordingly the preferred "spokesperson" for the welfare of the child.

Proposition 4. The teaching profession holds the technical expertise relevant to schooling and is best qualified to make decisions about the organization and administration of educational services.

Proposition 5. Societal concerns are paramount where there are significant spillover benefits from education and where there are redistributive and intergenerational considerations.

Proposition 6. Centralization of authority over education policy decisions reduces the realization of individual interests, increases social stress, and makes decision-making and implementation more complex.

Proposition 7. Decentralization of authority over education policy increases inequity in the allocation of human and economic resources to the provision of educational services.

Proposition 8. Decentralizing authority over education policy increases heterogeneity and reduces social integration, but decentralizing decision making may enhance efficiency.

Proposition 9. Policies that promote equality have their greatest impact when they are established at a high level of social aggregation, but centralized authority is likely to lead to greater bureaucratization and to a reduction in system efficiency.

Proposition 10. The policy objectives of equity (equality) and fraternity require the involvement of government in decisions related to the allocation of resources and curriculum definition.

Proposition 11. The policy objectives of liberty and efficiency can best be realized through market-like mechanisms such as school choice and school-based decision making.

Proposition 12. Realization of the policy objective of efficiency may be furthered when the teaching profession plays a prominent role in making decisions about how educational services will be produced and how school-level resources will be deployed through the process of school-based decision making.

A better understanding of the outcomes when various propositions are implemented is essential to the development of informed policy with respect to education. Analyses and evaluations of the many "natural experiments" that take place around the world constitute an important part of the research that is needed. Because most developed Western nations face similar social and economic pressures, but with different policy priorities and government structures, important insights into relationships among structures of governance, policy priorities, and policy outcomes can be gained through cross-country comparisons. Education policy makers should also continue to be alert to, and to be guided by, the experiences of other information-age organizations in the public and private sectors.

SUMMARY

In this chapter, we described the social and economic forces that launched the current education reform movement and their impact on priorities given to core national values that affect education policy. Our intent has been to reframe the debate over the appropriate allocation of power and authority to make education decisions. We want to move the discussion beyond simplistic doctrine-driven disputes and to focus on the critical questions of what should be loosely organized and what should be tightly controlled at various levels of the system. Agreeing on acceptable allocation patterns of authority is a dynamic process, that varies over time and among cultures according to the priorities that these cultures assign to fundamental social and personal values. The nature of values and their impact on individual and societal decision making was discussed.

A framework presented for analyzing the allocation of power and authority in a system of schools provided a vehicle for evaluating alternative patterns of power distribution. The model depicts the political–economic structure as a grid of decisions (who gets what, when, and how) and decision makers (society/government, the teaching profession, and the family/client). The model was applied to the historical evolution of education governance in the United States and to the current situations in England, New Zealand, and Australia. The analysis suggested a number of propositions as guides to policy formulation concerning the design of formal structures for making decisions about education and the allocation of ultimate authority among decision makers within these structures.

ACTIVITIES

1. Examine the education decision matrix at the center of the generic model of education policy development (Figure 1.3). Fill in each blank cell with the decisions that can best be made by each category of decision maker for each decision type: For example, indicate which resource allocation decisions can best be made by society, which by the teaching profession, and which by the family.
2. Numerous proposals have been put forth for reforming education. Discuss each of the following proposals in terms of the generic model of the political–economic system of education policy development presented in Figure 1.3. For each proposal, describe the change from the status quo in the allocation of decision-making authority and in the relative priorities of the five values: liberty, equality, fraternity, efficiency, and economic growth.
   - Family choice of public schools.

   - Unconstrained educational vouchers.
   - Tax credits or deductions for private school tuition.
   - Professional control over admission to the profession.
   - Career ladders for teachers.
   - School-based decision making.
   - Full state funding of schooling.
   - State achievement testing to determine successful completion of high school.
3. Locate data on changing demographic characteristics of people served by schools within a large district or a state. What social and economic trends exert pressure on schools to alter programs in ways to improve student achievement in this setting?
4. If you are studying school finance with classmates from other nations, compare experiences and responses to Activities 1 and 2 from the perspectives of policy makers in those nations.
5. McGinn and Street (1986, cited on pages 28–29) wrote,

   > [C]ompetition and markets can contribute to social justice in circumstances where there is a relatively equitable balance of powers among the participants in the competition or market. . . . A strong state must first achieve some minimal degree of social equity so that decentralization can lead to genuine participation.

   - Describe policies that a strong state might pursue to "achieve some minimal degree of social equity so that decentralization can lead to genuine participation."
   - McGinn and Street used the term *state* in a generic sense. With respect to the United States, at what level can the "minimal degree of social equity" be guaranteed most effectively: federal, state, or local? What is the rationale for your answer?

REFERENCE LIST

Anderson, D. S. (1993). Public schools in decline: Implications of the privatization of schools in Australia. In H. Beare & W. L. Boyd (Eds.), *Restructuring schools: An international perspective on the movement to transform the control and performance of schools* (pp. 184–199). Washington, DC: Falmer.

Archer, M. S. (1984). *Social origins of educational systems*. London: SAGE Publications.

Bacharach, S. B., & Shedd, J. B. (1989). Power and empowerment: The constraining myths and emerging structures of teacher unionism. In J. Hannaway & R. Crowson (Eds.), *The politics of reforming school administration* (pp. 139–160). New York: Falmer.

Banfield, E. C. (1970). *The unheavenly city: The nature and future of our urban crisis*. Boston: Little, Brown.

Banfield, E. C. (1974). *The unheavenly city revisited*. Boston: Little, Brown.

Beare, H., & Boyd, W. L. (1993). Introduction. In H. Beare & W. L. Boyd (Eds.), *Restructuring schools: An international perspective on the movement to transform the control and performance of schools* (pp. 2–11). Washington, DC: Falmer.

Berne, R., & Stiefel, L. (1983). Changes in school finance equity: A national perspective. *Journal of Education Finance, 8*, 419–435.

Benson, C. E. (1978). *The economics of public education* (3rd ed.). Boston: Houghton Mifflin.

Boyd, W. L. (1984). Competing values in educational policy and governance: Australian and American developments. *Educational Administration Review, 2* (2), 4–24.

Boyd, W. L. (1987). Balancing public and private schools: The Australian experience and American implications. In W. L. Boyd & D. Smart (Eds.), *Educational policy in Australia and America: Comparative perspectives* (pp. 163–183). New York: Falmer.

Bridge, R. G. (1976). Parent participation in school innovations. *Teachers College Record, 77*, 366–384.

Butterworth, G., & Butterworth, S. (1998). *Reforming education: The New Zealand experience, 1984–1996*. Palmerston North, New Zealand: Dunmore.

Butts, R. F. (1955). *Assumptions underlying Australian education*. Melbourne, Australia: Australian Council for Educational Research.

Caldwell, B. J. (2001). *Setting the stage for real educational reform in Australia*. Paper presented at the First International Conference on Education Reform, organized by the Office of the National Education Commission of Thailand, Bangkok, July 30–August 2.

Caldwell, B. J. (1998). *Administrative and regulatory mechanisms affecting school autonomy in Australia*. Canberra, Australia: Department of Employment, Education, Training and Youth Affairs.

Caldwell, B. J. (1993). Paradox and uncertainty in the governance of education. In H. Beare & W. L. Boyd (Eds.), *Restructuring schools: An international perspective on the movement to transform the control and performance of schools* (pp. 158–173). Washington, DC: Falmer.

Caldwell, B. J., & Spinks, J. M. (1998). *Beyond the self-managing school*. London: Falmer.

Callahan, R. E. (1962). *Education and the cult of efficiency: A study of the social forces that have shaped the administration of the public schools*. Chicago: University of Chicago Press.

Chubb, J. E., & Moe, T. M. (1985). *Politics, markets, and the organization of schools* (Project Report No. 85-A15). Stanford, CA: Stanford University School of Education, Institute for Research on Educational Finance and Governance.

Chubb, J. E., & Moe, T. M. (1990). *Politics, markets and America's schools*. Washington, DC: The Brookings Institution.

Clune, W. H. (1993). The shift from equity to adequacy in school finance. *The World and I, 8* (9), 389–405.

Clune, W. H. (1995). Accelerated education as a remedy for high-poverty schools. *University of Michigan Journal of Law Reform, 28*, (3), 655–680.

Cohn, E. (1997). The rate of return to schooling in Canada. *Journal of Education Finance, 23*, 193–206.

Coleman, J. S., & Hoffer, T. (1987). *Public and private high schools: The impact of communities*. New York: Basic Books.

Coons, J. E., & Sugarman, S. D. (1978). *Education by choice: The case for family control*. Berkeley, CA: University of California Press.

Cremin, L. A. (1976). *Public education*. New York: Basic Books.

Cummings, W. K., & Riddell, A. (1994). Alternative policies for the finance, control, and delivery of basic education. *International Journal of Education Research, 21*, 751–828.

Department of Education and Science. (1978). *The Department of Education and Science—a brief guide*. London: The Department.

Dewey, J. (1916). *Democracy and education*. New York: Macmillan.

Drucker, P. F. (1980). *Managing in turbulent times.* New York: Harper & Row.

Drucker, P. F. (1989). *The new realities: In government and politics, in economics and business, in society and world view.* New York: Harper & Row.

Easton, D. A. (1965). *A systems analysis of political life.* New York: Wiley.

The education reform act. (1988). London: Her Majesty's Stationery Office.

Elmore, R. F. (1993). School decentralization: Who gains? Who loses? In J. Hannaway & M. Carnoy (Eds.), *Decentralization and school improvement* (pp. 33–54). San Francisco: Jossey-Bass.

Elmore, R. F., & McLaughlin, M. W. (1988). *Steady work: Policy, practice, and the reform of American education* (Report No. R-3574-NIE/RC). Santa Monica, CA: The RAND Corporation.

Farrar, E., DeSanctis, J. E., & Cohen, D. K. (1980, Fall). Views from below: Implementation research in education. *Teachers College Record,* 77–100.

Fiske, E. B., & Ladd, H. F. (2000). *When schools compete: A cautionary tale.* Washington, DC: The Brookings Institution Press.

Foster, W. P. (1986). *Paradigms and promises: New approaches to educational administration.* Buffalo, NY: Prometheus.

Galbraith, J. K. (1992). *The culture of contentment.* Boston: Houghton Mifflin.

Getzels, J. W. (1957). Changing values challenge the schools. *School Review, 65,* 91–102.

Getzels, J. W. (1978). The school and the acquisition of values. In R. W. Tyler (Ed.), *From youth to constructive adult life: The role of the school* (pp. 43–66). Berkeley, CA: McCutchan.

Guthrie , J. W., Garms, W. I., & Pierce, L. C. (1988). *School finance and education policy: Enhancing educational efficiency, equality and choice.* Englewood Cliffs, NJ: Prentice-Hall.

Hancock, G., Kirst, M. W., & Grossman, D. L. (Eds.). (1983). *Contemporary issues in educational policy: Perspectives from Australia and USA.* Canberra, Australia: Australian Capital Territory Schools Authority.

Hodgkinson, C. (1983). *The philosophy of leadership.* Oxford, England: Basil Blackwell.

Hodgkinson, H. (1991). Reform versus reality. *Phi Delta Kappan, 73,* 9–16.

Hodgkinson, H. (1993). Keynote address. In S. Elam (Ed.), *The state of the nation's public schools: A con-*ference report (pp. 194–208). Bloomington, IN: Phi Delta Kappa.

Hogan, M. (1984). *Public vs. private schools: Funding and direction in Australia.* Ringwood, Victoria, Australia: Penguin.

Hoy, W. K., & Miskel, C. G. (1991). *Educational administration: Theory, research and practice* (4th ed.). New York: McGraw-Hill.

Hughes, P. (1987). Reorganization in education in a climate of changing social expectations: A commentary. In W. L. Boyd & D. Smart (Eds.), *Educational policy in Australia and America: Comparative perspectives* (pp. 295–309). New York: Falmer.

Iannaccone, L. (1985). Excellence: An emergent educational issue. *Politics of Education Bulletin, 12,* 1–8.

Iannaccone, L. (1988). From equity to excellence: Political context and dynamics. In W. L. Boyd & C. T. Kerchner (Eds.), *The politics of excellence and choice in education* (pp. 49–65). New York: Falmer.

Kahne, J. (1994). Democratic communities, equity, and excellence: A Deweyan reframing of educational policy analysis. *Educational Evaluation and Policy Analysis, 16,* 233–248.

Koppich, J. E., & Guthrie, J. W. (1993). Ready, A.I.M., Reform: Building a model of education reform and "high politics." In H. Beare & W. L. Boyd (Eds.), *Restructuring schools: An international perspective on the movement to transform the control and performance of schools* (pp. 12–28). Washington, DC: Falmer.

Kuhn, T. S. (1970). *The structure of scientific revolutions* (2nd ed.). Chicago: University of Chicago Press.

Ladd, H. F., and Hansen, J. S. (Eds.). (1999). *Making money matter: Financing America's schools.* Washington, CD: National Academy Press.

Langemann, E. C. (1999). The changing meaning of a continuing challenge: Will the scholarly unraveling of education's "black box" enlarge the concept of access? *Education Week, 18* (20), 47–49.

Lawton, D. (1992). *Education and politics in the 1990s: Conflict or consensus?* London: Falmer.

Lawton, S. B. (1993). A decade of reform in Canada: Encounters with the octopus, the elephant, and the five dragons. In H. Beare & W. L. Boyd (Eds.), *Restructuring schools: An international perspective on the movement to transform the control and performance of schools.* (pp. 86–105). Washington, DC: Falmer.

Levacic, R. (1999). *New Labour education policy with respect to schools: Is the Third Way coherent and dis-*

tinctive? Paper presented at the University of Melbourne, Australia.

Levin, B. (1987). The courts as educational policy-makers in the USA. In W. L. Boyd & D. Smart (Eds.), *Educational policy in Australia and America: Comparative perspectives* (pp. 100–128). New York: Falmer.

Locke, J. (1690/1956). *The second treatise of government.* Oxford, England: Basil Blackwell.

Louden, L. W., & Browne, R. K. (1993). Developments in education policy in Australia: A perspective on the 1980s. In H. Beare & W. L. Boyd (Eds.), *Restructuring schools: An international perspective on the movement to transform the control and performance of schools* (pp. 106–135). Washington, DC: Falmer.

Macpherson, R. J. S. (1993). The reconstruction of New Zealand education: A case of "high politics" reform? In H. Beare & W. L. Boyd (Eds.), *Restructuring schools: An international perspective on the movement to transform the control and performance of schools* (pp. 69–85). Washington, DC: Falmer.

McGaw, B. (1994). Effectiveness or economy. *Australian Council for Educational Research (ACER) Newsletter Supplement*, March.

McGinn, N., & Street, S. (1986). Educational decentralization: Weak state or strong state? *Comparative Education Review, 30,* 471–490.

McNeil, L. M. (1986). *Contradictions of control: School structure and school knowledge.* New York: Routledge, Chapman and Hall.

Ministerial Council on Education, Employment, Training and Youth Affairs (MCEETYA). (1998). *National report on schooling in Australia 1998.* Melbourne, Australia: Author.

Mitchell, D. E. (1989). Alternative approaches to labor–management relations for public school teachers and administrators. In J. Hannaway & R. Crowson (Eds.), *The politics of reforming school administration* (pp. 161–181). New York: Falmer.

Morris, W. (Ed.). (1969). *The American heritage dictionary of the English language.* New York: American Heritage.

Murphy, J. T. (1983). School administrators besieged: A look at Australian and American education. In G. Hancock, M. W. Kirst, & D. L. Grossman (Eds.), *Contemporary issues in educational policy: Perspectives from Australia and USA* (pp. 77–96). Canberra, Australia: Australian Capital Territory Schools Authority and Curriculum Development Centre.

Naisbitt, J. (1982). *Megatrends: Ten new directions transforming our lives.* New York: Warner.

Naisbitt, J., & Aburdene, P. (1990). *Megatrends, 2000: Ten new directions for the 1990s.* New York: Morrow.

National Commission on Excellence in Education. (1983). *A nation at risk: The imperative for educational reform.* Washington, DC: U.S. Department of Education.

National Center for Education Statistics. (Various years). *Digest of education statistics.* Washington, DC: U.S. Department of Education.

Nyberg, D. (1977). Education as community expression. *Teachers College Record, 79,* 205–223.

Nyberg, D. (1981). *Power over power: What power means in ordinary life, how it is related to acting freely, and what it can contribute to a renovated ethics of education.* Ithaca, NY: Cornell University Press.

Nyberg, D. (1993). *The varnished truth: Truth telling and deceiving in ordinary life.* Chicago: University of Chicago Press.

OECD (Organization for Economic Cooperation and Development). (1994). *School: A Matter of Choice.* Paris: OECD.

Paquette, J. (1991). Why should I stay in school? Quantifying private educational returns. *Journal of Education Finance, 16,* 458–477.

Parsons, T. (1951). *The social system.* New York: Free Press.

Partridge, P. H. (1968). *Society, schools and progress in Australia.* Oxford, England: Pergamon Press.

Picot, B. (1988). *Administering for excellence*, Report of the Task Force to Review Education Administration (Brian Picot, chairperson). Wellington, New Zealand: Government Printer.

Pierce, B., & Welch, F. (1996). Changes of structures of wages. In E. A. Hanushek & D. W. Jorgenson (Eds.), *Improving America's schools: The role of incentives* (pp. 53–73). Washington, DC: National Academy Press.

Potts, A. (1999). Public and private schooling in Australia: Some historical and contemporary considerations. *Phi Delta Kappan, 81* (3), 242–245.

Poverty and education. (1992). *Education Week, 11,16,* 5.

Ravitch, D. (1985). *The schools we deserve: Reflections on the educational crises of our times.* New York: Basic Books.

Rokeach, M. (1973). *The nature of human values.* New York: Free Press.

Samuelson, P. A., & Nordhaus, W. D. (1989). *Economics* (13th ed.). New York: McGraw-Hill.

Slater, R. O. (1993). On centralization, decentralization and school restructuring: A sociological perspective. In H. Beare & W. L. Boyd (Eds.), *Restructuring schools: An international perspective on the movement to transform the control and performance of schools* (pp. 174–183). Washington, DC: Falmer.

Smith, M. S., and O'Day, J. O. (1991). Systemic school reform. In S. H. Fuhrman and B. Malen, (Eds.), *The politics of curriculum and testing: The 1990 politics of education yearbook* (pp. 233–267). New York: Falmer.

Toffler, A. (1980). *The third wave*. New York: Bantam.

Toffler, A. (1990). *Powershift: Knowledge, wealth, and violence at the edge of the 21st century*. New York: Bantam.

Tyack, D. B. (1974). *The one best system: A history of American urban education*. Cambridge, MA: Harvard University Press.

Tyack, D. B. (1993). School governance in the United States: Historical puzzles and anomalies. In J. Hannaway & M. Carnoy (Eds.), *Decentralization and school improvement* (pp. 1–32). San Francisco: Jossey-Bass.

U.S. Bureau of the Census. (2000a). *Current population reports*. Washington, DC: U.S. Government Printing Office.

U.S. Bureau of the Census. (2000b). *March current population surveys, 1998*. Washington, DC: U.S. Government Printing Office.

Weiler, H. N. (1993). Control versus legitimation: The politics of ambivalence. In J. Hannaway & M. Carnoy (Eds.), *Decentralization and school improvement* (pp. 55–83). San Francisco: Jossey-Bass.

Whitty, G., Power, S., & Halpin, D. (1998). *Devolution and choice in education: The school, the state, and the market*. Melbourne, Australia: The Australian Council for Educational Research.

Wirt, F. M. (1987). National Australia–United States education: A commentary. In W. L. Boyd & D. Smart (Eds.), *Educational policy in Australia and America: Comparative perspectives* (pp. 129–137). New York: Falmer.

Wise, A. E. (1979). *Legislated learning: The bureaucratization of the American classroom*. Berkeley, CA: University of California Press.

Wise, A. E. (1988). Two conflicting trends in school reform: Legislated learning revisited. *Phi Delta Kappan, 69*, 328–332.

chapter 2

EDUCATION DECISION MAKING
IN A MIXED ECONOMY

Issues and Questions

- *Achieving High Standards with Equity and Efficiency*: What political and economic forces are at work encouraging and impeding the realization of high standards for all children?
- *Private- and Public-sector Decisions*: What economic and political processes are employed by the public and private sectors in making decisions about investments in education and about the nature of educational services to be provided?
- *Human-capital Theory*: Why are people motivated to invest in their own development, and in that of their children to improve marketable knowledge and skills?
- *Education as Both a Private and a Public Good*: Do the benefits that derive from schooling accrue solely to the individual, or are there also societal benefits that justify public support?
- *Economic Decisions*: In what ways do households and businesses influence decisions about what goods and services are produced, how these commodities are produced, and for whom goods and services are produced?
- *Political Decisions*: Why are policies needed to govern individual and societal behavior, and what theories and models enhance our understanding of public policy making?
- *Policy Analysis*: What methods are borrowed from social science research to help us understand school finance policy goals and effects?

Education deals with matters related to the heart and soul of the individual citizen, and these same matters are critical to the political and economic welfare of the nation and its security. To ensure that both individual and societal demands for schooling are met, decisions about the provision of education are made in both the public and the private sectors. Decisions are made in the public sector through political processes within governments, whereas decisions are made in the private sector by individuals through markets. Although the actors are the same, decisions made through governments are quite different from those made through markets because the influence is distributed among actors quite differently in the two sectors.

Politics is the process by which values are allocated within society (Easton, 1965) whereas *economics* is the study of the allocation of scarce resources. Economics is concerned with the production, distribution and consumption of commodities (Samuelson & Nordhaus, 1989). Achieving efficiency in the use of resources is the objective of economics, efficiency being defined as securing the highest level of social satisfaction at the least cost of scarce resources. Obviously, one's value priorities strongly influence one's judgment about what is an efficient allocation of material resources. Because these priorities vary greatly among individuals, there is a continuing interaction between economics and politics, the public finance of education being a major point of interaction. Decisions about the public finance of education are made in political arenas, but the decisions made in those arenas have strong economic implications for individuals and businesses as well as for communities, states, and the nation. Individuals and businesses respond independently to political decisions by deciding whether to participate in government programs (such as schooling) or to supplement government programs—or even substitute for them—by purchasing services provided by the private sector.

It is not possible to fully understand the financing of elementary and secondary schooling without also understanding how decisions about school finance are made and how public and private resources are transformed into the realization of societal and individual aspirations through education. It is the purpose of this chapter to provide a basis for such understanding by describing the functioning of the economic and political arenas in which those decisions are made and implemented. The issues of when and how governments should become involved in the process are also considered. We begin with a discussion of the theory of human capital. This theory explains why individuals invest in improving themselves and why governments invest in improving population quality in general. In addition, human-capital theory provides a major rationale for keeping education high on the public policy agenda.

THE THEORY OF HUMAN CAPITAL

Classical economists attributed physical output to three factors of production: land, labor, and capital. Modern economists have either treated land as a constant or subsumed it under capital, leaving labor and capital as the variables in their formulas for predicting the gross production of an economy and for assessing its efficiency. *Labor* represents the human resource that goes into production. *Capital* is the produced means of production, such as computers, school buildings, and infrastructure (e.g., roads and utilities).

In their analyses, economists had originally measured only the quantitative aspects of the two factors of production (that is, aggregate hours for labor and aggregate hours for equipment used in production). In effect, they considered each factor to be qualitatively homogeneous. Theodore W. Schultz (1963, 1981), who received the Nobel Prize in economics in 1979 for his work with developing countries, challenged this assumption, claiming that it is essential to see the heterogeneity of labor and capital and how they complement one another in production. He noted that particular forms of material capital increase the demand for particular human skills. Schultz's work sparked renewed interest in human-capital theory and focused attention on the economic importance of education. The *human-capital* approach assumes that schooling endows an individual with knowledge and skills that enable him or her to be more productive and thereby to receive higher earnings. This is, of course, beneficial to the individual. The accumulation of benefits derived by all workers is beneficial to society as a whole through greater total production, higher tax yields, and spillover benefits that contribute to a generally improved quality of life for all.

Schultz (1963, p. viii) observed that the concepts commonly used at the time to "measure capital and labor were close to being empty in explaining the increases in production that occur over time." He was referring to the fact that quantitative increases in labor and physical capital explained less than one-third of the rate of economic growth in the United States between 1929 and 1957; moreover, the trend of their explanatory power was downward.

In attempting to explain the cause of the remaining two-thirds of U.S. economic growth, called "the residual," Schultz drew an analogy between additions of stock to physical capital and increases in the amount of education available in the population at large. Schultz's (1963) thesis was that traditional measures of labor and capital understated the true investment. He concluded that the unexplained economic growth "originates out of forms of capital that have not been measured and consists mainly of human capital. . . . [T]he economic capabilities of man are predominantly a produced means of production and . . . most of the differences in earnings are a consequence of differences in the amounts that have been invested in people" (pp. 64–65).

Schultz was not the first to observe the relationship between earnings and personal skills. Indeed, human capital has been recognized as essential to economic progress since the beginning of economics as a field of study. In his *Wealth of Nations*, published in 1776, Adam Smith included this concept in his definition of fixed capital. In referring to the acquired abilities of all members of the society, he wrote,

> The acquisition of such talents, by the maintenance of the acquirer during his education, study, or apprenticeship, always costs a real expense, which is a capital fixed and realized, as it were, in his person. Those talents, as they make a part of his fortune, so do they likewise of that of the society to which he belongs. The improved dexterity of a workman may be considered in the same light as a machine or instrument of trade which facilitates and abridges labour, and which, though it costs a certain expense, repays that expense with a profit. (Smith, 1993, p. 166)

Smith concluded that "The difference between the wages of skilled labour and those of common labour is founded upon this principle" (p. 98).

Despite the early recognition of the concept of human capital, and of education as a formal means for developing it, the investment aspects of education were almost completely neglected by economists through the nineteenth and the first half of the twentieth centuries (Blaug, 1970). Alfred Marshall (1961), in his *Principles of Economics* (first published in 1890), rejected the notion of including the acquired skills of a population as part of the wealth or capital of an economy because of the difficulties in measuring them. He did, however, accept Smith's analogy of an educated person being like an expensive machine, claiming that the motives that induce people to invest principal capital *in* their children's education are similar to those that inspire the accumulation of material capital *for* their children (Marshall, 1961, p. 619). Marshall also supported the spending of public and private funds on the education of the masses. Without it, he felt that there would be an underinvestment in education as long as the financial means to acquire education were unequally distributed among the population.

In the twentieth century, Maynard Keynes linked national output to the behavior of households and enterprises as distinct economic agents. The precise nature of the goods purchased by these two agents was irrelevant to his purpose, which led to the widely held view that the contrast between consumption and investment depends on which agent makes the decision to purchase, rather than on the type of good being purchased. Thus national income accounting, an outgrowth of Keynesian macroeconomics, treated education as consumption because it is an expenditure made by households or by government acting on their behalf out of taxes collected from them (Blaug, 1970).

The contemporary interest in human-capital theory brings us full circle; education is again treated as investment. This reorientation was possible because early modern proponents of the theory, such as T. W. Schultz (1963), Becker (1964), Dennison (1962), and Kuznets (1966), found satisfactory means for measuring investment in human capital. Through their work, the importance of education as a vehicle of economic development and national economic policy has become firmly established.

More recently, Hanushek and Kim (1995) took Schultz's qualitative differentiation theory one step further. In addition to the quantity of education achieved by a country's population, they investigated the impact of differences in the quality of that education on national economic growth. They used as their quality measures comparative tests of mathematics and scientific skills of school children from thirty-nine countries participating in various international testing programs over the past three decades. They concluded that quality of education has a "consistent, stable, and strong influence on economic growth . . . . [T]he impact of quality indicates that one standard deviation in mathematics and science skills trans-

lates into one percentage point in average annual real growth" (p. 34).

These studies show that education contributes significantly to national economic growth, but they do not address the *adequacy* of investment in education. To address the adequacy issue, economists use another analytical procedure: rate-of-return analysis. With respect to education, rate-of-return analysis is intended to inform policy makers about whether to spend on different kinds of programs (Benson, 1978, p. 91). Rate-of-return analysis compares the profit (increased earnings) to the expense of acquiring knowledge and skills, including earnings forgone in the process.

In a free market, when supply and demand for persons possessing a particular set of knowledge and skills are in equilibrium, the rate of return approximates that which is generally expected from other types of investments. If the rate is much higher, there is an apparent shortage of persons with these skills, and this enables them to command higher than expected wages. This encourages more people to acquire similar training and enter the workforce until wages and the rate of return drop to the expected level. If, on the other hand, the rate of return is much lower than that which can be obtained from other investments, there is a surplus of persons with similar skills—more than the market can absorb. Competition for employment drives wages down, discouraging people from acquiring such skills until supply again equals demand and the rate of return from earnings over expenditures equals the expected. Market effects may be dampened by constraints placed on them through such vehicles as union contracts, which are quite common among public school enterprises.

Evaluating social policy by computing internal rates of return for investments in education was the focus of the pioneering work by Becker (1964). He estimated the social rate of return for white male college graduates to be between 10 and 13 percent. Assuming that rates for college dropouts and nonwhites would be lower, he estimated the rate for all college entrants to be between 8 and 11 percent. Becker (1964, p. 121) concluded, "The rates on business capital and college education seem, therefore, to fall within the same range." Rates of return for high school graduates were higher, and they were highest for elementary school graduates. Becker cautioned, however, that adjustments for differential ability would probably reduce or eliminate the differences in rates among levels of schooling. As noted in Chapter 1, recent analyses by Pierce and Welch (1996) and Paquette (1991) suggest that higher rates of return are experienced primarily by persons holding a baccalaureate degree or higher.

Investments in human capital can be made privately by individuals or collectively by governments. No matter how the investments are made, some of the benefits received will be experienced personally by individuals, and other benefits will improve the general welfare collectively. In the next section, we examine the collective and private benefits of education and seek guidance for determining whether, when, and how governments and markets should be involved in the investment process.

EDUCATION: A PUBLIC AND A PRIVATE GOOD

It is consistent with human-capital theory to view education as both a public and a private good because it brings important benefits for society as well as for the individual. If public benefits were simply the sum of individual benefits, this would not constitute a problem. However, this is not the case. Frequently there are substantial differences between societal and individual interests. As noted by Marshall, full public interest would not be realized if provision of education were left solely to private vendors and to the ability of individuals to pay for education. Conversely, it is unlikely that the full private or individual interest would be satisfied if education were left solely to public

provision. Public provision through taxation is warranted when social benefits exceed private benefits. When private benefits predominate, user fees or full-cost tuition becomes appropriate.

Private Goods

Private goods are divisible, and their benefits are left primarily to their owners. If an individual desires a particular item or service, he or she can legally obtain it by negotiating an agreed-upon price with the current owner. The new owner can enjoy the item or service while those unable or unwilling to pay the price cannot. A good is "private" if someone who does not pay for it can be excluded from its use and enjoyment. This is known as the exclusion principle. Such goods are readily provided through the market system—that is, the private sector.

The private (or individual) benefits of education, whether it is provided by the public sector or the private sector, include the ability to earn more money and to enjoy a higher standard of living and a better quality of life. As part of this, educated persons are likely to be employed at more interesting jobs than are the less well educated. Schooling opens up the possibility of more schooling, which in turn leads to even better employment possibilities; long-term unemployment is much less likely. Similarly, educated persons, through knowledge and understanding of the arts and other manifestations of culture, and with greater resources at their disposal, are likely to have more options for the use of leisure time and are likely to use such time in more interesting ways. As informed consumers, they are likely to get more "mileage" out of their resources. Finally, better-educated persons are likely to enjoy a better diet and to have better health practices. This is likely to result in less sickness and in a longer productive life.

It would be possible for those unable or unwilling to pay for them to be excluded from educational opportunities. Thus schooling could be provided exclusively through the private sector, as it was before the organization of public schools during the nineteenth century. But there would be a number of socially undesirable external effects, because the public (or societal) benefits of publicly provided education would be lost or at least severely diminished.

Public Goods

Public goods are indivisible, yielding large and widespread benefits to the community and to society as a whole. Because these benefits are such that they cannot be limited to individuals willing to pay the price, it is unlikely that they would be provided fully through the market system in a satisfactory fashion. In other words, "public" or "collective" goods are those that violate the exclusion principle.

The public (or societal) benefits of the availability of both publicly and privately provided education include enlightened citizenship, which is particularly important to a democratic form of government. In projecting a common set of values and knowledge, schools can foster a sense of community and national identity and loyalty among a diverse population. A public school system can provide an effective network for identification and development of talent, spurring the creation of both cultural and technological innovations and providing the skilled workforce required for the efficient functioning of society. These results are believed to contribute to economic growth, higher tax revenues, and in a generally more vital and pleasant life for everyone.

These benefits are considered so important that public funds are used to provide for the schooling of nearly all of the school-age population in most developed countries. At the same time, parents who are not satisfied by public schools have the option of seeking alternative means of educating their children by paying tuition to private agencies while still paying taxes in support of the public schools.

Conflicting Concerns

Structuring the decision-making process for education becomes particularly complex because education is both a public and a private good. Procuring educational services incurs costs and produces benefits that accrue to individuals independently and, at the same time, incurs social costs and produces benefits that accrue to society collectively. Levin (1987) concluded that there is a potential dilemma when schools are expected to provide both public and private benefits:

> Public education stands at the intersection of two legitimate rights: [1] the right of a democratic society to assure its reproduction and continuous democratic functioning through providing a common set of values and knowledge and [2] the right of families to decide the ways in which their children will be molded and the types of influences to which their children will be exposed. To the degree that families have different political, social, and religious beliefs and values, there may be a basic incompatibility between their private concerns and the public functions of schooling. (p. 629)

A century earlier, Marshall (1961, p. 216) had observed, "There are few practical problems in which the economist has a more direct interest than those relating to the principles on which the expense of education of children should be divided between the State and the parents."

If education were exclusively a private good, it could be provided through the market without governmental intervention. Because education has many attributes of a public good, however, it is provided through publicly controlled institutions as well as through the market.

DECISION MAKING IN THE MARKET PLACE

In this section, we describe how resource allocation decisions are made through the market.

The section following this one describes political processes through which such decisions are made by governments.

The Private Sector

Five fundamental economic decisions that any society must make were incorporated into the generic model of the policy development process presented in Chapter 1 (Figure 1.3). These decisions are: (1) setting goals and objectives for the enterprise, (2) determining for whom services are to be provided, (3) determining the level of investment, (4) allocating resources to and among goods and services and (5) determining the means of production (Benson, 1978). In a capitalistic economy, the preference is to make such decisions through unrestrained or self-regulating markets. Figure 2.1 illustrates the circular flow of a monetary economy between two sets of actors, households and producers (or enterprises, to use Keynes's term). It is assumed that households own all resources (capital), whereas producers have the capacity to convert resources into finished goods and services.

Both households and the producers have something the other wants and needs. Producers need the resources controlled by households in order to produce finished goods and services. Households need the goods and services provided by the producers for survival (in the case of food and shelter) and for improved quality of life (in the case of many other goods). To facilitate the exchange, markets provide a means of communication. Producers (for example, private schools) acquire the resources they need through resource markets by making money income in the form of wages, rents, interest, and profits available to households (which include persons qualified to be teachers, bus drivers, maintenance workers, and so on). Households in turn use the money acquired through the sale of resources to purchase finished goods and services (such as private schooling) in product markets. It is these sales that provide producers with money to purchase resources from the households. And so the cycle continues.

Through markets, households and producers negotiate prices to be paid for resources and finished goods and services. The outcomes of these negotiations ultimately determine the five fundamental economic issues listed at the beginning of this section. Resources are scarce and unevenly distributed among households,

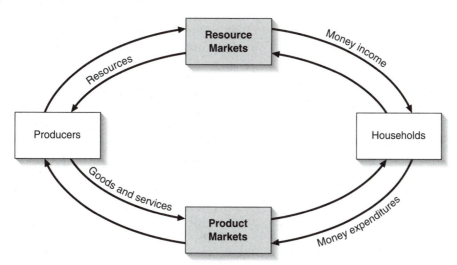

FIGURE 2.1. The Circular Flow of Resources in a Monetary Economy

whereas household wants are unlimited. This means that each household must prioritize its wants and satisfy as many of them as possible within the constraints of the resources it controls and the value of those resources. The value or price of resources (and products) depends on supply and demand.

Figure 2.2 illustrates the interaction between supply and demand as related to the number of teachers employed by schools and the amount paid for their services. The demand curve shows that there is an inverse relationship between the level of teacher salaries and the number of teachers that school districts are willing to employ. Conversely, the supply curve shows that the number of persons willing to take jobs as teachers is high when salaries are high and is low when salaries are low. Thus, if salaries are at P_1 as illustrated in Figure 2.2, there is a gap (Q_1 to Q_3) between the number of persons willing to work at that wage and the number of teachers that school districts want to employ. To close the gap, school districts must raise salaries to P_3 in order to attract the desired number of teachers (Q_3) or strike a compromise whereby the number of teachers to be employed is reduced to Q_2, for example, and the point that represents salaries

that districts willing to pay is raised to P_2. This requires a shift in strategy for organizing schools in the district. One strategy is to substitute technology for teachers. As teacher salaries increase, technological substitutes become relatively less expensive; thus, fewer teachers in large classes using sophisticated instructional technology may produce results similar to those of more teachers in small classes using little information technology. Alternatively, rather than purchasing instructional technology, a district may provide low-cost teacher aides to assist teachers in managing their large classes.

In the private sector, producers will produce only that on which they can make a reasonable profit, with prices established through the market serving as signals to producers and consumers alike. Profit depends on the amount of a good or a service that is sold, the price, and the cost of production. If the demand for a product is not sufficient for the producer to sell all units produced at a price above the cost of production, no profit can be made. Under such circumstances, the producer has three options: reduce the cost of production by adopting more efficient means, shift production to another product that can be sold for a profit, or go out of business. When conditions permit an above average profit for producing a given good, more producers are attracted into the field. The number of units produced increases to the point where supply equals demand. Competition forces prices down, returning the rate of profit to a normal range.

Each dollar controlled by each consuming household is a potential vote to be cast in favor of the production of one good or service over another or in favor of the product of one producer over the product of a competitor. The influence of a household over producers is directly proportional to the value of the resources controlled by the household. This poses ethical dilemmas about the distribution of wealth. The rich can make expenditures for improving the quality of their lifestyle while

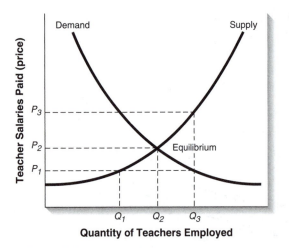

FIGURE 2.2. Supply and Demand Curves

the poor lack basic necessities. Also, development of highly efficient, low-cost technologies leads to reduction in the demand for labor, causing reductions in wages and/or widespread unemployment. The design and operation of highly sophisticated instruments and techniques is usually done by well-educated persons; thus the burden of unemployment and low wages is likely to fall disproportionately on those with little formal education. The issue of equity with respect to allocation of resources for education is discussed in Chapters 10 and 11.

The Public Sector and the Market

We do not rely solely on market mechanisms to make economic decisions, however. Over 40 percent of our gross national product (GNP) is distributed according to political decisions made by governments, such as municipalities and school districts. Governmental units differ from households and producers in the ways in which they answer economic questions and the criteria they use in arriving at their answers. Downs (1957, p. 282) identified government as the agency in the division of labor that has as its

proper function the maximization of social welfare. When results generated by free markets are ethically or economically unsatisfactory, government can be used as a tool of intervention to set things right (p. 292). Governments have the unique power to extract involuntary payments, called taxes, from households and producers, and the federal government controls the money supply on which both public and private sectors depend. Governmental programs and agencies are not profit-oriented and they rarely "go out of business." When they do, it is the result of political decisions and not of market forces, although conditions in the market may influence the political decision. Efficiency has not traditionally been an overriding objective of the public sector as it is in the private sector, although growing numbers of people think that it should be, given that governments collectively determine how more than 40 percent of the GNP is used in the United States. Thus efficiency of educational operations (which consume about 7 percent of the GNP) has become an important criterion in evaluating the progress of school reform.

Figure 2.3 inserts government (the public sector) into the center of the circular flow of a

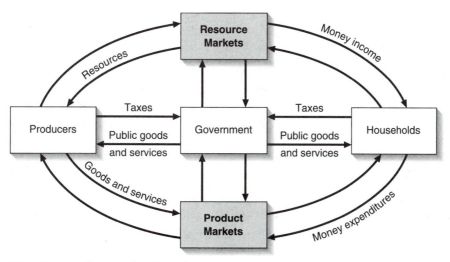

FIGURE 2.3. The Circular Flow of Resources, Including Government (the public sector)

monetary economy. As noted, government obtains money for its operations by levying taxes on producers and households. With this money, government acquires human and physical resources through resource markets and acquires goods and services through product markets. There are no separate markets for the private and public sectors. In the establishment of prices, government demands are factored into the resource and product markets along with private-sector demands. Thus there is not a unique market for school personnel, for example; school districts compete with businesses, professions, and other governmental units for desired human services. When the federal government borrows heavily from the financial market, interest rates go up for everyone alike—for the school district borrowing to build a schoolhouse and for the individual borrowing to buy an automobile or a home.

Governments produce some goods and services that are desired by households and producers. These include public schooling, national defense, fire and police protection, airports, harbor facilities, and roads. Typically, such services are neither distributed through the market nor "priced" through the market. The "price" of such goods and services is equivalent to their "cost," a political decision. "Efficiency" of public schools becomes an issue only when the electorate makes it an issue. By serving 90 percent of the potential clientele and having access to the power of taxation to meet their revenue needs, public schools take on many characteristics of a monopoly.

When government budgets are balanced at full employment, government purchases do not affect overall prices, even though prices for the specific goods purchased may increase as a consequence of the change in demand. If government is reckless in printing money (which only the federal government can do) or in borrowing for current operations (which, again, only the federal government can do), the resulting inflation from excess demand will distribute the burden of government to households in an unknown (though probably regressive) manner through inflation. Long-term borrowing by governments can be justified only for assets lasting more than a year and, in the case of the federal government, when the economy is at less than full employment and needs stimulating.

Because public-sector decisions are political and, ideally, political power is distributed evenly among the electorate (one person, one vote), the answers given to the five economic questions cited earlier differ markedly from the answers that would apply if the decisions were made through the private sector (market), where influence is distributed in proportion to the amount of resources controlled (that is, the rich have much influence and the poor have little). The greater relative power of the poor in the public sector than in the private sector leads to an equalitarian bias in decisions made in the public sector. The private sector has a bias toward efficient use of resources, as well as a libertarian bias to permit the exercise of individual preferences within the limits of resources available to each individual.

In making decisions about education, natural tensions exist between households, members of the teaching profession, and society. To the extent that decisions are made in the private sector, individuals and families can maximize their personal aspirations within the limits of their economic resources and according to individual value preferences. Professionals are free to provide or withhold services and to determine the nature of those services. But when decisions are made through the political process, individuals and groups of varying value orientations must negotiate a single solution, and their value preferences are likely to be compromised in the process.

Proponents of school-based decision making (to be discussed in Chapter 14) and family choice of schooling (to be discussed in Chapter 15) share the view that too many educational decisions are being made by government. Some of these proponents believe that this has led to an unwarranted emphasis on social values such as equity, making it hard to realize a variety of privately held values through public education; others believe that governmental operation of public schools has resulted in the inefficient use of resources committed. In contrast, supporters of governmental operation of schools fear that educational services would be even more inequitably distributed than they are now if schooling enterprises were privatized and that the sense of community (or fraternity) that binds us together as a people would be weakened.

POLITICAL DECISION MAKING

Any functioning group—be it the United States government, a state government, a business or industry, a voluntary or charitable association, a local school district, or a school—needs to agree on a set of rules under which it will operate. These rules are called *policies*, a concept that includes statutes in the case of government when the policies are formally adopted through a prescribed legislative process and local school board decisions that govern the behavior of employees, students, and members of the general public. Rules and regulations generated by a government agency, including school officials, under authorization of a law are also considered to be policies.

Policies establish the parameters within which the organization will function. They specify the activities that the organization will or will not do. Policies act to guide coherent action by channeling the thinking of employees and other members of the organization. They set constraints within which discretion can be exercised. They ensure that all partners in an endeavor have the same "marching orders," visions, and intentions (Kaufman & Herman, 1991).

The state and federal constitutions specify the formal procedures to be followed in adopting laws. But laws are usually written in quite broad terms, and they must be interpreted in

order to be implemented. The interpretation begins with the bureau within the executive branch of government given the responsibility for administering the law, such as state education departments and the U.S. Department of Education. Decisions made by bureaucrats to guide actions at lower levels of authority, and written in the form of regulations, are as much policy as the laws themselves. State law specifies general procedures to be followed by local school districts in formulating policy, although variation is permitted within prescribed limits. School districts may specify procedures to be followed by schools in setting policy, or they may let the schools establish their own procedures subject to district review and approval. Private organizations may go through formal incorporation, which specifies a corporate procedure to be followed in making decisions, or they may agree on a set of by-laws to guide corporate decision making. In the public sector, policies are usually (and preferably) written. Policies may, however, be informal, unwritten, and unstated agreements (norms) by which members of an organization are bound when they act on behalf of the organization.

Although constitutions, laws, charters, and by-laws spell out the formal steps to be followed in arriving at group decisions (that is, at policy), the human interactions in carrying out those steps are not specified. Often these interactions involve elaborate strategies, power plays, and intrigue that individuals and subgroups united by common interests employ to shape an organization's (or a government's) decisions. These interactions, whether simple or elaborate, can be referred to as "politics." Indeed, Hodgkinson (1983) has described politics as "administration by another name." Both the structure of the policy-making process and the politics employed within the structure are believed to influence policy outcomes (Dye, 1987).

In the United States, about 90 percent of the boys and girls enrolled in elementary and secondary schools are in schools operated by government (public schools). The other 10 percent are in schools operated independently or by religious and other not-for-profit organizations, but even these schools are monitored to varying degrees by governmental agencies and are formally chartered or incorporated by a governmental unit. Public schools, on the other hand, are strongly influenced by what goes on in the nongovernment sector through their dealings in "the market" and through formal and informal pressures brought to bear on governmental decision-making processes by individuals and private interest groups.

There is no overarching general theory of political decision making but, rather, a "grab bag" of heuristic theories and contrasting methods (Wirt & Kirst, 1982). Heuristic theory is a method of analytically separating and categorizing items in experience. Among the most useful theories for understanding policy related to school governance are institutionalism, incrementalism, group theory, elite theory, rationalism, and systems theory. These theories and models are complementary to one another. Each emphasizes a particular aspect of the policy-making process. Taken together, they provide a rather complete picture of the total process. Although these theories were developed primarily to describe policy formulation at the national level, they are fully applicable at the state level and can provide much insight into the making of policy at the school district level—and the school building level as well.

Institutionalism

Institutionalism focuses on the structure of the policy-making process in the belief that variations in structure result in variation among decisions made (Grodzins, 1966; Elazar, 1972; Walker, 1981). The discussion in Chapter 1 about the differences in policy making between parliamentary and executive governments is an example of the thinking of institutionalists.

Unlike most of the rest of the world, where education is the responsibility of the national government, education in the United States is characterized by the primacy of state governments and the delegation of authority to school districts. On the positive side, this arrangement has produced educational systems that are quite diverse, dynamic, and responsive to local conditions. On the negative side, the structure has resulted in gross financial and curricular inequities. Some districts operate schools that are unequaled in quality throughout the world; others operate schools that are an embarrassment to the profession and to the nation (Kozol, 1991). The devolved nature of school governance has, during the past several decades, impeded state and federal efforts to equalize educational opportunities in terms of finance, curricular offerings, and the integration of students and staff with respect to race, ethnicity, and national origin.

But the structure of educational governance has changed over the years, and it continues to change. An aspect of this change is reflected in Table 2.1, which shows the gradual increase of state and federal participation in the financing of public education and the decrease in reliance on local resources in the United States since 1920. During the early part of the twentieth century, state governments paid on average less than 20 percent of the cost of elementary and secondary education; school districts and/or local governments provided the rest. The state share grew steadily after 1930. By 1980, the total aggregate state aid of the 50 states exceeded revenue raised from local sources for the first time. Federal participation grew from virtually nothing at the beginning of the century to nearly 10 percent in 1980. Federal aid has since declined to 6.8 percent of all revenues for public schools, with states providing 48 percent and localities 45 percent (National Center for Education Statistics, 2001, Table 158).

Although financial support for schools is now shared nearly equally between state governments and school districts, schools are still operated by local school boards. In recent

TABLE 2.1.
Revenue Sources for Public Elementary and Secondary Schools, 1920–1998

Year	Total Revenue Sources (millions)[1]	Percentage of Total		
		Local	State	Federal
1920	$970	83.2	16.5	0.3
1930	$2,089	82.7	16.9	0.4
1940	$2,261	68.0	30.3	1.8
1950	$5,437	57.3	39.8	2.9
1960	$14,747	56.5	39.1	4.4
1970	$40,267	52.1	39.9	8.0
1980	$96,881	43.4	46.8	9.8
1990	$207,753	46.8	47.1	6.1
1998	$325,976	44.8	48.4	6.8

[1]In current dollars.

Source: National Center for Education Statistics (2001). *Digest of Education Statistics 2000.* Washington, DC: U.S. Department of Education.

years, however, state and federal grants-in-aid have become significant factors in shaping district policies. This evolving influence was described in Chapter 1 through the lens of the generic model of educational policy making. The growing participation of state and federal governments in the financing of schools parallels their growing interest in and influence over educational policy in general. State governments have become particularly active in the prescription of basic curricula, monitoring student progress through mandatory testing programs and the certification of teachers (Darling-Hammond & Barry, 1988; Elmore & McLaughlin, 1988). State education departments and the U. S. Education Department have increased in size and influence (Moore, Goertz & Hartle, 1983; Murphy, 1982).

According to Wirt and Kirst, (1982, p. v), "The 1970s will be remembered as an era when the previous hallmark of American education—local control—became fully a myth." Local superintendents have lost their once-preeminent position in setting the school district agenda and controlling decision outcomes. The discretionary range of superintendents and

school boards has been narrowed at the top by federal and state action and at the bottom through collective bargaining with employee unions. The more recent trend toward school-based management is narrowing the range even further, to the point where some are beginning to question the efficacy of school districts. Nevertheless, local school districts continue to exert a considerable, though declining, amount of influence on educational policy (Odden & Marsh, 1989).

Other structural changes that are taking place in political institutions have an impact on the decision-making process and the ultimate nature of decisions made. Small districts have consolidated and large districts have decentralized. Progress is being made toward the professionalization of teaching, and the practice of letting parents choose the schools their children attend is gaining in popularity. Adoption of policies such as educational vouchers and tax credits will further change the face of educational governance, increasing the role of private providers. The changes in the school governance structures in Chicago (Hess, 1991) and Kentucky (Guskey, 1994) are dramatic examples of institutionalism's premise that the nature of the structure of the decision-making process influences the quality of its decisions and the efficiency of its operations.

Systems Theory

The most comprehensive of the models represents an application of *systems theory* to the political process. A system is made up of a number of elements that are interrelated. An open system, as is characteristic of political systems, draws resources from its environment, processes them in some fashions and returns the processed resources to the environment. All systems tend toward entropy (disorganization) and must consciously combat this tendency in order to maintain equilibrium. A key tool for combating entropy is feedback—that is, continual monitoring of a system's internal operations and its relationship with the environment. Accurate feedback is particularly critical to a system's health in that the system depends on the environment for resources without which the system would shrink and die. Equilibrium is maintained by modifying or adapting system structures and processes on the basis of analysis of feedback (cybernetics). Maintaining equilibrium is a dynamic process leading to growth and evolution of the system in harmony with its environment.

Easton (1965) was among the first to apply general systems theory to political systems. His model, which is illustrated in Figure 1.2, served as a prototype for the generic model of education policy making (Figure 1.3) around which this book is organized. The reader is referred to the discussion of these two models in Chapter 1 for an elaboration of the application of systems theory to education decision making.

Incrementalism

Lindblom (1959) described the public policy process in the United States as a continuation of past government activities with only incremental modifications. He insightfully labeled the process "muddling through." Although some deplore his exaltation of the process as a theory of *incrementalism*, one of his most ardent critics credits him with presenting "a well considered theory fully geared to the actual experience of practicing administrators" (Dror, 1964, p. 153). Incrementalism is perhaps more representative of American governance (division of powers) than of parliamentary forms of government, as noted in the cross-national analysis in Chapter 1.

Lindblom (1968, p. 32) took issue with the popular view that politics is a process of conflict resolution. He argued that "governments are instruments for vast tasks of social cooperation" and that "conflicts are largely those that spring from the opportunities for cooperation that have evolved once political life becomes orderly." Within this context, he described the "play of power" as a process of cooperation among specialists. It is gamelike, normally proceeding according to implicitly accepted rules. "Policy analysis is incorporated as an instrument or weapon into the play of power, changing the character of analysis as a result" (Lindblom, 1968, p. 30).

The focus of the play of power is on means (policy) not ends (goals or objectives). This, according to Lindblom, is what permits the political system to work. Because of the overlap in value systems among interested groups, and because of the uncertainty of the outcomes of any course of action, partisans across the value spectrum are able to come to agreement on means where agreement on ends would be impossible.

Because, according to Lindblom (1968, p. 33), agreement on goal priorities is impossible in a pluralistic society, the type of analysis appropriate to the political process is termed "partisan analysis." It is analysis of a relatively limited set of values or ends, conducted by advocates (organized interest groups) such as teacher associations, taxpayer groups, and religious and patriotic organizations. Comprehensiveness is provided by the variety of partisans participating in the political process. The responsibility for promoting specific values thus lies in the hands of advocates of those values (pressure groups and lobbyists) and not in the hands of some "impartial" analyst (as would be the case with rationalism, to be discussed later).

The net result of this advocacy process is incremental rather than revolutionary changes in policy. In light of our general ignorance about the relationships between public policy and human behavior, Lindblom viewed incremental policy decisions as being well justified. Incrementalism permits the expansion of policies that prove successful, while limiting the harm caused by unsuccessful policies. Within the context of strategic planning, incrementalism can ensure that each increment leads toward desired goals while minimizing organizational disruption. Incrementalism preserves the system while changing it.

In the next two sections we discuss group theory and elite theory. Both provide explanations of how incrementalism may work in practice.

Group Theory

Truman (1951), a leading proponent of *group theory*, saw politics as the interaction among groups (as opposed to individuals) in the formulation of public policy. Individuals band together into formal or informal groups, similar to Lindblom's partisans, to confront government with their demands. The group is the vehicle through which individuals can influence government action. Even political parties are viewed as coalitions of interest groups. Elected and appointed officials are seen as being continually involved in bargaining and negotiating with relevant groups to work out compromises that balance interests.

Group theory, as portrayed by Dye (1987), is illustrated in Figure 2.4. Public policy at any point in time represents the equilibrium of the balance of power among groups. Because the power alignment is continually shifting (e.g., toward Group B, in Figure 2.4, as it gains supporters or partners in coalition on a particular issue), the fulcrum of equilibrium also shifts, leading to incremental changes in policy (in the direction desired by Group B, as illustrated).

Stability in the system is attributed to a number of factors. First, most members of the electorate are latent supporters of the political system and share in its inherent values, (a concept similar to Easton's input assumptions). This latent group is generally inactive but can be aroused to defend the system against any group that attacks it. Second, there is a great

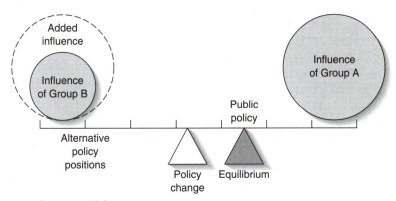

FIGURE 2.4. Group Theory Model.

Source: T. R. Dye (1987). *Understanding Public Policy* (6th ed.). Englewood Cliffs, NJ: Prentice-Hall, p. 27. Reprinted by permission of Pearson Education, Inc., Upper Saddle River, NJ.

deal of overlap in the membership of groups; a given individual is likely to be a member of several. This tends to discourage any group from taking extreme positions because, although the group as a whole may be focused on a single issue, its membership is much more broadly oriented. The third factor promoting system stability results from group competition. No single group constitutes a majority in American society. Coalitions are easily formed to counter the influence of any group that seems to gain undue influence. As a result, the political process is characterized by evolution, as in incrementalism, rather than by revolution.

Elite Theory

Elite theory focuses on actions by a select group of influential elite citizens. Elite theory (Dye & Zeigler, 1981) characterizes the general public as apathetic, ill informed, and uninterested about public policy—not unlike the latent group in group theory. This leaves a power vacuum that is happily filled by an elite. The elites do more to shape the opinion of the masses on public issues than the general public does to shape the opinions of the elite, although influence is reciprocal (e.g., civil rights legislation [Dye, 1987, chap. 3]). According to this theory, policy is developed by the elites amid the trappings of democratic government.

Elites tend to be drawn from upper socioeconomic levels. They are not necessarily against the general welfare of the masses, as in the case of civil rights legislation, but they approach the welfare of the masses through a sense of *noblesse oblige*. They may not agree on all issues, but the elite share a consensus on basic social values and on the importance of preserving the system. The masses give superficial support to this consensus that provides a basis for elite rule. When events occur that threaten the system, elites move to take corrective action. According to elite theory, changes in public policy come about when elites redefine their own positions, sometimes

as a result of external pressures. Because elites maintain a conservative posture with respect to preserving the system, policy changes tend to be incremental.

Rationalism

Adherents of *rationalism* seek to shape the policy-making process in such a way as to ensure the enactment of policies that maximize social gain. According to Dror (1968), the assumptions of pure rationality are deeply rooted in modern civilization and culture and are the basis of certain economic theories of the free market and of political theories of democracy. He characterized the pure-rationality model as having the six phases that are organized sequentially in Figure 2.5:

1. Establishing a complete set of operational goals, with relative weights allocated to the different degrees to which each may be achieved.
2. Establishing a complete inventory of other values and of resources, with relative weights.
3. Preparing a complete set of alternative policies open to the policy maker.
4. Preparing a complete set of valid predictions of the costs and benefits of each alternative, including the extent to which each will achieve the various operational goals, consume resources, and realize or impair other values.
5. Calculating the net expectation of each alternative by multiplying the probability of each benefit and cost for each alternative by the utility of each, and calculating the net benefit (or cost) in utility units.
6. Comparing the net expectations and identifying the alternative (or alternatives, if two or more are equally good) with the highest net expectation. (p. 132)

In theory, rationalism involves all individual, social, political, and economic values, not just those that can be converted into dollars and

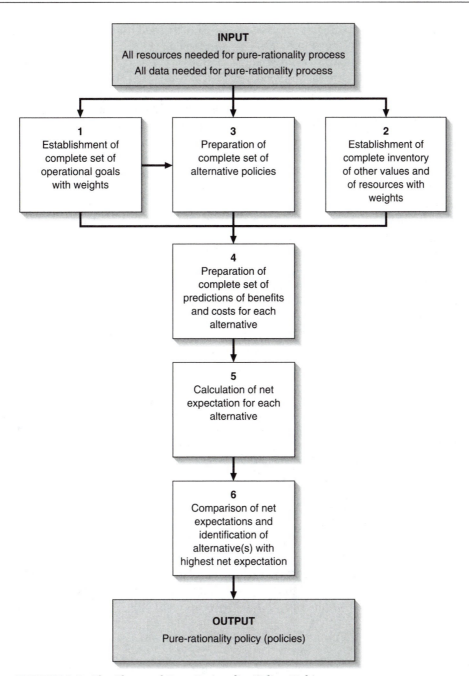

FIGURE 2.5. The Phases of Pure-Rationality Policy Making.

Source: Y. Dror. (1968). *Public Policy-Making Reexamined*. San Francisco: Chandler, p. 134.

cents. In reality, measurement difficulties make the inclusion of values other than economic values unlikely. Thus this model elevates economic efficiency above other potential societal objectives, such as equity, fraternity, and liberty.

Political realists argue that decisions in the public sector, including public education, are made on the basis of political rationality rather than economic rationality. To them, "rationalism" is at best irrelevant and can be downright dysfunctional to the political process (C. L. Schultz, 1968). To "know" all that would be required to select a policy "rationally"— all of society's value preferences and relative weights, all available policy alternatives, and the consequences of each alternative—is what Lindblom (1959, p. 88) termed "superhuman comprehensiveness." In essence, rationalism attempts the impossible by quantifying all elements of the political process and of human behavior and expressing the decision-making function in mathematical terms (Lavoie, 1985). Wise (1979) referred to persistent bureaucratic rationalization when the relationship between means and ends is not known as "hyperrationalization"—that is, an effort to rationalize beyond the bounds of knowledge (this concept is developed further in Chapter 9). Imperfect as it is, the representative legislature (such as school boards and Congress) is a political mechanism for approximating "all of society's value preferences and relative weights."

Rational techniques that are based on economic principles and procedures should be an important factor in budget development; however, Cibulka's (1987) research found that rationalism played a relatively small role even here. Wildavsky (1964) also argued that pure rationality is an illusion. He emphasized the political nature of the budgetary process: "If one looks at politics as a process by which the government mobilizes resources to meet pressing problems, then the budget is the focus of these efforts . . . . In the most integral sense, the budget lies at the heart of the political process (pp. 4–5).

Similar conclusions emerged from studies by Bigenwald (1977), Demmin (1978), and Hitzges (1988) of factors influencing decisions about school district resource allocation. Socioeconomic status, crises, and aggressive professionals and laity were found to be determining forces in budget construction.

Rationalism was a key principle behind the comprehensive centralized planning schemes of socialist and communist countries. With the collapse of many of the latter, and with the routine failure of five-year plans in socialist—mostly developing—countries, rationalism has lost much of its credibility (Carlson and Awkerman, 1991; Agarawala, 1984; Weiler, 1980).

Nevertheless, rationalistic philosophy has had an important impact on policy analysis and, indirectly, on policy decision making. Its bias of economic efficiency is a value that is all too frequently neglected in the traditional political process. The spirit of rationalism has fostered such management devices as "planning programming budgeting" systems (PPBS), Zero Based budgeting (ZBB), management by objectives (MBO), and operations research (OR), as well as cost–benefit and cost–effectiveness analysis. The terms *accountability* and *assessment* are now a part of the schooling vernacular, and teacher, pupil, and program evaluations are accepted procedures. Local school boards and state and federal governments are adding to their long-standing concerns over the quantity and quality of school inputs a similar concern over school outputs through mandatory evaluation and testing programs— that is, "standards-based education." All of this is done with the intent of introducing greater economic rationality into decisions made about education and schooling.

Whereas tools of rational analysis have had some effect on the educational decision-making process, rationalistic approaches have fallen short of the expectations of their supporters and have met with strong opposition from some segments of the traditional educational decision-making process. A major source of resistance to the use of analysis in schools is the teaching profession itself. In addition to their vested interests as employees, teachers are acutely aware that it is nearly impossible to quantify all the complex variables associated with educational inputs and outputs and with the learning process.

The most ardent supporters of rational analysis are economic purists who seek economic efficiency in the public sector. Within the private sector, the market provides powerful mechanisms to weed out inefficiencies. Indeed, one of the roles of government is to police the marketplace, keeping in check those forces that would impede the functioning of these mechanisms. Few, if any, similar mechanisms operate in the public sector.

Unlike incrementalism, which focuses on means, rationalism requires agreement on outcomes, which is unlikely in pluralistic organizations (such as state and federal governments and large urban school districts). Because of the reduced number of conflicting interest groups at the school level (which may also be the case with small, homogeneous school districts), such agreement is frequently obtained, and rationalism can become functional at that level. Indeed ,this is customarily a requirement of school-based management models.

ISSUES INVOLVING GOVERNMENTAL INTERVENTION

Up to this point, we have sketched the functioning of the economic and political systems separately and have indicated how decisions made in the two sectors are likely to differ. Each sector is capable of answering the policy issues posed, but as individuals and as a society, we would probably be quite unhappy with the results if *all* decisions were made through either sector acting alone. Given the general preference of a capitalistic society for the private sector as a venue for making decisions, we would like now to address the matter of when governments should intervene in private-sector decision making and how they should do so.

When Should Governments Intervene?

Eckstein (1967) identified four situations wherein market mechanisms fail and government intervention is necessary: collective goods, external economies (that is, divergence between private and social costs or benefits), extraordinary risks, and natural monopolies. Education as a collective or "public" good was discussed earlier.

External Economies

The market works well when the prices charged reflect the total costs involved in producing goods or services. There are instances, however, where a producer can escape paying the full cost of production with the consumer benefiting in terms of lower prices, or where a producer cannot charge the full value of that which is produced. These are known as external economies or diseconomies. When external economies occur, the good or service is not fully provided by the private sector; education is a case in point. Although there are profit incentives to provide educational programs with a specific focus, such as occupational education and college preparation, there are few profit incentives to provide universal education in the private sector—especially to the poor and to the disabled.

External economies are illustrated by paper manufacturing. Without environmental protection legislation, paper manufacturers were likely to dump highly toxic waste generated by the manufacturing process into adjacent rivers and streams, killing wildlife and fouling the air. Requiring the detoxification of waste prior to returning it to the environment increases the cost of production and raises the cost of paper products to the consumer. Prior to protective legislation, manufacturers were able to escape paying a portion of the true costs of production. Part of the price was paid by those living near the mill in the form of low quality of life and low property values because of the pollution.

Similarly, when pupils drop out or are forced out of school, there is a high probability that they will become wards of society in one form or another. They are much less likely to be regularly employed than are persons who complete their schooling and are more likely to receive government assistance in the form of unemployment insurance payments, welfare, and Medicaid. School dropouts are also more likely to turn to crime and be incarcerated in penal institutions. The resources saved by some school districts in not fully educating such persons are lost many times over by society at large, which must provide them with social services, later in life, financed largely at the federal and state levels.

Until federal and state governments intervened, many people with severe mental and physical disabilities were denied access to schooling because of the high cost of special education. This meant that they were institutionalized their entire lives. Now, having had access to schooling, many are able to work and live independently or with minimal supervision. The increased expenditures for education are paying dividends in terms of lower costs for social services and a better quality of life for persons with disabling conditions.

Extraordinary Risks

The term *extraordinary risks* refers to situations wherein the probable return, or pay-off, on investment is low. The development of atomic energy, space exploration, and cancer research are examples. Investments in research on learning, teaching, and curriculum may also fall into this category. The growing global economy requires investment in retraining low-skilled workers to prevent the development of a permanent underclass as a result of free-trade agreements: a social problem, but not necessarily an economic one.

Natural Monopoly

A natural monopoly is an enterprise that exhibits a continually falling cost curve. In other words, the cost to produce a unit becomes less and less as the number of units produced or served increases. Thus, because of economies of scale, the largest firm has a distinct competitive advantage, eventually driving smaller firms out of business. Electricity, gas, and water utilities are examples. The technology governing most businesses and industries is such, however, that economies of scale are realized only up to the point where diseconomies of scale set in—that is, the cost per unit increases as the number of units produced or serviced increases. This yields a U-shaped cost curve, nullifying any advantage of large firms over small ones and preserving competition.

There is a general misperception that there are substantial economies of scale in providing educational services, and this misperception often encourages states to enact school consolidation policies. But in reality, economies of scale affect only the very smallest of schools and school districts, as demonstrated in Chapter 12. On the other hand, there is convincing evidence of diseconomies of scale in education in large schools and school districts (also discussed in Chapter 12). Despite this, schooling has been organized as a near public monopoly.

Other Reasons for Intervention

Government intervention also takes place for other reasons. The federal government has assumed a responsibility for controlling business cycles and inflation and, to a limited extent, the redistribution of wealth. Schooling and training frequently become means through which such control is exercised. All governments use the power of eminent domain, whereby they can force the sale of private property for public use, as in the construction of interstate highways—or of schools.

If There Is Government Intervention, How Might It Occur?

Once the decision to intervene is made, there are numerous modes of intervention. Public schools are currently owned and operated by government. So are police and fire departments and the United States armed forces. Ownership is not the typical type of government intervention, however. Governments may also oversee the public interest through regulation, licensure, taxation, subsidies, transfer payments, and contracts.

Most communication systems, utilities, and intercity transportation enterprises in the United States are privately owned, yet they are carefully monitored and regulated. Restaurants are regularly inspected for health code violations. Governments license professionals, even though most professionals, an important exception being teachers, work in the private sector. State government agencies also regulate private schools and home schooling.

Governments can attempt to influence human behavior by changing the price paid for specific items through subsidies or taxation. Consumption of cigarettes, alcoholic beverages, and gasoline is discouraged through excise taxes that increase the cost to consumers with the intent of reducing demand. On the other hand, the government may pay subsides to farmers to encourage them to increase (or decrease) production of specific products, or to businesses to enable them to remain in operation in the face of foreign competition. Similarly, subsidies and scholarships that reduce the cost of higher education encourage families and individuals to pursue education beyond high school. Complete subsidization makes universal elementary and secondary education possible.

Governments also contract for services from private companies. Federal, state, and local governments rely on contractors to build their buildings, highways, and parks. Although the federal government coordinates space exploration, privately contracted vendors conduct research and development and manufacture space vehicles. During periods of rapid enrollment increases, school districts may rent or lease space from private vendors. Instead of providing their own services, many school districts contract with private vendors for transportation, cleaning, and cafeteria operations. Recently, some school districts have contracted for the operation of individual schools, for specific administrative services, and (in a couple of cases), for the administration of the entire business of the district.

Many governmental responsibilities are met through transfer payments to individuals. Social security, Aid for Dependent Children (that is, welfare), unemployment insurance, food stamps, and educational vouchers are examples. Through transfer payments, the government can equalize the distribution of resources, while permitting the individual maximum discretion as to how to use the funds. For example, before social security, elderly indigents were institutionalized in facilities owned and operated by local government, as schools are today. Now, with monthly payments from the social security system, recipients have many options open to them such as living in their own home, in a smaller apartment, in a retirement community, in a residence for the elderly, in a nursing home, or with relatives. The public policy of providing all senior citizens with at least a subsistence living standard is realized without prescribing their lifestyles. The G.I. Bill, which paid the tuition of World War II and Korean War veterans to postsecondary institutions not limited to public institutions, is an example of education vouchers. A few large cities are beginning to make limited use of vouchers at the elementary and secondary levels.

Choosing the Appropriate Level of Government to Intervene

Within any given context, significantly different patterns of allocation of authority among levels of government and potential decision makers can be structured, depending on the relative priorities given to policy objectives (Kirst, 1988; Theobald & Malen, 2000). Extreme centralization of authority is characterized by making all decisions collectively and by administering them through public institutions. Extreme decentralization of authority is characterized by having no public schools and no subsidies, leaving the production and distribution of educational services to be determined solely by market forces. This position enhances the potential for realizing values of efficiency and personal freedom, but it has severe negative implications for the realization of other societal values such as equity.

Increasing centralization of authority was used in the post–World War II years as a vehicle for promoting equity considerations, but the flood of national criticism during the last two decades of the twentieth century, and the resulting reform movement, suggested that the efficiency and effectiveness of the educational system had been impaired. To promote values of efficiency and liberty while retaining considerable control over equity, some states have adopted policies permitting cross-district enrollments, and some school districts have taken modest steps in enhancing families' choice of schools by creating magnet schools and/or permitting open enrollment among all schools. Many states have taken the more radical step of authorizing charter schools, and a few states and districts have authorized publicly funded vouchers that can be used in private schools. Other districts have delegated substantial policy-making authority to schools and teachers, paving the way for school-based decision making and teacher empowerment. Centralizing policy proposals aimed at improving efficiency in the educational system include setting state standards for student academic performance, adopting state curricula, administering achievement tests, raising high school graduation requirements, and raising state standards for entering the teaching profession.

Wirt and Kirst (1982) diagnosed centralization/ decentralization tensions as a function of the inherent conflict between "individualism and majoritarianism." They saw the political stress in today's society as stemming from the emphasis that we, as a society, place on translating private preference and need into public policy. In acknowledging that all persons are regarded as important, government, if it is to survive, must mediate conflicts arising out of diverse individual desires so that the conflicts remain at tolerable levels. Majority rule is an integral part of democratic governance. Individualism, on the other hand, is reflected in our economic system and in the bills of rights in our national and state constitutions designed to protect individuals from the "tyranny of the majority." Friedman (1962) analyzed the situation as follows:

> The widespread use of the market reduces the strain on the social fabric by rendering conformity unnecessary with respect to any activities it encompasses. The wider the range of activities covered by the market, the fewer are the issues on which explicit political decisions are required and hence on which it is necessary to achieve agreement. In turn, the fewer issues on which agreement is necessary, the greater the likelihood of getting agreement while maintaining a free society. (p. 24)

There are legitimate concerns about education at all levels of the sociopolitical hierarchy; the critical issue is achieving the best balance among legitimate interests. The best balance will vary from society to society and over time within a society as contexts, value definitions, and priorities change (Wirt, 1986).

SUMMARY

In this chapter, we have described how educational decisions are made. Because education provides benefits that are highly valued by individuals and society, often in different ways, the process is particularly complex and involves both government and the market.

We began the chapter with a discussion of human-capital theory. This perspective offers an explanation of why individuals are motivated to invest in themselves and in their children to improve their marketable knowledge and skills. Because the skills of any individual affect the well-being of others (spillover effects), and because many do not have sufficient resources to invest in their own education, human-capital theory also provides a rationale for public intervention to ensure universal education. Thus we showed that education has attributes of a private good, subject to the exclusion principle, and of a public good with indivisible benefits.

We described the allocation of scarce resources through markets and several models of political decision making. We identified five education issues that any society must address either through the political process of government or through market transactions. Because the political process is biased toward the metavalue of equity and the market holds biases toward metavalues of personal freedom and efficiency, preferences for the resolution of these issues are quite different, depending on sector. We provided guides for determining when issues should be resolved by government and when they should be left to individual initiatives through the market. A range of ways for structuring government involvement and the implications of vesting authority in local, state, and federal bodies were presented.

ACTIVITIES

1. Identify the attributes of education that are in the nature of consumption and those that are in the nature of investment.
2. Identify the attributes of education that make it a public good and those that make it a private good.
   a. List separately the public and private benefits of education.
   b. Are any public benefits derived from private schools? If so, what are they, and can public financing of private schools be justified to the extent of the value of those public benefits?
3. Describe the process by which fundamental economic decisions about education are made.
   a. What groups are involved in making the fundamental economic decisions with respect to education that are listed on p. 43?
   b. Indicate how might schools be organized to serve more efficiently the needs of:
      • students with no severe impediments to learning
      • children who have disabilities
      • gifted children
      • adults
      • preschool children
   c. What policies would be needed to facilitate the implementation of the school organizations described in Activity 3b?
4. Discuss the strategies that are available to government for intervening in issues of financing, organizing, and distributing educational services.
   a. Does the goal of enabling all children to meet high academic standards justify the continuation of today's near public monopoly in the provision of elementary and secondary education? List separately the arguments supporting affirmative and negative responses to this question.
   b. What alternative structures have been proposed for organizing elementary and secondary education to enable all children to meet high academic standards? Which, if any, do you consider the most viable? Why?
5. Study the political policy-making process at the local level with respect to education.
   a. Interview your superintendent of schools and/or members of your board of education about how educational policy is developed and who influences the process in your school district.

b. On the basis of information gathered from the foregoing interview(s), describe situations that illustrate each of the policy-making models listed on page 48.

6. Identify aspects of education wherein private investment is unlikely because of uncertain payoff.

a. Does research on teaching, learning, and curriculum development represent an activity where the probable payoff of private investment is so low as to justify government involvement? List the arguments in support of your response.

b. Ideally, how should education research be organized and financed?

COMPUTER SIMULATIONS: REVENUE FOR EDUCATION

Computer simulations are available on the Allyn & Bacon website **http://www.ablongman .com/edleadership.com**. The computer simulations for this chapter are introductory activities that are designed for the new user of spreadsheet software. Experienced spreadsheet users need not do these simulations. The simulations focus on the following objectives:

- To understand the degree to which public education relies on various levels of government for revenue.
- To become familiar with computer spreadsheet programs.
- To develop beginner computer skills such as entering data, moving material, copying, and entering formulas.

REFERENCES

Agarawala, R. (1984). *Planning in developing countries: Lessons of experience,* World Bank staff working papers, No. 576. Washington, DC: The World Bank.

Becker, G. S. (1964). *Human capital: A theoretical and empirical analysis, with special reference to education.* New York: National Bureau of Economic Research.

Benson, C. S. (1978). *The economics of public education* (3rd ed.). Boston: Houghton Mifflin.

Bigenwald, M. M. (1977). *An extension of Thorstein Veblen's "The Theory of the Leisure Class" to contemporary consumption of educational services.* Buffalo, NY: Unpublished doctoral dissertation, State University of New York at Buffalo.

Blaug, M. (1970). *An introduction to the economics of education.* Middlesex, England: Penguin Books.

Carlson, R. V., & Awkerman, G (Eds.). (1991). *Educational planning: Concepts, strategies, and practices.* New York: Longman.

Cibulka, J. G. (1987). Theories of education budgeting: Lessons from the management of decline. *Educational Administration Quarterly, 23,* 7–40.

Darling-Hammond, L., & Barry, B. (1988). *The evolution of teacher policy* (Report No. JRE-01). Santa Monica, CA: The RAND Corporation.

Demmin, P. E. (1978). *Incrementalism in school budgeting: Patterns and preference ordering in resource allocation.* Buffalo, NY: Unpublished doctoral dissertation, State University of New York.

Dennison, E. F. (1962). *The sources of economic growth in the United States.* New York: Committee for Economic Development.

Downs, A. (1957). *An economic theory of democracy.* New York: Harper & Row.

Dror, Y. (1964). Muddling through—"science" or inertia? *Public Administration Review, 24,* 153–157.

Dror, Y. (1968). *Public policy-making reexamined.* San Francisco: Chandler.

Dye, T. R. (1987). *Understanding public policy* (6th ed.). Englewood Cliffs, NJ: Prentice-Hall.

Dye, T. R., and Zeigler, H. (1981). *The irony of democracy.* Monterey, CA: Brooks/Cole.

Easton, D. A. (1965). *A systems analysis of political life.* New York: John Wiley & Sons.

Eckstein, O. (1967). *Public finance* (2nd ed.). Englewood Cliffs, NJ: Prentice-Hall.

Elazar, D. J. (1972). *American federalism.* New York: Harper & Row.

Elmore, R. F., & McLaughlin, M. W. (1988). *Steady work: Policy, practice, and the reform of American education* (Report No. R-3574-NIE/RC). Santa Monica, CA: The RAND Corporation.

Friedman, M. (1962). *Capitalism and freedom.* Chicago: University of Chicago Press.

Grodzins, M. (1966). *The American system.* Chicago: Rand McNally.

Guskey, T. R., Ed. (1994). *High stakes performance as-*

sessment: Perspectives on Kentucky's educational re-form*. Thousand Oaks, CA: Corwin.

Hanushek, E. A., & Kim, D. (1995). *Schooling, labor force quality, and economic growth* (Working Paper 5399). Cambridge, MA: National Bureau of Economic Research.

Hess, G. A., Jr. (1991). *School restructuring, Chicago style*. Thousand Oaks, CA: Corwin.

Hitzges, R. A. (1988). *Analyzing professional staff allocation decision process in selected public schools*. Buffalo, NY: Unpublished doctoral dissertation, State University of New York at Buffalo.

Hodgkinson, C. (1983). *The philosophy of leadership*. Oxford, England: Basil Blackwell.

Kaufman, R., & Herman, J. (1991). *Strategic planning in education: Rethinking, restructuring, revitalizing*. Lancaster, PA: Technomic.

Kirst, M. W. (1988). Recent educational reform in the United States: Looking backward and forward. *Educational Administration Quarterly, 24,* 319–328.

Kozol, J. (1991). *Savage inequalities: Children in America's schools*. New York: Harper Perennial.

Kuznets, S. (1966). *Modern economic growth*. New Haven, CT: Yale University Press.

Lavoie, D. (1985). *National economic planning: What is left?* Cambridge, MA: Ballinger.

Levin, H. M. (1987). Education as a public and private good. *Journal of Policy Analysis and Management, 6,* 628–641.

Lindblom, C. E. (1959). The science of muddling through. *Public Administration Review, 19,* 79–88.

Lindblom, C. E. (1968). *The policy-making process*. Englewood Cliffs, NJ: Prentice-Hall.

Marshall, A. (1948/1961). *Principles of economics* (8th ed.). New York: Macmillan.

Moore, M. K., Goertz, M., & Hartle, T. (1983). Interaction of federal and state programs. *Education and Urban Society, 4,* 452–478.

Murphy, J. (1982). The paradox of state government reform. In A. Lieberman & M. McLaughlin (Eds.). *Educational policy-making*. The 81st Yearbook of the National Society for the Study of Education. Chicago: University of Chicago Press.

National Center for Education Statistics. (2001). *Digest of education statistics 2001*. Washington, DC: U.S. Department of Education.

Odden, A., & Marsh, D. (1989). State education reform implementation: A framework for analysis.

In J. Hannaway & R. Crowson (Eds.), *The politics of reforming school administration* (41–59). New York: Falmer.

Paquette, J. (1991). Why should I stay in school? Quantifying private educational returns. *Journal of Education Finance, 16,* 458–477.

Pierce, B., & Welch, F. (1996). Changes of structures of wages. In E. A. Hanushek & D. W. Jorgenson (Eds.), *Improving America's schools: The role of incentives* (pp. 53–73). Washington, DC: National Academy Press.

Samuelson, P. A., & Nordhaus, W. D. (1989). *Economics* (13th ed.). New York: McGraw-Hill.

Schultz, C. L. (1968). *The politics and economics of public spending*. Washington, DC: The Brookings Institution.

Schultz, T. W. (1963). *The economic value of education*. New York: Columbia University Press.

Schultz, T. W. (1981). *Investing in people: The economics of population quality*. Berkeley, CA: University of California Press.

Smith, A. (1993, originally published 1776). *An inquiry into the nature and causes of the wealth of nations*. Oxford, England: Oxford University Press.

Theobald, N. D., & Malen, B. (2000). *Balancing local control and state responsibility for K–12 education* (2000 Yearbook of the American Education Finance Association). Larchmont, NY: Eye on Education.

Truman, D. B. (1951). *The governmental process*. New York: Knopf.

Walker, D. B. (1981). *Toward a functioning federalism*. Cambridge, MA: Winthrop Press.

Weiler, H. N. (Ed.). (1980). *Education planning and social change*. Paris: UNESCO: International Institute for Educational Planning.

Wildavsky, A. (1964). *The politics of the budgetary process*. Boston: Little, Brown.

Wirt, F. M. (1986). *Multiple paths for understanding the role of values in state policy*. Paper presented at the Annual Meeting of the American Education Research Association, San Francisco, CA. (ERIC Document Reproduction Service No. ED-278086)

Wirt, F. M., & Kirst, M. W. (1982). *Schools in conflict: The politics of education*. Berkeley, CA: McCutchan.

Wise, A. E. (1979). *Legislated learning: The bureaucratization of the American classroom*. Berkeley, CA: University of California Press.

part II

Acquiring Resources for Schools

In Part II, we turn to the sources of funds that have historically sustained public education and to current issues that challenge policy makers. In Part I we developed the broader political–economic context within which educational decision making occurs. Public policy making evolves as legislators and school boards respond to shifts in circumstances and to the priorities that they, and the public they represent, assign to different values. We now draw on this context in presenting revenue sources. We focus on basic principles of taxation and the primary revenue sources of federal, state, and local governments.

Before we look at specific taxes, we examine the federated tax structure in which different levels of government have authority to govern and to raise revenue. Federal, state, and local governments rely to varying degrees on the tax bases of wealth, income, consumption, and privilege. The intents and consequences of different taxes can be analyzed in relation to several criteria: yield, equity, neutrality, elasticity, and administrative burden. We introduce these criteria in Chapter 3. Then we use them to evaluate the revenue sources available to federal and state levels of government (Chapter 4), and to local jurisdictions, including school districts (Chapters 5 and 6).

PRINCIPLES OF TAXATION

Issues and Questions

- *Achieving High Standards with Equity and Efficiency*: What principles underlie the choices made to adopt tax systems that generate revenue to support improvements in public education?
- *The Federated Tax Structure*: Are there advantages and disadvantages in having multiple governance structures overseeing and raising revenue for public education?
- *Tax Bases*: What forms of individual and business activities are subjected to wealth-, income-, consumption-, and privilege-based taxes?
- *Criteria for Assessing the Merits of Various Taxes*: What insights do criteria of yield, equity, neutrality, elasticity, and administrative burden give policy makers as they consider which revenue sources to adopt?
- *Tax Incidence and Impact*: Who pays the taxes, and what are the relative burdens on those groups of taxpayers?
- *Balancing Values in Designing Tax Systems*: How do policy makers weigh the foregoing criteria and the competing values of liberty, equality, fraternity, efficiency, and economic growth as they decide which taxes best meet public goals?

OVERVIEW OF THE FEDERATED TAX STRUCTURE

Public finance in the United States is influenced greatly by the separation of powers among federal, state, and local levels of government. Multiple layers, it is believed, can more efficiently and effectively finance and deliver public services. The division is not a strict one, however, because there is considerable sharing of tax sources and substantial flow of money from federal and state governments to local subdivisions of government such as counties, townships, municipalities, and school districts.

A highly decentralized system ties costs to the jurisdiction that provides services. A loose federation among levels of government is believed to stimulate a stronger economy, wherein goods and services and the factors of production move freely in response to differing levels of taxes and benefits (Musgrave & Musgrave, 1989, p. 469). On the other hand, a highly decentralized system tolerates inequities in the nature and extent of goods and services provided among jurisdictions. Two school districts with differing levels of property wealth or personal income, for example, have very different capacities to raise desired revenue from these tax bases. For this reason, higher levels of government might intervene to equalize tax capacity or revenue among jurisdictions at lower levels in order to ensure the provision of adequate public services.

For much of the twentieth century, fiscal federalism was characterized by a trend toward greater centralization. That is, a larger proportion of governmental revenue was raised at federal and state levels later in the century, and this trend was accompanied by an increase in grants-in-aid to states and localities. The centralization of revenue sources and growth in revenue sharing from federal and state to local governments nonetheless left the provision of public services largely the responsibility of localities. This arrangement continues to justify the property tax as the primary means

of providing financial support for local schools. The broader-based tax systems of federal and state governments are better suited to their mission of redistributing wealth and expanding opportunities for access to public services. The federated system of taxation and governance recognizes advantages of both centralized and decentralized units and promotes interactions among all levels.

Because local governments have no tax authority other than that granted by the state, the state is in a superior position to coordinate tax policy. For example, many states (as well as the federal government) permit income taxpayers to deduct the value of local property taxes before computing their income tax liability, and several others grant income tax rebates for a portion of property taxes paid by low-income and elderly persons. Although the federal government has no constitutional responsibility to coordinate tax systems, federal provisions can also influence tax structures at lower levels of government. States that have income taxes rely to a large extent on federal income tax policy to reduce administrative costs and ease the burden on taxpayers as they compute taxes and file returns. Similarly, reform of the federal income tax in 1986 eliminated the deduction of state and local sales taxes and thereby affected tax collection and policy development for states and localities.

Interdependence indeed characterizes the loosely federated structure of governance and finance in the United States. It is within this framework of understanding that we present several bases on which taxes can be assessed and some criteria for judging the appropriateness of various revenue sources.

Primary Tax Bases

Measures of taxpayer *ability to pay* for public services and taxpayer *use of services* are at the foundation of government tax collection. Wealth, income, consumption, and privilege are primary tax bases. Taxes on real estate property, personal property, or accumulations of property at the time of death reflect taxation of different forms of *wealth* at a given moment. In contrast, income taxes represent a portion of the *income* earned by an individual or business during a period of time, such as the calendar or fiscal year.

Taxes based on *consumption* apply to commodities purchased, without reflecting taxpayer wealth or income. Excise taxes are levied on particular items such as gasoline and cigarettes, whereas general sales and gross receipts taxes are less selective in their application. Yet even these sales taxes usually exempt the purchase of food, housing, and other necessities, rather than applying to all consumption. Taxes on legalized gambling and lotteries in some states are based on individual consumption, as well as on the privilege of participating in these games.

Privilege-based taxes permit individuals and businesses to engage in certain activities or make use of public facilities. For example, teachers and other professionals obtain licenses, national park patrons pay entrance fees, and ranchers pay the government to to be allowed to graze cattle on open lands. There are many privilege taxes related to transportation; vehicle owners pay registration fees, drivers obtain licenses, and specific users pay tolls for traveling on restricted-access highways.

Policy makers deliberate about the extent to which it is appropriate to rely on each of these different tax bases and specific objects of taxation. Once it is decided to tax people's economic well-being, some legislators consider which tax objects (such as wages, income from investments, purchases, or other indicators of monetary "flow") are most appropriate. Other policy makers prefer to tax property, accumulated capital, inventory, net worth, estates, and other measures of the "stock" of wealth (Mac-Phail-Wilcox, 1984, p. 325). The outcomes of these public policy deliberations form a maze of different taxes that are relied on to finance public services.

ASSESSING THE MERITS OF REVENUE SOURCES

Government reliance on the different tax bases is related to goals of tax policy and to several criteria for judging their appropriateness. Providing an adequate yield of money is one, but not the only, reason to adopt a particular revenue plan. Taxes serve a number of other purposes, including redistributing wealth and power, creating an economic climate that supports the growth of business, discouraging the consumption of certain products, and encouraging various social and economic policies. Many goals take into account what group of people or business is to be affected by a particular tax—and in what ways. Five criteria for evaluating taxes—yield, equity, neutrality, elasticity, and administrative burden—further our understanding of the goals of taxation and assist in assessing the merits of current and potential revenue sources.

Yield

The flow of revenue from a tax affects the financial health of government. Without an adequate yield, government might not be able to provide public services, balance budgets, and avoid unnecessary debt. Among governments, only the federal government can legally run a deficit in operating its budget. Provisions in all state constitutions require that state and local governments balance their budgets for current operations and that they raise sufficient revenue from other levels of government and their own tax sources to maintain public services. Obviously, as the benefits of alternative sources of tax revenue are compared, a tax that provides a large yield is more favorable than a tax that offers a lesser yield.

The yield of a tax is calculated as the product of the tax base (e.g., the amount of income or the value of goods purchased or property owned) and a tax rate. A governing body or the voting public decides this rate. Government can increase its tax yield either by expanding the size of the tax base through economic growth or by raising the tax rate on a given tax base.

Equity

Fairness is an important principle in tax policy. It is generally believed that all individuals in society should contribute to the public good and be treated in uniform ways. However, not all taxpayers are in the same financial condition when taxes are due. The determination of actual tax payments invokes conflict between foundations of *ability to pay* and *use of services*. Equity is the most complex of the five criteria and the most difficult to measure. This section considers principles that underlie the concept of equity, including benefits received, ability to pay, equal sacrifice, and horizontal and vertical equity.

Benefits-Received Principle

The benefits-received principle states that taxpayers should contribute to government in accordance with benefits derived from public services, just as they do when they make purchases in the private sector. For example, fees charged for municipal transportation and national parks collect the same amount from all beneficiaries—users of services—without regard to individual income or wealth. To some degree, it might be argued that all tax and expenditure policies within democracies reflect a benefit principle: "People, or some majority thereof, would not be willing to sustain a fiscal program if, on balance, they did not benefit therefrom" (Musgrave & Musgrave, 1989, p. 220).

However, the relationship between benefits received and taxes paid is not always clear. It is difficult to determine who benefits and to what degree from such public services as libraries and parks that are shared generally by residents (and many nonresidents) of a tax jurisdiction. Furthermore, taxes on or fees for the use of services might not entirely cover the costs of such services. Some mismatching of benefits and costs inevitably occurs. Thus, for general services, including schools, ability to pay is considered a more appropriate principle in evaluating tax policy than is a benefits-received standard.

Ability-to-Pay Principle

The ability-to-pay theory states that taxpayers should contribute in accordance with their economic capacity to support public services. Rather than demanding absolute equality in tax payments, this principle calls for an examination of individual abilities to contribute. Adam Smith advanced this standard as early as 1776:

> The subjects of every state ought to contribute towards the support of the government, as nearly as possible, in proportion to their respective abilities: that is, in proportion to the revenue which they respectively enjoy under the protection of the state. . . . In the observation or neglect of this maxim consists what is called the equality or inequality of taxation. (Smith, 1993, p. 451)

The "revenue" to which Smith refers might include any return from property or investments. Income has become the best measure of ability to pay taxes "for it determines a person's total command over resources during a stated period, to consume, or to add to his wealth" (Eckstein, 1967, p. 60). However, the difficulty of agreeing on adjustments to income as appropriate recognitions of differences in ability to pay creates policy dilemmas and a sense of unfairness in taxation.

Equal-Sacrifice Principle

In the interest of maintaining relative equity in the distribution of tax burdens, higher-income earners are expected to pay in taxes not merely higher dollar amounts but also higher proportions of their income. This requirement is justified under the equal-sacrifice principle, which ties differing abilities to pay with the economic view of diminishing marginal utility.

Under this theory, consumers seek to maximize their total satisfaction, or utility, from their income through the acquisition of various goods and services. For example, an initial purchase of an automobile provides a large degree of utility (U_1 in Figure 3.1) in the form of basic transportation. More benefits come from successive purchases of automobiles, but the addition to overall utility is smaller with each new sacrifice of personal resources for transportation. Additional vehicles may give independence of movement to other family members or serve a specialized function such as recreation. At some point, however, the value of additional vehicles in terms of utility diminishes. Buying a fifth automobile brings a smaller addition to total utility (from U_4 to U_5) than did prior automobile purchases.

Conversely, when an automobile is taken away from an individual who owns five, there is less sacrifice, or reduction in utility, than when an automobile is taken away from an individual who owns a single vehicle. To apply this principle to taxation, the reduction of income by a given tax payment represents a greater sacrifice for individuals with less income. An "equal"-sacrifice rule, then, implies that individuals with different income levels should contribute different amounts to the government, in such a way that they forgo similar amounts of utility.

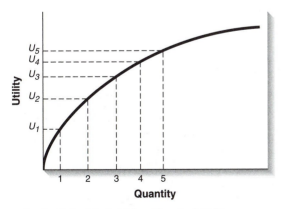

FIGURE 3.1. Diminishing Marginal Utility

Horizontal-Equity Principle

Equality under the law is reflected in the concept of horizontal equity. This principle, as practiced, frequently includes the assumption that people who are in similar economic circumstances have an equal ability in terms of wealth or income. Therefore, each person should contribute the same amount of taxes (i.e., equal treatment of equals). For example, taxpayers with equal annual incomes should pay equal amounts of income tax.

Vertical-Equity Principle

Vertical equity calls for differing amounts of taxes from individuals who have different abilities to pay (i.e., unequal treatment of unequals). This principle as practiced in federal income taxation, for example, requires that taxpayers who have higher annual incomes pay higher amounts of income tax. The higher amounts of tax reflect both more dollars and a greater proportion of income. Fairness in the treatment of tax burdens is attempted by requiring unequal tax payments—that is, people who have greater ability to pay are expected to contribute more and in greater proportion than people who have less ability to pay.

Neutrality

Taxes should be neutral so that there are no undesirable side effects on the operation of the economic system: "A tax system that introduces distortions into the functioning of the economy typically imposes a loss of welfare on consumers over and above that resulting from the tax payments themselves; this extra welfare loss is the excess burden of the tax" (Oates, 1972, p. 121). A neutral tax (or, alternatively, an efficient tax) does not alter individual or business behavior in response to the tax. It does not distort consumer spending patterns, and it has neither positive nor negative effects on work incentives or choices of alternative means of production.

Taxes may alter methods of production and uses of resources, reducing the potential efficiency of both. For example, an excise tax that raises the price of products may cause a shift in consumer preferences, encouraging manufacturers to divert resources to the production of other commodities. Consumption-based taxes frequently result in reallocations of human and capital resources—as a consequence not of free-market conditions but of indirect government involvement (Webb, McCarthy, & Thomas, 1988, p. 80).

Decisions of individual taxpayers about work, investments, and residential locations are often reactions to actual or perceived tax burdens. Society suffers a loss if taxes diminish the willingness of people to work, to accept more responsible positions, to gain education necessary for professional work, or to take risks (Due, 1976, p. 258). Owners of low-rent housing in urban areas may decide to abandon the property or allow it to deteriorate if reassessments for property improvements translate into higher tax burdens. Changes in tax structures may also influence decisions whether to relocate; this has been one outcome of California's Proposition 13 whereby property tax rates are based on valuation at the time a home is purchased rather than on its current market value.

Similarly, businesses consider tax burdens when making location and investment decisions. Differences among states, counties, or municipalities in sales or property taxes or in taxes on corporate income can encourage businesses to consider locations that are less than optimal in terms of production efficiency. Investment incentives in tax policy affect decisions that firms make about expanding into new markets. Not only do taxes alter behavior, but distortions also reduce revenue and require higher overall tax rates.

In contrast to potential negative effects of taxation, some taxes purposely create "desirable distortions" (Levin, 1987, p. 431) and are enacted because of their economic or social effects. Sumptuary taxes deter the consumption of such products as cigarettes and liquor. Duties on imported goods protect domestic producers by making foreign products more expensive. At the same time, however, consumers may pay higher prices and product quality may fall because domestic producers need not introduce the most efficient production techniques.

Elasticity

A tax's elasticity determines the stability or flexibility of its yield in relation to movements of the economy, usually measured by changes in gross national product (GNP) or total personal income. An *elastic* tax is one in which the tax base increases at a greater rate than the rate of economic growth or one in which the base is stable but the tax rate structure is progressive. In either case, the yield of an elastic tax grows more quickly than some measure of economic change. Conversely, an *inelastic* tax is one in which the rate of revenue growth is less than the rate of economic growth. If rates of change for tax yield and for the economy are the same, the revenue source has an elasticity of *unity*.

To obtain a coefficient of elasticity, one divides the percentage of change in tax *yield* between two points in time (t_1 and t_2) by the percentage change in state or national *income* during the same period:

$$\text{Elasticity} = \frac{\dfrac{\text{yield } t_2 - \text{yield } t_1}{\text{yield } t_1}}{\dfrac{\text{income } t_2 - \text{income } t_1}{\text{income } t_1}}$$

For example, assume that income in a given region has grown from \$800 million to \$1 billion, while the amount of individual income tax collections levied at a uniform rate has increased from \$50 million to \$70 million. In this case, the income tax is highly elastic, given the resulting coefficient of 1.6. If sales tax revenue had grown from $18 million to $22.5 million during this time frame, the resulting coefficient of 1.0 would indicate an elasticity of unity. In contrast is the relatively inelastic property tax, whose yield has increased from $13.6 million to $16.66 million, with a resulting coefficient of 0.9.

The yield from a stable tax (with an elasticity coefficient of less than 1.0) grows more slowly than the rest of the economy unless there are increased tax rates. On the other hand, yield does not decline as rapidly during periods of recession. This stability provides a degree of dependability that is essential for planning government functions and budgeting to pay for them. The large and predictable yield of the relatively inelastic property tax makes it a particularly suitable revenue source for local governments.

> It is desirable to have a revenue source that does not suffer from large year to year fluctuations, especially for school districts, who have limited authority to borrow. The property tax is often viewed as being a stable revenue source, especially relative to income and sales taxes. The stability results from the relative insensitivity of property assessments to changes in cyclical economic conditions. (Netzer & Berne, 1995, p. 52)

Revenue growth associated with elastic taxes (with an elasticity coefficient of more than 1.0) during periods of economic expansion enables governments to expand programs and services and to balance budgets without the frequent adjustments in rates required by stable or inelastic taxes. But during recession, a time when governmental assistance is more likely to be needed by the general population, tax yields from elastic taxes drop at a greater rate than the rate of the general economic decline. A tax with a relatively high coefficient of elasticity, such as the income tax, produces revenues that fluctuate with economic conditions. This flexibility, or responsiveness, may be advantageous if the economy is expanding, but it may constrain governmental services during a reces-

sion. A more stable tax offers predictable revenue yields—even in an uncertain economy.

Administrative Burden

The costs of tax administration and compliance can generally be thought of as administrative burden. Operating processes for collecting a tax are necessary but costly for governments in monetary and other ways. A good tax system should be certain, with no hidden taxes on families and businesses. The tax system must also ensure nonarbitrary administration, and the administrative costs must be low enough to make possible a sufficient relative yield while also discouraging tax evasion. Similarly, processes imposed on taxpayers to determine what they owe should be understandable and should not cause a nuisance. Because compliance and administrative costs detract from yield and taxpayer acceptance, they should be minimized.

Taxation should have clearly stated obligations for individuals and businesses. Stability in government and in the private sector depends in part on a tax system in which payments are predictable. Businesses must be certain about taxes when they make investments, and individuals must be secure against unpredictable taxes being levied on their incomes (Eckstein, 1967, p. 58).

Some critics might call into question the fairness of property taxation because of exemptions granted to charitable institutions, government-owned properties, veterans, and Native American reservations. Other critics might find fault with different assessment ratios applied to business, agricultural, and vacant property classifications. Political pressure and outright corruption sometimes interfere with the application of uniform procedures called for in tax codes.

Taxpayer acceptance of tax burden depends to a large extent on ease of compliance. Such methods as payroll deductions for income taxes, inclusion of property tax collections with home mortgage payments, and sales tax collections on goods at the time of purchase reduce compliance costs. In contrast, the time and expense of income tax preparation place a costly burden on taxpayers because of the complexity of federal and state tax codes.

Enforceability is important in the structure of a good tax system. Tax *avoidance* is a legal activity to maximize after-tax income. Individuals and businesses consider tax provisions as they plan expenditures or decide on the most advantageous investments. Tax *evasion* is illegal noncompliance with tax code provisions. All tax systems require the government to locate and place a value on taxable objects. Evasion or avoidance may result if it is easy to hide certain forms of property or income, if it is difficult for assessors to appraise them, or if it is easy to overestimate particular income tax deductions.

Audits that help ensure accurate reporting of property value or taxable income are very costly to government agencies, individuals, and businesses in terms of personnel and technologies. If auditing processes are overly invasive or intrusive, the taxing agency may evoke more dissatisfaction with the tax system than it is worth for the additional revenue gained from the process. On the other hand, relaxed audit procedures may tempt otherwise honest taxpayers to take advantage.

MEASURING THE IMPACT OF TAXES AND TAX STRUCTURE

Taxpayers and governments are concerned about the economic impact of tax structures and about their overall fairness. Crucial in understanding the impact of taxes on taxpayers and the economy are questions related to the ways in which taxpayers are classified, the selection of measures of economic ability, and the relative burdens of taxes on different groups. In this section, we discuss the concept of incidence and several measures of the impacts of taxation.

The person or business that bears the initial impact of a given tax is not always the point of ultimate *incidence*, the "settling, or coming to rest, of the tax" (Seligman, 1927, p. 2). An increased tax on a corporation, for example, may be shifted *forward* to consumers who pay higher prices for goods. Alternatively, the burden may fall *backward* to investors who derive smaller dividends or to employees who receive smaller salaries.

A first concern in understanding incidence is defining the group that is the focus of analysis. A narrowly defined group of taxpayers (defined, for example on the basis of race or occupation), would offend the concept of equity even though all members of a given class might be taxed the same. The more appropriate classification for examining tax treatment is income, and of concern is the relative impact of taxation on different income groups who bear the ultimate incidence.

An *indirect* tax is one in which the burden is easily transferred. For example, excise taxes on tobacco products, initially imposed on manufacturers who pay the government, are shifted wholly or in part to consumers (depending on market conditions). It is more difficult to shift a *direct* tax that is imposed on individuals who are meant to bear the burden (such as the property tax on an owner-occupied residence or a tax on personal income). Even an income tax can be shifted, as may occur when individuals are transferred to higher-income-tax jurisdictions and higher salaries are granted to offset the increased tax burden. Employers might then attempt to shift the additional tax burden to consumers through higher prices. The alternative is to suffer lower profits and pay lower dividends to investors.

Some states can shift, or export, tax burdens to residents of other states. This occurs most dramatically in the case of energy-rich states that fund their governments through severance taxes, which are ultimately paid by persons in energy-consuming states. Similarly, the sales tax in states that enjoy high levels of travel and tourism trade can provide state revenues borne largely by out-of-state visitors.

A second concern is identifying the basis for judging how tax burdens are related to the economic positions of taxpayers. Because taxes are ultimately paid from income, tax burdens are most often compared in relation to personal income. A *progressive* tax is one, such as the federal income tax, in which the proportion of income paid to the government increases as income rises. A tax system that collects $240 and $500 from taxpayers with incomes of $30,000 and $50,000, respectively, is progressive. A larger percentage of income (0.8 percent and 1.0 percent, respectively) is collected from the higher-income group. If the proportion collected decreases as income levels rise, the tax is *regressive*. For example, assuming the same amount of property tax is levied on similar homes in a given area of a commu-nity, some households may pay 8 percent of their incomes in taxes, whereas others with twice the income pay only 4 percent of their in-comes. A *proportional* tax demands the same percentage of income from all income groups. The burden of a payroll tax that assesses the same flat rate on all earned income (e.g., a 2 percent citywide payroll tax on gross income) is proportional.

Relative tax burdens are evident in state and local taxes paid in relation to family incomes in selected cities (see Table 3.1). New York City provides an example of a progressive tax system. The burden grows from 8.6 percent of income for families earning $25,000 to the considerably greater 14.1 percent for those with a $100,000 income. In contrast is the slight regressivity noted in Philadelphia, a city

TABLE 3.1.

Total State and Local Taxes[a] Paid as a Percentage of Income in Selected Cities, 1998

City	Family Income[b]			
	$25,000	*$50,000*	*$75,000*	*$100,000*
Albuquerque, NM	6.4	7.3	8.4	8.9
Atlanta, GA	7.0	8.5	9.7	10.0
Baltimore, MD	7.1	10.7	11.2	11.2
Chicago, IL	10.8	10.5	11.0	10.7
Columbus, OH	8.3	8.7	9.5	9.9
Detroit, MI	9.6	9.9	10.6	10.6
Indianapolis, IN	8.0	7.6	7.8	7.7
Kansas City, MO	8.9	9.0	9.6	9.6
Memphis, TN	6.0	4.9	5.3	5.2
Milwaukee, WI	9.9	11.2	11.7	11.6
New York City, NY	8.6	11.7	13.4	14.1
Philadelphia, PA	13.0	12.2	12.2	11.9
Portland, ME	10.7	12.1	13.5	13.7
Seattle, WA	8.3	7.0	7.2	6.8
Washington, DC	8.6	9.3	10.5	10.9
Median (51 cities)	7.7	8.3	9.4	9.6

[a] Includes state and local sales, income, auto, and real estate taxes.

[b] Mean income for family of four with two wage earners, owning their home and living in the city where taxes apply.

Source: U.S. Department of Commerce, Bureau of the Census. (2000). *Statistical Abstract of the United States: 2000*. Washington, DC: U. S. Government Printing Office, Table 516.

in which the burden falls more heavily on lower-income groups. The tax burdens in Baltimore, Detroit, and Kansas City are progressive through an income of $75,000, at which point they become proportional. In addition to these comparisons among income levels, the range in tax burdens among cities reveals differences in tax policies and practices. At the $50,000 income level, for example, the proportion of income paid in taxes in Memphis (4.9 percent) is substantially less than half of that paid in Philadelphia (12.2 percent).

The conclusions drawn from more sophisticated comparisons of revenue sources and distributions of tax burdens depend in part on the assumptions made about tax incidence. In his analyses of incidence, Pechman (1985) contrasted combined federal, state, and local tax burdens under eight variants, or sets of assumptions. All variants assigned individual income taxes to taxpayers and general sales and excise taxes to consumers; differences in incidence came through the treatment of corporate income, property, and payroll taxes. His least progressive variant, variant 3b, appears in Table 3.2. Under this variant, property taxes are divided in such a way that taxes on land fall on landowners, whereas taxes on buildings and other improvements fall on consumers. This variant also allocates to consumers half the corporate income tax and half the payroll tax on employers. Under Pechman's most progressive set of assumptions, variant 1c in Table 3.2, all property taxes are assigned to owners of capital, and corporate income taxes are divided between stockholders and owners of capital.

Effective tax rates provide an expression of the amount of tax that is assumed to be paid *after* shifting incidence as a proportion of income. Table 3.2 compares effective tax rates for 1966 and 1985 under the two sets of inci-

TABLE 3.2.

Percentage of Income Paid in Federal, State, and Local Taxes under Two Incidence Assumptions, 1966 to 1988

Group (Income decile)	Variant 3b (least progressive) (%)		Variant 1c (most progressive) (%)		
	1966	1985	1966	1985	1988[a]
First[b]	27.5	24.0	16.8	17.0	16.4
Second	24.8	20.1	18.9	15.9	15.8
Third	26.0	20.7	21.7	18.1	18.0
Fourth	25.9	23.2	22.6	21.2	21.5
Fifth	25.8	24.4	22.8	23.4	23.9
Sixth	25.6	25.0	22.7	23.8	24.3
Seventh	25.5	25.5	22.7	24.7	25.2
Eighth	25.5	26.2	23.1	25.4	25.6
Ninth	25.1	26.7	23.3	26.2	26.8
Tenth	25.9	25.0	30.1	26.4	27.7
All deciles	25.9	25.3	25.2	24.5	25.4

[a] Projected from 1985 on the basis of estimates of changes in effective federal tax rates.

[b] Includes only the sixth to tenth percentiles.

Source: J. A. Pechman. (1985). *Who Paid the Taxes, 1966-85?* Washington, DC: The Brookings Institution, Table 5-2, p. 68, with revisions obtained from the author; reprinted with the permission of the Brookings Institution; J. A. Pechman. (1989b). *The Case Against the Value Added Tax. Statement before the U.S. Senate Finance Committee*, p. 7.

dence assumptions just described and for the most progressive variant through 1988. With the exception of the lowest-income earners, who bear a heavier burden than those in the second decile, the overall tax system is somewhat progressive. The burden was nearly proportional through the middle range of income (the fourth to seventh deciles) in 1966 under each variant. By 1985 there was greater progression for the second through ninth deciles.

Under the most progressive set of assumptions, which Pechman (1989b) accepted as the most realistic, there had been a substantial decline in the burden of the highest-income decile. In 1985 effective rates were 17 percent for individuals earning less than $7,300 and 26.4 percent for those earning over $60,000. In 1966 the burden was similar for the lowest-income group (16.8 percent), but there was a much higher burden (30.1 percent) for the highest-income decile. Changes in effective rates between 1966 and 1985 favored wealthy taxpayers. The rate for the top 5 percent of income earners declined from 32.7 percent to 26 percent, and the rate for the top 1 percent of income earners declined even more dramatically, from 39.6 percent to 25.3 percent. Pechman attributed this decline to reductions in personal income tax rates (from a cap of 70 percent to a cap of 50 percent in this time period) and in effective corporate rates (from 32.8 percent to 16 percent).

Estimates for effective tax rates in 1988 for the most progressive assumptions, reported in Table 3.2, reveal effects of increases in social security tax rates (which are highly regressive) since 1985 and of revisions in income taxation brought about by the Tax Reform Act of 1986. These latter changes in the personal income tax eliminated the tax advantages of some tax shelters and raised personal exemptions and the standard deduction. Despite lower rates, collections from the corporate income tax increased under the Tax Reform Act. This legislation redefined the tax base and removed loopholes (Pechman, 1989b). Overall, tax bur-

dens declined somewhat in the first three income deciles and increased in the top seven, making the tax system more progressive between 1985 and 1988. However, despite restoration of some of the progressivity between 1966 and 1985, the highest-income decile continues to benefit from lower effective rates than those paid in 1966. Galper and Pollock (1988) also found greater progressivity in simulations of changed tax burdens between 1986 and 1987 in both federal and individual state systems.

Shifts in burdens among income groups are also evident in Table 3.2. The aggregate tax burden did not change over the two decades; the average proportion of income paid in taxes remained about 25 percent. However, burdens on middle and upper income earners (the fifth to ninth deciles) grew, whereas those born by people in the lowest four deciles and in the highest-income group declined. Thus a shifting in tax burdens occurred at both extremes of income.

Consideration of the presence of income transfers provides additional insight into relative tax burdens. Welfare, food stamp, social security, unemployment insurance, and other such social programs have the effect of shifting monies from higher-income groups to poorer families, thus making the tax system less regressive (or more progressive). Pechman's analyses that included transfer payments show that families in the lowest three deciles receive more transfers than they pay in taxes, whereas those in the other deciles pay more taxes than they receive in transfers. He concludes that the "tax-transfer system is, therefore, highly progressive" (Pechman, 1989a, p. 23).

TRADE-OFFS AMONG VALUES AND CRITERIA

Weighing the advantages and disadvantages of various proposals for new taxes or for reform in current tax structures involves value judgments to be resolved in the political arena. The values of liberty, equality, fraternity, efficiency, and economic growth discussed in Part I are affected by modifications in tax systems. The development of tax policy is an evolutionary process that seeks balance among these often conflicting values: "Taxation is an art and a technique as well as a science, and it always needs to be judged against the conditions of time and place" (Groves, 1974, p. 24).

Conflicting goals of taxation demand trade-offs among these values and among criteria presented in this chapter. The goal of maximizing revenue yield by raising a given tax rate, for example, must be balanced with the principle of neutrality and its goal of minimizing social and economic disruptions. Similarly, a reform proposal designed to improve equity by shifting the burden to high-income groups may inadvertently be a strong incentive for some taxpayers or businesses to behave differently. Reforms driven by equity goals may also add excessive administrative burden, resulting in higher costs of compliance and enforcement. Increased import duties, which may be justified by the goals of protecting domestic producers and promoting economic development, can be criticized for reducing the incentive for production efficiency.

In reality, legislative bodies operate somewhere between a deliberate consideration of just and equitable taxation in relation to these goals and what Johns, Morphet, and Alexander (1983, p. 94) present as the eclectic principle. This approach, referred to as a "social expediency theory" of taxation, recognizes that taxes are obtained most easily when they affect groups least likely to object: "Pluck the goose that squawks the least." Politicians recognize the political liability of raising taxes on groups that complain vigorously. However, the consequences can be minimized by increasing taxes gradually, rather than in big jumps, and by making a strong case that tax increases are essential to maintain or dramatically improve services (Gold, 1994, p. 6).

The politics of public policy making is played out to the fullest when proposals are entertained to tip the balance among tax sources. Diverse interest groups, including public school personnel, exert pressure on policy makers when a tax bill is being considered. Governmental agencies and special-interest groups such as teacher unions and school board associations seek revenue to raise salaries or sponsor new programs. Some organizations promote policies to shift tax burdens to induce greater equity in tax structures without raising revenue. Still other industries desire favorable tax treatment and reduced burdens to stimulate investments and economic productivity. The same groups that argue for reform in tax policy are likely to resist changes that would negatively affect their social or economic positions. Despite these diverse forces, or perhaps because of them, revenue systems of state and federal government change very slowly, and a delicate "balance" is achieved among the burdens placed on various tax bases.

The result is a mix of revenue sources that differs among levels of government and that is unique to each state. The particular taxes that fuel federal and state government are the subject of Chapter 4.

SUMMARY

The principles of taxation enumerated in this chapter shape the mosaic of tax policies that define the means by which funds are derived from private-sector households and businesses for use in the public sector. The federated system of governance and finance in the United States illustrates that some forms of taxation are better suited to some governmental jurisdictions than to others. There is no distinct division of authority over tax policy among levels of government in a federated system. Changes in tax structure and administration at one level of government affect tax policy and yield at other levels of governmental jurisdiction.

Policy makers must continually assess the potential of various tax bases—including wealth, income, consumption, and privilege—for raising the revenue necessary to delivering public services while maintaining a fair system of taxation. Criteria of yield, equity, neutrality, elasticity, and administrative burden are useful constructs for understanding policy intents and consequences. Taxes are designed to raise government revenue while also serving various economic and social goals that affect individuals and businesses. Tax policy development is extremely complex because of underlying real and perceived threats to liberty, equality, fraternity, efficiency, and economic growth: "Relief for one class of citizens may mean overburden for another, and how these tensions are balanced by tax policies affects the social and economic progress of individuals and the nation" (MacPhail-Wilcox, 1984, pp. 318–319). The effectiveness of the tax system depends to a large extent on actual and perceived fairness of treatment for all taxpayers. Analyses of tax incidence and relative burdens conclude that the overall government revenue system in the United States is progressive, particularly when transfers of money to poor people are considered.

We turn next to the merits of various tax sources in relation to the goals of taxation and criteria presented in this chapter. Chapter 4 focuses on federal and state tax policies. The property tax and other revenue sources for local school districts are the subjects of Chapters 5 and 6.

ACTIVITIES

1. What are the justifications, if any, for permitting each level of government to draw on any available tax base for obtaining necessary revenue? For what reasons might each level be limited to one or two specific tax bases?
2. In what ways might the values introduced in Part I and the principles of taxation presented in this chapter be considered when designing mechanisms for coordinating tax structures and policies among federal, state, and local governments?
3. Record the per capita income and tax receipts from selected sources in a given state over the past ten years, and calculate the elasticity of these taxes relative to income growth. (Using an electronic spreadsheet will greatly expedite the calculations.)
4. Define the concept of neutrality as it is related to tax systems, and debate the advantages and disadvantages of using tax policy to influence the economic and social behavior of individuals and private-sector businesses.

REFERENCES

Due, J. F. (1976). Alternative state and local tax sources for education. In K. Alexander & K. F. Jordan. (Eds.), *Educational need in the public economy* (pp. 257–298). Gainesville: University Presses of Florida.

Eckstein, O. (1967). *Public finance* (2nd ed.). Englewood Cliffs, NJ: Prentice-Hall.

Galper, H., & Pollock, S. H. (1988). Models of state income tax reform. In S. D. Gold (Ed.), *The unfinished agenda for state tax reform* (pp. 107–128). Denver, CO: National Conference of State Legislatures.

Gold, S. D. (1994). *Tax options for states needing more school revenue*. Westhaven, CT: National Education Association.

Groves, H. (1974). *Two hundred years of thought in Great Britain and the United States*. Madison: University of Wisconsin Press.

Johns, R. L., Morphet, E. L., & Alexander, K. (1983). *The economics and financing of education* (4th ed.). Englewood Cliffs, NJ: Prentice-Hall.

Levin, H. M. (1987). School finance. In G. Psacharopoulos (Ed.), *Economics of education: Research and studies* (pp. 326–436). Oxford, England: Pergamon Press.

MacPhail-Wilcox, B. (1984). Tax policy analysis and education finance: A conceptual framework for issues and analysis. *Journal of Education Finance, 9,* 312–331.

Musgrave, R. A., & Musgrave, P. B. (1989). *Public finance in theory and practice* (5th ed.). New York: McGraw-Hill.

Netzer, D., & Berne, R. (1995). Discrepancies between ideal characteristics of a property tax system and current practice in New York. In D. H. Monk (Ed,), *Study on the generation of revenues for education, Final report* (pp. 31–47). Albany, NY: State Education Department.

Oates, W. E. (1972). *Fiscal federalism.* New York: Harcourt.

Pechman, J. A. (1985). *Who paid the taxes, 1966–85?* Washington, DC: The Brookings Institution.

Pechman, J. A. (1989a). *Tax reform, the rich and the poor* (2nd ed.). Washington, DC: The Brookings Institution.

Pechman, J. A. (1989b). The case against the value added tax. Statement before the U.S. Senate Finance Committee.

Seligman, E. R. A. (1927). *The shifting and incidence of taxation.* New York: Columbia University Press.

Smith, A. (1993, originally published 1776). *An inquiry into the nature and causes of the wealth of nations.* Oxford, England: Oxford University Press.

U.S. Department of Commerce, Bureau of the Census. (2000). *Statistical abstract of the United States: 2000.* Washington, DC: U.S. Government Printing Office.

Webb, L. D., McCarthy, M. M., & Thomas, S. B. (1988). *Financing elementary and secondary education.* Columbus, OH: Merrill.

Chapter **4**

REVENUE SOURCES FOR FEDERAL AND STATE GOVERNMENTS

Issues and Questions

- *Achieving High Standards with Equity and Efficiency*: To what extent do state and federal government rely on the primary tax bases and intergovernmental transfers to support public services, including education, and what reforms might improve the tax capacity and effort made to raise revenue for education?
- *Assessing the Merits of State and Federal Taxes*: What are the advantages and disadvantages of personal and corporate income taxes, excise and sales taxes, lotteries, severance taxes, estate and gift taxes, and payroll taxes in relation to the criteria presented in Chapter 3?
- *Achieving a Balanced Tax System*: Why is it beneficial for government to rely on multiple, broad-based revenue sources?

As state and federal government shares of school resources grew rapidly during the 1960s and 1970s, and as public dissatisfaction with property taxation intensified during the 1980s and 1990s, educators became increasingly interested in the revenue sources that fueled state and federal government. This chapter continues with the discussion of taxation, turning from the general principles presented in Chapter 3 to a review of the primary revenue sources that state and federal governments use to support schools and other public services. Local government is discussed only briefly in this chapter. Local reliance on property taxation and other revenue sources is the focus of Chapters 5 and 6.

PRIMARY REVENUE SOURCES

The total revenue raised by all levels of government in 1995 was $2.759 trillion. Included in this grand total is the $1.418 trillion that financed state and local governments (U.S. Department of Commerce, 2000, p. 301). Federal, state, and local levels of government rely on specific revenue sources to very different degrees in raising these monies.

The proportions of revenue collected from intergovernmental transfers and from each level of government's own tax sources are presented in Table 4.1. Grants-in-aid flow from federal to state governments to provide almost one-quarter of state revenue. Similar transfers from federal and state to local levels constitute about one-third of the total revenue of school districts, municipalities, and special districts. These intergovernmental transfers grew in total throughout the twentieth century, but as shown in Table 4.1, between 1980 and 1995 there was a decline in the proportion of intergovernmental transfers used to fund local government.

Property taxation provides no federal funds and negligible state funds and has declined in relative importance at local levels. Between 1970 and 1995, the importance of property taxes diminished from about 37 percent to about 20 percent of total revenue for all local government units. Although the property tax remains the primary source of revenue that is readily available to local school districts, this reliance has been questioned, and many states and localities want other sources to replace this revenue. Michigan voters, for example, sup-

TABLE 4.1.

Revenue for Federal, State, and Local Government (percentage of total revenue)

Source	Federal			State			Local		
	1970	*1980*	*1995*	*1970*	*1980*	*1995*	*1970*	*1980*	*1995*
Taxes									
Property	0.0	0.0	0.0	1.1	1.1	1.1	37.1	25.6	19.8
Individual income	43.7	43.2	37.5	10.1	13.4	13.9	2.2	1.9	1.6
Corporate income	16.0	11.5	10.0	4.5	4.7	3.2	0.0	0.0	0.2
Sales or gross receipts	8.7	5.7	4.8	30.3	24.5	21.7	3.4	4.7	5.3
Total taxes[a]	68.4	62.1	53.7	46.0	49.5	44.0	42.7	33.3	34.5
Charges and miscellaneous	8.3	11.9	10.8	10.1	11.6	13.7	14.6	17.1	20.6
Intergovernmental	0.0	0.4	0.2	22.5	23.1	23.8	33.7	39.5	34.2
Other revenue	33.3	25.6	35.3	21.4	15.8	18.5	9.0	11.2	10.7
Total revenue	100.0	100.0	100.0	100.0	100.0	100.0	100.0	100.0	100.0

[a] Includes taxes not listed separately.

Source: U.S. Department of Commerce, Bureau of the Census. (2000). *Statistical Abstract of the United States: 2000.* Washington, DC: U.S. Government Printing Office, Table 493.

ported an increase in the sales tax from 4 percent to 6 percent in order to offset local property tax revenues that were lost through a 1993 legislative action.

The federal government derives the bulk of its revenue from individual income taxation. State reliance on this source grew from about 10 percent to about 14 percent of total tax receipts between 1970 and 1995. The proportion of total tax receipts generated from sales taxes and gross receipts taxes, however, fell from about 30 percent to about 22 percent during the same period. These taxes nonetheless remain the single most important source of state revenue. The corporate income tax is declining relative to other tax sources at both federal and state levels. In contrast, user charges and miscellaneous other revenues are growing in importance at state and local levels of government. At the local level, user fees and sales taxes grew as the proportion raised by intergovernmental transfers and property taxes decreased.

The international comparison of tax receipts presented in Table 4.2 indicates the degree to which the United States (including all levels of government) relies on available tax sources in relation to other nations. Canada relies on the personal income tax about as much as the United States; Sweden is the only other nation that relies on the personal income tax for over one-third of its revenue. Japan and the United Kingdom place the heaviest burden among these nations on corporate income taxes. Six nations collect a higher percentage of tax receipts for social security than does the United States.

There is substantially lighter use of consumption-based taxes in the United States than in all countries except for Japan. The European nations are generally higher than others in consumption-based taxes, placing a value-added tax on goods in all stages of production. All countries except Japan exhibit a preference for general consumption taxes over taxes on specific goods and services. The category "other revenue" in Table 4.2 includes property tax receipts, which produces varying proportions of revenue in these countries. The

TABLE 4.2.

Distribution of Total Government Tax Receipts for Selected Countries, 1997 (percentage of total)

Country	Individual Income	Corporate Income	Social Security	General Consumption[a]	Excise Tax on Specific Goods and Services[b]	Other Revenue[c]
Canada	38.0	10.3	13.4	13.9	8.4	16.0
France	14.0	5.8	40.6	17.8	8.8	13.0
Germany	23.9	4.0	41.6	17.6	9.0	3.9
Italy	25.3	9.5	33.5	12.6	9.7	9.4
Japan	20.5	15.0	36.9	7.0	7.6	13.0
Netherlands	15.6	10.5	40.9	16.0	9.5	7.5
Sweden	35.0	6.1	29.2	13.6	8.0	8.1
United Kingdom	24.8	12.1	17.2	19.5	13.9	12.5
United States	39.0	9.4	24.2	7.8	6.8	12.8

[a] Primary value-added and sales taxes.

[b] For example, alcohol, tobacco, and gasoline.

[c] Includes property taxes, other payroll taxes, and miscellaneous taxes not shown separately.

Source: U.S. Department of Commerce, Bureau of the Census. (2000). *Statistical Abstract of the United States: 2000.* Washington, DC: U.S. Government Printing Office, Table 1375.

Advisory Commission on Intergovernmental Relations (1992, p. 27) reported property tax collections in 1989 ranging from 9.1 percent at state and local levels in Germany to 100 percent of local revenue in the United Kingdom. Italy and Sweden do not use this revenue source, and this tax generated 31.7 percent of state and local revenue in the United States. Differences among nations in reliance on the taxes included in Table 4.2 reflect the structure of the various economies, including the degree of fiscal centralization, the importance of the corporate sector, and varying tax policies and attitudes (Musgrave & Musgrave, 1989, p. 322).

Revenue for the Federal Government

Trends in revenue collections of the United States government are evident in Table 4.3. Individual income taxation increased from about $90 to $952 billion dollars between 1970 and 2000. In total dollars, all sources of federal government tax receipt grew during the 30-year period. The relative importance of individual income taxation remained about the same over the decades; income taxes accounted for 46.9 percent of total receipts in 1970 and for 48.6 percent in 2000. Relative to other sources, reliance on corporate income taxation diminished, from 17.0 percent to 9.8 percent during the same time period.

Payroll tax collections, including social security and unemployment insurance, grew dramatically during these decades. The proportion of total federal revenue gained from these payroll taxes rose from 23.0 percent to 33.2 percent. Excise taxes, on the other hand, dropped to less than half of their relative importance—from 8.1 percent to 3.5 percent—between 1970 and 2000.

Revenue for State Government

Because public schools depend heavily on state general revenue funds for their support, sources of revenue available to state legislatures are of particular importance to educators. The fifty states vary greatly in the extent to which they rely on different revenue sources.

As indicated in Table 4.4, from 1970 to 1990, the total amount collected by states from

TABLE 4.3.

Federal Government Tax Receipts, 1970 to 2000

Source	Amount (billions)				Percentage of Total			
	1970	*1980*	*1990*	*2000[a]*	*1970*	*1980*	*1990*	*2000[a]*
Individual income	$90.4	$244.1	$466.9	$951.6	46.9	47.2	45.2	48.6
Corporation income	32.8	64.6	93.5	192.4	17.0	12.5	9.1	9.8
Social security and unemployment	44.4	157.8	380.0	650.0	23.0	30.5	36.8	33.2
Excise	15.7	24.3	35.3	68.4	8.1	4.7	3.4	3.5
Miscellaneous receipts	9.4	26.3	56.3	93.9	5.0	5.1	5.5	4.8
Total	192.8	517.1	1032.0	1956.3	100.0	100.0	100.0	100.0

[a] Estimated.

Source: U.S. Department of Commerce, Bureau of the Census. (2000). *Statistical Abstract of the United States: 2000*. Washington, DC: U.S. Government Printing Office, Table 534.

consumption-based taxes was larger than that collected from income-based taxes. This relationship changed over the last decade. By 2000, the combined revenue from general sales taxes and specific excise taxes on motor fuels, alcohol, and tobacco products was $217,051 billion, whereas the total collected from individual and corporate income taxes was $226,785 billion. The change in relative proportions of total collections is also evident in Table 4.4. General sales tax collections increased only slightly between 1970 and 2000 (from 29.6 percent to 32.3 percent); personal income taxes increased sharply (from 19.1 percent to 36.0 percent) during the same time period. In addition, excise taxes on motor fuels, vehicle and license fees, and alcohol and tobacco products declined in relative importance. This decline reflects, in part, the nature of the tax base. For example, excise taxes are typically applied per unit (e.g., per gallon of gasoline), whereas sales and income taxes are based on the value of items or earnings.

The higher rate of growth in income taxes reflects both their greater elasticity and a general preference among states for imposing income-based rather than consumption-based taxation. The rate of change in amounts collected just from personal income taxes (a 1037 percent increase from $9.2 billion in 1970 to $104.6 billion in 1992) exceeded the rate of change in general sales taxes (an increase of 659 percent from $14.2 billion in 1970 to $107.8 billion in 1992). With elasticity at about unity, sales tax revenue grows at about the rate of change in inflation. Thus rates were altered, and the scope of coverage was expanded to encompass additional goods and services, in order to stimulate the 659 percent revenue growth (ACIR, 1995, p. 89–94). At the same time, income tax rates were indexed to slow the rate of growth to about that of inflation—suggesting that the rapid change noted is due largely to factors other than the generally greater elasticity of income taxes. States expanded their use of income taxes; indeed, four states (New

TABLE 4.4.

State Government Tax Receipts, 1970 to 2000 (millions)

Source	Amount (billions)				Percentage of Total			
	1970	*1980*	*1990*	*2000*	*1970*	*1980*	*1990*	*2000*
General sales and gross receipts	$14,177	$43,168	$99,702	$174,450	29.6	31.5	33.2	32.3
Individual income	9,183	37,089	96,076	194,461	19.1	27.1	32.0	36.0
Motor fuels	6,283	9,722	19,379	30,117	13.1	7.1	6.4	5.6
Corporation net income	3,738	13,321	21,751	32,324	7.8	9.7	7.2	6.0
Motor vehicle and operators' licenses	2,728	5,325	10,675	16,517	5.7	3.9	3.6	3.1
Alcohol and tobacco products	3,728	6,216	8,732	12,484	7.8	4.5	2.9	2.3
Estate and gift	996	2,035	3,832	7,998	2.1	1.5	1.3	1.5
Other taxes	7,129	20,199	40,342	71,289	14.9	14.7	13.4	13.2
Total	47,962	137,075	300,489	539,640	100.0	100.0	100.0	100.0

Source: U.S. Department of Commerce, Bureau of the Census. (1990). *State Government Tax Collections: 1990*. Washington, DC: U.S. Government Printing Office, GF-90-1; U.S. Department of Commerce, Bureau of the Census. (2001). *State Government Tax Collections: 2000*. Washington, DC: U.S. Government Printing Office, State Tax section.

Jersey, Ohio, Pennsylvania, and Rhode Island) adopted income taxes during this time period. One might conclude from the higher rate of growth in income taxes evident in this table that income taxation will become a more important revenue source for states in the future. On the other hand, the 1994 decision of Michigan voters to adopt a sales tax rather than have an income tax imposed by the legislature suggests a preference for consumption-based taxation.

The proportionate reliance on different tax sources presented in Table 4.5 illustrates the varied pattern of state tax policies. The yield of state tax collections, ranging from $927 million in South Dakota to $83.8 billion in California, varies with state populations. All but five states derive revenue from general sales taxation, and the states that have this consumption-based tax range, in proportion of total collections, from just 14.6 percent in Vermont to 61.6 percent in Washington. All states collect excise

TABLE 4.5.

Sources of State Government Tax Collections, 2000

| | | | | | *Percentage of Total Collections* | | | |
State	Total Collections (millions)	General Sales and Gross Receipts	Motor Fuels	Alcohol and Tobacco Products	Individual Income	Corporation Net Income	Motor Vehicle License Fees	Other Taxes[a]
AL	$ 6,438	26.4	7.8	2.9	32.2	3.8	3.0	23.9
AK	1,423	0.0	3.0	4.3	0.0	30.8	2.5	59.5
AZ	8,101	44.8	7.3	2.6	28.3	6.5	1.9	8.6
AR	4,871	35.0	8.0	2.5	30.2	4.9	2.4	17.0
CA	83,808	28.0	3.6	1.8	47.2	7.9	2.1	9.3
CO	7,075	26.1	7.7	1.3	51.4	4.7	2.5	6.2
CT	10,171	33.6	5.3	1.7	39.1	4.2	2.3	13.8
DE	2,132	0.0	4.9	1.8	34.4	11.3	1.5	46.1
FL	24,817	60.5	6.5	4.1	0.0	4.8	3.7	20.4
GA	13,511	34.3	4.7	1.7	47.1	5.3	1.7	5.3
HI	3,335	46.1	2.2	2.4	31.9	2.3	2.3	12.8
ID	2,377	31.4	8.8	1.5	40.6	5.3	4.6	7.9
IL	22,789	28.1	6.0	2.6	33.5	9.9	4.5	15.5
IN	10,104	35.4	6.9	1.2	37.1	9.2	1.6	8.6
IA	5,185	33.2	6.7	2.1	36.5	4.1	6.5	10.9
KS	4,865	35.8	7.3	2.6	38.3	5.6	3.0	7.4
KY	7,695	28.2	5.7	1.1	35.1	4.0	2.5	23.4
LA	6,512	31.6	8.4	2.2	24.3	3.4	1.7	28.3
ME	2,661	31.8	6.8	4.1	40.5	5.6	2.6	8.6
MD	10,354	24.1	6.3	2.3	44.6	4.2	1.7	16.9
MA	16,153	22.1	4.0	2.1	56.0	8.1	1.4	6.3
MI	22,756	33.7	4.7	3.2	31.6	10.5	3.6	12.7
MN	13,339	27.9	4.6	1.9	41.6	6.0	4.8	13.2
MS	4,712	49.5	8.9	2.0	21.4	4.8	2.4	11.0
MO	8,572	32.5	8.1	1.6	41.4	3.1	2.8	10.4
MT	1,412	0.0	13.4	2.2	36.6	7.1	3.9	36.9
NE	2,981	34.5	9.4	2.1	39.4	4.7	2.8	7.1
NV	3,717	52.2	7.0	2.2	0.0	0.0	3.1	35.5
NH	1,696	0.0	6.9	6.3	3.9	18.4	3.8	60.7
NJ	18,148	30.4	2.8	2.6	39.7	7.4	1.9	15.2

TABLE 4.5.

(Continued)

State	Total Collections (millions)	General Sales and Gross Receipts	Motor Fuels	Alcohol and Tobacco Products	Individual Income	Corporation Net Income	Motor Vehicle License Fees	Other Taxes[a]
		Percentage of Total Collections						
NM	3,743	40.1	6.2	1.6	23.5	4.3	3.8	20.4
NY	41,736	20.5	1.2	2.0	55.6	6.6	1.5	12.5
NC	15,216	22.1	8.0	1.6	46.6	6.5	2.8	12.4
ND	1,172	28.2	9.4	2.4	16.9	6.7	3.7	32.7
OH	19,676	31.8	7.1	1.9	41.9	3.2	3.1	11.0
OK	5,852	24.6	6.9	2.3	36.5	3.3	11.1	15.3
OR	5,946	0.0	8.0	3.4	68.9	6.8	6.2	6.7
PA	22,467	31.4	3.4	2.2	30.1	7.6	3.5	21.7
RI	2,035	30.5	6.4	3.4	40.7	3.7	2.5	12.7
SC	6,381	38.5	5.8	2.5	38.3	3.6	1.7	9.6
SD	927	52.6	13.5	3.2	0.0	4.9	4.2	21.6
TN	7,740	57.4	10.2	2.0	2.3	7.9	3.0	17.0
TX	27,424	51.1	9.8	3.8	0.0	0.0	3.4	31.9
UT	3,979	35.8	8.3	1.8	41.5	4.4	2.0	6.2
VT	1,471	14.6	4.1	1.9	29.4	3.0	2.4	44.6
VA	12,648	19.5	6.4	1.1	54.0	4.5	2.4	12.0
WA	12,567	61.6	6.2	3.5	0.0	0.0	2.3	26.4
WV	3,343	27.4	7.2	1.2	28.9	6.5	2.6	26.2
WI	12,643	27.7	7.2	2.4	47.1	4.6	2.4	8.5
WY	964	38.3	8.4	1.2	0.0	0.0	5.4	46.7
Total	$539,640	32.3	5.6	2.3	36.0	6.0	3.1	14.7

[a] Includes taxes and license fees not shown separately.

Source: U.S. Department of Commerce, Bureau of the Census. (2000). *State Government Tax Collections: 2000.* Washington, DC: U.S. Government Printing Office.

taxes on such specific goods and services as motor fuel, tobacco, and alcoholic beverages, but these sources of revenue make relatively small contributions to total revenue. All but seven states support public services through personal income taxes. This revenue amounts to almost 70 percent of total collections in Oregon. Corporate income taxes are used by all but four states, but the yield is low (6 percent overall) relative to other tax sources.

In addition to the primary taxes presented in Tables 4.4 and 4.5, states rely to different degrees on other sources of income, such as inheritance taxes, severance taxes, lotteries, and user fees. These sources and other taxes ac-

count for a large proportion of revenue in many states, including Alaska, Montana, and Wyoming, which rely heavily on severance taxes; Delaware, which relies on user charges and license fees; and Nevada, which turns to taxes on gambling. The varied proportions of state tax collections in Table 4.5 clearly illustrate the great variation in state reliance on different tax bases, but they do not reveal to what degree states make use of potential tax sources.

There are several ways to depict the relative effort that states exert to generate tax revenue from available sources. Congress created the Advisory Commission on Intergovernmental Relations (ACIR) to monitor and recommend improvements in tax practices and policies. This agency is now named the American Council on Intergovernmental Relations. ACIR reports (1) the proportions of family incomes that are spent on taxes, and (2) data on the degree to which each state makes use of available tax capacities. This latter method of assessing relative effort is more sensitive to the diversity of tax sources and the ability of states to shift burdens to nonresidents.

The ACIR's Representative Tax System (RTS) provides an index of each state's tax base, using the national average rate for each of twenty-seven commonly used levies. Fiscal *capacity* is the relative per capita amount of tax revenue that a given state would raise if its tax system made use of all these levies. Measurements of capacity are useful in monitoring trends in states' fiscal health and providing perspectives on regional economic trends. Tax *effort*, which is measured as a state's actual tax revenue relative to its hypothetical fiscal capacity, indicates the overall tax burden placed on that base. Measures of effort can be used to compare the degrees to which states use available tax bases. These measures of capacity and effort could be employed to target aid to states that have less ability to raise revenue from their own sources or to target federal aid through grant formulas that reflect tax efforts. Policy makers can determine easily whether a state is "underutilizing" or "overworking" particular tax sources relative to the national average. However, ACIR cautions analysts interpreting these "descriptive" data as follows: "They are not meant to imply that a state should or should not have a particular tax effort or revenue mix. Furthermore, state rankings in fiscal capacity do not imply better or worse services or revenue systems, or more or less efficiency in taxation." (ACIR, 1993, p. 9).

States' actual tax revenues from state and local sources expressed as percentages of personal incomes in 1992, and ACIR's indices of states' tax capacities and efforts in 1991, are shown in Table 4.6. These data provide infor-

mation about individual states and reveal regional differences. For example, Wisconsin's capacity is 10 percent below the national average, but the effort index of 118 shows that its capacity is taxed well above average. This effort is also apparent in the 12.2 percent of personal income that is collected in state and local taxes. In contrast is New Hampshire, a state whose capacity is 10 percent above the national average. This state's effort lags at 16 percent below average, and it collects a lower than average 9.6 percent of income in taxes. Nevada and Wyoming also exhibit low effort despite their large tax capacities; New Hampshire does not employ sales taxes, and the other states do not make use of personal income taxation.

The states with the highest relative capacities are Alaska, Hawaii, Wyoming, Connecticut, Nevada, Delaware, New Jersey, Massachusetts, and California. Those exerting the highest efforts are New York, Alaska, Wisconsin, Rhode Island, Minnesota, New Jersey, Michigan, Maryland, and Arizona. Washington, D.C. also has high capacity and effort. Alaska, the state with the highest relative capacity, also appears to exert one of the highest levels of effort. This state's collections of 17 percent of personal income—a large proportion despite having no sales or income taxes—are derived primarily from severance taxes on the extraction of natural resources. Thus the point of incidence of this tax is not the residents of the state but, rather, out-of-state businesses and individuals who are consumers of energy and products made from extracted minerals. The revenue gained through these taxes enables Alaska to make annual rebates available to residents instead of charging them income taxes.

In general, states in the Great Lakes and Plains regions have higher than average effort, relative to capacity. Many states in New England and the Far West exhibit relatively higher capacities than their rankings in tax effort. Many states in the Southeast (Arkansas, Alabama, and Tennessee in particular) exhibit low capacity and low relative effort. With a

TABLE 4.6.

Regional Variation in Tax Revenue as a Percentage of Personal Income and in Tax Capacity and Effort

States by Region	State and Local Taxes as Percentage of Personal Income (1992)	Capacity (1991)			Effort (1991)		
		Score	Rank	1988–1991 Change	Index	Rank	1988–1991 Change
New England							
Connecticut	11.3	130	4	−13	99	18	9
Maine	11.8	95	24	−3	102	11	−3
Massachusetts	10.8	117	9	−12	101	13	7
New Hampshire	9.6	110	11	−16	84	43	18
Rhode Island	11.1	89	38	−10	115	5	11
Vermont	12.1	105	15	0	97	21	−3
Mideast							
Delaware	11.3	125	6	1	80	49	−4
Washington, DC	14.7	123	7	0	157	1	3
Maryland	10.0	106	14	−3	103	9	−5
New Jersey	11.2	119	8	−5	112	6	11
New York	14.7	103	16	−6	156	2	4
Pennsylvania	10.6	96	23	2	95	25	−2
Great Lakes							
Illinois	10.1	102	19	3	100	14	−2
Indiana	9.7	90	36	3	93	31	0
Michigan	11.1	94	26	−1	107	8	−5
Ohio	10.2	93	28	2	96	23	−1
Wisconsin	12.2	90	36	0	118	4	−1
Plains							
Iowa	11.1	93	28	10	100	14	−13
Kansas	10.1	93	28	2	100	14	−4
Minnesota	12.1	101	20	−3	112	6	0
Missouri	8.8	91	32	1	85	42	−1
Nebraska	10.7	95	24	5	99	18	1
North Dakota	10.3	91	32	5	92	33	1
South Dakota	9.1	86	42	8	83	44	−12
Southeast							
Alabama	8.7	81	48	5	81	47	−3
Arkansas	9.7	78	49	4	82	45	−2
Florida	9.8	103	16	−1	86	40	4
Georgia	9.8	91	32	−3	95	25	6
Kentucky	10.6	83	43	2	100	14	12
Louisiana	10.4	89	38	6	89	37	−1
Mississippi	9.4	68	51	3	92	33	−2
North Carolina	10.2	93	28	2	87	38	−6
South Carolina	9.8	83	43	4	90	36	−6
Tennessee	8.3	82	45	−2	82	45	−1
Virginia	9.5	103	16	−1	91	35	0
West Virginia	10.6	77	50	−1	102	11	14

(continued)

TABLE 4.6.

(Continued)

States by Region	State and Local Taxes as Percentage of Personal Income (1992)	Capacity (1991)			Effort (1991)		
		Score	Rank	1988–1991 Change	Index	Rank	1988–1991 Change
Southwest							
Arizona	11.6	94	26	–5	103	9	7
New Mexico	11.6	87	40	4	96	23	–3
Oklahoma	10.0	87	40	–2	93	31	4
Texas	10.1	97	22	1	87	38	–1
Rocky Mountain							
Colorado	9.8	109	12	2	86	40	–3
Idaho	10.7	82	45	6	94	29	–3
Montana	10.9	91	32	6	78	50	–24
Utah	10.9	82	45	4	94	29	–12
Wyoming	12.5	134	3	11	81	47	–13
Far West							
Alaska	17.4	178	1	19	119	3	–8
California	13.2	115	10	–1	95	25	1
Hawaii	14.1	146	2	32	95	25	–17
Nevada	9.4	128	5	–7	73	51	4
Oregon	11.3	100	21	9	97	21	–2
Washington	10.9	108	13	10	99	18	–3
U.S. Average	10.8	100			100		

Source: ACIR. (1994). *Significant Features of Fiscal Federalism, Vol. 2: Revenues and Expenditures.* Washington, DC: Advisory Commission on Intergovernmental Relations, Tables 51, 98–99, pp. 92–93, 182–183.

few exceptions, states in the Mideast are higher than average on both measures. Interestingly, the relationship between capacity and effort does not appear to be an indirect one as might be expected. That is, states with higher relative capacities are able to provide the same services at lower levels of effort than other states. Indeed, many of the wealthier states appear to be willing to expand and improve the quality of services by exerting higher relative efforts than other states. Many of these states exert greater effort to offset the large costs associated with their urbanization.

This table also indicates the change in RTS scores over the period from 1988 to 1991, re-

vealing changes in the economy and state tax systems over time. Although large relative shifts in fiscal capacity are evident in the positive increases noted in Hawaii, Alaska, Wyoming, Iowa, and Montana, these states also evidence a negative change in relative tax effort. In contrast are New Hampshire and Rhode Island, which experienced negative changes in capacities but large positive shifts in tax effort. The former states chose not to increase tax efforts to improve or expand public services in a manner commensurate with their rapid growth in capacities, whereas the latter states exerted larger tax efforts than might have been expected from their relative declines in fiscal capacity.

Changes in state tax policies in recent years offer insights into directions that other state legislatures may follow in the future. In 1993, substantial tax reforms occurred in states: Arkansas, Ohio, and Washington included new services within the base of the sales tax. Iowa, Minnesota, Missouri, Nebraska, and Ohio increased the progressivity of their income taxes by adding new brackets or changing the definition of income subject to taxes. Wisconsin increased its standard deduction for low-income taxpayers, and Minnesota expanded the earned-income tax credit. Illinois repealed an unpopular tax on nursing homes and increased cigarette taxes to replace lost revenue. Hawaii, Utah, and West Virginia enacted new health care provider tax programs. New Hampshire enacted a broad-based business enterprise tax that made corporate taxation more equitable. Nebraska enacted a state lottery. Nine states increased motor fuel taxes. And fifteen states increased cigarette taxes, including a rate hike from 26 to 51 cents per pack imposed by Massachusetts voters (Mackey, 1993).

Changes in personal income taxes dominated the 1994 reforms: New Jersey, Michigan, Arizona, and New Mexico cut tax rates. Massachusetts, New Mexico, New York, and Pennsylvania expanded or created new programs for easing the burden on low-income taxpayers. Six other states targeted tax relief to the elderly or families. And New York and South Carolina postponed scheduled tax cuts to maintain revenue flow. Other reforms were also enacted: Michigan raised its sales tax rate from 4 percent to 6 percent and enacted a state-level property tax to offset lost local tax revenue. Pennsylvania planned to reduce its corporate net income tax from the nation's highest rate (12.25 percent) to 9.99 percent over three years. Kentucky and Missouri increased their gasoline tax rates, whereas New Mexico cut its gasoline rate. And Michigan and Idaho increased cigarette taxes (National Conference of State Legislatures, 1994). The total revenue change from all reforms and from im-

proving economic conditions in 1993 and 1994 brought net tax increases of $4.1 billion and $3.8 billion in state tax revenue for fiscal years 1994 and 1995, respectively.

MERITS OF SPECIFIC TAXES

The comparisons of government revenue sources detailed above reveal that some tax sources (e.g., individual income and sales taxes) are relied on heavily, whereas others (e.g., excise and estate taxes) yield relatively small amounts. The criteria described in Chapter 3 reflect the advantages and disadvantages of these different taxes and explain why policy makers rely more heavily on some revenue sources than on others. Here we present income and sales taxation in considerable detail, given their prevalence across tax systems. Then we turn to lotteries, severance taxes, estate and gift taxes, and payroll taxation.

Personal Income Taxation

All taxes are ultimately paid from individual income. Income is the most widely accepted measure of ability to pay, and taxes on earnings are generally considered the most equitable of the major tax sources. A progressive personal income tax has long been thought to moderate the disparities in welfare, opportunity, and economic power that arise from unequal distributions of income (Simons, 1938, pp. 18–19).

In colonial America, a "faculty" (meaning ability to pay) tax was collected in varying amounts depending on people's skills and occupations. Although this tax countered the effects of duties on goods, which imposed higher relative burdens on lower-income consumers, income-based taxes were discontinued for many years. The new nation relied on tariffs to finance activities of the federal government, at least until the revenue demands of the Civil War necessitated a temporary income tax.

Industrialization and various social movements in the late 1800s revived interest in progressive taxes. An amendment to an 1894 tariff bill would have imposed a federal income tax, but the U.S. Supreme Court declared it unconstitutional (*Pollock* v. *Farmers' Loan and Trust Co*, 1895). The court's concern, which was related to the proposed unequal distribution of revenue among states, was clearly addressed in the Sixteenth Amendment to the U.S. Constitution. Ratified in 1913, this amendment empowered Congress to collect taxes on "incomes, from whatever source, without apportionment among the several states, and without regard to any census of enumeration."

The first federal income tax was "born of a partisan movement to achieve social justice" (Waltman, 1985, p. 6). It was a response to regressive tariffs and included a sufficiently large personal exemption to relieve low-income earners. A flat 1 percent tax applied to incomes above $4000, and a graduated tax was levied on earnings above $20,000. Through the 1900s, the tax was expanded to cover nearly all income earners. A more progressive rate structure and higher overall burdens financed military expenses of two world wars, several "police actions" in Southeast Asia, and an expanding federal government. During the 1960s, the highest rate was 91 percent of income on earnings over $400,000.

Public demands for tax relief in the 1980s initially reduced federal tax rates from 14 percent to 11 percent at the bottom and from 70 percent to 50 percent at the top of the income scale. The Tax Reform Act of 1986 reduced the fourteen income brackets to two income divisions with taxes of 15 percent and 28 percent, eliminated deductions for state sales tax payments and for interest other than home mortgages, and removed the distinction between ordinary income and capital gains. A temporary 5 percent surcharge made the top rate 33 percent on earnings between $78,400 and $162,700 until changes in 1990 created a three-bracket schedule with rates of 15 percent, 28 percent and 31 percent. The Revenue Reconciliation Act of 1993 increased the highest rate to 36 percent for joint returns over $140,000 and single-taxpayer incomes over $115,000. A 10 percent surtax on incomes over $250,000 created a marginal rate of 39.6 percent, thus establishing a five-bracket income tax (Research Institute of America, 1993, p. 9). The Economic Growth and Tax Relief Reconciliation Act of 2001 lowered these rates. The highest marginal rate in 2002 was 38.6 percent of taxable incomes over $307,050. This rate declines to 37.6 percent in 2004 and to 35.0 percent in 2006 (Research Institute of America, 2001, p. 18).

The state individual income tax is a *graduated* tax, collecting a higher percentage from higher-income earners, in the District of Columbia and in thirty-three of the forty-four states that tax income. For example, Iowa relies on seven brackets that range from 0.4 percent on income below $1060 to 9.98 percent on incomes over $47,700 (ACIR, 1995, p. 49). Five other states (CT, IL, IN, MI, and PA) apply a *flat* rate to all incomes; four states (CO, ND, RI, and VT) levy a percentage of taxable income determined by federal income tax procedures; and two states (NH and TN) have a very limited tax on interest and dividend earnings. Seven of the income tax states derive over 40 percent of their tax receipts from the income tax, including almost 70 percent in Oregon. Another seven states do not employ any form of personal income taxation.

Over 3000 localities in eleven states (2500 of these localities are in Pennsylvania) levy an income tax (ACIR, 1995, p. 70). In addition to many cities in these states, counties in Indiana, Kentucky, and Maryland and school districts in Iowa, Ohio, and Pennsylvania collect income taxes.

Merits of Personal Income Taxation

Federal and state governments raise substantial amount of money through the income tax (see Tables 4.3 and 4.4). This yield was highly elastic prior to *indexation* in the mid-1980s. This policy linked growth in revenue to the rate of inflation. The coefficient of elasticity of the federal income tax, estimated by Galper & Pollock (1988, p. 125) to have declined from 1.95 to 1.80 following the 1986 reforms, indicates the power of this tax to grow at a rate much greater than that of increases in national income. The rampant inflation of the 1970s raised families' incomes in current dollars, pushing them into higher tax brackets and higher taxes, while their actual purchasing power declined. Termed "bracket creep," these increases in tax liability were not based on gains in real income and added substantially to tax coffers without enabling legislation (MacPhail-Wilcox, 1984, p. 327).

Beginning in 1985, tax rates and personal exemptions were indexed to tie their growth to changes in the general level of prices, as determined by the consumer price index (CPI). Slower growth in federal revenue resulted from the restructured and indexed tax brackets. At the same time, social security and military retirement benefits were raised to keep pace with the growing cost of living. Diminished yields, but larger commitments, contributed to the growing federal deficit. The return to a more progressive structure in the 1990s reversed this trend (Gold, 1994, p. 21).

Equity goals are more fully realized through income taxation than through consumption- or wealth-based taxes (see the discussion of equity in Chapter 3). *Exemptions, deductions, credits*, and a *progressive rate structure* recognize that taxpayers have differing abilities to pay. For example, the personal exemption of the federal income tax of $2900 for calendar year 2001, coupled with the standard deduction of $4550 for the same year, promises single taxpayers with incomes below $7450 zero income tax liability (U.S. Department of the Treasury, 2002a). Having this exemption and deduction removes low-income earners entirely from tax obligations. Other exemptions adjust the tax base to reflect family size, blindness, and senior citizen status. Standard deductions increase to $6650 for heads of households and $7600 for

married couples. Itemized deductions can also be applied for persons with larger financial burdens to reduce taxable income for purposes of taxation. For example, in calculating itemized deductions as an alternative to the standardized deduction, taxpayers can consider medical and dental expenses, state and local income taxes paid, real estate taxes paid, home mortgage interest, gifts, unreimbursed employee expenses, and tax preparation fees (U.S. Department of the Treasury, 2002b).

The progressive tax rate structure moves upward from 15 percent on taxable income below $27,050; to 27.5 percent below $65,550; to 30.5 percent below $136,750; to 35.5 percent below $297,350; and to 39.1 percent at and above $297,350. These graduated brackets and rates are the schedule for single taxpayers. Heads of households and married couples are subject to the same tax rates, but the graduated steps of taxable income are higher (U.S. Department of the Treasury, 2002a). Finally, tax credits reduce income tax liability on such bases as relatively low income, costs of child care and education, conditions of being elderly or disabled, and encouragement of specific types of investments. Because of these exemptions, deductions, and credits, the personal income tax has been progressive over the income scale, with only slight regressivity at the very top (Pechman, 1985, p. 53). Many state income tax policies further relieve the burden on the poor through more liberal exemptions and additional deductions. Income taxes are also used as a mechanism for property tax relief in thirty-four states.

These provisions help achieve the goal of vertical equity. However, adjustments to income erode the tax base and raise concerns about preferential treatment for some groups of taxpayers. What is designed to be a legitimate recognition of an individual's economic well-being or tax capacity is often termed a loophole by those who do not benefit or who deem the adjustment to be unfair or unjustified. For example, the tax code includes income tax shelters and deductions, which are intended to influence taxpayer behavior by encouraging saving for retirement and enable individuals to defer taxation legitimately until they are in lower income tax brackets. Effects of income tax policy thus differ from the unintended effects that are often realized when consumption or property tax policies are altered, particularly at local and state levels. Income-based taxes are considered more neutral in social and economic effects than other taxes, because changes in personal income taxation do not as directly intervene in market activities.

The absolute cost of income tax administration and compliance is high for taxpayers and governments alike. This is the only major tax in which taxpayers are responsible for assessing their own tax liability. Regulations and interpretations of the tax code by the Internal Revenue Service (IRS) guide taxpayers. The cost of tax consultation services provided by private vendors is high, as are the expenses occasioned by audits and dispute resolution by the IRS and tax courts. Nevertheless, the relative cost of administration is estimated to be only about 0.5 percent of revenue (Pechman, 1983, p. 61).

The elaborate system of deductions and credits complicates the income tax and often motivates creative tax avoidance on the part of taxpayers. Taxpayers must keep detailed records and often must turn to accountants and tax consultants to prepare returns, which raises the estimated cost of compliance to 7 percent of total revenue (Musgrave & Musgrave, 1989, p. 279). On the other hand, the practice of withholding estimated tax payments through payroll deductions distributes the burden of tax payment throughout the year. Those states that base their income tax collections on a given proportion of federal tax liability streamline administrative costs and minimize taxpayer cost of compliance. However, these states also relinquish control over decisions about exemptions and deductions that can greatly affect state revenue.

There are many advantages of federal and state income taxation, but taxation at the local level has been criticized on a number of grounds (Due, 1970, p. 320). Income is often earned in one locality by residents of another. This multiple taxation by communities creates problems and raises the costs of administration and audits. If there is strong incentive for individuals and businesses to migrate to localities that have no income tax, economic distortions result.

Reform of Income Taxation

Ever-present calls for reform in income taxation center on tax simplification to reduce its complexity and the high compliance costs it entails. Although the many preferences expressed in deductions and tax credits help achieve vertical equity, they also interfere with horizontal equity because it dampens taxpayer morale when persons with the same gross income ultimately pay lower taxes. Critics advocate the elimination of such adjustments, favoring a flat tax of about 15 percent to 20 percent of all income to improve fairness and increase yield.

Analyses of *effective rates*—the percentages of income paid in taxes after exemptions and deductions—reveal that the federal tax system lost revenue prior to reform in 1986 because of its many tax preferences. In 1985, effective rates ranged from 0.7 percent on incomes below $5000 to 26.4 percent for incomes between $500,000 and $1,000,000 (Pechman, 1984a, p. 16–17). In comparison, incomes over $1,000,000 were taxed at an effective rate of only 23.1 percent, far below the 50 percent rate then called for in the tax code. Eliminating all personal deductions, exclusions, and investment incentives would broaden the tax base, permitting the same revenue to be raised with lower rates and a higher personal exemption: "A personal income tax conforming strictly with the 'equal treatment' principle would apply to all income from whatever source derived, making allowances only for the taxpayer and his dependents" (Pechman, 1986, p. 45). The 1986, 1990, and 1993 reforms were partially successful in meeting this goal.

Musgrave and Musgrave (1984) would also define income broadly. They suggest including all accretion, with no consideration for whether it is saved or consumed, and call for a meaningful and consistent criterion of equity: "In the absence of such a norm, technical issues of taxable income definition applicable to particular cases cannot be settled in a consistent and equitable fashion and the ever-present pressures for loophole snatching cannot be resisted" (p. 351). Providing for the deduction of home mortgage interest rather than having a housing allowance, for example, favors higher-income homeowners over renters, who tend to be lower-income earners.

Capital gains taxation has been a major source of complication and economic distortion in income taxation. In principle, each year's appreciation in value (i.e., the dollar gain that exceeds relative changes in the cost of living) should be taxed as it accrues. In practice, gains were taxed for many years only when sales of properties or stocks occurred and at substantially reduced rates to promote investment and risk taking. Most gains escaped taxation, and ordinary income was often converted into capital gains to take advantage of reduced rates. Changes in the code in 1986 treated realized capital gains the same as ordinary income for tax purposes (without considering inflation), but strong pressure to maintain the incentive for investment limited the tax rate on gains to 28 percent for individuals and 35 percent for most corporations. These limits became more important to investors as higher brackets (up to 39.6 percent) were instituted in the 1993 reform. A subject of continuing debate is the treatment of unrealized gains—those not converted to cash—from investments. By delaying taxation until the gain is realized, the government is in effect granting an interest-free loan to higher-income earners (Musgrave & Musgrave, 1989, p. 337).

Many changes in income taxation have occurred since ratification of the Sixteenth Amendment. The process of reform is a political one, however, and those individuals and businesses that are treated favorably resist dramatic change. Goals of equity and economic efficiency are often set aside to accommodate other social and economic objectives. For example, wealthy taxpayers benefit greatly from the exclusion of municipal bond interest from ordinary income on the premise that one government level should not tax the financial instruments of another. At the same time, however, construction of schools and other public facilities would be more costly without tax incentives for these investments.

Corporate Income Taxation

Taxation of corporate income once contributed a quarter of federal revenue, but now it accounts for less than one-tenth of the total. All states except Nevada, Texas, Washington, and Wyoming derive revenue from a form of this tax, and this revenue source accounts for over 10 percent of collections in four states (see Table 4.5). Michigan repealed its corporate income tax in 1976, replacing it with a single modified value-added tax on businesses (ACIR, 1995, p. 35).

Benefits received by businesses have been tied to costs of public services for many years. Congress levied an excise tax on the privilege of engaging in business when the constitutionality of the federal personal income tax was questioned in the late 1880s. The initial 1 percent rate became a graduated tax to meet growing revenue needs. Since 1987, corporate incomes below $50,000 have been taxed at 15 percent and those between $50,000 and $75,000 at 25 percent. Corporations earning over $75,000 pay a 34 percent tax to the government; the 1993 tax reforms increased (to between 35 and 39 percent) the rates on corporations with larger incomes (Research Institute of America, 1993, p. 24).

Rates generally apply to a corporation's taxable income, which is defined as sales revenue less costs of production, interest and rent payments, depreciation on capital equipment and facilities, and state and local taxes. This corporate profit is the base taxed in forty-five states, many of which also base the tax on the value of capital stock or net worth; three states tax gross receipts. Credits and incentives reduce tax owed and serve economic and social goals. For example, investment credits encourage businesses to acquire new equipment to raise productive efficiency, energy credits urge conservation, and various education credits in fifteen states offset a portion of the costs of vocational training and employer-sponsored child care programs. Tax incentives help businesses contribute to employees' pension plans, hire disadvantaged persons, and participate in public–private partnerships (ACIR, 1995, pp. 78–87).

Tax policy development poses problems that are similar to those identified for personal income taxation. Each deduction and credit reduces the tax base. It is difficult to have agreement on which costs of business should be deductible expenses and which incentives are important enough to be included as credits to reduce taxes paid. The corporate tax differs from individual income because it is a tax on profits rather than on income during the year.

The effective rate—the tax as a percentage of profits before deductions and other tax preferences—has fallen. In 1965, when the corporate income tax rate was 48 percent and profits were $80.4 billion, the effective tax rate was 34.5 percent. By 1982 the effective rate had declined to 13.1 percent, but the nominal rate was 46 percent and profits were $238.3 billion (Pechman, 1984b, p. 144).

Merits of Corporate Income Taxation

The relatively high and elastic yield of the corporate income tax offers advantages of growth potential for federal and state governments. The burden of this and other taxes on businesses is hidden from taxpayers; it is often exported from the community to other parts of the country or world (Gold, 1994, p. 15). Because it has few direct effects on voters, and because of the widely held perception that it is a tax on the rich, corporate income taxation is politically popular. Not all shareholders are wealthy, however, particularly in the case of workers whose retirement plans are invested heavily in corporations. When we consider that the burden of corporate taxes falls on consumers who pay higher prices or on employees who receive reduced wages, then the basis for an assumption of progressivity disappears (Pechman, 1985, p. 57) and, indeed, this tax burden might be regressive. Tax burden is further compounded when individuals pay a number of times from the same income—first directly through individual income taxes on earnings and then indirectly through corporate and sales taxes on their purchases.

Costs of administration are minimal relative to yield, but interstate commerce brings with it problems in allocating corporate income among states. Multiple taxation of this income is minimized among states that have adopted uniform systems for reporting income and allocating collections to the respective states. Compliance costs are high for corporations that plan expenditures carefully and maintain complete records to minimize tax liability.

Excise and Sales Taxation

Consumption-based taxes have been an important source of support for federal and state governments, and they are gaining popularity at the local level. Excise taxes are charged either on a per-unit basis (e.g., per gallon of motor fuel or distilled spirits) or on an ad valorem basis (e.g., percentage of airline ticket cost or telephone charges). These taxes on selected goods are often defended as substitutes for service charges, given the close relationship between the tax and the benefits received. Many governments view gasoline taxes and vehicle registration fees, for example, as user charges to support highway maintenance, and they dedicate this revenue for that purpose.

Unlike tariffs and excise taxes on specific commodities, state and local sales taxes apply more broadly as general taxation on the retail value of many goods and services. Falling property and income tax receipts during the depression of the 1930s led states to adopt emergency sales taxes. These taxes became more entrenched during World War II, and sales tax rates have risen steadily since that time (ACIR, 1990, p. 74; Due, 1982, p. 273). Only five of the thirty-six states with a sales tax in 1962 levied a rate of 4 percent, then the highest rate. The most common rate in 1994 was 5 percent (14 states), and only Colorado had a 3 percent rate. Fourteen states levied between 3 percent and 4.9 percent, and fifteen states and the District of Columbia had a rate higher than 5 percent. Mississippi and Rhode Island had the highest rate (7 percent) in 1994 (ACIR, 1995, p. 93). Alaska, Delaware, Montana, New Hampshire, and Oregon do not rely on general sales tax revenue (see Table 4.5).

Thirty-one states permit localities, including school districts in Louisiana, to levy a sales tax (ACIR, 1995, pp. 95–99). For example, the addition of city and county sales taxes to statewide rates results in total rates of over 8 percent in twenty-two large cities.

Merits of Excise and Sales Taxes

The yield of consumption-based taxes is substantial. Sales and gross receipts taxes account for more than 50 percent of tax revenue in Florida, Nevada, South Dakota, Tennessee, Texas, and Washington (see Table 4.5). All states levy an excise tax on motor vehicle fuel; in fact, three states raise more than 10 percent of their total revenue from this source. Tobacco products are taxed in all states, and alcoholic beverages provide tax revenue in thirty-four states, but no state grosses more than 10 percent of total revenue from these excise taxes. Taken together, consumption-based

taxes account for over 40 percent of total state collections.

Growth in the amount of state sales and excise tax revenue between 1970 and 2000 was presented in Table 4.4. Collections from selective excise taxes on motor fuels and on alcohol and tobacco products more than tripled, while general sales and gross receipts taxes increased more than tenfold. There has also been an increase in local dependence on sales taxes (see Table 4.1). Sales and gross receipts taxes accounted for 3.4 percent and 5.3 percent of local government tax revenue in 1970 and 1995, respectively. Some of this increase in state and local taxes can be accounted for by the financial demands of recent educational reforms. For example, Michigan increased general sales taxation (from 4 to 6 percent) and excise taxes on cigarettes (from 25 to 75 cents per pack) to replace revenue lost as a consequence of property tax reductions.

Consumption-based taxes are less sensitive to equity goals than are income taxes, because they are levied *in rem* (on things) rather than *in personam* (on the person). The amount of tax owed does not account for conditions of individual taxpayers other than their patterns of purchases. Manufacturers and retailers may bear the initial impact of excise and gross receipts taxes, but the ultimate burden falls upon consumers. Rates applied to the value of purchases are the same for all consumers regardless of income level, and there are no deductions or progressive rate schedules. Only the exemption of basic necessities—including food, shelter, and medicine—in many state plans makes general sales taxes less regressive, because these items represent a higher proportion of the budgets of the poor. Interestingly, the prevalence of consumption-based taxes in many other nations (see Table 4.2) makes their tax systems less progressive than those that rely more heavily on income-based taxation (Pechman, 1989, p. 14).

Individuals with the same income but with different consumption habits pay varying amounts of sales and excise taxes; thus horizontal equity is not satisfied. People with different incomes also have dissimilar spending and saving patterns. As incomes rise, consumption declines as a percentage of income, and higher-income earners divert more money to housing and investments, both of which are exempt from this taxation. Because sales and excise taxes place a heavier burden on lower-income groups with little or no tax relief, vertical equity is not satisfied. Pechman's (1985) analysis, discussed in Chapter 3, reveals that the lowest-income decile paid an effective rate of 18 percent of income in sales tax, whereas the highest-income group paid only 1 percent.

Sales tax policy has been sensitive to this regressivity by exempting necessities or providing a credit on the amount of income tax owed in the form of a *circuit breaker*. In 1994, the District of Columbia and all but two of the forty-five states that imposed a sales tax exempted prescription drugs; twenty-six of these jurisdictions exempted food but not restaurant meals; and a portion of electric and gas utility costs was not taxed in thirty-one states (ACIR, 1995, pp. 89–92). Only eight states exempted telecommunication services (e.g., telephone), but thirty-five states excluded personal services (e.g., hair styling). Rent is universally excluded from the sales tax.

These exemptions are thought to improve the sales tax's equity. However, having more personal services fall within general sales taxation may improve its vertical equity. This is because the consumption of services is more elastic with respect to income than is the consumption of goods since people tend to use more services as incomes rise (Howard, 1989). It might be argued, for example, that applying a sales tax to legal, medical, and educational services would reduce its regressivity. On the other hand, the taxation of services may introduce undesirable distortions, encouraging highly mobile companies to move in order to avoid taxes and inducing other businesses to provide their own services rather than purchase them (Gold, 1994). Nevertheless, in order to increase revenue, and perhaps to improve tax equity, a growing number of states are expanding the list of personal and business services subject to sales taxation (ACIR, 1995, p. 89–92).

Despite the political appeal and reduced tax burdens, exemptions cause substantial revenue loss (estimated between 20 and 25 percent of potential tax yield), complicate retailers' collection and states' enforcement of the tax, and exclude many expenditures of middle- and upper-income groups (Due, 1982, p. 273). For example, placing a ceiling on the amount of tax to be collected on purchases of automobiles and other vehicles makes the tax more regressive and reduces revenue. Eliminating all exemptions, even for food and prescription drugs, would simplify administration and raise greater revenue. A preferred approach for reducing regressivity may be through a circuit breaker, the mechanism that eight states use to relieve sales tax burdens (ACIR, 1995, pp. 89–90). Some state income taxes are reduced by a flat dollar credit per family member regardless of income; others apply a declining rate as income rises; still others provide a separate refund program. Although a cash refund might be available for those low-income earners who have no tax liability, they might also neglect to file necessary income tax forms.

Consumption-based taxes are not neutral and often have severe economic and social impacts. Shopping habits of consumers may be affected, particularly if sales tax rates differ within a relatively small geographic area. Decisions about the location of shopping plazas and automobile dealerships might be influenced by rate differences among municipalities and counties, or even across state lines. Easing geographic rate differentials would make the tax more neutral. In addition, better controls over interstate transactions would recapture lost revenue from exemptions made for goods ordered by mail and shipped across state lines.

Higher rates on demerit (i.e. censurable) goods may discourage consumption of alcohol and tobacco. These excise taxes are often justified on the basis of costs to society that can result from excessive use of the products and on sumptuary grounds—that is, because their consumption is considered immoral and unhealthful. If these taxes were effective, however, both consumption and tax revenue would decline (Musgrave & Musgrave, 1989).

The relatively simple tax structure of sales and excise taxes minimizes administration and compliance costs. Manufacturers pay excise taxes according to the quantity produced, and retailers charge consumers general sales taxes at the time sales are made. Computerized cash registers simplify sales tax procedures, reducing clerks' errors (these once were a problem, particularly in states with exemptions of certain goods). Costs of auditing retailers' accounts are minimal, estimated to be about 1 percent of the revenue collected (Due, 1970, p. 305).

Personal Expenditure and Value-Added Taxes as Alternatives

Personal expenditure and value-added taxes offer very different approaches to consumption-based taxation. A personal expenditure tax, also referred to as a consumption expenditure tax, is based on an individual's aggregate spending (Courant & Gramlich, 1984; Musgrave & Musgrave, 1989). Unlike sales and excise taxation, this tax is levied on consumers rather than on actual goods and services purchased. As an alternative to the income tax, its structure may also provide exemptions or deductions, and it may have graduated rates.

Tax liability is determined by (1) adding income from all sources to assets at the beginning of the tax year, (2) increasing this amount by net borrowing and decreasing it by net investments during the year to give an indication of funds available for personal expenditures, (3) subtracting accumulated assets from this total at the end of the year, which yields the annual amount of consumption, and (4) applying the

appropriate tax rate. Designed to replace income and general sales taxes, an expenditure tax offers some of the advantages of both. Including personal exemptions, deductions, and progressive rates would protect low-income groups who consume with higher proportions of their income. In contrast to the income tax's weakness in discouraging investments, an expenditure tax would encourage saving and discourage consumption (Pechman, 1989, p. 112). However, the costs of administration and compliance would increase greatly, given the need for annual valuations of assets.

A value-added tax (VAT) has also been suggested as an alternative to retail sales taxation. This tax recognizes that goods increase in value at various production stages and that their final prices reflect the sum of these increments in value. Used successfully in many countries, the VAT is the basic instrument of tax coordination among nations in the European Union. Large deficits in the United States during the 1980s brought attention to this tax as a means to generate revenue, stimulate investments, and improve the balance of payments in international trade.

The invoice method of tax calculation that is used in most countries is an indirect form of taxation in that it does not actually calculate the value and apply a tax rate to that base, as happens with income, sales, and property taxes (Tait, 1988, pp. 4–5). Instead, the rate is applied to the gross receipts of a business (i.e., output) minus the value of intermediate materials and other production costs (i.e., input). Tax liability results from applying the VAT rate to this base and then crediting against the gross tax the amount of VAT already paid by suppliers of intermediate and capital goods.

Opponents view the value-added tax as a hidden and regressive tax that has high administrative costs (Aaron, 1981; McClure, 1984, p. 185; Tait, 1988, pp. 400–403). The initial impact is on producers, but because the tax is shifted forward as prices increase, the burden (incidence) falls ultimately on consumers. Like the general sales tax, regressivity might be reduced through exemptions for necessities or income tax credits. Such measures would moderate the VAT's regressivity, making it proportional to income for the lower half of the income distribution, but it would continue to be regressive for upper income levels (Pechman, 1989, p. 8). Costs of administration for the government and the costs for businesses to comply would be much greater under a VAT than are the costs incurred with general sales taxes.

The division of revenue among government levels would need to be considered in the development of a VAT policy. If a federal government VAT replaced state general sales taxes such that industrial states benefited from taxes imposed at the production stage, many other states would lose tax revenue currently collected at retail levels. Similarly, states could forfeit revenue currently gained from the sales of imported automobiles and other products.

For the VAT to be justified, it must be argued either that the tax system is too progressive or that substantial revenue is needed to fund a major new federal direction or to close an intolerable deficit. In today's political environment, state and local officials are concerned about a federal tax on consumption. There are concerns that as many businesses would be hurt as would be helped. Such an environment would not support a VAT (Aaron, 1984, p. 217; Tait, 1988, p. 34). Because of its disadvantages and potential complications for the current tax structure, it is not likely that a value-added tax will be adopted in the United States.

Lottery as Taxation

A lottery has been defined as a game in which "chances to share in a distribution of prizes are sold" (Commission on the Review of the National Policy toward Gambling, 1976). A governmental-sponsored lottery is a voluntary tax that can be classified as either a consumption- or a privilege-based tax. If the portion paid in prizes is considered to be a product sold by the state, then the remaining revenue, less operating expenses, is an excise tax on that product (Guthrie, Garms, & Pierce, 1988, p. 95). This revenue is an "implicit" tax collected from a portion of the proceeds (Clotfelter & Cook, 1989, p. 219). It might also be considered a privilege-based tax, like that derived from casino games in an increasing number of states, in which the government collects a fee for permitting people to participate in and wager on games of chance.

Lotteries have been used throughout history to resolve disputes objectively and to raise funds for churches and governments. About fifty colleges and three hundred elementary/secondary schools benefited from lottery revenue through the Civil War (Ezell, 1960). However, the revenue that lotteries can generate has been overshadowed by political corruption and by claims that any form of gambling encourages immoral behavior, fraud, and bribery. Abuses in the late 1800s led to federal legislation against using postal services for transporting lottery materials. Although charitable organizations continued to sponsor legalized social play (e.g., raffles, bingo games) for many years, the government has been hesitant to sanction more addictive and commercialized forms of gambling (e.g., casinos). Today's state-sponsored lotteries fall in the middle of the continuum that runs from social, low-wager play to higher-stakes gambling (Jones & Amalfitano, 1994, p. xvii).

The lottery was revived in the mid-1960s in New Hampshire and New York. By 1992, 37 states and the District of Columbia had operating lotteries. Nine states reported yields in excess of $1 billion: California, Florida, Illinois, Massachusetts, Michigan, New Jersey, New York, Ohio, and Pennsylvania (ACIR, 1995, pp. 106–107). The highest revenue producer was Florida ($2.1 billion), and its proceeds accounted for 4.8 percent of total state general revenue (p. 108). Of the $19.17 billion collected nationwide in 1991, $10.35 billion (54 percent) was paid in prizes, and another $1.15

billion (6 percent) was diverted to administrative expenses, leaving $7.67 billion (40 percent) in tax revenue.

Federal legislation in 1988, the Charity Games Advertising Clarification Act, permits not-for-profit and commercial organizations to operate lotteries in accordance with state laws and to advertise lotteries and list prize winners in adjoining states' media (P.L. 100–625, 18 USCS 1301). Various forms of the lottery include "instant games," in which players rub a waxy substance off tickets to determine winnings; "numbers," in which players place bets on a three- or four-digit number via computer terminals and learn later of winning numbers through the media; "lotto," which generally has players select 6 of 36 numbers and holds a weekly drawing to determine winners; and "video lottery" play, which resembles slot machines in casinos. Jones and Amalfitano (1994, p. 42) note that many observers expect this latter form (which was legalized in only five states in 1991) and interactive television lottery to be the fastest-growing forms of play in the future.

Proponents argue that the revenue gained outweighs the lottery's disadvantages. Unlike many unpopular taxes, only the willing pay this "painless" tax (Clotfelter & Cook, 1989, p. 215). These voluntary games provide some degree of enjoyment for participants, and this public entertainment raises state revenue without increasing other taxes. A portion of the prize money is also a revenue source, because winnings are subject to income taxation. However, much revenue is lost through the exemption from withholding or reporting of cash payments up to $600. The lottery provides an example of double taxation; the money used to purchase tickets was previously taxed as income. Because no new income is generated for society through the lottery, it might be argued that there should be no income tax on winnings.

Ease of compliance (there are no tax forms to complete and low-cost tickets are readily ac-

cessible) is one advantage that this revenue source offers. However, the cost of administration is high relative to the yield, raising concerns about the efficiency of this tax mechanism. This tax accounts for less than 7 percent of state revenues, and the costs of marketing, printing tickets, and paying off winners are high. Operating costs consumed between 3 percent (New York and Pennsylvania) and 29 percent (Montana) of 1991 collections. This administrative burden compares to less than 5 percent for other tax yields (Thomas & Webb, 1984, p. 303). As a result, the proportion of lottery proceeds that remains to fund government programs ranges between 20 percent (Montana) and 67 percent (South Dakota) of receipts.

This average tax rate, the proportion of sales that becomes revenue to states (40 percent), is higher than other excise taxes, including those charged for alcohol and tobacco products. Like other consumption-based taxes, the price of the lottery ticket is the same for all. The burden is on the poor, who spend a higher proportion of their income for tickets, and it is argued that the lottery is more regressive than general sales or excise taxes (Mikesell & Zorn, 1986). Clotfelter and Cook (1989, p. 223) concluded, from their review of studies of the regressivity of this tax, "Without exception, the evidence shows that the implicit tax on lotteries is regressive." If the lottery tax rate were lower to be more comparable with other such taxes, prizes could be higher and the tax burden would be lower, but the government's share would decline.

The moral and public policy dilemmas raised by lotteries can be cast within the criterion of neutrality as they alter people's behavior. Opponents contend that lotteries catch states in a dilemma of enticing the citizenry into previously forbidden and immoral activities in order to raise needed revenue and that legalized gambling encourages organized crime, political corruption, and fraud by reducing the stigma of playing. In response, advocates argue that governmental-sponsored games offer a legal gambling alternative to, and thus compete with and deter, organized crime (Jones & Amalfitano, 1994, pp. 59, 64–68).

Twenty-two of the lottery states earmark proceeds for public education, senior citizen programs, or other specific purposes. These designations encourage ticket sales and enhance political appeal, but earmarking this revenue may make little difference in overall financial support. There is evidence that money previously allocated is often diverted to support other programs, so earmarking lottery proceeds does not always benefit statutory recipients (Borg & Mason, 1990; Stark, Wood & Honeyman, 1993). Jones and Amalfitano (1994) found that neither the presence of a state lottery nor the earmarking of revenue for education explained the variation among states in levels of support or effort for public education. They concluded, both from analyses of revenue effects and from the moral and policy dilemmas, that states should be more judicious in sponsoring lotteries, providing "truth in advertising," or ensuring that the revenue derived from lotteries benefits private charities exclusively.

States have turned to this voluntary tax despite its regressivity, low yield, high administrative costs, and opposition from groups concerned about its social effects. The success and current popularity of lotteries, as well as the emergence of a new generation of automated and interactive games, suggest that they will continue to grow in importance as an alternative to traditional state revenue sources. Educators are cautioned, however, that this additional revenue does not necessarily benefit public schools.

Severance Taxes

Thirty-eight states collect severance taxes for the privilege of extracting natural resources from land or water (ACIR, 1995, p. 122–129). Production, license, and conservation taxes are levied on such resources as coal, natural gas, minerals, forest products, and fish. Oil and gas production accounts for over 80 percent of these taxes. Energy-related industry also brings revenue to states and localities through rents and royalties on mineral leases for energy production on public land, corporate income taxes, and local property taxes.

Severance taxes are either specific rate, based on the quantity of resources removed (e.g., $0.45 per ton of coal in Missouri), or *ad valorem*, based on market value of goods (e.g., 3 to 5 percent of the value of fish products in Washington). Differing extraction processes complicate the task of valuation for tax purposes. In some cases, a very large investment must be made to extract very little mineral (as with diamonds); in others, a low-cost extraction process yields much return (as with natural gas).

Collections from severance taxes grew rapidly following the 1973 oil embargo and subsequent deregulation of the oil and gas industries, but they fell during the 1980s. The uncertain yield of this tax is evident in its steady growth from $800 million in 1972 to $7.4 billion in 1983, its decline to $4.1 billion in 1987, and its subsequent increase to $4.9 billion in 1993 (U.S. Department of Commerce, 1995, Table 492). Severance taxes accounted for over 50 percent of state taxation in Alaska and for 39 percent of state revenue in Wyoming in 1993 (U.S. Department of Commerce, 1995, Table 492).

States, counties, and school districts with energy revenues are better able to finance public services, and they can export a large share of the tax burden to nonresidents (Cuciti, Galper, & Lucke, 1983, p. 17). In order to curtail this shifting of incidence, several reforms have been suggested to limit severance taxation to a given percentage of production value or to a certain level of total revenue per capita. State policies might require those producing counties (and school districts) to share some portion of tax revenue with energy-consuming regions. But the counterargument can be made that severance taxes are fair compensation for the environmental damage associated with many extraction processes.

Estate and Gift Taxation

The base of gift, estate, and inheritance taxes is wealth. Federal and state governments tax estates for the privilege of transferring money or other property to heirs, and many states collect an inheritance tax on the privilege of receiving a bequest. These taxes reallocate a portion of very large wealth accumulations on the theory that a wealthy and politically powerful aristocracy might otherwise disrupt free enterprise and that large inheritances might cause heirs to lead less than productive lives (Pechman, 1989, p. 121). Many universities and private foundations have benefited from tax policies that exempt donations to charitable institutions from estate taxation.

Tax reform in 1976 joined federal estate and gift taxes under a "unified" rate schedule to reduce the incentive to give away a person's wealth to avoid taxation at death. Estates below $600,000 are exempt from taxation at the federal level. The gift tax exclusion permits annual transfers of up to $10,000 for each qualified recipient without a tax obligation on either party. Gift taxes paid during the donor's life are credited against estate taxes due at the time of death. Tax reform in 1981 increased the exemption from 60 percent to 100 percent of an estate for a surviving spouse. The rates applied to remaining taxable estates range from 18 percent for those under $10,000 to 55 percent on those over $3 million (ACIR, 1995, p. 29). The large exemptions diminish collections, which account for less than 1 percent of total federal revenue.

All states benefit from a portion of the federal tax. Six states levy an additional tax on estates, 17 states tax inheritances, and six states impose an additional gift tax during a donor's life (ACIR, 1995, p. 147). These death and gift taxes provided 1.5 percent of total state revenue in 2000 (see Table 4.4).

Payroll Taxation

Unlike the foregoing revenue sources, which yield money for general government expenses, payroll deductions are earmarked specifically to finance two federal insurance programs: social security and unemployment compensation. Initiated by the Social Security Act of 1935, programs today reduce the financial burdens inflicted by old age, premature death of family providers, medical expenses, and long-term unemployment. These required payroll taxes supplement other retirement and insurance programs available to educators.

The Old-Age, Survivors, Disability, and Health Insurance (OASDHI) program, as it has been called since the addition of health benefits in 1965, is the largest program sponsored by the federal government. The original intent of Congress was to establish a fully funded insurance program. Payroll taxes were to be invested in a trust fund to guarantee future benefits. The inclusion of unemployment benefits in 1939 altered the investment approach, creating a pay-as-you-go system of financing (Davies, 1986, p. 169). Despite increased collections between 1970 and 1980, the trust fund failed to keep pace with demands placed on the system. Cost-of-living adjustments began in 1975 to keep inflation from eroding the value of benefits. This increase reached 14.3 percent in 1980 and then declined annually along with the consumer price index, to 2.8 percent in 1995. Legislation in 1983 improved the trust fund by partially taxing social security benefits, accelerating tax rate increases in recent years, and gradually increasing the retirement age from sixty-five to sixty-seven by the year 2017. Collections have outpaced benefit payments in recent years, and balances are not likely to be exhausted before 2050 (Pechman, 1989, p. 183).

The social security program began in 1937 as a 1 percent tax, collecting a maximum of $30 on the covered earnings base of $3000 (ACIR, 1995, p. 27). This earnings base, which has been raised annually since 1972 to keep pace with average wages, was $84,900 in 2002 (RIA, 2001, p. 20). The 7.51 percent tax collected on earnings below $45,000 in 1988 increased to 7.65 percent for 1990 and thereafter. This rate includes the 1.45 percent Medicare tax on all earned income. The total tax is over 15 percent, including the matching contributions of employers. In addition, employers pay 6.0 percent of the first $7000 of each employee's income for the unemployment compensation tax. These taxes represent a sizable annual expense for school districts in states participating in the national program. Total collections represent a very large proportion of federal revenue—in fact, about one-third (see Table 4.3).

Payroll taxes are nearly proportional for income levels up to the covered earnings base. They are regressive for upper-income groups, however, because these groups do not contribute beyond this point. The benefit schedule is more progressive. Low-income earners receive relatively higher proportions of the taxes they pay into the system (Davies, 1986, p. 171). Furthermore, beneficiaries with incomes over $44,000 (married) or $34,000 (single) pay income taxes on 85 percent of their social security benefits.

Increased rates and the raised earnings base in recent years eased concerns that earlier retirement ages, longer life expectancies, cost-of-living adjustments for beneficiaries, and unpredictable rates of unemployment would jeopardize the fund. It has been estimated that only two workers would support each retiree after 2000, in comparison to a 3-to-1 ratio in the mid-1980s. In order to maintain solvency and reduce regressivity, more drastic reforms may be necessary: raising the ceiling on contributions, supporting health insurance programs such as Medicare with income taxes, reducing cost-of-living allowances, or permitting workers to invest a portion of social security contributions in private accounts.

ADVANTAGES OF MULTIPLE, BROAD-BASED TAX SOURCES

Relying exclusively on any one of the taxes we have discussed would accentuate its disadvantages and place a large burden for supporting government services on one segment of society. The tables in this chapter offer evidence that governments choose multiple sources and depend on specific taxes to differing degrees. Designing revenue systems to include several forms of taxation that broaden the base from which revenue is collected offers advantages to governments.

Gold (1994) noted the importance of a balanced tax system that relies on broad-based taxes. Tapping multiple sources helps keep tax rates low for any given tax, thus stimulating economic development, and stabilizes government because overall revenue is not subject to fluctuations in yields of any one tax. Furthermore, including more than one tax minimizes distortions in the economy because the defects of each tax are averaged out. A broad-based tax system is also more neutral: it minimizes distortions in location decisions and improves horizontal equity.

These advantages, and the trade-offs among values noted in Chapter 3, explain why a number of revenue sources constitute the total picture of financial support for government. School districts, which derive much of their revenue from higher levels of government, thus indirectly depend on multiple taxes in addition to their historical reliance on the property tax.

SUMMARY

The revenue sources detailed in this chapter provide money for federal, state, and (to some degree) local governments. Personal income taxation provides high revenue yield that responds well to the economy, contributes to vertical equity, causes minimal social and economic disruption, and has a relatively low cost of administration. However, its complexity and high compliance costs, along with perceptions that loopholes unfairly advantage some taxpayers, fuel calls for reforms. The simplified structures of excise and sales taxes, which have no deductions or exemptions based on taxpayer income, minimize administrative and compliance costs. However, these consumption taxes result in economic distortions of true consumer preferences and, unless provisions are made for exempting necessities or allowing income tax credits, work against equity goals. These two primary sources of tax revenue offer federal and state governments different advantages that argue for augmenting their role in tax policy. Their weaknesses offer opportunities for tax policy reform.

Corporate income taxes, lotteries, severance taxes, estate and gift taxes, and payroll taxes also contribute to government resources. Because they rely on very different tax bases, these taxes offer ways to diversify tax policy. States rely to very different degrees on income, consumption, wealth, and privilege taxes because of particular conditions of population, geography, natural resources, economy, and tradition. It is best to have a balanced tax system that relies on broad-based taxes.

The next chapter addresses the structure and administration of property taxation. Unlike the taxes examined in this chapter, the property tax has been the principal revenue source for local governments and school districts in particular.

ACTIVITIES

1. Trace the history of one tax revenue source, identifying the initial rationale, any changes in provisions that might have al-

tered the original purpose, and trends in rates and collections over time.

2. Debate the advantages of income-based taxes over consumption-based taxes in relation to criteria of yield, equity, neutrality, elasticity, and administrative burden.

3. Investigate the primary state-level taxes that support schools in a selected state. Indicate what proportion of revenue is derived from each of the following tax sources: personal income, corporate income, excise, sales, lottery, severance, inheritance, and other taxes. What modifications might you suggest to make this state's revenue system more responsive to tax criteria of yield, equity, neutrality, elasticity, and administrative burden?

4. Do states with high capacities or effort spend comparatively more on education than states with lower abilities or willingness to tax? Compare the rankings in state capacities and efforts (Table 4.6) with their revenues per pupil for education (see Table 7.1 of Chapter 7).

5. Design an instrument to survey residents or policy makers of your community or state to determine their preferences for reform in tax policy in the coming decade.

COMPUTER SIMULATIONS: REVENUE SOURCES FOR STATES

Computer simulations related to the content of this chapter are available on the Allyn & Bacon website, **<http://www.ablongman.com/ed-leadership.com>**. They focus on graphing and on using alternative types of graphs to present data and information. Objectives for the exercise are

- To understand the relative reliance of states on various tax sources.
- To identify trends in the proportions of government tax collections over time.
- To use spreadsheet graphics capability in the analysis of school finance policy.

REFERENCES

Aaron, H. J. (Ed.). (1981). *The value-added tax: Lessons from Europe, Studies of government finance.* Washington, DC: The Brookings Institution.

Aaron, H. J. (1984). The value-added tax: A triumph of form over substance. In C. E. Walker & M. A. Bloomfield (Eds.), *New directions in federal tax policy for the 1980s* (pp. 217–240). Cambridge, MA: Ballinger.

ACIR. (1990). *Significant features of fiscal federalism,* Vol. 1: Washington, DC: Advisory Commission on Intergovernmental Relations.

ACIR. (1992). *Significant features of fiscal federalism,* Vol. 2: Washington, DC: Advisory Commission on Intergovernmental Relations.

ACIR. (1993). *RTS 1991: State revenue capacity and effort.* Washington, DC: Advisory Commission on Intergovernmental Relations.

ACIR. (1994). *Significant features of fiscal federalism, Vol. 2: Revenues and expenditures.* Washington, DC: Advisory Commission on Intergovernmental Relations.

ACIR. (1995). *Significant features of fiscal federalism, Vol. 1: Budget processes and tax systems.* Washington, DC: Advisory Commission on Intergovernmental Relations.

Borg, M. O., & Mason, P. M. (1990). Earmarked lottery revenues: Positive windfalls or concealed redistribution mechanisms? *Journal of Education Finance, 15,* 289–301.

Clotfelter, C. T., & Cook, P. J. (1989). *Selling hope: State lotteries in America.* Cambridge, MA: Harvard University Press.

Commission on the Review of the National Policy toward Gambling. (1976). *Gambling in America.* Washington, DC: U.S. Government Printing Office.

Courant, P., & Gramlich, E. (1984). The expenditure tax: Has the idea's time come? In J. A. Pechman et al., *Tax policy: New directions and possibilities* (pp. 27–36). Washington, DC: Center for National Policy.

Cuciti, P., Galper, H., & Lucke, R. (1983). State energy revenues. In C. E. McLure & P. Mieszkowski (Eds.), *Fiscal federalism and the taxation of natural resources* (pp. 11–60). Lexington, MA: Lexington Books.

Davies, D. G. (1986). *United States taxes and tax policy.* Cambridge: Cambridge University Press.

Due, J. F. (1970). Alternative tax sources for education. In R. L. Johns et al. (Eds.), *Economic factors affecting the financing of education* (pp. 291–328). Gainesville, FL: National Education Finance Project.

Due, J. F. (1982). Shifting sources of financing education and the taxpayer revolt. In W. W. McMahon & T. G. Geske. (Eds.), *Financing education: Overcoming inefficiency and inequity* (pp. 267–289). Urbana, IL: University of Illinois Press.

Ezell, J. S. (1960). *Fortune's merry wheel: The lottery in America.* Cambridge, MA: Harvard University Press.

Galper, H., & Pollock, S. H. (1988). Models of state income tax reform. In S. D. Gold (Eds.), *The unfinished agenda for state tax reform* (pp. 107–128). Denver, CO: National Conference of State Legislatures.

Gold, S. D. (1994). *Tax options for states needing more school revenue.* Westhaven, CT: National Education Association.

Guthrie, J. W., Garms, W. I., & Pierce, L. C. (1988). *School finance and education policy: Enhancing educational efficiency, equality, and choice.* Englewood Cliffs, NJ: Prentice-Hall.

Howard, M. A. (1989, Summer). State tax and expenditure limitations: There is no story. *Public Budgeting and Finance, 9,* 83–90.

Jones, T. H., & Amalfitano, J. L. (1994). *America's gamble: Public school finance and state lotteries.* Lancaster, PA: Technomic.

Mackey, S. R. (1993). *State tax actions 1993.* Denver, CO: National Conference of State Legislatures.

MacPhail-Wilcox, B. (1984). Tax policy analysis and education finance: A conceptual framework for issues and analysis. *Journal of Education Finance, 9,* 312–331.

McLure, C. E. (1984). Value added tax: Has the time come? In C. E. Walker & M. A. Bloomfield (Eds.), *New directions in federal tax policy for the 1980s* (pp. 185–213). Cambridge, MA: Ballinger.

Mikesell, J. L., & Zorn, C. K. (1986, July/August). State lotteries as fiscal savior or fiscal fraud: A look at the evidence. *Public Administration Review, 46,* 311–320.

Musgrave, R. A., & Musgrave, P. B. (1984). *Public finance: Its background, structure, and operation* (4th ed.). New York: McGraw-Hill.

Musgrave, R. A., & Musgrave, P. B. (1989). *Public finance in theory and practice.* New York: McGraw-Hill.

National Conference of State Legislatures. (1994). *State budget and tax actions 1994: Preliminary report.* Denver, CO: Author.

Pechman, J. A. (1983). *Federal tax policy.* Washington, DC: The Brookings Institution.

Pechman, J. A. (1984a). Comprehensive income tax reform. In J. A. Pechman et al. *Tax policy: New directions and possibilities* (pp. 13–18). Washington, DC: Center for National Policy.

Pechman, J. A. (1984b). *Federal tax policy* (4th ed.). Washington, DC: The Brookings Institution.

Pechman, J. A. (1989). *Tax reform: The rich and the poor* (2nd ed.). Washington, DC: The Brookings Institution.

Pechman, J. A. (1985). *Who paid the taxes, 1966–85.* Washington, DC: The Brookings Institution.

Pechman, J. A. (1986). *The rich, the poor, and the taxes they pay.* Brighton, Sussex, England: Wheatsheaf Books of the Harvester Press.

Research Institute of America (1993). *1994 RIA federal tax handbook.* New York: Author.

Research Institute of America (2001). *Federal tax handbook.* New York: Author.

Simons, H. C. (1938). *Personal income taxation: The definition of income as a problem of fiscal policy.* Chicago: University of Chicago Press.

Stark, S., Wood, R. C., & Honeyman, D. S. (1993). The Florida education lottery: Its use as a substitute for existing funds and its effects on the equity of school funding. *Journal of Education Finance, 18,* 231–242.

Tait, A. A. (1988). *Value added tax: International practice and problems.* Washington, DC: International Monetary Fund.

Thomas, S. B., & Webb, L. D. (1984). The use and abuse of lotteries as a revenue source. *Journal of Education Finance, 9,* 289–311.

U.S. Department of Commerce, Bureau of the Census. (1990). *State government tax collections: 1990.* GF-90-1. Washington, DC: U.S. Government Printing Office.

U.S. Department of Commerce, Bureau of the Census. (1995). *Statistical abstract of the United States: 1995.* Washington, DC: U.S. Government Printing Office.

U.S. Department of Commerce, Bureau of the Census. (2001). *State government tax collections: 2000.* Washington, DC: Author. Available at: www.census.gov /govs/www/statetax00.html

U.S. Department of Commerce, Bureau of the Census. (2000). *Statistical abstract of the United States: 2000.* Washington, DC: U.S. Government Printing Office.

U.S. Department of the Treasury, Internal Revenue Service. (2002a). *1040 Instructions, 2001.* Cat. No. 11325E. Washington, DC: U.S. Government Printing Office.

U.S. Department of the Treasury, Internal Revenue Service. (2002b). *Schedule A—Itemized deductions, 2001.* Cat. No. 11330X. Washington, DC: U.S. Government Printing Office.

Waltman, J. L. (1985). *Political origins of the U.S. income tax.* Jackson, MS: University Press of Mississippi.

chapter 5

THE PROPERTY TAX
IN SUPPORT OF SCHOOLS

Issues and Questions

- *Achieving High Standards with Equity and Efficiency*: In what ways has local reliance on property taxation contributed to the disparities in spending for, and the quality of, programs and facilities among communities?
- *The Property Tax Base*: How has benefit theory resulted in the taxation of tangible real property for supporting local services, including education?
- *Determining the Amount of Tax Owed*: What procedures are employed for assessing the value of real property, for relieving the tax burdens of certain taxpayers, and for calculating the amount owed by individuals and businesses?
- *Tax Capacity and Effort*: How do states differ in the size of their property tax bases, the tax rates applied to that base, and the revenue collected?
- *Strengths and Weaknesses of the Property Tax*: How does this revenue source measure up on the criteria of yield, equity, neutrality, elasticity, and administrative burden?
- *Limitations on Revenue and Expenditures*: What constitutional or statutory limitations, particularly those imposed through citizen initiatives, affect state and local abilities to increase taxes or constrain the growth of revenue and spending?
- *Local Autonomy and the Property Tax*: Why have communities resisted attempts to elevate the property tax from a local to a regional or state revenue source, given the potential benefits of broader-based taxation in financing educational reforms?

The property tax has traditionally been the financial mainstay of local governments, including school districts. This tax continues to provide the bulk of local funds. At the same time, the public expresses concern about its fairness, and policy makers consider proposals to replace property tax revenue with broader-based income or sales taxes.

The property tax persists as the primary source of local government revenue for several reasons. This local tax permits public governing boards and administrators to predict annual revenue flow accurately as they plan for and deliver public services to citizens. The property tax has close ties with local governmental autonomy, and it is a visible link between public services and their costs to individuals and businesses. Because county and state administrative mechanisms have been in place for many years, the cost of property tax collection is relatively low.

Despite these advantages, property taxation is severely criticized. The public rates it as the least popular form of taxation (ACIR, 1988, p. 97), and it has been described as "the most wretchedly administered tax" (Shannon, 1973, p. 27). Perceptions of unfair and differentially applied assessment policies give this tax a poor public image. It is often the most painful tax for businesses and homeowners to pay. Challenges to continued use of property taxes cite the following disadvantages: the regressive burden placed on the poor; the contribution to the deterioration of urban housing; the inability to capture the real fiscal capacity of communities; and the inequities created in educational opportunities for children in different school districts.

We devote a full chapter to property taxation because of its historical significance in financing schools and because of its continuing role as an important revenue source in nearly all states.

THE PROPERTY TAX BASE

Property taxes are imposed on wealth in the form of tangible personal property, intangible personal property, and tangible real estate property. Tangible personal property consists of such objects as machines, inventories, livestock, and equipment owned by businesses, as well as individually owned jewelry, furniture, vehicles, and personal computers. Intangible personal property—stocks, bonds, savings, and other investments—has no physical existence beyond the accounts or certificates that represent its value.

Tangibles are a more common tax base in states because they are more readily identifiable, often through licensing processes, than are intangibles. Only nine states include intangibles within local tax bases. In comparison, eighteen states tax business inventories, seventeen states tax household personal property, and eighteen states include motor vehicles (U.S. Department of Commerce, 1994, p. VI, VII). Thus the majority of states exempt tangible and intangible personal property from taxation.

The bulk of property taxation today falls on tangible real estate property. This classification includes land and what are referred to as "improvements" in the form of houses, commercial buildings, swimming pools, and so on. Table 5.1 shows that locally assessed real estate property exceeded $5.8 trillion in 1991. This amount overshadowed the $589 billion of assessed personal property. With an additional $286 billion assessed by states, the total net assessed value available to localities was over $6.6 trillion. The growth in the real property portion of this tax base was dramatic during the 1970s. There was a 335 percent increase between 1971 and 1981. The rate of growth slowed during the decade of the 1980s, rising 141 percent from $2.4 trillion to $5.8 trillion. It is this portion of the property tax base that is of prime concern in school finance. Thus the term *property* refers to real property in the remainder of this text.

The rationale for property taxation to support local government evolved from the principle of benefits received (see Chapter 3). The extent of police and fire protection, libraries

TABLE 5.1.
Assessed Values of Real and Personal Property, 1961 to 1991 (billions of dollars)

Kind of Property	1961	1971	1981	1991	Percentage Change 1971–1981	Percentage Change 1981–1991
Locally assessed property	326.1	641.1	2678.4	6395.8	318	139
Real property	269.7	552.7	2406.7	5806.7	335	141
Personal property	56.5	88.3	271.7	589.0	208	117
State-assessed property	27.8	53.5	159.0	285.8	197	80
Total assessed property (net locally taxable)	354.0	694.6	2837.5	6681.6	309	135

Source: U.S. Department of Commerce, Bureau of the Census. (1994). *1992 Census of Governments*, Vol. 2: *Taxable Property Values*. Washington, DC: U.S. Government Printing Office, Table C, p. XIV.

and schools, parks and museums, and other public services and amenities within a community increases the value of properties. It is assumed that individuals who receive the benefits of such services should pay the associated costs. It is also assumed that benefits are roughly proportional to property values (Musgrave & Musgrave, 1989, p. 411).

In accordance with benefit theory, property owners and tenants should be willing to pay higher taxes directly, or indirectly through rent, in communities with more extensive and better public services. However, relationships among benefits, property values, and levels of taxation are not as direct as they once were. Owners of real estate do not necessarily benefit from local services in proportion to the ascribed values of property. Indeed, many business and rental property owners do not even live within the community. And individuals who do not reside in a given tax jurisdiction may benefit from city parks, libraries, and museums that are financed by the local property tax base. For these reasons, researchers grapple with the problem of expanding or changing local property tax bases (Monk & Brent, 1997) while preserving appropriate degrees of local and community control over education (Theobald & Malen, 2000).

Refinements to the traditional property tax structure are further complicated by school choice policies that permit families to cross school district lines. As this practice continues to expand, both within and across public and private sectors, traditional "benefits theory" linkages among educational benefits, local property tax bases, and funds available for school programs and facilities will become more tenuous. Meanwhile, we have seen that the fundamental structure of property taxation is slow to change and that its elimination is unlikely for a number reasons presented throughout this chapter.

Property taxation is a general tax in that it applies to all community residents, regardless of whether direct benefits accrue to households; this approach is based on the assumption of a general distribution of benefits. Accordingly, this tax source assumes that public education serves broader public goals than would justify a specific charge assessed only of families with children enrolled in schools. Furthermore, the amount of property tax payments in the United States is based on the value of property owned rather than tied to individual taxpayer income, wealth, or some other measure of ability to pay. In England and some other countries, the tax is levied on the actual rental income, or on rental value in the case of owner occupancy, to better reflect taxpayers' abilities to pay. How the value of the tax base is determined affects not only the amount of revenue derived but also the perceived fairness of the tax.

PROPERTY VALUATION AND TAX DETERMINATION

We must understand the processes used to assess property values and to calculate the amount of taxes owed before we discuss property taxes in relation to the criteria presented in Chapter 3.

Assessing Real Property

Counties, municipalities, special-purpose districts, and fiscally independent school districts levy *ad valorem* property taxes according to the value of land and improvements. The amount of equity (the portion of property that represents the owner's wealth) is not of concern. For example, a bank or other holding company may have title to the largest share of a property's value, but an individual or business is liable for the full tax on its total value.

Statutes that authorize local governments to levy taxes call for an assessment of property to determine its value. An appointed or elected official, usually at the county, city, or town level of government, is responsible for discovering, listing, and valuing each taxable property in the jurisdiction. Statutes might specify an assessment cycle, a period of time during which the assessor must review the value of each parcel. For example, the assessment cycle is six years in Ohio (Ohio Department of Taxation, 2001, p. 130), ten years in Connecticut, and annually in Missouri. Other state statutes indicate a fraction of the jurisdiction to be reappraised each year. For example, one-fifth of the property is reappraised annually in Idaho (U.S. Department of Commerce, 1994, p. D-1).

The ideal appraisal is a recent sales price. *Fair market valuation*, often stated as true or full value, is defined as the amount that a willing seller of property would receive from a willing buyer in an open-market setting. Residen-

tial property and vacant land are generally appraised according to sales of comparable properties. However, because business and industrial properties do not change hands frequently, current market values are not readily available. Their appraisals are more often based on their income-earning capacity or on the cost of replacing the property (Oldman & Schoettle, 1974, chap. 3).

Subjectivity is the primary limitation of the following three commonly used appraisal methods. It is also the basis for many tax disputes. Relying on market data assumes that the value of a given parcel may be estimated from sales of other properties of somewhat similar age, condition, location, and style. A cost approach depends on estimates of land value, current costs of replacing buildings and other improvements, and depreciation. The income method estimates the remaining life of the property and an appropriate capitalization rate in calculating the present value of future income to be derived from the property. The limitations of each method are offset by the advantages of others, so the fairest valuations are those assigned by appraisers who can objectively apply several methods.

Advances in technology offer opportunities for greater objectivity and more frequent valuations. Scientific appraisals rely on statistical techniques to relate actual (or estimated) selling prices of homes and businesses with a large array of characteristics, including location, land acreage, square footage, type of heating and ventilating system, and number of fireplaces. Current technologies make it possible to maintain assessments that are closer to full value and to reappraise all properties annually without actual inspections. Additional revenue from more current and accurate valuations may be used to offset the increased cost of scientific appraisals, particularly during periods of rapidly changing real estate markets. But taxpayers might express concern with what they view to be unwarranted increases in property values.

The *assessed valuation* is the value given to a piece of property by an official appraiser. It is generally a percentage of fair market value, even in states that call for full valuation. Assessment ratios, which express the relationship between assessed and full values, often differ among classifications of property. Because the same tax rate is later applied to all properties in a jurisdiction, the effect of classification schemes is legally to shift the tax burden from some groups of taxpayers to others. This differentiation of properties became widespread in the 1970s, following judicial determination that prior assessment practices unfairly placed additional tax burdens on businesses. At that time, many local assessors had used their own "extra-legal" (Shannon, 1973, p. 29) systems of classification to deviate from uniformity mandates. Under legitimate classification plans, assessment ratios vary according to an accepted and consistently applied criterion, such as the current use of parcels.

Assessment ratios are illustrated in Table 5.2. Full market valuation is called for in twenty-three states, including Nebraska. Another eleven states, such as Connecticut and Indiana, specify a single percentage of full valuation to be applied to all taxable property. The remaining sixteen states, including Arizona and Tennessee, assign different ratios to various classes. Higher ratios for assessments of industrial, commercial, utility, and transportation property than for agricultural and residential property are common.

Property is valued on the basis of its "highest and best" use, in accordance with the application naturally suited to the site and likely to maximize its potential monetary return. Several assessment methods provide incentives to hold agricultural, recreational, open and historic land from development. For example, certain agricultural lands in Ohio are granted preferential treatment, whereas all other classes of property are assessed at 35 percent of market value (Ohio Department of Taxation, 2001, p. 130). A preferential assessment approach was employed by twenty-seven states in 1991 (U.S. Department of Commerce, 1994, p. IX). This practice gives a low assessment based on current income or use rather than on the true market value of the land. The assessment continues until the qualified use ends without any later penalty.

A deferred taxation approach is followed by thirty-one states. This approach also offers a preferential use assessment, but it requires a penalty (e.g., recoupment of back taxes and interest) when land use changes. Another method, employed by fourteen states, calls for a restrictive agreement in which a contract between the landowner and the local government holds land in qualified use for a specified period of time in exchange for lower assessment or deferred taxation. For example, agricultural reserves and not-for-profit conservation trusts maintain farm and open land in exchange for lower or forgiven taxes.

Musgrave and Musgrave (1989, p. 417) argue that sound property tax administration demands "uniform assessment at full market value." However, imprecise assessment practices and the desire to maximize taxpayer satisfaction with tax systems often justify residential assessments that are below fair market values. The public is less likely to complain about these lower assessments or to vote for a change in local politicians. Similar practices reduce business assessments to attract manufacturing or commercial activity or to discourage industry from leaving the locality. On the other hand, residential and business properties that do not receive preferential assessments must absorb tax burdens deferred or exempted from properties receiving preferential treatment. This causes them to pay higher taxes than they would if all properties were subject to the same standards. To the degree that the subjectivity of assessment practices permits easy deviation from established policies or standards, favoritism or political cronyism may result. These activities are discussed more fully as a cost of administration.

TABLE 5.2.

Assessment Ratios and Classifications of Real Property in Selected States, 1991

Arizona	13 classes:	a.	Mines and timber, 30%
		b.	Telephone, gas, and utility services, 30%
		c.	Commercial and industrial, 25%
		d.	Agricultural and vacant, 16%
		e.	Residential, not-for-profit, 10%
		f.	Residential, leased or rented, 10%
		g.	Railroad and airline, ratio of assessed value of property in classes *a*, *b*, and *c* to the market value of such property
		h.	Historic, 5%
		i.	Historic, commercial, and industrial portion, modification of class *c* ratio
		j.	Historic, leased or rented portion, modification of class *f* ratio
		k.	Livestock, aquatic animals, bee colonies, 8%
		l.	Possessory interests (e.g., lease on transportation facilities), 1%
		m.	Producing oil or gas company, 100%
Connecticut	All property at 70% of market value		
Indiana	All property at 33⅓% of market value		
Nebraska	All property at 100% of market value		
Tennessee	3 classes:	a.	Public utilities, 55%
		b.	Industrial and commercial, 40%
		c.	Farm and residential, 25%

Source: U.S. Department of Commerce, Bureau of the Census. (1994). *1992 Census of Governments*, Vol. 2: *Taxable Property Values*. Washington, DC: U.S. Government Printing Office, Appendix A.

Because state allocations of financial aid to school districts are generally tied to local property wealth (see Chapter 7), states should oversee local assessment practices. Netzer and Berne (1995) discussed the importance of interjurisdictional equalization of property values:

Equalization is necessary both for the implementation of statewide policies (in state school-aid calculations and for determining tax and debt limits) and for the determination of the tax liabilities of individual taxpayers whenever there are overlapping taxing and assessing jurisdictions, like state agency assessment of the value of utility property or school district boundaries that are not coincident with the boundaries of the assessing jurisdiction. The equalization process should be understandable, it should yield results that truly do equalize among jurisdictions, and it should be seen as essentially fair. (p. 34)

A state-level equalization board determines an *equalization ratio* for each tax jurisdiction. Dividing the assessed values of properties by the respective equalization ratio yields an estimate of market values. This practice brings all assessments in a state to a common basis. In Ohio, this occurs every six years, during the third year that follows a 6-year reappraisal conducted by county officials (Ohio Department of Taxation, 2001, p. 130). The school district depicted in Table 5.3 overlaps four assessing jurisdictions, such as towns or counties. Jurisdiction A has the highest equalization ratio, not because it is the wealthiest town, which it

TABLE 5.3.

Illustration of Equalization Ratios for Several Tax Jurisdictions within a School District

Jurisdiction	Assessed Value	Equalization Ratio	Equalized Value
A	$324,000,000	1.20	$270,000,000
B	85,000,000	0.85	100,000,000
C	45,000,000	0.50	90,000,000
D	21,000,000	0.15	140,000,000
Total	$475,000,000		$600,000,000

is, but because of its practice of assessing properties 20 percent above market value. Jurisdiction D has the lowest assessed value, but its equalized value is higher than that of either B or C. This is because jurisdiction D assesses its property at only 15 percent of market value, whereas jurisdictions B and C assess parcels at 85 percent and 50 percent, respectively.

This example illustrates the role that the state may play to mitigate differences in local assessment practices. This intervention may reduce taxpayers' presumptions of unfairness in property taxation. Moreover, using equalized values for each jurisdiction permits a fairer allocation of state funds in relation to local tax capacities. Without a system of equalized assessment ratios, tax jurisdictions may underassess properties to make their wealth appear to be lower in order to gain more state revenue.

Exemptions and Tax Relief

Local tax bases are diminished by total exclusions or partial exemptions of several classifications of property: (1) schools, universities, and governments; (2) religious and welfare organizations, including churches, chambers of commerce, fraternal organizations, and labor unions; (3) heads of households, senior citizens, veterans, volunteer firefighters, and persons with disabilities; and (4) incentives to rehabilitate housing or to attract industry. Tax

relief may also be granted through a credit against income tax payments to individuals whose property taxes exceed a given percentage of their income.

Exemptions are defended on the basis of desired social values. It is assumed that the benefits that not-for-profit organizations provide the community offset the cost of public services that are in effect given to them without tax payments. When the Supreme Court examined claims of unconstitutional aid to religion, tax exemptions for churches survived scrutiny under the First Amendment: "Elimination of exemption would tend to expand the involvement of government by giving rise to tax valuation of church property, tax liens, tax foreclosures, and the direct confrontations and conflicts that follow in the train of those legal processes" (*Walz* v. *Tax Commission of the City of New York*, 1970).

On the other hand, exemptions are criticized because of the diseconomies they create. For example, income-producing office buildings, hotels, and medical centers might otherwise be located on exempt church and university land. Manufacturing plants that are leased by counties to private corporations might be constructed on exempt public land. Even facilities constructed on private land often fall within designated enterprise zones that receive tax breaks to encourage economic development. Industries located in these tax enclaves benefit from paying no taxes or enjoy favorable tax rates in the short run, generally not exceeding ten years. Moreover, these businesses and other residents gain long-term benefits from the enlarged tax base that reduces future tax burdens or makes possible the eventual expansion of public services.

Many exemptions and tax breaks provide governmental subsidies for diverse interest groups. Other residents and businesses must then pay higher taxes. The loss of tax base to support local governments can be substantial. The exempt portion was less than 5 percent of the gross assessed valuation in all but twelve states in 1991. For example, $3.9 billion (nearly 12 percent) of the total locally assessed value is tax exempt in Indiana. For many large cities, the loss may be even greater. Over one-third ($438 million) of assessed property is exempt in New Orleans (U.S. Department of Commerce, 1994, pp. XI, 17, 42).

Municipalities and urban school systems suffer from policies that exempt these properties. They would benefit from state reimbursement of lost revenue, similar to the way the federal government provides financial payments to school districts impacted by tax-exempt military installations, public housing, and Native American reservations (see Chapter 9). In this manner, individuals who do not reside in the community but who use public libraries, parks, universities, and other facilities would share the cost of exemptions. A second way to spread the tax burden requires exempt organizations to pay user charges for selected governmental services. For example, many universities make payments to municipalities to offset large public service costs and to maintain community goodwill.

Nearly all states give some individual taxpayers relief from property taxes. These *homestead exemptions* came into being during the depression of the 1930s. They were granted to homeowners regardless of income. Since then, exemptions have also been granted to elderly homeowners, veterans, and disabled persons.

This relief reduces assessed valuations or provides a credit toward tax liability. For example, Georgia homesteaders' valuations are reduced $2000. Elderly taxpayers receive exemptions of $4000 generally and of $1000 on education assessments. Disabled veterans' valuations are reduced $32,500 (ACIR, 1995, p. 138). Similar exemptions are granted to elderly and disabled taxpayers in Ohio, but their exemption amounts are adjusted for income and taxable property value (Ohio Department of Taxation, 2001, p. 131). Such exemptions are criticized because they reduce the tax base, complicate tax administration, and might provide a subsidy for individuals who are otherwise able to pay taxes (Shannon, 1973, p. 35–37).

Circuit breakers in thirty-five states and the District of Columbia permit a credit against state income taxes for property tax payments that exceed a specified proportion of income for elderly and low-income homeowners and, in some cases, renters. For example, Pennsylvania offers relief ($500 maximum) against taxes due from homeowners and renters over sixty-five and from disabled taxpayers. These credits range from 100 percent for incomes under $5500 to 10 percent for incomes greater than $13,000 and give an average benefit of $257 per household (ACIR, 1995, p. 135).

Circuit breakers, which maintain the local tax base and provide income redistribution at the state level, are preferable to general homestead exemptions. However, this approach might not help all low-income earners. Property owners and renters who have little or no taxable income for the year still qualify for rebates of property taxes paid. But as in the case of income tax credits to offset sales taxes on food and necessities, these low-income families might not file for property tax relief. Renters, who currently qualify for circuit breakers in twenty-eight states, should be eligible if it is assumed that tenants bear the full property tax burden.

Aaron (1973) noted that because circuit breakers do not fully ease the burden on low-income taxpayers, the singling out of this one household expenditure (i.e., property tax) for relief might be due to its political acceptability. He advocated a housing allowance. This practice might be a more effective mechanism, assuming that property taxes affect housing costs. It might also be argued that exempting all taxes paid over a given fraction of income would more appropriately recognize that property and other taxes excessively burden low-income households.

Calculating the Property Tax

The technical function of assessment that we have examined determines the value of properties in a jurisdiction—that is, the capacity of the tax base. A political decision sets the tax rate. The tax rate reflects the level of tax effort the community is willing to exert to support public services.

The local tax amount (*levy*) to be collected is expressed as the difference between projected expenditures for programs (*costs*) for a given fiscal year and the amount of funds (*revenue*) anticipated from federal, state, and other local sources:

$$\text{Levy} = \text{costs} - \text{revenue}$$

This levy is divided by the aggregate *assessed value* or, in some states, the *equalized value*, of

properties in the tax jurisdiction to yield a *tax rate*:

$$\text{Tax rate on assessed value} = \text{levy/assessed value}$$
$$\text{Tax rate on equalized value} = \text{levy/equalized value}$$

Tax rates are often expressed in terms of mills. A mill is defined as one-tenth of a cent (0.001). A rate of 10 mills places a 1 percent tax on the assessed value of property. This rate might be expressed in a decimal form (0.01) or, as is common in many states, as a tax of $10 for each $1000 of assessed valuation. In other states, this rate is expressed as 10 cents per $100 of valuation. For example, the school district depicted in Table 5.3 has a total equalized valuation of $600 million. If a levy of $15 million is necessary for local support of school operations, the required tax rate is 0.025 (calculated as $15,000,000/$600,000,000). This 25-mill tax is equivalent to a rate of $25 per thousand, $2.50 per hundred, or a 2.5 percent tax on assessed values.

The calculations of tax levies in Table 5.4 apply this 25-mill tax rate to the four assessing jurisdictions presented in Table 5.3. The rate for the total district divided by the four respective equalization ratios yields tax rates that may be applied to the initial assessed values. The resulting tax levies for the four jurisdictions total the required $15 million for district operations.

TABLE 5.4.

Illustration of Tax Rates and Levies for Tax Jurisdictions within a School District

Jurisdiction	Tax Rate on Equalized Value	Equalization Ratio[a]	Tax Rate on Assessed Value[a]	Assessed Value[b]	Tax Levy[b]
A	25.00	1.20	20.83	$324,000,000	$6,750,000
B	25.00	0.85	29.41	85,000,000	2,500,000
C	25.00	0.50	50.00	45,000,000	2,250,000
D	25.00	0.15	166.67	21,000,000	3,500,000

[a] See Table 5.3.
[b] Rounded.

Once tax rates have been established for jurisdictions, a tax bill is prepared for each property. The constant tax rate is multiplied by the appraised value of each parcel on the tax roll to determine the amount of property tax owed:

Tax owed = rate × assessed value

Calculations of property taxes for the four parcels in Table 5.5 illustrate the application of this formula and the effect of exemptions such as those for homesteaders, senior citizens, or veterans. The properties have the same market value, $80,000. However, because the equalization ratios are different for the two jurisdictions, the assessed values for parcels 1 and 2 are different from those for parcels 3 and 4. Even though parcels 1 and 3 have different assessed values and tax rates, their owners pay the same amount of taxes and have the same effective tax rates. Parcels 2 and 4 benefit from exemptions and pay less taxes than parcels 1 and 3. Because exemptions are applied to assessed values, and because parcel 4 is assessed at a smaller ratio than is parcel 2, the effect of the exemption is greater for parcel 4, which pays

the lowest taxes and has the lowest effective tax rate.

In addition to school districts, property taxes may be levied in support of overlapping branches of local governments independently or in combination. These include county, town, or city governments; community colleges and public libraries; fire protection, water districts, and sewer districts; and road districts. A given piece of property is usually assessed by only one jurisdiction. However, an entity such as a school district may encompass several assessing authorities, as in the example above, and this necessitates the use of equalization ratios. It is thus possible for taxes to be collected by an authority, such as county government, other than the school district or other governmental unit that levies the tax.

The political decision that establishes a tax rate is not left entirely to government officials. Increases in tax rate are very often subject to *referenda*. School districts in many states confront the reality of public willingness to support government when seeking approval for program expansion or facility construction. For

TABLE 5.5.
Determining Net Tax and Effective Tax Rate

	Jurisdiction B		Jurisdiction C	
	Parcel 1	*Parcel 2*	*Parcel 3*	*Parcel 4*
Net Tax				
Market Value	$80,000	$80,000	$80,000	$80,000
Equalization ratio	0.85	0.85	0.50	0.50
Assessed value	$68,000	$68,000	$40,000	$40,000
less exemption	– 0	– 5,000	– 0	– 5,000
Taxable value	$68,000	$63,000	$40,000	$35,000
by tax rate[a]	× 0.2941	× 0.2941	× 0.05000	× 0.0500
Net tax owed	$2,000	$1,853	$2,000	$1,750
Effective tax rate (per $1000 market value)	$25.00	$23.16	$25.00	$21.88

[a] From Table 5.4. In Table 5.4, the tax rates are expressed in dollars per $1000 of assessed value. For computation purposes, they are expressed here as a ratio.

example, government officials can unilaterally impose only a 10-mill tax in Ohio; public support is required to establish a more realistic tax rate, such as the 51.91 mills collected in 1999 (Ohio Department of Taxation, 2001, p. 130). Public support of tax rate increases cannot be taken for granted. An antitax mood was blamed for New York State voters' rejecting 33 percent of 501 school district budgets in the spring of 1994 (Lindsay, 1994b). A more positive report was made one year later. At that time, the majority of district budgets or tax referenda were approved by voters in New York (80 percent), New Jersey (72 percent), and Ohio (63 percent) (Lindsay, 1995).

Variations Among States in Property Tax Capacity and Effort

Disparities in property tax bases and tax rates among states and local tax jurisdictions reveal differences in abilities and willingness to tax real estate property. Table 5.6 presents tax capacity, effort, and revenue collected in states.

The Advisory Commission on Intergovernmental Relations (ACIR) defines *capacity* as including (1) estimated market values of residential and farm properties and (2) net book values of commercial/industrial and public utility properties. Table 5.6 lists the states' capacities in four categories of properties. Many of

TABLE 5.6.

Property Tax Capacity and Revenue per Capita, 1991

	Capacity per Capita				Tax Effort		
State	*Residential*	*Farm*	*Commercial/ Industrial*	*Public Utility*	*Revenue per Capita*	*Index*	*Rank*
Alabama	$287.48	$14.06	$136.75	$47.10	$170.78	35	49
Alaska	550.12	0.00	244.50	17.65	1212.64	149	7
Arizona	484.37	19.31	125.36	40.06	661.86	99	24
Arkansas	252.89	35.52	128.72	55.88	244.20	52	45
California	679.55	12.79	183.30	28.50	639.38	71	39
Colorado	585.29	28.37	165.25	30.41	689.77	85	32
Connecticut	667.39	3.82	229.57	38.80	1137.61	121	13
Delaware	517.31	13.30	324.00	48.86	311.05	34	50
District of Columbia	543.55	0.00	280.34	48.90	1474.71	169	3
Florida	500.71	12.36	115.31	36.65	687.15	103	20
Georgia	315.73	13.26	157.60	47.55	506.41	95	26
Hawaii	1135.32	15.01	139.12	27.00	430.46	33	51
Idaho	300.97	61.33	119.95	40.63	426.81	82	33
Illinois	358.88	24.97	203.28	49.85	785.40	123	11
Indiana	287.12	26.15	189.77	56.68	570.81	102	23
Iowa	395.81	97.89	131.83	41.54	686.28	103	21
Kansas	289.04	63.29	156.94	61.15	691.46	121	12
Kentucky	275.62	25.79	157.98	39.76	276.82	55	44
Louisiana	275.08	13.52	213.34	58.64	275.50	49	46
Maine	463.98	8.10	136.82	33.29	796.43	124	10
Maryland	505.57	7.18	135.08	40.20	616.52	90	28
Massachusetts	571.42	2.89	187.49	32.59	829.90	104	19
Michigan	345.11	8.83	199.29	42.16	893.83	150	6
Minnesota	371.88	41.71	189.70	36.09	717.89	112	17
Mississippi	238.88	26.69	118.96	42.11	344.23	81	34

TABLE 5.6.

(Continued)

State	Capacity per Capita				Tax Effort		
	Residential	Farm	Commercial/ Industrial	Public Utility	Revenue per Capita	Index	Rank
Missouri	293.10	28.66	161.12	40.12	377.37	72	38
Montana	287.43	128.44	120.75	68.67	524.20	87	31
Nebraska	392.41	116.04	127.50	20.40	743.92	113	16
Nevada	460.74	10.71	154.92	52.99	455.76	67	41
New Hampshire	511.74	6.73	150.30	39.00	1341.23	190	1
New Jersey	545.83	3.89	239.28	38.30	1256.94	152	5
New Mexico	313.89	46.67	108.95	59.38	221.80	42	48
New York	395.47	3.39	196.45	31.07	1100.63	176	2
North Carolina	424.40	12.63	165.21	45.45	382.18	59	43
North Dakota	214.11	165.67	105.07	27.33	505.27	99	25
Ohio	363.76	12.33	191.52	43.53	540.84	88	29
Oklahoma	252.70	35.66	173.23	57.71	250.43	48	47
Oregon	490.30	25.07	145.19	29.77	877.05	127	9
Pennsylvania	403.26	8.40	182.04	49.45	561.80	87	30
Rhode Island	375.48	2.41	133.50	17.70	879.63	166	4
South Carolina	320.58	9.78	140.20	46.09	423.42	80	35
South Dakota	251.42	156.25	96.86	27.08	579.92	109	18
Tennessee	265.27	17.46	153.99	16.43	329.10	73	37
Texas	310.60	25.83	209.61	51.93	679.39	114	15
Utah	405.89	18.16	132.68	32.24	416.21	71	40
Vermont	591.81	21.46	134.79	32.44	925.00	119	14
Virginia	499.94	12.94	152.34	38.69	638.34	91	27
Washington	621.86	17.96	157.99	22.11	625.11	76	36
West Virginia	199.76	9.07	132.59	109.06	272.91	61	42
Wisconsin	333.33	21.39	167.55	37.41	796.78	142	8
Wyoming	472.20	81.70	211.01	127.07	912.22	102	22
U.S. Total	$431.58	$18.88	$174.70	$40.76	$665.93	100	

Source: ACIR. (1993). *RTS 1991: State Revenue Capacity and Effort*. Washington, DC: Advisory Commission on Intergovernmental Relations, Tables 4–25 to 4–27, pp. 100–102. RTS = representative tax system.

the states with consistently low per capita tax bases, including Arkansas, Mississippi, and West Virginia, are located in the South. Very high valuations of per capita farm capacities offset the relatively low residential and commercial/industrial capacities in Montana and the Dakotas. In contrast, the states with the highest residential tax bases, such as Hawaii, California, and Connecticut, have relatively lower farm capacities. The states with the highest commercial/industrial tax capacities are

Delaware, Alaska, and New Jersey. Wyoming, West Virginia, and Montana have high public utility tax bases, in contrast to Alaska, Rhode Island, and Tennessee.

Per capita tax capacities reveal the revenue that could be raised via property taxation if states taxed themselves at the national average rate. Not all states, however, tax their capacities at that level, and others exceed the national average by a considerable amount. Table 5.6 also gives property tax revenue raised by states in 1991 and an index of relative tax effort. This *effort* index expresses the relationship between actual revenue produced and each state's capacity. The District of Columbia collects the most revenue per capita. This jurisdiction exerts a very high effort, as do many other cities in the nation. New Hampshire, New York, and Rhode Island have the highest effort indices. Alaska is ranked relatively high in effort, but this state exports much of its energy-related property taxes to other states. Connecticut exerts somewhat less effort but collects a similarly high revenue per capita because of its high tax capacity. With their relatively low capacities and very low efforts, Alabama, Arkansas, New Mexico, and Oklahoma collect low revenue per capita from property taxes.

New England has traditionally relied more heavily on property taxes than have other regions (Gold, 1979, pp. 298–303). There has been a strong commitment to local control, a high degree of fiscal decentralization, low levels of state-financed relief, and few state-imposed limitations on local taxes and spending. States in the Plains and Great Lakes area, once near the top of the nation in terms of tax burdens, have led other states in adopting circuit breakers and shifting burdens through local income taxation and limitations on property tax increases.

Southeastern states have traditionally had low property taxes because their fiscal centralization brings more state grants-in-aid. Localities in the Southeast rely more heavily on user charges and sales taxes, and their property classification schemes and homestead exemptions reduce tax collections. It is more difficult to generalize about states in Rocky Mountain, Southwest, or Far West regions.

In addition to these variations in tax capacities and efforts among states are extreme disparities in property valuations, and very often in tax rates, among school districts. More will be said in subsequent chapters about these conditions in relation to state funding formulas.

MERITS OF PROPERTY TAXATION

The criteria we looked at in Chapter 3—yield, equity, neutrality, elasticity, and administrative burden—provide a framework for us to assess the advantages and disadvantages of property taxation as a revenue source.

Yield and Elasticity

State and local revenue from property taxation totaled $209 billion in 1996. The yield had increased from $156 billion in 1990 and from $68 billion in 1980. The importance of this revenue source is evident in the amount of yield in relation to that of other taxes. Property taxes collected at state and local levels in 1996 rivaled revenue from sales and gross receipts taxes ($249 billion) and far exceeded personal and corporate income taxes ($147 billion and $42 billion, respectively) (U.S. Department of Commerce, 2000, Table 502). Despite this large amount, reliance on the property tax has declined over the years. Expressed as a percentage of state and local taxes, the property tax's share of these governments' revenue diminished from 45 percent in 1956–1957 to 36 percent in 1976–1977 (U.S. Department of Commerce, 1994, p. XIV). This share dropped further to about 30 percent of state and local taxes in 1996 (U.S. Department of Commerce, 2000, Table 502).

Even when we examine just local tax collections, we find that communities depend less on this tax. Table 5.7 indicates that local property tax revenue grew from about $12.6 billion to about $188.8 billion between 1956–1957 and 1993–1994. However, its contribution to local government declined both in relation to total revenue received (from 43 percent to 30 percent) and in relation to total local tax revenue (from 87 percent to 74 percent) during the period. Property taxes also add to state revenue (about $8.4 billion in 1993–1994), and their proportionate contributions also declined relative to other funds received by states.

TABLE 5.7.
Revenue from Property Taxes, 1956–1957 to 1993–1994 (dollar amounts in millions)

Year	State Governments			Local Governments		
	Property Tax Revenue	*Percentage of Revenue from All Sources*	*Percentage of Tax Revenue*	*Property Tax Revenue*	*Percentage of Revenue From All Sources*	*Percentage of Tax Revenue*
1956–57	$ 479	1.9	3.3	$ 12,618	43.4	87.0
1961–62	640	1.7	3.1	18,416	42.6	87.9
1966–67	862	1.4	2.7	25,186	41.3	86.6
1071–72	1257	1.1	2.1	41,620	38.0	83.7
1976–77	2260	1.3	2.2	60,267	34.3	80.5
1981–82	3113	1.2	1.9	78,805	30.0	76.0
1986–87	4700	1.2	1.9	116,618	28.8	73.7
1990–91	6228	1.2	2.0	161,705	30.8	75.3
1993–94	8386	1.3	2.2	188,754	30.2	74.8

Source: American Council on Intergovernmental Relations. (1998). *Significant Features of Fiscal Federalism*, Vol. 2: *Revenues and Expenditures 1995*. Bethesda, MD: American Council on Intergovernmental Relations, Table 36, p. 78.

The property tax is generally not considered an elastic tax because "as income increases, the full value of property does not increase proportionately" (Netzer & Berne, 1995, p. 52). Assessed valuations, the legal base of the tax, do not necessarily reflect market values, and coefficients of elasticity appear to be below unity. The inclusion of business properties in particular reduce the elasticity, whereas residential property assessments more closely respond to changes in the economy. For this reason, Netzer (1966, pp. 184–90) argued that elasticity is best determined by the change in property tax yield in relation to change in the underlying tax base, which is the market value of properties, rather than in terms of personal income. He reported on studies that examined elasticity in relation to market values or to state-equalized tax bases. These calculations revealed a somewhat elastic tax, with coefficients between 1.0 and 1.2.

Assessments respond slowly to changes in the general economy, which accounts for property tax stability. This is both a strength and a weakness of property taxation. On the one hand, stability is important to local officials who must plan budgets and balance expenditures with available revenue. On the other hand, assessments are slow to respond to fluctuations in prices and incomes. Unlike income and sales tax rates, which are adjusted less frequently, property tax rates must be reexamined annually and placed before voters when changes are deemed necessary. With improvements in assessment practices and more frequent valuations of properties, rising assessments reflect growing market values, particularly during periods of inflation. As the yield grows in relation to the economy, tax rates need to be adjusted less frequently. However, the efficiency and currency of assessment mechanisms have contributed to taxpayer complaints and eventually to legal limitations on the growth of valuations in California and elsewhere (Musgrave & Musgrave, 1989, p. 418).

Without an expanding tax base between the Great Depression through World War II, school expenditures lagged behind the growth rate of the general economy. Growth in assessments and strong public support for education permitted increases in property tax yield and rates during the 1950s and 1960s, a period of rapid expansion of public schooling. The general economic recession during the 1970s brought with it restricted governmental growth, regardless of the tax source. Federal and state governments, with their heavier reliance on more elastic taxes, faced potentially large shortfalls. School districts that relied heavily on property taxation were in many cases at a relative advantage because of the stability of the tax and the dependability of its yield. In contrast, many school systems suffered financial losses in terms of stagnant annual growth during the economic slowdown of the early 1990s and early 2000's, partly because of their greater dependence on state revenue sources.

Equity

Land ownership was closely tied to wealth, income, and power in an agrarian society. It also was a better proxy for benefits received from government. Real estate property was then a good indicator of individual ability to pay taxes. In information and industrial societies, land ownership is only one form of wealth, and equal treatment under tax codes is generally measured in terms of income (see Chapter 3). Moreover, with the exclusion of many forms of wealth (e.g., investments and most personal property) from property taxation, there is little relationship between taxpayer wealth and income and the amount of taxes paid. Horizontal equity is violated, because individuals with the same income do not necessarily pay the same amount of tax.

To determine the degree to which this revenue source satisfies vertical equity—the unequal treatment of unequals—we must first consider who bears the burden of the tax and then identify its relationship to taxpayers' incomes. Occupants typically pay the taxes on housing. The property tax is a direct tax on homeowners who might be able to recoup a portion of taxes paid when houses are later

sold for appreciated values. It becomes an indirect tax when owners of rental property are able to raise rents and shift tax increases to tenants who cannot later recoup any portion of taxes paid.

Under the traditional view of incidence, tax burdens are assumed to be higher for people with low incomes. In the case of renters, residential taxes fall on tenants rather than on property owners. Property taxes on businesses fall on consumers rather than on owners or stockholders. Assuming lower relative valuations of higher-priced houses and a higher proportion of income spent on housing by low-income families, a tax on residential property has been considered regressive (Netzer, 1966, p. 131).

A second approach to determining incidence considers the property tax to be a tax on capital, such that its incidence is upon owners. Thus taxes on commercial and industrial property are distributed in line with income from capital rather than on the basis of consumption expenditures (Aaron, 1975). If property owners are assumed to bear the burden, then the tax is more progressive. This conclusion rests on the presumed close relationship between ownership of capital and the distribution of income.

We discussed the overall tax burdens under these two sets of assumptions in Chapter 3 (see Table 3.2). Except for the lowest income level, which bears a relatively heavy burden, the proportion of income paid in all taxes in 1985 rose slowly with income under either set of assumptions. Even assuming the property tax burden itself to be regressive, it does not appear to make overall tax burdens regressive. Homestead exemptions and circuit breakers based on income serve to reduce property tax regressivity in many states.

Neutrality

Property taxes are not neutral. They often discourage owners from maximizing the potential use of property, contribute to the deterioration of urban areas, influence choices of geographic location for residences and businesses, and cause disparities in educational programs.

Communities engage in "fiscal mercantilism" (Netzer, 1966, pp. 45–59) to maximize tax bases in relation to demand for public services. Lower tax rates become incentives for individuals and businesses to migrate from cities to suburbs and from northern to southern and western states. Tax benefits and restrictive zoning regulations that define land use encourage formation of industrial enclaves. High-income families are similarly attracted to communities with higher residential wealth, whereas low-income families, who do not contribute to the tax base but who increase public service costs, are discouraged from residing in such communities.

The practice of valuing buildings and other improvements within the taxation of real property, as it is presently structured and administered by localities, may discourage owners from making substantial investments. Site value taxation, which would simplify property valuation by reducing the property tax base to include only land without improvements, would make the tax more neutral. By definition, a neutral tax has little or no effect on the mix of resources in production processes (i.e., land, labor, and capital). It has been argued for many years that taxing the land itself, without valuing improvements, would not hinder production: "the whole value of land may be taken into taxation, and the only effect will be to stimulate industry, to open new opportunities to capital, and to increase the production of wealth" (George, 1879, p. 412). This approach would stimulate the development of real estate to its full potential, particularly in deteriorating central cities, because it is in owners' interests to maximize the use of land (Peterson, 1973). However, site value taxes might discourage investors from keeping older buildings, single-story structures, parking lots, and other improvements that do not maximize land use.

Because land values are underassessed and improvements are overassessed, land may be withheld from its most productive use in deteriorating sections of cities. Upgrading properties in generally blighted neighborhoods does not necessarily bring larger rents, but such investments would certainly result in higher taxes, given the higher assessments that accompany improvements. The overassessment of poor neighborhoods creates tax delinquency, and many cities are slow in enforcing tax collections (Peterson, 1973, p. 10).

Yinger, Borsch-Supan, Bloom, and Ladd (1988), found strong evidence that differences in effective property tax rates are, to some extent, capitalized into the price of housing. This is because, all else being equal, buyers are willing to pay more for homes with low taxes than for comparable houses with high taxes. Yinger et al. conclude

> Because households compete with each other for access to housing in jurisdictions with low tax rates, jurisdictions with relatively low tax rates will have relatively high house values, and vice versa. In equilibrium, households must be exactly compensated for higher property tax rates by lower housing prices. (p. 56)

Full capitalization of the property tax would impose the same burden on each unit of housing, regardless of the actual tax levied. However, effective tax rates are not fully capitalized. The studies by Yinger et al. found the degree of capitalization to range between 16 and 33 percent. Not only can property tax rates be capitalized into the price of housing, but Wyckoff (2001) asserts that state equalizing aid can also be capitalized into housing prices for similar reasons. These differing treatments of property taxes and state equalization attempts as related to the price of homes may influence the selection of homes and communities.

Property taxes contribute to disparities among school districts in funds available for daily operations and facility construction. In most states, the level of resources available for each pupil's education depends to some degree on the wealth of the local community and on the level of effort that taxpayers exert to support schools. The more local school districts depend on the property tax for their financial support, the greater will be the disparity in funding levels among school districts. This is particularly true with regard to funds for capital improvements, which are largely dependent on property taxation with little or no assistance from state revenue sources.

The property tax itself, however, does not cause many of these economic distortions. The problem lies with the fragmentation of the local governance structure. If another revenue source such as the income or sales tax had been tied traditionally to local governments, then similar disparities would be evident: "large differentials in the rates of any major local tax among neighboring and competitive jurisdictions are likely to be bad rather than good" (Netzer, 1966, p. 172). Systemic mechanisms, such as state aid to school programs, are meant to overcome these economic distortions, but they are often compromised by political realities. Although new ways of raising local revenue (see Chapter 6; Addonizio, 2001; Monk & Brent, 1997; Pijanowski & Monk, 1996) are meant to shift the burden away from the property tax, they are likely to compromise equalization efforts further and contribute to disparities that are not caused by the property tax.

Administrative Burden

Criticism of the property tax is often centered on its administration and perceptions (or the reality) of unfairness in assessment practices. Revenue is maximized, as are taxpayer acceptance and support, when valuation and collection procedures are administered efficiently and fairly.

Unlike the case with income taxes, individual taxpayers do not determine their liability for property taxes. Property assessment and tax

calculation are the responsibility of local public officials, and compliance costs are nearly nonexistent. However, many assessors are poorly trained in appraisal procedures, serve only part-time, and are often concerned about their reelection or advancement in the local or state political arena. Problems of tax administration are epitomized by the conflict faced by assessors who must raise assessments to keep pace with inflation and property improvements, while maintaining favor in the local power structure. For this reason, progressive jurisdictions are appointing assessors as civil servants. This practice reflects an earlier recommendation that abandoning elections in favor of appointments on the basis of demonstrated ability to assess properties contributes to the professionalization of the assessment function (ACIR, 1973, p. 69).

The cost of property tax administration is low relative to its yield and in comparison with the costs of other major revenue sources. However, this low cost is indicative of deficiencies in assessment practices that relate to inefficiencies of small units of government. Making full disclosure of local assessment practices and improving appeals procedures offer the advantages of reducing inequities and political interference with the system, while increasing public confidence. It would be possible to have good property tax administration at a cost of about 1.5 percent of tax collections, an acceptable amount when compared with administrative costs for income and sales taxes (Netzer, 1966, p. 175).

In states where voter approval is necessary to change tax rates, the administrative burden on local officials and school districts can be quite high. Although unmeasured, multiple levies for operations, emergencies, and facilities; unfavorable public votes that require school leaders to go back to the drawing board; and repeated public relations campaigns to pass property tax levies all imply considerable burden. These burdens, although they are indirect costs to administration and compliance, intensify with greater degrees of public dissatisfaction. The public's dissatisfaction with the increased size and cost of government generally—and with larger property assessments and tax bills more specifically—culminated in tax limitation initiatives over the past several decades in many states.

LIMITATIONS ON TAXATION AND GOVERNMENT EXPENDITURES

Tax and spending limitations restrict government capacity to deliver public services with the intention of encouraging fiscal responsibility. Officials who are overzealous in their desire to meet demands of constituents might raise taxation and indebtedness to dangerous levels. The Revolutionary War was fought to ensure that the citizenry would have a voice in decisions about government taxation. Two subsequent movements addressed the large debt that local governments incurred (the late 1800s) and the growth in both state and local government spending and taxes (the 1970s to the present). In this chapter we discuss the limitations imposed by the more recent movement because of their direct effects on local property taxation and school district operations. These limitations also affect state revenues and expenditures.

Limits on Local Government Debt and Tax

State constitutions and statutes that define the structure of local governments also limit their fiscal powers. Localities are typically restricted with regard to the type of taxes or the maximum tax rates that they may levy. Limits on indebtedness define the maximum percentage of the local government's property tax base that may be obligated for future payments. Table 5.8 illustrates provisions for limiting tax rates, assessments, revenues, and expenditures of school districts in several states. Many

states limit tax rates that are expressed in terms of millage (e.g., Michigan and Ohio) or dollars per hundred of valuation (e.g., North Carolina). In contrast, Colorado and Wisconsin essentially limit revenue and spending with reference to a budgeted formula or prior spending levels. Where tax rate limitations are in place, the treatment of assessed valuation plays an even greater role. For example, assessment increases in Michigan are limited to the rate of inflation or 5 percent, whichever is less; assessment increases in Ohio are countermined by tax rate decreases to produce the same amount of revenue, without adjustments for inflation.

As is reflected in Table 5.8, states employ a great variety of methods to limit property taxation and revenue growth. The role of voters in this process also varies considerably among states. For example, voter support is required in Colorado, Michigan, and Ohio for operations spending above some established baseline amount, even with limitations in place. In contrast, North Carolina procedures call for public hearings, but voter approval is not required. Wisconsin calls for public meetings and seeks voter approval, but government authorities can adjust tax levies to meet educational requirements (NCES, 2001).

Similar limitations in many states restrict long-term borrowing for capital outlay for constructing buildings and purchasing school buses. Open-disclosure laws require hearings and referenda prior to creation of debt or the raising of indebtedness above a given level. Additionally, school boards of fiscally dependent districts cannot themselves incur debt.

Movements to Restrict Growth in Taxation and Spending

With the growth of municipalities during an inflationary period following the Civil War, current expenses were paid by floating debt carried forward each year, rather than through increased taxes. Many jurisdictions overex-

TABLE 5.8.

Limitations on Property Taxation and Revenue Growth for Current Expenses in Selected States

State	Type of Limitation	Provisions
Colorado	Revenue and Spending	Growth in revenue and spending is limited by a cap of 20% of formula or $200,000.
		Districts can choose the greater of the two limits, but voter approval is required.
Michigan	Tax rate and Assessment	Several tax rate limitations are in place, but they can be overridden up to 50 mills by voter approval.
		Assessed values are limited to the rate of inflation or 5%, whichever is less.
North Carolina	Tax rate	A maximum tax rate of $1.50 per $100 of valuation has been established.
		Voter approval is not required.
Ohio	Tax rate and Revenue	A maximum tax rate of 10 mills can be imposed without voter-approval; there is no limit on voter approved millage.
		As assessed values increase, tax rates decrease correspondingly to produce the same yield.
Wisconsin	Revenue and Spending	Annual increases in revenue and spending from state aid and property taxes are limited, with or without voter approval.
		The amount of increase was limited to $208.88 per pupil for fiscal year 1999, to be adjusted for inflation in future years.

Source: National Center for Education Statistics. (2001). *Public School Finance Programs of the United States and Canada, 1998–99*. NCES 2001-309. [J. Dayton, C. T. Holmes, C. C. Sielke, A. L. Jefferson (compilers); W. J. Fowler, Jr. (project officer).] U.S. Department of Education, Washington, DC: Author.

tended their tax bases prior to the recession of the 1870s, and states responded with measures to limit debt and public services in relation to local revenue. By 1880, ten states had limitations on taxes, and half of the states had imposed limits on debt incurred by cities (Wright, 1981, p. 42).

A century later, public perceptions of uncontained growth and inefficiency in government spawned a similar movement to contain taxes and expenditures. Confidence and trust in government waned in the 1970s, and it was claimed that reducing revenue would necessitate efficiency in the delivery of essential services. This tax revolt responded to the rapid growth in federal, state, and local governments during the 1950s and 1960s: "The votes are votes against inflation and irritating regulations

and government actions, not just against taxes" (Due , 1982, p. 281). Taxation became the focal point, however, and the public called for tax and expenditure limitations of two forms: (1) reducing the existing size of government, a limitation predicated on the beliefs that tax burdens are too heavy and that government is not a good investment, and (2) containing the growth of government, a limitation predicated on the belief that government is as large as it should be relative to the rest of the economy (Palaich, Kloss, & Williams, 1980, pp. 1–2). These two goals are illustrated in initiatives in several states.

The movement began in California in 1978. Proposition 13 was a citizen initiative to reach the first goal, that of cutting the size of government by reducing revenue and thus expenditures. This constitutional change limited local property tax rates to 1 percent of 1975–1976 fair market values and restricted annual increases in assessments to a maximum of 2 percent. Assessments would reflect current values only when property changed ownership or was newly constructed. Proposition 4, passed one year later by a wider margin of California voters, illustrates the goal of containing government growth. This measure limited growth in state and local appropriations from tax revenue to the rates of increases in the cost of living and population. This referendum also made it possible for a simple majority of voters to adjust the spending limit of any government unit and called for full state reimbursement of the costs of mandates associated with any new or upgraded program.

The effect of these limitations on property taxes can be seen in trends in effective tax rates. Table 5.9 shows a slower growth in taxation relative to the value of houses in nearly all states. Effective tax rates represent tax liability as a percentage of the market value of homes financed through the Federal Housing Authority. The average rate in the nation grew from 1.34 percent in 1958 to 1.70 percent in 1966. However, with the tax revolt and concurrent shift in revenue burdens to states, this trend was reversed. Effective rates diminished to 1.16 percent in 1986. In all but eight states, there was a higher rate in 1966 or 1977, and a

TABLE 5.9.

Average Effective Property Tax Rates[a]

State	1958 (%)	1966 (%)	1977 (%)	1986 (%)	Rank[b]
Alabama	0.56	0.66	0.74	0.39	49
Alaska	1.12	1.42	NA	0.82	41
Arizona	2.14	2.41	1.72	0.68	45
Arkansas	0.86	1.09	1.49	1.09	25
California	1.50	2.03	2.21	1.06	28
Colorado	1.72	2.20	1.80	1.09	24
Connecticut	1.44	2.01	2.17	1.46	12
Delaware	0.71	1.14	0.88	0.73	43
District of Columbia	1.08	1.37	NA	1.17	21
Florida	0.76	1.09	1.13	0.89	39
Georgia	0.84	1.30	1.27	0.90	36
Hawaii	0.62	0.81	NA	0.51	48
Idaho	1.14	1.23	1.46	0.91	35
Illinois	1.35	1.96	1.90	1.59	9
Indiana	0.84	1.64	1.66	1.28	19
Iowa	1.34	2.12	1.76	1.96	8
Kansas	1.65	1.96	1.37	1.06	29
Kentucky	0.93	1.03	1.25	1.10	22
Louisiana	0.52	0.43	0.61	0.25	50
Maine	1.50	2.17	1.65	1.21	20
Maryland	1.47	2.05	1.69	1.30	18
Massachusetts	2.21	2.76	3.50	1.08	27
Michigan	1.45	1.81	2.63	2.26	5
Minnesota	1.57	2.14	1.39	1.03	31

(Continued)

TABLE 5.9.

(Continued)

State	1958 (%)	1966 (%)	1977 (%)	1986 (%)	Rank[b]
					(continued)
Mississippi	0.66	0.93	1.10	0.77	42
Missouri	1.12	1.64	1.59	0.89	38
Montana	1.32	1.70	1.31	1.32	17
Nebraska	1.90	2.67	2.48	2.21	7
Nevada	1.06	1.47	1.71	0.61	46
New Hampshire	1.81	2.38	NA	1.55	10
New Jersey	1.77	2.57	3.31	2.33	1
New Mexico	0.93	1.30	1.65	1.01	32
New York	2.09	2.40	2.89	2.22	6
North Carolina	0.90	1.31	1.35	NA	33
North Dakota	1.54	1.81	1.26	1.37	15
Ohio	1.07	1.44	1.26	1.08	26
Oklahoma	0.86	1.11	0.95	0.90	37
Oregon	1.55	1.98	2.25	2.26	4
Pennsylvania	1.50	1.88	1.85	1.37	16
Rhode Island	1.67	1.96	NA	1.49	11
South Carolina	0.48	0.60	0.82	0.70	44
South Dakota	2.01	2.64	1.79	2.31	2
Tennessee	0.97	1.37	1.40	1.04	30
Texas	1.36	1.62	1.84	1.44	13
Utah	1.05	1.52	1.03	0.93	34
Vermont	1.63	2.27	NA	NA	NA
Virginia	0.90	1.13	1.21	1.42	14
Washington	0.92	1.14	1.75	1.10	23
West Virginia	0.56	0.71	NA	0.88	40
Wisconsin	1.82	2.31	2.22	2.27	3
Wyoming	1.17	1.34	0.87	0.57	47
U.S. Total	1.34	1.70	1.67	1.16	

[a] Effective rates are for existing FHA-insured mortgages only, which represent varying percentages (by state) of total single-family homes.

[b] In cases where 1986 data were not available, rank was based on data for the most recent year.

NA = not available.

Source: ACIR. (1987). *Significant Features of Fiscal Federalism, 1987 edition.* Washington, DC: Advisory Commission on Intergovernmental Relations, Table 30, p. 70.

smaller rate was evident by 1986. Effective rates in California, for example, increased from 1.50 percent in 1958 to 2.21 percent in 1977, the year before Proposition 13. Then effective rates declined to 1.06 percent in 1986. In a more recent comparison of fifty-one major cities, Los Angeles had one of the lowest effective property tax rates in 1998, 0.79 percent. Its rate was higher than that of Honolulu, which had the lowest rate of 0.46 percent, but substantially lower than those of the three cities with the highest rates: 4.59 percent in Bridgeport,

CT; 3.99 percent in Newark, NJ; and 3.33 percent in Manchester, NH (U.S. Department of Commerce, 2000, Table 517).

Diminishing effective rates during the years depicted in Table 5.9 do not necessarily mean that there were declines in actual millage rates levied on appraised value or in tax amounts collected. Rapidly rising market values bring increases in tax payments (assuming similar increased assessments) even if millage rates remain the same or decline somewhat. For example, taxes on a house appraised in 1966 for $22,000 would be $374, given the average effective rate of 1.70 percent. If this same house were appraised in 1986 at $45,000, it would be taxed $522, given the national average rate of 1.16 percent. The increased tax owed reflects growth in the appraisal, despite the substantial decline in effective rate.

Much has been written about the aftermath of Proposition 13 in California. The feared reductions in government spending and services did not materialize initially. Some said that the state's economy was strengthened in the short run by the tax cuts (Adams, 1984, pp. 171–174). Increased user fees for public swimming pools, golf courses, marina docking, and so on placed the burden for services directly on beneficiaries. Business property turned over at a faster rate than was anticipated, and newly raised assessments shifted the burden for property taxation from residences to businesses. With respect to schools, Proposition 13 resulted in the replacement of property tax revenue with state financial aid; this narrowed disparities in expenditures per pupil among school districts.

On the other hand, many unintended economic effects occurred. The greatly increased dependence on state revenue resulted in a loss of local autonomy and a weakening of citizen participation in decision making. Reductions in property taxes were not always passed on to consumers and renters. Beneficiaries of the revolt included businesses, large oil companies, and property owners (Due, 1982, pp. 281–

283). Having newly constructed or newly purchased property taxed differently from property that had not changed hands created inequities in effective rates for properties within neighborhoods. Californians paid higher federal income taxes because of the lower deductions they could claim for property taxes. With the shift to user fees, homeowners still had to pay for services. But they lost the federal income tax deductions for which they would have qualified if the services had been paid for through property tax.

Even with the state paying proportionately more for public education, there was a large drop in total revenue for schools relative to other states. In per-pupil spending for schools California dropped from among the top ten in the nation prior to Proposition 13 to a low of thirty-fifth. By the end of the 1980s its rank had stabilized at twenty-fifth (Verstegen, 1988, p. 85). The effects of this reform include a dramatic reduction in the tax base because valuations are tied to the price of property at the time it is sold. The tax burden shifts to younger, lower-income taxpayers, which makes the tax more regressive: "The result of California's Proposition 13 or switch to an acquisition-based system of property tax assessment was to significantly lower the tax base over time and violate horizontal equity in directions that make the property tax even more regressive overall" (Odden & Picus, 2000, p. 137).

The 1980 Massachusetts Proposition $2\frac{1}{2}$ served both to reduce taxes and to contain the growth of government. It limited property tax rates to $2\frac{1}{2}$ percent of "full and fair cash value," required jurisdictions that were previously taxing above that level to reduce levies, and held revenue from real estate to a $2\frac{1}{2}$ percent annual growth rate. By the early 1980s, thirty states had adopted expenditure or revenue limits. Most of these actions tied increases in tax collections to changes in the cost of living, to a fixed percentage increase over prior years, or to a fixed percentage of property value (Wright, 1981, pp. 29–30).

The movement to limit taxes and expenditures slowed in the 1980s, and only six of the twenty-four states with active revenue or spending limitations noted by ACIR (1994, pp. 14–19) had adopted the restrictions after 1982. Proposition 9, defeated by California voters in June 1980, proposed a constitutional amendment to halve state income tax rates, index rates to stem bracket creep, and abolish the state's inventory tax. In the same year that the Massachusetts proposition passed, initiatives failed in another five states. In 1988, tax or expenditure limitation measures were placed before voters in three states, but they all failed.

Property tax revenue, which had fallen nationally from $66.4 billion in fiscal 1978 to $64.9 billion a year later, grew substantially thereafter. It reached $209 billion in fiscal year 1996 (U.S. Department of Commerce, 1994, p. VI; 2000, Table 502). In the late 1980s, public opinion shifted once again in support of public services, especially those related to expenditures for education. Quality and excellence were desired. The public voiced its willingness to raise state and local taxes to finance improved schools. The drive to ensure adequate funds for public education brought another California initiative. Proposition 98, approved by voters in 1988, amended the state constitution such that public education would receive the larger of 40 percent of any new state revenue or the previous year's allocation increased by the rate of inflation and enrollment growth. State money that could not otherwise be spent because of spending limits imposed by Proposition 4 was also diverted to support education.

The movement may have slowed with the realization that limitations might not be effective in constraining government growth. Howard's (1989) study of the effectiveness of limitations found them to play only a minor role in constraining state revenue or expenditures.

The overall condition of state economies and structure of state tax systems, in combination with the sensitivity of policymakers to anti-tax sentiment, have done more to limit state spending than have imposed restrictions. (p. 83)

She explained their limited effectiveness by noting that a large proportion of state-appropriated funds (over 50 percent in six of seventeen states studied) is exempt from limitations; that restrictions are less effective when they are tied to personal income growth, because state tax systems are not highly elastic; and that some states that have exceeded limits have been pressured to assume financial responsibilities previously met by localities.

Enactments in a number of states, including most of those appearing in Table 5.8, revived the movement in the 1990s (Fulton & Sonovick, 1992). Oregon voters approved a constitutional amendment to limit property taxes to 15 mills for school districts. As this local burden declined to 5 mills, greater responsibility for school finance shifted to the state. Six states adopted limitation measures in 1992. Florida limited tax increases for residential property, and Rhode Island limited overall state spending. Arizona and Colorado limitations imposed the need for a two-thirds vote by legislators to enact tax increases. The Oklahoma constitutional provision required a three-quarters vote either by the state legislature or by voters. The Colorado initiative also required voter approval for increases in spending that exceed the rate of change in population and the consumer price index (CPI) in the case of state and local governments or the percentage change in enrollments and the CPI in the case of school districts.

The 1994 elections included over two hundred initiatives, seventy-eight of which resulted from citizen petition drives (Lindsay, 1994a). A revenue cap approved in Florida restricted state revenue growth to that of personal income. However, this constitutional amendment exempted property taxes and lottery revenue, both of which finance schools. Nevada voters gave initial approval to an amendment that requires a two-thirds legislative vote to enact tax increases. But voters must approve amendments twice before they are effective. Voters defeated similar proposed constitutional amendments to limit increases in revenue or property valuations in Missouri, Montana, Oregon, and South Dakota.

In reviewing reasons for the success or failure of citizen initiatives in seven states, Whitney (1993) noted that "education finance measures are more likely to succeed when expenditures are tied to specific educational improvements that are carefully explained to the public" (p. vii). Distrust of local government, or the real or perceived unnecessary tax burden, leads to initiatives to curtail the growth of property tax revenue. Then local officials seek additional state assistance. The property tax was once a large source of local funds for some districts. It has declined in importance as policy makers have shifted to the state the burden supporting schools.

PROPERTY TAXES AND STATE-LEVEL REVENUES

When the property tax is weighed against criteria of yield, equity, neutrality, elasticity, and administrative burden, there is no overriding consideration that argues for its elimination. When the financing of educational programs and facilities in communities depends heavily on property taxation, however, people do object. They argue that a shift from local to either state or regional property taxation, or the replacement of this revenue with broader-based taxes, would be more equitable. Others contend that the property tax is an important part of local community control of schools.

State Assumption of Property Taxation

For many years people have argued that continuing to place a large burden on small local governmental units to finance schools is inconsistent with the goals of equity and effi-

ciency in resource allocation (Netzer, 1973, pp. 13–24). Giving the state a larger role in school finance would equalize educational opportunities. This goal recognizes the geographic spillovers that occur when the mobility of labor among localities distributes the positive and negative consequences of varying school quality among communities. Similarly, efficiency in tax administration might be better served through state or regional control of tax policy, rather than county or school district control. These alternative tax structures are examined extensively by Monk and Brent (1997) and Brent (1999).

Judicial decisions, tax study commissions, and other pressures to meet equity goals led many states to deemphasize local property taxation during the finance reform movement of the 1970s. When state and federal governments assumed increased responsibilities for financing elementary and secondary education, this eased the burden on local revenue (see Table 2.1). Greater fiscal federation promised a broader base of support, equalization of local district capacities to finance schools, and improved assessment practices (ACIR, 1973, p. 77). Inequities persisted, however. Some questioned the role of property taxation in the context of educational reforms that would ensure higher standards for all students and eliminate the extreme disparities in spending, programs, and facilities depicted by Kozol (1991). At the same time, the systemic reform movement of the late 1980s and throughout the 1990s directed attention once again to the advantages of maintaining control over many decisions at the district or school level (Theobald & Malen, 2000). Control over fiscal affairs is an important part of control over programs. In fact, even in the midst of litigation and fiscal uncertainty, stakeholders and policy makers clearly value retaining local control and decision making (Monk & Theobald, 2001).

Having access to a substantial revenue source is important to the autonomy of local governments. The property tax has traditionally been the revenue source best suited to local governments. It is symbolic of the autonomy of local government, and any move to have the state assume property taxation is resisted. Shannon (1973, p. 28) contended that this revenue source "serves as the sheet armor against the forces of centralization." Although decisions about school programs could be made locally even if all funds were allocated from higher levels, access to this revenue source enables local officials to determine the total level of resources and services to be provided, at least at the margin. Furthermore, Thompson and Wood (2001) pointed out that when revenue sharing among levels of government falls short of supporting educational requirements, local school authorities have little choice other than to rely on property taxation.

Gold (1994) observed that "the real root of inequality is reliance on *local revenue*, not the property tax itself. Disparities would generally be even worse if the local income or sales tax were used instead of the property tax" (p. 9). Rather than eliminating property taxation, states' finance policies typically consider the amount of funds that are raised locally in distributions of financial aid. These formulas thus equalize local communities' tax capacities and make levels of school expenditures more comparable among districts (see Chapter 7). In effect, larger tax bases, including utilities and industrial properties, are spread among more localities. Tax-based disparities and service disparities are thus greatly reduced. To the extent that this equalization does not occur, local initiatives to increase local revenues perpetuate inequalities.

Even in states that have assumed a large financial involvement, property tax administration remains, for the most part, a local government responsibility. But states use equalization ratios and exercise more control over assessment practices. Some states have explored the benefits of regional school taxing units, in which collections from high-wealth districts are shared with others. This approach improves uniformity of fiscal effort and enhances taxpayer equity within regions, without turning property taxation into a state responsibility (Clark, 1995). The Texas Supreme Court, however, declared this practice to be unconstitutional (*Carrollton* v. *Edgewood*, 1992). Nonetheless, there still exist a number of possibilities for expanding property tax bases or at least their nonresidential portions (Monk & Brent, 1997; Brent, 1999). Meanwhile, it makes more sense for states to consider the level of revenue that is collected locally in determining state allocations or to turn to state-level resources to accomplish equalization goals.

Replacing Property Taxes with Broader-Based Taxes

In the mid-1990s, several states entertained proposals to reduce dramatically the burden on property taxes and shift to broader-based sales or income taxes (NCSL, 1994). The Michigan legislature imposed a statewide property tax to raise $1.02 billion to offset the loss of $4.4 billion when it repealed nearly all local support for schools. When asked about a suitable alternative to raise additional state-level funds, voters approved a constitutional amendment that increased the sales tax rate from 4 to 6 percent rather than permitting an automatic increase in the state income tax, as was called for in the legislation. This amendment and the subsequent statutory changes also required a three-fourths vote by the legislature to increase the tax rate, capped annual assessment increases at the lesser of 5 percent or the rate of inflation, increased the cigarette tax from 25 to 75 cents per pack, and imposed a 0.75 percent tax on the sale of homes and businesses. The initial legislative action eliminated property taxes for schools. But the burden placed on state revenue resulted in continued property taxation to finance "systemic educational reforms" (Addonizio, Kearney, & Prince, 1995). Whether for tax limitation or equalization purposes, Michigan policy makers and voters sought to eliminate property taxation. They found other tax bases for revenue; however, they also found it necessary to rely on property taxes and allow for unequal property tax revenues among districts.

The Wisconsin legislature raised the state share of school funds from 40 percent to 60 percent by severely cutting property taxes and turning to broader-based state revenue. Voters in Rhode Island passed a constitutional amendment that required the legislature to craft a school finance plan that would reduce property taxes while increasing state aid. In contrast, other states rejected legislative proposals to decrease reliance on property taxation in 1994. Colorado, Nebraska, and New Hampshire are notable examples. The court system, however, increasingly calls upon states to reduce reliance on local property taxation. Fenwick (1998) notes this and cites Kentucky, Ohio, and Tennessee as examples.

Financing for school facilities has relied largely on local property taxation. As courts persist in assessments of equity and adequacy, justices have placed greater emphasis on financing school facilities (see Chapter 10). For example, litigation in New Jersey led to increased state funding for school facilities (Erlichson, 2001). Texas litigation led to the expenditure of millions and the appropriation of billions for school facilities (Clark, 2001). In Ohio, billions are required, and legislators have been working since 1991 to meet financial demands for school facilities (Edlefson & Barrow, 2001). Pressures for higher levels of state funding for school operations and facilities build the case for broader-based taxes. These pressures also open the door for experimentation with school revenues derived from bases other than real estate property.

The choice of a suitable broader-based revenue source appears to be limited to income- or consumption-based taxes to replace the large yield of the property tax. Busch and Stewart (1992) noted that when Ohio voters were first given an opportunity in 1989 to enact local-option income taxes for supplementing school support, they enacted the measures in seventeen school districts. In their study of voters' attitudes, they found a slim margin of support for a local income tax over the property tax. They concluded that the income tax is a viable source of school funds. Today, 123 Ohio school districts have elected to have the local-option income tax (Ohio Department of Taxation, 2001, p. 119), but overall support for the tax and the yield of the tax fall far short of property taxation. For example, only 20 percent of districts employ the income tax. Districts receive a total of $141.6 million from this tax, compared to over $8.1 billion from real estate property taxation.

Unlike the Michigan experience, where greater reliance was established on consumption-based taxes, Ohio voters rejected a sales tax increase in 1998. Even though the trend in the nation since the 1800s has been to ease the burden on local tax revenue, state-level policy makers and local-level decision makers are running out of options. Given continuing public dissatisfaction with government and its taxes, legislated and constitutional property tax limitations, and increased demand for government resources, Odden and Archibald (2001) may be correct in contending that a large influx of resources for schools will not be forthcoming and that greater attention needs to be paid to resource allocation. Whatever developments and outcomes present themselves, the necessity of collecting property taxes at state, regional, or local levels is bound to persist, even if broad-based revenue sources are secured across the nation.

The trend in the nation since the 1800s has been to ease the burden on local tax revenue. There is little question that the recent movement among legislatures and voters to turn from property taxation toward broader-based sales and income taxes will continue. This is true if we assume that other policies protect local school and community autonomy with regard to decisions about programs.

SUMMARY

Wealth-based taxation of real property brings a stable and productive revenue source to local governments. Its productive yield and stability have effectively countered arguments against property taxation. Its stability offers predictability, enabling local officials to plan municipal and school district programs within balanced budgets. The property tax is inelastic relative to income- and consumption-based taxes, because assessed values used in determining tax yield respond slowly to changes in the economy. As valuation practices improve, such that the tax base more closely reflects market values, the yield will grow with fewer annual adjustments in tax rates, if we assume that property values also keep pace with the economy.

Property tax structure and administration vary considerably from state to state. Assessment and equalization ratios, exemptions, revenue and expenditure limitations, and tax relief mechanisms affect tax bases and yields. Many of these policies, along with arbitrary assessment practices, interfere with equity and neutrality. Some provisions shift tax burdens from one group to another. These shifts lead to misallocations of economic resources and to inequities among taxpayers of different incomes. Careful policy development, including use of circuit breakers to ease tax burdens on low-income families, makes this tax less regressive. Other provisions affect the purchase and rehabilitation of houses, the location of businesses and industry, and the development of vacant and farm land. Urban redevelopment is discouraged, and businesses and upper-income families are encouraged to migrate to localities with lower tax rates but better services.

Property taxation in most states enables localities to expand educational programs beyond the minimal offerings financed by state aid programs. However, disparities in tax bases (capacity) and tax rates (effort) among communities often result in or exacerbate program inequities. State or regional responsibilities and standards for valuing properties might ease inequities in taxation and reduce extreme disparities in programs. If properties such as utilities and industrial plants that serve broad regions were removed from the local tax base and taxed only by the state, then the tax capacities of localities would be more evenly distributed, and many of the negative social and economic effects of property taxation would be reduced.

However, these reforms must be balanced against the strong historical precedent for preserving local autonomy. Assessment practices can be improved and local governments can exercise some degree of independence if we continue to place the responsibility for setting tax rates at the local or regional level. A primary goal for states and localities in the next decade should be to strengthen the integrity of property taxation through continued improvements in its structure and administration. As more states entertain proposals for curtailing or eliminating this revenue source, a crucial policy question will be how much local autonomy will be maintained.

With the resurgence of tax and spending limitations, and with the continuing movement to ease or eliminate the burden on property taxation for school finance, education must rely more on state revenue and there must be a more equitable distribution of money among districts. Tax and spending initiatives were intended to curtail the growth of government or induce greater efficiency. They may have succeeded to some degree. However, there has been a concurrent push for localities to secure new revenues to maintain or expand levels of service.

In the next chapter, we explore several strategies for tapping local resources in support of school districts. Borrowing and investments bring new money to construct facilities and ensure continuous school operations. Partnerships and volunteers offer opportunities for schools to gain new talent at minimal cost.

ACTIVITIES

1. At the same time that the state legislature is considering abolishing property taxation for supporting school operations, a school district board of education is proposing to raise the local tax rate to finance expansion of programs or facilities in your school district. During a public meeting at which you are describing the project, you are asked why the property tax is an appropriate revenue source for this purpose. How might you respond?

2. Contact your tax assessor and inquire about the current tax rates for school districts, municipalities, and other special districts served by this tax jurisdiction. When were properties last assessed and when will they next be appraised? Which of the three valuation methods—market, cost, and income—are most likely to be used to appraise residential, business, and agricultural property? What proportion of appraised value is exempt from taxation? What might you recommend to improve the fairness of property assessment practices?

3. Develop a rationale for tax incentives in the form of lower assessments to attract new industry or commercial development. Keep in mind that taxes will increase for currently operating businesses if expansions in municipal and educational services are necessitated by this new development.

4. Prepare a chart that contrasts the strengths and weaknesses of property taxation with those of income- and consumption-based taxes, referring to yield, equity, neutrality, elasticity, and administrative burden. List the five criteria along the left margin. Label three columns across the top for the primary tax bases: wealth, income, and consumption. In each cell, place the names of the primary revenue sources discussed in Chapters 4 and 5 that correlate most closely with the designated base and criterion.

5. Describe provisions in one state's constitution or statutes that limit local governments' power to tax or that contain growth in revenue or spending. Design a study to determine the views of legislators and superintendents on the value of such limitations.

6. Clarify your beliefs about local control over school finance and programs and about the relationship between such autonomy and the policies that govern taxes to support schools. To what degree are these beliefs consistent with proposals for (a) shifting more control over property taxation to the state level, or (b) replacing property taxes with broader-based revenue sources?

EXERCISES

1. Express a tax rate of 23.2 mills in terms of dollars per thousand, in terms of dollars per hundred, and as a percentage of assessed valuation. Given this rate, what is the tax on a house that is assessed at $64,000?

2. Find the equalized value and the amount of property tax owed by a business that has a market value of $1.6 million, is located in a jurisdiction with an equalization ratio of 0.25, and faces a school levy of $3.50 per hundred of equalized valuation (use the decimal form or mathematical equivalent of this rate as it is commonly used in your state).

3. Two school districts, each enrolling 5000 pupils, have aggregate market valuations of $510 million and $360 million, respectively. Assume that they are located in a state that assesses all properties at one-third of market value.
   (a) Determine the total assessed valuation of each school district and the amount that each district raises per pupil from a 28-mill levy.
   (b) How much more or less is raised in each district if the tax rate remains the

same but the state assessment ratio is increased to 40 percent?

(c) What tax rate in mills is needed in each district to raise $1428 per pupil, given the assessment ratio of 40 percent?

(d) Explain the source(s) of inequities in the amount of funds that these districts are able to generate per pupil from the property tax.

COMPUTER SIMULATIONS: PROPERTY TAXATION

Computer simulations related to the content of this chapter are available on the Allyn & Bacon website <**http://www.ablongman.com/ed-leadership.com**>. They focus on calculating property tax rates and levies as well as measuring the impact of property tax exemptions. Objectives for the exercise are

- To develop an understanding of the concepts of equalization ratios, exemptions, and effective tax rates and their impact on the ability of school districts to raise revenue from the property tax
- To develop an understanding of the impacts of increasing the tax rate on individual tax jurisdictions and parcels of property.

REFERENCES

Aaron, H. J. (1973). What do circuit-breaker laws accomplish? In G. E. Peterson (Ed.). *Property tax reform* (pp. 53–64). Washington, DC: The Urban Institute.

Aaron, H. J. (1975). *Who pays the property tax: A new view*. Washington, DC: The Brookings Institution.

ACIR. (1973). *Financing schools and property tax relief—A state responsibility*, Report A-40. Washington, DC: Advisory Commission on Intergovernmental Relations.

ACIR. (1987). *Significant features of fiscal federalism, 1987 edition*. Washington, DC: Advisory Commission on Intergovernmental Relations.

ACIR. (1988). *Changing public attitudes on government and taxes*. Washington, DC: Advisory Commission on Intergovernmental Relations.

ACIR. (1993). *RTS 1991: State revenue capacity and effort*. Washington, DC: Advisory Commission on Intergovernmental Relations.

ACIR. (1994). *Significant features of fiscal federalism, 1994 edition*, Vol. 1. Washington, DC: Advisory Commission on Intergovernmental Relations.

ACIR. (1995). *Significant features of fiscal federalism, 1995 edition*, Vol. 1. Washington, DC: Advisory Commission on Intergovernmental Relations.

Adams, J. R. (1984). *Secrets of the tax revolt*. New York: Harcourt.

Addonizio, M. F. (2001). New revenues for public schools: Blurring the line between public and private finance. In S. Chaikind, & W. J. Fowler, Jr. (Eds.), *Education finance in the new millennium* (pp. 159–171). Larchmont, NY: Eye on Education.

Addonizio, M. F., Kearney, C. P., & Prince, H. J. (1995, Winter). Michigan's high wire act. *Journal of Education Finance, 20*, 235–269.

American Council on Intergovernmental Relations. (1998). *Significant features of fiscal federalism*, Vol. 2: *Revenues and expenditures, 1995*. Bethesda, MD: American Council on Intergovernmental Relations.

Brent, B. O. (1999, Winter). An analysis of the influence of regional nonresidential expanded tax base approaches to school finance on measures of student and taxpayer equity. *Journal of Education Finance, 24*, 353–378.

Busch, R. J., & Stewart, D. O. (1992, Spring). Voters' opinion of school district property taxes and income taxes: Results from an exit-poll in Ohio. *Journal of Education Finance, 17*, 337–351.

Carrollton-Farmers Branch ISD v. *Edgewood ISD*, 426 S.W.2d 488 (1992).

Clark, C. (1995). Regional school taxing units: The Texas experience. In D. H. Monk, *Study on the generation of revenues for education: Final report* (pp. 75–88). Albany: New York State Education Department.

Clark, C. (2001). Texas state support for school facilities, 1971 to 2001. *Journal of Education Finance, 27*, 683–700.

Due, J. F. (1982) Shifting sources of financing education and the taxpayer revolt. In W.W. McMahon & T.G. Geske (Eds.), *Financing education: Overcoming inefficiency and inequity* (pp. 267–289). Urbana, IL: University of Illinois Press.

Edlefson, C., & Barrow, R. (2001). The impact of litigation on school facilities funding in Ohio. *Journal of Education Finance, 27*, 701–712.

Erlichson, B. A. (2001). New schools for a new millennium: Court-mandated school facilities construction in New Jersey. *Journal of Education Finance, 27*, 663–682.

Fenwick, J. (1998). Funding public education: The constitutionality of relying on local property taxes. *Journal of Law and Education, 27*, 517–523.

Fulton, M., & Sonovick, L. (1992). Tax and spending limitations—An analysis. *ECS Issuegram*. Denver, CO: Education Commission of the States.

George, H. (1879). *Progress and poverty*. Garden City, NY: Doubleday, Page & Company.

Gold, S. D. (1979). *Property tax relief*. Lexington, MA: Lexington Books.

Gold, S. D. (1994). *Tax options for states needing more school revenue*. Westhaven, CT: National Education Association.

Howard, M. A. (1989, Summer). State tax and expenditure limitations: There is no story. *Public Budgeting and Finance, 9*, 83–90.

Kozol, J. (1991). *Savage inequalities*. New York: HarperCollins.

Lindsay, D. (1994a, November 2). Educators buck giving the public say on taxes. *Education Week*, pp. 1, 20–21.

Lindsay, D. (1994b, June 15). N.Y. lawmakers tap surplus in approving 5% boost in school aid. *Education Week*, p. 13.

Lindsay, D. (1995, May 24). Tide turns for the better in N.J., Ohio budget votes. *Education Week*, pp. 12, 15.

Monk, D. H., & Brent, B. O. (1997). *Raising money for education: A guide to the property tax*. Thousand Oaks, CA: Corwin.

Monk, D. H., & Theobald, N. D. (2001). A conceptual framework for examining school finance reform options for the State of Ohio. *Journal of Education Finance, 27*, 501–516.

Musgrave, R. A., & Musgrave, P. B. (1989). *Public Finance in theory and practice* (5th ed.). New York: McGraw-Hill.

National Center for Education Statistics. (2001). *Public school finance programs of the United States and Canada, 1998–99*. NCES 2001-309. [J. Dayton, C. T. Holmes, C. C. Sielke, A. L. Jefferson (compilers); W. J. Fowler, Jr. (project officer).] Washington, DC: Author.

NCSL. (1994). *State budget and tax actions 1994: Preliminary report*. Denver, CO: National Conference of State Legislatures.

Netzer, D. (1966). *Economics of the property tax*. Washington, DC: The Brookings Institution.

Netzer, D. (1973). Is there too much reliance on the local property tax? In G. E. Peterson (Ed.). *Property tax reform*. Washington, DC: The Urban Institute.

Netzer, D., & Berne, R. (1995). Discrepancies between ideal characteristics of a property tax system and current practice in New York. In D. H. Monk, *Study on the generation of revenues for education: Final report* (pp. 31–47). Albany: New York State Education Department.

Odden, A. R., & Archibald, S. (2001). *Reallocating resources: How to boost student achievement without asking for more*. Thousand Oaks, CA: Corwin.

Odden, A. R., & Picus, L. O. (2000). *School finance: A policy perspective* (2nd ed.). New York: McGraw-Hill.

Ohio Department of Taxation, Tax Analysis Division. (2001). *Ohio's taxes: A brief summary of major state and local taxes in Ohio, 2001*. Columbus, OH: Author.

Oldman, O., & Schoettle, F.P. (1974). *State and local taxes and finance: Text, problems and cases*. Mineola, NY: The Foundation Press.

Palaich, R., Kloss, J., & Williams, M. F. (1980). *Tax and expenditure limitation referenda.* Report F80-2. Denver, CO: Education Commission of the States.

Pijanowski, J. C., & Monk, D. H. (1996). Alternative school revenue sources: There are many fish in the sea. *School Business Affairs, 62*, 4–10.

Peterson, G. E. (Ed.). (1973). *Property tax reform*. Washington, DC: The Urban Institute.

Shannon, J. (1973). The property tax: Reform or relief? In G. E. Peterson (Ed.) *Property tax reform* (pp. 25–52). Washington, DC: The Urban Institute.

Theobald, N. D., & Malen, B. (Eds.). (2000). *Balancing local control and state responsibility for K–12 education*. Larchmont, NY: Eye on Education.

Thompson, D. C., & Wood, R. C. (2001). *Money and schools* (2nd ed.). Larchmont, NY: Eye on Education.

U.S. Department of Commerce, Bureau of the Census. (1994). *1992 Census of Governments*, Vol. 2: *Taxable Property Values*. Washington, DC: U.S. Government Printing Office.

U.S. Department of Commerce, Bureau of the Census. (2000). *Statistical Abstract of the United States: 2000*. Washington, DC: U.S. Government Printing Office.

Verstegen, D. (1988). *School finance at a glance.* Denver, CO: Education Commission of the States.

Walz v. *Tax Commission of the City of New York.* 397 U.S. 664 (1970).

Whitney, T. N. (1993). *Voters and school finance: The impact of public opinion.* Denver, CO: National Conference of State Legislatures.

Wright, J. W. (1981). *Tax and expenditure limitation: A policy perspective.* Lexington, KY: The Council of State Governments.

Wyckoff, P. G. (2001). Capitalization and the incidence of school aid. *Journal of Education Finance, 27,* 585–608.

Yinger, J., Borsch-Supan, A., Bloom, H. S., and Ladd, H. F. (1988). *Property taxes and house values: The theory and estimation of intra-jurisdictional property tax capitalization.* San Diego, CA: Academic.

Chapter **6**

EXPANDING SCHOOL RESOURCES THROUGH USER FEES, CASH FLOW MANAGEMENT, CAPITAL OUTLAY, PARTNERSHIPS, AND VOLUNTEERS

Issues and Questions

- *Achieving High Standards with Equity and Efficiency*: What opportunities are there for schools and school districts to enrich their resources for school improvement?
- *User Charges*: Should families and community groups who directly benefit from school-related programs, transportation, and facilities pay fees for such services?
- *Investing and Borrowing Funds*: What are the options for investing excess or idle funds to gain interest earnings until payroll and other payments are due? What short-term strategies are available to districts to meet financial obligations until they receive other federal, state, and local revenues?
- *Capital Outlay*: How does long-term borrowing through the sale of bonds enable districts to construct facilities and purchase costly equipment?
- *Partnerships, Educational Foundations, and Voluntarism*: In what ways might involving the community and the private sector in public schools expand resources and political support for school improvement efforts?

School officials increasingly seek nontraditional sources of support. The effort to identify new monies is in some states a response to restrictions placed on the growth of property taxes and in other states a response to the resistance of taxpayers to increasing local taxes to support operating budgets or expand programs. Constraints on state and federal revenue available for education, given competing demands placed on these governments, also encourage school boards and administrators to look elsewhere.

In the previous chapter, we presented the property tax as providing the greatest amount of funds within the control of localities. However, school systems are not limited to this revenue. They can expand their resource bases by collecting fees from students and other patrons and by carefully managing their cash flow, which includes making timely decisions to invest and borrow funds. They also secure capital outlay financing for large projects. The creative use of partnerships, foundations, and volunteers also taps valuable resources and invites parents and communities to support and participate actively in school programs.

USER CHARGES FOR EDUCATIONAL PROGRAMS

Privilege-based taxation, which we introduced in Chapter 3, includes fees assessed for users of specific governmental services. This form of taxation is justified on the benefits-received principle; the amount charged to beneficiaries is tied to the presumed value of the "privilege." In actuality, the fee rarely covers the entire cost of the service, and other forms of taxation subsidize the program.

In states where these fees are permitted, schools may assess students fees for extracurricular activities, summer schools, before- and after-school programs, lunches, field trips, elective courses, textbooks, and supplemental supplies. In addition, nonstudent users of school facilities—for example, community groups that sponsor social functions in gymnasiums—often pay charges to cover the costs of utilities and maintenance. The fees charged external groups have caused little difficulty for schools, and we do not discuss them further. The focus of this section is the prevalence and legality of charges for student access to school programs.

In 1996–1997, charges for school lunch programs and other activities amounted to $4.5 billion and $2.9 billion, respectively, across the nation (U.S. Department of Commerce, 2000, p. 14). Expressed as a proportion of all revenue received by school districts from local sources, these sources averaged only 3.26 percent and 2.09 percent of monies, with a range in the "other activities" category from zero percent in Delaware to 12.0 percent in Alabama.

User charges are typically a minor source of school support. But a study of fees in seven districts surrounding Vancouver, Canada, revealed a wide range in fees charged students. The highest fees included $1000 for a technical studies course, $1500 for extracurricular activities, $110 for graduation, and $12,000 for an international program (Brown & Bouman, 1994). Wassmer and Fisher (2000) asserted that in the United States, costs of auxiliary services could be financed with fees, potentially paying for 13 percent of public school expenditures. Indeed, charges for particular activities and services can offer potential revenue growth for schools (Monk & Brent, 1997), but these charges also pose challenges for policy makers and administrators.

This tax is likely to spur debate between school personnel and the public over the degree to which the burden for paying program costs should be shifted from taxpayers to parents and other users. Parents and the courts raise many issues: "Should schools be able to charge some students for some services, if their parents can afford to pay? Should schools be able to deny other children certain activities based on the fact that their parents cannot or will not pay? If so, what are the limits?" (Jones & Amalfitano, 1994, pp. 142–143).

These questions involve several of the criteria of taxation noted in Chapter 3, particularly the equity principle and its dimension of ability to pay, neutrality, and administrative burden. A fundamental issue is whether fees may legally be charged in public schools whose programs are supposed to be free and accessible to children of all economic levels. Another issue is the degree to which charges have any unintended consequences, such as the diminished participation of students and negative public relations as parents oppose these additional taxes. Finally, user charges create a number of difficulties in enforcing compliance and overseeing waiver policies.

Legal Status and Inequities

Because education is a provision of state constitutions and statutes, federal courts defer to state authorities for resolving this and other school finance issues. Challenges to fees as violations of state constitutions' guarantees of free public education have yielded mixed results. Some decisions have interpreted constitutional provisions as permitting fees for textbooks and instructional supplies; others have denied them. As a result, thirty-four states permit at least one type of student fee, and fifteen states and the District of Columbia prohibit fees (Hamm & Crosser, 1991). In many cases, the acceptability of user fees is related to whether the activity or item of expenditure is a "necessary or integral part" of the educational program. For example, an Illinois court determined that a lunchroom supervision fee could be charged students because it supported a noneducational service (*Ambroiggio* v. *Board of Education*, 1981).

Instructional programs appear at first glance to fall within this standard, because it prohibits fees for essential components of students' education. State constitutions or statutes governing education prohibit public schools from charging tuition for instructional programs during the academic year, other than for stu-

dents who enroll out of district. In this case, tuition charges offset differentials in local tax collections. Although charges have historically been permitted for summer school programs (*Washington* v. *Salisbury*, 1983), there are circumstances for which required fees may be challenged. The U.S. Court of Appeals for the Fifth Circuit ensured that year-round services would be available for students with disabilities. Otherwise, the interrupted schooling would deny an appropriate education under what is now the Individuals with Disabilities Education Act (*Alamo Heights Independent School District* v. *State Board of Education*, 1986). A similar circumstance, discussed by Dayton and McCarthy (1992), resulted in a challenge to the Kentucky State Department's demand that private school students pay for required summer remediation. The objection rested on the 1990 Education Reform Act mandate of free summer programs for students who do not pass minimum-competency tests required for promotion.

Fees for elective courses are common. Although these fees have been upheld in several decisions (e.g., *Norton* v. *Board of Education*, 1976), a California review prohibited assessment of fees for any school-related course or extracurricular activity (*Hartzell* v. *Connell*, 1984). This decision concluded that under the state's constitution, "access to public education is a right enjoyed by all—not a commodity for sale" (p. 44), despite the financial pressures placed on districts following passage of Proposition 13.

Only eight states permit textbook fees: Alaska, Illinois, Indiana, Iowa, Kansas, Kentucky, Utah, and Wisconsin (Hamm & Crosser, 1991). There are mixed interpretations by the courts concerning the permissibility of charges for required textbooks. For example, *Cardiff* v. *Bismark Public School District* (1978) disallowed fees for textbooks in North Dakota. In contrast, *Marshall* v. *School District* (1976) upheld a Colorado district's book fee but required financial assistance for indigent students. Supplemental instructional materials such as workbooks, dictionaries, and paperback books have been treated differently from required textbooks; charging for them is often permitted (e.g., *Sneed* v. *Greensboro Board of Education*, 1980). Other courts have held that all school textbooks and supplies are covered within guarantees of free education (e.g., *Bond* v. *Ann Arbor School District*, 1970).

States generally do not consider extracurricular activities a necessary or integral part of educational programs. Twenty-three states assess fees for participation in clubs, and twenty-one states permit fees for athletic teams (Hamm & Crosser, 1991). In an early decision, the Supreme Court of Idaho disallowed a general fee assessed against all students—half of this fee supported extracurricular activities—but upheld a fee charged participants only (*Paulson* v. *Minidoka County School District*, 1970). A Michigan Appeals Court permitted fees for interscholastic athletics, because these activities are not a fundamental part of the state's educational program and because a confidential waiver enabled indigent students to participate (*Attorney General* v. *East Jackson Public Schools*, 1985). One year prior to this ruling, the *Hartzell* (1984) decision denied schools the ability to assess fees for any activities.

Transportation fees may become more common as bus routes are extended to enable children to attend the schools of their choice outside neighborhoods and across district lines. In one of the few federal reviews of user fees, the U.S. Supreme Court narrowly (in a 5-to-4 decision) upheld a North Dakota statute that permitted districts to charge a transportation fee (*Kadrmas* v. *Dickinson Public Schools*, 1988). Districts could waive fees for low-income families under the statute, but they were not obligated to do so. The challenge claimed that students who were unable to pay the fee were deprived of minimum access to education, in violation of the Fourteenth Amendment's equal protection clause. Like the court's analysis in the *San Antonio* v. *Rodriguez* (1973) decision, which denied a similar argument relative

to differing levels of overall finances among districts, the majority would not overturn the fee, because those who were deprived of transportation did not constitute a "suspect class," nor was there a fundamental right to education under the Constitution. Because the equal protection clause did not require free transportation, and because the state successfully defended the rational relationship between the statute and its goal of encouraging districts to provide bus service, the court permitted the fee.

State court decisions have also upheld districts' transportation fees. A Michigan court examined fees for busing to school in relation to a constitutional provision: "The legislature *may* provide for the transportation of students . . ." (emphasis added). Interpreting this phrase to permit rather than mandate busing, the court upheld fees for this nonessential part of schooling (*Sutton* v. *Cadillac Area Public Schools*, 1982). The California Supreme Court found transportation to be a "supplemental service," unlike those activities that are a fundamental part of the education program for which fees are not permitted. The court also denied an equal protection challenge, because the statute that permits transportation fees included an exemption for indigent students (*Arcadia* v. *Department of Education*, 1992).

User charges may be necessary to provide basic educational services or to extend extracurricular programs in districts having less money available from traditional state and local revenues. However, families in these districts may be the least able to afford additional charges. These taxes are regressive in that they are not always determined by a family's ability to pay, nor do schools adjust fees according to the number of children from a family paying fees. Furthermore, fees reflect in part community and state abilities to fund schools adequately. The states with low per-pupil expenditures are the ones that assess academic fees (Hamm & Crosser, 1991).

Because governments do not consider revenue from user charges in funding formulas, fees may interfere with efforts to equalize financial support for schools in rich and poor districts. However, Wassmer and Fisher (2000) contended that equity goals might be enhanced through the use of fees, provided that fees were assessed only on auxiliary services, not on standard curriculum services.

Fee Waivers

In response to concerns about inequities when parents with differing abilities to pay are assessed the same charges, schools have created waiver and scholarship programs to encourage students from low-income families to participate in activities and elective courses. The administrators who grant waivers of fees and partial reductions through scholarships depend on family income and family size, generally using the same criteria as those that define eligibility for free and reduced-price lunches.

There are conflicting judicial opinions in state courts about the legal status of fee waivers (Dayton & McCarthy, 1992). An adequate waiver policy, including assurances of confidentiality and a timely notice of benefits and procedures to parents, was a constitutional prerequisite for upholding fees in North Carolina (*Sneed* v. *Greensboro Board of Education*, 1980). In contrasting decisions, courts in several states, including California, denied waivers along with fees for constitutionally required education. The *Hartzell* (1984) decision that denied any charge for public education programs also found a "constitutional defect in such fees [that] can neither be corrected by providing waivers to indigent students, nor justified by pleading financial hardship" (p. 44). Local district policies may not be more restrictive than those of the state, according to a Utah court. This decision disallowed a district's partial waiver of fees for books, materials, and activities. The state board's rules allowed assistance to anyone unable to pay fees (*Lorenc* v. *Call*, 1990).

Neutrality

The criterion of neutrality was presented in Chapter 3 as a consideration of social, economic, and other effects of taxation. Fees are often criticized for discouraging student participation in curricular and extracurricular activities. They diminish the education of those students who encounter fiscal barriers to opportunities for developing athletic, social, artistic, or other skills. Even with a system of waivers or scholarship assistance, disadvantaged students may feel diminished self-worth and may be induced by social stigma to decline to participate in school programs. Indeed, fees may actually counter other societal efforts to create positive programs through which young people can experience academic and athletic success and avoid gang-related or other dysfunctional activities.

Charges can also create unnecessary negative responses from parents. They often view fees as imposing an unnecessary double tax. In addition, charges for space utilization, specifically for advertising (Cooper, 1996; Pijanowski & Monk, 1996), can affect neutrality and public relations. Financial gains from user fees and charges must be weighed against the possibility of diminished student participation and potential damages to district public relations efforts.

Administrative Burden

The amount that users pay must provide a sufficiently large yield to offset some portion of the costs of services provided. The smaller the charge in relation to program costs, the larger the burden on the general fund or other revenue to provide the activity and pay administrative expenses incurred in collecting the fee. However, larger fees may increase the likelihood that students will avoid the activity, may raise costs of collection, and may diminish public and student support of school activities.

There are administrative difficulties in overseeing both the compliance of those expected to pay fees and waiver policies (Brown & Bouman, 1994). Hidden costs of enforcement can appear in different forms as teachers delay activities, coaches deny practice sessions or game participation, students are not permitted to register, principals contact parents, and office personnel send reminders and withhold report cards and transcripts. Collections may become a discipline problem if students see fees as a focus for rebellion against authority. The waiver policy itself adds another set of administrative costs and problems: advertising its benefits and procedures to parents, monitoring who qualifies, maintaining confidentiality of those who are granted waivers, and defending denial of waivers to those who do not qualify.

Because of these additional administrative costs of relying on user fees to support activities, schools may seek assistance for the expansion of programs from businesses and other donors. Later in this chapter, we explore opportunities for schools to obtain resources through partnership activities. We now turn to ways in which schools and districts supplement traditional revenue via interest earnings and loans.

MANAGING CASH FLOW THROUGH INVESTMENTS AND BORROWING

The financing of school systems introduces large amounts of monies on a monthly and annual basis. Wise investment decisions lead to high yields of interest earnings when funds accumulate before expenditures are due. At other times, it is necessary to borrow funds. This may happen when anticipated revenue from local taxes or state and federal aid is delayed or is not sufficient to meet current expenditures. The first of these cash flow scenarios brings opportunities for investing school resources. The second makes borrowing necessary.

Nonrevenue receipts, including short-term loans and long-term bond issues (see the discussion of capital outlay), do not constitute additional new monies for schools. This is because the amount borrowed plus interest must be repaid in time from anticipated revenue. Nonrevenue receipts differ from revenue receipts, which generate monies through taxes, federal and state aid payments, gifts, investment earnings, and tuition and fees. Nonrevenue monies are important to school systems because they enable finance officers to maintain an even flow of district funds to meet payrolls, pay vendors, and make other expenditures on schedule. They also constitute a growing debt owed by school districts. They amounted to $63.7 billion in 1990–1991, including $60.5 billion in outstanding long-term debt (i.e., for more than one year) and $3.2 billion in short-term debt (U.S. Department of Commerce, 1993, p. 21). Five years later, this debt had nearly doubled. In 1996–1997, the total was $125.7 billion, including about $123.2 billion in outstanding long-term debt and $2.5 billion in short-term debt (U.S. Department of Commerce, 2000, Table 10).

Investments of District and School Funds

School districts, particularly fiscally independent districts, expand their resources by investing revenue and nonrevenue money. Schools have traditionally been able to invest funds in interest-bearing accounts to acquire additional monies for student organizations. They are now investing larger amounts of monies within the control of administrators and teachers under school-site management.

Large revenue payments, especially proceeds from the property tax, are concentrated at one or more times of the year. In contrast, operating expenditures are more evenly distributed throughout the year. For example, when district fiscal years run July 1 to June 30, tax collection amounts can be received in July and February. Borrowing can be minimized because money is collected early in two semiannual portions of the budget year, freeing large amounts of idle cash that can be invested for a substantial period of time (Ray, Hack, & Candoli, 2001). Tax collections, state and federal aid payments, proceeds from bond issues or bond anticipation notes, and monies carried forward from one year to the next all create large cash balances and opportunities to generate additional revenue through investments. These investments can include U.S. Treasury bonds and notes; federal government agency bonds; certificates of deposit, money market savings and passbook savings accounts; repurchase agreements; and, to a much lesser degree, commercial paper issued by corporations (Ray, Hack, & Candoli, 2001).

Investments in the form of cash deposits and securities are presented by state in Table 6.1. The state with the greatest amount of holdings was California in 1996–1997 (over $10 billion),

TABLE 6.1.
Cash and Security Holdings of Public School Systems[a] (millions of dollars)

State	1977–78	1985–86	1990–91	1996–97	Percentage Increase (Decrease) from 1990–91 to 1996–97
Alabama	98.7	220.9	299.6	935.1	212.1
Alaska	[b]	[b]	[c]	[c]	NA
Arizona	353.7	741.9	925.6	1,242.6	34.3
Arkansas	120.5	238.1	266.5	436.4	63.8
California	1,725.0	3,223.6	5,302.0	10,447.8	97.1
Colorado	342.8	615.9	1,524.8	1,662.7	9.0
Connecticut	8.0	3.8	20.6	124.7	505.3
Delaware	3.5	13.0	16.0	44.9	180.6
District of Columbia	[b]	[b]	[c]	[c]	NA
Florida	726.9	1,761.5	3,216.3	4,177.1	29.9
Georgia	326.3	656.2	1,776.2	1,997.7	12.5
Hawaii	[b]	[b]	[c]	[c]	NA
Idaho	44.4	107.3	153.8	292.2	90.0
Illinois	1,338.4	2,449.5	7,025.8	7,154.3	1.8
Indiana	458.6	559.9	635.4	1,745.2	174.7
Iowa	205.7	281.4	536.6	803.2	49.7
Kansas	293.0	561.1	802.1	425.1	(47.0)
Kentucky	82.1	181.8	161.4	391.4	142.5
Louisiana	315.9	851.2	885.5	1,325.0	49.6
Maine	7.2	55.2	53.9	66.7	23.8
Maryland	[b]	[b]	3.7	[c]	NA
Massachusetts	58.2	67.7	96.7	98.2	1.6
Michigan	947.4	1,375.6	2,785.1	4,457	60.0
Minnesota	490.9	830.4	2,018.2	3,051	51.2
Mississippi	92.9	225.8	276.1	617.5	123.7
Missouri	353.3	563.6	1,734.9	1,571.6	(9.4)
Montana	171.0	149.3	307.9	191.2	(37.9)
Nebraska	164.2	318.0	778.0	607.3	(21.9)
Nevada	15.9	137.0	612.9	1,029.6	68.0
New Hampshire	11.7	36.5	59.5	84.7	42.4

(continued)

TABLE 6.1.

(Continued)

State	1977–78	1985–86	1990–91	1996–97	Percentage Increase (Decrease) from 1990–91 to 1996–97
New Jersey	346.2	610.7	968.1	1,498.5	54.8
New Mexico	60.8	189.1	278.6	388.9	40.0
New York	550.1	1,540.1	2,905.4	3,395.9	16.9
North Carolina	b	b	4.0	c	NA
North Dakota	47.7	180.2	156.3	150.4	(3.8)
Ohio	1,013.3	1,006.2	1,764.3	2,847.2	61.4
Oklahoma	245.0	698.5	640.0	973.5	52.1
Oregon	325.7	360.0	406.5	1,071.4	163.6
Pennsylvania	721.9	1,489.7	3,172.9	5,706.2	79.8
Rhode Island	0.1	0.8	—	3.9	NA
South Carolina	145.4	280.1	418.2	740.0	77.0
South Dakota	75.7	120.8	170.3	258.5	51.8
Tennessee	7.8	8.5	19.5	32.6	67.2
Texas	1,356.3	4,243.6	4,615.0	8,035.8	74.1
Utah	183.5	302.1	93.9	649.9	592.1
Vermont	18.4	67.8	68.7	57.2	(16.7)
Virginia	b	b	c	c	NA
Washington	392.4	875.4	1,313.2	2,068.6	57.5
West Virginia	186.1	322.9	296.7	283.0	(4.6)
Wisconsin	337.0	776.5	1,121.7	2,199.0	96.0
Wyoming	80.5	279.1	220.4	190.5	(13.6)
U.S. Total	14,850.2	29,614.9	50,908.8	78,531.5	54.3

[a]Holdings of retirement funds are excluded.

[b]Holdings of dependent school systems are not reported.

[c]Zero or rounds to zero.

NA = not available.

Sources: U.S. Department of Commerce, Bureau of the Census (1980), *Finances of Public School Systems in 1977–78*, Series GF/78-10, Washington, DC: U.S. Government Printing Office, p. 12; U.S. Department of Commerce, Bureau of the Census (1988), *Finances of Public School Systems in 1985–86*, Series GF/86-10, Washington, DC: U.S. Government Printing Office, p. 10; U.S. Department of Commerce, Bureau of the Census (1993), *Public Education Finances: 1990–91*, Series GF/91-10, Washington, DC: U.S. Government Printing Office, p. 12; U.S. Department of Commerce, Bureau of the Census (2000), *Public Education Finances: 1997*, Series GC97(4)-1, Washington, DC: U.S. Government Printing Office, p. 1.

followed by Texas (over $8 billion), Illinois (over $7 billion), and Pennsylvania (over $5 billion). This table reports little or no investments for Alaska, the District of Columbia, Hawaii, Maryland, North Carolina, and Virginia. Some districts, however, are financially dependent on other units of government that are likely to manage large investment portfolios on behalf of schools and other divisions. The total holdings indicated for these school years grew substantially over two decades, from $14.9 billion in 1977–1978 to $78.5 billion in 1996–1997. From 1990–1991 to 1996–1997, cash and security holdings increased 54.3 percent. These data illustrate that massive amounts of school monies are available for investment and emphasize the importance of positive cash flow management.

Investments are an important part of cash management. Dembowski and Davey (1986) defined *cash management* as "the process of managing the moneys of a school district to ensure maximum cash availability and maximum yield on investments" (p. 237). Goals of monitoring cash flow include (1) *safety*, protecting the school district's assets against loss; (2) *liquidity*, the ability to convert investments to cash without such penalties as the loss of interest, so that there is sufficient money available to meet daily needs; and (3) *yield*, earning the maximum return on investments. These goals may conflict when longer terms to maturity give higher interest and yield but the lost liquidity might necessitate short-term loans to cover expenses. Similarly, some degree of risk might yield higher interest, but the safety of the public's money might be jeopardized. The failure of the Orange County, California, investment pool in 1994, for example, threatened nearly $1 billion of twenty-seven school districts' operating revenue. Counties maintain district investments in this state, and some of these districts had previously taken low-interest loans to increase the amount invested in the higher-yield fund. The county borrowed extensively to triple its investments and buy less secure derivatives. This aggressive investment strategy was partially to blame for the fund's collapse and the county's filing for bankruptcy protection (Lindsay, 1994).

The way districts manage their cash flow also contributes to several important nonfinancial goals. Sound financial management builds trust and goodwill within the taxpaying and business communities, promotes favorable business relationships with vendors and banks, and ensures the orderly conduct of financial aspects of district operations (Dembowski, 1986). There are legal and ethical considerations, and careful cash flow strategies diminish the potential for charges of embezzlement and graft. The public visibility of spending and investment decisions compels personnel to follow

procedures specified in law, including any limitations placed on investments (Ray, Hack, & Candoli, 2001). For example, many states require collateral for school investments (e.g., FDIC insurance on the first $100,000 of deposits), but banks pay lower interest rates when they must maintain assets as collateral rather than diverting them to more lucrative purposes (Dembowski & Davey, 1986). Finance officers exercise caution when proposed interest rates are higher than anticipated, which may signal that a bidder is on the brink of insolvency and desperately needs to attract investors.

Several short- and long-term investment strategies are available to school districts. Savings accounts offer the advantage of immediate liquidity. Withdrawals are possible without prior notification, and interest is earned on a daily basis. However, interest earnings are lower from savings than from other investments. Interest on money market accounts fluctuates with economic conditions, offering opportunities to improve yield during periods when interest rates are rising. There may, however, be limits on the number of withdrawals each month, so money market accounts are less flexible than ordinary savings accounts. Certificates of deposit also offer security but tend to pay higher interest. Interest rates increase as the term lengthens for deposits. Districts gain investment flexibility when they coordinate investment terms (between one week and one year) with projected dates for planned expenditures. Early withdrawals bring a penalty of lost interest, making these instruments less liquid.

United States government securities are among the safest long-term investments, offering both high security and liquidity. The government guarantees these investments, which are sold at a discount from stated face values. The full value is paid at maturity; the difference represents the interest earned by the investor. The liquidity of these securities results from a strong and receptive secondary market. Other investors will purchase them on the open market before they are mature. Thus a school district may liquidate when necessary.

Investments in federal agency securities offer similar safety. These, however, are not legal obligations of the government. For example, securities made available by the Federal Land Bank, the Federal Home Loan Bank, the Banks for Cooperatives, the Federal Intermediate Credit Bank, and the Federal National Mortgage Association offer higher yields than Treasury securities because of their low marketability.

Districts may enter into repurchase agreements, referred to as "repos," to earn relatively large returns in a short period. They purchase Treasury or other government securities under an agreement to sell them back to the issuing bank in the future. This strategy gives districts the opportunity to invest idle funds in a safe, high-yield investment for as short a period as one day.

A cash flow schedule (Dembowski & Davey, 1986, p. 240) tracks incoming revenue and outgoing expenditures to help district- or school-level personnel plan the most productive cash management strategy. Administrators invest deposits as soon as they receive the funds. Today's electronic transfers of funds speed transactions, especially for the deposit of large state and federal aid payments. Disbursements are timed to remove cash from district and school accounts at as close a time as possible to when payments are owed to vendors. When checking and savings accounts are maintained with a balance large enough only to meet current expenses, cash resources of separate funds can be pooled to yield potentially higher earnings from longer-term investments that require large deposits.

This pooling is common in districts that allocate monies to the control of individual buildings. Investments are centralized, and the interest gained by pooled investments is dispersed to individual accounts in the same proportion as the original contributions. Small school districts can gain similar advantages by pooling investment funds. They may do this through a Board of Cooperative Services or some other form of intermediate unit of government, to maximize yield and minimize paperwork for finance officers.

Obtaining Loans to Cover Shortfalls

Sound financial management often relies on short-term loans to meet current obligations before receiving anticipated funds. By borrowing, districts can avoid such potentially severe consequences as disruptions in school operations; increased costs of future purchases of needed materials as suppliers' faith in prompt payment declines; and deteriorated morale of their employees as payrolls and scheduled acquisitions of supplies are delayed. Short-term loans are limited to the amount of future revenue due to the district. Repayment is generally scheduled to occur within the fiscal year during which the district collects taxes or receives aid payments.

Several mechanisms are available to ease an interim cash deficit (Dembowski & Davey, 1986). *Revenue anticipation notes* permit districts to borrow against future revenues other than property taxes (e.g., the intergovernmental transfers discussed in Chapter 7). *Tax anticipation notes* bring needed money to meet general operating expenses before the actual receipt of property or local income taxes. A *budget note* that raises funds to assist with an unforeseeable emergency is repaid during the following fiscal year. *Bond anticipation notes* enable districts to initiate a construction project or obtain buses or other equipment in advance of the issuance of bonds, following voter approval. Entering into this long-term debt to finance capital outlay is the subject of the next section.

FINANCING CAPITAL OUTLAY

School systems require more funds than they typically have at their immediate disposal in order to construct new facilities, renovate older buildings, and purchase buses and large equipment. Many districts would find it difficult to proceed with large projects without the authority to issue bonds to spread payments over a long period. At the same time, states regulate borrowing to ensure responsible use of debt. They thus prevent districts from defaulting on obligations or incurring large long-term deficits.

Capital outlay funds repay the principal and interest necessary to retire bonds issued to finance buildings and equipment that have useful lives extending beyond a single school year. Although school systems may allocate capital outlay funds within their annual budgets to make small equipment purchases, they generally finance major projects through other sources. The local property tax base has traditionally been burdened with repayment of the resulting long-term debt. The long-term debt is defined to include debt payable more than one year after the date of issue. Despite the increased reliance on state revenue for financing annual school operations, only a few states assume responsibility for constructing the facilities within which school programs are delivered.

The previously cited amount of total outstanding debt in 1996–1997 ($125.7 billion) reflects this burden on school districts and local tax bases. During that year, capital outlay totaled $32.4 billion, including $22.5 billion for construction, $1.5 billion for land and existing structures, and $8.4 billion for equipment (U.S. Department of Commerce, 2000, Table 9). In addition to expenditures for capital outlay, interest payments on outstanding debt exceeded $6.5 billion, whereas relief from intergovernmental transfers was less than $1.1 billion. Although school systems were able to retire almost $10.3 billion of outstanding long-term debt in 1996-1997 (Table 10), tremendous capital outlay and interest expenditures and new long-term debt issues exceeding $22.5 billion demonstrate the burden on school districts and local tax bases.

Districts derive funds to meet capital outlay needs primarily through state and local governments. The burden for financing elementary and secondary school construction in 1990–1991 fell most heavily on local governments. This level of government funded nearly all (98 percent) of the total $19.8 billion spent throughout the country (see Table 6.2). Fiscally independent school districts assumed the bulk of capital outlay costs (81 percent of the total). Other school systems derived funds

TABLE 6.2.

State and Local Government Expenditures for Capital Outlay for Elementary and Secondary Education, 1990–1991 and 1998–1999 (millions of dollars)

	Total	*Local Portion*	*State Portion*
1990–1991 Amount	$ 19,852	$ 19,424	$ 428
1990–1991 Percent	100	97.8	2.2
1998–1999 Amount	$ 40,768	$ 40,160	$ 608
1998–1999 Percent	100	98.5	1.5
Increase (1990–1991 to 1998–1999)	$ 20,916	$ 20,736	$ 180
Percent Increase	105.4	106.8	42.1

Source: U.S. Department of Commerce, Bureau of the Census (1993), *Public Education Finances: 1990–91*, Series GF91-10, Washington, DC: U.S. Government Printing Office, Table 1, p. 2; U.S. Department of Commerce, Bureau of the Census (2001), *United States State and Local Government Finances by Level of Government: 1998–99*. Washington, DC: U.S. Government Printing Office, p. 2. Available at **http://www.census.gov/govs/estimate/9900us.html**

through county, municipal, or special district governments. State legislatures contributed $428 million for capital outlay, including $374 million toward the construction of facilities (U.S. Department of Commerce, 1993, p. 2). The growth in this aspect of school finance is evident in the rise in the proportion of all state and local expenditures for elementary and secondary schools that was devoted to capital outlay. During fiscal year 1980, the proportion was 6.8 percent. By 1998, the proportion of funds for capital outlay had grown to 10.8 percent (NCES, 2001, Table 162).

Current emphasis on the improvement of school facilities and student learning conditions might explain some of this growth. Other possible explanations for this growth include increases in the number of construction projects;

higher construction costs, due in part to prevailing wage rates (Keller & Hartman, 2001); and fluctuations in interest rates. As noted earlier, intergovernmental transfers for capital outlay are modest. Congress allocates a very limited amount of federal capital outlay funds for elementary and secondary education annually. These funds are primarily devoted to school construction for Native American reservations and areas affected by military installations (see Chapter 9).

Table 6.3 presents greater detail on expenditures for capital outlay projects by elementary and secondary school systems during the 1996–1997 school year. Of the $32.4 billion spent across the nation, the largest proportion (69 percent) was devoted to construction of new facilities, including additions and site im-

TABLE 6.3.

Elementary and Secondary Expenditures for Capital Outlay, 1996–1997 (per-pupil expenditures in dollars; others in thousands of dollars)

State	Construction	Equipment	Land and Existing Structures	Total	Per Pupil
Alabama	261,414	130,787	27,869	420,070	562
Alaska	126,594	15,241	10,495	152,330	1172
Arizona	418,794	214,645	45,354	678,793	849
Arkansas	109,182	74,817	8,205	192,204	420
California	1,963,005	808,550	317,119	3,088,674	543
Colorado	437,318	226,518	14,795	678,631	1008
Connecticut	103,513	57,842	32,865	192,204	368
Delaware	52,503	21,443	—	73,946	669
District of Columbia	43,690	9,416	—	53,106	675
Florida	1,536,931	500,920	73,598	2,111,449	942
Georgia	789,453	236,790	30,273	1,056,516	784
Hawaii	109,277	3,258	11,169	123,704	659
Idaho	146,080	32,623	—	178,703	729
Illinois	1,017,654	580,420	—	1,598,074	810
Indiana	370,770	279,049	17,209	667,028	679
Iowa	168,145	124,741	2,672	295,558	588
Kansas	59,266	115,326	13,564	188,156	404
Kentucky	200,374	119,305	4,688	324,367	494
Louisiana	122,022	100,230	27,643	249,895	315
Maine	26,167	27,615	17,843	71,625	335

TABLE 6.3.

(Continued)

State	Construction	Equipment	Land and Existing Structures	Total	Per Pupil
Maryland	425,086	146,447	21,192	592,725	724
Massachusetts	357,900	81,373	—	439,273	470
Michigan	913,794	425,406	139,750	1,478,950	877
Minnesota	616,031	148,986	34,137	799,154	943
Mississippi	156,073	88,028	—	244,101	484
Missouri	313,152	196,815	42,338	552,305	613
Montana	32,903	23,232	3,581	59,716	363
Nebraska	85,657	120,676	7,339	213,672	732
Nevada	299,727	57,929	11,873	369,529	1310
New Hampshire	106,175	18,564	44,738	169,477	855
New Jersey	650,191	169,686	118,656	938,533	764
New Mexico	154,684	46,023	48,963	249,670	751
New York	2,283,303	259,285	18,542	2,561,130	901
North Carolina	561,782	235,743	50,703	848,228	701
North Dakota	22,257	22,317	3,418	47,992	400
Ohio	617,036	417,276	41,194	1,075,506	583
Oklahoma	142,264	122,781	17,577	282,622	455
Oregon	294,811	86,925	13,705	395,441	735
Pennsylvania	1,189,620	202,972	7,581	1,400,173	776
Rhode Island	7,749	14,104	—	21,853	144
South Carolina	343,397	155,543	10,693	509,633	781
South Dakota	4,497	58,695	—	63,192	441
Tennessee	326,830	140,889	12,448	479,484	530
Texas	2,372,945	673,713	100,427	3,147,085	822
Utah	171,970	88,682	22,175	282,827	587
Vermont	74,570	13,273	8,322	96,165	904
Virginia	534,688	287,312	9,898	831,898	759
Washington	639,737	212,683	44,717	897,137	921
West Virginia	62,864	48,085	33,260	144,209	474
Wisconsin	588,558	145,001	27,631	761,190	866
Wyoming	52,668	29,517	2,045	84,230	850
U.S. Total (or per-pupil average)	22,465,071	8,416,814	1,552,264	32,434,149	711

Note: —means zero or rounds to zero.

Source: U.S. Department of Commerce, Bureau of the Census (2000), *Public Education Finances: 1997*. [Series GC97(4)-1] Washington, DC: U.S. Government Printing Office, Tables 9, 18, pp. 9, 172.

provements. Another 26 percent went for purchases of equipment such as motor vehicles and office machines with a life expectancy of more than five years. Five percent was used to acquire land and existing structures. Per-pupil expenditures for capital outlay varied widely. They ranged from $144 in Rhode Island to $1310 in Nevada, where there has been rapid growth in student enrollments. Possible explanations for such variation in expenditure include shifts in population among states, lower costs of living in some states, and varying costs of construction.

Despite this large and growing outlay of funds for facilities, schools in many communities are inadequate and need extensive renovation for twenty-first-century needs. A survey of facility needs by the American Association of School Administrators (Hansen, 1991) revealed that one-third of currently used schools were built prior to World War II. Another 43 percent were constructed during the expanding enrollment years of the 1950s and 1960s. Relatively few were constructed in the 1970s (14 percent) and between 1980 and 1993 (11 percent). About 13 percent of schools had poor learning environments. An earlier survey judged the condition of one-quarter of schools to be inadequate, a majority of schools to require major repairs (61 percent), many to have uncorrected environmental hazards (43 percent), and 13 percent to be structurally unsound (Education Writers Association, 1989).

On the basis of responses from a sample of school officials throughout the nation, the United States General Accounting Office (GAO) (1995a) estimated that one-third of schools needed extensive repair or replacement and that about $112 billion was required to upgrade school facilities to a "good" overall condition. Of this amount, $11 billion would help districts comply with prior federal mandates to make all programs accessible to students with disabilities and to remove or correct hazardous substances such as asbestos, lead in water or paint, materials in underground storage tanks, and radon. A subsequent GAO survey revealed that most schools do not fully use modern technology. About 40 percent of schools do not meet requirements of laboratory science even moderately well. Over half do not have the flexibility to implement many effective teaching strategies. Two-thirds are not equipped to meet requirements of before- or after-school care or day care (U.S. General Accounting Office, 1995b). This report also observed, "Overall, schools in central cities and schools with a 50 percent or more minority population were more likely to have more insufficient technology elements and a greater number of unsatisfactory environmental conditions—particularly lighting and physical security—than other schools" (p. 2).

The most recent estimate of capital outlay required for schools is more than double the $112 billion estimated in 1995. Crampton, Thompson, and Hagey (2001) placed the estimated need for funding at $266.1 billion. The purpose of their study was "to develop estimates of unmet funding need for school infrastructure on a state-by-state basis" (p. 644). Their estimation model also included future projections, such as anticipated changes in student enrollment and policies to reduce student class size. According to the estimate, the states requiring the greatest influx of funding were: New York ($47.6 billion), California ($22.0 billion), Ohio ($20.9 billion), and New Jersey ($20.7 billion). Vermont and New Hampshire required the least amount of funding, $220.1 million and $409.5 million, respectively (Table 1). The national average requirement per pupil was estimated at $1100 over five years or $600 over ten years in this study. Moreover, the authors asserted that immediate and short-term remedies would not be sufficient to cover investment requirements of this magnitude. Rather, permanent structures of funding, such as those that exist for state operating aid to schools, were essential (Crampton, Thompson, & Hagey, 2001).

The poor condition of the nation's schools might reflect the unwillingness of voters to invest in this aspect of public education. Alternatively, the inadequacy may result from the traditional methods of financing capital outlay. These have placed a heavy burden on local resources. In fact, Sielke (2001) found that in 39 states voter approval is necessary for the district to issue bonds that support school infrastructure requirements. Moreover, only one state, Hawaii, provided full state funding, and twelve states provided no state funding for school infrastructure in 1998-1999. Perhaps most disturbing is the gap that exists between state funding for capital outlay and infrastructure and estimated requirements. Sielke (2001) found that from 1993-1994 to 1998-1999 state funding increased from $4.1 billion to $10.9 billion. Although this increase was substantial, the underlying dollar amounts pale in comparison to two estimates of the resources needed for school construction: $112 billion (U.S. General Accounting Office, 1995a) and $266.1 billion (Crampton, Thompson, & Hagey, 2001). In the absence of monumental state— and perhaps federal—investment interventions, local capital outlay requirements will need to be satisfied by more traditional means of capital outlay finance.

Although some states make loans available to districts or provide partial or full state assumption of capital costs, the vast majority of districts must rely on a number of methods to finance capital projects. Examples include pay-as-you-go plans, sinking funds to save for future construction projects, and issuance of long-term bonds. Other approaches to acquiring needed facilities include assessing fees on developers of new housing, lease-purchasing, and joint venturing. The following methods of financing capital outlay draw from or are discussed in greater detail by Ortiz (1994), Thompson, Wood, and Honeyman (1994), Kowalski (2001), and Thompson and Wood (2001).

Current Revenue and Construction Funds

Districts in fifteen states receive no state-level assistance for capital outlay. Even in those states that do provide a portion of funds, localities typically pay the lion's share of projects (Education Writers Association, 1989). Paying for major projects from current revenue receipts is rare because of their large costs and the many other demands on annual budgets. It is possible in only the wealthiest and largest

school districts. This pay-as-you-go approach offers the advantages of avoiding interest costs and discouraging districts from making extravagant facility improvements that they might make if state allocations financed the full cost of projects. However, this approach makes large increases in property tax rates necessary in most districts in order to meet such expenditures as they are incurred. Districts must turn to some form of savings or borrowing to keep tax rates more consistent from year to year.

"Construction" or "sinking" funds are special accounts created for accumulating reserves over a period of time in anticipation of future construction needs. Some states permit such funds. These savings accrue interest to expand the reserves even more; they encourage long-range planning of future needs as the reserves grow. The advantage of this approach is that districts accrue interest on the "sinking" fund and eliminate the large interest costs associated with borrowing. However, savings may not be adequate for financing remodeling of facilities or new construction as schools age or for purchasing sufficient numbers of buses in times of extraordinary population growth. In addition, school boards and taxpayers are reluctant to pledge funds for uncertain future projects. This is especially true when districts do not meet current instructional needs or when school board elections or administrative appointments alter the priorities for the use of funds.

The Issuance of Bonds

Rather than delaying improvements until savings have accrued, districts may sell bonds to make funds available for specific projects when they are needed. Several advantages of this form of borrowing offset the additional cost of a project due to the interest that must be paid to investors. First, the debt created is paid by the actual users in future years, which is consistent with the benefits-received principle discussed in Chapter 3. Otherwise, it would have been paid from taxes placed in a sinking fund over a period of years before the project was begun. Second, facilities that are constructed at today's costs may actually spell savings for the district. This is because the low-interest bonds are paid with future tax revenue, which is generally worth less because of inflation.

Districts raise over 75 percent of capital outlay funds to finance improvements at the local level by issuing bonds (Ortiz, 1994, p. 40). Salmon and Thomas (1981) define a *bond* as "a written financial instrument issued by a corporate body to borrow money with the time and rate of interest, method of principal repayment, and the term of debt clearly expressed" (p. 91). State statutes enable school districts and other public entities to incur debt that is paid either by future gate receipts (as may be the case for sports facilities) or by anticipated property tax revenue. Unlike home mortgages and other forms of long-term debt that rely on the property itself as collateral, *general obligation bonds* are secured by a public entity's pledge of its "full faith and credit." Because they obligate the district, or in some cases the state, to raise taxes for repayment, and because debt obligations often have the first claim on state aid, there is little fear that the district will default on future payments. Furthermore, because the interest earned from investments on public projects is exempt from federal and state income taxation, these school district bonds are attractive to investors.

Governing boards, in the case of fiscally dependent school districts, or school district voters, in the case of fiscally independent districts, decide whether to issue bonds and levy property taxes for a fixed term to pay the principal and interest. Some states conduct school bond sales themselves to take advantage of their stronger taxing power and credit rating. In this way, they may obtain even lower interest rates. In these cases, local districts may petition the state to participate in bond sales after voters approve a project. Alternatively, the state may assume liability for all local bond debt (Thompson, Wood & Honeyman, 1994, p. 568).

Bonds are marketed through competitive bidding to bond underwriters, who in turn make the bonds available to investors. Municipal and school district bonds are marketed at substantially reduced interest rates. These rates are low because of the bonds' high security and because the interest paid to bond holders is tax exempt. On the other hand, taxes must be paid on loans to finance commercial construction projects. The cost of public-sector capital projects is thus reduced. Those school districts with excellent credit ratings are at a further advantage because they can market bonds at very low interest rates. Professional bond-rating companies, such as Moody's Investor Service and Standard and Poor's, consider such factors as local property valuation, outstanding debt, current tax rates, and enrollment trends in informing potential investors about the relative security of a bond issue. A prospectus (Wood, et al., 1995) communicates to the financial community the purpose of the bond issue; the type and denomination of the bond issue; full disclosure of the financial condition of the district, including outstanding debt; any pending litigation that might affect the bond sale; and other information about the school district. This information, compiled by the bond underwriter, and the current national economy influence the actual interest rates paid to investors (Education Writers Association, 1989, p. 31).

Serial bonds are the most common form for financing school construction. They structure repayment so that a portion of the debt is retired on periodic (e.g., annual) maturity dates; the total debt is paid over the period of issue (e.g., ten, twenty, or thirty years). Interest rates are lower for short amortization periods than for long ones. Investors and school districts alike are cautious about defining interest rates over a long period. They hesitate because fluctuations in the economy may mean either a sharply lowered return for investors or excessive interest payments for districts. Districts less often use *term bonds*, which specify a particular date on which the principal and interest are due.

Callable bonds include provisions under which bonds can be reissued after a specified number of years. These bonds offer districts the opportunity to take advantage of lower interest rates in the future. Noncallable bonds protect the investor and thus carry more favorable rates. But with noncallable bonds, districts are unable to control the amount of interest paid as the economy fluctuates. Callable bonds are most likely to be considered when interest rates are relatively high. Even when a school district appears to be saddled with a high interest rate on a noncallable bond issue, advanced refunding can offer the potential of lowering the total net cost of borrowing. Advanced refunding is not legal in some states. In this mechanism, new bonds are issued at a lower interest rate, and funds are invested with maturity just before the original bond issue's payment date.

Issuing bonds is primarily a local mechanism for raising capital outlay funds. States, however, regulate the use of monies and the bonding process itself. Districts borrow funds to acquire land and construct new facilities, to make additions to or remodel existing buildings, and to purchase equipment. But these funds cannot be diverted to school operations. Once a school board has approved plans for construction and (in most cases) has received clearance from the state to proceed, it releases a public notice about the project and holds an open hearing. In fiscally independent school districts, a referendum may be required to authorize the borrowing of money and the repayment of bonds by a tax rate increase. The nature of bonds to be issued is also regulated by the state. Regulations may specify acceptable types of bonds, lengths of time to maturity, and maximum interest rates.

States may specify the maximum amount of debt to be incurred by local governments. A *debt ceiling* is often imposed to prohibit school districts from overcommitting their tax bases

and to ensure favorable credit ratings in the future. The ceiling may take the form of a maximum tax rate to raise capital outlay funds or a given proportion (e.g., 6 percent) of property valuation (see Chapter 5). Many poor districts are unable to meet capital outlay needs because their limited bonding capacity restricts the amount to be raised for facility construction and remodeling. Debt ceilings allow wealthier districts to raise more funds through bond issues than less wealthy districts, even though these restrictions bear no relationship to district facility needs (Augenblick, 1977, p. 12).

State Loans and Grants-in-Aid

Whereas state courts and legislatures have been concerned about equalizing disparities in per-pupil revenues for school operations (see discussions in Chapters 7 and 10), they have not demanded policies to ease the large inequities in facilities that result from heavy reliance on local tax bases to finance capital outlay. Loans and direct grants have provided some state-level assistance. But the funds appropriated have not been sufficient to meet capital needs.

Localities can create a pool of state funds from which loans can be made for approved projects without needing to market bonds. Loans of state money enable many communities to have sufficient facilities despite debt ceilings that would otherwise limit available funds. Loan funds are derived from reserves in retirement programs, direct legislative appropriations, permanent funds set aside with interest used for this purpose, or state-level borrowing. Salmon et al. (1988, p. 9) reported that seven states make low-interest loans available to districts. The Education Writers Association (1989, p. 27) listed five such states.

The use of loans that require repayment is thus limited. In contrast, the majority of state legislatures appropriate capital outlay funds and distribute them according to such measures of need as the cost of approved projects, the number of students or instructional units, fiscal capacity, or tax effort. Only Hawaii assumes complete support of capital outlay. Full state financing has limitations in that local control over decisions is lost, and project approval and funding restrictions constrain states' abilities to meet all their needs for facilities (Augenblick, 1977, pp. 7–8; Salmon & Thomas, 1981, p. 96). Many states have adopted an approach to help finance school construction that is sensitive to the varying fiscal abilities of districts. A majority of states that provide partial assistance do so according to a foundation or percentage equalizing formula (see Chapter 7) that takes into account local property valuations and, in some cases, tax effort (Gold, Smith & Lawton, 1995, pp. 48–52).

Several states permit public corporations to be formed for financing capital improvements. Building authorities were first created in the early 1900s to circumvent debt restrictions on municipalities and school districts. They are subject to their own taxing and debt limitations. Camp and Salmon (1985) reported that as many as nineteen states have experimented with building authorities. But they continue to operate at either state or local levels in only eight states. For example, New York City's Educational Construction Fund represents an innovative local approach to financing school facilities for large cities. This authority constructs buildings on school-owned land. Schools occupy only portions of the facilities, and rental of the remaining space to businesses pays the debt. Four states operate bond banks (Education Writers Association, 1989, p. 27) to consolidate bond issues. They thus take advantage of lower interest rates than would be available for individual district projects. Camp and Salmon (1985) suggested that multicounty public authorities and regional bond banks may offer financial advantages and economies of scale that are similar to those achieved by cooperatives for delivering educational services.

A larger state role in financing capital outlay offers a number of advantages. When poorer districts can access broader-based tax revenue for expanding and improving facilities, there is greater equalization of educational opportunity. School districts realize savings in debt service costs. This is true whether bonds are issued using states' higher credit ratings or there are direct grants without borrowing. Furthermore, guidelines and standards for approval of projects to receive state funding often outline cost-effective construction practices, influence the design and location of school buildings, and contribute to energy conservation (Johns et al., 1983, p. 286; King & MacPhail-Wilcox, 1988).

On the other hand, a larger state role has disadvantages. When power and control become more centralized, local citizens may support public education less. If facility designs and functions become uniform across a state, innovations and the recognition of unique local needs may be inhibited. Finally, there may be delays in addressing local needs, given the intense competition for resources at the state level (Salmon & Thomas, 1981, p. 96).

Developers' Fees, Lease–Purchase, and Joint Venturing

Ortiz (1994) described several other mechanisms for expanding local resources to meet facility needs. Suburban districts—primarily in rapidly growing areas of California, Colorado, and Florida—assess an *impact fee* directly on developers of new housing and businesses. This approach differs from general property taxation throughout the district in that it places a portion of the burden (from 10 to 15 percent of construction costs) for financing new buildings and expanded services on developers as building permits are approved. These privilege-based taxes are ultimately shifted to residents or owners of commercial buildings who will benefit most directly from economic development in rapidly growing communities. As attractive as impact fees are to citizens who desire to shift this burden, Bauman (1995) warns school officials to prepare for greater scrutiny from community and business leaders who are most affected by the fees.

Lease–purchasing is a form of borrowing that has been used for many years to construct facilities for institutions that cannot incur debt (e.g., Boards of Cooperative Educational Services) and to acquire large equipment and portable classroom buildings. An underwriter generally sells leases to investors, and the district uses the proceeds to acquire needed equipment. *Joint venturing* can use many of the previously discussed forms of financing to bring several government or private agencies together with school districts that acquire or construct, and then share, facilities. Joint occupancy arrangements with other public entities maximize facility use and reduce construction costs. In particular, recreation facilities such as swimming pools and tennis courts are often constructed in concert with municipalities and senior citizen organizations.

In the future, communities will increasingly need capital outlay funds to replace or expand facilities. This is particularly true in rapidly growing school districts. Other districts will remodel or close older buildings as they deteriorate. Those school systems that experience declining enrollments will sell underused buildings or convert them for other purposes. Public school facilities will increasingly house early-childhood and prekindergarten activities, before- and after-school programs for students, and continuing-education and community college classes for adults during evenings and weekends. Restructured elementary, middle-grades, and secondary organizational patterns, as well as new uses of instructional and information technologies, will also create pressures for remodeled buildings or for very different original construction. Localities will respond to these demands with increased taxes, calls for state assistance, impact fees, or other financing mechanisms.

PARTNERSHIPS, FOUNDATIONS, AND VOLUNTARISM

Schools have historically relied on private resources to supplement public monies. Citi-zens—students' parents in particular—once contributed substantial time, talent, and money through tuition and special fees, fund-raising social activities, direct donations, and volunteer time. However, individuals and the private sector became less involved in building the resource base, other than through property taxation, in many districts during the 1960s and 1970s, for several reasons. Changes in family structures and priorities for the use of time meant fewer hours to devote to school activities. Rapidly expanding communities and centralized school systems created large distances and altered relationships between parents and school personnel. A larger and more specialized profession displaced volunteers, and states assumed a greater share of the responsibility for financing public education. A major consequence of these changes was an increasing separation of schools from home, work, and community. As Mathews (1996, 1997) put it, schools lost legitimacy in the public eye. Schools no longer exhibited organizational characteristics of being part of or for the public that created them.

New attitudes toward encouraging greater privatization and entrepreneurship within public education have developed in recent years. Efforts in many states to limit taxation threatened to reduce local revenue. These efforts stimulated schools to turn once again to private sources of human and monetary inputs. The private sector was concerned about economic growth and international competitiveness. It encouraged school districts to involve businesses and communities not only in acquiring resources but also in planning future educational structures and learning outcomes.

Individuals have enriched schools or financed broader reform efforts through donations and challenge grants, which require recipients to raise matching funds. In 1990, Ross Perot's $500,000 challenge grant stimulated other fund raising to support Teach for America and its recruitment of college graduates into the profession. The largest private gift ever to public education was Walter Annenberg's $500 million pledge in 1994. A portion of this donation was in the form of challenge grants to attract matching public and private investments for school reform efforts through the New American Development Corporation, the Education Commission of the States, the Annenberg Institute for School Reform at Brown University, and several of the nation's largest urban school districts (Annenberg Institute for School Reform, 1995).

In the early years of the recent movement to form partnerships, the private sector and public schools forged adopt-a-school programs. Corporations lent executives to improve school leadership and management skills. They hired teachers during the summer to acquaint them with the needs of business and sponsored career days for students. They financed advertising campaigns to raise consciousness about the need for school improvement and to discourage students from dropping out. Adult and continuing-education programs shared school space, and municipalities jointly financed the construction of special-use facilities. Educational foundations stimulated individuals and corporations to donate funds. Senior citizens and parents volunteered in classrooms. As the movement expanded, the private sector became more aggressive in contracting with public school boards for the operation of individual schools or for providing chief executive officers to oversee district operations (see Doyle, 1994).

In this section, we examine entrepreneurial activities in the form of partnerships, educational foundations, and voluntarism. These activities offer school districts opportunities for securing additional capital and human resources, both as incentives to improve instruction and as enrichments to the dialogue about curriculum and policy (see King & Swanson, 1990). These activities began because partnerships to provide individual schools needed human and financial resources. They have evolved into more meaningful public–private relationships directed at system-level restructuring and renewal efforts.

Public-Private Partnerships

Formal and informal relationships between school districts or individual schools and businesses accomplish a number of things. The private sector desires a better-educated workforce to boost productivity, reduce on-the-job training costs, and improve international competitiveness. Interest in school improvement derives in part from the realization that tomorrow's labor market is in schools today and that business can work with educators in developing needed skills: "The sharing of expertise is the bedrock for effective relationships" (Hoyt, 1991, p. 451). This investment in developing human capital is explored more fully in Chapter 2. It yields returns to business and society alike.

Schools have traditionally represented a large market for the sale or donation of goods and services. Businesses profit from direct sales. Schools benefit from private-sector research and development undertaken to provide more efficient products and technologies. Private-sector involvement is also motivated by tax benefits that derive from donations of money and products to public schools (Wood, 1990).

In return for investments in schools, the private sector expects improved school performance. In contrast to school systems' desires for more resources to expand offerings and produce better results, Doyle (1989) stated that the premise often underlying business involvement is that results will produce more resources:

> Business should expect of the schools precisely what it expects of itself and what its customers expect of it: performance. Schools must be able to describe and defend what they do in terms of value added. What difference does going to school make? In what measurable ways is a student better off having gone to school? (p. E100)

School–business collaborations that yield improved schooling offer returns in the form of resources *and* results for both parties.

Public–private interactions occur in several forms. Among them are the categories of donor, shared, and enterprise activities identified by Meno (1984). *Donor activities* are directed to soliciting goods, services, and money. *Shared or cooperative activities* permit schools to pool resources with community organizations, colleges and universities, or government agencies to reduce costs. *Enterprise activities* involve school districts in many revenue-producing services: providing food preparation, data processing, and transportation services for other organizations; leasing surplus buildings for alternative community uses, athletic fields to professional athletic teams, or facility space to profit-making enterprises such as credit unions; driver education and swimming instruction, which generate user fees and service charges; and the sale of access to school markets such as food service rights and vending machines. This latter concept of enterprise has broadened recently with the expanded search for alternative revenue. Parents and students actively solicit financial support and engage in numerous fundraising events; Whittle's Channel One brings news programs and corporate advertising into classrooms; and districts in some states sell commercial advertising space on school walls, athletic uniforms, newsletters, and buses (Bauman & Crampton, 1995). These donor, shared, and enterprise activities enrich district and school resources in diverse ways. Each is predicated on the belief that schools and the communities they serve benefit greatly through collaborative arrangements.

Partnerships at the school level offer opportunities for directly affecting classrooms. There are countless examples of private sponsorship of school programs. Businesses may stimulate innovations by funding directly or by issuing challenge grants. They donate computers and other equipment, finance artistic performances, sponsor academies to model reforms and market-driven innovations, create programs for connecting families with social service agencies, encourage academic and social suc-

cess for low-income children, sponsor counseling and preemployment experiences for school dropouts, and raise money to guarantee high school graduates employment or financial assistance for college. Businesspeople also partner by working in schools—teaching classes for students and workshops for teachers, serving on planning committees, and strategizing ways to attract and work effectively with other partners (Sammon & Becton, 2001). Glenn (2001) asserted that the most successful partnerships are community-based and involve a continuous improvement process that includes planning and development, implementation and management, monitoring and evaluation, and planning for the future (p. 12).

Higher education has also formed partnership agreements with elementary and secondary schools. The Chelsea, Massachusetts, public schools turned to Boston University for assistance in implementing educational reforms. State legislation in 1989 enabled the university to manage the school system for ten years. The presidents of the University of Texas at El Paso and El Paso Community College joined with other leaders to form a collaborative aimed at improving academic achievement in the area's public schools (Navarro & Natalicio, 1999). The State University of New York College at Purchase and Westchester County public schools collaborated to increase the pool of qualified college students, foster vitality in the teaching profession, raise standards, strengthen career counseling, develop leadership, and improve teaching and learning in secondary schools (Gross, 1988). Many colleges of education have joined with public schools to create professional development schools to improve the skills of current and future teachers. High school students can often attend college courses for credit, and college personnel can teach courses in schools (Ziegler, 2001).

Partnerships are generally created within local school districts. State reform legislation, however, often encourages or mandates linkages between businesses and schools in analyzing and planning school improvements. In addition, several national-level efforts have encouraged business involvement in school-based activities, systemwide policy development, and state-level reform efforts. The 1993 National Partnerships in Education Program brought federal encouragement. The National Association of Partners in Education (NAPE), formed in 1988, recognized the value of public–private partnerships for educational improvement.

The Public Education Fund Network (PEFNet) includes sixty urban school districts in its effort to link many locally based not-for-profit partnership organizations (Bergholz, 1992; Muro, 1995). The goals and strategies of members of this network have shifted over the years (Useem & Neild, 1995). The fund was created to seek political and financial support from business and civic leaders to help impoverished school systems. The initial tactics were providing resources, improving public relations, nurturing adopt-a-school programs, and facilitating school-based projects through minigrants for teacher and staff development. The public relations goal in particular was critical to eliciting the support of civic and business leaders in an era of middle-class flight from urban schools. Concomitant with changes in educational reform efforts, the role of partnerships has evolved in many urban districts to involve the private sector more directly in district-level policy debates and whole-school change initiatives: "In a number of the longer-lived funds, their dominant role has shifted from being just a resource-provider and relatively uncritical supporter of a district to that of catalyst and agent of long-term change willing to speak frankly about the need for systemic reform" (Useem & Neild, 1995). Not only are they raising questions about the organization, conducting studies of administrative arrangements and operational efficiencies, and making recommendations for changed policies, but they are also following through with assistance in implementing reforms.

This new wave of partnership activities is typified by projects that have stimulated school restructuring, studied organizational problems, or encouraged state-level reform (Useem & Neild, 1995). Examples of restructuring with partners' involvement include: site-based restructuring in all 600 Los Angeles schools through the LEARN initiative, teacher-driven curricular changes and restructuring of schools with an emphasis on the arts or math and sciences in Philadelphia, adoption of the Paideia philosophy in curriculum and teaching in Chattanooga, and the creation of a principals' study group on restructuring with funds to implement projects in San Francisco. Several partnerships have studied organizational problems and formed policy recommendations. For example, the New York City chancellor's strategic working groups brought about systemwide change in mathematics curriculum and altered graduation requirements. The Denver-area Public Education Coalition sponsored a management efficiency audit to assess organizational health in five districts. Finally, state-level reform can be an outgrowth of partnership activities, as occurred when the Education Reform Act of 1993 was modeled after recommendations of the Massachusetts Business Alliance for Education.

A survey of fifty private-sector coalitions located in twenty-six states by the Indiana Education Policy Center (Hamrick, 1993) examined influences of partnership activities on state-level policies. Coalitions included in the study had to perceive themselves as change agents for statewide education reform and to promote their priorities for change by influencing state-level education policy makers and elected officials. The highest-ranked priorities of these coalitions were improving student performance and changing the power structure through citizen and parent involvement, revised state education governance structures, reducing or eliminating state regulations, site-based management, and teacher participation in decision making. Although these organizations represented private-sector interests, school choice, vouchers, and tuition tax credits were among the lowest-rated priorities of coalitions in the nation, except for those located in western states. State government representatives viewed these coalitions as effective or somewhat effective and linked their effectiveness to the groups' success in developing relations with state offices, in promoting specific legislative proposals, and in building public support. Hamrick concluded that private-sector influence is strong and increasing and that coalitions are a key strategy for exerting that influence.

A number of lessons have been learned through these and other initiatives to improve school programs. Business leaders become familiar with operations. They raise questions about the distribution of power when they examine district policies and initiate whole-school change. They are frustrated by such structural roadblocks as union contracts, teacher-hiring policies, schedules in secondary schools, and standardized test requirements (Useem & Neild, 1995, p. 7). For example, the New York City fund, which launched the New Visions Schools in 1993, eventually negotiated an agreement with the district and union to permit teachers to be hired at the school site without regard for the contract's seniority provisions (Lief, 1992). From their review of partnership activities stimulated under the Public Education Fund, Useem and Neild (1995, pp. 17, 21) concluded that their effectiveness depends on three key factors: (1) the superintendent's encouragement and support, (2) visible and strong support from the business community that is channeled through the fund's board or through other organizational vehicles that collaborate with the fund, and (3) the negotiating and coalition-building skills of the fund's staff members. They also noted the importance of frequent communications among participants at all stages of activities, and of delicate handling of critical assessments of district practices, which is "almost always done through the vehicle of a broadly representative commission or task force that is quasi-independent of the fund" (p. 19).

The advantages of these public–private partnerships are numerous. They are designed to be nonbureaucratic, nonpartisan and less politicized, flexible, innovative, and entrepreneurial. They are simultaneously inside organizations (they have commitments to work over time with specific school systems and their administrations and teacher unions) and outside organizations (they have independent governing boards and funding sources) (Useem & Neild, 1995).

The scope and visibility of these large urban projects overshadow those in smaller districts, which may indeed have less need for formalized partnerships. Inman (1984) and Mann (1987b) discussed reasons why school–business partnerships are less likely to form in rural areas than in larger, more urbanized districts. The presence of strong preexisting connections, dispersed economies, a local culture of thrift, and the unintended consequences of competition in rural communities either remove the need for alliances or make creating them undesirable. Rural school districts do not have so large an economic base. Thus contacting businesses for donations of funds or supplies may be unwise when they are also asked to raise taxes to support the school system budget. Smaller districts enjoy better communications among schools, businesses, and community agencies. The lack of these linkages is often a motivation for partnerships in cities. Urban school districts are the largest beneficiaries of partnership activities, in part because businesses tend to support schools located within the same community.

Partnership activities grew rapidly in the 1980s. McLaughlin (1988) reported that 64 percent of 130 major corporations listed elementary and secondary education as their number 1 community affairs concern. Nevertheless, only about 3 percent of corporate contributions to education are directed to precollegiate public education (Timpane, 1984). Hess (1987) surveyed sixty-two Chicago-based funding organizations and found they made 446 grants that totaled $7.7 million. However, this represented just 4.6 percent of their total giving. Corporate downsizing in the 1990s affected giving. For example, Atlantic Richfield reduced its total philanthropic donations from a high of $37 million in 1983 to $12.5 million in 1993 (Sommerfeld, 1994). Despite projections by corporate leaders that charitable giving would increase along with increased profits, the Foundation Center projected that philanthropy would remain flat through the 1990s in part because of uncertainty about potential effects of changes in federal tax treatment of corporate giving (Sommerfeld, 1995).

The amount of business donations may reflect their limited role in school activities and policies. Mann's (1987a, 1987b) studies of 108 school systems, including twenty-three large cities, found that only 17 percent of the schools visited had developed relationships that exhibited all four features of "new style" business involvement: a coordinating structure, multiple purposes, multiple players, and stability. Mann (1987a) stated that the modest role of businesses in addressing school improvement needs is understandable:

> After having designed a system of limited government in order to minimize the abuse of power, after having vested most control in professionals, and after having inserted boards between the schools and their communities, why should we be surprised that no one—least of all the business community—has much power to solve problems? (p. 126)

Many partnerships avoid areas of conflict, and businesses restrict their involvement to helping schools acquire funds and materials. According to Timpane (1984), business reluctance to become involved in schools stems from feelings that the sponsorship of isolated projects is not likely "to improve the performance of school systems caught in webs of program-matic, managerial, and financial control created by years of governmental inaction at local, state and federal levels" (p. 391). However, their limited partnership roles do not enable educators to take advantage of business expertise, leadership, and political clout as reform directions are forged at local and state levels.

In contrast to these reports of limited roles for business is a study of effective schools in which collaborative efforts are shown to have made a large difference in school programs. Wilson and Rossman's (1986) investigation of programs and policies of 571 exemplary secondary schools revealed several common themes. These schools actively recruited human resources from the community and used aggressive public relations campaigns that relied on parent volunteers who served as promoters, communicators, and decision makers. The schools successfully attracted financial resources from individuals and businesses. Schools and communities benefited mutually. Communities made extensive use of school facilities, and schools formed positive identities with their communities. What set these schools apart from other schools? The frequency of cooperation between schools and communities, the high level of participation, and the degree to which these activities were considered central to the schools' missions and programs.

Partnership activities that offer more than cosmetic changes in school programs hold much potential for school improvement. The nature and extent of the partners' involvement may be an important distinguishing feature of effective restructured schools. Rather than approaching partnerships as singular, task-specific undertakings, the trend is toward integrating partners into the school mission as part of a comprehensive initiative that includes multiple stakeholders and volunteers.

Educational Foundations

Privately financed, not-for-profit school foundations expand the capacity of individual school fund-raising efforts (Addonizio, 2000; Monk & Brent, 1997; Pijanowski & Monk, 1996). Many districts have taken advantage of this form of partnership to coordinate and encourage giving from individuals and businesses. An *educational foundation* can support general educational goals, or it can create special-purpose funds to attract donations for specific school programs, athletics or other activities, or facility construction. Funds from foundations finance an array of special projects, including science and computer laboratories, field trips locally and abroad, grants for teachers to improve instruction, endowed teaching chairs, athletic facilities, and incentives for students to complete high school or enroll in colleges. Targeting specific groups, such as alumni, industries that employ graduates, or wealthy residents of the community, has been an effective foundation strategy. Long-term development activities encourage estate planning to establish endowments from which future income will be derived to support teaching positions or student scholarships.

Foundations may benefit schools throughout a state or within specific school systems. Statewide reform efforts are best exemplified by the efforts of the Edna McConnell Clark Foundation in stimulating collaboration on policy changes in Kentucky (McKersie & Palaich, 1994). The largest foundation gift ever made to a single school district was the MacArthur Foundation's pledge of $40 million over ten years to Chicago schools beginning in 1990. The I Have a Dream Foundation provides incentives for at-risk students in thirty-two cities to complete school by ensuring later support of higher education. The Minneapolis Five Percent Club relies on peer pressure among businesses to stimulate giving (McLaughlin & Shields, 1987). Many smaller school districts (Ballew, 1987; Havens, 2000; Neill, 1983; Nesbit, 1987) have also created foundations to solicit and manage donations.

The previously described national Public Education Fund Network (PEFNet) succeeded the Public Education Fund, which was created in 1983 through a $6 million Ford Foundation grant. A study of the activities sponsored by fifty foundations through this network between 1983 and 1988 found that they sponsored "small, high visibility" projects through mini-grants to teachers (an average amount of $662). They also urged public relations efforts to support district goals (Olson, 1988). The potential of this movement is evident in the size of PEFNet's largest educational foundations: the Fund for New York City Public Education (an annual budget of $9.7 million in 1994), the Los Angeles Educational Partnership ($8.2 million), and the Philadelphia Partnership for Education ($4 million) (Bergholz, 1992; Useem & Neild, 1995).

An appraisal of foundation efforts urges them to assume leadership roles in initiating and supporting educational reforms: "Systemic reforms based on a convergence of policy sectors—governmental, for-profit, nonprofit, and philanthropic—will have more success than systemic reforms based on a single policy sector." (McKersie & Palaich, 1994) The initiatives cited previously as examples of the expanded roles of partnerships suggest the potential of foundations in reform efforts.

Federal and state statutes define the legal structures of foundations as either charitable trusts or not-for-profit corporations (Wood, 1990). Because they generally operate as self-governed entities, foundations may limit school boards and personnel to advisory roles. In this role, school personnel help external groups set priorities for the use of resources and decide the appropriateness of gifts of equipment and teaching materials. In addition, they should monitor cash flow to avoid any suspicion of fund misuse. An example of this need is the financial mismanagement and fraud that forced the Dallas public schools to bring legal action against the Foundation for Quality Education in the late 1970s (Wood, 1990).

Foundation activities offer businesses and individuals an opportunity to support public education without devoting large amounts of time. On the other hand, this banking or "checkwriting" mode of philanthropy (McLaughlin, 1988) falls short of broader partnership goals because it does not directly involve donors in school activities. For this reason, intermediary organizations such as PEFNet try to reduce the distance between donors and recipient schools. For example, when the John Hancock Insurance Company donated $1 million through the Boston COMPACT, company executives served on a committee to review teachers' proposals for the use of grants. McLaughlin (1988) concluded, "These intermediary organizations thus foster knowledge, understanding, and identification, rather than alienation or distancing from the public schools" (p. 69). This observation suggests that the nature and extent of donors' involvement, like those of volunteers, are as important to school improvement as is the amount of the donation.

Linkages between donors as partners with schools are likely to improve as public school foundations are established for specific school districts and schools. According to Havens (2001), the number of public school foundations has grown and probably exceeds 3000. Moreover, nearly every school district in Florida and Oklahoma has a foundation. Some schools individually have foundations in San Diego, California, and Pocatello, Idaho. Addonizio (1998) found that 153 foundations were established by school districts in Michigan to increase revenue and support school–community linkages. Indeed, as we noted in our discussion of partnerships, the trend in expanding local resources through foundations is toward establishing relationships with the community that involve human and social resources rather than just money.

Voluntarism

Parents, community residents, and other individuals directly support schools when they volunteer their time and ideas. Over 16 percent of the adults responding to a survey conducted nationally by the Gallup Organization in 1992 reported that they had volunteered services to schools during the past year. This figure was second only to the 28 percent volunteering in religious organizations (National Center for Education Statistics, 1995, p. 308). In 1996, 39.6 percent of parents reported that they had volunteered at school. Private schools fared better with these volunteer parents, with 66.4 percent of parents volunteering as compared to 35.4 percent of parents in the public schools (National Center for Education Statistics, 2001, p. 30).

In enacting the Goals 2000: Educate America Act in 1994, Congress affirmed the importance of building closer relationships with parents. This goal expanded the goals originally adopted by the nation's governors: "Every school will promote partnerships that will increase parental involvement and participation in promoting the social, emotional, and academic growth of children." Just as the role of partnerships and foundations has changed in recent years, so too has schools' involvement of volunteers.

Brown (1998) defined school *voluntarism*, or benevolence, as follows: "the donation of time, from a person external to a school, to a school itself. It implies no certain return but it requires a positive interest on the part of the donor for the welfare of the student(s)" (p. 27). People's motivations for giving freely of their time and money vary widely, but schools stand to benefit from this altruism. Brown advocated voluntarism as an opportunity to lessen three problems facing schools: the paucity of resources available at the school level to educate children; the problem of autonomy—the inability to make school-level decisions to address local priorities; and the problem of integration—the need to provide sufficient care or social support especially for students. He also viewed voluntarism to be a substantial part of school structure and spoke of the *voluntary pub-*

lic school. Brown (1998) defined such a school as "one that is mainly supported by public funds but receives a substantial amount of its resources in the form of gifts" (p. 95). He proposes that gifts supply 10 percent of school resources.

Voluntarism appears in diverse forms as individuals and groups lend invaluable support for instruction, extracurricular activities, and fund-raising efforts. Parents, college students, and senior citizens become involved in classrooms and field trips, reducing the pupil-to-adult ratio so that greater individual attention can be given to students. Booster clubs lend support to athletic teams, band and choral groups, and debate and drama activities. The Parent–Teachers Association was initiated in 1897 and is today the largest voluntary organization in the country (Brown, 1998). It supports schools in numerous ways, including sponsoring carnivals and saving grocery receipts and coupons to acquire instructional and playground equipment. In an innovative approach, the Chapel Hill–Carrboro, North Carolina, school district benefits from substantial proceeds of stores that sell donated clothing and furniture. Each school receives a portion of these funds for discretionary purposes. Allocations are based on student enrollments as well as the number of volunteer hours posted by parents and students from respective buildings.

The Dedicated Older Volunteers in Educational Service (DOVES) coordinates activities in which Springfield, Massachusetts, residents serve as tutors, mentors, guest speakers, and library assistants in the public schools (Gray, 1984). The Golden Sage program in Pottstown, Pennsylvania, integrates senior citizens into school activities and provides them with a $500 school tax deduction (Ziegler, 2001). This program begins with senior citizens working for the tax deduction, but then many seniors remain in the school as volunteers. A recent study of fifty-seven elementary schools that was conducted by Brent (2000) revealed that 14 percent of volunteers were age fifty-six and over.

In recent years, voluntarism has been encouraged to create opportunities for community members to affect instructional goals and management efficiency. Advisory or decision-making committees and strategic planning teams rely on elected representatives or persons who are appointed by school administrators because of their particular expertise or positions of leadership in the community. Residents share their expertise in staff development programs. Corporations lend executives to give advice on management practices or conduct performance audits. Brown (1990) observed that additional local resources strengthen school site management: "voluntarism may be regarded as a variation on the theme of decentralization since it permits discretionary decision making with private resources in a similar way that school-based management permits flexibility with public dollars" (p. 1). In addition, by giving greater responsibility to parents and other volunteers, schools are able to close the growing distance between schools and homes (Sandfort, 1987; Brown, 1998). Principals who participated in Brent's (2000) study overwhelmingly maintained that volunteers benefit schools by improving relationships with the community (98 percent).

Successful, institutionalized volunteer programs share a number of characteristics (Gray, 1984). The superintendent, school board, and business leaders give strong and visible support. This support includes the formal adoption of a policy of support, which then helps school staff overcome traditional barriers to voluntarism. A systemwide manager coordinates volunteer services and facilitates information sharing. Building-level coordinators assess needs and identify potential resource people. The emphasis is on attracting people who bring personal talents and commitment, rather than on procuring money. There are many ways for volunteers to assist in instruction, counseling of pupils, and school management. Collaborative, long-range planning involves volunteers in seeking ways to improve schools. Unfortunately, many volunteer programs that have been implemented across the country do not share these institutionalized characteristics. Specifically, well-developed training programs for volunteer tutors, instructional materials for tutors and students, and guidelines for evaluation of tutoring programs are lacking in many places (Wasik, 1997).

The expansion of voluntarism and the influx of innovations in this area continue. In fact, what began as attempts to increase monetary resources for schools has been overtaken by human resources in the multiple forms of labor, expertise, and community building. Evidence is mounting that voluntarism connects parents to schools and schools to communities in mutually reciprocating ways. Business partnerships with schools increasingly build networks of expertise, coordination, and community engagement through donations of employee and executive time rather than donations of money, equipment, and supplies. Even the progress made through and with school foundations plays down the detached-donor mentality and emphasizes donors as stakeholders and members of the schooling community. It is important to remember, however, that whereas the nonpecuniary benefits of voluntarism are evident, its economic consequences must be carefully considered (King & Swanson, 1990; Swanson, 2000).

Benefits and Costs of Partnership Activities

To appraise these activities fairly, we must weigh the many benefits derived from greater involvement of the private sector and volunteers in schools against the potential costs to public education. Our discussion of partnerships, foundations, and voluntarism notes such returns as enriched programs, academic learning, parental advocacy, and political support. However, some suggest that these gains are concentrated in wealthy school districts. They say that privatization may negatively affect current revenue sources and decisions about public education.

It is difficult to determine the monetary value of many partnership and volunteer activities. Weisbrod (1988) valued volunteer efforts devoted to nonprofit organizations, including schools, as worth 50 percent more than the amount of money donated. Wilson and Rossman (1986) suggested that involving the community, opening schools to other organizations, and building political support across constituencies are more important than financial supplements to school budgets:

> It builds commitment and loyalty. It creates a special identity for the school that includes the surrounding community. The ethic of mutual caring that is created multiplies the effectiveness of the school and integrates the school into its community. (p. 708)

Opening schools to the community improves relationships and contributes to *social capital*, which consists of the diverse social relationships that foster children's growth and development (Coleman, 1990). Schools, families, and society generally benefit from investments in social capital as they gain in productivity from greater investments in the development of human capital. Coleman and Hoffer (1987) discussed this concept as it enriches private schools' capabilities:

> The social capital that has value for a young person's development does not reside merely in the set of common values held by parents who choose to send their children to the same private school. It resides in the functional community, the actual social relationships that exist among parents, in the closure exhibited by this structure of relations and in the parents' relations with the institutions of the community. (pp. 225–226)

In a similar manner, partnerships and voluntarism can pay large dividends in public schools regardless of the socioeconomic backgrounds of children served. Coleman (1991) asserted that social capital grows in public schools in which parents join educators to establish standards for behavior, enforce rules that are consistent among families, and support one another's children. Brown (1998) noted the presence of *rich schools in poor neighborhoods*—that is, schools that have considerable amounts of physical, human, and social capital: "In general, it appears that high levels of voluntarism tend to occur under two conditions—when neighborhoods are upper-middle-income and/or when schools are administered to welcome and support volunteers" (pp. 54–55). There must also be efforts to make opportunities available for families of disadvantaged children to volunteer:

> [T]here is strong evidence that low-income and poorly educated parents *want* to play a role in their children's education. Indeed, these parents seek a role even when they believe that their children will fail or do poorly in school. Conventional wisdom to the contrary, parents who lack knowledge themselves do not necessarily lack interest in the schools their children attend. What's lacking, in most schools and school districts, [is] appropriate strategies or structures for involving low-income parents. (McLaughlin & Shields, 1987, p. 157)

As the public's feelings of responsibility and ownership for *their* schools grow, the local resource base expands, schools have greater opportunities for improvement, and students are the ultimate beneficiaries. The movement to restructure schools is premised on such hopes.

On the other hand, although these many material and intangible benefits may be enticing, the literature on partnerships suggests three problem areas. Substantially increased reliance on partnerships, foundations, and voluntarism can have detrimental effects on current revenue sources, decisions about resource use, and equity goals.

First of all, if citizens and businesses view requests for additional donations of goods and services from the private sector as another tax, although voluntary, to support schools, one consequence may be opposition to various forms of public support. If increased voluntarism means that fewer certified professionals or teaching assistants are required for program delivery and fewer office staff are needed, teachers unions and support staff unions might express concerns about possible displacements by unpaid workers (Brown, 1993, p. 197). Partnerships may enable school systems to ease the burden on local taxes. Similarly, states may consider these additional local resources in reducing state aid allocations. School systems may factor school fund-raising efforts into their distributions of money or personnel allotments among schools. These developments would reduce the incentive for districts and schools to obtain external support (King & Swanson, 1990).

Although support from traditional sources could be reduced if there was substantial private support in the future, the above concerns may be overstated. Corporate involvement is minimal in relation to the total financial support of public education. Community and individual involvement in schools is on too low a level to threaten traditional sources. Rather than negatively affecting support, additional monetary and human resources tapped through partnership activities can satisfy teachers' desires for more instructional materials, smaller classes, and released time for team planning and participation in decision making. Because the many benefits of partnerships exceed any potential threats to current resources and staffing patterns, there is no reason to discourage schools from seeking and accepting private-sector involvement.

Second, some worry that increased support of public schooling by individuals and the private sector may give these elements undue influence over educational decisions to the detriment of traditional school board governance. Meno (1984) warned that as nontraditional finance activities grow, educators and policy makers will have to decide whether fiscal benefits are worth the potential modifications in present practices. Indeed, greater parental involvement in decision making can lead to frustrating and time-consuming efforts to reach consensus, to an erosion of trust in professionals, and to an atmosphere of fear among teachers (Yaffe, 1994). In contrast, McLaughlin (1988) argued that corporations respect educators' expertise and that donors, primarily small businesses, are unable to influence school decisions.

Business interests will be represented in formal processes of school- or district-level decision making because of their partnership activities, just as they continue to be expressed on governing boards. It might be argued that direct and indirect pressure to alter educational policy to receive partnership assistance is not necessarily negative. Educators need to be comfortable in deciding whether it is advantageous to form partnerships or receive gifts, especially when they have concerns about effects on school policy and curricula. To limit conflicts of interest, there should be school- and district-level consideration of the relationship between the acceptance of goods and services and subsequent decisions about their use. This concern, however, is not sufficient reason for schools to discourage participation by the private sector.

The third problem area—equity—is of greater concern than the potential effects of partnerships and voluntarism on traditional resources or decision making. Schools and school districts differ in the opportunities they have to form business partnerships and in their abilities to raise funds within communities (Monk, 1990). Just as varying property valuations have enabled school districts to raise different levels of tax revenue, variations in socioeconomic status give school districts and schools within them unequal settings to obtain private resources. If partnerships become a potent force for raising funds in the future, disparities in educational programs and extracurricular activities will be perpetuated. Wood (1990) discusses privatization in relation to the goal of equalizing educational opportunities:

To allow public school districts to pursue outside sources of fiscal support, however noble in the intent to support public education, is to allow the districts to engage in *laissez-faire* self interest. . . . This agenda is indifferent to local resources or lack thereof, the educational or fiscal needs, and the allocation of resources to this goal. Within this system, every school district is capable of seeking to maximize its present assets in a manner competitive with all other school districts. (p. 60)

Even though many small and rural school districts cannot take advantage of private resources to the same degree as larger and wealthier districts, potential effects on equity goals might be overstated. McLaughlin (1988) commented that dollars made available through these activities are small in comparison with total school district budgets and do not underwrite inequalities of the scale that result in judicial challenges (see Chapter 10). Where the scale of private resources warrants intervention, Swanson (2000) contended that state distributions of aid to districts as well as district distributions to schools could be adjusted by policy makers. If the focus of partnership assistance is entirely on individual schools, they will benefit to very different degrees. However, not all private-sector supports should target the individual school as recipient. Some activities and foundations are more appropriately maintained at centralized—district, regional, or state—levels to permit distributions that are sensitive to equity goals. For example, the Los Angeles Educational Partnership gives bonus points to applications for grants from teachers in inner-city schools and supports programs that benefit the district as a whole through workshops, incentive programs for students, and math/science collaboratives. These arrangements hold promise for other districts as they allocate funds among restructured schools.

School improvement depends in large part on the active involvement of communities and businesses, regardless of the amount of monetary support they are able to provide. Educators are also called to action to participate with the private sector, especially as business interests are communicated through legislatures and school boards to restructure public education. Every school and district has the potential to benefit from partners and volunteers.

SUMMARY

School districts have many opportunities to expand their resources beyond traditional reliance on the property tax and other local taxes. User fees apply a privilege-based charge to students for some portion of the costs of services and activities. Careful planning and management of the flow of money through school district accounts at times requires borrowing to increase available cash. At other times, this management frees idle cash to be invested. Partnerships, foundations, and volunteers enhance monetary and human resources as well as offering needed political support as educators reconsider the role and structure of public education.

Schools that want to charge students for instructional materials, elective courses, extracurricular activities, transportation, and other services should consider the legal, financial, and educational implications. Fees raise concerns about inequities in access to free public education. They limit opportunities for all children to participate in curricular or extracurricular programs. They also bring administrative costs. Fees are likely to be supported in the courts when they apply to activities that are not necessary and integral to the educational process and when the fee policy includes a confidential waiver that enables children of low-income families to participate.

Districts can add considerably to their revenue by planning their short- or long-term investments around the flow of revenue and nonrevenue money into the district in relation to future expenditures. It also makes sense to minimize checking account balances and to pool small accounts to maximize investments.

Districts select strategies for investing periodic surplus funds according to their potential yield, the safety or amount of risk entailed, and their liquidity (the ease of accessing funds without loss of interest).

Nonrevenue money obtained through short- and long-term borrowing helps districts maintain an even flow of funds and construct school facilities. Short-term borrowing through tax and revenue anticipation notes enables districts to pay employees and outside vendors on schedule when there is a revenue deficit. When pay-as-you-go financing is not feasible, capital outlay financing to retire general obligation bonds permits the construction or remodeling of facilities and the purchase of equipment. However, basing capital outlay financing on local property valuations results in large disparities among communities in the nature of school buildings. State-sponsored loan programs, direct grants of state funds, and public bonding authorities ease the burdens on local tax bases and help districts reach the goal of providing adequate, if not equal, educational opportunities.

Tax limitation and education reform movements have encouraged districts to garner private resources through partnerships, educational foundations, and volunteers. These activities can yield discretionary money and other goods and services for schools. They also enrich linkages among schools, businesses, community agencies, and parents. The potential for enlarging the local resource base is substantial. The meaningful involvement of individuals and groups can improve instruction and school leadership. These activities may be beneficial in many predominantly urban and suburban districts. However, some people worry that supplements to school resources might not reach relatively poor and small school systems.

The chapters that follow in Part III examine the principles and mechanisms for transferring funds raised through state and federal sources to local authorities for the operation of schools.

ACTIVITIES

1. Discuss how the various financial and human resources presented in this chapter might expand the ability of schools and school districts to improve schools.

2. Investigate the restrictions that state policies place on charging fees for required courses, elective offerings, and extracurricular activities in your state. If fees are permitted, determine the extent to which students pay fees to support various school programs and activities in several districts that differ by size and wealth.

3. Discuss the management of cash flow, including the timing of borrowing and investments, with a school district finance officer. What opportunities exist for school-level decisions to borrow and invest funds?

4. In what ways do state-imposed limits on borrowing and investments strengthen financial management practices? In what ways do these limitations reduce the flexibility that districts need in order to maximize the benefits of these cash flow strategies?

5. Debate the appropriateness of the state or federal government assuming a larger role in financing capital outlay.

6. Investigate to what extent private resources supplement schools and school districts in a given locality or state. What demographic or organizational conditions present within schools appear to be related to the amount of resources gained from partnerships, foundations, and voluntarism?

7. Determine how extensively business partnerships are involved in a given school district. To what extent do partnerships exhibit the four characteristics of "new style" involvement identified by Mann (1987a): a coordinating structure, multiple purposes, multiple players, and stability?

REFERENCES

Addonizio, M. F. (1998). Private funding of public schools: Local education foundations in Michigan. *Educational Considerations, 26,* 1–7.

Addonizio, M. F. (2000). Salvaging fiscal control: New sources of local revenue for public schools. In N. D. Theobald & B. Malen (Eds.), *Balancing local control and state responsibility for K–12 education* (pp. 245–278). Larchmont, NY: Eye on Education.

Alamo Heights Independent School District v. *State Board of Education,* 790 F.2d 1153 (5th Cir. 1986).

Ambroiggio v. *Board of Education,* 427 N.E.2d 1027 (IL App. Ct. 1981).

Annenberg Institute for School Reform. (1995). *Walter H. Annenberg's challenge to the nation: A progress report.* Providence, RI: Author.

Arcadia Unified School District v. *Department of Education,* 5 Cal. Rptr.2d 545 (1992).

Attorney General v. *East Jackson Public Schools,* 372 N.W.2d 638 (MI Ct. App. 1985).

Augenblick, J. (1977). *Systems of state support for school district capital expenditure.* Report No. F76–8. Denver, CO: Education Commission of the States.

Ballew, P. (1987, November). How to start a school foundation. *Executive Educator, 9,* 26–28.

Bauman, P. C. (1995). Searching for alternative revenues: The political implications of school impact fees. *Journal of School Business Management, 7,* 38–49.

Bauman, P., & Crampton, F. E. (1995, July). When school districts become entrepreneurs: Opportunity or danger? *NCSL State Legislative Report, 20.*

Bergholz, D. (1992). The public education fund. *Teachers College Record, 93,* 516–522.

Bond v. *Ann Arbor School District,* 178 N. W. 2d 484 (MI Sup. Ct. 1970).

Brent, B. O. (2000). Do classroom volunteers benefit schools? *Principal, 80,* 36–43.

Brown, D. J. (1993). Benevolence in Canadian public schools. In S. L. Jacobson & R. Berne, (Eds.), *Reforming education: The emerging systemic approach* (pp. 191–208). Thousand Oaks, CA: Corwin.

Brown, D. J. (1990). *Voluntarism for public schools.* Paper presented at the annual conference of the American Education Finance Association, Las Vegas.

Brown, D. J. (1998). *Schools with heart: Voluntarism and public education.* Boulder, CO: Westview.

Brown, D. J., & Bouman, C. (1994). *Policies on fees in public schools.* Vancouver, Canada: University of British Columbia.

Camp, W. E., & Salmon, R. G. (1985, Spring). Public school bonding corporations financing public elementary and secondary school facilities. *Journal of Education Finance, 10,* 495–503.

Cardiff v. *Bismark Public School District,* 263 N.W.2d 105 (ND Sup. Ct. 1978).

Coleman, J. S., & Hoffer, T. (1987). *Public and private high schools: The impact of communities.* New York: Basic Books.

Coleman, J. S. (1991). *Parental involvement in education.* OERI Document #65-000-00459-3. Washington, DC: U.S. Government Printing Office.

Coleman, J. S. (1990). *Foundations of social theory.* Cambridge, MA: Harvard University Press.

Cooper, T. (1996). Buses and advertising: A unique way to raise funds. *School Business Affairs, 62* (7), 31–34.

Crampton, F. E., Thompson, D. C., & Hagey, J. M. (2001). Creating and sustaining school capacity in the twenty-first century: Funding a physical environment conducive to student learning. *Journal of Education Finance, 27,* 633–652.

Dayton, J., & McCarthy, M. (Fall, 1992). User fees in public schools: Are they legal? *Journal of Education Finance, 18,* 127–141.

Dembowski, F. L. (1986). Cash management. In G. C. Hentschke, *School business management: A comparative perspective* (pp. 214–245). Berkeley, CA: McCutchan.

Dembowski, F. L., & Davey, R. D. (1986). School district financial management and banking. In R. C. Wood (Ed.), *Principles of school business management* (pp. 237–260). Reston, VA: ASBO International.

Doyle, D. P. (1989, November). Endangered species: Children of promise. *BusinessWeek,* Special Supplement, E4-E135.

Doyle, D. P. (1994, October). The role of private sector management in public education. *Phi Delta Kappan, 76,* 128–132.

Education Writers Association. (1989). *Wolves at the schoolhouse door: An investigation of the condition of public school buildings.* Washington, DC: Author.

Glenn, J. M. L. (2001). The giving and the taking: Business–education partnerships come of age. *Business Education Forum, 55,* 6–13.

Gold, S. D., Smith, D. M., & Lawton, S. B. (Eds.). (1995). *Public school finance programs of the United States and Canada, 1993–94.* Albany, NY: American Education Finance Association and The Center for the Study of the States.

Gray, S. T. (1984, February). How to create a successful school/community partnership. *Phi Delta Kappan, 65,* 405–409.

Gross, T. L., (1988). *Partners in education: How colleges can work with schools to improve teaching and learning.* San Francisco: Jossey-Bass.

Hamm, R. W., & Crosser, R. W. (1991, June). School fees: Whatever happened to the notion of a free public education? *American School Board Journal, 178,* 29–31.

Hamrick, F. (1993, April). Private-sector coalitions and state-level education reform. *Policy Bulletin.* Bloomington, IN: Indiana Education Policy Center.

Hansen, S. (1991). *Schoolhouses in the Red.* Reston, VA: American Association of School Administrators.

Hartzell v. *Connell,* 679 P.2d 35, 201 Cal. Rptr. 601 (CA Sup. Ct. 1984).

Havens, M. M. (2000). *Dream big: Creating and growing your school foundation.* Rockville, MD.

Havens, M. M. (2001). Beyond money: Benefits of an education foundation. *School Administrator, 58,* 16–21.

Hess, G. A. (1987). *1985 education survey.* Chicago: Donors Forum of Chicago.

Hoyt, K. (1991, February). Education reform and relationships between the private sector and education: A call for integration. *Phi Delta Kappan, 72,* 450–453.

Inman, D. (1984, Fall). Bridging education to industry: Implications for financing education. *Journal of Education Finance, 10,* 271–277.

Johns, R. L., Morphet, E. L., & Alexander, K. (1983). *The economics and financing of education.* (4th ed.). Englewood Cliffs, NJ: Prentice-Hall.

Jones, T. H., & Amalfitano, J. L. (1994). *America's gamble: Public school finance and state lotteries.* Lancaster, PA: Technomic.

Kadrmas v. *Dickinson Public Schools,* 487 U.S. 450 (1988).

Keller, E. C., & Hartman, W. T. (2001). Prevailing wage rates: The effects on school construction costs, levels of taxation, and state reimbursements. *Journal of Education Finance, 27,* 713–728.

Kowalski, T. J. (2001). *Planning and managing school facilities* (2nd ed.). Westport, CT: Greenwood.

King, R. A., & MacPhail-Wilcox, B. (1988, Spring). Bricks-and-mortar reform in North Carolina: The state assumes a larger role in financing school construction. *Journal of Education Finance, 13*, 374–381.

King, R. A., & Swanson, A. D. (1990, Summer). Resources for restructured schools: Partnerships, foundations and volunteerism. *Planning and Changing, 21*, 94–107.

Lief, B. (1992). The New York City case study: The private sector and the reform of public education. *Teachers College Record, 93*, 523–535.

Lindsay, D. (1994, December 14). Counting their losses in wealthy Orange County. *Education Week, 14*, 3.

Lorenc v. *Call*, 789 P.2d 46 (Utah App. 1990).

Mann, D. (1987a, October). Business involvement and public school improvement, part 1. *Phi Delta Kappan, 69*, 123–128.

Mann, D. (1987b, November). Business involvement and public school improvement, part 2. *Phi Delta Kappan, 69*, 228–232.

Marshall v. *School District*, 553 P.2d 784 (CO Sup. Ct. 1976).

Mathews, D. (1996). *Is there a public for public schools?* Dayton, OH: Kettering Foundation.

Mathews, D. (1997). The lack of a public for public schools. *Phi Delta Kappan, 78*, 740–743.

McKersie, B., & Palaich, R. (1994, May 4). Philanthropy and systemic reform: Finding a cross-sector blend of risk-taking and political will. *Education Week, 13*, pp. 33, 48.

McLaughlin, M. L. (1988). Business and the public schools: New patterns of support. In D. H. Monk & J. Underwood (Eds.), *Microlevel school finance: Issues and implications for policy* (pp. 63–80). Cambridge, MA: Ballinger.

McLaughlin, M. W., & Shields, P. M. (1987, October). Involving low-income parents in the schools: A role for policy? *Phi Delta Kappan, 69*, 156–160.

Meno, L. (1984). Sources of alternative revenue. In L. D. Webb & V. D. Mueller. (Eds.), *Managing limited resources: New demands on public school management* (pp. 129–146). Cambridge, MA: Ballinger.

Monk, D. H. (1990). *Educational finance: An economic approach*. New York: McGraw–Hill.

Monk, D. H., & Brent, B. O. (1997). *Raising money for education: A guide to the property tax*. Thousand Oaks, CA: Corwin.

Muro, J. J. (1995). *Creating and funding educational foundations: A guide for local school districts*. Boston, MA: Allyn & Bacon.

National Center for Education Statistics (NCES). (1993). *Digest of educational statistics*. Washington, DC: Office of Educational Research and Improvement.

National Center for Education Statistics (NCES). (1995). *Digest of educational statistics*. Washington, DC: Office of Educational Research and Improvement.

National Center for Education Statistics (NCES). (2001). *Digest of education statistics, 2000*. Washington, DC: Office of Educational Research and Improvement.

Navarro, M. S., & Natalicio, D. S. (1999). Closing the achievement gap in El Paso: Collaboration for K–16 renewal. *Phi Delta Kappan, 80*, 597–601.

Neill, G. (1983). *The local education foundation: A new way to raise money for schools*. NASSP Special Report. Reston, VA: National Association of Secondary School Principals.

Nesbit, W. B. (1987, February). The local education foundation: What is it, how is it established? *NASSP Bulletin, 71*, 85–89.

Norton v. *Board of Education*, 553 P.2d 1277 (N.M. 1976).

Olson, L. (1988, April 20). Public-school foundation effort surpasses expectations. *Education Week, 7*, 4.

Ortiz, F. I. (1994). *School housing: Planning and designing educational facilities*. Albany, NY: State University of New York Press.

Paulson v. *Minidoka County School District*, 463 P.2d 935 (Idaho Sup. Ct. 1970).

Pijanowski, J. C., & Monk, D. H. (1996). Alternative school revenue sources: There are many fish in the sea. *School Business Affairs, 62*, 4–10.

Ray, J. R., Hack, W. G., & Candoli, I. C. (2001). *School business administration: A planning approach*. Boston, MA: Allyn & Bacon.

Piele, P. K., & Hall, J. S. (1973). *Budgets, bonds and ballots: Voting behavior in school financial issues*. Lexington, MA: Heath.

Salmon, R., & Thomas, S. (1981, Summer). Financing public school facilities in the 80s. *Journal of Education Finance, 7*, 88–109.

Salmon, R., Dawson, C., Lawton, S. & Johns, T. (Eds.). (1988). *Public school finance programs of the*

United States and Canada, 1986–87. Blacksburg, VA: American Education Finance Association.

Sammon, G., & Becton, M. (2001). Principles of partnerships. *Principal Leadership, 1*, 32–35.

San Antonio Independent School District v. *Rodriguez*, 411 U.S. 1 (1973).

Sandfort, J. A. (1987, February). Putting parents in their place in public schools. *NASSP Bulletin, 71*, 99–103.

Sielke, C. C. (2001). Funding school infrastructure needs across the states. *Journal of Education Finance, 27*, 653–662.

Sneed v. *Greensboro City Board of Education*, 264 S.E.2d 106 (NC Sup. Ct. 1980).

Sommerfeld, M. (1994, September 7). ARCO cuts unsettle corporate-giving field. *Education Week, 14*, 12.

Sommerfeld, M. (1995, September 27). Corporate giving predicted to increase 3% this year. *Education Week, 15*, 7.

Sutton v. *Cadillac Area Public Schools*, 323 N.W.2d 582 (MI Ct. App. 1982).

Swanson, A. D. (2000). Book review of D. J. Brown, Schools with heart: Voluntarism and public education (Boulder, CO: Westview, 1998). *Educational Administration Quarterly, 36* (4), 633–642.

Thompson, D. C., & Wood, R. C. (2001). *Money and schools* (2nd ed.). Larchmont, NY: Eye on Education.

Thompson, D. C., Wood, R. C., & Honeyman, D. S. (1994). *Fiscal leadership for schools: Concepts and practices*. White Plains, NY: Longman.

Timpane, M. (1984, February). Business has rediscovered the public schools. *Phi Delta Kappan, 65*, 389–392.

U.S. Department of Commerce, Bureau of the Census. (1980). *Finances of public school systems in 1977–78*. Series GF78, No. 10. Washington, DC: U.S. Government Printing Office.

U.S. Department of Commerce, Bureau of the Census. (1988). *Finances of public school systems in 1985–86*. Series GF86, No. 10. Washington, DC: U.S. Government Printing Office.

U.S. Department of Commerce, Bureau of the Census (1993). *Public education finances: 1990–91*, Series GF/91-10. Washington, DC: U.S. Government Printing Office.

U.S. Department of Commerce, Bureau of the Census (2001). *United States state and local government finances by level of government: 1989–1999*. Washington, DC: U.S. Government Printing Office.

U.S. Department of Commerce, Bureau of the Census (2000). *Public education finances: 1997*, Series GC97(4)-1. Washington, DC: U.S. Government Printing Office.

National Center for Education Statistics [NCES]. (2001). *Digest of education statistics, 2000*. U.S. Department of Education, Washington, DC: U.S. Government Printing Office.

U.S. General Accounting Office (1995a). *School facilities: America's schools not designed or equipped for 21st century*, GAO/HEHS-95-95. Washington, DC: Author.

U.S. General Accounting Office (1995b). *School facilities: Condition of America's schools*, GAO/HEHS-95-61. Washington, DC: Author.

Useem, E., & Neild, R. C. (1995, July). Partnerships. *Urban Education, 30*.

Washington v. *Salisbury*, 306 S.E.2d 600 (SC Sup. Ct. 1983).

Wasik, B. A. (1997). Volunteer tutoring programs: Do we know what works? *Phi Delta Kappan, 79*, 282–287.

Wassmer, R. W., & Fisher, R. C. (2000, February). *Interstate variation in the use of fees to fund K–12 public education*. Unpublished manuscript in review. California State University at Sacramento and Michigan State University.

Weisbrod, B. (1988). *The nonprofit economy*. Cambridge, MA: Harvard University Press.

Wilson, B. L., & Rossman, G. B. (1986, June). Collaborative links with the community: Lessons from exemplary secondary schools. *Phi Delta Kappan, 67*, 708–711.

Wood, R. C., Thompson, D. C., Picus, L. O., & Tharpe, D. I. (1995). *Principles of school business management* (2nd ed.). Reston, VA: ASBO International.

Wood, R. C. (1990). New revenues for education at the local level. In J. E. Underwood & D. A. Verstegen (Eds.), *The impacts of litigation and legislation on public school finance: Adequacy, equity, and excellence* (pp. 59–74). New York: Harper & Row.

Yaffe, E. (1994, May). Not just cupcakes anymore: A study of community involvement. *Phi Delta Kappan, 75*, 697–704.

Ziegler, W. (2001). School partnerships: Something for everyone. *Principal Leadership, 2*, 68–70.

part **III**

Allocating State and Federal Funds for Schools

We began this exploration of school finance policy with a discussion of the extent to which society should become involved in the provision of education. Our attention turned in Part II to revenue sources, the means by which federal, state, and local governments acquire monies to support public services. We now focus on the policies available to higher levels of government for distributing dollars to school systems. Part III explores this flow of funds from state and federal governments to finance school programs at the local level.

Chapter 7 opens with a discussion of the rationale for intergovernmental transfer payments and of differences among general, block grant, and categorical aid programs. State-level policy is the primary focus of the analysis. We present general models and actual state funding plans to illustrate alternative ways of structuring aid formulas. Chapter 8 refines the discussion of state policy by detailing how formulas for making allocations take characteristics of students and school districts into account. Finally, in Chapter 9 we discuss the influence that federal government exerts on educational policy through mandates and financial incentives.

Chapter 7

INTERGOVERNMENTAL TRANSFER PAYMENTS AND MODELS FOR ALLOCATING STATE AID

Issues and Questions

- *Achieving High Standards with Equity and Efficiency*: In what ways do higher levels of government promote these goals as they fund public education?
- *Rationale for Intergovernmental Transfers*: Why do state and federal governments finance educational programs that are provided at the local level?
- *General Aid, Block Grants and Categorical Aid*: To what extent should federal and state governments dictate the purposes of grants-in-aid and oversee their use at the local level?
- *Adequacy, Division of Fiscal Responsibilities, Capacity, and Effort*: Why and how do state aid formulas differ in their consideration of these four concepts?
- *General Models of Financial Aid Formulas*: What structures have states adopted to allocate funds for school programs and operations?

In this chapter we discuss policies that govern transfers of funds from state and federal governments to school districts. We explore the rationale for these grants-in-aid and the extent to which policies may dictate purposes or pupils to be served. We discuss a number of models for basic school support and review their application by selected states. We contrast these models in terms of how they consider local property wealth and tax effort.

JUSTIFICATION FOR TRANSFER PAYMENTS

In Chapter 3 we introduced the division and overlap of responsibilities among multiple layers of government in the context of taxation. Some societal needs, such as highways and national defense, are appropriately provided through higher levels of government. However, this centralization of authority is not always justified. The benefits of local control over such public services as law enforcement within communities justify decentralized delivery. Transfer payments channel money raised at federal and state levels to localities. This revenue sharing serves a number of purposes in financing schools.

First, state governments have a constitutional responsibility for creating and maintaining systems of public education. Accordingly, state legislatures outline how schools are to be financed throughout the state and typically provide about half of the money for their support. In contrast, the United States Constitution does not place a similar burden on Congress. The Tenth Amendment reserves responsibility for education to the states. However, the Constitution's General Welfare clause and the Fifth and Fourteenth Amendments permit federal intervention when the national interest warrants legislative action. For example, the federal government provides financial support for national defense, enacts legislation to protect civil rights, and directs financial assistance for selected educational programs (see Chapter 9).

Second, leadership and financial assistance from higher levels of government can ensure that essential services, including public education, are made available throughout the nation or state. Theobald and Bardzell (2001) differentiate among assistance-oriented, persuasive, and regulatory approaches. In the first of these strategies, federal and state governments provide financial incentives to enable local governments voluntarily to sponsor programs that conform to national or state goals. Virtually all federal school aid is of this nature. If local governments depended solely on their own revenue-generating abilities, then many decisions about the level and quality of services would reflect expected returns to the locality rather than to the larger society. Financial aid programs, for example, help define and reach equity goals by encouraging schools to expand educational opportunities.

In the persuasive approach, the president or governors make use of the "bully pulpit" to urge changes in local policies and educational practices without any transfer of funds or additional personnel. Similarly, no funds accompany many mandates issued under the regulatory approach, but this strategy requires local governments to do something they might not have done on their own or might have done inadequately. Persuasion and mandates play a particularly critical role in challenging localities to raise the standards all students are expected to meet. First (1992) stressed this role in terms of holding schools accountable for educational outcomes:

> The battles for equal access to education and equal treatment in U.S. schools have been fought, and to a large extent, won. The battle for equal outcomes is now being fought, as is the battle for excellence in education, but it must be excellence for all, and herein lies the importance of the states' role. (p. 134)

Third, a central government (state or federal) can take advantage of broader tax bases and economies of scale to improve the effectiveness and efficiency of schools in all localities. Allocations make possible a higher basic level of education, expand educational opportunities, and broaden course offerings in communities that may have little tax base or are unwilling to raise sufficient revenue.

In many ways, state and federal leadership and financial resources can improve the quality of education. On the other hand, the mandates imposed without financial assistance, and the regulations that accompany some financial aid programs, are often viewed as unwarranted interventions into the affairs of local government. Rather than promoting efficiency and economies of scale, mandates may stifle educators' abilities to address particular needs of pupils and communities. Therefore, higher levels of government take varying approaches when legislators design financial aid policies. Sometimes they offer financial incentives to influence school programs. At other times they provide revenue without conditions so that school boards can respond to community priorities and school personnel can meet pupils' educational needs.

GENERAL AID, CATEGORICAL AID, AND BLOCK GRANTS

Transfer payments are described as general aid, categorical grants, or block grants, depending on the degree of latitude given to recipients. *General* financial aid flows from federal and state governments with few limitations on governing boards of municipalities and school districts. Local school boards and educators largely determine specific educational programs and related expenditures within broad guidelines. Later in this chapter, we describe the general aid that states allocate via basic finance formulas. This general aid accounts for the largest proportion of state support for school operations.

In contrast, a *categorical* aid program links grants to specific objectives of the government providing the funds. To qualify for such aid, a district or school must comply with program requirements. Thus, unlike general aid, categorical grants can be used only for a certain group of students (e.g., those with disabilities), a specific purpose (e.g., to improve literacy), or a particular project (e.g., construction of a school building).

Federal and state categorical aid is an important policy instrument to communicate legislative priorities. These appropriations restrict local control and constrain program design. For example, the federal government allocates money to broaden the educational opportunities of children who are economically disadvantaged or have disabilities. An *entitlement* program directs funds to school districts according to the number of qualifying pupils; no detailed application is required. In contrast, a *competitive* categorical grant requires school personnel to develop a proposal specifying program goals in relation to plans for spending funds. For example, a school improvement grant program may require applicants to include detailed plans for program delivery and evaluation in their proposals.

A categorical aid program brings about greater centralization of decision making and more complex administration at all levels. In place of local discretion, legislatures set priorities. State and federal bureaucracies then oversee programs and ensure that funds are used in accordance with legislative intent. They develop guidelines for entitlement programs, request and review proposals for competitive grants, monitor the use of money, and require appraisals of results. Nearly all federal aid to education is categorical in nature.

Administering categorical aid, particularly for competitive grants, is also far more involved for local officials than administering general operating aid. School personnel must maintain a separate account to restrict expenditures to designated programs and targeted groups. A large burden may be placed on project coordinators to show that grants are spent to *supplement,* rather than to *supplant* (replace), state and local revenue. Whereas general aid flows to schools each year with little administrative attention, many categorical aids call for annual applications, regular documentation of expenditures, and frequent program evaluations. Because the paperwork involved in administering competitive categorical aids places small and rural districts at a disadvantage in competing for funds, many categoricals are allocated as entitlement programs. In recent years, block grants have absorbed prior categoricals to reduce the burden, ease centralized control, and increase local discretion.

General aid and categorical grants occupy the ends of a continuum of funding types in terms of the degree of control by higher levels of government. *Block grants* define a middle ground. State and federal block grants allow a range of services within a broad set of government purposes. Requirements for planning, implementing, and assessing programs are also less distinct than those for categorical aid.

The federal government popularized the block grant approach when Congress combined a number of former categorical programs in the early 1980s. Chapter 2 of the Education Consolidation and Improvement Act of 1981 enhanced local control over federal programs (see Chapter 9). Under this block grant, states received funds according to their total number of pupils rather than through a competitive application process. In turn, state-developed formulas factored in enrollments as well as other measures of need in making allocations to school districts. This block grant program initially outlined several broad purposes. The 1994 revisions gave school district personnel even greater discretion in program design.

Local school boards, administrators, and teachers generally prefer unrestricted grants that minimize administrative processes and permit latitude to meet local priorities. However, special-interest groups and many educators are concerned about diluted programs under less restrictive approaches. They argue that policy intents should be defined at broader

state and federal levels. The political reality once favored equity goals through strict categorical funding. It turned in the 1980s and 1990s to support liberty and efficiency goals through block grants and greater local initiative. Clearly, the degree of control over the use of funds differentiates these three approaches for designing policies that transfer funds between government levels.

State finance policies direct general aid to school districts for most operating expenses. The remainder of this chapter focuses on state policy for distributing these funds through a finance formula. We discuss categorical aid and block grants more fully in Chapters 8 and 9.

MODELS FOR STATE FINANCE PROGRAMS

Funding formulas for allocating general state aid follow several prototypes, or models. Formulas evolved as state legislatures assumed a larger role in ensuring that all districts had resources to provide at least a minimal level of education. School finance formulas became increasingly complex as legislatures sought to equalize educational opportunities, achieve efficiency by attaining high standards at a reasonable cost to taxpayers, and respect local boards' and voters' desires to decide priorities for school programs.

The prototypes presented in this section depict the formula structures that blend local and state revenue to finance school operations. There are four key concepts that apply to all models: adequacy, division of fiscal responsibility, ability, and effort. *Adequacy* reflects whether the total amount of money available is sufficient to permit educators and students to meet high academic expectations (see Chapter 11). This support has traditionally been measured in terms of operating revenue per pupil or per classroom unit. The *division of fiscal responsibility* determines relative shares of state and local contributions toward the desired revenue or spending level. The *capacity*, or ability, of the community to raise taxes in support of education is defined as property valuation or personal income per pupil. Local *effort* often reflects the willingness of taxpayers to raise funds for schools. Effort is defined as the tax rate to be applied to the value of property or income. We present the general features of prototypes, sketch selected states' applications of several models, and suggest exercises and computer simulations to help readers understand how these four concepts are related to actual aid structures.

The primary finance approaches through which states fund basic school operations appear in Table 7.1 as they are presented by the National Center for Education Statistics.[1] In 1998–1999, a total of thirty-six states financed school districts through a foundation program. Five states employed a percentage equalization approach, and two followed a guaranteed tax base model. Four states adopted a full state funding model, and three states directed a flat amount of aid per pupil to districts. Six states with a flat grant or foundation plan also

TABLE 7.1.

States' Basic Support Programs, 1998–1999, and Per-Pupil Revenue and Percentage of Revenue by Source, 1999–2000

| State | Finance Program | Revenue | | Source of Revenue | | |
		Per Pupil	Rank	Federal (%)	State (%)	Local (%)
Alabama	FND	$ 5,596	47	10.4 %	64.5 %	25.0 %
Alaska	FND	8,694	8	12.5	63.6	23.9
Arizona	FND	5,170	48	7.3	49.2	43.5
Arkansas	FND	5,792	45	8.2	62.9	28.9
California	FND	7,284	25	7.7	62.9	29.4
Colorado	FND	6,039	42	5.5	44.6	49.9
Connecticut	PCT[b]	11,014	1	4.7	42.7	52.6
Delaware	FLT[c]	8,887	5	7.4	66.0	26.6
Florida	FND	7,453	21	8.1	50.8	41.1
Georgia	FND[d]	6,383	36	6.6	51.5	41.9
Hawaii	FULL	7,288	24	9.8	87.8	2.3
Idaho	FND	6,134	41	7.0	60.9	32.0
Illinois	FND	6,890	31	6.5	27.3	66.2
Indiana	GTB[e]	8,197	16	4.5	50.7	44.8
Iowa	FND	7,078	29	4.3	52.8	42.9
Kansas	FND	7,152	27	6.2	64.4	29.4
Kentucky	FND	7,316	23	8.0	63.2	28.8
Louisiana	FND[d]	6,354	38	11.7	50.8	37.5
Maine	PCT[b]	7,952	17	6.2	46.3	47.6
Maryland	FND	8,324	12	5.4	39.9	54.8
Massachusetts	FND	9,532	4	5.0	43.0	52.0
Michigan	FND	8,863	6	6.7	72.2	21.1
Minnesota	FND	8,307	13	4.7	60.0	35.3
Mississippi	FND	5,166	49	14.0	54.7	31.3
Missouri	FND[f]	7,348	22	6.8	37.7	55.5

(Continued)

TABLE 7.1.

(Continued)

State	Finance Program	Revenue Per Pupil	Rank	Federal (%)	State (%)	Local (%)
Montana	FND[d]	6,765	32	11.1	44.8	44.1
Nebraska	FND	6,608	34	5.3	43.3	51.5
Nevada	FND	6,654	33	5.0	30.5	64.5
New Hampshire	FND	7,185	26	3.7	8.5	87.8
New Jersey	FND	10,182	3	3.2	38.1	58.7
New Mexico	FULL	6,445	35	12.6	74.7	12.7
New York	PCT	10,745	2	6.6	45.7	47.6
North Carolina	FLT	6,312	39	7.6	68.6	23.9
North Dakota	FND	6,024	43	11.5	40.3	48.2
Ohio	FND	8,236	15	5.8	43.3	50.9
Oklahoma	FND[d]	6,200	40	8.7	61.5	29.9
Oregon	FULL	7,519	19	6.3	57.0	36.7
Pennsylvania	PCT	8,557	9	5.5	41.0	53.5
Rhode Island	PCT[g]	7,931	18	4.4	38.1	57.6
South Carolina	FND	7,110	28	7.9	51.3	40.8
South Dakota	FND	6,355	37	10.4	36.6	53.1
Tennessee	FND	5,710	46	9.0	48.1	42.9
Texas	FND[d]	6,999	30	8.4	44.0	47.6
Utah	FND	5,076	50	6.9	62.4	30.7
Vermont	FLT[d]	8,514	10	4.5	76.6	19.0
Virginia	FND	5,871	44	5.4	37.8	56.7
Washington	FULL	7,474	20	7.7	65.8	26.5
West Virginia	FND	8,289	14	9.0	62.8	28.2
Wisconsin	GTB	8,862	7	4.6	53.4	42.0
Wyoming	FND	8,439	11	7.6	52.1	40.3
United States[h]		7,574		6.9	50.7	42.4

[a] FLT   Flat grant   GTB   Guaranteed tax base
   FND   Foundation   GY   Guaranteed yield
   FULL   Full state funding   PCT   Percentage equalization

[b] Although Connecticut and Maine describe the basic support plans as foundation programs, the plans are considered to be PCT because the calculation of basic support aid depends on a ratio of local to state tax capacities.

[c] Delaware has a small equalization program (8% of appropriations) beyond the flat grant.

[d] Second tier of funding (PCT, GTB, or GY) above the flat grant or foundation program.

[e] The second tier of the Indiana GTB formula is a GY program.

[f] Missouri incorporates a GTB within the foundation formula.

[g] Rhode Island's PCT program was suspended in 1998–1999; all districts received the same amount of aid as in the prior year under the PCT structure.

[h] Includes District of Columbia ($9,317 revenue per pupil; 16.6% federal, 83.4% local).

Sources: National Center for Education Statistics. (2001). *Public School Finance Programs of the United States and Canada, 1998–99* **http://www.ed.gov/pubsearch/pubsinfo.asp?pubid=2001309**; National Education Association (2001). *Public School Revenue per Student in Fall Enrollment, 1999–2000*, Table F-2, **www.nea.org/publiced/edstats/00rankings/f-2.html** (accessed 10/15/01), reprinted with permission of National Education Association; U.S. Department of Commerce, *Statistical Abstract of the United States, 1996–1999* (2001). Washington, DC: U.S. Government Printing Office, Table H, p. 93, **www.census.gov/prod/www/statistical-abstract-us.html**

allocated funds to districts through one of the tax-base-equalizing models as a second tier of funding.

Table 7.1 also indicates per-pupil revenue and relative proportions of funds derived from federal, state, and local levels in 1999–2000. New Hampshire, for example, relied heavily on local revenue (87.8 percent) in its foundation plan. School districts in Illinois and Nevada also derived 60 percent or more of their revenue from local sources. In contrast, Hawaii's large percentage of state funds (87.8 percent) reflected its organization as a single school district. The percentage of revenue from state-level sources also exceeded 65 percent in Delaware, Michigan, New Mexico, North Carolina, Vermont, and Washington. A number of finance plans divided support for schools nearly equally (within ten percentage points) between state and local sources: Arizona, Colorado, Florida, Indiana, Maine, Massachusetts, Montana, Nebraska, New York, North Dakota, Ohio, Tennessee, and Texas. The average percentages for the United States indicate that states (50.7 percent) provide the majority of

revenue. Local revenue accounts for somewhat less (42.4 percent), and the federal government's share is substantially less (6.9 percent).

The percentage mix of state and local resources is often misconstrued in relation to the adequacy of overall revenue. People often think that more money is available to districts in states that have a higher percentage of state funds. This is not the case. Figure 7.1 graphically shows the distribution of states by the percentage of funds derived from state sources and the average revenue per pupil (using data in Table 7.1). The ranges in revenue per pupil (from $5,076 in Utah to $11,014 in Connecticut) and in the percentage of funds from state revenue (from 8.5 percent in New Hampshire to 87.5 percent in Hawaii) are large. The relationship between the two variables, which is represented by the regression line on the graph, is somewhat negative (correlation of −0.05453). This low correlation coefficient and the nearly horizontal regression line indicate that there is virtually no relationship between expenditure levels and the percentage of revenue derived through state sources. The

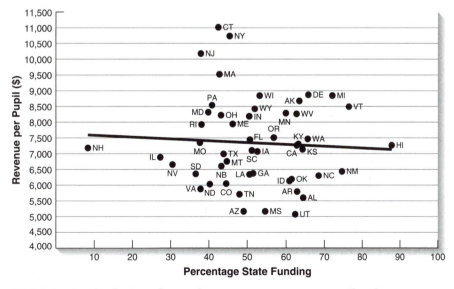

FIGURE 7.1. Distribution of States by Average Revenue per Pupil and Percentage of State Funding

average revenue per pupil in the twenty-eight states with a percentage of state funding over 50 percent is $7,221. This compares with $7,550 for the twenty-two states that provide less than 50 percent of total school funds.

Parrish and Fowler (1995) noted the same pattern in their analyses of disparities in school resources among geographic regions. Western states, which had the lowest overall adjusted revenue per student, received the greatest share of support from state sources (an average of 60.5 percent). In contrast, states in the Northeast (average share from state, 40.4 percent) and Midwest (41.5 percent) had higher levels of overall revenue. States that continue to rely on local tax bases generally have somewhat higher revenue than those that finance education primarily through state resources.

The total amount of money made available to school systems depends on the per-pupil valuation of various tax bases (i.e., capacity) and on the willingness of legislators, school boards, and voters to tap these sources in support of public education (i.e., effort). The simplified models presented in this section illustrate that the total per-pupil operating revenue (PPOR) can vary greatly, or can be virtually equal, among districts. However, they do not address whether there is an adequate amount of PPOR available in a given district or across the state to enable students to meet high standards. The models take school districts' fiscal capacity and tax effort into account in determining state aid allocations. They also communicate priorities assigned to the values of equality and liberty in their approaches to dividing responsibilities between state and local levels. The six prototypes range in scope from complete local financing with no state assistance to full state funding of education.

No State Involvement

Even though states had assumed constitutional responsibility for public education, there was not a large state role in financing schools until the twentieth century. States created school districts in the eighteenth and nineteenth centuries to encourage the spread of formal education at a time when attendance was voluntary. Minimal state aid supplemented revenue raised by county or district property taxes and through private contributions.

The small and typically homogeneous school districts had very different funds available for school programs under this first prototype. Per-pupil revenue depended on the wealth of individuals, the capacity of tax bases, and the willingness of individuals and taxpayers to divert funds to schooling. Thus the adequacy of revenue (defined at that time as the level of support deemed essential for meeting locally determined goals), and consequently the adequacy of school programs, closely reflected local property assessments and tax rates (see Chapter 5). Districts with large capacity (i.e., large per-pupil valuations) could raise needed PPOR even with low effort (i.e., tax rates). However, districts with low capacity could not finance an adequate program even with high tax effort. Equalization of opportunities (in terms of financial inputs) was only within, and not among, districts.

These conditions prevailed at the turn of the century, when Cubberley (1906) advocated a state role in school finance:

> [W]hile it may be possible to maintain schools entirely or almost entirely by local taxation, the doing so involves very slight efforts on the part of some communities, and very excessive burdens for other communities . . . . [T]hese excessive burdens, borne in large part for the common good, should be in part equalized by the state. To do this some form of general aid is necessary. (p. 250)

Even today, when state aid enables all districts to sponsor at least a minimum educational program, raising the funds for constructing school buildings quite often relies on local property capacity and effort. When there is little or no state involvement in financing facilities, great inequities result (see discussion of capital outlay in Chapter 6 and Kozol, 1991).

Matching Grants

One of the first forms of state aid was matching grants. In this second prototype, state funds stimulate local taxation by requiring localities to match state contributions. This may be done on an equal dollar-for-dollar basis or in terms of a proportionate match, whereby localities must raise, say, $100 for each $500 of state money.

Although a matching grant may effectively motivate voters to raise taxes, the total amount of funds received depends on local fiscal capacity and effort. These grants work against goals of equalizing capacity, because they favor wealthy districts that are best able to raise the required local share with little tax effort. Further amplifying disparities in expenditure levels among districts, matching grants promote "inequalities in educational opportunities or burdensome local school taxes" (Burke, 1957, p. 395).

Matching grants no longer provide general state aid for school districts, and this model is not listed in Table 7.1. Nevertheless, some states call for matching funds to construct school facilities or to offer an incentive for school improvement. For example, Indiana school corporations (districts) dedicate $1 for each $2 received from the state for remediation programs to serve students who do not meet state proficiency standards. The federal government promotes vocational and technical education through matching grants (see Chapter 9). Donors may also adopt this strategy when they issue challenge grants to stimulate local fund-raising activities (see Chapter 6).

Flat Grants

States abandoned matching grants as a structure for general aid in favor of strategies that could better extend educational opportunities to districts that were unwilling to exert tax effort and/or had little capacity. In this third prototype, states allocate funds on a per capita basis—that is, according to a count of students or teachers. These flat grants ignore local fiscal capacity and effort.

This finance approach presumes that an appropriate state role is to guarantee each student a minimum level of schooling. Thus the state achieves a form of fairness by distributing equal monies to educate all students. Responding to the complete reliance on local property tax bases early in the century, Cubberley (1906) argued that the state should "equalize the advantages to all as nearly as can be done with the resources at hand" (p. 17). Although it was the state's duty to secure for all pupils as high a minimum of education as possible, he cautioned against reducing all education to this level. Thus local control of schools remained a priority. States would provide only "the central support necessary to the health of the program without detriment to the local operating unit" (Mort & Reusser, 1941, p. 375).

The value of liberty is realized through this flat grant approach insofar as the structure leaves to local boards or voters decisions about programs beyond the minimum. Through permissive property taxation, this model allows communities to rise above the base presumed adequate. If equality is defined in terms of minimum program standards, then the variations in total expenditures resulting from local optional taxes are not viewed as being inequitable.

Figure 7.2 illustrates the flat grant plan, as it might be applied in the hypothetical state of the computer simulation accompanying this chapter. Unequal amounts raised by optional local taxes supplement the uniform per-pupil allocations of state aid (e.g., $6,000). Voters in the relatively wealthy district, Sommerset, agree to supplement the uniform state grant with $2,719 of local funds to reach a desired total per-pupil spending of $8,719. Dividing this local supplement ($2,719) by the property valuation ($617,100) determines the tax rate (4.41 mills).[2]

Even though Ellicott and Redrock levy heavier tax rates (5.52 and 12.57 mills, respectively),

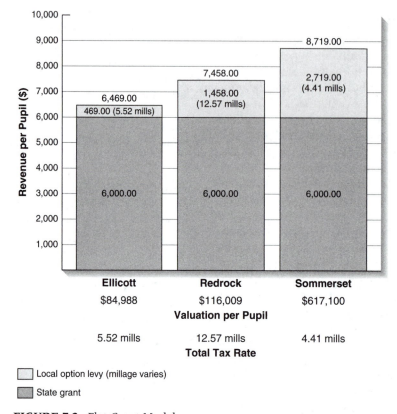

FIGURE 7.2. Flat Grant Model

their total revenues ($6,469 and $7,458) are less. Clearly, the total funds available under this plan vary greatly among districts when there is a relatively large reliance on local-option taxes. By increasing the size of the base allocation relative to these supplements, or by placing a cap on local discretionary taxes, the state can induce greater equalization of total revenue. If a state chose to disallow any local leeway, the plan would have fully equalized per-pupil revenue (see Figure 7.11).

Local capacity and effort are not considered in the base amount of PPOR. Simply dividing the total amount of state funds available for school operations by the number of pupils or instructional units results in the flat grant amount. However, in a variation of this proto-type, a *variable flat grant* approach permits dif-ferent funding levels according to particular needs of pupils or classes. Weighted pupil or in-structional unit techniques (discussed fully in Chapter 8) enable the state to adjust the size of grants to account for varying costs of educa-tional programs and services.

Three states, Delaware, North Carolina, and Vermont, have a variable flat grant model (see Table 7.1). Vermont provides a general state support block grant ($5,010 in 1998–1999) per weighted pupil. Because this flat grant is the same in all districts, the block grant offsets dif-fering levels of total spending desired by local voters. North Carolina allocates personnel al-lotments that specify a state-determined ade-quate number of positions to be filled. This plan's features appear in Figure 7.3. The per-sonnel allotments reflect characteristics of

North Carolina's Flat Grant Program

The state allocates funds to districts according to personnel allotments. The number of allotted positions depends on average daily membership. Localities may supplement the flat grants through local-option property taxation.

State Funding of Base Program

There is no required local contribution to the basic support program in this finance plan, which has remained virtually unchanged since it was enacted in 1933. The state fully funds what it considers a district's current expense requirement. Personnel allotments depend primarily on the number of students in average daily membership. The variable grants reflect state-adopted class size ratios for respective grade levels: grades K–2, 1:20; grade 3, 1:22.23; grades 4–6, 1:22; grades 7–8, 1:21; grade 9, 1:24.5; grades 10–12, 1:26.64.

Allotments vary according to teacher experience and training through a statewide salary schedule. The number of pupils enrolled also determines position allotments for instructional support personnel, teacher assistants, and central office and building administrators. Other positions (e.g., superintendent) are allocated on a district basis.

Local Support beyond the Basic Program

All but 2 of the 117 school districts are fiscally dependent. County commissioners may levy an additional tax, up to $1.50 on $100 appraised valuation, without voter approval. These optional levies provide funds to hire personnel beyond the state's allotments and to supplement state minimum salary levels. The statewide average for these local contributions to current expenses is 23.4 percent of the total annual budget. Local taxes also fund the construction and maintenance of facilities.

FIGURE 7.3. Variable Flat Grants in North Carolina

Source: J. K. Testerman & C. L. Brown (2001). North Carolina. In National Center for Education Statistics, *Public School Finance Programs of the United States and Canada, 1998–99.* **http://www. ed.gov/pubsearch/pubsinfo.asp?pubid=2001309**

teachers and class sizes related to particular programs. However, allotments do not vary in relation to any measure of local capacity or effort. Districts may supplement the state's basic allocations with local resources, primarily from property taxation. Disparities in total spending among districts have traditionally been small because of the percentage of state funds is relatively high (64.3 percent in 1999–2000).

Even when one of the other models form the basis of the state's plan for financing school district operations, wealthy districts may be guaranteed at least a minimum amount of state aid via a flat grant. For example, all California districts receive a constitutionally mandated $120 per pupil. In addition, many categorical programs rely on flat grants. Illinois funds special education through a flat grant of one-half the teacher's salary up to $1,000 per pupil served or $8,000 per teacher, whichever is less. Districts also receive a flat $8,000 for psychologists and specialists.

Foundation Programs

In a foundation plan, as in the flat grant model, the state legislature defines a funding level associated with a basic education, and localities are free to fund additional programs. The difference between these prototypes appears in responsibilities for financing the base or foundation level. Under a flat grant, the state alone funds the uniform per-pupil or per-classroom amount. In a foundation plan, the state and each school district form a partnership to finance the required program cost. The state determines the required level of local participation. All but fourteen of the states use this fourth prototype in designing finance policies.

Strayer and Haig (1923) devised this plan for sharing educational costs between states and localities. School districts or counties levy a uniform statewide tax rate "sufficient to meet the costs only in the richest district" (p. 176). State subventions make up the differences between this foundation level and what is raised locally in all other districts. Under the required levy, effort is controlled and fiscal capacity dictates relative shares of local and state funds that apply to the foundation. Beyond the equalized guarantee, local leeway satisfies liberty interests of districts much as it did in the flat grant prototype.

A graphical display of this model, drawn from the computer simulation, appears in Figure 7.4. The total amounts of revenue available to districts are the same as those depicted for the flat grant model (Figure 7.2). These diagrams differ in the sources of revenue that make up the base. The guaranteed per-pupil revenue (in this case, $6,000) appears as a horizontal line. This foundation level, or base level, is often referred to as a "Strayer–Haig line" in the model. Below this minimum foundation of spending per pupil or per instructional unit, revenue from the required local effort (RLE of 7.55 mills) blends with state funds.

Districts with greater tax capacity contribute proportionally more. Thus the poorer dis-

tricts, Ellicott and Redrock, receive more state dollars per pupil ($5,358 and $5,124) than the wealthier district, Sommerset ($1,341). In addition to the required effort of 7.55 mills, voters in these districts approve optional taxes—just as they did under the flat grant model. Local option taxes vary substantially according to voters' willingness to pay for program enhancements and property valuations. In this depiction, a larger effort (12.57 mills) is required in Redrock to increase its spending by only $1,458, compared to the 4.41 mills levied in Sommerset to raise $1,719 per pupil. Despite the equal foundation level, there are inequities in overall spending and tax rates. Sommerset has the highest revenue but the lowest total ef-

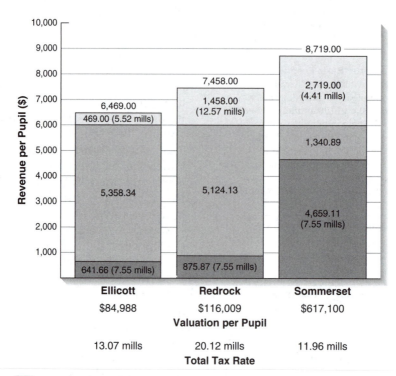

FIGURE 7.4. Foundation Model

fort (11.96 mills) relative to the levies in Elli-cott and Redrock (13.07 mills and 20.12 mills, respectively).

The local effort required of districts in this model is not so high as the amount that would be levied under the foundation plan conceived by Strayer and Haig. From a strict equalization standpoint, Sommerset would receive no state aid, and the uniform levy would be 9.72 mills ($6,000/$617,100). However, legislative ac-tions result from political compromises among any number of goals. An important goal of leg-islatures that adopt a foundation plan is to use state aid to relieve local tax burdens and to broaden the tax base through state-level taxa-tion. The result is therefore a lower required levy, even if complete equalization of local wealth is not achieved.

The *guaranteed funding* of the foundation level theoretically corresponds to the state's minimum educational standards or to an edu-cational plan that includes "all the activities the state wishes to assure the communities of least ability to support schools" (Mort and Reusser, 1951, p. 397). Establishing this guar-antee is often a political decision dictated by available revenue, rather than a rational de-termination of educational needs and costs. If it is too low, there may not be adequate PPOR in those districts that have a small tax base or in those that choose not to levy additional taxes. The state may claim that its responsibil-ity is fulfilled. However, the minimum may be insufficient to support a basic educational pro-gram, let alone enable all students to reach high academic standards. The level of funding available in all districts of a state may become an issue in judicial reviews and in analyses of adequacy (see Chapters 10 and 11).

Johns, Morphet, and Alexander (1983) sug-gested that the state should provide a relatively large percentage—at least 75 percent—of the guarantee. Placing this burden on the state would take advantage of broader-based taxes and recognize the heavy reliance that localities place on property taxes for capital outlay and program supplements. As Table 7.1 shows, state participation in finance plans has a wide range for foundation plans. New Hampshire, with a minimal percentage of revenue from the state (8.2 percent), contrasts with Ken-tucky's relatively large (68.0 percent) state contribution.

The required local effort (RLE) is in essence a state-imposed property tax. If the RLE is set such that the foundation level is met by local money in the wealthiest district, as conceived originally by Strayer and Haig, then the state effectively leverages property taxes to create a higher funding base than could be obtained under a flat grant program. However, state leg-islatures are reluctant to deny any district state aid. Actual state implementation of this plan then diminishes the equalizing potential of the foundation plan in several ways. First, the foundation guarantee is maintained at a high level while the state reduces the RLE. In that case, more state dollars flow to all districts, but especially to the wealthiest. Second, some states build a foundation plan upon a flat grant guarantee. In this way, even the wealthiest dis-tricts that would otherwise receive no state funds are assured a minimum grant. Third, the local effort specified in statute or regulations may not be required. Very often, the amount that should be raised is a "chargeback" against the foundation level when districts are unwill-ing to raise the expected local levy. Thus there are spending disparities within the foundation amount that the legislature deems to be ade-quate. This is because the anticipated local funds that should be raised in accordance with the computational tax rate are deducted from the state allocations.

The optional levy depicted in the model (see Figure 7.4) is referred to as a *voter override*. This permissive tax that allows local leeway is re-ferred to as a mill levy increase in some states. The yield of this optional levy builds upon the base foundation level for school operations. The foundation amount satisfies goals of equal-ization. By permitting district voters to determine what they believe to be an adequate level for financing school programs and helping students meet expectations, the finance structure satisfies liberty goals. The resulting disparities in spending above the foundation guarantee reflect not only the differing tax efforts and desires of local voters, but also the differing tax capacities to which rates are applied.

Voter overrides are rooted in earlier finance plans that relied heavily on local revenue and on continuing desires to involve the community in school finance. In view of the way the early matching grants stimulated local effort, finance theorists argue that local voter involvement encourages innovation and efficiency without constraints of state-defined levels of adequacy. This "adaptability," or propensity of districts to change with the times (Mort, 1933), enables lighthouse districts to experiment (*Fleischmann Report*, 1973; Jones, 1985). Once demonstrated in these lighthouses, a program adaptation such as full-day kindergartens or reduction in class size may be disseminated to other school systems. Districts then pressure the legislature to raise the foundation level so that all localities can take advantage of a successful program's benefits.

Thirty-six states employ a foundation plan for basic operating expenses (see Table 7.1). The majority of these states require a specific local levy for the base plan. The others permit districts to set a tax rate and then adjust the foundation level (impose a chargeback) when a lower-than-expected levy prevails. The Michigan foundation program, as summarized in Figure 7.5, establishes a per-pupil foundation allowance (base) for each district. The revenue to pay for this guarantee includes local tax revenue raised through a uniform levy (18 mills on nonhomestead property) and state allocations. The latter share equalizes the locally raised property tax by distributing more funds to localities with lower assessed valuations. The state earmarks 60 percent of its prior sales tax (a 4 percent rate) and 100 percent of the voter-increased sales tax (2 percent) for education. In

addition, the state collects a 6-mill levy on all property to raise revenue for schools (see Michigan's property tax reforms in Chapter 5). Local voters may supplement the equalized guarantee by approving an optional levy of up to 3 mills on all property.

Tax-Base-Equalizing Programs

Several forms of tax base equalization represent a fifth prototype. Rather than having the state determine a guaranteed funding level for all districts, as occurs in flat grants and foundation approaches, these plans stress local determination of a desired level of spending. Once local officials or voters set an expenditure goal, the state equalizes school districts' abilities to raise the necessary funds.

Updegraff and King (1922) argued the importance of giving localities a dominant role in finance decisions:

> Efficiency in the conduct of schools should be promoted by increasing the state grants whenever the true tax-rate is increased and by lowering it whenever the local tax is decreased. (p. 118)

In their view, an appropriate state role was one of helping school systems deliver educational programs fashioned by local educators. The state should also neutralize the disparities in local tax bases as determinants of spending goals.

Like the foundation plan, three variations of the tax-base-equalizing prototype contribute to states' goals of financial equalization. The difference between these models and the foundation plan is the involvement of localities in determining the level of state support. Even though disparities in overall spending result, these tax-base-equalizing plans satisfy the criterion of fiscal neutrality that was urged in several judicial reviews of school finance policies (see Chapter 10). *Fiscal neutrality* demands that resources for public education be a function of the wealth of the state as a whole rather than a function of the wealth of localities. Coons,

Michigan's Foundation Program

Basic foundation aid for general operating funds considers a locally raised property tax on nonhomestead property. The legislature determines this tax rate, and state revenue from a sales tax, a statewide property tax, and other sources equalizes the amounts raised locally. In addition, voters may enact local enhancement levies on all property to supplement the foundation guarantee.

Local/State Shares

The state guarantees each district a basic level of funding per pupil. This foundation allowance, which was established at $5,000 per pupil in 1994–1995, increases annually. However, not all districts are funded at this level, and the actual foundation allowance varies from $4,200 to $6,500 under a plan to level up lower-spending districts without leveling down others. Lower-spending districts have larger annual increases according to a sliding scale.

The local share of a district's foundation allowance is raised by a required levy (18 mills) on nonhomestead property (property other than owner-occupied residences and qualifying agricultural property). The state share is the difference between the foundation allowance and the amount raised by the required levy (18 mills) on nonhomestead property.

A 6 percent statewide sales tax is the major source of state revenue. Sixty percent of the revenue from the first 4 percent tax and all revenue from the additional 2 percent tax on general sales are constitutionally earmarked for the School Aid Fund. Portions of other state revenue contributing to school aid include the 6-mill state property tax, the personal income tax, tobacco and liquor taxes, taxes on commercial and industrial facilities, and the lottery.

High-revenue districts (those with a foundation allowance above $6,500 in 1994–1995) levy hold-harmless millage—above the local levy of 18 mills on nonhomestead property and the state-level tax (6 mills) on homestead property.

Local Support beyond the Equalized Program

The 555 school districts are fiscally independent. Voters may approve local enhancement levies of up to 3 mills on all property above the required levies. The state does not equalize this optional levy.

FIGURE 7.5. Foundation Program in Michigan

Source: M. F. Addonizio, E. M. Mills & C. P. Kearney (2001). Michigan. In National Center for Education Statistics, *Public School Finance Programs of the United States and Canada, 1998–99.* **http://www.ed.gov/pubsearch/pubsinfo.asp?pubid= 2001309**

Clune, and Sugarman (1970) articulated this concept and identified two essential characteristics of an acceptable system of state aid:

> First, any right of subunits of the state to be relatively wealthy for educational purposes is denied. The total financial resources of the state should be equally available to all public school children. Ultimate responsibility for public schools is placed squarely with the state. Second, on the other hand, *the units should be free, through the taxing mechanism, to choose to share various amounts of the state's wealth* (by deciding how hard they are willing to tax themselves). (pp. 201–202, emphasis added)

In this conception, a fiscally neutral finance plan ensures that communities have the financial ability to raise funds to support schools at their chosen spending level. Because the spending level is locally determined, however, the total amount of funds may not be sufficient to enable all students to meet the state's high standards for academic performance.

Three mathematically equivalent variations of tax base equalization are evident in state policies: percentage equalization, guaranteed tax base, and guaranteed yield. Seven states (see Table 7.1) include these forms of tax base equalization as the primary funding mechanism. Six others rely on this form of equalization as a second tier of funding that builds on a flat grant or foundation program.

Percentage Equalization

In a percentage equalization formula, local and state shares of locally determined expenditures are a function of school district wealth (tax capacity) relative to the wealth of the state as a whole. State aid in this plan is calculated by the following formula:

$$\text{State aid ratio} = 1 - c \times \left[\frac{\text{school district tax capacity}}{\text{state average tax capacity}} \right]$$

The school district tax capacity and the state average capacity change every year according to assessment rolls and equalization ratios (see

Chapter 5). The legislature determines the value of the constant *c*, which represents the portion of expenditures to be financed by a district of average wealth. Assuming that this required percentage local share is 50% (that is, *c* is 0.50) and that the state average wealth is $159,951 per pupil, the formula becomes:

$$\text{State aid ratio} = 1 - 0.50 \times \left[\frac{\text{school district tax capacity}}{\$159,951} \right]$$

Figure 7.6 shows state and local shares of PPOR for selected school districts in the computer simulation. The three scenarios depict percentage equalization plans with constants of 0.25, 0.50, and 0.75, respectively. Scenario B, for example, assumes that local resources in a district of average wealth finance 50 percent of desired expenditures. The state allocates the remaining 50 percent of the necessary revenue to meet the district's spending goal. Calculation of the aid ratio follows the percentage equalization formula (see above) to compare local property valuation with the state average valuation ($159,951).

A higher aid ratio (73.4 percent) is evident in the poorer-than-average Ellicott (per-pupil valuation of $84,988). In this district, and in any other district in the state that has the same valuation, the locality pays 26.63 percent of the desired expenditures chosen by the school board or voters. Thus district resources provide only $1,722 of the spending goal ($6,469), and the tax rate is 20.26 mills (computed as $1,722/ $84,988). In comparison, Redrock's aid ratio is 63.7 percent. This district receives $4,747 from the state. When this aid blends with the $2,711

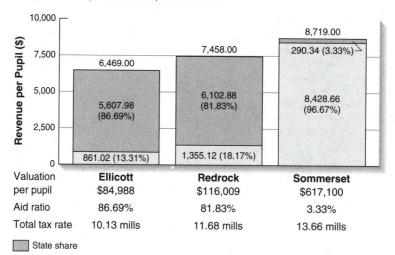

Scenario A

Equivalent forms of this model are as follows:

Percentage equalization, constant of 0.25; guaranteed tax base, GTB of $638,364; and guaranteed yield, $638.36 per mill levied.

	Ellicott	Redrock	Sommerset
Valuation per pupil	$84,988	$116,009	$617,100
Aid ratio	86.69%	81.83%	3.33%
Total tax rate	10.13 mills	11.68 mills	13.66 mills

State share

Local share (optional spending level or millage)

FIGURE 7.6. Tax-Base-Equalizing Models (Calculations are rounded to hundredths. Any discrepancies in results among the percentage equalization, guaranteed-tax-base, and guaranteed-yield models are due to this level of rounding.)

Scenario B

Equivalent forms of this model are as follows:

Percentage equalization, constant of 0.50; guaranteed tax base, GTB of $319,182; and guaranteed yield, $319.18 per mill levied.

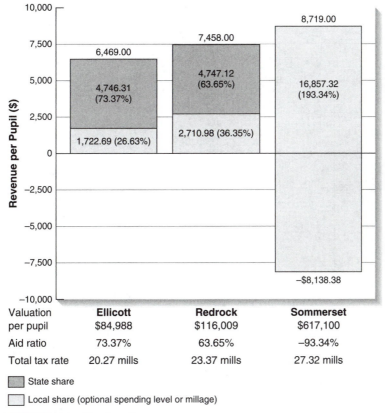

FIGURE 7.6. *(Continued)*

raised locally from the 23.37 mill levy, the district attains the desired per-pupil spending ($7,458.00).

Continuing the conditions in Scenario B, districts with valuations exceeding the state average per-pupil valuation ($159,591) have aid ratios below 50 percent. A district having a valuation of $319,912 does not receive state money at any level of expenditure (the aid ratio is 0.0 percent under the percentage equalization formula). Districts that exceed this valuation have negative aid ratios. These districts

would remit to the state any property tax receipts in excess of their identified spending levels. For example, Sommerset has a valuation of $617,100 per pupil and a computed aid ratio of –93.3 percent. Given the desired spending ($8,719) and the negative aid ratio, the computed state aid is a negative $8,138.00 ($8,719 × –0.9334). In order to collect $16,857 (the sum of the spending level and the negative aid), the district must levy 27.32 mills. In all, then, the district raises the equivalent of 193.34 percent of the desired spending. The state col-

Scenario C

Equivalent forms of this model are as follows:

Percentage equalization, constant of 0.75; guaranteed tax base, GTB of $212,788; and guaranteed yield, $212.79 per mill levied.

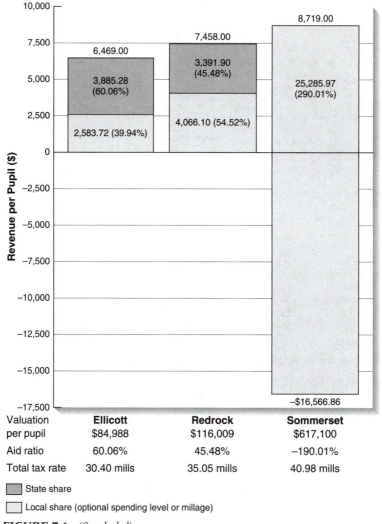

Valuation per pupil	**Ellicott** $84,988	**Redrock** $116,009	**Sommerset** $617,100
Aid ratio	60.06%	45.48%	−190.01%
Total tax rate	30.40 mills	35.05 mills	40.98 mills

▢ State share

▢ Local share (optional spending level or millage)

FIGURE 7.6. *(Concluded)*

lects the negative aid for distribution to poorer districts.

This practice of redistributing locally raised property taxes, which is known as *recapture*, occurs in several states' policies. State legislators are reluctant to take money from districts,

and political realities typically ensure that all districts receive some aid. A number of states have adopted recapture features at one time in either their foundation or their tax-base-equalizing approaches. Whereas state courts in Kansas, Montana, Texas, and Vermont upheld recapture provisions, this policy was found to violate the Wisconsin state constitution (see Chapter 11).

A strategy more commonly applied when states implement a percentage equalization plan is to provide a *floor*, or a minimum amount of state aid for all districts. A flat grant, either as a dollar amount or as a minimum aid ratio, ensures that even the wealthiest districts receive some state assistance. Another common modification to a pure application of tax base equalization is placing a *ceiling*, or upper limit, on per-pupil expenditures that will be aided by the state. This limits the state's total financial obligation. If the ceiling is set below what most school districts are spending, the formula is ineffective in meeting pupils' educational needs in all districts. The greatest negative impact of a ceiling is on poor districts. If states fail to recapture excess revenue and impose floors and ceilings, then tax-base-equalizing approaches do not neutralize the relationship between wealth and spending (Phelps & Addonizio, 1981). In this case, percentage equalization formulas take on the same inequities as flat grant and foundation programs that do not ensure that all districts have adequate resources for students to meet high academic standards.

Scenarios A and C of Figure 7.6 illustrate the effect of adjusting the constant. If the constant were reduced to 0.25 (the state meets 75 percent of PPOR in the district of average wealth), virtually every district would qualify for state aid (see Scenario A). The three districts' aid ratios would be 86.69 percent, 81.83 percent, and 3.33 percent, respectively. Because the state shares under this lower constant are larger than those depicted in Scenario B, local contributions to the respective per-pupil expenditures are reduced. The districts' tax rates thus decline to 10.13 mills, 11.68 mills, and 13.66 mills to raise the respective local shares.

In contrast, Scenario C illustrates the effect of raising the constant to 0.75 (the state meets

one-quarter of the PPOR in the district of average wealth). This policy would lower the percentage of state aid (or increase the amount of recapture). When the constant is 0.75 and desired spending levels remain the same for each district, Ellicott's aid ratio declines to 60.06 percent, and the state aid diminishes ($3,885). Redrock's ratio falls to 45.48 percent ($3,392). The state would recapture more of Sommerset's money under the negative aid ratio (−190 percent). This district must generate $25,285.86 in property taxes to pay the state $16,566.86 per pupil. The respective tax rates rise substantially to 30.40 mills, 35.05 mills, and 40.98 mills under this larger constant.

Lowering the constant is beneficial for all districts, but especially for districts of high wealth. Of course, lowering this percentage to come from local resources is very expensive from the state's perspective. Raising the constant lowers aid to all districts. But this policy change reduces the overall commitment of state funds and shifts the financial burden from broad-based state revenues to the local property tax. States can equalize revenue in the poorest districts with a relatively small commitment of state funds if they keep the value of the constant high. Adjustments in the constant make it possible for any state, regardless of the amount of revenue that is devoted to schools, to afford this plan.

If voters in all three districts chose the same spending level, their aid ratios would dictate differing shares of state and local money. Scenario D (see Figure 7.7) assumes equal spending at the level initially selected by Sommerset's voters ($8,719) and a constant of 0.50. Note that the districts have the same millage rate (27.32 mills). Thus the effort is equalized along with the spending goal. Scenario D makes it clearer that the policy of recapture is essential in a fully operational percentage equalization plan. Otherwise, wealthy districts retain a large advantage because they can achieve their spending goals at far less effort. States must then search elsewhere for revenue

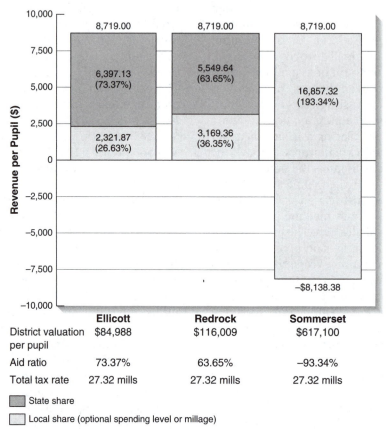

Equivalent forms of this model are as follows:

Percentage equalization, constant of 0.50; guaranteed tax base, GTB of $319,182; and guaranteed yield, $319.18 per mill levied.

	Ellicott	Redrock	Sommerset
District valuation per pupil	$84,988	$116,009	$617,100
Aid ratio	73.37%	63.65%	−93.34%
Total tax rate	27.32 mills	27.32 mills	27.32 mills

■ State share

□ Local share (optional spending level or millage)

FIGURE 7.7. Equal Spending under Tax-Base-Equalizing Models (Calculations are rounded to hundredths. Any discrepancies in results among the percentage equalization, guaranteed-tax-base, and guaranteed-yield models are due to this level of rounding.)

to enable poorer districts to attain desired spending levels.

A summary of the New York percentage equalization program appears as Figure 7.8. Fiscal capacity is defined by both real property and personal income (see the discussion of fiscal capacity in Chapter 8). Each district's aid ratio considers the property valuation and adjusted gross income of residents relative to state averages for those tax bases. Total operating aid is a function of the number of aidable pupil units, the aid ratio, and the desired expenditure level. Several modifications in this plan illustrate deviations from the percentage equalization model. First, a flat grant floor ensures that all districts receive at least a minimum ($400 per pupil) in state assistance. Second, a ceiling on the amount of local spending to be equalized makes the plan function like a foundation program. Finally, a save-harmless provision guarantees state funding at the level set in prior years. Thus the amount of aid that most dis-

New York's Percentage Equalization Program

Operating aid depends on an aid ratio that compares the wealth of each district to the wealth of the state as a whole. Local wealth considers property valuation and per capita income. No district receives less than $400 per pupil, and a ceiling is placed on the expenditures to be equalized. Districts may spend above the ceiling, because there is no recapture provision.

Local/State Shares

The average daily attendance (ADA) of resident and nonresident students determines the total aidable-pupil units (TAPU). Additional weights include those for high school pupils with special educational needs as defined by scores on state examinations and for pupils with disabilities. The pupil count and applicable weights constitute the total wealth pupil units (TWPU) in the formula.

There are 682 districts that employ eight or more teachers and are eligible for regular aid. The five largest cities are fiscally dependent. The shares of locally determined spending vary according to districts' combined wealth ratios (CWR). This measure of ability to pay is the sum of two ratios: 50% of the equalized actual valuation (AV) of property per TWPU in relation to the state average, and 50% of the adjusted gross income (INC) of resident taxpayers per TWPU in relation to the state average. Given a statewide average actual valuation per TWPU of $246,400 and an average adjusted gross income per TWPU of $86,400 in 1998–1999:

$$\text{CWR} = \frac{(0.5 \times \text{district AV/TWPU})}{\$246,400} + \frac{(0.5 \times \text{district INC/TWPU})}{\$86,400}$$

The state operating aid ratio (OAR) for a district is the larger of four calculations, but not more than 0.90 nor less than 0.00:

$$1.37 - (1.23 \times \text{CWR}) \qquad 0.80 - (0.39 \times \text{CWR})$$
$$1.00 - (0.64 \times \text{CWR}) \qquad 0.51 - (0.22 \times \text{CWR})$$

The district receives the larger of $400 per TAPU (a minimum flat grant that ensures aid to all districts regardless of wealth) or the result of the per-pupil basic operating aid (BOA) formula:

$$\text{BOA} = [3,900 + 0.05 \times (\text{district expense/TAPU})] \times \text{state operating aid ratio}$$

The district expense in this formula is its approved operating expense (AOE). The ceiling amount is $3,900 plus an amount equal to the product of (i) the lesser of $8,000 or the base-year AOE per TAPU for those less than $3,900, and (ii) the greater of 0.075 or 0.075/CWR.

For example, a district of average wealth has a CWR of 1.00 and the state pays 41% of its expenditures under the third OAR formula:

$$\text{OAR} = 0.80 - (0.39 \times 1.00) = 0.41$$

The state's share is $1,665, assuming that the district's per-pupil AOE is $6,050:

$$\text{BOA} = [3,900 + 0.075 \times (\$6,050)] \times 0.41 = \$1,665$$

This amount of state aid is multiplied by the number of aidable-pupil units (TAPU). The local share in this example is $4,385, or 59% of its chosen expenditure level.

A large number of districts (627) were off formula in 1998–1999. Many districts should have received more aid, but limited state funds inhibited the full state share. These districts received transition aid that gradually moves them on the formula. Others received save-harmless aid that guaranteed no less than the amount of operating aid provided in the base year.

Local Support beyond the Equalized Program

There is no recapture provision (the aid ratio may not be below 0.0). Taxes raised in many districts enable them to spend beyond the ceiling used in determining operating aid.

FIGURE 7.8. Percentage Equalization in New York

Source: B. O. Brent (2001). New York. In National Center for Education Statistics, *Public School Finance Programs of the United States and Canada, 1998–99*. **http://www.ed.gov/pubsearch/pubsinfo.asp?pubid=2001309**

tricts receive is not a function of fiscal capacity, pupils' educational needs, or local effort alone.

Connecticut, Maine, Pennsylvania, and Rhode Island also employ a percentage equalization formula for determining state aid (see Table 7.1). In addition, Louisiana includes this plan in a second tier of funding. This approach may be used to fund particular programs beyond basic school operations. For example, New York uses districts' combined wealth ratios in determining support for special-education programs. Along with Massachusetts and Montana, the five states (CT, ME, NY, PA, and RI) using this approach for the first tier of basic aid also provide state assistance for school construction according to a percentage equalization formula.

Guaranteed Tax Base

In this variation of tax base equalization, districts are guaranteed a state-defined valuation per pupil to achieve their spending goals. As in the percentage equalization plan, school districts determine spending levels. Both the tax effort and the amount of state aid grow proportionately with desired increases in expenditures.

The desired budget per pupil divided by the guaranteed tax base (GTB) yields the tax rate a district must apply to its property valuation:

$$\text{Tax rate} = \text{spending} / \text{GTB}$$

State resources finance the difference between the amounts that would be raised under the GTB and the amounts actually raised under the local assessed valuation (AV):

$$\text{State aid} = (\text{rate} \times \text{GTB}) - (\text{rate} \times \text{AV})$$

Given the same parameters as for percentage equalization in Scenario B (see Figure 7.6), each district's tax rate is computed as the desired spending divided by the legislatively determined guaranteed tax base. In this case, the GTB is $319,182, which is double the average state wealth. Given Ellicott's budget, the tax rate is 20.27 mills (calculated as $6,469/

$319,182). State and local shares are determined by the foregoing formula. For example, Ellicott's state aid is $4,747.31. This state share is the difference between what the district would raise under the GTB ($0.02027 \times \$319,182$) and the local revenue derived from the rate applied to the actual per-pupil valuation ($0.02027 \times \$84,988$). The results mirror those obtained under the percentage equalization model with a constant of 0.50 (any differences are due to rounding). The consequences of increasing or lowering the state GTB are evident in Scenarios A and C, respectively.

Although percentage equalization and guaranteed-tax-base plans are equivalent mathematically, the GTB focuses attention on districts' taxation rather than on spending. In essence, the GTB plan, as illustrated in Scenario B, guarantees all districts a tax base of $319,182. Those districts whose voters desire per-pupil expenditures of $8,719 must levy 27.32 mills ($8,719/$319,182), just as is depicted in Scenario D (see Figure 7.7). If a district has above-average wealth, as Sommerset does, the tax base yields a higher amount at this levy ($16,857.32). Thus the state recaptures the difference between this revenue and the amount that is raised by the GTB.

As in percentage equalization plans, ceilings are usually applied to limit the amount of state commitment. Moreover, floor funding levels ensure that all districts receive some state aid, regardless of their wealth. In such cases, the plan fully equalizes only those districts whose tax bases are less than the state GTB and whose expenditures are below the ceiling (Reilly, 1982).

Indiana and Wisconsin relied on a guaranteed-tax-base formula in 1998–1999 (see Figure 7.1). In the Wisconsin GTB displayed in Figure 7.9, three guaranteed valuations correspond to expenditure levels. A high GTB ($2,000,000 for K–12 districts) for primary costs brings aid to all but one wealthy district for the first $1,000 spent per pupil. The lower guaranteed valuations for secondary costs between $1,000

Wisconsin's Guaranteed-Tax-Base Program

The state compares each school district's per-pupil property valuation with the state's guaranteed tax base (GTB) at three different spending levels to determine equalization aid. Some revenue is recaptured in wealthy districts.

Local/State Shares

The average of pupil membership counts on two count days, plus enrollments in summer school programs, determines the ADM for aid. Full property valuation per member defines the fiscal capacity of the 426 fiscally independent districts (370 K–12, 47 K–8, 10 high school districts). Aid is based on membership (ADM), equalized property valuation, amount of shared cost, the state's guaranteed valuation (GTB), and the total amount of funds available for schools.

The formula has three tiers of cost sharing, with the guaranteed valuations defined by grade level structure and expenditure level. In 1998–1999, the per-pupil GTBs for expenditures up to the primary cost ceiling ($1,000), for secondary costs (between $1,000 and $6,285) and for tertiary shared costs over that level were as follows:

District Type	Primary Costs	Secondary Costs	Tertiary Costs
K–12	$ 2,000,000	$ 676,977	$263,246
K–8	3,000,000	1,015,465	394,869
High school	6,000,000	2,030,931	789,738

A district receives aid for each cost level on the basis of the following formula:

$$\text{State aid} = \text{district cost} \times \left[\frac{\text{district tax base}}{\text{guaranteed tax base}} \right]$$

The total state share equals per-pupil aid calculations for primary, secondary, and tertiary costs times ADM. The 227 districts spending above the secondary-cost ceiling received aid for those expenditures on the basis of the lower guaranteed valuation for tertiary costs. If tertiary aid is negative because the district tax base is larger than the guaranteed base, it is subtracted from any secondary aid. If total secondary and tertiary aid is negative, there is no reduction of primary aid.

For example, a K–12 district with per-pupil property valuation of $225,659 has a ratio of local valuation to the state GTB of 0.113 ($225,659/$ 2,000,000). The state's percentage of primary costs is 88.7% (1 – 0.113 = 0.887). If per-pupil spending is $5,600, the primary-costs aid amounts to $887 per ADM (88.7% of $1,000). The ratio of local valuation to the GTB for secondary costs is 0.333 ($225,659/$676,977). Thus the remaining costs ($4,600) are aided at 66.7% (1 – 0.333). This secondary aid amounts to $3,068.20. There is no tertiary aid, and the district receives a total of $3,955.20 per ADM in state aid.

The high GTB for the primary-costs level ensures state aid to all but one district. A hold-harmless special adjustment eases the effect of reductions in aid (85% of the prior year's aid minus $1,000,000).

Local Support beyond the Equalized Program

The formula recaptures negative aid under the tertiary guarantee formula up to the secondary-cost limit. Wealthy districts can spend revenue raised by tax bases that exceed this level.

FIGURE 7.9. Guaranteed Tax Base in Wisconsin

Source: M. Larsen & D. Loppnow (2001). Wisconsin. In National Center for Education Statistics, *Public School Finance Programs of the United States and Canada, 1998–99*. **http://www.ed.gov/pubsearch/ pubsinfo.asp?pubid=2001309**

and $6,285 ($676,977) and for tertiary ($263,246) costs over $6,285 bring more aid to poorer districts. Although the state Supreme Court disallowed an earlier recapture provision (*Buse* v. *Smith*, 1976), the current GTB plan includes a form of recapture. When there is negative aid in wealthy districts under the tertiary-costs formula, the state subtracts this amount from districts' secondary aid. Thus there is no transference of property tax revenue from wealthy districts to the state, as might occur under a strict policy to recapture excess local revenue.

Guaranteed Yield

This third form of tax base equalization focuses on local effort (tax rate). Instead of guaranteeing a tax base, the state specifies and guarantees a revenue yield for each mill of tax levied locally.

An illustration of the guaranteed yield (GY) model has the same parameters as those in Scenario B of Figure 7.6. A state guarantees that all districts have a yield of $319.18 per pupil for each mill levied. A tax rate of 20.27 mills yields PPOR of $6,469 (0.02027 × $319.18). This is approximately the amount desired by Ellicott in previous examples (any deviations from prior calculations are due to rounding). Similarly, a tax rate of 23.37 mills guarantees PPOR of $7,459.24, and a tax of 27.32 mills yields $8,720 per pupil—regardless of actual local capacity. Once the level of desired spending is determined, the associated tax rate is applied locally. The state finances the difference between this local contribution and the desired spending level. In contrast to a foundation plan, which also involves a state–local partnership, the choice of effort is a local option. In addition, the state's shares vary in relation to both the tax capacity and the chosen tax effort.

If a wealthy school district generates an amount in excess of the spending guarantee under a fully operational GY model, as advocated by Coons et al. (1970), the state recaptures the excess yield. In the foregoing example,

the tax rate (27.32 mills) specified for districts spending $8,720 raises an additional $8,139 in Sommerset. This amount is eligible for recapture. When a district remits these funds to the state, the integrity of a fiscally neutral plan, one in which all districts choosing a given level of tax effort have the same PPOR, is maintained. Although recapture (or negative aid) is a part of formulas in several states, the presence of floors and ceilings means that no state currently has a guaranteed-yield plan fully implemented in its ideal form.

Indiana, Georgia, Montana, Oklahoma, Texas, and Vermont include a guaranteed-yield formula as a second tier of funding. Districts in Georgia, for example, levy a required 5 mills under the foundation plan. The state equalizes up to 3.25 mills above this levy in districts that are below the ninetieth percentile in property wealth per pupil. Thus state aid is the difference between the amount of money generated by the local tax base and the amount that would be raised by the district at the ninetieth percentile. In addition, districts can levy up to 15 mills over the 5-mill RLE. There is no recapture of amounts raised by wealthy districts that have capacity above the ninetieth percentile. The second tier of Vermont's finance structure guarantees a yield (about $42 in 1999) for each locally voted percentage point (1.1 cents per hundred of valuation) increase in the tax rate. The state recaptures revenue generated above this guarantee.

The second tier of the Texas finance structure illustrates the GY approach (see Figure 7.10). The state guarantees a revenue yield ($21 per weighted student unit) for each cent of local property tax. Districts exerting the same effort are guaranteed the same revenue up to a ceiling (1.50 per $100 of valuation). Under the recapture policy, wealthy districts (over $280,000 per weighted student) have five options for reducing their excess wealth: consolidating with another district to form a new district, detaching property that then is attached to a poorer district, purchasing atten-

Texas's Guaranteed-Yield Program

This reward-for-effort plan guarantees a revenue yield for each cent of local taxes in the second tier of funding. Revenue raised in the first tier is equalized under the foundation program. Under the recapture policy, wealthy districts have five options for redistributing revenue raised by taxes on property values that exceed the equalized wealth level.

Local/State Shares

A multitier system permits local determination of tax rates and provides state aid to the 1,042 fiscally independent school districts in inverse proportion to local wealth. The first-tier foundation program considers the number of students in average daily attendance (ADA). The required local effort (RLE) is $0.86 per $100 of valuation toward a basic allotment ($2,396 in 1998–1999). State aid makes up the difference.

The second-tier guaranteed-yield plan considers weighted students (WADA). Program weights include special education, compensatory education, bilingual education, vocational programs, and education for the gifted and talented. The state guarantees a yield ($21 in 1998–1999) per WADA for each penny of tax. The state places a limit on this effort ($1.50 per $100 valuation); thus districts levied an average of 47.9 cents for the second tier (i.e., above the RLE of 86 cents).

Districts with the same desired spending exert the same level of effort. The state makes up the difference between the guarantee and the revenue raised locally only for those districts that have up to $210,000 in taxable property. Districts with wealth between $210,000 and $280,000 per WADA generate this $21 yield entirely with local taxes. Districts with wealth in excess of this equalized wealth level ($280,000 in 1998–1999) per weighted student must reduce district property tax wealth to this level.

Local Support beyond the Equalized Program

The state does not fully recapture local revenue that is raised above the guaranteed yield. Districts with valuations between $210,000 and $280,000 per WADA retain any amount raised above the guaranteed $21 per WADA per penny of tax.

A hold-harmless provision permits high-wealth districts to retain as much local wealth in excess of the equalized wealth level as is necessary to maintain revenue at the 1992–1993 level at a tax rate of $1.50. In addition, all districts benefit from distributions of interest on the permanent school fund and 25 percent of collections from the motor fuels tax.

FIGURE 7.10. Guaranteed Yield in Texas

Source: C. Clark (2001). Texas. In National Center for Education Statistics, *Public School Finance Programs of the United States and Canada, 1998–99.* **http://www.ed.gov/pubsearch/ pubsinfo.asp?pubid=2001309**

dance credits (remitting per-WADA revenue to the state), paying the cost of educating a student in another district, or consolidating tax bases with another district to pay for operations in both. The ninety-three districts subject to this provision chose either the third or the fourth option. In addition to the guaranteed yield for this second tier of aid for operations, a GY formula guarantees that Texas districts can raise funds for facilities. This yield was $28 per student for each penny of tax in 1998–1999.

Full State Funding

The complete state assumption of all costs in this sixth prototype contrasts with the shared state–local partnership evident in foundation and tax-base-equalizing plans. This approach parallels the flat grant program, except that there is no local-option tax permitted beyond the state guaranteed PPOR level.

In order to promote uniformity in education across school units, Morrison (1930) proposed state administration and full financial support of schools that serve public, or social, goals. He reasoned that local autonomy should yield because education and citizenship training are state concerns. Proponents of this approach believe that the level of funds available for designing educational programs to enable students to meet high academic standards should not in any way rely on districts' fiscal capacity or effort. The *Fleischmann Report's* (1973) recommendation of full state funding for New York State considered several benefits:

> Full state funding makes possible, though it does not automatically provide, more effective controls over expenditures. It permits the state to invest in improvement in quality at a rate consonant with the growth of the overall economy of the state. It eliminates the present competition among wealthy districts for the most elaborate schoolhouse and similar luxuries. (p. 56)

The simplified full state funding prototype (see Figure 7.11) shows that the state equalizes

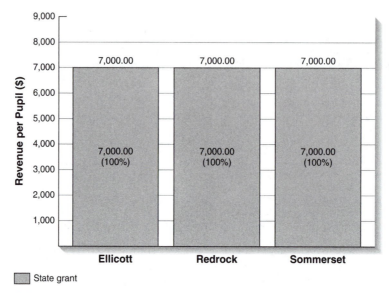

FIGURE 7.11. Full State Funding Model

all revenue, whether from state or local sources. The relatively poorer Ellicott and Redrock districts and their wealthier counterpart, Sommerset, have the same level of funds ($7,000) available for each pupil. Either the state takes into account all property tax revenue, or the plan is financed solely by state-level taxes. The legislature, rather than local school boards and voters, sets the uniform PPOR. There is no voter override to supplement the state-established funding level. In this fiscally neutral plan, neither local fiscal capacity nor tax effort affects spending for schools.

Because Hawaii consists of one school district, there is a fully state-financed, and a heavily state-controlled (Thompson, 1992), educational system. The Oregon finance plan, which is evolving toward full state funding, is described in Figure 7.12. Voters in Oregon enacted two measures in the 1990s to limit the growth of property taxation and to shift the burden for funding schools to state revenue. Districts cannot raise taxes to exceed the constitutionally limited tax rate for operations.

Ultimately, when all districts are leveled up or down to the guaranteed PPOR level, the formula will be fully equalized. Even though local property taxes and income from forest reserves raise about 30 percent of revenue, the state takes these funds into account in making allocations of state funds. The funding structure also creates a framework in which the relationship between costs and performance can be determined (see Chapter 13).

California, New Mexico, and Washington are also included in Table 7.1 as evolving toward full state funding. However, these states permit some degree of local leeway. California's foundation plan approaches full state assumption as a result of a judicial decision requiring a fiscally neutral finance structure and a subsequent movement to limit taxes and expenditures. Even with 30.6 percent of revenue coming from local resources, local property taxes are directly controlled by the state. Basic education in Washington is nearly fully funded by the state as a consequence of a judicial decision that the prior finance plan denied equal and

Oregon's Full State Funding Program
The state takes into account all revenue raised locally for school operations in the 198 school districts.

Local/State Shares
In enacting two initiatives during the 1990s, voters placed a strict constitutional limit on property valuations and property tax growth. In 1990 voters approved Measure 5 to limit taxes for schools to $5 per $1,000 of valuation. In 1997 Measure 50 imposed a fixed, permanent rate for school operations and rolled back assessed valuations to the 1995–1996 level less 10 percent. This maximum valuation cannot grow more than 3 percent annually.

These initiatives required the state to replace local property tax losses with state revenue. The state takes into account a County School Fund, timber revenues, and a State Common School Fund in the distribution formula to reduce the state's contribution. Thus the control of local taxes and forest reserve revenue has effectively moved to the state. The state provides approximately 70 percent of basic operational funds under the formula.

The legislature determines a "target grant" amount annually. This guarantee is adjusted for each district according to the difference between the district's average teacher experience and the statewide average experience. The adjusted target grant amount then is multiplied by the number of weighted students in ADM and by a funding percentage to determine the state share of this base.

The process of equalizing local revenue through both leveling up and leveling down over several years is nearly complete. About 96 percent of the inequity existing prior to the initiatives and formula changes has been eliminated.

Local Support beyond the Basic Program
District voters may not approve property taxes to rise above the level specified under Measures 5 and 50 to enhance school programs. Districts depend on local revenue for school construction.

FIGURE 7.12. Full State Funding in Oregon
Source: F. P. McNamara (2001). Oregon. In National Center for Education Statistics, *Public School Finance Programs of the United States and Canada, 1998–99*. **http://www.ed.gov/pubsearch/ pubsinfo.asp?pubid=2001309**

adequate levels of funding in all districts (see Chapter 10). Voters may approve "special levies" up to 24 percent of a district's state and federal revenue. A local-effort assistance program provides a guaranteed tax base for those districts passing this special levy with property tax rates above the state average. The New Mexico foundation program permits districts to spend very little revenue on school operations beyond the state guarantee. Until recently, school districts retained 5 percent of the 0.5-mill property tax, federal impact aid, and forest reserve revenue. This percentage increased to 25 percent, but the difference can be spent only on school construction and capital improvements.

Full state funding illustrates the tension between goals of equality, liberty, and efficiency that we discussed in Chapter 2. This plan equalizes PPOR, attains fiscal neutrality, shifts the burden for education finance to broader state taxes, and provides the revenue the state deems essential to meet high standards. On the other hand, more uniform finances and policies might bring a regimented education that is inefficient and heavily controlled by an impersonal bureaucracy. Diminished local involvement in policy and finance could constrain responsiveness to unique community needs. The restriction on fiscal flexibility could inhibit the abilities of districts to support and stimulate innovation. Unless there were sufficient revenue to raise all districts at least to the level that was available in the highest-spending units prior to adoption of a full state funding formula or to levels deemed adequate, it would be difficult for any state to satisfy demands in all localities. An alternative is to reallocate currently available local tax revenue through recapture. However, the consequence would be a politically unpopular strategy of leveling down spending in many districts.

In some states, including those in which general school operations are not fully state-financed, the state assumes the complete cost of various categorical programs. For example, the state fully supports the excess costs of special education in Nebraska, Oregon, and Washington and approved pupil transportation expenses in Delaware, Georgia, New Mexico, and Washington.

SUMMARY

Transfers of funds from federal and state governments to localities ensure the provision of basic public services in all communities. Financial assistance encourages localities to expand programs to meet pupils' educational needs fully and enable them to reach high performance expectations. This revenue sharing equalizes districts' fiscal capacities through the broader tax bases available to central governments. The degree to which these transfers constrain local decision making depends on whether they are general, categorical, or block grant aids. These three approaches differ in the government level at which program goals are defined, in the degree to which funds are targeted by group or purpose, in the burdens placed on personnel to develop proposals and monitor programs, and in the structure of fund accounting.

A blend of state general aid and local revenue funds school operations. We introduced four concepts for understanding state financial assistance for per-pupil operating revenue: the adequacy or level of support, which reflects decisions by legislatures or voters about the desired level of educational programs and funding in relation to academic standards; the division of fiscal responsibility between state and local governments; local capacity, defined as property valuation or personal income per pupil; and local effort, the tax rate that is applied to the value of property or income. If local fiscal capacity and effort alone determined the availability of financial resources for education, there would be large variations in per-pupil operating revenue (PPOR) and inadequate resources in many districts. State finance plans take into account variations in capacity and effort. In so doing, they moderate disparities in PPOR among districts.

We presented six prototypes for distributing general aid. These models differ in their consideration of communities' tax capacities and efforts. Matching grants favor wealthier districts, because allocations respond directly to capacity and effort. The state share of a flat grant does not take either local capacity or effort into consideration. State allocations in a foundation plan control local effort and direct funds in inverse relation to fiscal capacity. Optional levies permit localities to supplement the base PPOR in a flat grant or foundation plan. Although these levies enable voters to define the level of adequacy deemed appropriate to enable students to meet academic standards, these voter overrides are not equalized and result in varying overall expenditures as they reflect tax capacities and rates. In the different forms of tax base equalization, state allocations respond to local effort, but capacity is fully equalized. Localities determine spending levels, and the state equalizes the ability of school districts to reach their spending goals and local definitions of an adequate program. Because full state funding controls both fiscal capacity and effort, there is no variation in PPOR among school districts. In this state-controlled finance plan, the state determines what is adequate in terms of programs and funding for all school districts.

In the next chapter, we discuss state finance policies more fully. We explore how states measure and consider the different needs of pupils and examine several ways in which districts make adjustments in these basic finance approaches. We then examine measures of local capacity and effort that states use in determining the blend of local and state revenue for financing school operations.

ENDNOTES

1. Examples of states' policies cited in the chapter are abstracted from descriptions of state finance plans; see National Center for Education Statistics (2001). J. Dayton, T. Holmes, C. Sielke, and A. Jefferson prepared this volume for the American Education Finance Association and the National Education Association. W. Fowler, Jr., served as project officer for NCES. It is available through NCES, either on CD-ROM or at **http://www.**

ed.gov/pubsearch/pubsinfo.asp?pubid=
2001309. Unless otherwise noted, the finance formulas and funding amounts affected school districts in the 1998–1999 school year. Additional
information on state finance formulas is available
on the National Conference of State Legislators
website: **www.ncsl.org/programs/educ/ed_
finance/edudata**.

2. For illustrative purposes, calculations of mill levies
are rounded to the nearest hundredth throughout
the chapter. In reality, state funding formulas may
carry calculations to four or more decimal places.

ACTIVITIES

1. Locate and compare statutes or regulations
   that outline purposes and provisions of
   at least two state or federal aid programs.
   Identify language that supports your classification of these policies as general, categorical, or block grant assistance.

2. Obtain documents that fully describe the
   finance plan for one state. Compare the
   basic support program with the six general
   prototypes presented in this chapter. What
   other approaches does the state use to finance special programs and services beyond the base program?

3. Review reports of school finance commissions, state agencies, or policy analysts as
   published in professional journals to identify strengths and shortcomings of the
   finance plan in place in a given state's finance system. What policy changes, if any,
   do these assessments suggest regarding the
   plan's consideration of fiscal capacity and
   tax effort, disparities in revenue among
   districts, and the adequacy of funds to help
   students achieve high academic standards?

4. A committee of legislators and educators is
   considering alternative finance plans for
   equalizing educational opportunities while
   also encouraging districts to adopt innovations. Discuss the dilemma presented in
   the committee's task in terms of equality
   and liberty goals, and present a rationale
   for the committee to advance one of the

general finance models described in this
chapter.

5. Using the computer simulation accompanying this chapter as a guide, create an
   electronic spreadsheet for the formula that
   distributes revenue for a state's basic support program. Enter data for all districts
   (or a sample), and modify several of the
   plan's parameters to examine the effects
   on allocations of state aid.

EXERCISES

1. A state legislature allocates $8,812,500,000
   for the education of its 2,350,000 pupils. (a)
   What is the amount of a uniform flat grant
   distribution? (b) If two districts supplement
   this state aid with a tax of 10 and 15 mills
   on their respective per-pupil valuations of
   $240,000 and $180,000, how much total
   per-pupil revenue is available in each district? (c) What are the effects of raising the
   flat grant by $600 per pupil and placing a
   cap of 12 mills on local leeway? (Assume
   that both districts then tax at this rate.)

2. A school district has a total assessed valuation of $600 million and 2,000 pupils. (a)
   If the state requires a local levy of 4.5 mills
   and guarantees $3,400 per pupil, how
   much does the state contribute per pupil in
   this district under a foundation plan? (b)
   If the district levies a total tax of 14 mills
   (including the RLE), what total per-pupil
   amount is available, including the state
   transfer payment and local option tax?

3. Assume that the district of average wealth
   ($220,000 per-pupil valuation) contributes
   48 percent of its spending in a percentage
   equalization plan. (a) Calculate state aid as
   a percentage of spending in three districts
   having per-pupil valuations of $160,000,
   $250,000, and $520,000. (b) If each of
   these districts spends $4,800 per pupil,
   how much state aid is forthcoming or how
   much local revenue might be recaptured
   by the state?

COMPUTER SIMULATIONS: MODELS FOR STATE AID

Computer simulations related to the content of this chapter are available on the Allyn & Bacon website **<http://www.ablongman.com/edleadership>**. They focus on distributing state aid through foundation programs, distributing state aid through percentage equalization programs, and distributing state aid through guaranteed-tax-base programs. Objectives for the exercise are

- To develop an understanding of the basic structures of three common formats for distributing state aid to school districts: foundation programs, percentage equalization programs, and guaranteed-tax-base programs.
- To introduce students to the hypothetical state database.
- To conduct "what if" analyses on selected state aid models.

REFERENCES

Addonizio, M. F., Mills, E. M., & Kearney, C. P. (2001). Michigan. In National Center for Education Statistics, *Public school finance programs of the United States and Canada, 1998–99*. **http://www.ed.gov/pubsearch/pubsinfo.asp?pubid=2001309**

Brent, B. O. (2001). New York. In National Center for Education Statistics, *Public school finance programs of the United States and Canada, 1998–99*. **http://www.ed.gov/pubsearch/pubsinfo.asp?pubid=2001309**

Burke, A. J. (1957). *Financing public schools in the United States*. (Rev. ed.). New York: Harper & Brothers.

Buse v. Smith (1976). 247 N.W. 2d 141.

Coons, J. E., Clune, W. H., & Sugarman, S. D. (1970). *Private wealth and public education*. Cambridge, MA: The Belknap Press of Harvard University Press.

Clark, C. (2001). Texas. In National Center for Education Statistics, *Public school finance programs of the United States and Canada, 1998–99*. **http://www.ed.gov/pubsearch/pubsinfo.asp?pubid=2001309**

Cubberley, E. P. (1906). *School funds and their apportionment*. New York: Teachers College, Columbia University.

First, P. F. (1992). *Educational policy for school administrators*. Boston, MA: Allyn & Bacon.

The Fleischmann report on the quality, cost, and financing of elementary and secondary education in New York State. (1973) Vol. I. New York: Viking Press.

Johns, R. L., Morphet, E. L., & Alexander, K. (1983). *The economics and financing of education*. (4th ed.). Englewood Cliffs, NJ: Prentice-Hall.

Jones, T. H. (1985). *Introduction to school finance: Technique and social policy*. New York: Macmillan.

Kozol, J. (1991). *Savage inequalities: Children in America's schools*. New York: Crown.

Larsen, M., & Loppnow, D. (2001). Wisconsin. In National Center for Education Statistics, *Public school finance programs of the United States and Canada, 1998–99*. **http://www.ed.gov/pubsearch/pubsinfo.asp?pubid=2001309**

McNamara, F. P. (2001). Oregon. In National Center for Education Statistics, *Public school finance programs of the United States and Canada, 1998–99*. **http://www.ed.gov/pubsearch/pubsinfo.asp?pubid=2001309**

Morrison, H. C. (1930). *School revenue*. Chicago: University of Chicago Press.

Mort, P. R. (1933). *State support for public education*. Washington, DC: American Council on Education.

Mort, P. R., & Reusser, W. C. (1941). *Public school finance: Its background, structure, and operation*. New York: McGraw-Hill.

Mort, P. R., & Reusser, W. C. (1951). *Public school finance* (2nd ed.). New York: McGraw-Hill.

National Center for Education Statistics. (2001). *Public school finance programs of the United States and Canada, 1998–99*. NCES 2001-309. (J. Dayton, C. T. Holmes, C. C. Sielke, & A. L. Jefferson, compilers; W. J. Fowler, Jr., project officer.) Washington, DC: U.S. Department of Education, Office of Educational Research and Improvement. Available on CD-ROM or **http://nces.ed.gov/pubsearch/pubsinfo.asp?pubid=2001309.**

Parrish, T. B., & Fowler, W. J. (1995). *Disparities in public school district spending, 1989–90*. Washington, DC: U.S. Government Printing Office.

Phelps, J. L., & Addonizio, M. F. (1981, Summer). District power equalizing: Cure-all or prescription? *Journal of Education Finance, 7,* 64–87.

Reilly, G. J. (1982, Winter). Guaranteed tax base formulas in school finance: Why equalization doesn't work. *Journal of Education Finance, 7,* 336–347.

Strayer, G. D., & Haig, R. M. (1923). *The financing of education in the State of New York, Report of the Educational Finance Inquiry Commission.* Vol. 1. New York: Macmillan.

Testerman, J. K., & Brown, C. L. (2001). North Carolina. In National Center for Education Statistics. *Public school finance programs of the United States and Canada, 1998–99.* **http://www.ed.gov/pubsearch/pubsinfo.asp?pubid=2001309**

Theobald, N. D., & Bardzell, J. (2001). Introduction and overview: Balancing local control and state responsibility for K–12 education. In N. D. Theobald & B. Malen (Eds.), *Balancing local control and state responsibility for K–12 education* (pp. 3–18). Larchmont, NY: Eye on Education.

Thompson, J. A. (1992, Spring). Notes on the centralization of the funding and governance of education in Hawaii. *Journal of Education Finance, 17,* 286–302.

U.S. Department of Commerce. (2001). *Statistical abstract of the United States, 1996–1999.* Washington, DC: U.S. Government Printing Office, **www.census.gov/prod/www/statistical-abstract-us.html**

Updegraff, H., & King, L. A. (1922). *Survey of the fiscal policies of the state of Pennsylvania in the field of education.* Philadelphia: University of Pennsylvania.

chapter **8**

ADJUSTING STATE AID PROGRAMS FOR DIFFERENCES IN STUDENT AND DISTRICT CHARACTERISTICS

Issues and Questions

- *Achieving High Standards with Equity and Efficiency*: In what ways do legislatures modify the basic school finance models to achieve this goal?
- *Measuring Educational Needs*: What characteristics of pupils and special programs do states consider as having legitimate cost implications when allocating funds?
- *Offsetting Cost Differences among School Districts*: Do characteristics of districts—including size, personnel, and the cost of delivering education—warrant consideration within funding formulas?
- *Measuring District Wealth and Tax Effort*: Are there advantages in blending property valuation and other measures of the capacity of school districts to pay for education? How is tax effort defined to identify the extent to which state legislatures and local voters make use of available tax bases in supporting schools?

In this chapter we continue the discussion of state school finance policy. We turn from the basic structure of finance plans to consider a number of measurement issues related to the educational and financial conditions of school systems. When state legislatures modify simple per-pupil distributions of funds to all districts, their goal is to recognize financial capacities and educational costs fairly. Some of the costs are beyond the control of local school boards. Failure to make such modifications would diminish the funds that would otherwise be available for classroom instruction in some districts.

School finance formulas have become very sophisticated and complex in the years since Mort (1924) argued early in the twentieth century that states should consider causes of variation in costs over which local communities had little or no control. Today's formulas are tailored to provide different levels of funds to enable districts to offer programs appropriate to the learning abilities and educational needs of pupils. Many states consider these additional costs within the equalized aid program. Others address special needs through categorical funds. When states allocate funds outside the basic funding formula, they often offset costs in all districts regardless of local capacity to pay.

Once the educational needs of pupils have been defined, states consider whether to moderate the variations in the costs of delivering educational programs in terms of school district characteristics. In making allocations, states may take into account the size of the district or the sparsity of population, the costs of living and education, and characteristics of personnel. After determining the total cost of the program to be financed, the funding structure determines the blend of state and local revenue to finance school operations. In Chapter 7 we discussed different ways in which state finance plans take local revenue sources into account. We now explore problems of measuring fiscal capacities of districts and the effort taxpayers make to finance school operations.

It should be noted that the measures of need, fiscal capacity, and effort in state aid programs are typically approximations of the intended concepts. In many cases, they are the most valid indicator available. In other cases, perhaps because of political compromises, a program may adopt one measure as a proxy for another closely related, but not easily measured, variable.

MEASURING PUPILS' EDUCATIONAL NEEDS

The scope of public education is crudely expressed in terms of the number of the students served. This measure of the school district's need is closely tied to the size of the teaching force, to the extent of programs and facilities, and, ultimately, to the amount of money required. In addition, state governments are concerned with the nature and cost of programs designed to meet particular educational needs of students. We explore the ways in which states count pupils, consider these counts as weighted units in funding formulas, and reimburse excess costs of meeting pupil needs. We then offer examples of special programs and priorities funded by state legislatures and the various mechanisms used to offset all or a portion of the additional costs.[1]

Pupil Count

Governments determine how much money they need to finance education primarily on the basis of the number of students served. Early in the century, allocations relied on a full census that accounted for all school-age children. Alternatively, there was a count of only the pupils who attended a public or private school. The first of these techniques, the full census, offered little incentive for keeping children enrolled in schools. The second approach resulted in the overfunding of many communities in which a large percentage of pupils attended private schools.

Today's state aid plans provide better estimates of costs associated with the number of pupils actually enrolled in or attending public schools. About half of the states determine the *average daily membership* (ADM) by calculating the average number of pupils enrolled in schools over a particular period. Twelve states accept the actual *enrollment* (ENR) on a given date. Eight states calculate the *average daily attendance* (ADA) from the number of pupils actually in attendance during specific weeks of the school year. Few states base allocations on the number of teachers or instructional units to be funded. Even this method ultimately reflects the number of pupils enrolled or in attendance. Specific dates (e.g., tenth-day enrollment) or periods of time (e.g., average attendance in the months of October and March) are often established in statute for collecting pupil counts for funding purposes.

The choice between measuring enrollment and measuring attendance has implications for politics, pedagogy, and efficiency. ADM and ENR recognize that costs of school operations continue regardless of the actual presence of pupils on a daily basis. However, there may be inefficiencies with these approaches if districts are not held accountable for reducing absenteeism and truancy. ADA-based funding reinforces compulsory-attendance laws and the belief that pedagogical goals are maximized when absenteeism is reduced. Approaches relying on enrollments work to the financial advantage of large cities that often have higher absence rates. In contrast, ADA shifts the available state aid to suburban and rural school systems that typically have higher attendance.

The majority of the states base funding on pupil counts during the current year. In this approach, states provide aid on the basis of an estimate of pupil enrollment or attendance as the fiscal year begins. Subsequent adjustments reflect the actual counts of students enrolled or in attendance on one or more count days. Other states base aid on prior-year enrollment or attendance data. The advantage of this strategy is having accurate counts and revenue identified when preparing budgets and hiring personnel. However, shifts in pupil counts before the school year begins may create unanticipated difficulties.

The need for an adjustment in the method of counting pupils is most apparent in communities that face growth or decline as a consequence of boom-and-bust cycles of local economies. In particular, rapidly declining enrollments mean reduced funding even though personnel and facility costs remain somewhat fixed, at least in the short run (Edelman & Knudsen, 1990). For this reason, some school finance formulas include a *hold-harmless (or save-harmless)* clause to guarantee the same count to ease the impact of sudden aid reductions. For example, hold-harmless provisions in Missouri, Nevada, and North Dakota guarantee payment for 100 percent of the previous year's enrollment. Some states determine a percentage of a prior year's pupil count or a rolling average of several years' counts to cushion the impact. Florida funds 50 percent of the decline in pupils from the previous year. Michigan's pupil membership count is a blend of enrollment in February of the prior school year (20 percent of the count) and that in October of the current year (80 percent). Ohio school districts receive funding based on either the current ADM or the average of the current and the two prior years' pupil counts.

If districts with declining enrollments are able to continue prior years' pupil counts for aid purposes, there is a more predictable resource base for planning programs and making personnel commitments. However, save-harmless clauses that result in no loss of funds unnecessarily protect districts from confronting the implications of a reduction in enrollment (Leppert & Routh, 1978). They may also introduce inequities by channeling funds to some districts with little need for a cushion and induce inefficiencies by discouraging local economizing (Goettel & Firestine, 1975). Policies that include percentage reductions in student units, short terms for phasing in reductions, or an average of several years' enrollments more effectively encourage planning and efficiencies than do provisions that continue inflated pupil counts into the future.

States' finance plans may also make adjustments for the rapid increases in costs associated with a large growth in student enrollment. Kentucky districts experiencing growth during the first two months of the school year receive additional funds. Wyoming recalculates district entitlements to compensate for growth in those districts that have increases of over 10 percent from the prior year during the first 60 days, or increases of over 15 percent by February 1.

Grade Levels and Special Programs

The simplified models of state finance plans that we discussed in Chapter 7 may create the impression that the same level of funding is tied to each pupil. In reality, the amount of aid varies considerably depending upon student characteristics that policy makers agree warrant special and more expensive programs. The resulting cost differentials are due to smaller classes and more support personnel, as well as specialized equipment and instructional materials. As is consistent with the concept of vertical equity (the unequal treatment of unequals), state finance policy pegs allocations to higher costs of education at different grade levels and for specified categories of students. States adopt one or both of the following approaches to account for these characteristics of students, teachers, or special programs.

Weighted Units

School finance formulas in the majority of states consider *weighted-pupil* or *weighted-classroom units.* Mort (1926) conceived this approach in his refinement of early foundation plans. His weighted-pupil and typical-teacher units provided objective measures of educational need

to give "extra weight to the actual number of pupils in those situations where the true per pupil cost of a given educational offering is high" (p. 15). This method of adjusting operating aid within the base program assigns weights for grade levels and special programs relative to a base that defines the lowest-cost instruction. A typical child, usually in grades 3–6, counts as a unit of 1.0. Students in higher-cost programs are assigned additional weights.

The weights listed in Table 8.1 for South Carolina's foundation program correspond to anticipated average costs for each grade level and program relative to those of fourth through eighth grades. For example, the weight of 2.04 recognizes that educational and support services for emotionally and orthopedically disabled children cost twice as much as those for students in grades 4–8 who are not placed in a special program. Similarly, there is a greater weight for students in primary grades and high schools than for the lowest-cost grade levels.

Because some students are served for only a portion of a school day, the concept of full-time equivalency (FTE) is often used to express pupil counts. For example, Minnesota supports half-day kindergartens with a per-pupil weight of 0.53. A school having 128 kindergarten students would be funded for 64 FTEs, and the funding formula would include the weight of 1.06 for each FTE student.

To determine financial need under a weighted-pupil approach, the numbers of FTE students in each grade level and applicable special program are multiplied by respective weights specified in the statute. The resulting products for all grade levels and programs are then totaled to obtain a composite measure of educational need. This weighted measure of pupils' needs is entered into any of the general finance models presented in Chapter 7. In a foundation plan, for instance, the dollar guarantee established by the legislature for a given year is multiplied by the total number of weighted-pupil units. Likewise, when a district's fiscal capacity

TABLE 8.1.

Weighted-Pupil Categories in South Carolina

Category	Weight
Grade Levels	
Kindergarten (full-day program)	1.30
Primary (grades 1–3)	1.24
Elementary (grades 4–8)	1.00
High school (grades 9–12)	1.25
Vocational Programs	
Vocational (three levels)	1.29
Special Education	
Learning disabilities	1.74
Educable mentally handicapped	1.74
Trainable mentally handicapped	2.04
Emotionally handicapped	2.04
Orthopedically handicapped	2.04
Autism	2.57
Visually handicapped	2.57
Hearing handicapped	2.57
Speech handicapped	1.90
Homebound	2.10

Source: D. R. Tetreault & D. Chandler. (2001). South Carolina. In National Center for Education Statistics, *Public School Finance Programs of the United States and Canada, 1998–99.* **http://nces.ed.gov/pubsearch/pubsinfo.asp?pubid=2001309**

is measured, its valuation is divided by the total number of weighted-pupil units.

Some states assign weights to instructional units. These weights are determined by dividing the total number of students by a legislatively defined typical classroom size. The ratio of pupils to teachers provides a measure of grade level and special program needs. For example, the Tennessee formula allocates teacher units as follows: 1 per 20 ADM pupils in K–3, 1 per 25 ADM in 4–6, 1 per 30 ADM in 7–9, and 1 per 26.5 ADM in 10–12. The twelve categories for special education in the Delaware plan specify class sizes that range from four to fifteen pupils. In either a weighted-pupil or a weighted-classroom approach, higher weights reflect traditionally larger expenditures in secondary grades and in vocational and special education programs.

The weights generally mirror cost differences that prevail in schools (i.e., what is). They are not grounded in studies of what funding would most appropriately finance educational programs to meet the needs of pupils (i.e., what should be). Mort (1924) recommended weights for high schools, for example, on the basis of costs associated with the typical practice of assigning more teachers per pupil in high school grades than in elementary grades and on the basis of these teachers' higher salaries. As planners accepted the rationality of average practice, that procedure became the benchmark to be applied when assigning state aid. Similarly, the National Education Finance Project (Johns, Alexander, & Jordan, 1971) based its indices of average per-pupil cost on actual costs of grade levels and special program offerings within selected school districts, rather than on true measures of need. New York's *Fleischmann Report* (1973) addressed the disadvantage of accepting average practice in aid formulas:

> The pedagogical wisdom of weighting secondary students more heavily than elementary students is questionable; we suspect that in many instances it might be good policy to spend more money per student in the elementary grade than in the secondary, but the present weighting factor has a psychological effect of suggesting that all districts should spend more money on secondary students. (p. 64)

In a later section of this chapter, we describe practices that states apply to adjust formulas for the higher costs of small classes. This recent drive to reduce the student–teacher ratio in elementary schools suggests that policy makers are becoming more inclined to address educational needs than to continue to let average costs of past practices dictate future allocations.

Reimbursement of Excess Costs

Another approach to funding special programs is to reimburse districts for excess costs incurred. According to this procedure, the state partially or fully subsidizes those expenditures that exceed a given level for specified programs.

By paying these costs, states encourage local districts to expand programs to serve qualifying students, such as those enrolled in vocational or special education offerings. States provide aid for pupils in these programs twice, first under the basic formula and second under the excess cost formula. The amount of assistance received may depend only on the actual cost of programs, or it may reflect district wealth. If the excess cost is reimbursed in all districts (e.g., through a flat grant), this categorical aid may work against goals of equalization. In states in which the amount of aid is inversely related to local wealth, more aid flows to poorer districts. The total revenue then provides special programs that many of these districts could not otherwise afford. A report of the National Con-

ference of State Legislatures (1994) noted the trend of states to increasingly earmark revenues for specific purposes, "so a growing share of state support is outside the general fund" (p. 9).

Although they were designed to provide additional dollars to meet educational needs determined locally, weighted-unit and excess cost reimbursement methods may in practice create incentives to misclassify pupils. They may influence decisions to remove students unnecessarily from regular classrooms to earn additional state aid. Reimbursement plans that partially finance excess costs offer the least incentive to misclassify pupils because they demand local contributions for students placed in special programs (Hartman, 1980).

Offsetting Costs of Special Programs

State legislatures use weighted-pupil unit or excess cost reimbursement approaches in funding numerous special programs. We present examples of state policies for funding a portion or all of the costs of special education, gifted and talented education, vocational education, compensatory education, early-childhood education, bilingual education, and pupil transportation. In addition, we illustrate legislative priorities that are expressed through funds for class size reduction, electronic technologies, and alternative and charter schools.

Special Education

Few states fully reimburse the excess costs of programs and services for students with disabilities. If a state assumes all expenses above the average cost of educating nondisabled students, as occurs in Nebraska and Oregon, there may be little incentive for districts to operate efficient programs. For this reason, most states partially reimburse excess costs, and local funds pay the difference.

This aid may come to districts through an equalization formula that considers weighted units and local wealth. A large number of states, including South Carolina and Delaware as we have noted, fund programs through the basic support program. This occurs most often by weighting different categories of pupils, instructional units, or services. Alternatively, the number of pupils served may trigger categorical aid for special education outside the funding formula. A flat grant may offset a portion of costs; for example, Indiana students with more severe needs justify larger grants ($7,285) than do students with moderate ($1,977) or less severe ($469) disabilities. In a different approach, Wisconsin differentiates the proportion reimbursed in terms of the following costs: 63 percent of salaries and transportation, 51 percent of psychologists and social workers, and 100 percent of lodging and transportation for nonresident students. New Hampshire provides 80 percent of special education expenses that exceed 3.5 times the state average per-pupil expenditure. This reimbursement is limited to a maximum of 10 times the statewide average per-pupil cost. Similar catastrophic aid in Kansas reimburses 75 percent of actual per-pupil costs over $25,000 for the most severely disabled students.

Gifted and Talented Education

Some states fund the learning needs of gifted and talented pupils by including additional pupil weights within the formula. Others provide flat dollar amounts for eligible students, variable competitive grants for innovative programs, or support for residential high schools for exceptional students.

Oklahoma provides an additional weight of 0.34 for districts to design programs for identified gifted pupils. California provides a sliding scale of funds according to the number of identified gifted and talented students: 1–10 pupils, $161 per pupil served; 11–25, $147; 26–50, $125; and for those with more than 50 pupils, $681 times the total district ADA. The Accelerated Learning Program in Utah finances three approaches: gifted and talented programs on a per-pupil basis, advanced placement courses according to the hours completed and tests passed, and concurrent enrollment for high school students who also earn college credit. Michigan assists efforts of intermediate school districts to support teachers in gifted and talented programs, finances summer institutes for pupils, and provides districts or consortia of districts up to $50 per pupil for up to 5 percent of their enrollments. Several states fund specialized high schools for academically gifted pupils. Virginia sponsors regional and residential Governor's Schools. Maine and Mississippi fully fund residential schools for mathematics and science.

Vocational Education

There is similar diversity in the ways in which states fund vocational and technical education. Categorical support for approved programs continues to be the predominant funding method. Weighted-pupil and weighted-instructional-unit approaches consider the number of students in vocational and technical education programs within equalization formulas.

Delaware's finance plan calls for one classroom unit for every 27,000 minutes in which pupils are enrolled in vocational classes per week. Florida's weighted-pupil plan includes a weight of 1.24 for those students in vocational education in grades 6–12. The Pennsylvania subsidy varies according to districts' aid ratios under the percentage equalization formula. Michigan districts are reimbursed up to 75 percent of the additional costs of approved programs. New Hampshire funds twenty regional vocational centers for eleventh- and twelfth-graders by paying tuition aid and transportation.

Compensatory Education

Many states finance special programs for educationally disadvantaged students from low-income families. The criteria for determining who is served often mirror those used for federal assistance for compensatory education.

Some states include broader measures to identify students who are at risk of academic failure.

Many states tie eligibility to family income, following federal guidelines for defining Aid to Families with Dependent Children or for free and reduced-price lunches under the National School Lunch Program (see the Title I criteria discussed in Chapter 10). Vermont school districts receive support for preschool programs through a weighted-pupil formula that adds 0.25 for each student whose family qualifies for food stamps. Minnesota's compensatory revenue varies directly with the concentration of poverty. Schools with at least 80 percent of pupils qualifying for free or reduced-price lunches earn the maximum allocation, which is 60 percent of the formula allowance. New Jersey distributes Demonstrably Effective Program aid through a flat grant to schools with low-income enrollments. Schools with between 20 percent and 40 percent qualifying pupils receive $316 per pupil, and those with at least 40 percent receive $448 per pupil.

Maryland's School Accountability Funding for Excellence (SAFE) supports several programs serving at-risk pupils. Targeted improvement grants flow in relation to the number qualifying for free and reduced-price lunches. Schools with over 25 percent of eligible students receive an $8,000 teacher development grant. Urban schools benefit from teacher mentoring programs and effective-schools programs. The Indiana at-risk factor draws on data from the decennial census. Consideration is given to the percentage of families with incomes below the poverty level, to the percentage of single-parent families, and to the percentage of the community population that is over 19 years of age and has not graduated from high school.

Other states consider academic performance in determining who qualifies for aid. The percentage of New York State students who score below minimum competence on the state Pupil Evaluation Program warrant an additional 0.25 weighting. Washington fully funds a Learning Assistance Program that is based on the district's poverty percentage and the number of pupils scoring in the lowest quartile on the state's fourth- and eighth-grade basic skills tests. Districts in North Carolina must sponsor state-funded remediation programs for students who fail parts of the state's standardized test.

The different determinants of need in these compensatory and at-risk adjustments have limitations. Some at-risk measures assume a correlation between family income and educational deficiencies. Others that are designed to compensate for low academic performance may inadvertently reward schools for their poor performance.

Early Childhood Education

In addition to funding full- or half-day kindergartens, some states finance programs for preschool students. A survey of states by Editorial Projects in Education (2002) indicated that eight states require districts to offer full-day kindergartens. Thirty-three states require districts to offer half-day programs, and the remaining nine states do not require districts to provide kindergartens. A total of twenty-five states fund full-day programs in districts that provide them.

Thirty-nine states finance prekindergarten programs for three- to five-year-olds who are identified as being at risk. Twenty-one supplement federal aid to serve additional children through Head Start (see Chapter 9). Georgia, New York, and Oklahoma fund universal prekindergarten programs for four-year-olds. These programs are universal in the sense that they serve all children who qualify solely on the basis of their age. Only Georgia requires districts to sponsor programs, and the state lottery provides the funds. New York's Universal Pre-Kindergarten Aid flows to districts on a wealth-equalized basis. Districts receive between $2,700 and $4,000 for each eligible four-year-old child.

South Carolina districts must offer at least half-day programs for four-year-olds with significant readiness deficiencies. These programs are developed in collaboration with the Interagency Coordinating Council on Early Childhood Development and Education. Grants to Illinois districts enable screening programs to identify children who are potentially at risk of academic failure. Eligible three- and four-year-olds count in the Texas foundation plan to fund half-day kindergartens for children who cannot speak and comprehend English, are homeless, or are from low-income families.

Several states finance programs for parenting education. Matching grants in Kansas provide state and local funds to give new parents information on parenting and child development for up to two years. The Minnesota Early Childhood Family Education program combines parenting education with other interagency services. This program is designed to enhance the ability of parents to provide for their children's optimal learning and development through education and support from birth to kindergarten. The maximum revenue is $113.50 times the greater of 150 and the actual number of children under five years of age who reside in the district. In addition, learning-readiness funds for coordinated child development services vary according to a formula that considers the number of four-year-olds and the number of the district's students who qualify for free or reduced-price lunches. School boards also receive $25 per child for a mandatory early-childhood health and development screening for those between three and four years old.

Bilingual Education

Many states finance programs for students with limited English proficiency (LEP) through a flat grant, a weighted-pupil approach, or reimbursement of excess costs. The Maryland flat grant is $1,350 per pupil in programs for students with no or limited English proficiency. The Florida weight is 1.201 for students en-

rolled in English for Speakers of Other Languages programs. Illinois reimburses districts for excess costs of transitional bilingual education, which is required when there are twenty or more qualifying pupils. Minnesota considers the following costs within the basic skills revenue of the funding formula: 68 percent of one teacher's salary for every forty LEP students, 47 percent of the cost of supplies and equipment up to $47 per qualifying pupil, and additional concentration revenue of $190 times the percentage of the total enrollment that participates in LEP programs (to a maximum of 11.5 percent).

Pupil Transportation

Nearly all states offset all or a portion of the costs of transporting students to and from school. This assistance is typically in the form of categorical aid, which may also include school bus purchase and replacement. State reimbursements depend on allowable per-student costs—usually the actual expenses plus the cost of bus replacements divided by the number of eligible students in a given district (Thompson, Wood, & Honeyman, 1994). Determinations of expenses rest upon such factors as the miles traveled with students onboard, the extent of home-to-school transportation for special education students, a density index that calculates the number of students transported divided by the total mileage for bus routes, road conditions, altitude, and the cost and age of buses. The state aid may be determined within the equalization formula to take into consideration local wealth, or transportation aid may be allocated by variable flat grants.

Delaware, Washington, and Wyoming fully fund allowable transportation costs. Alaska pays about 90 percent of transportation costs, including travel by airplane for students to participate in athletic and cultural events. Colorado funds approved costs at the rate of 37.87 cents per mile, plus 33.87 percent of the amount by which actual costs exceed this mileage reimbursement, to a maximum of 90 percent of total costs. Massachusetts districts receive partial payment for general school transportation, for students who use mass transit, for transportation to achieve racial balance, for increments for bilingual and special-needs riders, for non-public-school pupils, and for students transported to occupational programs. Wisconsin pays a flat amount per transported pupil. This flat grant varies according to the distance transported, with a range from $12 per pupil for less than 2 miles when there are hazardous conditions to $85 per pupil for over 18 miles.

Indiana districts receive reimbursements according to an equalization formula. Transportation costs reflect the density of school corporations (i.e., the number of eligible pupils divided by the total round-trip mileage). The state reimburses the difference between the allowable costs and the levy raised by a tax of $0.42 per $100 of assessed valuation. The Kansas equalization formula includes a weighting factor that is based on a density/cost analysis and the number of pupils transported more than 2.5 miles to school. New York's formula considers the district's aid ratio (see Figure 7.8), a sparsity factor, and approved expenses for transporting students to public and nonpublic schools.

Reduction in Class Size

State legislatures began during the 1990s to provide incentives to reduce student–teacher ratios. In some cases, the reduction applied to all schools. Other states targeted funds to low-performing schools.

The Class Size Reduction program requires California districts to diminish pupil–teacher ratios in early elementary grades. Districts receive incentive grants of $800 per pupil in classes of twenty or fewer in grades K–3 and a one-time grant of $40,000 per new or renovated classroom. Michigan's Small Class Size program provides competitive grants to reduce classes in grades K–3 to an average of seventeen pupils, with not more than nineteen in

any one class. Eligible districts include those that meet criteria for at-risk funding and have an elementary school in which over 50 percent of students are eligible for free lunches. Florida's allocation establishes a priority of reducing class size to a ratio of sixteen students to one teacher in grades K–3 in schools that are designated as critically performing. South Carolina funds districts that choose to reduce class size to a ratio of fifteen students to one teacher in grades 1–3. Schools receiving low ratings on the accountability measures (see Chapter 13) have priority for allocations based on ADM. Other schools receive funds on the basis of the number of students qualifying for free or reduced-price lunches. Schools receiving funds must analyze the impact of smaller class sizes on participants' academic performance for three years.

Electronic Technologies

State legislatures allocate funds to encourage districts to adopt computer and distance learning technologies. Schools purchase equipment and software, and teachers participate in professional development programs to learn about the integration of electronic technologies into the curriculum.

The Iowa School Improvement Technology Program provides flat grants with a minimum of $15,000 per district for equipment, software, and staff development. Georgia finances specialists in each district to assist teachers in the use of computer technologies. The number of funded positions ranges from one in districts with thirty-two or fewer schools to ten positions in districts with over one hundred schools. The Classroom-Based Technology Fund in Louisiana helps schools achieve the goal of giving all teachers and learners access to technologies that are effective in improving achievement. West Virginia's Student Utilization of Computers in the Curriculum (SUCCESS) initiative finances staff development and hardware to give all secondary school students access to a networked computer. The Electronic Classroom program creates a satellite delivery network to offer middle and high school credit courses, primarily in languages and mathematics, and to deliver staff development opportunities in Virginia. New Jersey's Distance Learning Network provides $41 per pupil for the acquisition of technologies and professional development.

Alternative and Charter Schools

Many states provide funds to support alternative schools within the public school system. A few states' policies enable parents to choose among public and private schools. An increasing number of states empower districts, and perhaps other entities, to issue charters to encourage site-based decision making and parental choice among public schools (see Chapters 14 and 15).

In addition to school boards creating magnet schools that have a special curricular emphasis, state legislatures may finance alternative secondary schools for disruptive or expelled students. Oregon provides for alternative education to help students achieve in a manner consistent with their learning styles and needs. Districts must provide, and make parents aware of, options for students who are expelled, have recurring discipline problems, or have erratic attendance that keeps them from benefiting from the regular program. Students may enroll in an appropriate and accessible public or private alternative program of instruction that is registered with the state department of education. The resident district funds the student's placement and claims the student for state reimbursement. Pennsylvania helps districts develop appropriate programming for disruptive students with funding for up to 2 percent of a district's secondary school enrollment. The goals are to protect the learning environment, provide special programming for students who are dangerous or violent, and ensure positive reentry into the regular school.

For many years, Maine and Vermont have provided public funds to support private school options. School administrative units in Maine that do not operate schools in some or all grades may pay tuition for resident pupils to enroll in nearby public or approved private schools. There are five quasi-private academies that historically served as high schools for regions in Vermont. They were founded as religious schools, but in the 1960s they secularized their curricula to continue receiving public funds. In addition, towns that do not operate schools may pay tuition, up to the average public school expenditure level, for students to attend private schools. There are no requirements for participating private schools, and parents may choose schools that are located out of state and out of the country.

Several states fund voucher programs (see Chapter 16) for students of low-income families. The Wisconsin program permits up to 15 percent of Milwaukee's students to attend, at no charge, private sectarian or nonsectarian schools located in the city. The state pays the participating school Milwaukee's equalization aid per pupil or the private school's operating cost per pupil, whichever is less. In 1998–1999, 5.6 percent of the district's enrollment attended 87 private schools under this program. In 1999 the Florida legislature included in the A-Plus Accountability and School Choice Program the possibility of students in low-performing schools receiving an Opportunity Scholarship. If a school is designated as an "F" school and has two years of poor performance in a four-year period, then parents may request a scholarship for the child to attend a private school. A state court declared this provision to be unconstitutional under the education article that requires the legislature to provide a system of free public schools (Herrington & Weider, 2001). The program continued during the state's appeal of this decision. In addition to vouchers for students in low-performing schools, the Florida legislature in 2001 enacted a scholarship program for students with disabilities (Fine, 2001). This program does not premise vouchers on a school's receiving a failing grade. Parents of students with disabilities who believe that schools are not meeting students' needs are eligible for vouchers to pay private school tuition.

Charter schools provide an alternative for students, and greater autonomy for school personnel, within the public school system. As of 2000, 36 states' statutes permitted school districts, universities, and other entities to grant charters to autonomous governing boards (U.S. Department of Education, 2000). Depending on the state, per-pupil revenue for charter schools may be based on the state average spending level, on the local district revenue or expenditures, or on a funding level negotiated between the school and chartering agency. In addition to base funding, schools typically are allocated funds to offset extra costs associated with children with special needs. The governing board may purchase services (such as special education and personnel services) from the district or other private agencies.

Minnesota, which was the first state to permit charter schools, provides schools with the state average general education revenue per pupil without any local contribution. In addition, the schools qualify for basic skills revenue according to the number of at-risk and LEP pupils. New charter schools are eligible for two years for start-up aid equal to $500 per pupil or $50,000, whichever is greater. Connecticut allocates a flat grant of $6,500 per student enrolled in charter schools that are authorized by the State Board of Education. New Jersey requires the sending district to pay a charter school an amount equal to 90 percent of the regular education expenditure, plus any categorical aid attributable to the pupil. Colorado school districts include charter school students in the pupil count of the foundation plan. The school's base budget is at least 95 percent of the district's per-pupil operating revenue, and the remaining 5 percent (or greater) is a negotiable amount to purchase services from the district or outside vendors.

Arizona school districts, the State Board of Education, or the State Board for Charter Schools may sponsor charter schools. District-sponsored schools receive the same revenue as that generated by the foundation program, including the local contribution. Those chartered by the two state boards receive the full amount of the foundation guarantee from the state, but they do not benefit from local override elections. Michigan also permits other agencies than local boards, including universities and intermediate school units, to charter public school academies. Here the foundation allowance for all academies is the same as that for the district in which they are located, up to a maximum of $5,962.

Funding for Other Priorities

Categorical aid or additional weights within formulas finance an array of other educational programs. The following examples illustrate ways in which states offset expenses and give incentives for districts to adopt legislative priorities for desegregating schools, reducing violence and dropout rates, and strengthening home schools.

Indiana, Massachusetts, Michigan, Minnesota, Missouri, and New York provide integration aid to finance voluntary inter- and intradistrict transfers of pupils to improve racial balances. Desegregation settlement aid in Wisconsin directs funds to full-day kindergartens for low-income students, private day care center, alternative education programs for families receiving welfare, and an extended-day pilot program.

Pennsylvania's Center for Safe Schools makes grants available for districts to develop innovative strategies to reduce violence. Tennessee allocates grants for innovative violence prevention programs, conflict resolution, management of disruptive behavior, improved school security, peer mediation, and employee training. Several states, including Florida, Louisiana, Maryland, Michigan, Missouri, and Virginia, finance programs to reduce high school dropout rates.

South Carolina provides a weighting factor (0.25) in the foundation plan for students who are home-schooled. Districts may expend funds for activities designed for the overall supervision, coordination, and direction of home schooling. California and Iowa fully fund students who are dual-enrolled in a home school and the public school. In addition, a formula weight (0.6) provides partial funds for Iowa students who are home-schooled and desire a teacher to work with parents. Alaska includes the cost of home-schooled students in funding correspondence courses.

The measures of pupil needs and various special programs are important determinants of the revenue needed for school support. In the next section, we discuss additional adjustments in the total pupil or instructional unit count to reflect other characteristics of school districts.

RECOGNIZING SCHOOL DISTRICT CHARACTERISTICS

State finance policies consider aspects of communities that have cost implications beyond the control of local school officials. If formulas considered only the needs of pupils, significant inequities would result. Adjustments in state aid plans most often take into account the size of the district, the cost of personnel, and the cost of living in school districts.

School and District Size

The sizes of districts and individual schools vary widely. Some urban districts are large both geographically and in terms of pupil enrollment. Up to a point, large and densely populated school systems may benefit from economies of scale (see Chapter 12). On the other hand, some rural districts cover many sparsely populated square miles. State finance plans often include corrections in pupil or instructional units to account for cost considerations associated with size.

Sparsely populated rural districts and densely populated cities may both have high expenditures. Swanson (1966) observed that their schools are costly for very different reasons. Small rural districts experience higher costs due to smaller classes, diseconomies resulting from the division of some expenses (e.g., superintendent and principal salaries) among fewer students, and additional salaries to attract teachers, particularly in subject fields experiencing shortages. Urban schools and districts face different challenges. Their high per-pupil costs are due to the expanded services and additional personnel to meet the needs of large at-risk populations. Urban schools may also incur more costs associated with disruptive behavior and vandalism. Thus both large urban districts and small rural schools and districts tend to have higher per-pupil costs for basic educational services than do suburban schools and districts. This is true even though suburban districts may spend as much or more to provide a higher level of services.

Table 8.2 illustrates that states' adjustments for indicators of population sparsity and the small number of pupils served by rural school districts vary greatly. Plans may provide for additional pupil weights or instructional units, additional flat grants, or proportionately more funds to compensate for size-related costs. Adjustments may be keyed to enrollments, as in Montana and South Dakota; tax capacity and enrollments, as in Pennsylvania; population sparsity and bus distances, as in Texas; or the existence of remote and necessary small schools, as in California and Washington. This latter criterion enables small, isolated schools to serve students close to their residences, despite a high per-pupil cost. States determine whether a small school is essential on the basis of such factors as the terrain and any road conditions that create safety problems. They may also consider the length of bus routes (in miles or hours) to the nearest larger school.

It is not just sparsely populated regions that experience higher costs. Needs and costs in

TABLE 8.2.

Adjustment in Selected States for Small Size

California	Additional funding for geographically isolated necessary small schools in districts that have below 2,501 ADA and an elementary school under 101 ADA and/or a secondary school under 301 ADA.
Pennsylvania	Poorer districts whose ratio of market value and personal income to respective state averages is 0.50 or greater, and that have an ADM of 1,500 or fewer, qualify for an additional $75 per pupil.
Montana	Per-pupil entitlements are inversely related to school size, with higher per-pupil support for elementary districts with fewer than 1,000 pupils and for high school districts with fewer than 800 pupils.
South Dakota	Pupil count is adjusted as follows: 1.2 times ADM in districts with 200 or fewer pupils; 2.98 times ADM raised to the power of 0.8293 in districts with between 200 and 600 pupils; and 1.0 times ADM in districts with 600 or more pupils.
Texas	Districts with under 1,600 ADA receive a small district adjustment, with additional weight for those under 300 square miles. A midsize adjustment applies to those under 5,000 ADA. A sparsity adjustment applies by grade levels: a K–12 district with fewer than 130 pupils receives aid based on 130 ADA if it has at least 90 ADA or is 30 or more miles by bus from the nearest high school district; K–8 districts that have at least 50 ADA or are at least 30 miles by bus from the nearest high school district receive aid for 75 ADA; K–6 districts that have at least 40 ADA or are at least 30 miles by bus from the nearest high school district receive aid for 60 ADA.
Washington	Additional instructional staff units for districts with "remote and necessary" schools as follows: K–8 schools with under 100 FTE; 9–12 schools with under 25 FTE; no high schools and between 50 and 180 FTE; or not more than two high schools and under 300 FTE in each school.

ADA = Average daily attendance

ADM = Average daily membership

FTE = Full-time equivalent

Source: National Center for Education Statistics, *Public School Finance Programs of the United States and Canada, 1998–99.* **http://nces.ed.gov/pubsearch/pubsinfo.asp?pubid=2001309**

large cities may also justify additional state funds. Formulas may include adjustments for density or large size. In making these corrections, states recognize that demands on local tax bases for competing public services (referred to as overburden) create fiscal stress in cities (Sjogren, 1981). Other states may determine that the additional weighted units or reimbursements of excess cost that are provided for students who qualify for compen-satory education and for programs for students with limited proficiency in English, as well as state and federal aid paid directly to municipalities, sufficiently offset the higher urban expenditures.

Few states consider this burden in school finance formulas. The Colorado size adjustment factor recognizes higher costs in both very small and very large school districts. Smaller districts (fewer than 5,650 pupils) and larger districts (at least 32,193 pupils) warrant the largest size adjustments in the foundation plan. New York provides Shared Services Aid to the five largest city school districts to help cover the cost of instructional support services. These districts are not eligible for the state assistance granted to small and suburban districts participating in Board of Cooperative Educational Services (BOCES) programs.

Debates about the appropriateness of state aid provisions for small and large districts focus on the extent of participation and the amount of aid. Policy makers disagree about which communities are to be eligible for additional funds. Adjustments for small size should not encourage the creation or perpetuation of unnecessary and inefficient districts (Johns, 1975). States should ensure that educational opportunities are adequate in necessarily small schools and that adjustments apply only when mergers are not feasible. Otherwise, size adjustments may become "allocative disincentives" (Cohn, 1975, p. 216), encouraging schools and districts to remain small. Explicit penalties and incentives within state aid plans may provide stimuli for changing school organization when there is considerable waste of resources (Cohn, 1974). Penalties reduce state aid by a portion of the cost savings that would be realized had the district operated schools with more nearly optimal enrollments. Under incentive systems, districts that undertake grade-level reorganization and district consolidation receive additional general aid and assistance with capital projects.

In debating size adjustment for large districts, policy makers are sensitive to how much aid is essential to offset only those costs that are beyond the control of school systems. These legitimate cost burdens may include the following: maintenance related to crime and vandalism; larger salaries and benefits packages to attract teachers to difficult situations; desegregation; and disproportionate numbers of language-deficient, disabled, and disadvantaged students. Other formula adjustments tied to pupil needs and personnel costs may already recognize these burdens. Furthermore, because people choose to live in communities that offer the kinds of public services they desire and are willing to pay for (Tiebout, 1956), state intervention may not be warranted.

Personnel Costs

Allocations of additional funds to small schools that have lower pupil–teacher ratios, and thus higher personnel costs per pupil, emerged initially as an alternative form of sparsity correction. In addition to size factors, some states' formulas today are sensitive to costs driven by qualifications of certified employees and that offset costs of staff development.

Early in the century, Cubberley (1906) argued that "the real unit of cost is the teacher who must be employed to teach the school, and not the children who may or do not attend . . ." (p. 252). Placing teachers in a prominent place in apportionment plans would reflect personnel costs and efforts made by communities to support schools. It was also believed that this focus on teachers, regardless of their level or subject area, would stimulate the development of innovative programs. Updegraff and King (1922) later refined the concept of the "teacher unit" to account for other community characteristics. Like a sparsity or density factor, different ratios of average daily attendance per teacher would compensate for costs incurred in rural and urban communities, in elementary and secondary schools, and for special subjects.

Adjustments for personnel costs now present in state policies rely primarily on the two traditional determinants of salaries. The training and the experience of teachers, counselors, administrators, and other certified personnel are reflected in minimum-salary schedules. Some states adopt these schedules to fund personnel costs through formulas based on instructional units. Arizona, Minnesota, New Mexico, and Oregon recognize personnel costs through formulas that account for teacher training and/or experience. The Oregon Teacher Experience Adjustment increases (or decreases) each district's base funding per student by $25 for each year the district's average teacher experience exceeds (or falls short of) the statewide average.

In the New Mexico weighted-pupil formula, a matrix identifies weights associated with personnel characteristics to determine the average level of training and experience in each district (see Figure 8.1). School systems that have low weights because of a concentration of teachers with only bachelor's degrees and few years of experience generate fewer additional weighted-pupil units than districts that have many highly experienced and trained professionals. The former districts thus receive less enhancement in state aid.

Without state assistance for this aspect of need, districts that have difficulty financing adequate salaries might deny tenure or stimulate rapid turnover as teachers gained experience and graduate degrees. This scenario is less likely when there are teachers unions and state legislative guarantees of due process in removal procedures. The diversion of funds from other instructional and administrative budgets to raise salaries to competitive levels is more likely. This assistance for personnel costs may make greatest sense in poorer school systems. However, the net effect of this aid is often to help wealthy districts maintain their competitive edge in attracting and holding the highest-quality teachers (Cohn, 1974). Teachers in high-socioeconomic-status (high-SES) communities tend to possess higher levels of formal training and more years of experience, and SES

New Mexico's Training and Experience Index

Each district's instructional staff training and experience (T&E) index is calculated as follows:

1. Multiply the number of FTE instructional staff in each academic classification by the numerical factor in the appropriate Years of Experience column of this matrix:

Academic Classification	Years of Experience				
	0–2	*3–5*	*6–8*	*9–15*	*Over 15*
Bachelor's degree or less	0.75	0.90	1.00	1.05	1.05
Bachelor's plus 15 credit hours	0.80	0.95	1.00	1.10	1.15
Master's or bachelor's plus 45 credit hours	0.85	1.00	1.05	1.15	1.20
Master's plus 15 credit hours	0.90	1.05	1.15	1.30	1.35
Post-master's or master's plus 45 credit hours	1.00	1.15	1.30	1.40	1.50

2. Divide the total of the products obtained in step 1 by the total number of FTE instructional staff. No district's factor shall be less than 1.00.

The resulting T&E index is multiplied by the total units derived from early-childhood, grades 1–12, special education, and bilingual education programs.

FTE = full-time equivalent

FIGURE 8.1. Training and Experience Index in New Mexico

Source: S. S. Ball & J. P. Garcia. (2001). New Mexico. In National Center for Education Statistics, *Public School Finance Programs of the United States and Canada, 1998–99.* **http://nces.ed.gov/pubsearch/pubsinfo.asp?pubid=2001309**

explains much of the variation in salaries among districts (King, 1979). In addition to a given district's relative wealth, the willingness of local communities to support education is critical in determining salaries relative to salaries paid in neighboring districts (Kirby et al., 1993). Thus legislatures should examine closely the "disequalizing effect on local school finances" (Leppert et al., 1976, p. 19) when states assist districts with costs incurred for salaries of personnel.

Unlike adjustments driven by training and experience, the education reforms of the 1980s brought allocations of state funds to upgrade teaching quality. Career ladders and performance- and skill-based compensation plans expand or replace traditional criteria for salary enhancement (see Chapter 13). Various forms of aid stimulate induction programs for new teachers and professional development programs throughout a career. For example, Oklahoma funds a teacher consultant, or mentor, to supervise, advise, and evaluate first-year teachers. An Idaho mentor program funds developmental assistance for first-year teachers and administrators. Similarly, the Louisiana Teacher Assessment program assigns a mentor to coach and prepare first-year teachers for later assessments on measures of effective teaching. West Virginia's Teacher Mentorship Program provides a $600 grant to mentors to assist first-year teachers.

Massachusetts districts are required to spend at least $100 per pupil from state funds for professional development of current teachers and administrators. In addition, the state's Comprehensive Teacher Incentive plan includes signing bonuses for outstanding candidates, loan reimbursement for new teachers, and tuition remission for high school seniors who graduate in the top 25 percent of their class and agree to teach at least four years after college. Georgia makes funds available for teachers and other employees to correct identified weaknesses, gain skills in areas where the district need more strength, and improve individual

competencies. Oregon's staff development funds enable schools and districts to design programs for improving curriculum and instructional methodologies. Kentucky allocates $15 per pupil for a series of state-sponsored professional development programs for certified personnel.

Cost-of-Living and Cost-of-Education Indices

Indices tied to the cost of living or to the cost of delivering education recognize that additional resources are necessary to fund schools in some geographic regions. Efforts to determine the cost of living in different districts involve comparing the cost of purchasing the same "market basket" of consumer goods. It is more difficult to determine the cost of education because a higher percentage of costs is due to personnel (Fowler & Monk, 2001). Wendling (1981) argued that a cost-of-living index for educational purposes should include multiple determinants of salaries: personal characteristics, professional environment, fiscal capacity, student characteristics, school district characteristics, and regional characteristics.

Several states recognize the cost of living within equalization formulas. For example, Ohio calculates the Cost of Doing Business Factor by county. This adjustment in the foundation amount varies according to regional differences in the cost of living, the cost of procuring goods, and prevailing wages in the public sector. The Alaska formula considers regional cost-of-living differentials. Colorado's cost-of-living adjustment reflects the cost of housing, goods, and services. This factor applies to the portion of a district's base funding that reflects personnel costs. Such formula adjustments may be most essential when finance plans are almost fully state-funded. For example, Florida's highly equalized foundation plan includes a Price Level Index in which a three-year average of consumer prices determines cost differentials for counties. This index considers many factors (such as housing, food, transportation, health, and recreation) that influence salary levels.

For several reasons, few states have adopted cost-of-living corrections. The adjustments for teacher characteristics discussed previously may ease this need. A high proportion of school budgets is related to personnel costs that tend to be higher in high-SES communities. In addition, demands for state aid to supplement salaries in high-cost areas of the state may receive little attention in the political arena. The presence of cultural amenities, opportunities for advanced education, and generally higher quality of public services in metropolitan districts may counter demands for additional aid. Moreover, districts with the greatest fiscal capacity tend to be located in metropolitan areas. This may mean that cost-of-living adjustments work against goals of equalization. However, adjustments are justified to offset the higher costs of educating the most needy students in urban school districts.

A cost-of-education index takes into account differences in the actual costs that schools incur in purchasing specific instructional supplies and personnel. States assume that helping districts purchase these material inputs makes a difference in learning in accordance with the production function we introduce in Chapter 12. One of the first forms of this adjustment, a resource–cost model, assesses the extent to which differences in the costs of educational services reflect variations in prices paid for comparable resources, pupils' programmatic needs, and the scale of school and district operations (Chambers, 1980; Chambers & Parrish, 1986). Chambers and Fowler (1995) included teacher characteristics (gender, ethnicity, experience, and education), working conditions (class size), and salary information in their Teacher Cost Index. Chambers's (1998) Geographic Cost of Education Index included several additional inputs, such as administrators and noncertified personnel. Monk and Walker (1991) urged the refinement of cost indices within state finance plans:

> As progress is made toward clarifying goals for educational systems, toward gaining knowledge about educational production realities, and toward developing criteria for which modes of production are and are not acceptable, we can aspire to developing a truly comprehensive cost of education index, one that accounts for differences in a wide range of phenomena currently handled on a largely ad hoc basis within funding formulae. (p. 176)

Ideally, state aid should give all districts the purchasing power to provide the same kinds and combinations of resources that are appropriate to students' educational needs. In concert with the definition of adequacy (see Chapter 11), a well-constructed index may bring all districts the resources required to enable all students to reach performance expectations. Yinger (2001) emphasized both resource inputs and performance expectations in defining educational costs: "A school district's educational cost is the amount it must spend per pupil to obtain a given level of student performance, based on factors outside its control." His comprehensive education cost index considers the impacts of labor market conditions and the presence of at-risk students in determining educational costs. Reschovsky and Imazeki (2000) developed a statistical approach to measuring education costs and integrating cost information into school aid formulas to provide the funding necessary to give students an adequate education.

The Texas cost-of-education index emphasizes resource inputs, whereas the Wyoming approach begins with an assessment of educational needs. The Texas index considers geographic variations in known resource costs due to factors beyond the control of school districts. Indices are sensitive to enrollments, the concentration of low-income students, and salaries of teachers in neighboring districts. Wyoming's finance structure considers the cost of education in response to the state Supreme Court's holding that the prior policy was unconstitutional (see Chapter 9). The court ordered the state first to define the "basket" of education that every student should receive. Cost-of-education studies would then determine the actual cost of providing the basket in the various sizes and types of school districts, taking into account the needs of different kinds of students. Finally, the legislature would fund the basket accordingly. The adopted Education Resource Block Grant Model specifies the instructional and operational resources necessary for an equal opportunity for a quality education regardless of locality. The model determines the competitive market costs of five categories of operating resources for each district: personnel, including a teacher seniority adjustment with a cap of twenty years of experience; supplies, materials, and equipment; specialized services, including student activities, professional development, and district operations and maintenance; special student characteristics, to account for special education, gifted students, students with limited English proficiency, and economically disadvantaged youth; and special school/district/regional characteristics, including sparsity adjustments.

Pupil counts, special programs to meet educational needs, and characteristics of districts are important considerations in allocating state funds. Once the funding mechanism determines the cost of the educational program and applicable adjustments, formulas determine what shares of local and state revenue need to be applied to meet those needs. This dimension of the funding structure rests largely on measures of local capacity and effort. We explore these concepts in the next section.

DEFINING FISCAL CAPACITY AND TAX EFFORT

In previous chapters, we have discussed the fiscal inequities caused by the extreme decentralization of the school district pattern of governance. The financial ability of districts, and the willingness of elected officials or voters to deliver more resources to education, often dictate the amount of available funds. If finance policies failed to consider these conditions, there would be inequities in educational opportunities because of the extreme differences in per-pupil wealth among districts (Johns, 1975; Kozol, 1991).

In Chapter 7, we discussed a number of approaches for neutralizing these inequities. Basic to all finance formulas except flat grants and full state funding is an accurate measure of the school district tax base.

Measurement of Fiscal Capacity

Fiscal capacity (also referred to as fiscal ability) "represents the resources of a government or taxing jurisdiction that are available for taxation" (Sparkman, 1976, p. 302). The best way to compare the fiscal capacities of different jurisdictions is to compute the ratio of fiscal capacity to a measure of the demand for public services. State school finance plans have traditionally considered property valuation as the measure of fiscal capacity because of the historical reliance on this tax base. They have accepted the number of pupils, typically weighted to consider various needs and cost differences, as the measure of demand for services:

$$\text{Fiscal capacity per pupil} = \frac{\text{district property valuation}}{\text{weighted-pupil units}}$$

Over the years, states have developed greater sophistication in measuring both the numerator and the denominator of this ratio. These considerations assess fiscal capacity more accurately and inject greater equity into state distribution policies.

Problems in measuring the fiscal capacities of large cities illustrate the shortcomings of relying on property valuation alone. Urban areas such as Atlanta, Denver, New York, and San Francisco have very large commercial and industrial tax bases to draw on for school support. However, this property-based wealth is a poor indication of local money available for schools, given competing demands for public funds and services. Because state aid flows in inverse proportion to local wealth, and because localities are expected to draw on their property tax base for the remainder, equalization formulas assume that all school districts have equal access to property tax bases. This assumption works to the disadvantage of urban centers.

Other cities, such as Baltimore, Buffalo, and St. Louis, faced large-scale migration of businesses and higher-income families to suburbs during the past several decades. With deteriorated tax bases and diminished economic activity, these cities are less financially able to provide adequate municipal services *and* public education. At the same time, growing concentrations of low-income families increase the percentage of children in need of high-cost education programs.

The heavier costs of services and the demands on property tax bases in cities (referred to as municipal overburden) urge a broader view of fiscal capacity. Many states have modified their finance plans to

- Expand property wealth measures to include other economic indicators.
- Measure capacity on a per capita rather than a per-pupil basis.
- Adjust the per-pupil denominator in wealth measures to reflect educational needs of students (Goertz, 1981; Odden 1977).

The majority of the states consider assessed (or equalized) valuation only. However, nearly half of the states expand the definition of fiscal capacity beyond simply property valuation. Some add a personal income measure, and others include various revenue sources but not personal income. Two states (Hawaii and North Carolina) do not consider local fiscal capacity in making state allocations. New York's percentage equalization formula considers both prop-

erty wealth and personal income (see Figure 7.8). Operating aid in Maine also takes into account personal income (adjusted for local cost of living) in determining 15 percent of a district's fiscal capacity, the remaining 85 percent being based on property value. Similarly, New Jersey adjusts local property wealth by both an income multiplier and a property wealth multiplier. When a state includes other sources of revenue actually received by the district or various indicators of economic health that may not be subject to local taxation, it gains a more accurate picture of districts' ability and willingness to raise local revenue. Despite their complexities, such indices offer a more accurate measure of capacity (Gurwitz, 1977; Ladd, 1975).

Measures that include income strengthen state assessments of fiscal capacity. This is particularly true in districts that receive local income tax revenue. However, even when income taxes are collected, there may be difficulties with accounting for applicable revenue. This may happen in states where school district boundaries are not coterminous with county or municipal boundaries. For example, a study of income as a partial measure of capacity in New York revealed many problems due to inaccurate, incomplete, and untimely reporting of income tax revenue to be credited to school districts (Dembowski et al., 1982). Nevertheless, defining capacity in terms of income per pupil reflects both financial ability and pupils' educational needs (Adams & Odden, 1981). Most indices are additive (i.e., the sum of ratios of property valuation and income to the number of weighted-pupil units) rather than multiplicative (i.e., the product of per-pupil valuation and per capita income). Adams and Odden (1981) argued that a multiplicative factor would allocate more aid to low-income districts and improve the equity of the school finance system.

When both property valuation and personal income are taken into account in finance plans, urban areas appear poorer. Cities have relatively high per-pupil property values and relatively low incomes. Because they have high personal incomes, suburban districts appear to be wealthier. In Connecticut, for example, property wealth is adjusted through a comparison of each town's per capita income and median household income with these income levels in the state's highest-income town. This adjustment makes the computed fiscal capacity of many cities lower. They then receive more state aid than they would under a property-tax-based formula (Goertz, 1981).

Per capita measures, rather than per-pupil measures, of fiscal capacity increase the denominator of the wealth-to-size ratio. More state aid flows to districts with a smaller than average proportion of their population enrolled in public schools. This is often the case for cities in which a large number of pupils enroll in nonpublic schools. In addition, the proportion of households without children is higher in cities than in suburban areas. Including total population yields a better measure of the ability of municipalities to raise revenue to support multiple public services. However, per capita factors also direct more aid to districts with large percentages of pupils enrolled in nonpublic schools. Thus these factors do not account for the increased abilities of these districts to support the remaining pupils (Odden, 1977). Several other states, in addition to Connecticut use per capita measures of capacity. Virginia's Composite Index of Local Ability to Pay includes property valuation, personal income, and taxable sales on both a per-pupil and a per capita basis.

We addressed the importance of correcting pupil counts according to educational needs in a previous section. Several states also modify the definition of local tax bases to reflect the needs of pupils. Adjusting fiscal capacity in this way gives cities an advantage because of their disproportionate enrollment of students in high-cost programs. For example, New York's Total Wealth Pupil Units considers the number of pupils with special educational needs as determined by achievement tests and a weighted count of students with disabilities.

Measurement of Effort

The amount of effort put forth to determine local contributions to the support of school programs works in concert with fiscal capacity. Tax effort is defined as the "extent to which government is actually using the resources available to it for tax purposes" (Sparkman, 1976, p. 302). Two school districts may have the same fiscal capacity; the one that exerts the greater effort has the higher level of revenue for school operations.

Measures of tax effort involve a ratio of local tax revenue to some measure of fiscal capacity:

$$\text{Effort} = \frac{\text{tax revenue}}{\text{fiscal capacity}}$$

This ratio often serves as a proxy for the willingness of school boards or voters to support their schools. Effort often reflects the voters' attitudes toward public schools and their perceptions about the use of taxation to support public services generally. The effect that district effort has on spending is most apparent when funding relies totally on local revenue. This often occurs in financing capital outlay (see Chapter 6). The effect is also apparent when local option taxes are not capped in a flat grant or foundation plan and when there is insufficient state funding of the tax-base-equalizing plans we discussed in Chapter 7.

Expenditure levels are often used to approximate effort, but they are an unsatisfactory measure, because spending in wealthier districts is exaggerated. These districts can raise and expend large amounts of local revenue with little actual tax effort because of their large fiscal capacities. Locally determined tax rates express the ratio of revenue to property valuation. These rates are commonly used indicators of voters' sacrifice to support schools.

The fairest comparison of the property tax effort among school systems is effective tax rates. If tax rates are related to full market or equalized values, differing assessment practices are taken into account (see Chapter 5).

Measures of fiscal capacity may be broadened to include personal income and other indicators of economic status. Analyses of local effort may be similarly enriched. Revenue may be expressed as a percentage of personal income (per capita or per pupil) to compare effort among states in relation to ability to pay. Similarly, the representative tax system we discussed in Chapter 4 examines actual tax receipts in relation to available (whether used or not) tax bases to compare effort (see Table 4.6).

Local fiscal capacity and tax effort are important constructs in the reform of finance structures. Disparities in educational opportunities are most often a function of differing levels of capacity and effort. States, however, have traditionally viewed local property tax yield as a means to increase the total revenue available. It is easy to agree that local fiscal capacity and effort are important components of nearly all states' finance plans. It is less clear what measures of each dimension provide fair indicators of available wealth and the public's willingness to support education.

The politics of school finance comes alive in debates about the most appropriate measures of capacity and effort within state aid formulas. Potentially large shifts in state aid accompany any change in the definitions of fiscal capacity and tax effort. Winning and losing school districts express their positions in the policy arena. Strong rationales for revisions and accurate projections of the impacts of alternative measures are essential to counter arguments made solely to protect resources granted under less effective measures. The resulting effects of these policies on the amount of revenue available in districts are often the subject of challenges in state and federal courts.

SUMMARY

State finance policies allocate resources to augment the capabilities of school systems to meet pupils' educational needs. The measurement of needs has expanded greatly from simply counting students enrolled to considering student characteristics, educational goals, and resource requirements by grade levels and special programs. States have adopted weighted-pupil and instructional-unit approaches to finance anticipated costs within school finance formulas. Some also allocate flat grants or reimburse a portion of the excess costs of education for students with special needs. States adopt either method to finance programs for students with disabilities, programs for gifted and talented students, vocational offerings, compensatory education, early-childhood education, and bilingual education. Legislatures also offset costs (and communicate priorities) when funding class size reduction, technologies, alternative and charter schools, and other programs.

State aid mechanisms also recognize that the cost of school operations reflects community and school district characteristics. Size adjustments respond to economies (and diseconomies) of scale related to small (and large) districts in terms of pupil enrollments and community populations. Personnel training and experience affect the costs of program delivery. State aid helps districts meet salary obligations and pay the costs of staff development. Factors may be designed to adjust pupil units within equalization formulas for districts in which the general cost of living and other costs of educational resources are unusually high.

The many adjustments in finance plans that we have discussed in this chapter can offset legitimate costs that would otherwise burden localities or diminish the amount of funds available for instruction. However, states must guard against the possibility that formula adjustments favor politically powerful districts and interest groups. These adjustments may divert funds from meeting more pressing needs. In addition, states should be aware that the trend to offset costs increasingly through categorical aid programs that fund excess costs in all districts may unnecessarily reduce the amount of money available to equalize poorer districts' abilities to finance educational programs.

Measures of fiscal capacity and tax effort are indicators of the ability and willingness of localities to support public education. Most state aid plans include local contributions. These allocation plans are strengthened by expanded measures of capacity that include both property valuation and personal income and by effort measures that consider the local revenue actually raised in relation to that capacity.

Financial capacity and tax effort define local contributions to state aid plans designed to meet the educational needs of pupils and to offset costs incurred by districts. This local–state partnership provides nearly all the funds to support public schools, the remainder being provided by federal financial assistance. We next turn our attention to the primary ways in which the federal government has influenced state and local policies and curricula through legislation and appropriations.

ENDNOTE

1. Examples of states' policies cited in the chapter are abstracted from descriptions of state finance plans in National Center for Education Statistics (2001). This volume is available through NCES, either on CD-ROM or at **http://www.ed.gov/ pubsearch/pubsinfo.asp?pubid=2001309**. Unless otherwise noted, the finance formulas and funding amounts affected school districts in the 1998–1999 school year. Additional information on state finance formulas is available on the National Conference of State Legislatures website: **www.ncsl.org/programs/educ/ed_finance/ edudata.html**

ACTIVITIES

1. Define need, capacity, and effort of school districts and list several measures of each.

In what ways might the inclusion of multiple measures of each concept contribute to the effective functioning of state school finance structures?

2. If enrollments (e.g., ENR or ADM) recognize pupil costs associated with the number of students, why do some states adopt ADA to count pupils? Describe the school systems that would most benefit from approaches that use enrollment rather than attendance data.

3. Differentiate a weighted-pupil strategy from a full or partial excess cost reimbursement approach to compensating districts for the higher costs of instructional programs required to meet pupils' educational needs. What incentives are implicit in each approach? What are the advantages that each method is likely to offer?

4. Debate the merits of including adjustments to pupil counts within funding formulas that take into account enrollment decline or growth, small schools or districts, cost of living or cost of education, teacher experience or training, and so on. How might you research whether these modifications provide legitimate recognition of needs and costs of school districts or whether they merely serve the interests of politically powerful communities?

5. Obtain the statute(s) governing the financing of school districts in a given state, or locate the description of the state's plan on the NCES website (see endnote 1). Identify the provisions for counting pupils or instructional units, adjusting that count for special learning needs and programs, taking into account district size or cost of living, and making other adjustments for student needs or district characteristics.

6. Examine a state's policy for defining the wealth of school districts in its finance plan. Collect data and compare the effects of changing the definition (a) to blend property valuation and income, or (b) to include per capita or per-pupil measures of

fiscal capacity. Which measures work to the advantage of rural school districts, which to the advantage of suburban school districts, and which to the advantage of urban school districts?

COMPUTER SIMULATIONS: ADJUSTING STATE AID FORMULAS

Computer simulations related to the content of this chapter are available on the Allyn & Bacon website <**http://www.ablongman.com/ edleadership**. They focus on changing the measure of school district wealth in the percentage equalization program, changing the measure of school district need from average daily membership (ADM) to average daily attendance (ADA), and changing the measure of school district need from average daily membership (ADM) to weighted average daily membership (WADM). Objectives for the exercise are

- To develop an appreciation of the importance of how elements of state aid formulas are measured.
- To understand the differential impact on the distribution of state aid when:
  a. District ability is measured using property value per pupil, personal income per pupil, or some combination of these.
  b. District need is measured using average daily membership (ADM) or average daily attendance (ADA).
  c. District need is calculated using weights to indicate the relative costs of educating students with differing characteristics.

REFERENCES

Adams, E. K., & Odden, A. (1981). Alternative wealth measures. In K. F. Jordan & N. H. Cambron-McCabe (Eds.), *Perspectives in state school support programs* (pp. 143–165). Cambridge, MA: Ballinger.

Ball, S. S., & Garcia, J. P. (2001). New Mexico. In National Center for Education Statistics, *Public school finance programs of the United States and Canada, 1998–99.* **http://nces.ed.gov/pubsearch/ pubsinfo.asp?pubid=2001309**

Chambers, J. G. (1998). *Geographic variations in the prices of public school inputs.* Washington, DC: U.S. Department of Education, National Center for Education Statistics (NCES 98–04).

Chambers, J. G. & Fowler, J. J., Jr. (1995). *Public school teacher cost differences across the United States.* Washington, DC: U.S Department of Education, National Center for Education Statistics (NCES 95–758).

Chambers, J. G. (1980, Winter). The development of a cost of education index. *Journal of Education Finance, 5,* 262–281.

Chambers, J. G., & Parrish, T. B. (1986). *The RCM as a decision making process.* Stanford, CA: Stanford Education Policy Institute.

Cohn, E. (1974). *Economics of state aid to education.* Lexington, MA: Lexington Books.

Cohn, E. (1975, Fall). A proposal for school size incentives in state aid to education. *Journal of Education Finance, 1,* 216–225.

Cubberley, E. P. (1906). *School funds and their apportionment.* New York: Teachers College, Columbia University.

Dembowski, F. L., Green, M. & Camerino, J. (1982). Methodical issues in the use of income in the allocation of state aid. *Journal of Education Finance, 8,* 73–92.

Edelman, M. A., & Knudsen, J. J. (1990, Winter). An analysis of selected school aid compensation options for school districts with declining enrollment. *Journal of Education Finance, 15,* 319–332.

Editorial Projects in Education (2002). Building blocks for success: State efforts in early-childhood education. *Education Week, 21,* 58–59.

Fine, L. (2001, August 8). Florida's "other" voucher program taking off. *Education Week, 20,* 28, 35.

The Fleischmann report on the quality, cost and financing of elementary and secondary education in New York State. (1973). Vol. I. New York: Viking .

Fowler, W. J., & Monk, D. H. (2001). *A primer for making cost adjustments in education.* Washington, DC: National Center for Education Statistics.

Goertz, M. (1981). School finance reform and the cities. In K. F. Jordan & N. H. Cambron-McCabe,

(Eds.), *Perspectives in state school support programs* (pp. 113–142). Cambridge, MA: Ballinger.

Goettel, R. J., & Firestine, R. E. (1975, Fall). Declining enrollments and state aid: Another equity and efficiency problem. *Journal of Education Finance, 1,* 205–215.

Greenwald, D. (Ed.). (1994). *McGraw-Hill encyclopedia of economics* (2nd ed.). New York: McGraw-Hill.

Gurwitz, A. (1977). *The financial condition of urban school districts: A federal policy perspective.* Santa Monica, CA: The Rand Corporation.

Hartman, W. T. (1980, Fall). Policy effects of special education funding formulas. *Journal of Education Finance, 6,* 135–159.

Herrington, C. D., & Weider, V. (2001, Summer). Equity, adequacy and vouchers: Past and present school finance litigation in Florida. *Journal of Education Finance, 27,* 517–534.

Johns, R. L., Alexander, K., & Jordan, K. F. (Eds.). (1971). *Planning to finance education.* Vol. 3. Gainesville, FL: National Education Finance Project.

Johns, R. L. (1975). An index of extra costs of education due to sparsity of population. *Journal of Education Finance, 1,* 159–204.

King, R. A. (1979, Winter). Toward a theory of wage determination for teachers. *Journal of Education Finance, 4,* 358–369.

Kirby, P., Holmes, C. T., Matthews, K. M., & Watt, A. D. (1993). Factors influencing teacher salaries: An examination of alternative models. *Journal of Education Finance, 19,* 111–121.

Kozol, J. (1991). *Savage inequalities: Children in America's schools.* New York: Crown.

Ladd, H. F. (1975, June). Local education expenditures, fiscal capacity and the composition of the property tax base. *National Tax Journal, 28,* 145–158.

Leppert, J., Huxel, L., Garms, W., & Fuller, H. (1976). Pupil weighting programs in school finance reform. In J. J. Callahan & W. H. Wilken (Eds.), *School finance reform: A legislators' handbook.* Washington, DC: Legislators' Education Action Project, National Conference of State Legislatures.

Leppert, J., & Routh, D. (1978). An analysis of state school finance systems as related to declining enrollments. In S. Abramowitz & S. Rosenfeld (Eds.), *Declining enrollment: The challenge of the coming decade* (pp. 187–208). Washington, DC: National Institute of Education.

Monk, D., & Walker, B. D. (1991, Fall). The Texas cost of education index: A broadened approach. *Journal of Education Finance, 17,* 172–192.

Mort, P. R. (1924). *The measurement of educational need: A basis for distributing state aid.* New York: Teachers College, Columbia University.

Mort, P. R. (1926). *State support for public schools.* New York: Teachers College, Columbia University.

National Center for Education Statistics. (2001). *Public school finance programs of the United States and Canada, 1998–99.* NCES 2001–309. (J. Dayton, C. T. Holmes, C. C. Sielke, & A. L. Jefferson, compilers); W. J. Fowler, Jr., project officer.) Washington, DC: U.S. Department of Education, Office of Educational Research and Improvement. Available on CD-ROM or at **http://nces.ed.gov/pubsearch/pubsinfo.asp?pubid=2001309**

National Conference of State Legislatures. (1994). *State budget and tax actions 1994.* Denver, CO: Author.

Odden, A. (1977, Winter). Alternative measures of school district wealth. *Journal of Education Finance, 2,* 356–379.

Reschovsky, A., & Imazeki, J. (2000). *Achieving educational adequacy through school finance reform.* No. RR-045. Philadelphia, PA: Consortium for Policy Research in Education.

Sjogren, J. (1981). Municipal overburden and state aid for education. In K. F. Jordan & N. H. Cambron-McCabe (Eds.), *Perspectives in state school support programs* (pp. 87–111). Cambridge, MA: Ballinger.

Sparkman, W. E. (1976). Tax effort for education. In K. Alexander & K. F. Jordan (Eds.), *Educational need in the public economy* (pp. 299–336). Gainesville, FL: University Presses of Florida.

Swanson, A. D. (1966). *The effect of school district size upon school costs: Policy recommendations for the state of New York.* Buffalo: Committee on School Finance and Legislation.

Tetreault, D. R., & Chandler, D. (2001). South Carolina. In National Center for Education Statistics, *Public school finance programs of the United States and Canada, 1998–99.* **http://nces.ed.gov/pubsearch/pubsinfo.asp?pubid=2001309**

Thompson, D. C., Wood, R. C., & Honeyman, D. S. (1994). *Fiscal leadership for schools: Concepts and practices.* White Plains, NY: Longman.

Tiebout, C. M. (1956, October). A pure theory of local expenditures. *Journal of Political Economy, 65,* 416–424.

Updegraff, H., & King, L. A. (1922). *Survey of the fiscal policies of the state of Pennsylvania in the field of education*. Philadelphia: University of Pennsylvania.

U.S. Department of Education. (2000*). The state of charter schools 2000: Fourth year report*. Washington, DC: Office of Educational Research and Improvement **<http://www.ed.gov/pubs/charter4thyear/>**.

Wendling, W. (1981, Spring). The cost of education index: Measurement of price differences of education personnel among New York State school districts. *Journal of Education Finance, 6*, 485–504.

Yinger, J. (2001). *Fixing New York's state education aid dinosaur: A proposal*. Policy Brief No. 21/2001. Syracuse, NY: Center for Policy Research.

chapter **9**

THE FEDERAL ROLE IN FINANCING PUBLIC EDUCATION

Issues and Questions

- *Achieving High Standards with Equity and Efficiency*: In what ways are federal government program requirements and financial assistance intended to help schools achieve high standards with equity and efficiency?
- *Justifying a Federal Role*: What national interests warrant federal legislative mandates and incentives that shape state and local policies, standards, and curricula?
- *Programs and Financial Assistance*: What purposes and allocation strategies characterize federal programs?
- *Amounts of Assistance*: What priorities are evidenced in allocations of federal funds for education?
- *The Future Federal Role*: Given historical shifts in prevailing views of federalism, and given the nation's continuing concern for high standards, what directions and priorities are likely to be adopted in the future?

Many educational programs created by the United States government reflect the primary themes of this text—high standards, equity, and efficiency. Congress and the courts promote equity goals by extending educational opportunities to all citizens regardless of race, ethnicity, gender, or disability. Programs that improve state and local governments' abilities to prepare the nation's workforce at a low per-pupil investment reflect a concern for efficiency. Encouraging states to strengthen curricular standards and enable all students to meet those expectations is also intended to improve the efficiency of schools.

Despite the many federal programs promoting these goals, the federal government's role in financing education has been quite limited. The federal government does not provide a system of schools in the United States. Public education is a responsibility of states and local school districts. These levels of government provide all but about 7 percent of revenue to support schools (see Table 7.1). The influence of the federal government on educational policies and curricula, however, exceeds its modest contribution to the financial support of schools. This influence comes in part through what has been termed a "bully pulpit." The president and the secretary of education use this highly visible national forum and their virtually instant access to the media to urge school reform at state and local levels. In addition to the executive leadership of the president and department of education, congressional actions and appropriations of money very often shape priorities for the use of state and local educational funds.

In this chapter, we discuss the principles of intergovernmental transfers introduced in Chapter 7 in relation to the federal role in educational policy and finance. We trace the history of federal financial assistance and discuss the priorities expressed in the relative amounts of funds allocated to specific programs.

FEDERALISM AND FUNDING STRATEGIES

Several views of federalism have historically shaped debates about the division of power between national policy makers and state and local governments. On the one hand, the Tenth Amendment within the Bill of Rights of the United States Constitution reserves decisions about such matters as education to states and to the people. The authority for providing schooling rests with state government, which delegates much of this responsibility to local school districts. Beliefs that local officials can best respond to parents, determine students' educational needs, and conceive innovations argue for giving affected populations the authority to make decisions about programs and services (Elazar, 1972). When local officials are accountable to the constituencies who pay for and use public services, greater efficiency and responsiveness may result (Levin, 1982). *General grants-in-aid*, which do not specify purposes or restrict fund use, and *block grants*, which give localities some discretion in defining priorities within broad federal guidelines, are consistent with this view of federalism.

On the other hand, some argue that the extent and quality of education provided throughout the nation depend on the federal government's leadership. This is particularly true when schools serve students who are economically disadvantaged or have disabilities. Whereas local and state resources are often committed to maintaining existing efforts, the "federal government, free of such constraints, can attempt to pinpoint its resource inputs on the margins of change" (Milstein, 1976, p. 126). Federal policies can thus target financial assistance to purposes or population groups that states and localities have been unable or unwilling to serve, perhaps because of limited resources or political considerations (Verstegen, 1987, 1994). *Categorical grants*, which restrict the use of funds to particular purposes or identify certain groups to be served, enable the government to influence educational priorities in line with this view of federalism.

The large number of federal categorical programs developed during the 1960s and 1970s evidenced legislators' preferences at that time for focused interventions. However, the policies that fragmented the system and isolated qualifying students in "pull-out" programs were ineffective in closing the achievement gap among socioeconomic groups. In the last several decades of the twentieth century, the support for categorical programs waned as demands grew to return control over education to localities . Congress adopted the block grant approach, combining former categorical aid programs to give greater discretion to state and local policy makers. This policy approach may also bring smaller federal allocations on the premise that fewer programs and regulations ease state and local administrative costs and promote greater efficiencies. Verstegen (1990) noted that the government adopted this approach in the 1980s to achieve federalism objectives, reduce spending, and end inflation.

Intergovernmental transfers for specific purposes recognize that local governance does not always serve broader state and national interests. Just as state intervention influences local priorities and tries to equalize fiscal abilities, the early basis for federal aid was "to stimulate the correction of weaknesses in state school systems, particularly in those areas in which national interest had evolved" (Mort & Reusser, 1941, p. 473). Congress responds to constituents, to the judiciary (see Chapter 10), and to many special-interest groups. In this way, legislators determine programs and funding priorities to serve what they and others see as the national interest. In addition, they justify these actions by invoking Article 1, Section 8 of the U.S. Constitution. This provision grants Congress the authority to provide for the "general Welfare of the United States." Thus Congress may enact legislation that affects public education in concert with what legislators view to be improving the general welfare and broad interests of the nation.

Shifting views of federalism and pressure by the public to serve ever-changing national interests result in varied policies and funding strategies. The expanding federal role in public education during much of the 1900s responded to urgent social needs and desires to extend educational opportunities to all children. In accordance with the first view of federalism presented above, the control of education became more centralized at federal and state levels during much of that century. The second view of federalism, which is characterized by deregulation and decentralized decision making, guided policy development in the 1980s. As the century ended, however, this movement to diminish the federal presence and budget for education yielded to pressing concerns about the quality of education.

Following the leadership of the states' governors, Congress adopted eight National Education Goals in the 1990s. The reauthorization of many federal categorical aid programs urged school districts and states to raise expectations for pupil performance and to upgrade curricula through voluntary content and performance standards. At the same time, violent incidents became more common within schools. The dawn of the new millennium brought increasing concerns over international terrorism. People became somewhat more willing to yield individual freedoms to gain greater personal security for themselves and their children. School personnel welcomed state and federal regulation of weapons and statutes to mandate expulsion, and the public looked to the federal government to ensure airport security. Nevertheless, enactment of the No Child Left Behind Act of 2001 to reauthorize many federal programs gave schools greater flexibility in the use of federal funds. This easing and subsequent tightening of governmental control of school policies and curricula over the years clearly illustrate different views of federalism.

The prevailing view of federalism and policy makers' interpretations of the national interest have historically shaped the nature and extent of federal involvement in public education. In the following section, we examine congressional actions in the context of six themes to illustrate national interests that have promoted federal financial assistance for schools over time.

NATIONAL INTERESTS AND FEDERAL EDUCATION PROGRAMS

Public education is not among the powers and responsibilities granted to the federal government by the U.S Constitution. Unlike many other countries, the United States has no national education system. Nor is there a strong federal-level governance body that oversees educational policy. Yet even though the federal government can assume only the duties expressly granted by the Constitution, the implied powers under the general welfare clause and judicial interpretations of constitutional provisions (see Chapter 10) shape the federal role in education.

Congress exerts great influence over education policies through its power to make laws and appropriate funds. For example, the purpose of Title I of the No Child Left Behind Act of 2001 communicates a national concern for strengthening education for all students:

> The purpose of this title is to ensure that all children have a fair, equal, and significant opportunity to obtain a high-quality education and reach, at a minimum, proficiency on challenging State academic achievement standards and state academic assessments. (P.L. 107–110, Sec. 1001)[1]

The history of legislation affecting elementary and secondary schools (National Center for Educational Statistics, 2001, pp. 393–402) represents different aspects of the national interest in education. The following discussion categorizes legislation within six themes:

strengthening the nation and boosting its productivity; improving defense and international relations; expanding educational opportunities; promoting reform and the capacity to improve schools; improving student nutrition, safety, and health; and advancing educational research and development.

Strengthening the Nation and Economy

Before the nation formed, the Continental Congress communicated the importance of a well-educated citizenry to the developing democracy: "Religion, morality and knowledge being necessary to good government and the happiness of mankind, schools and the means of education shall forever be encouraged." Ordinances of 1785 and 1787 set aside one section of land in each newly settled township from which would be derived income to support public schooling. Committing national resources for vocational and technical education and for various curricular improvements helps strengthen the economy.

Economic Development and Vocational Education

The government's desire to strengthen the nation's economy provided the first rationale for direct financial assistance to public education. New programs and funds often coincided with economic, political, and social changes. For example, the Civil War and, later, industrialization and urbanization stimulated government programs to improve farm and factory production. The Morrill Acts of 1862 and 1890 allocated public land from which states and territories would derive income for colleges to advance instruction and research in agricultural and mechanical arts. Today's sixty-nine land grant colleges and universities continue to derive earnings from land holdings. The Smith–Lever Act of 1914 financed teacher training in agriculture and home economics and provided extension services by home demonstration agents, 4-H leaders, and county agricultural agents.

Two world wars and the Great Depression enlarged the federal role in education. The Vocational Education Act of 1917 provided funds for trade-related programs in high schools. Unemployment during the Depression led to establishment of the Federal Emergency Relief Administration (1933) to sponsor adult education and vocational rehabilitation; the Public Works Administration (1933) to construct public buildings, including schools; and the Civilian Conservation Corps (1933–1943) to provide work and education for youth in restoring depleted natural resources. World War II stimulated the 1943 Vocational Rehabilitation Act and the Vocational Education Act of 1946. The former assisted disabled veterans, and the latter expanded support for school programs.

Domestic conditions prompted federal actions to upgrade vocational and technical skills in the latter part of the twentieth century. An enlarged Vocational Education Act of 1963 created work–study opportunities for students, developed programs for out-of-school youth, and provided funds for the construction of area vocational schools. The 1966 Adult Education Act encouraged people to acquire new job skills, and the 1968 Vocational Education Act increased funds to states and established the National Advisory Council on Vocational Education. The 1973 Comprehensive Employment and Training Act (CETA) created employment and training opportunities for economically disadvantaged and unemployed persons.

In recent years, Congress made vocational education more accessible on a nondiscriminatory basis and urged higher standards in programs. Four set-asides created in the late 1970s allocated 50 percent of basic state grants for vocational programs to serve disadvantaged, disabled, postsecondary, and bilingual populations. The Perkins Vocational Education Act of 1984 also addressed this concern for ending discrimination. Although the 1990 reauthorization of this act deleted the specified alloca-

tions for special-needs students, provisions targeted funds to districts with higher proportions of qualifying students, gave local districts greater flexibility, and designed program evaluations to ensure that such needs were appropriately served. These changes advanced another national interest—that of expanding educational opportunities to previously underserved groups. The 1998 Carl D. Perkins Vocational and Applied Technology Education Amendments revised the program extensively (American Vocational Association, 1998). Congress gave states and districts greater flexibility to upgrade and integrate academic and vocational standards. However, states receiving funds must develop and implement a statewide system of core standards and measures of performance for secondary, postsecondary, and adult vocational education programs.

Vocational and technical education provided the first direct federal assistance to schools in the United States. The current legislation and appropriations are described in Figure 9.1. Of the fiscal year (FY) 2002 appropriation of $1.9 billion, over $1.2 billion funded various vocational and tech-prep programs, and $591 million financed adult education and literacy programs.

Curricular Improvements to Strengthen Productivity

In addition to vocational and technical education, numerous federal programs that are explored in this chapter influence school goals and curricula in ways that are related to workforce skills. Programs have encouraged students to continue formal education, increased their awareness of occupational choices, improved adult and student literacy, formed public–private partnerships, and created national skill standards.

The 1974 Juvenile Justice and Delinquency Prevention Act developed programs to prevent students from dropping out of school and to limit unwarranted expulsions. The Youth Employment and Demonstration Projects Act of

Improving Vocational and Technical Skills

Program Intent:	To make the nation competitive in the world economy by developing more fully the academic and occupational skills of all segments of the population.
Congressional Action:	Originally the Smith–Hughes Act (1917). The Vocational Education Acts of 1946 and 1963 increased financial assistance to secondary schools. The goal of the Carl D. Perkins Vocational and Applied Technology Education Act of 1984, as amended in 1998, is to develop students' academic, vocational and technical skills by building on state and local efforts to develop academic standards; promoting activities that integrate academic, vocational, and technical instruction; increasing state and local flexibility in providing services; and disseminating research and providing professional development and technical assistance.
Appropriations:	$ 1.934 billion in FY 2001, including basic grants of $1.2 billion for vocational education, $108 million for tech-prep education, and $591 million for adult education.
Distributions:	Dollar-for-dollar matching grants encourage a high level of state financial commitment. Grants flow through State Educational Agencies (SEAs), which may withhold up to 5% or $250,000, whichever is greater, for administration of the state plan. State boards for vocational education oversee the development, implementation, and evaluation of states' plans. Local advisory councils assess needs and submit proposals to SEAs. States allocate at least these proportions of basic funds: the Secondary School Vocational Education and the Postsecondary and Adult Education programs, 75%; Program for Single Parents, Displaced Homemakers and Single Pregnant Women, 7%; Sex Equity Program, 3%; and State Programs and State Leadership Activities, up to 8 ½%. Districts receive allotments in proportion to receipts of ESEA Title I (70%) and IDEA (20%) funds and enrollments in vocational programs (10%).
Restrictions:	Federal assistance for vocational and applied technology education is categorical in that funds are targeted by purpose. Programs must include competency-based applied learning that contributes to academic knowledge, higher-order reasoning and problem-solving skills, work attitudes, and the occupational skills necessary for economic independence. States have discretion in developing plans. Primary state projects are professional development for teachers and counselors, program improvement, and curriculum development to integrate vocational and academic standards and performance assessments. To promote equitable participation of special populations, districts must coordinate programs with ESEA Title I, IDEA, and those programs for students with limited English proficiency.

FIGURE 9.1. Vocational and Technical Education

Sources: 20 USC 2301; 34 CFR 400; Final fiscal 2001 and fiscal 2002 appropriations (2002), pp. 26–27.

1977 promoted literacy training, vocational exploration, and on-the-job skills training. The desire to help elementary and secondary students understand potential careers stimulated the 1978 Career Education Incentive Act.

The purposes of the Education for Economic Security Act of 1984 were to improve the quality of mathematics and science instruction and to promote careers in these fields, as well as in engineering, computers, and foreign languages. Funds encouraged the formation of partnerships among the business community, institutions of higher education, and elementary/secondary schools. Presidential awards recognized teaching excellence, and competitive "Excellence in Education" grants urged quality improvements. The 1988 Education and Training for American Competitiveness Act cited challenges to the nation's "preeminence in international commerce" as the rationale for grants to improve instruction in mathematics, science, foreign languages, and technologies and to help functionally illiterate adults and out-of-school youth obtain skills. One section of this legislation, the Educational Partnerships Act, encouraged involvement of the private and not-for-profit sector in enriching education and students' career awareness.

Reducing adult illiteracy and improving the education of homeless children were goals of the Homeless Assistance Act of 1988 and the McKinney–Vento Homeless Education Assistance Improvements Act of 2001. The School Dropout Prevention and Basic Skills Improvement Act of 1990 and the Dropout Prevention Act of 2001 urged schools to adopt programs to reduce dropout rates, increase reentry, and improve graduation rates through division of schools into smaller learning communities, alternative schools, and linkages to career skills and employment. Illiteracy was also the focus of the National Literacy Act of 1991, which established the National Institute for Literacy and the Interagency Task Force on Literacy. The 1994 School-to-Work Opportunities Act created a system for easing the transition from

high school to employment or further training. The National Skills Standards Act of 1994 stimulated the development of a voluntary system of standards and assessments for job training programs in secondary and postsecondary institutions that "will result in increased productivity, economic growth and American economic competitiveness." The Reading Excellence Act of 1999 promoted the ability of children to read independently by the third grade and helped districts to reduce class sizes in early grades.

Many provisions of the No Child Left Behind Act of 2001 influenced curriculum, particularly with regard to academic standards (see the discussion in the section on education of disadvantaged students), reading, and advanced placement courses. The Reading First Initiative within this act provided financial assistance for "establishing reading programs for students in kindergarten through grade 3 that are based on scientifically based reading research, to ensure that every student can read at grade level or above not later than the end of grade 3" (Section 1201). This legislation also tripled (from $300 million to $900 million in FY 2002) the appropriations for improving several aspects of reading instruction, including strengthening preservice teacher preparation and in-service professional development, developing instructional materials, selecting and administering assessments, and coordinating school and family literacy programs. The Early Reading First Program supported early language, literacy, and prereading development of preschool children, particularly those from low-income families. The Goodling Even Start Family Literacy Programs under this 2001 act integrated early-childhood, adult literacy, and parenting education programs into a unified family literacy approach.

The Access to High Standards Act within this 2001 reauthorization promoted state and local efforts to raise academic standards through advanced placement programs. Financial assistance encouraged states and schools to demonstrate that larger and more diverse groups of students can succeed in these programs, to develop pre-advanced-placement programs in middle schools, to give low-income and other disadvantaged students access to highly trained teachers, to increase the availability of on-line courses, and to pay the costs of fees for advanced placement tests.

Ever since the founding of the nation, when there were concerns for a strong democracy, the federal government has played a role in public education. This interest expanded to include improving the nation's economic productivity. Supporting and stimulating reforms in vocational education, adult and student literacy programs, advanced placement courses, and other areas of schools' curricula have been designed to serve these national interests.

Improving Defense and International Relations

The federal government has a constitutional duty to provide for the national defense. Kaestle and Smith (1982) observed that times of national crisis foster expansions in the federal role in education: "Wars both threaten and unite a nation, creating reasons for large scale mobilization of talent and resources that tend to outweigh traditional resistance to centralized control of education" (p. 391). Thus it is not coincidental that the launching of many of the vocational education programs described in the previous section coincided with wars.

Federal support of defense-related education is best illustrated by governmental sponsorship of military academies. The U.S. Military Academy (established in 1802), the Naval Academy (1845), the Coast Guard Academy (1876), and the Air Force Academy (1954) are almost fully funded by the federal government. Reserve Officer Training Corps (ROTC) programs are federally sponsored in high schools and postsecondary institutions. In addition to military program support are funds to compensate federally affected public schools and to encourage

curricular changes that strengthen defense and international relations.

Aid for Impacted Districts

Federal impact aid assists school districts that suffer loss of property tax revenue as a consequence of the tax-exempt status of military bases, government buildings, and Native American reservations. The Lanham Act of 1941 initiated this indirect form of educational support for districts that were financially affected by the presence of military installations. In 1950, coincident with the Korean War, the School Assistance to Federally Affected Areas Act augmented this aid for school operations and construction of facilities. Programs expanded in subsequent decades to include families living on Native American reservations and in federally supported low-income housing. The provisions of impact aid are outlined in Figure 9.2.

Alterations to the impact aid program in 1994 targeted funds to the most severely affected districts. The formula assigns the greatest weights to children living on Native American lands and to those whose parents live and work on military installations (often referred to as *A* children). Less weight is assigned to children whose parents work for the government but do not reside on federal land (*B* children) and to those who reside in low-rent housing. The historically most controversial aspect of impact aid has been payments for *B* children. Many of these children attend schools in districts that have lost no property to federal installations (e.g., those residing in counties bordering the District of Columbia). Rather than being impacted financially, these districts may have been helped economically by their proximity to government activities. Attempts to discontinue this support have been frustrated in the political arena because of the large amount of aid available to districts in all states. Formula revisions in 1994 tightened eligibility requirements, granting assistance only if a district has 2,000 or more eligible students and if they exceed 15 percent of the district's total

Assisting Districts Subject to Federal Impact

Program Intent:	To provide financial assistance for public schools in areas affected by federal activities, including those serving students who reside on federal property and on Native American reservations, and to help federally connected students meet state content and performance standards.
Congressional Action:	School Assistance to Federally Affected Areas Act enacted in 1950 for school operations and school facility construction; reauthorized as Title VIII of the Improving America's Schools Act of 1994 and the No Child Left Behind Act of 2001.
Appropriations:	$993 million in FY 2002, including $982.5 million in basic support, $50 million for supplemental payments for children with disabilities, and $48 million for the construction of facilities.
Distributions:	A parent–pupil survey identifies the number of qualifying students by residence and place of parental employment. Applications for operational funds are made through State Education Agencies. A formula assigns weights for students who live on Native American land (1.25), whose parents live and work on federal property (1.00), who reside in low-rent housing (0.10), and whose parents are employed by the federal government but do not live on federal land (0.10). The latter category includes only the most severely impacted districts (those with over 1,000 eligible students who constitute over 10 percent of total average daily attendance). Additional weight (0.35) is granted the first two categories in districts with over 100,000 total average daily attendance (ADA) and at least 6,500 eligible pupils. Students with disabilities who qualify for both impact aid and IDEA services are given a weight of 1.00. The total eligible weighted-student count is multiplied by the greater of 50% of average per pupil expenditure for the state or nation, or by the comparable local contribution rate certified by the state. In years for which there are insufficient funds, allocations are made first to districts with high percentages of eligible students.
Restrictions:	Impact aid is general rather than categorical in nature, because it provides federal funds in place of lost property tax revenue. The exceptions are aid provided for children with disabilities and funds for school construction and modernization.

FIGURE 9.2. Impact Aid

Sources: 20 USC 7701; 34 CFR 222; Final fiscal 2001 and fiscal 2002 appropriations (2002), pp. 26–27.

pupil count. In addition, the amendments limited special education funding under impact aid to children with disabilities who are from military families and Native American reservations.

Impact aid supplements local and state resources, and districts decide priorities for this general aid—with two primary exceptions.

First, aid for children with disabilities is categorical, and regulations ensure that payments are expended for identified pupils. Second, states that successfully satisfy one of two fiscal-equity standards may apply impact aid receipts, just as they consider local property taxes, to reduce the state equalization allocations to districts. The wealth neutrality test demands that at least 85 percent of local and state operating revenue (i.e., the portion included in the state equalization program) be unrelated to local wealth. Few states (they include Arizona, Maine, Michigan, and Kansas) have satisfied this test. The disparity standard demands that the difference in general revenue for districts at the fifth and ninety-fifth percentiles of pupils (see the federal range ratio in Chapter 12) cannot exceed 25 percent. Only Alaska and New Mexico have satisfied this test. These two fiscal-equity standards were initially created to determine the "extent to which a state had removed from the local district one of the primary reasons for the federal aid—the loss of local taxable wealth" (Magers, 1977, p. 126). However, the definition of revenue to be included within the tests and the rigor of the standards have been questioned by some analysts in the context of school finance litigation and states' adoption of formulas to address equity, efficiency, and adequacy (Sherman, 1992).

Curriculum and International Relations

A number of federal initiatives advance the goals of strengthening defense and improving international relations. The Fulbright Act of 1945 and the Information and Education Exchange Act of 1948 sponsored programs to share elementary/secondary and higher-education faculty between the United States and other countries. The National Science Foundation was created in 1950 to "promote the progress of science; to advance the national health, prosperity and welfare; to secure the national defense; and for other purposes."

One year following the Soviet Union's launch of Sputnik, Congress enacted the National Defense Education Act (NDEA) of 1958. This broad program of financial assistance for science, mathematics, and foreign languages was designed to increase the supply of competent teachers and to improve instruction, guidance, and the use of television and other media. The curricular emphasis was placed on potentially high achievers, and school systems subsequently adopted policies to track capable students into advanced placement and honors classes.

As the cold war evolved into an era of economic competitiveness, the national interest again stimulated federal programs. Titles of several acts illustrate congressional concerns: the Education for Economic Security Act of 1984; the Education and Training for American Competitiveness Act of 1988; the Excellence in Mathematics, Science and Engineering Act of 1990; and the 1991 National Defense Authorization Act. The Foreign Language Assistance Act of 1994 supported the creation of model programs in elementary and secondary schools. This legislation was premised on the finding that "Multilingualism enhances cognitive and social growth, competitiveness in the global marketplace, national security, and understanding of diverse people and cultures" (Section 7202).

These diverse programs to finance military academies, education for children in federally impacted school systems, exchanges of people and ideas, and improvements in math, science, and foreign language curricula reflect the nation's interests in strengthened defense and international relations. Just like federal support of vocational and technical education, many of these programs have also enabled states and localities to enlarge access to schooling.

Expanding Educational Opportunities

The United States government ensures that all students have access to public education. Beginning in the 1780s, when land grants made possible schools in territories, this interest grew with creation of the Freedman's Bureau to advance educational opportunities for African Americans following the Civil War. The Morrill Act of 1890 urged land grant colleges to recognize students' civil rights. The GI Bill gave veterans opportunities for higher education in an effort not to overburden the job market following World War II.

The United States Supreme Court's *Brown* v. *Board of Education* (1954) decision that "separate but equal" schools are inherently unequal set the stage for subsequent legislation. Congressional actions prohibited discriminatory practices and compensated for economic and educational deprivation. Two provisions of the Civil Rights Act of 1964 and many subsequent statutes urged schools to cease discriminatory practices. Title VI concerned student behavior and prohibited discrimination on the basis of race, religion, or national origin in "programs and activities" receiving federal financial assistance. Title VII prohibited employment-related discrimination on the basis of these same characteristics as well as gender.[2]

Later enactment of Title IX of the Education Amendments of 1972 prohibited discrimination on the basis of gender in educational programs receiving federal funds. The Equal Pay Act (1963) and the Age Discrimination in Employment Act (1967) also extended protection from discriminatory policies and practices. The 1972 Emergency School Assistance Act (ESAA) rewarded school systems that had already desegregated and encouraged others to desegregate voluntarily. The Education of All Handicapped Children Act (1975), the Individuals with Disabilities Education Act (1991), and the Americans with Disabilities Act (1990) addressed discrimination in program participation and facility access. The Women's Educational Equity Act of 1994 provided grants to promote effective gender equity policies and to increase women's access to highly skilled, high-paying careers. The reauthorization of this act in 2001 noted that

> Federal assistance for gender equity must be tied to systemic reform, involve collaborative efforts to implement effective gender practices at the local level, and encourage parental participation; and . . . excellence in education, high educational achievements and standards, and the full participation of women and girls in American society,

cannot be achieved without educational equity for women and girls. (Section 5611)

The 1964 Civil Rights Act initiated the policy of withholding federal funds to encourage school districts to comply with mandates. The newly created Office of Civil Rights (OCR) within the Department of Education investigated reported denials of civil rights. This strategy of influencing change through such adverse consequences as legal actions and withholding transfer payments is said to hold a *stick* of enforcement over local officials. The reliance on sanctions to obtain results differs from a policy of financial incentives. Often referred to as *carrots*, these incentives have a subtle effect on schools. Directives, or so-called strings, attached to these categorical aid programs redirect state and local policies and curricula toward national priorities.

Federal categorical aid programs enacted during the decades of the 1960s and 1970s raised awareness of the role that formal education can play in improving particular groups' social and economic positions. These programs resulted in large increases in financial assistance for schools. The movement in the 1990s to restructure school curricula and assessments in line with national goals stimulated reforms in many of these programs to improve the education of all students. The No Child Left Behind Act that reauthorized many federal programs in 2001 was designed to improve all students' opportunities to meet high standards. This legislation required annual state assessments aligned with high standards; increased accountability for states, districts, and schools; gave states and districts flexibility in determining uses of federal funds; and permitted choice among supplementary services and among public schools for parents whose children attend low-performing schools.

In the following sections, we review the primary legislative acts that finance programs serving children with special needs, who have often been overlooked at state and local levels

(Verstegen, 1987, 1994). The primary targeted groups include Native Americans, the economically disadvantaged, children with disabilities, and students whose native language is not English. Many programs outlined in this section are *entitlements*, which means that available funds are allocated according to the numbers of qualifying students. Other *competitive* grants finance programs through an application process. Proposals identify intended goals, implementation strategies, and evaluation plans for programs to meet students' educational needs.

Education of Native Americans

Treaty provisions during the 1800s obligated the federal government to educate Native American children. In contrast to today's concern for the separation of church and state, the government initially supported church-related mission schools. By the turn of the century, financial support for sectarian schools ended, and the Bureau of Indian Affairs (BIA) assumed responsibility for administering boarding schools in remote areas and day schools in population centers. Public school districts whose boundaries overlap reservations serve the majority of Native American students today.

Federal programs to help finance Indian education in public schools began with the 1934 Johnson–O'Malley (JOM) Act. The Indian Education Act of 1972 expanded the federal role through research and demonstration projects that developed appropriate bilingual and curriculum materials. The Native American Language Act of 1990 provided grants to help ensure the survival of native languages and enhance the transfer of language skills among generations. Although school districts that serve reservations benefit from impact aid payments, these general funds need not be spent on programs for Native American students (see Figure 9.2).

Funds allocated under Title VII of the No Child Left Behind Act of 2001 addressed the "unique educational and culturally related aca-

demic needs" of American Indian, Native Hawaiian, and Alaska Native students. The purpose was to support local efforts "so that such students can meet the same challenging State student academic achievement standards as all other students are expected to meet" (Section 7102). The amount of funding was the greater of the average per-pupil expenditure of the respective state or 80 percent of the national average per-pupil expenditure.

Education of Economically Disadvantaged Students

Along with the Civil Rights Act of 1964, Congress created the Office of Economic Opportunity and financed a number of programs to improve the education of economically disadvantaged children and youth. The most visible of these programs were Job Corps, Volunteers in Service to America (VISTA), Head Start, Follow Through, and Upward Bound.

The largest program, Head Start, has a goal of providing comprehensive health, nutritional, educational, and social services for preschool children from low-income families. The 1994 reauthorization of Head Start created programs for children from birth to age three and devoted 25 percent of funding to upgrade the quality of personnel and operations. Congress also required a process for identifying and improving poorly performing programs. Those that failed to correct deficiencies within one year faced potential termination of funds. The Even Start Family Literacy Program also began in 1994 to integrate early-childhood programs with adult literacy and parental education programs. The 2001 reauthorization of this program, along with the Early Reading First initiatives (outlined earlier in our discussion of strengthening economic productivity), addressed continuing concern with reading instruction for preschool children, particularly those from low-income families.

Once educationally disadvantaged children enter school, they may be served by Title I programs. The initial purpose of Title I of the Elementary and Secondary Education Act (ESEA) of 1965 was to provide financial assistance to districts "serving areas with concentrations of children from low-income families . . . to expand and improve their educational programs." This federal program has also been referred to as Chapter 1, in reference to the reauthorization of this section of ESEA within the 1981 Education Consolidation and Improvement Act (ECIA). The program designation as Title I of ESEA reappeared within the Improving America's Schools Act of 1994. Under subsequent reauthorizations, Title I continued to target funds to schools having a percentage or number of qualifying poor students that is higher than the district average, or 36 percent, whichever is lower. Within a target school, remedial reading and mathematics programs serve pupils with low performance on standardized tests, regardless of family income. In addition, local education agencies (LEAs) direct funds to provide equitable services to eligible students in private schools.

The effects of Title I have been scrutinized and debated more than those of any other federal categorical aid program. A number of analyses reported success in raising cognitive levels of disadvantaged children, particularly for African American and Hispanic students (e.g., National Assessment of Educational Progress, 1981; Stonehill & Anderson, 1982; Stickney & Plunkett, 1983; Schorr & Schorr, 1988; U.S. Department of Education, 1999). However, other studies found evidence that effects are modest and are not sustained over time (e.g., Kaestle & Smith, 1982; Carter, 1984; Millsap, et al., 1992; Puma, et al., 1997). Wayson (1975) listed several factors that inhibited the potential of compensatory education. Pullout programs shifted the responsibility for students' success away from regular classroom teachers, and this fragmented school experience meant different teaching styles and different texts in regular and remedial classes. Organizational and political impediments, including the reluctance of local and state offi-

cials to accept Title I's major priorities and the failure of teachers and principals to support programs, worked against program success. The lack of full funding also inhibited the program's potential. Verstegen (1992, 1995) noted that only 60 percent of eligible Title I students have been served.

The reauthorizations of ESEA within the Improving America's Schools Act of 1994 and the No Child Left Behind Act of 2001 took into account many of these limitations. The latter legislation increased the appropriation substantially, brought greater accountability for academic achievement, and permitted flexibility in the use of many federal funds. Figure 9.3 summarizes the intent and provisions of Title I, which is the largest program of federal financial assistance provided under the Department of Education. Only the Department of Agriculture's allocations for school lunch programs exceeded the Title I appropriation of $12.3 billion in FY 2002. The 2001 legislation provided for appropriations to increase annually to $25 billion in FY 2007.

Across the nation, nearly 11 percent of all students enroll in Title I reading programs, and somewhat fewer (7 percent) participate in mathematics programs. These students are concentrated in elementary schools in central cities and in combined (K–12) schools in rural areas (National Center for Education Statistics, 2001, Table 59). Moore (2001) reported that about 92 percent of all districts take advantage of Title I funds in providing instructional services. Chambers et al. (2000) found that districts use Title I funds primarily for "instruction, supporting the hiring of additional teachers and teacher aides, providing instructional materials and computers, and supporting other instructional services and resources" (p. 98).

The 1994 amendments brought extensive changes in program requirements, uses of funds within schools, and accountability. Schools in which economically disadvantaged children account for at least 75 percent of all children in the attendance area have priority for available

---

Helping Disadvantaged Students Meet High Standards

Program Intent:	To improve teaching and learning in high-poverty schools to enable eligible students to meet states' challenging academic content and achievement standards.
Congressional Action:	Originally Title I of the Elementary and Secondary Education Act (ESEA) of 1965; revised as Chapter 1 of the Education Consolidation and Improvement Act (ECIA) of 1981; reauthorized as Title I of the Improving America's Schools Act of 1994 and the No Child Left Behind Act of 2001.
Appropriations:	$12.3 billion in FY 2001, including $10.3 billion in grants to states, $975 million for reading first initiatives, $396 million for migrant education, $250 million for Even Start, and $235 million for comprehensive school reform.
Distributions:	Funds flow through State Education Agencies (SEAs) to districts. Basic grants (86% of the total) are calculated by multiplying the number of eligible children (determined by family income) by 40 percent of the statewide average per-pupil expenditure (no less than 80 percent nor more than 120 percent of the national average). Concentration grants (14% of the total) direct additional funds to districts with more than 15% or 6,500 eligible students.
Restrictions:	Categorical aid is directed to public and private schools having concentrations of low-income children. Programs may be school-wide if there is high concentration (50% or over) of eligible students. In the past, only low-performing children received services. Schools may combine federal, state, and local funds in comprehensive efforts to upgrade the entire educational program. Schools are accountable for helping all students meet state academic content and achievement standards, with a goal of 100 percent of students achieving at the proficient level in 12 years on annual state assessments in mathematics and reading/language arts in grades 3 to 8. There are progress objectives for the performance of racial/ethnic, poverty, and limited-English-proficiency groups and national assessments of a sample of fourth- and eighth-grade students. Districts must provide parents of students in low-performing schools a choice of supplemental services, including private tutoring, extended day and summer schools, and transportation to other public schools. Schools that fail to make adequate yearly progress for five years may be reconstituted.

FIGURE 9.3. Education of Disadvantaged Students

Sources: 20 USC 6301; 34 CFR 200; Final fiscal 2001 and fiscal 2002 appropriations (2002), pp. 26–27.

funds. In order to advance equity goals, Concentration Grants direct funds to districts with either 6,500 or 15 percent of all children eligible for services. Although funds continued to be distributed to schools on the basis of poverty, the 1994 reauthorization no longer restricted participation to low-achieving students in many schools. Schools in which over 50 percent of students are from low-income families can involve all students in Title I programs. Chambers et al. (2000) noted that this *school-wide reform* occurs in nearly half of the nation's schools. The intent of this policy change was to "reduce the historically fragmented or categorical character of Title I programs and improve the effectiveness of entire schools rather than targeting services to meet the needs of the most disadvantaged subpopulations" (Wong & Meyer, 1998, p. 116). Minimizing the removal of Title I students from the regular classroom, serves to involve students in complex thinking and problem-solving experiences. Schools can also increase the amount and quality of learning time in an extended school day or year, in summer programs, or by offering other opportunities for enriched and accelerated curricula. Teachers gained greater decision-making authority and flexibility in exchange for assuming greater responsibility for student performance.

Under the 2001 reauthorization, state plans for Title I must ensure that there are "challenging academic content standards and challenging student academic achievement standards" (Section 1111). These standards for disadvantaged students must specify the same knowledge, skills, and levels of achievement that is expected of all students in at least mathematics, reading or language arts, and (beginning in 2005–2006) science. The *content standards* specify what students are expected to know and be able to do, contain coherent and rigorous content, and encourage the teaching of advanced skills. The *achievement standards* are aligned with the academic content standards, describe two levels of high achievement (proficient and advanced) that determine how well students are mastering the content, and describe a third level (basic) that monitors progress of lower-achieving students. A goal of the act was to close "the achievement gap between high- and low-performing children, especially the achievement gaps between minority and nonminority students, and between disadvantaged children and their more advantaged peers" (Section 1001).

The act required annual state *assessments* in third through eighth grades in reading and mathematics by 2005–2006 (and in science by 2007–2008). Schools are required to make reasonable adaptations and accommodations in assessments for students with diverse learning needs. In addition, states must assess in English the achievement of students who have limited English proficiency and have been in the country for three or more consecutive years. In addition to the state assessments, a sample of fourth- and eighth-graders would participate every other year in the National Assessment of Educational Progress (NAEP) in reading and mathematics to provide a cross-state verification of states' results on their own assessments. However, parents may withdraw their children from the federal assessment program.

This reauthorization brought greater *accountability* of states and schools "for improving the academic achievement of all students, and identifying and turning around low-performing schools that have failed to provide a high-quality education to their students, while providing alternatives to students in such schools" (Section 1001). Annual report cards to parents would indicate overall state assessment results, as well as progress of groups defined by family income, race and ethnicity, disabilities, and limited English proficiency. Reports would also include graduation rates and, at the state's discretion, such indicators as grade-to-grade retention rates, attendance rates, and participation in gifted and talented, advanced placement, and college preparatory courses.

States were required to monitor progress toward academic performance objectives annually. There would be *assistance* for poorly performing schools, *rewards* (state Academic Achievement Awards, bonuses, and recognition) for meeting annual progress goals, as well as *sanctions* for those not making "adequate yearly progress" (Section 1111). The act required states to achieve 100 percent proficiency, as defined by each state, over a 12-year period using 2001–2002 data as a starting point for measuring progress.

Students in schools that are not making adequate progress toward this goal for two consecutive years would be given the opportunity to transfer to better-performing public schools, including charter schools, with the district providing transportation. Schools would also receive federal assistance in offering supplemental educational services, to be selected by students' parents. These services could include tutoring by public or private providers and extended day school and summer school programs. Districts would spend up to 20 percent of Title I allocations to provide choice among schools and supplemental educational services for qualifying students. Schools continuing to make inadequate progress after five years would be identified for reconstitution. Sanctions could include replacing school personnel, revamping curricula, or converting to charter school status.

Along with this increased accountability for student academic performance, the 2001 reauthorization provided *flexibility* in the use of federal funds. The State and Local Transferability Act permitted states and districts to transfer up to 50 percent of federal funds under the following four programs to another program or to Title I without seeking permission: Teacher Quality, Educational Technology, Innovative Programs, and Safe and Drug-Free Schools. Districts could use these funds to reduce class size, hire additional teachers, increase salaries, or improve professional development. The State and Local Flexibility Demonstration Act financed up to 150 projects. Participating districts would have latitude in using federal funds for up to five years to improve student achievement in exchange for performance agreements.

States and districts are to coordinate programs for improving the academic performance of disadvantaged students with other federal programs, including the Perkins Vocational and Technical Education Act, the Head Start Act, and the Individuals with Disabilities Education Act. Recognizing that many condi-

tions outside of schools can adversely affect academic achievement, Title I provisions urge the coordination of services "with other agencies providing services to youth, children and families." Similarly, there should be "substantial and meaningful opportunities" for parents to participate in their children's education (Section 1001).

Many federal programs permit State Educational Agencies (SEAs) to retain a percentage of funds to finance administration, coordination, professional training, and technical assistance. This support grew rapidly with the enactment of ESEA. States could retain up to 1.5 percent of Title I funds for administration and school improvement activities. The impact of federal programs on the growth of SEAs is evident in a report that over 40 percent of SEA funding and staffing came from federal sources in the 1990s. The level of federal support ranged widely among states, from about 10 to about 80 percent, depending on the number and types of federal and state programs within the SEA's responsibility (U.S. General Accounting Office, 1994). Despite this substantial support, SEAs have been criticized for not providing needed programmatic leadership: "Staff sizes are small, other responsibilities already involve major time commitments, and staff members are much more comfortable with regulatory and fiscal matters than with curriculum and instruction in their dealing with school districts" (Millsap, et al., 1992, pp. ix–x). Nevertheless, SEA oversight of district curricula increased under recent amendments in Title I and other federal programs. In addition to guiding the development of content and achievement standards and aligned assessments, state agencies controlled corrective actions for low-performing schools.

The far-reaching modifications in the 2001 reauthorization of ESEA brought a blend of accountability via assessment results, flexibility in uses of funds, parental choice of supplemental services, and the ability of students to transfer to a better-performing public school for those states accepting Title I funds. As a consequence, the act is likely to bring greater federal influence over states' policies regarding standards, assessments, and accountability for academic performance of all students.

Education of Students with Disabilities

Expanding educational opportunities for children with disabilities became a federal priority during the 1960s and 1970s. Financial aid for educational programs began in 1965 with benefits granted by Title VI of the Elementary and Secondary Education Act (ESEA). In the same year, the National Technical Institute for the Deaf Act created Gallaudet University. This federally funded institution operates model elementary and secondary schools for deaf students.

The 1968 Handicapped Children's Early Education Assistance Act authorized preschool programs, and the Education of the Handicapped Act of 1970 created a Bureau of Education for the Handicapped. In several federal court decisions (e.g., *Mills* v. *Board of Education*, 1972), the federal judiciary declared that students with disabilities had a constitutionally protected right to a free public education.

Section 504 of the Vocational Rehabilitation Act of 1973 prohibited discrimination against physically, mentally, or emotionally handicapped persons. This civil rights legislation protects children who have one or more physical or mental impairments that substantially limit a major life activity. However, no funds accompany the mandate for schools to provide an educational experience that is comparable to that made available to students of the same grade and age who have no disabilities. For example, educators must make accommodations or modify facilities for students who are confined to a wheelchair but are able to learn academic material. Section 504 also guarantees services for students with AIDS, attention deficit disorder (ADD), substance abuse, and some childhood diseases that do not fall within the narrower definition of disabilities of the

legislation discussed in the following paragraphs (Anthony, 1994).

Enactment of the 1975 Education for All Handicapped Children Act, often referred to as Public Law 94-142, communicated a national commitment to educate students with disabilities in public schools. Its 1991 reauthorization as the Individuals with Disabilities Education Act (IDEA) ensured that eligible children could access "appropriate educational services which would enable them to have full equality of opportunity" (20 USC 1400). Figure 9.4 summarizes the provisions and appropriations of IDEA. One of the largest federal education programs, IDEA provided states and school districts with $8.7 billion in FY 2001 to pay a portion of the excess costs of special education and related services. About 7 percent of the nation's students receive special education services (National Center for Education Statistics, 2001). These students are about evenly divided between elementary and secondary schools and among urban areas, small cities, and rural districts.

Amendments to the original act in 1986 created demonstration projects for students with severe disabilities; research and technology; early-childhood education for children aged three to five; and early-intervention services for eligible children from birth to age two. The 1988 Technology-Related Assistance for Individuals with Disabilities Act helped states develop consumer-responsive statewide technology programs for disabled persons of all ages. A new federal initiative, the Families of Children with Disabilities Support Act, emerged within the 1994 reauthorization of ESEA. This legislation encouraged collaboration by developing "a family-centered and family-directed, culturally competent, community-centered, comprehensive, statewide system" of support for families. The competitive matching grants encouraged states to promote interagency coordination and create model demonstration projects. The Assistive Technology Act of 1998 addressed learning needs.

Educating Students with Disabilities

Program Intent:	To ensure that persons aged three to twenty-one with disabilities have a free appropriate public education that includes special education and related services to meet their unique needs and prepare them for employment and independent living.
Congressional Action:	Originally the Education of All Handicapped Children Act (P.L. 94-142) in 1975; reauthorized as the Individuals with Disabilities Education Act (IDEA) of 1991; amended by Title III of the Improving America's Schools Act of 1994; and reauthorized in 1997.
Appropriations:	$8.7 billion in FY 2002, including $7.5 billion for grants to states, $390 million for preschool programs, $384 million for infants and families, $90 million for personnel preparation, $38 million for technology and media services, and $78 million for research and innovations.
Distributions:	State education agencies (SEAs) submit an annual program plan on behalf of school districts. Grants equal the number of persons aged three to twenty-one with disabilities who receive special education and related services multiplied by a given percentage (IDEA authorizes up to 40%) of the national average per-pupil expenditure. SEAs may retain 25% of funds for administrative expenses, including financial and program audits; they allocate at least 75% to districts as flat grants.
Restrictions:	LEAs may spend IDEA funds only to pay the excess costs of providing special education and related services to children with disabilities. Instruction that is appropriate to students' unique needs occurs in the least restrictive environment. Eligible students have individual education plans (IEP) that identify present levels of educational performance, annual goals and short-term instructional objectives, special education and related services, the extent of inclusion in regular educational programs, and evaluation procedures to determine progress toward goals. State and local public agencies are responsible for ensuring that IEPs are prepared for private school children who receive special services from public agencies. Districts receiving funds coordinate IDEA with impact aid and ESEA Title I programs.

FIGURE 9.4. Education of Students with Disabilities

Sources: 20 USC 1400; 34 CFR 300; Final fiscal 2001 and fiscal 2002 appropriations (2002), pp. 26–27.

The Individuals with Disabilities Education Act (IDEA) requires a free appropriate public education, an individual education plan, and the least restrictive environment. States receiving financial assistance must ensure that a *free appropriate public education* (FAPE) is available to all students with disabilities. This requirement of FAPE extends to those students with disabilities who have been suspended or expelled from school. This principle has been the subject of litigation about schools' obligations to address needs of children with severe disabilities. For example, there was a responsibility to educate a multiply disabled student who was alleged to be unable to benefit from special education (*Timothy W.* v. *Rochester*, 1989). When the most appropriate placement is in a private school because public school programs cannot meet a child's needs, this education is provided at public expense. The U.S. Supreme Court ruled in 1993 that parents can be reimbursed for private school expenses even if that school is not approved by state officials and does not meet all federal regulations (*Florence v. Carter*, 1993).

IDEA defines special education as "specially designed instruction at no cost to the parents, to meet the unique needs of a child with a disability." An *individualized education plan* (IEP) outlines the nature of instruction and related services. The child-specific nature of this education implies that it can be accomplished in regular academic or vocational instruction, through community living skills or transition services to prepare the student for life after public schooling, or by whatever means a placement team deems appropriate. *Related services* encompass transportation and developmental, corrective, and other supportive services to help the child benefit from special education. These services include physical and occupational therapy, speech–language pathology and audiology services, counseling and psychological services, recreation, orientation and mobility services, and medical services for diagnostic or evaluative purposes. Several Supreme Court decisions clarified the extent to which such services must be provided. The court denied a parental request for a sign-language interpreter for a hearing-impaired child who was making satisfactory academic progress (*Board of Education* v. *Rowley*, 1982). In contrast, the administration of a catheterization procedure was ruled a related service to be performed by school personnel if the child would otherwise not be able to attend school (*Irving v. Tatro*, 1984). In 2000, the Supreme Court held a district to be responsible for the costs of a full-time nursing aide and other medical services for a physically disabled student (*Cedar Rapids Community School District* v. *Garret F.*, 1999).

IDEA's call for the *least restrictive environment* (LRE) requires a continuum of alternative placements. The placement team determines whether the regular classroom, special classes, home, hospital, or other institution is the appropriate placement. The choice is limited, however, by the requirement that to the greatest extent appropriate, students with disabilities be educated with children who are nondisabled. Special classes, separate schooling, or other removal from the regular classrooms and activities may occur only when "the nature or severity of the disability is such that education in regular classes with the use of supplementary aids and services cannot be achieved satisfactorily." As of 1994, the settings in which the student is educated must be specifically designated in the IEP or Section 504 plan. Costs can be among the many considerations applied in determining appropriate placements. For example, as it arrived at a ruling that a child with Down syndrome could be educated in the regular classroom with supplementary services (*Greer* v. *Rome*, 1991), the Court's test for determining whether inclusion was appropriate assessed the academic benefits in both placements and such nonacademic benefits as social development, effects on other students, and financial costs.

The movement toward inclusion brought greater social and academic integration of disabled and nondisabled students (Skrtic, 1991; Sage & Burrello, 1994). The National Association of State Boards of Education (1992) and a number of states adopted positions in support of *full inclusion*: educating all children in the general classroom and neighborhood school. Kauffman et al. (1995) defined an inclusive school system as "one that allows for a variety of placements that offer the conditions under which every individual feels safe, accepted, and valued and is helped to develop his or her affective and intellectual capacities" (p. 545). IDEA fosters full inclusion through efforts to ensure that state funding mechanisms do not result in restrictive placements, provision of leeway for districts to spend funds within regular classrooms, and formula revisions that remove incentives to place students in restrictive environments to increase revenue (Chaikind, 2001). Barriers to full inclusion include inadequate funds for training all teachers to address children's academic and physical problems, large class sizes, too few special educators spread too thinly among classrooms, principals' limited expertise in promoting inclusion in a participatory manner, and the paucity of research on effects of full inclusion on special and regular students' learning (Anthony, 1994).

The 1997 reauthorization (Public Law 105-17) shifted the focus from access rights to program quality. Changes ensured that the same curriculum, high standards, and assessments as those developed for students without disabilities would be available to most students with disabilities. Koretz and Hamilton (2000) described several options for inclusion in local and state assessments and distinguished between the terms *accommodation* and *alternate assessment*. Depending on the nature of the disability, many students could participate in general assessments of achievement without accommodations. Other students with disabilities could have accommodations, which are defined as changes in the presentation of the assessment or in the mode of the response to the examinee. These accommodations are designed to provide fairer and more valid estimates of performance. Other students who are not working toward the general educational standards but are attending public schools could be tested by an alternate assessment. This modification is a change in the content of the assessment itself.

Section 504 and IDEA requirements have successfully expanded educational opportunities for students with disabilities within public schools. However, the promise of federal funds to accompany those mandates has not been fulfilled (Council for Exceptional Children, 1999). Although IDEA authorizes federal assistance for 40 percent of the national average per-pupil expenditure, states and districts pro-

vide the bulk of funding. Parrish and Verstegen (1994) noted that federal aid for students with disabilities peaked at 12.5 percent of the national average per-pupil expenditure. This percentage declined to 8.2 percent in recent years. The Center for Special Education Finance (1994) urged full funding of the authorization level and suggested several formula changes. Basing allocations on states' overall student populations would provide disincentives for overidentification that may occur when funds flow according to the number of students who are diagnosed as eligible for special education programs. Adopting a poverty-based adjustment would direct additional allocations to states or districts with concentrations of poor families.

Vrestegen (2000) outlined the finance provisions of IDEA under the 1997 Amendments. The prior law based allocations to states on the number of students receiving special education and related services (i.e., a child count formula). The new formula bases increases above the prior base-grant level on the total school-age population in the state (85 percent) and the number of students from families in poverty (15 percent). A similar formula applied to increases in grants that states make to school districts. However, these allocations depended on the total number of students enrolled in public and private schools and thus do not include those who are home-schooled, those who reside in prisons or other institutions, or dropouts—all of whom are included when federal allocations are made to states. In addition to these changes in the formula to consider larger populations of students and poverty factors, the reauthorized IDEA established the amount of funds to be retained by states. This state set-aside for administration of programs and for other direct services and support is at least 25 percent of the total amount of the state grant in 1997. Annual increases in this amount depend on the rate of inflation or the percent change in the state grant, whichever is less. Any increases over the rate of inflation must be directed to capacity building and to improvements in districts' programs for students with disabilities and for other specified activities.

Despite these modifications, Parrish and Wolman (1999) advocated funding systems that would be equitable, adequate, accountable, and flexible. The issue of whether IDEA funding should continue to be discretionary within the congressional authorization (40 percent, as we have noted), or whether funding should be on the mandatory side of the federal budget, became an issue in recent debates about the reauthorization of IDEA (Sack, 2001). If the latter were to become law, then Congress would be required to increase appropriations substantially to fund 40 percent of states' excess costs under the law. This issue was not resolved at the time this text went to press.

Bilingual Education

Students whose native languages differ from English received attention in 1968 with passage of the Bilingual Education Act (Title VII of ESEA amendments). Following the Supreme Court's decision that denial of a "meaningful education" for non-English-speaking children violated Title VI of the Civil Rights Act (*Lau* v. *Nichols*, 1974), the Educational Opportunities Act of 1974 urged districts to provide equal opportunities regardless of language.

Programs have also helped immigrants and refugees gain facility in English. The 1962 Migration and Refugee Assistance Act and the 1975 Indochina Migration and Refugee Assistance Act authorized loans and grants for education and vocational training. The Emergency Immigrant Education Program within the 1994 reauthorized Bilingual Education Act provided financial assistance for improving educational programs in districts experiencing unusually large enrollment increases due to immigration.

Title III of the No Child Left Behind Act of 2001 reauthorized and modified the former Bilingual Education Act. The purpose of the renamed English Language Acquisition, Language Enhancement, and Academic Achievement Act was "to help ensure that children who are limited English proficient, including immigrant children and youth, attain English proficiency, develop high levels of academic attainment in English, and meet the same challenging State academic content and academic achievement standards as all children are expected to meet" (Section 3102). Funds appropriated under the act could enhance curricula and instructional materials, professional development, interagency coordination, and parental participation. This act eliminated a requirement that 75 percent of bilingual education funds support programs in which students were taught in their native languages.

Figure 9.5 describes the purpose and appropriation of $665 million in FY 2002 for bilingual and immigrant education. About 7 percent of pupils participate in bilingual programs and English as a second language (ESL) programs (National Center for Education Statistics, 2001). These programs serve primarily urban elementary school students.

Bilingual education has provoked controversy primarily in terms of the length of time, if any, that students should receive instruction in their native language while they learn English. Some specialists advocate teaching English as a second language (ESL), with students learning basic skills in their native languages until English is mastered. Others argue for a more rapid transition to learning in English and to enrolling in regular classes. A third group advocates an English-only approach with no native-language instruction in public schools. Districts have flexibility in designing instructional approaches. However, provisions of the 2001 reauthorization require state assessments in reading and language arts to be in English after a student is enrolled for three consecutive years in the United States.

The civil rights mandates and categorical aid programs presented in this section help the nation reach equity goals by expanding educational opportunities for diverse groups of

---

Educating Limited-English-Proficient Students

Program Intent:	To educate children and youth with limited English proficiency to meet state academic content and achievement standards expected of all students.
Congressional Action:	Title VII of the 1968 amendments to the Elementary Secondary Education Act; amended by the Bilingual Education Act of 1974; reauthorized by the Improving America's Schools Act of 1994; and renamed the English Language, Language Enhancement, and Academic Achievement Act as Title III of the No Child Left Behind Act of 2001.
Appropriations:	$665 million in FY 2002 for bilingual and immigrant education.
Distribution:	Funds are allocated on a discretionary rather than a formula basis. Districts apply directly to the Department of Education. States receive up to 5% of allocations to districts for coordination and technical assistance.
Restrictions:	The 2001 reauthorization consolidated bilingual education programs into one flexible initiative to ensure that students are able to meet content and achievement standards. Students must be included in state assessments in English after three years of enrollment. Funds may be used to upgrade curriculum, develop instructional materials and assessments, and improve professional development for teachers.

FIGURE 9.5. Education of Students with Limited English Proficiency

Sources: 20 USC 7401; Final fiscal 2001 and fiscal 2002 appropriations (2002), pp. 26–27.

students. Congress initially designed programs that would ensure access to public education. Since 1994, provisions within grant programs have urged states and schools to enable *all* students to achieve state academic content and achievement standards and have provided for some flexibility in uses of federal funds to meet student educational needs.

Promoting Reforms and the Capacity to Improve Schools

Previously described federal actions to improve economic productivity and expand educational opportunities often influenced local priorities in allocating funds and developing curricula. In addition, federal funds have enabled schools and districts to build instructional capacity via improved facilities, technologies, and professional knowledge and skills. National goals and financial incentives have also prompted local reforms in curricula, delivery of instruction, and choice among public schools.

Appropriations for many of the school improvement efforts described in this section appear in Figure 9.6. Of the $7.8 billion in congressional appropriations for FY 2002 to serve school improvements and innovations, nearly $2.9 billion would assist districts in improving teacher quality. Large appropriations would stimulate the creation of "21st Century Community Learning Centers," improvements in educational technologies, safe and drug-free schools and community programs, state assessments, and innovative educational program strategies. Charter schools, rural schools, small learning communities, and magnet schools would also receive financial assistance. Challenge Grants would encourage schools to improve American history, physical education, character education and counseling programs. Smaller appropriations would fund "star

---

Funding School Improvements and Innovations

For FY 2002, Congress appropriated a total of $7.2 billion for school improvement programs, including the following:

State grants for improving teacher quality	$2,850,000,000
21st Century Community Learning Centers	1,000,000,000
Educational technology	785,000,000
Safe and drug-free schools and communities	654,250,000
State assessments	387,000,000
Innovative education program strategies	385,000,000
Charter school grants	200,000,000
Rural education	162,500,000
Small learning communities	142,189,000
Magnet school assistance	110,000,000
Teaching of traditional American history	100,000,000
Education for homeless children and youth	50,000,000
Physical education for progress	50,000,000
Parental assistance information centers	40,000,000
Elementary and secondary school counseling	32,500,000
Community technology centers	32,475,000
Star schools	27,500,000
Education for native Hawaiians	30,500,000
Arts in education	30,000,000
Alcohol abuse reduction	25,000,000
Character education	25,000,000
Voluntary public school choice	25,000,000

Note: Includes programs with appropriations of at least $25 million

FIGURE 9.6. Appropriations for School Improvement Programs

Source: *Final Fiscal 2001 appropriations and President Bush's Fiscal 2002 Proposals.* Reprinted with permission from *Education Week*, Vol. 20, No. 36, (2001), pp. 26–27.

---

schools," education for homeless students, arts in education, and alcohol abuse reduction. Many of these grant programs comprise the Fund for the Improvement of Education.

Facilities, Instructional Materials, and Technologies

The federal government has assumed only a limited role in constructing schools. This costly aspect of the infrastructure for delivering instruction depends largely on local revenue (see Chapter 6). The federal government has played a more active role in updating instructional materials and technologies.

In 1930 Congress spent $47 million to build schools. The Disaster Relief Act of 1965 gave financial assistance to school districts "to help

meet emergency costs resulting from a national disaster." Recently, the School Facilities Infrastructure Improvement Act of 1994 linked the financing of facilities, including libraries and media centers, to the achievement of the National Education Goals. A number of other bills to increase federal financing of school construction have been defeated.

Financial incentives have encouraged teachers to develop materials and advance the use of technologies in instruction. Various titles of the 1965 Elementary and Secondary Education Act (ESEA) helped state agencies and schools improve library resources, develop curricula and instructional materials, initiate innovative programs, and assess educational progress. Schools broadened their use of television and other media under the 1962 Communications Act, the 1967 Public Broadcasting Act, and the 1976 Educational Broadcasting Facilities and Telecommunications Demonstration Act. The Children's Television Act of 1990 imposed controls over advertisements and programming to address the "educational and informational" needs of children.

The use of technologies in education expanded with the information age. The High Performance Computing Act of 1991 established a National Research and Education Network and created standards for high-performance networks. The potential benefits of integrating technology in instruction brought additional funding in several programs initiated in 1994 and reauthorized in 2001. The Enhancing Education Through Technology Act of 2001 promoted technology-enhanced curricula and instruction that is aligned with academic content and achievement standards, public–private partnerships to increase access to technologies, and distance learning and professional development via electronic means. The Star Schools Act advanced distance-learning strategies and telecommunication partnerships to improve instruction in mathematics, science, and foreign languages, particularly for disadvantaged and limited-English-proficient students. In 1998, the Federal Communications Commission began education rate (e-rate) discounts on Internet access and other telecommunication services to schools and libraries.

Chambers et al. (2000) concluded that federal funding contributed significantly to district spending on technology, providing nearly 25 percent of upgraded computers. These funds also addressed equity goals by providing 53 percent of new computers in schools serving areas high in poverty .

Professional Development and Instructional Improvements

The national government's concern about teachers' skills in developing and delivering curricula began in the late 1950s with the Na-

tional Defense Education Act. The 1965 Higher Education Act established the Teacher Corps and fellowships for teacher preparation. The Education Professions Development Act of 1967 was designed to improve the quality of teaching and to relieve the shortage of adequately prepared educators.

Nearly all of the subsections of the Improving America's Schools Act of 1994 and the No Child Left Behind Act of 2001 listed professional development as an important aspect of strengthening schools' abilities to enable students to meet state academic standards. The Eisenhower Professional Development Program to support efforts of states, districts, and teacher preparation institutions to improve the teaching and learning of all students. This program encouraged "sustained and intensive high-quality professional development" aligned with state content and performance standards and continuous improvement throughout schools. The 2001 act consolidated the class size reduction and Eisenhower programs into a combined Teacher Quality Program. State plans would identify strategies to ensure that all teachers were "highly qualified" by the end of the 2005–2006 school year. In addition, there would be flexibility in uses of up to 50 percent of other federal funds to hire teachers to reduce class size, increase salaries, and improve professional development. This reauthorization appropriated $2.85 billion for the Teacher Quality Program in 2002.

The Teacher and Principal Training and Recruiting Fund created in 2001 provided grants to school districts, state agencies for higher education, and eligible partnerships to "increase student academic achievement through strategies such as improving teacher and principal quality and increasing the number of highly qualified teachers in the classroom and highly qualified principals and assistant principals in schools" (Section 2101). Activities could include reforming certification (or licensing) requirements to be sure that teachers have adequate knowledge and skills in their respective academic subjects to help students meet standards; providing mentoring and reduced class schedules for beginning teachers; establishing alternative routes for certification of teachers and principals; reforming tenure systems and teacher testing for certification; and measuring the effectiveness of professional development in improving student achievement.

Federal programs have encouraged improvements in still other aspects of education. Legislation in 1984 created the National Talented Teachers' Fellowship Program, a Federal Merit Scholarship Program, and a Leadership in Educational Administration Program. Creation of the Fund for the Improvement and Reform of Schools and Teaching (1988) authorized grants to help at-risk children meet higher standards, strengthen school leadership and teaching, encourage school systems to refocus their priorities, and provide entry-year assistance to new teachers and administrators. The 1991 National Commission on a Longer School Year Act created a panel to study the relationship between time and learning. The Improving America's Schools Act of 1994 provided seed money for schools to increase substantially the amount of time spent in academic programs and to promote flexibility in schools' schedules.

National Goals

A movement that began in many states and local communities to reform education and upgrade expectations for pupil academic performance gained momentum early in the 1990s. The governors and the president urged Congress to adopt national education goals. The Goals 2000: Educate America Act of 1994 declared that *by the year 2000,*

1. All children in America will start school ready to learn.
2. The high school graduation rate will increase to at least 90 percent.
3. All students will leave grades 4, 8, and 12 having demonstrated competency over

challenging subject matter including English, mathematics, science, foreign languages, civics and government, economics, arts, history, and geography, and every school in America will ensure that all students learn to use their minds well, so they may be prepared for responsible citizenship, further learning, and productive employment in our Nation's modern economy.

4. The Nation's teaching force will have access to programs for the continued improvement of their professional skills and the opportunity to acquire the knowledge and skills needed to instruct and prepare all American students for the next century.
5. United States students will be first in the world in mathematics and science achievement.
6. Every adult American will be literate and will possess the knowledge and skills necessary to compete in a global economy and exercise the rights and responsibilities of citizenship.
7. Every school in the United States will be free of drugs, violence, and the unauthorized presence of firearms and alcohol and will offer a disciplined environment conducive to learning.
8. Every school will promote partnerships that will increase parental involvement and participation in promoting the social, emotional, and academic growth of children. (20 USC 5812)

The intent of making funds available through the Goals 2000: Educate America Act was to help participating states, districts, and schools prepare educational improvement plans. The act permitted flexibility in determining how funds would be used to achieve the eight goals and authorized waivers of regulations governing other federal programs when they impeded school improvement plans. Funding for these programs has ceased, but the focus on school improvement through academic standards and local flexibility in determining uses of federal funds continued as Congress crafted the No Child Left Behind Act of 2001.

Block Grants and Flexibility for School Improvements

Unlike restricted categorical funds, block grants enable states and districts to set their own priorities for school improvements. Chapter 2 of the Education Consolidation and Improvement Act (ECIA) of 1981 adopted a block grant approach to consolidate forty-three prior categorical aid programs. The goal was to give local education agencies discretion to direct funds where they judged improvements were most needed, while minimizing the federal presence, reducing paperwork, and eliminating prescriptive regulation and oversight. Block grants were available through states to public and nonpublic schools for activities related to basic skills development, school improvement and support services, and special purposes. This funding strategy shifted grant administration to states and decentralized, to district and school personnel, responsibility for designing and implementing programs within these broad purposes. However, funds were reduced over 25 percent from antecedent program levels, and redistributions of funds aided nearly all districts—to the detriment of poor and minority children primarily in urban districts (Verstegen, 1987).

Chapter 2 was reauthorized as ESEA Title VI of the Improving America's Schools Act of 1994. Funds continued for those states that participated in the Goals 2000: Educate America Act. Entitled "Innovative Education Program Strategies," this part of the act was more categorical in supporting districts' innovations that made possible achievement of the National Education Goals and states' content and performance standards. We noted previously that the 2002 reauthorization gave states and districts greater flexibility to transfer funds among selected programs or to Title I.

Charter and Magnet Schools

The 2002 reauthorization of ESEA encouraged states and school districts to enable parents and students to exercise greater choice among schools. In addition to enabling students in low-performing schools to transfer to better public schools (see the section on education of disadvantaged students), Title V of the act encouraged the creation of charter schools and magnet schools as alternatives within the public school system. (See Chapter 15 for a discussion of family choice and of these alternative public schools.)

The financial assistance provided to states for charter school grant programs was designed to make possible the planning, program design, and initial implementation of charter schools and the evaluation of their effects on academic achievement. Other goals of the act were to expand the number of high-quality charter schools across the nation and to encourage states to finance charter schools in an amount more nearly commensurate with the support provided to traditional public schools. The state plan would include a description of how information about the best or most promising practices of charter schools could be disseminated to each school district of the state.

The magnet school assistance program recognized the roles that these alternative schools have played in voluntary desegregation of school districts and as models for school improvement. The purposes of this grant program include reducing minority group isolation, achieving voluntary desegregation, and designing innovative practices to promote diversity of and choices among schools.

Many federal programs have directly or indirectly influenced what is taught in public schools and have helped schools expand their capacities for delivering instruction. Most recently, the federal government has urged school improvements to enable all students to meet states' academic content and achievement standards. Other congressional actions have confronted more basic concerns about students' health and safety.

Improving Nutrition, Safety, and Health

Government subsidies and programs address students' physical well-being in diverse ways. Recent federal programs that concern drug abuse prevention, school safety, and air quality followed earlier support of school food services.

Nutrition

The school lunch program under the Department of Agriculture was in part a response to concerns about children's nutrition. This program also evolved to relieve oversupplies of farm produce. The 1935 Agricultural Adjustment Act made commodities available for school lunches. The National School Lunch Act of 1946 provided funds on an equalized percentage matching basis to support facilities and purchase food. This effort expanded with the School Milk Program Act of 1954.

A major commitment to the welfare of children of low-income families coincided in the 1960s with educational programs for disadvantaged children. The 1966 Child Nutrition Act delivered breakfast and subsidized lunches for eligible students. Children in families with incomes below 130 percent of the poverty level (established by the Office of Management and Budget) are eligible for free lunches. Other low-income students qualify for reduced-price lunches if family incomes are within 185 percent. In 2001–2002, a family of four with an annual income of $22,945 qualified for the free-lunch program, and a family of the same size with an income of $32,653 met the guidelines for reduced-price meals. About one-third of all students, including 44 percent of students in large cities and 30 percent of students in rural communities, qualified for free or reduced-price lunches (National Center for Education Statistics, 2001, Table 373).

School Safety and Drug Abuse Prevention

The nation's fight against drug abuse emerged in the early 1970s. The Alcohol and Drug Abuse Education Act of 1970 brought grants for disseminating information, developing community education programs, and training teachers. Two years later, the Drug Abuse Office and Treatment Act established a special-action office for abuse prevention to coordinate planning and policy. This act also created the National Advisory Council for Drug Abuse Prevention and provided community assistance grants to support mental health centers for treating and rehabilitating drug abusers.

The 1986 Drug-Free Schools and Communities Act financed drug abuse education and prevention in coordination with community efforts. In the same year, the Omnibus Drug Abuse Prevention Act authorized teacher training and early-childhood-education programs. Schools and law enforcement agencies gained additional funding under the Anti-Drug Education and the Drug Abuse Resistance Education (DARE) Acts of 1990.

Along with concerns about drug abuse, the increased incidence of youth violence in schools and society prompted federal legislation. The Safe and Drug-Free Schools and Communities Act of the 1994 and the 2001 ESEA reauthorizations supported programs to involve parents and community resources in preventing violence and the illegal use of alcohol, drugs, and tobacco. One year earlier, school safety was the focus of the Gun-Free Schools Act of 1993. This legislation required states and districts that received financial assistance under ESEA to develop policies mandating a full-year expulsion for students who possess firearms on school property. District superintendents have the authority to modify this provision on a case-by-case basis.

The 2001 reauthorization of ESEA permitted students who are victims of crimes, or who attend public schools that states designate as unsafe, to transfer to a safe public school. It also provided that teachers and principals may take reasonable actions to discipline students for disruptive behavior without fearing subsequent frivolous lawsuits.

Environment and Air Quality

Diverse federal initiatives have raised awareness about the environment and the effects of air quality on children. The Environmental Education Acts of 1970 and 1990 provided funds for teacher training and community education, disseminated information about ecology, and created a federal Office of Environmental Education.

The 1980 Asbestos School Hazard Protection and Control Act mandated inspections and plans for eliminating or containing this material. Loans provided under the act assisted districts' efforts to remove hazardous asbestos. Air quality was also a concern of the Pro-Children Act of 1994. This federal legislation prohibited smoking in child care facilities, elementary and secondary schools, and libraries serving children.

Thus, the early federal role in improving student nutrition evolved into a societal concern for health and safety. Similarly, the scope of the government's agency for overseeing education evolved from a minimal data collection role into a cabinet-level office that sponsors research and development activities.

Advancing Educational Research and Development

The federal government plays an important role in stimulating, financing, and disseminating findings of educational research and development. Grant competitions establish priorities for researchers in school systems, state and federal agencies, universities, and independent institutes. Sponsored research furthers our understanding of current practice and innovations in teaching and learning, governance and decision making, school organization and leadership, finance and program equity, uses of technologies, and alternative assessments.

The initial U.S. Department of Education had a limited mission of collecting and disseminating statistics that "show the condition and progress of education." One year after its creation in 1867, the department became an office within the Department of the Interior. Reorganization in 1953 placed the Office of Education within the Department of Health, Education and Welfare. The federal interest in educational research and development—particularly that related to science and math curricula—increased in the late 1950s with NDEA and the creation of the National Science Foundation.

In 1965, ESEA Title IV authorized the Office of Education to sponsor regional laboratories, university-based research and development centers, the Educational Resources and Information Clearinghouse (ERIC), and graduate training programs for educational research (Timpane, 1982). Other programs funded applied research and demonstration in vocational education, special education, bilingual education, and library services during the 1960s and 1970s. Field experiments included the planned-variation evaluation designs for Head Start and Follow Through programs, the Experimental Schools program, performance contracting to involve private agencies in instruction, and voucher plans to encourage choice among schools. The National Institute of Education (NIE) was established in 1972 to house federal research activities in an independent agency. The National Center for Education Statistics (NCES) has coordinated data collection and dissemination since its creation in 1974.

The current Department of Education, which was created in 1979, has consolidated educational programs from several departments and agencies and has given educational issues greater visibility. An Office of Educational Research and Improvement (OERI) replaced NIE to coordinate and encourage educational research and development. The Educational Research, Development, Dissemination and Improvement Act of 1994 established the National Educational Research Policy and Priorities Board. OERI's Office of Reform Assistance and Dissemination provides technical and financial assistance for development and demonstration programs and coordinates the efforts of ten regional educational laboratories. OERI oversees five national institutes that promote research, development, dissemination of information, and evaluation in the following areas: Student Achievement, Curriculum and Assessment; Education of At-Risk Students; Educational Governance, Finance, Policy-Making and Management; Early Childhood Development and Education; and Postsecondary Education, Libraries and Lifelong Education. There is also a network of fifteen comprehensive regional assistance centers that coordinate activities with the department's regional offices, the regional educational laboratories, and state literacy and vocational resource centers. The National Diffusion Network (NDN) carries out state-based outreach, consultation, training, and dissemination programs and helps districts implement exemplary practices.

Provisions of the No Child Left Behind Act of 2001 called for research and development efforts in identifying effective instructional strategies that enable all children to meet states' content and achievement standards. There would be a national longitudinal assessment of Title I's impact on academic achievement in relation to the goal of having all students reach the proficient level on state assessments. The act also reauthorized the Fund for the Improvement of Education. This initiative promoted systemic education reform by encouraging research, development, and evaluation in such areas as student academic achievement, involvement of parents and the community, public school choice and school-based decision making, recognition for exemplary schools, and financial rewards for schools that close the achievement gap for students who

are farthest away from the proficient level on assessments.

In summary, these six themes capture the primary thrusts of federal involvement in public education. The many programs illustrate the willingness of Congress and executive agencies to influence specific dimensions of public education. Those programs that garner the greatest attention of educators and those that draw the most vehement attacks from critics of federal intervention are often those that receive the most funds.

FEDERAL FUNDS FOR SCHOOLS

The United States government spent $91 billion on education at all levels in fiscal year 2000 (National Center for Education Statistics, 2000, p. 6). The nearly half of this amount ($44 billion) that financed elementary and secondary education programs represented about 7 percent of all money spent at that level. In addition, postsecondary education benefited from $20 billion in federal assistance and from much of the $21 billion devoted to research. The remaining $6 billion fueled various other education programs.

The federal share of elementary and secondary school funds is much less than that of either state or local governments. We presented the proportions of revenue provided by federal, state, and local sources in Table 2.1. The federal share increased from under 1 percent prior to the 1930s to about 3 percent in 1950. At that time the federal government supported school lunch programs, vocational education, Indian education, and federally impacted districts. By 1970 this contribution had grown to 8 percent of total funds for schools, particularly as financial support became available for a wide range of programs to enlarge educational opportunities. In 1980 federal funds accounted for 9.8 percent of all revenue for education. This zenith occurred after a decade of program expansions, including large increases for the education of children with disabilities. By 1990 the federal share had declined to 6.1 percent of the total, as state and local revenue increased. By 1993–1994, the proportion of total elementary and secondary education revenue provided by the federal government reached 7.2 percent. However, by 1999–2000, this assistance had fallen to 6.9 percent of the total (see Table 7.1).

This average percentage of federal support varies greatly among states and school districts. In 1999–2000, eight states received over 10 percent of their revenue from the federal government, including a high of 14 percent in Mississippi. Federal revenue accounted for under 5 percent in nine states, including a low of 3.2 percent in New Jersey. States were affected to varying degrees by the decline in federal aid (an average of 14 percent after adjustments for inflation) between 1980 and 1990, with "four out of every five states experiencing double digit percentage reductions" (Verstegen, 1994, p. 109). There were declines of over 40 percent in Arizona, Michigan, and North Carolina. At the same time, federal assistance grew over 40 percent in Colorado, New York, and Vermont.

Allocations for the primary elementary and secondary programs over the latter part of the twentieth century are ranked by fiscal year 2000 outlays in Table 9.1. The trends reveal priorities in federal education policy. School lunch and milk programs accounted for the largest amount of federal aid to schools in each year except 1985. This support rose from $623 million to nearly $10 billion between 1965 and 2000 (reported allocations are not adjusted for inflation). Financial assistance for the education of economically disadvantaged students outpaced the funds for school food services in 1985. Enactment of ESEA in 1965 brought nearly $2 billion in aid by 1975 and steady growth to $8.4 billion, including Title I funds, in 2000.

Assistance for the education of children with disabilities amounted to $14 million in 1965. The 1975 passage of P.L. 94-142 prompted the increase of this allocation to $1 billion by 1985.

Special education funding reached $5.4 billion in 2000. The financing of Head Start programs in preschools had exceeded the amount for special education until 1985. This commitment grew from $96 million in 1965 to $5.3 billion in 2000. Allocations for school improvement efforts amounted to $72 million in 1965 and to $2.7 billion in 2000. The allocation of $1 billion in 2000 for the Goals 2000: Educate America Act encouraged participating states and localities to design programs around national goals.

Sponsorship of vocational education has been an important federal activity since the mid-1800s. However, its relative importance in school finance slipped between 1965 and 2000, as funds for this priority were directed toward community colleges. Financial support for vocational and adult education programs grew from $132 million in 1965 to $1.5 billion in 2000. A similar trend is noted for payments to federally impacted school districts. This commitment was second only to school lunch programs in 1965. This impact aid increased more slowly than other program funds, from $350 million to $1 billion by 2000. Funds for bilingual education programs rose from $93 million in 1975 to $496 million in 2000.

These trends in allocations reveal changes in the national interests to be served by the government's support for elementary and secondary education. There has been a continuing high level of assistance for school lunch programs and, indirectly, for the related interests of the agriculture industry. Shifts in other national interests are evident in relative levels of funding devoted to the defense-related impact aid and vocational education programs prior to the 1960s, compared with those directed to equalizing educational opportunities since the mid-1960s. The strong concern for equity is evident in the constellation of programs for economically disadvantaged students, special education, immigrant and migrant education, Head Start, Native American education, and bilingual education. The relatively low level of funds noted in Table 9.1 for school improve-

TABLE 9.1.

Federal Outlays for Selected Education Programs, Fiscal Years 1965–2000 (millions)

Program	1965	1975	1985	1990	1995	2000[a]
School lunch and milk[b]	$623	$1,884	$4,135	$5,529	$8,201	$9,856
Grants for disadvantaged	—	1,874	4,207	4,494	6,808	8,379
Special education	14	151	1,018	1,617	3,177	5,432
Head Start	96	404	1,075	1,448	3,534	5,267
School improvement programs	72	700	526	1,189	1,398	2,663
Vocational and adult education	132	655	658	1,307	1,482	1,547
Education reform, Goals 2000	—	—	—	—	61	1,125
Impact aid	350	619	647	816	808	1,034
Native American education	108	163	203	218	436	512
Bilingual education	—	93	158	189	225	496

Note: Dollar amounts are not adjusted for inflation.

[a] Estimated.

[b] Includes other Department of Agriculture subsidies for school food services.

Source: National Center for Education Statistics (2000). *Federal $upport for Education: Fiscal Years 1980 to 2000*. Washington, DC: U.S. Government Printing Office, Table D.

ment programs increased in recent years (see Figure 9.6). Influences on school curriculum itself, which remain the purview of states and localities, are becoming more evident as Congress directs funds toward educational reform and requires annual state assessments of student achievement. Raising expectations for all students to reach high academic standards is a continuing national priority.

FORGING AN APPROPRIATE FEDERAL ROLE IN PUBLIC EDUCATION

The primary federal programs serving public schools and students advance national interests, six of which were identified previously. The extent to which the federal government can promote the general welfare by influencing local and state educational efforts is often challenged. The growing federal presence in public education during much of the past half-century is viewed by some as an unwarranted intrusion into an area that is constitutionally reserved to the states or the people under the Tenth Amendment. Federal courts and Congress may have legitimate roles in guarding minority groups' access to education and in ensuring equitable treatment under the Fourteenth Amendment. However, the government's role in encouraging states to define standards and upgrade curricula is more tenuous constitutionally. We introduced concerns about the appropriate degree of federal control over education and its resources when we discussed taxation in Chapter 4 and transfer payments in Chapter 7. We raise it now in the context of the appropriate role of the federal government in influencing educational goals and programs.

Wise (1979) analyzed the expanded presence of the federal government during the 1960s and 1970s. He characterized the impacts of greater centralization on local control, institutional autonomy, and classroom activities as "legislated learning" and introduced the concept of hyperrationalization:

> As other and higher levels of government seek to promote equity and increase productivity in our educational institutions, important educational decisions are increasingly being determined cen-

trally. The discretion of local officials is limited by their need to conform to policy decisions. . . . To the extent that this process causes more bureaucratic overlay without attaining the intended policy objectives, it results in what I shall call the *hyperrationalization of the schools.* (pp. 47–48; emphasis in the original)

This hyperrationalization appeared in excessive prescription of inputs and outcomes of schools and in the proliferation of educational programs as solutions to the problems facing society. Policy makers and educators predicated new policies and programs on what they believed to be greater efficiency in meeting equity goals: "School systems which presumably did not previously have the knowledge or will or wherewithal to teach such children would, with federal funds, discover the knowledge, gain the will, and acquire the wherewithal to solve the problem" (Wise, 1979, p. 68).

Others believed that increasingly centralized control of educational policy without demonstrable results introduced inefficiencies. They urged deregulation and the block grant strategy early in the 1980s. The report of the National Commission on Excellence in Education (1983), which was entitled *A Nation at Risk*, raised the overriding issue of educational quality in relation to economic competitiveness. The nation's governors and Congress issued a challenge to states for upgrading public education in concert with the National Education Goals. Enacting the Goals 2000: Educate America Act urged states to reform education through voluntary state content and performance standards. Education became a national priority and a focus of attention in presidential politics.

Jennings (1998) contrasted the platforms of the predominant political parties in recent elections. Both parties stressed the importance of education to the nation, but they advocated different strategies for improving schools. The Republican agenda would repeal the Goals 2000 legislation, combine categorical programs within block grants to give states flexibility, create a voucher program to enable private

schools to educate low-income students, increase accountability of teachers and students, and limit the power of (or abolish) the Department of Education. These strategies would effectively alter the federal presence in defining educational goals and standards and in shaping curricula and assessments. This diminished federal role would probably strengthen state, local, and parental control of education. In this view of federalism, an appropriate role for the federal government is to facilitate and coordinate the efforts of states and schools rather than to design and closely monitor educational programs.

In contrast, Jennings (1998) described the Democratic agenda as increasing federal financial assistance for public school programs, expanding educational opportunities for all students through federal initiatives, increasing choice only among public schools, and strengthening performance expectations and professional development of teachers. These approaches would entail state and national standards and a larger federal role in financing programs to ensure that all students had opportunities to meet these high standards. This contrasting view of federalism argues for a stronger role of the government in public education. Advocates of a larger federal presence fear that reduced funding and eased regulations would diminish the willingness and capacity of many schools and districts to meet pressing needs. Politically powerless groups, including the growing numbers of poor children, might once again be denied adequate and appropriate education. Many state-level policy makers would welcome block grant flexibility. Those from large urban areas, however, express concern that education and social programs would suffer as less money was spread more thinly to compensate for reductions in funding other areas of state government.

Shortly after his election in 2000, George W. Bush urged changes in federal education programs. The reauthorization of ESEA by the No Child Left Behind Act, signed by President

George W. Bush early in 2002 represented several key strategies: accountability and testing, flexibility and local control over uses of federal funds, and expanded parental options for students in low-performing schools. States receiving Title I funds would have to administer state-selected assessments in reading and mathematics annually to all pupils in the third to eighth grades. In addition, a representative sample of fourth- and eighth-grade students would participate in administrations of National Assessment of Educational Progress (NAEP) tests in reading and mathematics. These expanded assessment requirements substantially increase federal influence over state education policies. States that continue to receive financial assistance for programs to educate economically disadvantaged students will have to alter their policies on standards, assessments, and accountability that affect *all* students. However, Riddle (2001) observed that these testing requirements are imposed in a context of increased state and local flexibility in the use of federal funds: "Under this strategy, accountability for appropriate use of federal aid funds would be established more on the basis of pupil performance outcomes, and less on prescribed procedures or targeting of resources, than currently" (p. 16).

The future role of the United States government in education will continue to reflect the struggle between these two views of federalism. As this text went to press, the nation had initiated a war against terrorism. The citizenry welcomed federal oversight of airport safety and homeland security, despite the fact that deficit spending and greater centralization of power would probably result. It is uncertain whether this tolerance for greater federal involvement and spending will carry over to educational programs. We pointed out early in this chapter that other international conflicts and economic crises have expanded federal support for vocational and technical education. The current initiative for upgrading academic standards for all students may thus be expanded to encompass upgraded standards for vocational and technical education.

Whatever policy evolves to strengthen the national economy and national defense early in the twenty-first century, we anticipate that the president and Congress will continue to provide leadership and some financial assistance for states, localities, and students to meet high standards with equity and efficiency.

SUMMARY

The federal government directs intergovernmental transfers of funds to help states and localities provide education in ways that satisfy broader societal goals. Although education is a state responsibility, the president can influence policies through the "bully pulpit," and Congress can invoke the general welfare clause to influence educational priorities in ways consistent with legislators' views of the national interest. Six themes that punctuate the history of federal education legislation capture the rationale for federal intervention and financial assistance: strengthening the nation and economy; improving defense and international relations; expanding educational opportunities; promoting reform and building capacity; improving student nutrition, safety, and health; and advancing educational research and development.

The preference for categorical funding of particular programs to achieve objectives was clearly established in the support of vocational education programs. It was not until Congress passed ESEA in 1965, however, that the level of federal aid was sufficient to affect school offerings significantly. This and other categorical aid programs influenced school priorities and created a new local–state–federal partnership. The 1980s brought reduced federal involvement, deregulation, and decentralization. A limited block grant strategy consolidated many former categorical aid programs.

With the encouragement of the nation's governors, Congress embarked on a more active federal role in education in the mid-1990s. The America 2000: Educate America Act codified the eight National Education Goals, and the Improving America's Schools Act provided the direction and funds to enable participating states to design content and performance standards for all students. The 2001 No Child Left Behind Act reauthorized ESEA in ways that promoted accountability via required state assessments; flexibility for districts in setting priorities for the use of federal funds; and availability, through parental choice, of supplementary educational services for students in low-performing schools.

The federated governance structure for education in the United States places control primarily at the state level. It is only when national interests and prevailing views of federalism favor assistance that the federal government exerts more influence in public education. Maintaining a proper balance among governance levels is a continuing dilemma of intergovernmental transfers: To what degree can and should state and federal governments intervene to shape school policies and practices without jeopardizing the benefits of local control?

This chapter concludes our examination of state and federal aid to education. The next part of the book examines ways in which the courts and policy analysts assess these finance structures against criteria of equity and efficiency.

ENDNOTES

1. The notation P.L. 107-110 indicates that this legislation was the 110th Public Law of the 107th session of Congress. Title I of the No Child Left Behind Act of 2001 can be found in the *United States Code* (20 USC 6301), and associated regulations are available in the *Code of Federal Regulations* (34 CFR 200). The entire act can be accessed at **http://thomas.loc.gov/cgi-bin/query/z?c107: h.r.l.enr:** (accessed January 26, 2002).
2. The term title refers to a section of a given statute. Thus there are many sections of federal law that

carry the designation Title I, Title II, and so on. We caution the reader to be aware of the particular statute when referencing a given section. For example, this paragraph refers to Titles VI and VII of the Civil Rights Act of 1964.

ACTIVITIES

1. Investigate thoroughly one of the federal aid programs cited in this chapter. Locate statutory provisions in the *United States Code* and implementing regulations in the *Code of Federal Regulations* (both can be found at **www.findlaw.com**). Interview a state and/or school system program coordinator to discuss compliance issues. What modifications do you recommend for improving this federal program?
2. Debate the advantages and disadvantages of the following modifications to the federal role in financing education: (a) increasing the proportion of revenue derived from national sources (e.g., one-fifth or one-third of the total) to relieve local and state tax bases; (b) redistributing current federal appropriations to equalize state and local fiscal capacities; (c) giving states or schools total control over the use of federal financial assistance.
3. Which, if any, of the six general themes identified in this chapter should provide the primary rationale for federal intervention and fiscal policy in education during the coming decade? Which view of federalism should guide the nature of grants and implementing regulations, in order to influence the degree to which this theme becomes important to state policy makers and school district personnel?
4. Interview district or school personnel who oversee federal programs. What do they see as the appropriate role for the government to play in helping states and schools meet high academic standards, ensure equity in educational opportunities, and improve efficiency?

5. Modify Simulation 14.1, which is a site-based budget, to assist in the management of federal funds. Rows should list specific projects and associated line-items, and columns should record the prior year's expenditures as well as the current year's revenue, budget, and expenditures to date and the remaining balance for each line-item.

REFERENCES

American Vocational Association, (1998). *The official guide to the Perkins Act of 1998*. Alexandria, VA: Author. (ERIC ED 435 807).

Anthony, P. G. (1994, Fall). The federal role in special education. *Educational Considerations, 22*, 30–35.

Board of Education of Hendrick Hudson School District v. *Rowley*. 458 U.S. 176 (1982).

Brown v. *Board of Education*, 347 U.S. 483 (1954).

Carter, L. (1984). The sustaining effects study of compensatory and elementary education. *Educational Researcher, 13*, 4–13.

Cedar Rapids Community School District v. *Garret F.*, 526 U.S. 66 (1999).

Center for Special Education Finance. (Fall, 1994). IDEA reauthorization: Federal funding issues. *The CSEF Resource, 2*. Palo Alto, CA: Author.

Chaikind, S. (2001). Expanding value added in serving children with disabilities. In S. Chaikind & W. J. Fowler (Eds.), *Education finance in the new millennium*. AEFA 2001 Yearbook (pp. 67–79). Larchmont, NY: Eye on Education.

Chambers, J., Lieberman, J., Parrish, T., Kaleba, D., Van Campen, J., & Stullich, S. (2000). *Study of education resources and federal funding: Final report*. Washington, DC: U.S. Department of Education, Planning and Evaluation Service.

Council for Exceptional Children, 1999). *Federal outlook for exceptional children: Fiscal year 2000*. Reston, VA: Author. (ERIC ED 435 151).

Elazar, D. J. (1972). *American federalism: A view from the states*. (2nd ed.). New York: Crowell.

Final fiscal 2001 and fiscal 2002 appropriations. (2002, January 30). *Education Week, 21*, 26–27.

Florence County School District v. *Carter*, 510 U.S. 7 (1993).

Greer v. Rome City School District, 950 F.2d 688 (11th Cir. 1991).

Irving Independent School District v. *Tatro*, 468 U.S. 883, 1984.

Jennings, J. F. (1998). *Why national standards and tests? Politics and the quest for better schools*. Thousand Oaks, CA: Sage.

Kaestle, C. F., & Smith, M. S. (1982, November). The federal role in elementary and secondary education, 1940–1980. *Harvard Educational Review, 52*, 384–408.

Kauffman, J. M., Lloyd, J. W., Baker, J., & Riedel, T. M. (1995, March). Inclusion of all students with emotional or behavioral disorders? Let's think again. *Phi Delta Kappan, 76*, 542–546.

Koretz, D., & Hamilton, L. (2000, Fall). Assessment of students with disabilities in Kentucky: Inclusion, student performance, and vitality. *Educational Evaluation and Policy Analysis, 22*, 255–272.

Lau v. *Nichols*, 414 U.S. 563 (1974).

Levin, H. M. (1982, November). Federal grants and educational equity. *Harvard Educational Review, 52*, 444–459.

Magers, D. A. (1977, Summer). Two tests of equity under impact aid Public Law 81-874. *Journal of Education Finance, 3*, 124–128.

Millsap, M., Turnbull, B., Moss, M., Brigham, N., Gamse, B., & Marks, E. (1992). *The Chapter 1 implementation study: Interim report*. Washington, DC: Office of Policy and Planning, U.S. Department of Education.

Mills v. *Board of Education*, 348 F. Supp. 866 (D.D.C., 1972).

Milstein, M. M. (1976). *Impact and response: Federal aid and state education agencies*. New York: Teachers College Press.

Moore, M. T. (2001). Prospects for Title I in the early 21st century: Are major changes in store? In S. Chaikind & W. Fowler (Eds.), *Education finance in the new millennium* (pp. 53–66). Larchmont, NY: Eye on Education.

Mort, P. R., & Reusser, W. C. (1941). *Public school finance: Its background, structure, and operation*. New York: McGraw-Hill.

National Assessment of Educational Progress. (1981). *Has Title I improved education for disadvantaged students? Evidence from three national assessments of reading*. Denver, CO: Education Commission of the States (ERIC ED 201 995).

National Association of State Boards of Education. (1992). *Winners all: A call for inclusive schools*. Alexandria, VA: Author.

National Center for Education Statistics (NCES). (2001). *Digest of Education Statistics: 2000*. NCES 2001-034. **http://nces.gov/pubs2001/2001034 .pdf** (accessed May 2001).

National Center for Education Statistics (NCES). (2000). *Federal $upport for education: Fiscal years 1980 to 2000*. Washington, DC: U.S. Government Printing Office.

National Commission on Excellence in Education. (1983). *A nation at risk: The imperative for educational reform*. Washington, DC: U.S. Government Printing Office.

Parrish, T. B., & Verstegen, D. A. (1994, Fall). The current federal role in special education funding. *Educational Considerations, 22*, 36–39.

Parrish, T. B., & Wolman, J. (1999). Trends and new developments in special education funding: What the states report. In T. B. Parrish, J. G. Chambers, & C. M. Guarino (Eds.), *Funding special education*. Thousand Oaks, CA: Corwin.

Puma, M. J., Karweit, N., Price, C., Riccuiti, A., Thompson, W., & Vaden-Kiernan, M. (1997). *Prospects: Final report on student outcomes*. Cambridge, MA: Abt Associates.

Riddle, W. C. (2001). *Educational testing: Bush administration proposals and congressional response*. Washington, DC: Congressional Research Service.

Sack, J. L. (2001, October 10). Lawmakers, Paige debate reform, funding as IDEA overhaul looms. *Education Week, 21*, 27.

Sage, D. D., & Burrello, L. C. (1994). *Leadership in educational reform: An administrator's guide to changes in special education*. Baltimore, MD: Brookes.

Schorr, L. B., & Schorr, D. (1988). *Within our reach: Breaking the cycle of disadvantage*. New York: Doubleday.

Sherman, J. D. (1992, Summer). Special issue: Review of school finance equalization under Section 5(d)(2) of P.L. 81-874, the impact aid program. *Journal of Education Finance, 18*, 1–17.

Skrtic, T. M. (1991). The special education paradox: Equity as the way to excellence. *Harvard Educational Review, 61*, 148–205.

Stickney, B. D., & Plunkett, V. (1983). Closing the gap: A historical perspective on the effectiveness of compensatory education. *Phi Delta Kappan, 65*, 287–290.

Stonehill, R. M., & Anderson, J. I. (1982). *An evaluation of ESEA Title I—Program operation and educational effects: A report to Congress*. Washington, DC: U.S. Department of Education.

Timothy W. v. *Rochester, New Hampshire, School District*, 875 F.2d 954 (1st Cir. 1989).

Timpane, M. P. (1982, November). Federal progress in educational research. *Harvard Educational Review, 52*, 540–548.

U.S. Department of Education. (1999). *Promising results, continuing challenges: The final report of the national assessment of Title I*. Washington, DC: Office of the Undersecretary, Planning and Evaluation Service.

U.S. Department of Education. (2001). *School improvement report: Executive order on actions for turning around low-performing schools*. Washington, DC: Author (**www.ed.gov/offices/OUS/PES/ lpschools.pdf**)

U.S. General Accounting Office. (1994). *Education finance: Extent of federal funding in state education agencies*. Washington, DC: Author.

Verstegen, D. A. (1987, Spring). Two hundred years of federalism: A perspective on national fiscal policy in education. *Journal of Education Finance, 12*, 516–548.

Verstegen, D. A. (1990, Winter). Education fiscal policy in the Reagan administration. *Education Evaluation and Policy Analysis, 12*, 355–373.

Verstegen, D. A. (1992). Economic and demographic dimensions of national education policy. In J. G. Ward & P. Anthony (Eds.), *Who pays for student diversity? Population changes and educational policy* (pp. 71–96). Newbury Park, CA: Corwin.

Verstegen, D. A. (1994, Summer). Efficiency and equity in the provision and reform of American schooling. *Journal of Education Finance, 20*, 107–131.

Verstegen, D. A. (1995). *Consolidated special education funding and services: A federal perspective*. Palo Alto, CA: Center for Special Education Finance.

Verstegen, D. A. (2000, Fall). Finance provisions under the Individuals with Disabilities Education Act 1997 amendments. *Educational Considerations, 28*, 32–38.

Wayson, W. (1975, November). ESEA: Decennial views of the revolution. Part II. The negative side. *Phi Delta Kappan, 57,* 151–156.

Wise, A. E. (1979). *Legislated learning: The bureaucratization of the American classroom.* Berkeley, CA: University of California Press.

Wong, K. K., & Meyer, S. J. (1998, Summer) Title I schoolwide programs: A synthesis of findings from recent evaluation. *Educational Evaluation and Policy Analysis, 20,* 115–136.

Rethinking School Finance Policy to Attain High Standards

In Part IV, we evaluate school fiscal policy from the perspectives of jurists (in Chapter 10) and policy analysts (in Chapters 11 and 12). We base these evaluations on the meta-values introduced and defined in Chapter 1: liberty, fraternity, equality (equity), efficiency, and economic growth.

Courts are the formal mechanisms created by society for evaluating social policy within parameters established by constitutional and statutory authority. Chapter 10 examines the assessments made by courts of school finance policy in the United States where equity and, more recently, adequacy are primary, but not exclusive, concerns. Chapter 11 views these closely related concepts from the perspectives of policy makers and policy analysts who are not constrained by the same parameters and procedures that obtain in judicial reviews. The findings of these policy studies are used as evidence in judicial proceedings, however.

Both judicial reviews and policy evaluation studies have shown that many schools are not effective in guiding children toward the goals society has set for them. This is particularly true for schools that primarily serve educationally at-risk children. But it is not only the children who are being harmed by this ineffectiveness. When the schools are not doing their jobs properly, citizens are not receiving a just return on the investments they make through taxes, and the entire national welfare is harmed.

Although the concepts of equity and adequacy on the one hand, and efficiency on the other, are quite different, we conclude in Chapters 10 and 11 that schooling cannot be truly equitable without also being efficient. In Chapter 12, we turn our attention to studies that use paradigms drawn from economics to seek ways of applying more efficiently the public resources already entrusted to schools.

We show that, as a nation, the United States is spending more per pupil than are most other advanced nations, especially its chief economic rivals. Most other nations, however, finance and administer their educational systems at the national level, and the resources committed are more evenly distributed throughout the school population than in the United States, where fifty states and thousands of school districts are involved. Much evidence is presented that the internal distribution of these resources to school districts and to schools is seriously flawed. Horizontal equity in the distribution of resources has improved over the years, but we are only beginning to grapple with the problem of vertical equity. Our early forays into vertical equity show that we have grossly underestimated the infusion of resources necessary to eliminate gaps in achievement between ethnic and socioeconomic groups. Thus we have a problem in the internal allocation of the total resources that the nation collectively commits to education.

We also have an efficiency problem. The evidence inspires little confidence that, given additional resources, schools and districts serving primarily at-risk children would use them in a manner that would improve student achievement. Studies of the use of resources by public schools and school districts consistently indicate that many—probably most—are not using their resources to full advantage. If there are to be improvements in educational outcomes, those improvements will depend not only on additional resources for the educationally at-risk population, but also on significant improvements in the internal efficiency of schools and districts.

chapter 10

JUDICIAL REVIEWS OF SCHOOL FINANCE POLICY

Issues and Questions

- *Achieving High Standards with Equity and Efficiency*: In what ways have judicial decisions influenced school finance structures to promote goals of equality and efficiency in enabling all students to meet performance expectations?
- *Role of the Courts*: What is the role of the judiciary in resolving challenges to school finance policy? How does the court's role differ from that of legislatures?
- *Criteria for Judicial Reviews*: What criteria have been derived from equal-protection clauses of federal and state constitutions and from education articles that call for state legislatures to provide public education?
- *Applying Criteria*: What have been the outcomes of federal and state court decisions that examine allocations of funds to school systems within the framework of constitutional provisions?
- *Future Litigation and Policy Development*: What implications might be drawn from the expanding judicial role in reviewing challenges to school finance policy?

The United States Constitution and fifty state constitutions provide a legal basis for the development of policy by the legislative branch of government. In turn, school finance policies that are enacted by state legislatures must be consistent with constitutional provisions calling for equal treatment, efficiency, and adequacy. The judicial branch of government is often called upon to decide whether policies and resulting distributions of state money satisfy federal or state constitutions.

Since 1968, there have been challenges of school finance systems in nearly all states. Plaintiffs who test state policies typically argue that aid formulas fail to allocate funds in a manner that enables property-poor districts to deliver educational opportunities similar to those available in wealthier school systems. They contend that inequities in resource inputs and in resulting student achievement are not permissible under constitutional provisions calling for equality, adequacy, and efficiency. In response, states often defend any disparities in spending among districts on the basis of the goal of promoting local control over public education. They argue that the appropriate role of the state is to ensure a base level of resources in all communities, with local voters determining any supplements. This argument is consistent with the value of liberty, which is satisfied when school boards and voters are free to identify educational needs and set related spending levels.

We begin this chapter by contrasting the nature of judicial decision making by the courts with the policy-making role of legislatures. We then discuss the criteria[1] of equality, adequacy, and efficiency that have evolved from court decisions. Finally, we examine four implications for future policy development, given constitutional provisions and judicial decisions in the context of demands for realizing expectations for high performance.

JUDICIAL AND LEGISLATIVE ROLES IN SHAPING POLICY

The judicial and legislative branches of government perform different functions in the formation of school finance policy. The state and federal aid programs presented in earlier chapters illustrate the products of legislative processes. The judiciary may be asked to test whether these fiscal policies satisfy societal expectations, or criteria, that are expressed in federal and state constitutions. This external review by the courts serves as a check on legislative actions. Furthermore, judicial interpretations often stimulate (or even compel) legislatures to alter school finance policy. Courts do not, however, initiate the subjects of judicial review. Instead, they react to conflicts and problems posed by affected citizens (i.e., plaintiffs who bring suits challenging government policies).

Holdings that clarified whether state policies affecting educational opportunity were consistent with the Fourteenth Amendment of the United States Constitution illustrate the role of the judicial branch of government. This amendment in part precludes state actions that "deny to any person within its jurisdiction the equal protection of the laws." In the landmark *Brown* v. *Board of Education* (1954) decision, the U.S. Supreme Court applied this equal-protection clause: "Such an opportunity, where the state has undertaken to provide it, is a right which must be made available to all on equal terms." The court concluded that educational opportunities must be provided in ways that satisfy a criterion of equality with regard to students' race.

Unlike this judicial interpretation regarding race, federal courts determined that the issue of inequities arising from finance structures was to be resolved in state legislatures and courts. Despite state court decisions favoring plaintiffs in many states, and despite pressures in nearly all states to reform finance policy to improve educational opportunities in property-poor districts, state legislatures were slow to respond. The nature of legislative processes, which are characterized by "give-and-take, negotiation, and compromise" (Fuhrman, 1978, p. 160), inhibited voluntary reform of states' finance structures. The movement to equalize tax bases and revenue slowed as consensus-building processes shaped the content of emergent policies.

The legislative policy arena gives primary attention to voters' preferences, school districts' interests, and consensus building. Social and political considerations influence voters' views, which in turn shape legislative actions:

> When given a choice, the majority will not opt to pay additional taxes and no parent will sacrifice funding at the school its child attends in order to secure additional funding for other schools. Of course, legislators must be responsive to these constituent interests and the contemporary social fabric is interwoven with historic valuations of fiscal liberty and local control of schools. (Sweetland, 2000, p. 98)

Legislators represent communities that are directly affected by proposed finance reforms. They are often more concerned with protecting interests of the school systems that they represent than with promoting equality in resources to improve education throughout the state. Because any redistributions of monies through changes in finance policy affect nearly all districts, it is essential that a majority benefit from reforms to ensure the necessary votes. Equality goals are often sacrificed in the bargaining and compromise essential to reaching agreement about policies that may alter current spending levels. Major consideration in the bargaining and compromise process is given to an assessment of which districts gain and which lose. In addition, school finance issues are not isolated from other matters before legislators, such as improving highways and prisons. Very often, lining up votes on a finance proposal depends on positions taken by legislators on prior and subsequent policy issues, rather than solely on the merits of equalizing educational opportunities (Brown & Elmore, 1982).

In contrast to these legislative concerns with voters' preferences, districts' interests, and competing demands, judicial reviews focus primarily on constitutional principles. Courts are more likely to consider inequities in the treatment of pupils under school finance policies. For example, decisions subsequent to *Brown* determined that exposing all students to the same program (i.e., an absolute equality of resources) denied equal educational opportunities to children with disabilities (*Mills* v. *Board of Education*, 1972) and children with limited English-language proficiency (*Lau* v. *Nichols*, 1974).

These decisions embody the principle of *equity*. This concept of fair treatment implies that children have a right of access to instructional programs that are appropriate to their individual learning potentials and needs. Equalizing educational opportunities does not necessarily mean equal dollars per pupil or equal dollars per program. In these contexts, "equal" treatment (i.e., equity) requires additional human and financial resources for programs that serve legitimate educational needs.

Many of the early challenges to school finance systems explored the concept of equality as it related to disparities in local wealth and the failure of state policy to enable the poorest districts to finance educational programs adequately. As the criterion of adequacy evolved, courts addressed the question of whether the goal of equity, as it is defined above, can be achieved if there are insufficient resources to permit the thorough and efficient provision of services. Recent decisions have also examined whether there are adequate resources to enable all students to meet standards of performance set by the state.

The court's role is one of interpreting constitutional principles in relation to previously enacted policy. In turn, this judicial role often sets the agenda for future policy development by legislatures.

EVOLVING CRITERIA FOR REVIEWS OF FINANCE POLICY

Individuals or groups may seek judicial redress when it is believed that principles of fairness are not served by government policies and actions. Plaintiffs in school finance suits contend that variations in spending that result from finance structures, as well as the inadequacy of resources provided, violate provisions of federal or state constitutions. Equal-protection clauses and the language of education articles within state constitutions convey society's expectations for legislative policy development. They also create criteria of equality, uniformity, efficiency, and adequacy for courts' reviews of school finance policy.

When plaintiffs first brought suits in the late 1960s, challenges failed because the courts lacked criteria against which to assess disparities in educational opportunities resulting from variations in property wealth (Alexander, 1982, p. 201). Federal district courts thus upheld school finance systems in Illinois (*McInnis* v. *Shapiro*, 1968) and Virginia (*Burruss* v. *Wilkerson*, 1969). In the absence of "discoverable and manageable standards" (*McInnis*, at 335), the courts deferred to state legislatures as the appropriate forum for policy development. For example, the *Burruss* court discussed educational needs and the limited abilities of courts to fashion appropriate remedies to ease inequities: "[T]he courts have neither the knowledge, nor the means, nor the power to tailor the public moneys to fit the varying needs of these students throughout the state" (at 574). The role of the courts would be only to ensure the outlays on one group would not be invidiously greater or less than those on another. Although these holdings were not successful for plaintiffs, the court's arguments urged a criterion of equality to determine the degree to which state funds should erase fiscal disparities and correct variations in educational needs.

Equal Protection

Like the Fourteenth Amendment's guarantee that no person may be denied "the equal protection of the laws," state constitutions ensure that government programs treat people in the same way. In other words, differential treatment is upheld only if classifications created by the law are not arbitrary or irrational. When it is alleged that varying treatment of children or taxpayers is contrary to equal-protection guarantees, one of three tests is applied to determine the reasonableness of the classification: the strict-scrutiny test, the rational-basis test, or the sliding-scale test (Underwood, 1989).

Courts employ a strict level of review to determine violations of equal protection when a policy treats some people differently solely because they belong to a "suspect classification" (e.g., race or national origin). Challenges involving a fundamental right guaranteed by the Constitution (e.g., religion or voting privileges) also invoke this rigorous test. In order to be upheld under the *strict-scrutiny test*, the classification or the denial of a constitutional right must be necessary to further a compelling objective of the state or federal government. In addition, the burden is on the government to show that there are no less intrusive methods to achieve the intended goal. A later section of this chapter cites state court decisions that interpreted education to be a fundamental right. Courts have also found that the heavy reliance on property taxation creates a suspect classification based on wealth. In this instance, the quality of educational opportunities in different districts rely too heavily on the wealth of localities. This argument was instrumental in the following decision, in which the California finance plan was found to violate the equal-protection clauses of both state and federal constitutions.

In the 1971 review, the California Supreme Court applied a narrower and more readily measurable criterion (the equality of dollar inputs) than the vague criterion of educational needs that was employed in the earlier *McInnis* and *Burruss* challenges. The question posed in *Serrano* v. *Priest* (1971) explored whether the finance plan discriminated inappropriately among districts on the basis of wealth. The state court examined inequities in expenditures that resulted from differing property wealth and tax burdens among school systems. The court declared that education was a fundamental right and that school district wealth created a suspect classification. Thus it placed the burden on the state to demonstrate a compelling reason for maintaining inequities. Because the state failed this strict scrutiny test, the court concluded that the policy violated both the state and federal equal-protection clauses. The court adopted the concept of *fiscal neutrality* as defined by Coons, Clune, and Sugarman (1970) to guide a legislative remedy: "The quality of public education may not be a function of wealth other than the wealth of the state as a whole" (p. 2). In the same year, a federal district court applied the same rationale to conclude that the Minnesota finance plan violated the Fourteenth Amendment (*VanDusartz* v. *Hatfield*, 1971).

In a second test for possible violations of the equal-protection clause, the judiciary exercises greater restraint. When neither a suspect classification nor a fundamental right is involved, the less stringent *rational-basis test* asks whether the classification is related to a legitimate objective. If the government satisfies this burden, the policy is upheld. The U.S. Supreme Court and many state courts adopted this test as the appropriate one for judging school finance challenges. These courts reasoned that finance structures, even when they permit program or fiscal disparities among districts, are constitutional if the policies are reasonably related to states' interests in promoting and preserving local control of education.

This rational-basis test was instrumental in the only school finance dispute to be fully reviewed by the U.S. Supreme Court (*San Antonio* v. *Rodriguez*, 1973). The rationale presented in this review of Texas school finance differed from that expressed in *Serrano*. First, education is not a fundamental interest because the right to a public education is not explicitly or implicitly guaranteed under the U.S. Constitution. The Supreme Court's previous holding to ban segregation by race recognized that education is "perhaps the most important function of state and local governments" (*Brown*, 1954). However, in the very close decision (a 5-to-4 vote of the justices) regarding Texas school finance, the court noted that education's importance did not elevate it to the level of other fundamental interests protected at the federal level. Second, the rights of a suspect class were not endangered as had been found with regard to race in *Brown*. Because poor people did not necessarily cluster in districts having low property values, a defined group had not been denied the benefits of public education. Without a fundamental right to an education or a clear disadvantage to a suspect class, the less stringent rational basis test was appropriate.

The Supreme Court concluded that there was a rational relationship between the funding plan and the state's interest in preserving local control over schools. A major consequence of this holding was to shift the attention of the finance reform movement from federal to state courts. State legislatures and courts were the appropriate venue to resolve conflicts over state statutes and constitutional provisions.

A federal district court followed the *Rodriguez* rationale in reviewing a claim that the distribution of state money to compensate school districts for lost revenue from railroad lands in Mississippi was inequitable. The Supreme Court's review found that a lower court's dismissal of the case was proper because "such differential funding was not unconstitutional" under *Rodriguez* (*Papasan* v. *Allain*, 1986, at 275). One year later, the Fifth Circuit Court of Appeals upheld Louisiana's school finance system. The court concluded that there was no violation of the equal-protection clause because the formula structure was "rationally related . . . to goals of providing each child in each school district with certain basic educational necessities and of encouraging local governments to provide additional educational support on a local level, to the extent that they choose to and are financially able to do so" (*School Board* v. *Louisiana State Board of Education*, 1987, at 572).

Finally, a mid-level scrutiny requires that classifications be substantially related to an important government interest. This *sliding-scale test* has been used in cases where courts are reluctant to declare a particular class (for example, one based on gender) suspect yet want to afford some protection (Underwood, 1989). The U.S. Supreme Court employed this test in its ruling that Texas could not deny free public education to the children of undocumented aliens (*Plyler* v. *Doe*, 1982). Under this test, a court may conclude that a school finance plan serves an important state objective even when the policy treats districts differently solely on the basis of their wealth.

The determination of which test is appropriate shapes the nature of a state's burden in defending school finance systems. We reference these tests in the later discussion of judicial reviews when plaintiffs challenge policies because of their denial of equal protection.

Uniformity, Efficiency, and Adequacy in Education Articles

In addition to or coincident with challenges based on equal-protection clauses are judicial reviews in state courts that focus on education provisions within state constitutions (McUsic, 1991; Sparkman, 1994). Education articles require state legislatures to establish and maintain public education for school-age children. These articles specify that education must be "uniform," "adequate," "thorough" and/or "efficient."

Challenges to the legality of states' finance plans contend that this constitutional language requires access to equal, efficient, and adequate educational opportunities. States respond that education articles require only that state resources provide a basic, or minimum, education in all districts. Defendants thus argue that the education article is satisfied even though policies permit local voters to spend more for programs or facilities than the minimum ensured by the state. Very often these conflicts center on the amount of discrepancy tolerated, particularly when the lowest-spending districts have inadequate resources to deliver educational programs to meet states' curricular standards. Courts in such cases may be more concerned with the adequacy of resources, programs, and services necessary to attain desired results (i.e., with efficiency) than they are with fiscal equity (Sparkman, 1983, p. 99).

McCarthy (1981) contrasted the concepts of equity and adequacy. *Equity* connotes fair and unbiased treatment, including unequal treatment for individuals who are not similarly situated. In contrast, *adequacy* connotes the state of being sufficient for a particular purpose (see Chapter 11). Wood (1995) stated the adequacy argument as one that questioned the degree to which local and state expenditures correlated with programmatic opportunities. Plaintiffs must demonstrate a substantive impact of available funds on students in terms of such factors as the "inability to update texts, hire teachers with advanced degrees, purchase school buses on a periodic basis, offer equal special education programs as compared with other school districts, support special education aid cuts, and so on" (p. 33).

It is difficult to achieve an "efficient" and "thorough" educational system if both equity and adequacy criteria are not satisfied. In the sections that follow, we illustrate the application of these criteria in state court decisions that invalidated or upheld finance systems.

STATE COURT REVIEWS OF SCHOOL FINANCE SYSTEMS

In addition to the early challenges to school finance policies in federal courts, there have been many state court reviews. Included in Table 10.1 are decisions of the highest level of court to review finance policies in forty-three states between 1968 and July 2002.[2]

Judicial reviews upheld state finance policies in twenty-nine states, including previous invalidations in Minnesota, Wisconsin, and

TABLE 10.1.

Reviews of School Finance Systems by Federal and State Courts

	Finance Systems Upheld		Finance Systems Invalidated	
Year	*Federal Courts*	*State Courts*	*Federal Courts*	*State Courts*
1968	Illinois			
1969	Virginia			
1971			Minnesota	California[b]
1973	Texas[a]	Arizona[b]		New Jersey[b]
		Michigan		
1974		Montana[b]		
		Washington[b]		
1975		Idaho[b]		
1976		Oregon[b]		Wisconsin[b]
1977				Connecticut[b]
1978				Washington[b]
1979		Ohio[b]		
		Pennsylvania[b]		
1980				Wyoming[b]
1981		Georgia[b]		
1982		Colorado[b]		
		New York[b]		
1983		Maryland[b]		Arkansas[b]
1984		Michigan		West Virginia[b]
1986	Mississippi[a]			
1987	Louisiana	Oklahoma[b]		
1988		South Carolina[b]		
1989		Wisconsin[b]		Kentucky[b]
				Montana[b]
				Texas[b]
1990				New Jersey[b]
1991		Oregon[b]		
1993		Minnesota[b]		Alabama[b]
		Nebraska[b]		Massachusetts[b]
				Missouri
				New Hampshire[b]
				Tennessee[b]
1994		Illinois		Arizona[b]
		Kansas[b]		New Jersey[b]
		North Dakota[b]		

(continued)

TABLE 10.1.

(Continued)

| Year | Finance Systems Upheld | | Finance Systems Invalidated | |
	Federal Courts	State Courts	Federal Courts	State Courts
1995		South Dakota Virginia[b] Maine[b] New York[b] Oregon Rhode Island[b] Texas[b]		Wyoming[b]
1996		Florida[b] Illinois[b]		Arkansas[b] Connecticut[b] Maryland
1997		Alaska[b]		Arizona[b] New Hampshire[b] New Jersey[b] North Carolina[b] Ohio[b] Vermont[b]
1998		Idaho[b] Louisiana Pennsylvania		New Jersey[b]
1999		Oregon		New Hampshire[b] South Carolina[b]
2000		Wisconsin[b]		Ohio[b]
2001				Alaska
2002		New York		

[a]Decision by United States Supreme Court.

[b]Decision by the highest state court. This is typically the state Supreme Court, but it may be designated by another name (e.g., Court of Appeals in New York).

Texas. Courts found finance systems to be unconstitutional in a total of twenty-four states. Nine of these states (Alaska, Arizona, Maryland, Montana, Ohio, South Carolina, Texas, and Washington) had successfully defended structures in earlier challenges. Included in Table 10.1 are five states (Illinois, Louisiana, Michigan, Missouri, and South Dakota) in which reviews have been heard only in lower courts. In one state (Mississippi), there has been no subsequent state court review after the U.S. Supreme Court upheld the finance structure. There has been no litigation testing the constitutionality of the school finance system in only seven states (Delaware, Hawaii, Indiana, Iowa, New Mexico, Nevada, and Utah).

Judicial decisions overturning or sustaining finance plans illustrate that the courts weigh provisions of those policies and the differing circumstances within states against criteria of equality, efficiency, and adequacy. In addition, the evolution of interpretations of the criteria over time, along with changes in judges and in legislative policy, explains what may appear to be a reversal of a previous holding within a given state.

Equality, Efficiency, and Adequacy in Successful Challenges

Judicial reviews of funding formulas in state courts centered initially on equal-protection clauses. Plaintiffs then expanded the basis for their challenges to include education clauses that required uniform, efficient, and/or adequate education. In this section we review decisions in favor of plaintiffs and the criteria for determining whether allocations of money for educational programs and facilities violate state constitutions.

Equality

Many of the early decisions invalidating finance plans (see Table 10.1) followed the *Serrano* rationale that was discussed previously. The Supreme Court of Connecticut, for example, applied the strict-scrutiny test after finding education to be a fundamental right guaranteed by the state constitution (*Horton* v. *Meskill*, 1977). The finance plan did not correct for large disparities in communities' wealth, which the court concluded were closely related to educational opportunities. A recent Connecticut Supreme Court decision reiterated the concern for equality. In 1996 the court found the existence of extreme racial and ethnic isolation in the Hartford schools to deprive children of a "substantially equal educational opportunity" (*Sheff* v. *O'Neill*, 1996).

The Wyoming Supreme Court determined that wealth constituted a suspect class and that education was a fundamental right when it struck down the state's finance plan (*Washakie* v. *Herschler*, 1980). Holding the distribution formula to be unconstitutional under the state's equal-protection clause and education article, the justices subsequently adopted a strong position on equality: "[T]his court will review any legislative school financing reform with strict

scrutiny to determine whether the evil of financial disparity, from whatever unjustifiable cause, has been exorcised from the Wyoming educational system" (*Campbell County School District* v. *State*, 1995, at 1266). They then outlined the legislative duty to fund an adequate education. This duty would entail determining what should be included in a "proper" education, analyzing the cost of its delivery in different districts, and adopting a finance plan.

An Arkansas Supreme Court decision illustrates that equal-protection challenges can be successful even when the judiciary applies the less stringent rational-basis test. We noted previously that the government has the burden of showing a justifiable relationship between the policy and some legitimate goal. The state did not convince the court that revenue disparities served a state interest: "Such a system only promotes greater opportunities for the advantaged while diminishing the opportunities for the disadvantaged" (*Dupree* v. *Alma*, 1983, at 93). In its analysis, the court gave the goal of equalizing educational opportunities greater weight than the goal of preserving local control. In 1996 the Arkansas Supreme Court dismissed the state's appeal of a lower court's holding (*Tucker* v. *Lake View School District*, 1996). The lower court had analyzed the finance system under the education article and concluded that the state did not provide a "general, suitable and efficient" educational system.

The degree of equality necessary to satisfy judicial review was the subject of the Vermont Supreme Court's holding (*Brigham* v. *State*, 1997). The court concluded that inequities in funding impeded equal educational opportunities as required by the state constitution's Education and Common Benefits clause. "Substantial equality" of educational opportunity, rather than absolute equality, would satisfy the constitution.

In addition to arguing violations of the equal-protection clause, plaintiffs in Pennsylvania and New York have recently challenged school finance policies as violating Title VI of the federal Civil Rights Act of 1964. This statute prohibits discrimination on the basis of a student's race or national origin in "any program or activity receiving Federal financial assistance." In 1999, plaintiffs claimed that Pennsylvania finance policies had a racially discriminatory effect. They argued that districts with high proportions of nonwhite students received proportionately less funding per pupil, in violation of Title VI. The Third Circuit reversed a lower court's dismissal of the case, ordering the trial court to determine whether there were disparate effects in violation of Title VI (*Powell* v. *Ridge*, 1999).

Similarly, in 2001 a lower court in New York reviewed the state's school finance structure as it affects students in New York City (*Campaign for Fiscal Equity* v. *New York*, 2001). Plaintiffs claimed that the state failed to ensure that the city's schools receive an adequate level of funding to afford their students a "sound basic education." The court concluded that the education provided "is so deficient that it falls below the constitutional floor set by the Education Article." In a second claim, the plaintiffs asserted that the funding mechanism had an adverse and disparate impact on minority students, who made up about 84 percent of enrollments. They claimed that this discrimination violated of Title VI of the Civil Rights Act of 1964. The court concluded that this disparate impact was not justified by any reason related to education. The court's order included "ensuring that every school district has the resources necessary for providing the opportunity for a sound basic education." Although an appellate court reversed this decision in 2002, the Pennsylvania and initial New York decisions suggest that Title VI may provide an avenue for plaintiffs to argue that unequal resources violate federal civil rights legislation.

Adequacy and Efficiency

Like *Serrano*, the foregoing rulings focused primarily on resource disparities and relied on equality as a criterion for review. Other state courts have considered arguments that there are insufficient funds to meet pupils' needs effectively and efficiently in all districts. This adequacy criterion is explicitly stated in or derived from language in state constitutions. The typical education article requires legislatures to establish and maintain a thorough and efficient system of public education in the state.

A series of New Jersey decisions illustrate the evolution of this adequacy criterion. One month after the U.S. Supreme Court's *Rodriguez* decision, the New Jersey Supreme Court interpreted the state constitutional requirement that the legislature ensure provision of a "thorough and efficient" educational system. The court clarified this mandate as providing "that educational opportunity which is needed in the contemporary setting to equip a child for his role as a citizen and as a competitor in the labor market" (*Robinson* v. *Cahill*, 1973, at 295). The finance policy did not enable all districts to deliver an adequate education as was required by this definition. A lengthy period of alternating legislative actions and judicial reviews sought an acceptable formula that would ensure both equity and adequacy.

In 1976 the court enjoined the New Jersey State Department from allocating aid to school districts. This action effectively closed schools until the legislature adopted a state income tax to fuel a new finance plan. A lower court's subsequent review of progress found that disparities had "steadily widened" because of the "proclivity of the equalization formula to perpetuate inequalities" (*Abbott* v. *Burke*, 1984, at 1284). The legislature responded by enacting the Quality Education Act in 1990.

Although this act equalized tax burdens, the New Jersey Supreme Court expanded its demand for adequacy in a 1990 decision. The finance system was found to be unconstitutional as it affected selected poor urban districts. Education in these settings was "tragically inadequate" in virtually all areas of curriculum, personnel, and facilities. In addition, there were unacceptable dropout and failure rates

(*Abbott* v. *Burke*, 1990, at 395–401). The court ordered amendments in the Quality Education Act to fund schools in poorer cities at the level of property-rich districts. Furthermore, there would be sufficient state funds so that spending would not depend on districts' wealth. There also had to be adequate funding "to provide for the special educational needs of these poorer urban districts in order to redress their extreme disadvantages" (at 363). However, Goertz (1993) observed that later revisions in the act effectively lowered the base foundation level and diverted funds from the equalization plan to provide property tax relief.

The court redefined adequacy in mandating unequal spending and supplemental programs and services:

> For these special needs districts, a thorough and efficient education—one that will enable their students to function effectively in the same society with their richer peers both as citizens and as competitors in the labor market—is an education that is the substantial equivalent of that afforded in the richer districts. (*Abbott* v. *Burke*, 1994, at 580)

The legislature responded with a comprehensive plan to link state funds to the cost of programs to meet content and workplace-readiness standards. However, plaintiffs prevailed once again in 1997 and 1998, because inadequate funds and facilities continued to impede the efforts of twenty-eight poor urban districts to conform to the plan necessary for students to achieve the standards. Holding that "adequate funding remains critical to the achievement of a thorough and efficient education," the Supreme Court ordered the state to fund improvements in programs and facilities (*Abbott* v. *Burke*, 1998, at 469). Goertz and Edwards (1999) noted that the measure of a thorough and efficient education had become the provision of programs and facilities necessary to meet the content standards at the level present in the wealthiest districts. The history of this state's experience in trying to achieve eq-

uity and adequacy illustrates the complexity of satisfying a constitution's "thorough and efficient" mandate.

The criterion of efficiency was at issue in the Texas Supreme Court's review of that state's school finance system. This challenge occurred two decades after the United States Supreme Court's landmark *Rodriguez* holding that education was not a right under the federal Constitution. In 1989 the state court interpreted the state constitution's mandate that there be "support and maintenance of an efficient system of public free schools" to foster a general diffusion of knowledge (*Edgewood* v. *Kirby*, 1989). In defining the term *efficient*, the court stated, " 'Efficient' conveys the meaning of effective or productive . . . results with little waste" (at 395). The extreme range in districts' wealth (from $20,000 to $14 million in property valuation per pupil) enabled rich districts to exert far less effort to raise necessary revenue. State allocations did not sufficiently equalize local revenue and related educational opportunities. Thus, the state Supreme Court concluded, "The present system . . . provides not for a diffusion that is general, but for one that is limited and unbalanced. The resultant inequalities are thus directly contrary to the constitutional vision of efficiency" (at 396).

The Texas court required full fiscal neutrality with a "direct and close correlation between a district's tax effort and the educational resources available to it" (at 397). The implicit link found by the court between goals of equality and efficiency was apparent in the order to make school resources fiscally neutral. An efficient system would recognize the value of local control in decisions about the amount of spending and would equalize districts' abilities to finance desired educational programs. The court subsequently concluded that the way in which the revised finance system took into account property tax collections made the local tax in reality a statewide *ad valorem* tax (*Carrollton-Farmers* v. *Edgewood*, 1992). Because this remedy violated the state constitution, the legislature then directed the wealthiest districts to transfer a portion of their wealth to poorer districts through one of five options: merging tax bases, consolidating districts, transferring property, contracting to educate nonresident students, or writing a check to the state. The state Supreme Court upheld this plan, including these forms of recapture. The reliance on local *ad valorem* taxes did not amount to the imposition of a state tax (*Edgewood* v. *Meno*, 1995).

An adequacy criterion underscored holdings in Tennessee and Massachusetts. The Tennessee Supreme Court noted that reliance on local funds inhibited poor districts' abilities to meet program standards of the 1990 state master plan. It found "a direct correlation between dollars expended and the quality of education a student receives" (*Tennessee Small School Systems* v. *McWherter*, 1993, at 144). Determining that the issues were "quality and equality of education" rather than equality of funding, the court concluded that the finance system was unconstitutional. Responding to a contention that substantially equal funding would "squelch innovation," the court noted, "Given the very nature of education, an adequate system, by all reasonable standards, would include innovative and progressive features and programs" (at 156). The Supreme Court subsequently ordered the state to equalize teachers' salaries as a part of the finance reform (*Tennessee Small School Systems* v. *McWherter*, 1995).

The Massachusetts Supreme Judicial Court, the state's highest court, similarly ruled the finance system to be inadequate and unconstitutional (*McDuffy* v. *Secretary*, 1993). Such deficiencies as inadequate teaching of the basics, neglected libraries, inferior teachers, lack of curriculum development, lack of predictable funding, administrative reduction, and inadequate guidance counseling contributed to the holding. In commenting on these inadequacies among districts, Underwood (1994) noted that plaintiffs can prevail under a "deprivation theory" (p. 147). This argument can be successful if there is evidence that students do not receive the

minimum level of education necessary to prepare them for responsibilities of citizenship.

Several decisions greatly expanded the role of the courts in promoting systemic reform. The judiciary closely examined the constitutionality of governance structures as well as finance systems under efficiency and adequacy criteria. West Virginia's Supreme Court of Appeals, the state's highest court, held that the "thorough and efficient system of free schools" requirement made education a fundamental right (*Pauley* v. *Kelly*, 1979). However, the court did not immediately declare the finance plan to be unconstitutional. Rather, the justices directed a lower court to determine whether any compelling state interest justified the classifications created under the policy. More significantly, the court desired an assessment of whether the school system's "high quality" educational standards were not met because of "inefficiency and failure to follow existing school statutes" or because of inadequacy of the existing system (at 878). The trial court then examined levels of resources in relation to standards for facilities, curriculum, personnel, materials, and equipment. Because all school systems, including the wealthiest, had deficiencies, the court invalidated both the educational system and the finance mechanism as not meeting the "thorough and efficient" requirement. A master plan would be necessary for the "constitutional composition, operation and financing" of the state's educational system. The Supreme Court of Appeals subsequently affirmed the State Board of Education's "duty to ensure delivery and maintenance of a thorough and efficient" educational system (*Pauley* v. *Bailey*, 1984).

Other state courts followed West Virginia's lead in demanding systemic reform. In 1989 the Kentucky Supreme Court declared that the "*entire system* of common schools is unconstitutional" (*Rose* v. *Council*, 1989). The court placed an absolute duty on the legislature to "re-create, re-establish" the entire system of public education:

This decision applies to the statutes creating, implementing and financing the *system* and to all regulations, etc. pertaining thereto. This decision covers the creation of local school districts, school boards, and the Kentucky Department of Education to the Minimum Foundation Program and Power Equalization Program. It covers school construction and maintenance, teacher certification—the whole gamut of the common school system in Kentucky. (at 215)

The concern for adequacy is apparent in the court's specification of seven competency areas, including academic content and vocational skills, that would enable students to compete in academics or in the labor market. In addition, the court specified clearly that any finance plan developed by the General Assembly would have to assess all property at 100 percent of market value and would necessitate uniform tax rates throughout the state. The far-reaching Kentucky Education Reform Act (KERA) of 1990 promoted systemic reform of governance, curricula, and finance. Critical elements included a foundation formula with restricted local supplemental levies, an increased minimum mill rate for district contributions and a larger state sales tax, financial rewards to schools with improvements in pupil performance, and reorganization of the state education department (Adams, 1993; King & Mathers, 1997).

In 1993 the Alabama Supreme Court clarified a lower court's decision that effectively struck down the entire educational system. The lower court had determined education to be a fundamental right, stating that "the Alabama system of public schools fails to provide plaintiffs the equal protection of the laws under *any* standard of equal protection review." The court also found that the state failed to provide appropriate and special services to children with disabilities. In reinforcing this decision, the Supreme Court required the legislature to "provide school children with substantially equitable and adequate educational opportunities" (*Opinion of the Justices*, 1993, at 165).

These decisions overturning state finance systems began in the 1970s with interpretations of the "thorough and efficient" requirements of state constitutions. As the application of these criteria evolved, the courts held states to the provision of adequate resources to make high minimum levels of education possible in all districts. The focus was primarily on the level of operating revenue available to school districts. Recent judicial reviews extended this reasoning to encompass the ability of local communities to construct school buildings.

Adequacy of Facilities

Local voters decide the extent to which property taxes are spent to construct and upgrade school buildings. Few state funding formulas provide equalization of local wealth in support of capital outlay. As a consequence, buildings in poorer districts in nearly all states are deficient and in need of extensive repairs (see Chapter 6). The condition of facilities was one of the indicators of adequacy or educational quality cited in several of the judicial decisions we have discussed. Recent Arizona and Ohio decisions focused particular attention on state responsibilities for financing school construction.

Arizona was the first state to declare the school funding system unconstitutional solely on the basis of the condition of school facilities. The state Supreme Court concluded that the financing of capital outlay did not satisfy the mandate to provide a "general and uniform" school system (*Roosevelt* v. *Bishop*, 1994). In particular, the court noted disparities in the condition and age of buildings and in the quality of classrooms and instructional equipment: "Some districts have schoolhouses that are unsafe, unhealthy and in violation of building, fire, and safety codes" (at 808). Disparities in facility quality resulted from "a combination of heavy reliance on local property taxation, arbitrary boundaries, and only partial attempts at equalization" (at 815). The Supreme Court subsequently ruled that several legislative acts failed to meet "an adequate capital facilities standard" (*Hull* v. *Albrecht*, 1997, at 1146).

The condition of facilities was one of the considerations in a recent review of Ohio school finance. An earlier decision by the state Supreme Court upheld the finance system as being rationally related to maintaining local control (*Board of Education* v. *Walter*, 1979). The 1997 reversal of this logic rested upon an adequacy criterion. The Ohio court declared the statewide education system to be unconstitutional in its failure to meet the "thorough and efficient" mandate. The court ruled that a thorough system is not starved for funds and an efficient system does not lack teachers, buildings, and equipment (*DeRolph* v. *State*, 1997). The court reiterated this holding in 2000 when plaintiffs complained that the state failed to provide funds to meet students' needs.

Like the differing interpretations of state constitutions over time in Arizona and Ohio, the South Carolina Supreme Court reached seemingly contradictory conclusions in 1988 and 1999. The former holding supported the finance policy as furthering legitimate state interests (*Richland County* v. *Campbell*, 1988). The latter decision favored plaintiffs by interpreting the education article to require the General Assembly to ensure a minimally adequate education and safe facilities (*Abbeville County School District* v. *State*, 1999).

The thirty years of school finance litigation favoring plaintiffs show an evolution in criteria from equality to adequacy of resources and facilities. In contrast to these decisions are judicial reviews in which states successfully defended challenges to finance structures.

Equality, Efficiency, and Adequacy in Decisions Upholding Finance Systems

Federal courts have upheld school support mechanisms in Illinois, Virginia, Texas, Mississippi, and Louisiana. We noted previously that the 1973 *Rodriguez* decision was the only

United States Supreme Court review of a school finance system. The court concluded that there is no fundamental right to an education under the U.S. Constitution and that the Texas policy did not disadvantage a suspect class. The holding made it clear that school finance policy was a matter for resolution within states.

Like the decisions in which courts overturned finance systems, the judicial reviews that validated finance policies (see Table 10.1) illustrate an evolution in the criteria applied by the courts. Early state decisions rested upon equal-protection clauses, whereas subsequent reviews examined policies in relation to the "efficiency and adequacy" requirements of education articles.

Equality

With a few exceptions, when asked to determine whether the state statute satisfied equal-protection clauses, state courts upholding school finance policies have declared that education was not a fundamental interest. Justices determined that the appropriate level of scrutiny was the less stringent rational-basis test. Under this level of analysis, states have successfully demonstrated a nexus between the finance plan and such goals as promoting local control over education. In 1973, for example, the Arizona Supreme Court declared that children are guaranteed a basic right to education, but it did not invalidate the finance system. Instead, the court determined that allocations need be "only rational, reasonable, and neither discriminatory nor capricious" (*Shofstall* v. *Hollins*, 1973, at 592). But the court reached a different conclusion in the 1994 *Roosevelt* decision cited previously.

The Supreme Courts of Colorado and Idaho concluded that education was not a fundamental right. Applying the rational-basis test, the courts found respective finance systems to further the states' interests in maintaining local control. The Colorado court emphasized the state's objective of fostering local control: "Taxation of local property has not only been the primary means of funding local education, but also of insuring that the local citizenry direct the business of providing public education in their school district" (*Lujan* v. *Colorado State Board of Education*, 1982, at 1021). This reasoning echoed an earlier decision by the Idaho Supreme Court (*Thompson* v. *Engleking*, 1975). When asked to review disparities in spending again in 1993, the justices ruled that the mandate of a uniform system in the education clause required only uniformity in curriculum, not uniformity in funding (*Idaho Schools* v. *Evans*, 1993). This conclusion became the justification for a later ruling that there need not be uniform funding for facilities. In 1998 the Idaho Supreme Court held that a thorough system includes the provision of facilities that offer a safe environment conducive to learning. However, this constitutional provision did not require the state to equalize funding for capital expenditures. The court upheld local override elections for facilities despite resulting disparities (*Idaho Schools for Equal Educational Opportunity* v. *State*, 1998).

The Oregon Supreme Court determined that the uniformity criterion applied to the general system of education, not to specific funding disparities. The constitution was satisfied even when districts exercised local control over decisions about spending for programs beyond the minimum level guaranteed by the state (*Olsen* v. *State*, 1976). The court's subsequent review in 1991 rested upon a finding that voters had approved a constitutional amendment that created a "safety net" for districts in financial difficulty. These districts could continue to operate under the prior year's levy without voter approval. Thus voters had endorsed the amendment and resulting disparities in taxation and in per-pupil levels of funding (*Coalition for Equitable School Funding* v. *State*, 1991).

The North Dakota Supreme Court relied on an "intermediate scrutiny analysis" in giving its finding of important substantive rights. This decision confirmed the trial court's declaration

that "the distribution method, as a whole, is unconstitutional." (*Bismarck* v. *State*, 1994, at 257) The Supreme Court agreed that "the present educational funding system seriously discriminates against some students and significantly interferes with their right to equality of educational opportunities" (at 262). Although a three-judge majority voted to invalidate the plan, it survived because the constitution required a vote by four justices to invalidate a statute. The court concluded that the education clause did not require absolute uniformity, only a basic level of education in all districts.

Plaintiffs in Alaska claimed that the different treatment of regional education attendance area school districts versus the city and borough school districts violated the right to equal protection. The state Supreme Court noted that the interest involved, freedom from disparate taxation, was at the lower end of the sliding scale of interests protected by the equal-protection clause. It thus needed to find only a "substantial relationship" between the finance policy and the goal of ensuring equitable educational opportunities. Because plaintiffs were unable to show that disparities in districts' contributions to the foundation level translated into disparities in educational opportunities, there was no denial of equal protection (*Matanuska-Susitna Borough School District* v. *State*, 1997).

Unlike the New Jersey holding in *Abbott* that called for remedies favoring poorer cities, judicial reviews by the highest courts in New York and Maryland would not broaden the concept of equity to include conditions of urban districts. However, recent lower-court holdings in both states determined that the school finance systems denied poor and minority students an adequate education.

New York's four largest cities joined poor school districts in challenging state aid distributions on two grounds. First, plaintiffs claimed in the lower court that the formula "arbitrarily and inequitably grants less and inadequate aid per pupil" in urban districts with the highest concentrations of pupils requiring compensatory schooling services (*Levittown* v. *Nyquist*, 1978, at 611). Second, they contended that the plan relied on an arbitrary and inadequate measure of local capacity by not considering the general poverty of residents or cities' higher levels of municipal and educational services. Plaintiffs claimed that the state failed to consider four urban conditions: municipal overburden, in which higher tax efforts are required to finance extensive public services; educational overburden, given the expense of educating disproportionate numbers of high-cost students; cost differentials, due to higher prices often paid for goods and services; and absenteeism overburden, in which revenue is lost under formulas that determine aid by average daily attendance (Goertz, 1981).

The Court of Appeals, which is New York's highest court, determined that the finance system did not deny equal protection or violate the constitution's education clause (*Levittown* v. *Nyquist*, 1982). Applying the rational-basis test, the court held that the "preservation and promotion of local control of education" was a legitimate state interest to which the finance system was reasonably related. Disparities in spending did not violate the education article, which did not require education across the state to "be equal or substantially equivalent." Finally, the court determined that "municipal dollars flow into cities' treasuries from sources other than simply real property taxes—sources similarly not available to non-municipal school districts" (at 649). The court reasoned that these alternative revenue sources countered the argument that the aid distribution plan denied equal protection.

In 1995 the Court of Appeals again denied plaintiffs' claims, despite finding even greater disparities among districts and unmet needs in poorer districts (*Reform Educational Financing Inequities Today* v. *Cuomo*, 1995). However, this court established clearly that the state constitution "imposes a duty on the Legislature to ensure a sound basic education to all the children of the State" (at 315). This duty became the basis for the previously discussed lower-court holding about the finance system as it affects students in New York City (*Campaign for Fiscal Equity* v. *New York*, 2001). However, an appellate court subsequently reversed this holding. The court noted that the State must ensure a "minimally adequate educational opportunity" rather than "some higher, largely unspecified level of education" (Gehring, 2002).

This pattern of judicial reviews involving urban plaintiffs parallels that experienced in Maryland. The state's highest court upheld the finance plan using justification similar to that given in the *Levittown* decision (*Hornbeck* v. *Somerset*, 1983). However, a lower court later ruled that Baltimore school students were deprived of their right to at least a minimum quality of education as guaranteed in the state constitution (*Bradford* v. *Board of Education*, 1996).

In a very different situation, Kansas plaintiffs challenged a funding formula that fully equalized local property taxation. The state district court had previously reasoned that the constitution's provision for education meant that the state should control and distribute all funds, including local property taxes, "regardless of current practices or concepts of local school control." The legislature revamped the school finance statute in 1992 to equalize local wealth. The Kansas Supreme Court upheld the plan, which included a statewide property tax and a recapture provision that applied to property taxes collected above a given level (*Unified School District* v. *Kansas*, 1994).

This decision upheld the policy of recapturing local revenue in an effort to promote greater equality in resources available in all districts (see Chapter 7). Plaintiffs in several other states have challenged the legality of this redistribution of property tax revenue from wealthy to poor districts. The Montana Supreme Court was one of the first to uphold a recapture feature (*Woodahl* v. *Straub*, 1974). The equalization formula called for wealthy districts to remit to the state any property tax proceeds in excess of the foundation funding level. The court rejected claims that the state-imposed tax discriminated against taxpayers who paid more than was necessary to support local schools. The court reasoned that the general property tax constituted "a rational method of providing for basic public education required by the Constitution" (at 777). In 1998 the Vermont Supreme Court similarly upheld the state's recapture provision (*Anderson* v. *State*, 1998). However, a 1976 Wisconsin Supreme Court decision stands in contrast to these decisions. This court found the state's redistribution of property tax revenue to equalize local revenue to be a violation of the state constitution (*Buse* v. *Smith*, 1976).

Efficiency and Adequacy

Courts in several states have denied challenges brought by plaintiffs on the basis of adequacy. This concept is derived from state constitutions' education articles that require legislatures to establish and maintain thorough, efficient, or adequate education. The Georgia Supreme Court determined that the term *adequate education* in the constitution did not "impose an obligation on the legislature to equalize educational opportunities." Nor did it prevent local districts from raising funds to improve education (*McDaniel* v. *Thomas*, 1981). The Minnesota Supreme Court discussed adequacy once it concluded that education was a fundamental right and that the finance system, including voter-approved tax supplements and debt service levies, satisfied the strict-scrutiny test (*Skeen* v. *State*, 1993). Disparities in overall funding were not objectionable, as long as the equalized base funding level provided an adequate education. The court noted that the term *adequacy* "refers not to some minimal floor but to the measure of need that must be met" (at 318).

The Supreme Court of Pennsylvania examined the finance plan and concluded that in the absence of any legal harm to a district or in-

jury to a student, there was no violation of the constitutional provision of a thorough and efficient educational system (*Danson* v. *Casey*, 1979). Plaintiffs were unsuccessful again in 1998 when they argued that the finance system violated the "thorough and efficient" provision by not providing adequate funds to meet unique needs of students at urban schools. The lower court noted that the state constitution placed responsibility for public school support in the legislature. Thus the court "will not inquire into the reason, wisdom, or expediency of the legislative policy with regard to education" (*Marrero* v. *Commonwealth*, 1998, at 965).

The Virginia Supreme Court accepted state minimum standards as the definition of adequacy in its decision that declared education to be a fundamental right and upheld the finance plan (*Reid Scott* v. *Commonwealth*, 1994). The constitution did not mandate "substantial equality of payments or programs" but guaranteed only that the State Board of Education's Standards of Quality be satisfied. Similarly, the Supreme Courts of Rhode Island and Florida upheld finance systems despite claims of unequal and inadequate resources. The Rhode Island court noted that money alone does not determine whether students receive "an equal, adequate and meaningful" education (*Pawtucket* v. *Sundlun*, 1995). The Florida court interpreted the state constitution as requiring only a system of schools that give students an equal chance to achieve basic educational goals (*Coalition for Adequacy and Fairness* v. *Chiles*, 1996).

The Wisconsin Supreme Court has upheld the finance structure in rulings that applied equality and adequacy criteria. Equality was at issue in 1989 when the court ruled that equal opportunity for an education is a fundamental right (*Kukor* v. *Grover*, 1989). However, this right did not necessitate absolute equality in financing. Disparities were rationally based on the goal of preserving local control, even if certain districts lacked funds to provide special programs to meet all children's needs. Adequacy of resources in relation to curricular standards became an issue in the recent 2000 decision. The Wisconsin court held that as long as the legislature provided sufficient resources to give all students an equal opportunity for a sound basic education, the school finance system would pass constitutional muster (*Vincent v. Voight*, 2000). The court defined a *sound basic education* as the opportunity for proficiency in mathematics, science, reading, writing, geography, and history and for exposure to the arts, social studies, physical education, health instruction, foreign language study, and vocational training.

The decisions upholding state plans illustrate judicial tolerance for spending disparities, particularly when they reflect voters' preferences. Early holdings of state courts found the promotion of local control of educational decisions to be a legitimate state interest. This finance policy advances the value of liberty as it was presented in Chapter 1. Subsequent challenges argued that finance plans did not meet an adequacy criterion, but courts upheld the policies when a base funding level enabled districts to provide an adequate educational program. Moran (1999) concluded that states prevail if they have "well developed content and performance standards, assessment systems, and rationally related funding formulas for ensuring that students meet proficient levels of performance" (p. 40).

IMPLICATIONS FOR SCHOOL FINANCE POLICY

This history of federal and state court holdings reveals differing interpretations of criteria derived from constitutional provisions and varying degrees of judicial activism in settling conflicts over school finance structures. These judicial reviews suggest a number of implications for the development of school finance policy.

1. Whereas the judicial branch of government may stimulate school finance reform,

policy development remains a legislative prerogative.

The judiciary provides a check on legislative actions, testing whether finance structures satisfy constitutional requirements. Court reviews also serve as a catalyst for policy change (Clune, 1992). Lehne (1978) describes the courts' role in advancing finance reform issues as an "agenda-setting" rather than a "decision-making" function. The courts specify which issues will be considered, rather than acting as institutions that develop concrete policies. The effect of the courts on policies is therefore obscured. However, there is some evidence that judicial decisions bring greater equalization, higher levels of funding for schools generally, and a shift in power from localities to states (Henderson, 1991; Hickrod et al., 1992). In addition, courts motivate change whether states are under direct orders to reform unconstitutional finance systems, have cases in process, or are threatened by the possibility of judicial reviews (Fuhrman, 1978, p. 162).

Courts are reluctant to assume the role of policy makers. A tradition of judicial deference to legislative processes ensures that a representative body develops policies involving taxation and allocations of public funds. The U.S. Supreme Court, for example, despite its conclusion in *Rodriguez* that the Texas finance system satisfied legal tests, commented that "ultimate solutions must come from the lawmakers and from the democratic pressures of those who elect them" (at 59). The Idaho Supreme Court refrained from convening "as a 'super-legislature,' legislating in a turbulent field of social, economic and political policy" (*Thompson* v. *Engelking*, 1975, at 640). The Minnesota Supreme Court noted that "the determination of education finance policy, in the absence of glaring disparities, must be a legislative decision because it involves balancing the competing interests of equality, efficiency, and limited local control" (*Skeen* v. *State*, 1993, at 318). However, courts do not avoid the issues because of this deference to policy makers. The Kentucky Supreme Court stated, "To avoid deciding the case because of 'legislative discretion,' legislative function,' etc., would be a denigration of our own constitutional duty" (*Rose v. Council*, 1989, at 209). We note below that in recent years, courts have become more activist in requiring legislatures to revamp governance, policy, and school finance mechanisms.

Many state court decisions validated finance policies when states demonstrated convincingly that local-control objectives fell within the prerogative of lawmakers, despite resulting variations in expenditures. In these states, advocates of reform must work within legislative processes, rather than rely on the judiciary, to further goals of equity and adequacy. For example, Colorado and Oregon lawmakers enacted equalization formulas *subsequent to* findings by respective state supreme courts that disparities in funding due to local voters' desires for schools were permitted under constitutional provisions.

Even in states in which courts declare finance plans to be invalid under constitutional mandates, the judiciary typically defers to legislatures to craft remedies. However, moving the reform agenda from the courts to the legislative arena means that finance policies will be shaped by individual legislators who represent special interests of school districts and respond to citizens' priorities (Sweetland, 2000). When principled decision making yields to political interests and compromises, goals of equalizing wealth and educational opportunities may be sacrificed. Plaintiffs may demonstrate successfully to a court that disparities in funds, programs, and facilities due to variations in wealth among school systems inhibit students' access to similar educational opportunities. But this may be only the first step in a lengthy process of reforming school finance policy.

2. Criteria of equality and adequacy continue to evolve as they are applied both to judg-

ing policy and to guiding the development of finance policies that bring sufficient resources to enable students to meet high performance expectations.

Constitutions provide broad statements about the protection of individual rights and the maintenance of public school systems. In the early decisions, courts struggled to find a means to relate disparities in districts' wealth or pupils' needs to equal-protection guarantees of federal or state constitutions. The *Serrano* court advanced the concept of fiscal neutrality, which asked policy makers to define the structure and parameters for making educational finance a function of state wealth. The criterion of equality has changed substantially over the years from an emphasis on redistributing revenue to one that broadens the concept to address fairness (i.e., equity) and the quality of students' education (i.e., adequacy).

Such vague criteria as "uniform," "adequate," thorough," and "efficient" in education articles have frustrated courts and legislatures. A number of state courts followed New Jersey's lead in *Robinson* and *Abbott*. They placed as great an emphasis on the adequacy of school resources and programs as they placed on equality. Once again, policy makers were given the task of determining what level of funding and what distribution plan would satisfy requirements for an adequate or a thorough and efficient educational system. The initial determination of whether a "thorough and efficient" mandate was satisfied depended on analyses of the degree to which finance structures resulted in unequal resource inputs and, ultimately, unequal student achievement.

The subsequent review of the revised New Jersey finance system extended the criterion of adequacy, requiring supplemental resources for programs and services to address urban students' needs and prepare them for citizenship and work responsibilities. Compensatory aid that raised spending above that of richer districts would satisfy the constitutional requirement of "a certain level of education, that which equates with thorough and efficient; it is that level that *all* must attain; that is the *only* equality required by the Constitution" (*Abbott v. Burke*, 1990, at 369). The court's mandate to finance program and facility improvements in urban schools adequately was meant to help all students meet the same standards as those present in wealthier communities.

Reviews in Alabama, Kentucky, North and South Carolina, Tennessee, and West Virginia also examined state expectations for educational quality in determining whether the level of revenue was adequate. Underwood and Sparkman (1991) observed that such decisions shifted the focus from equity litigation tied to spending levels to the broader concept of meeting students' needs in relation to academic expectations: "Focusing on the educational product and student needs changes the question from how much is spent to *how* it is spent and with what effects" (p. 543). Underwood (1994) amplified this altered judicial view of equity: "More courts are beginning to see the purpose of the funding formula to be the equitable provision of education to *all* children of the state. When this posture is taken, the court concludes that funding disparities do nothing to advance this state interest" (p. 145). Federal policy reforms in the mid-1990s and in 2001 (see Chapter 9) demanded that all children have access to programs enabling them to meet challenging state academic content and performance standards. If federal and state curricular expectations are to be realized in all districts, then courts and legislators will scrutinize resource adequacy in relation to student achievement. Enabling poor and at-risk students to achieve at high levels will require adequate levels of resources in all school districts.

In contrast, such decisions as those in Florida, Minnesota, North Dakota, Rhode Island, Virginia, and Wisconsin endorsed plans that ensured a base foundation level to enable all districts' educational programs to meet minimum standards. These reviews tolerated, in the name of local control, policies (such as voter override provisions) that resulted in disparities in total available revenue and that advantaged wealthier districts. Legislatures not under judicial directives to equalize resources have greater latitude to adopt plans that respect local districts' desires to supplement funding above a high minimum foundation.

The adequacy of facilities has often been cited as an indicator of students' access to equal educational opportunities. Supreme courts in Arizona, Ohio, South Carolina, Texas, and Wyoming noted the relationship between the quality of facilities and local property wealth. Their holdings urged state policy makers to equalize districts' access to adequate capital outlay funds. Few states' finance policies encompass this costly aspect of educational delivery at an adequate level. The limited state role in financing school construction in most states would likely fail to meet constitutional tests if courts were to include the access to capital outlay funds within guarantees of uniform, thorough and efficient, or adequate educational systems.

Many courts recognize that an equal or equitable distribution of resources alone does not improve educational programs and services. Equity is a necessary, but not a sufficient, condition for attaining equal educational opportunities. Minorini and Sugarman (1999) note that adequacy is becoming an important criterion for judging school finance policy in relation to constitutional provisions of equality and efficiency, particularly in the context of high performance expectations for students:

> What is most distinctive about the adequacy approach is that, unlike the traditional school finance cases, it does not rest on a norm of equal treatment. Indeed, the adequacy cases aren't about equality at all, except in the sense that all pupils are entitled to at least a high-minimum. In other words, adequacy is not a matter of comparing spending on the complaining group with spending on others. It is rather about spending what is needed (and its focus is in some respects

more on the school or the pupil than on the district). (p. 188)

Koski and Levin (2000) observed that judicial holdings embracing this criterion would assist legislative policy development: "This newer strategy has the advantage of assuring that equity is not achieved at a mediocre level of funding equality, and it eliminates a political source of opposition to educational funding reform by not threatening districts that are spending above this high minimum level" (p. 490). As states adopt rigorous standards and high expectations for academic results, there may be judicial interpretations that there is a *legislative duty* to provide commensurately high levels of resources in all school districts. For example, the Wyoming court declared a legislative duty to analyze the costs of a proper education and fund a plan to achieve this level of adequacy in respective districts. What is emerging from recent lower-court holdings in Pennsylvania, New York, and Maryland is a legislative duty for the state to provide a quality education for all students—particularly poor and minority students—to attain desired educational outcomes.

Unlike the early challenges that failed for lack of "manageable standards," courts will have no difficulty finding a basis for judging whether states' actions deny school districts equitable and adequate resources. Koski and Levin (2000) comment on courts' adoption of adequacy as a criterion: "Thus regardless of the difficulties in operationalizing the adequacy theory, advocates and courts armed with new state standards may nonetheless establish definitions and measures for adequacy that will be legal standards and, perhaps, legal rights" (p. 495). We anticipate that judicial holdings will reinforce this legislative duty to fund schools equitably and adequately in relation to the performance expectations placed on schools and students.

3. The goal of fiscal neutrality is not incompatible with goals of preserving and promoting local choice of spending levels or total tax effort.

The value of liberty is evidenced in many states' school finance policies that permit district voters to determine spending levels. The goal of maintaining local control has been accepted by federal and state courts as a legitimate interest in satisfying the rational-basis test. The school finance reform movement of the 1970s and 1980s encouraged states to adopt finance plans that stressed equality over liberty. However, this movement erased many of the benefits of school district autonomy. Ward (1990) observed that local voters had less discretion and school programs became more standardized: "Rather than increasing democratic participation in public decision making, the net effect of the school finance reform cases was increased centralization and bureaucratic decision making" (p. 246). The response to this movement in the 1980s and 1990s was to return control of educational decisions to school personnel, communities, and families (see Chapters 14 and 15). However, we noted previously that the standards movement, along with state and national assessments, has implications for judicial reviews of finance structures in relation to legislative requirements for districts to bring all students to high levels of achievement.

In requiring fiscal neutrality, courts in California, Texas, and Kansas proclaimed that the quality of a child's education may not be a function of wealth other than that of the entire state. Legislatures may choose to fully equalize local district spending to achieve this goal. But fiscal neutrality tolerates variations in tax effort and spending levels if the result is that districts choosing to exert the same effort have the same total per-pupil revenue available. Reformers have advanced model formulas to blend goals of fiscal neutrality and local control (see the various forms of percentage equalization presented in Chapter 7). For example, rich and poor districts desiring the same expenditure per pupil must tax local property at the same rate. The state then provides unequal amounts of aid to raise each district to that desired spending level. Under such a plan, total expenditures vary among districts. But the finance system is fiscally neutral because the state equalizes local wealth. As a consequence, disparities in overall funding are a function only of local decisions about educational programs.

The Texas Supreme Court concluded in *Edgewood* (1991) that goals of both equality and efficiency are satisfied when local control is encouraged within such an equalized finance plan. Similarly, the 1994 Kansas decision upheld legislative plans premised on full fiscal neutrality. Absolute equality of expenditures is not a necessary condition for states to achieve fiscal neutrality. Policies need only alter what has traditionally been a direct relationship between wealth and total spending for education.

4. In the absence of legislative action to promote equality, efficiency, and adequacy, courts may assume a more activist role.

When the New Jersey and Texas legislatures failed to agree on funding plans to satisfy criteria, their supreme courts threatened to withhold public funds for schools until policy makers resolved the issue. Lehne (1978) discussed the *Robinson* decision in relation to the growing activism of the judiciary and the dynamic role the courts play in policy debates:

> While judicial decisions have traditionally been negative statements proscribing specified actions, in recent decades, courts more frequently demand positive actions from government to achieve specified goals. The judiciary is now more likely to require the executive, the legislature, and the public to deal with an issue but also to leave them an uncertain latitude to determine exactly how to deal with it. (p. 16)

Bosworth (2001) claimed that state courts acted as policy makers in deciding remedies in Texas, Kentucky, and North Dakota. He characterized the role in terms of judicial activism:

> "Judicial activists" see their function as that of promoting the common good (however defined) through law. . . . [They] do not necessarily confine their activism to the discovery of constitutional wrongs, either; these judges are more likely to devise expansive remedies for these violations. (p. 3)

In contrast, "judicial restraintists" view the appropriate judicial role to be interpreting the law and applying it as closely as possible to the question before the court. Restraintists are critical of activists for substituting their own policy judgments for those of elected legislators.

Courts are becoming more activist, and some have assumed strong roles in defining criteria and designing remedies in recent school finance cases. This growing activism may be due to the vagueness of constitutional language calling for equal treatment, thoroughness, efficiency, and/or adequacy. It may also be a reaction to legislative resistance to change and to their proclivities to negotiation and compromise, which frustrate reformers' desires to reduce inequities. The New Jersey court eventually fashioned a remedy that required substantial compensatory aid to provide adequate education in urban districts. Even more dramatically, the Alabama, West Virginia, and Kentucky rulings indicate courts' willingness to effect change in educational governance structures and offerings, in addition to finance plans, to enable students to meet academic performance standards. Underwood (1994) concluded that the latitude to interpret vague constitutional language, particularly that of education articles, permits judicial activism and "some freedom to construe the language liberally to meet [the court's] own goals of reform" (p. 157).

The balance of power between these branches of government seems to have shifted toward the courts in Kentucky, New Jersey, Texas, and other states. However, legislators have the opportunity and responsibility to design educational policies in ways that ensure that students in all districts, regardless of wealth, can access adequately funded instructional programs and meet high performance expectations.

SUMMARY

Courts have played important roles in judging whether finance policies satisfy constitutional requirements, so they often play a strong role in stimulating change in school finance policy. Interpretations of constitutional provisions that guarantee equal protection and define legislative responsibilities for education establish criteria for later policy development. Federal court decisions and congressional actions that focused attention on equal educational opportunities in the 1960s and 1970s led to challenges of states' school finance systems. When they were denied access to federal courts for reviews of finance policies, plaintiffs turned to state courts.

Differing state court interpretations of equal-protection clauses depended in part on choices of the appropriate level of judicial analysis. A strict-scrutiny test is premised on findings that public education is a fundamental right or that disparities are a consequence of a suspect wealth-based classification. Such an analysis imposes a very difficult burden on states to justify spending variations among school districts. States have been more successful in satisfying the less stringent rational-basis test. They have often shown that disparities under finance systems are related to a legitimate objective, such as maintaining local control over educational decisions.

Judicial reviews may also rest on the education articles of state constitutions. These provisions typically require states to establish and maintain public educational systems that are uniform, thorough, efficient, and adequate. Interpretations of these mandates evolved from simplistic determinations of the degree of disparity in expenditures to judgments on the adequacy of available resources, programs, and facilities to enable all students to meet curricular standards. Recent reviews of state policies exhibit an expanding role of the courts in defining expectations for pupil performance in relation to content standards. Furthermore, the courts are interpreting these constitutional provisions as creating a duty for legislatures to develop funding mechanisms to provide adequate resources to ensure that all students can meet these standards. When several state courts were asked to review finance policies, they ultimately declared entire educational systems unconstitutional.

Judicial reviews represent one way to determine whether finance systems satisfy the goals of equality and efficiency. The next chapter continues to examine equality and adequacy, but from the perspectives of policy analysts.

ENDNOTES

1. We employ the term *criteria* to describe what are often referred to as judicial standards. In this way, we distinguish the criteria derived from constitutional provisions in reviews by the courts from the "standards" applied in describing student performance expectations.
2. State Supreme Court decisions not referenced in the text discussion include those in Illinois (*Committee for Educational Rights* v. *Edgar*, 1996); Maine (*School Administrative District* v. *Commissioner*, 1995); Montana (*Helena* v. *State*, 1989); Nebraska (*Gould* v. *Orr*, 1993); New Hampshire (*Claremont* v. *Governor*, 1993, 1997); North Carolina (*Leandro* v. *State*, 1997); Oklahoma (*Fair School Finance Council* v. *State*, 1987); and Washington (*Northshore* v. *Kinnear*, 1974; *Seattle* v. *State*, 1978).

ACTIVITIES

1. Locate the original report of at least two of the judicial reviews cited in this chapter (see the list of references). Identify one decision in favor of plaintiffs and another upholding a state's finance system. Contrast the holdings and rationales developed by the courts. If spending disparities were challenged under equal-protection clauses discuss the levels of scrutiny deemed ap-

propriate. If education articles were challenged, determine how the courts used the criteria of "uniform," "efficient," and/or "adequate" in reaching a decision.

2. What have been the roles of legislatures and courts in the development of educational finance policy in a selected state? Interview several individuals and read news accounts to investigate conditions that were (or may be in the future) related to an actual or threatened challenge to the finance structure. What legislative enactments, if any, responded to prior holdings in that state, or to pressure to reform when plaintiffs challenged the state's policies?

3. What are the implications of state standards and assessments for the development of school finance policy? Do these policies create a legislative duty to provide an equitable and adequate education for all students?

4. Speculate about the role of the judiciary in educational policy development in the coming decade. Relate your discussion to the willingness of the courts in Alabama and Kentucky to find entire public education systems unconstitutional, in Pennsylvania to find finance mechanisms to violate the federal Civil Rights Act, and in Arizona and Ohio to find disparities in facilities to be an important aspect of adequacy.

REFERENCES

Abbeville County School District v. *State*, 515 S.E.2d 535 (S.C. 1999).

Abbott v. *Burke*, 477 A.2d 1278 (1984); 495 A.2d 376 (1985); 575 A.2d 359 (N.J. 1990); 643 A.2d 575 (N.J. 1994); 693 A.2d 417 (1997); 710 A.2d 450 (N.J. 1998).

Adams, J. E. (1993, Spring). School finance reform and systemic school change: Reconstituting Kentucky's public schools. *Journal of Education Finance, 18,* 318–345.

Alexander, K. (1982). Concepts of equity. In W. W. McMahon & T. G. Geske (Eds.), *Financing educa-*

tion: Overcoming inefficiency and inequity (pp. 193–214). Urbana: University of Illinois Press.

Anderson v. *State*, 723 A. 2d 1147 (Vt. 1998).

Bismarck Public School District No. 1 v. *State*, 511 N.W.2d 247 (N.D. 1994).

Board of Education v. *Walter*, 390 N.E.2d 813 (Ohio 1979); cert. denied, 444 U.S. 1015 (1980).

Bosworth, M. H. (2001). *Courts as catalysts: State supreme courts and public school finance equity.* Albany, NY: State University of New York Press.

Bradford v. *Board of Education* (Md. Circuit Ct. 1996, unreported).

Brigham v. *State*, 692 A.2d 384 (Vt. 1997).

Brown, P. R., & Elmore, R. F. (1982). Analyzing the impact of school finance reform. In N. H. Cambron-McCabe & A. Odden (Eds.), *The changing politics of school finance* (pp. 107–138). Cambridge, MA: Ballinger.

Brown v. *Board of Education*, 347 U.S. 483 (1954).

Burruss v. *Wilkerson*, 310 F.Supp. 572 (1969); Affirmed, 397 U.S. 44 (1970).

Buse v. *Smith*, 247 N.W.2d 141 (Wis. 1976).

Campaign for Fiscal Equity v. *New York*, 719 N.Y.S.2d 475 (N.Y. Sup. Ct. 2001).

Campbell County School District v. *State*, 907 P.2d 1238 (Wyo. 1995).

Carrollton-Farmers Branch Independent School District v. *Edgewood Independent School District*, 826 S.W.2d 489 (Tex. 1992).

Claremont School District v. *Governor*, 635 A.2d 1375 (N.H. 1993); 703 A.2d 1353 (N.H. 1997); 725 A.2d 648 (N.H. 1998).

Clune, W. H. (1992, Spring). New answers to hard questions posed by *Rodriguez*: Ending the separation of school finance and educational policy by bridging the gap between wrong and remedy. *Connecticut Law Review, 24,* 721–755.

Coalition for Adequacy and Fairness in School Funding v. *Chiles*, 680 So.2d 400 (Fla. 1996).

Coalition for Equitable School Funding, Inc. v. *State*, 811 P.2d 116 (Or. 1991).

Committee for Educational Rights v. *Edgar*, 267 Ill.App. 3d 18 (Ill. 1994); 672 N.E. 2d 1178 (Ill. 1996).

Coons, J. E., Clune, W. H., & Sugarman, S. D. (1970). *Private wealth and public education.* Cambridge, MA: The Belknap Press of Harvard University Press.

Danson v. *Casey*, 399 A.2d 360 (Pa. 1979).

DeRolph v. *State*, 677 N.E. 733 (Ohio 1997); 728 N.E.2d 993 (Ohio 2000).

Dupree v. *Alma School District No. 30*, 651 S.W.2d 90 (Ark. 1983).

Edgewood Independent School District v. *Kirby*, 777 S.W.2d 391 (1989); 804 S.W.2d 491 (Tex. 1991).

Edgewood Independent School District v. *Meno*, 893 S.W.2d 450 (Tex. 1995); 917 S.W. 2d 717 (Tex. 1995).

Fair School Finance Council of Oklahoma v. *State*, 746 P.2d 1135 (Okla. 1987).

Fuhrman, S. (1978, Fall). The politics and process of school finance reform. *Journal of Education Finance, 4*, 158–178.

Gehring, J. (2002, July 10). N. Y. appeals court rebuffs lower court's school aid ruling. *Education Week, 21*,16.

Goertz, M. (1981). School finance reform and the cities. In K. F. Jordan & N. H. Cambron-McCabe (Eds.), *Perspectives in state school support programs* (pp. 113–142). Cambridge, MA: Ballinger.

Goertz, M. E. (1993, Spring). School finance reform in New Jersey: The saga continues. *Journal of Education Finance, 18*, 346–365.

Goertz, M., & Edwards, M. (1999). In search of excellence for all: The courts and New Jersey school finance reform. *Journal of Education Finance, 25*, 5–32.

Gould v. *Orr*, 506 N.W.2d 349 (Neb. 1993).

Helena Elementary School District No. 1 v. *State*, 769 P.2d 684 (Mont. 1989).

Henderson, R. L. (1991, Fall). An analysis of selected school finance litigation and its impact upon state education legislation. *Journal of Education Finance, 17*, 193–214.

Hickrod, G. A., Hines, E. R., Anthony, G. P., Dively, J. A., & Pruyne, G. B. (1992, Fall). The effect of constitutional litigation on education finance: A preliminary analysis. *Journal of Education Finance, 18*, 180–210.

Hornbeck v. *Somerset County Board of Education*, 458 A.2d 758 (Md. 1983).

Horton v. *Meskill*, 376 A. 2d 359 (Conn. 1977); 445 A.2d 579 (Conn. 1982); 486 A.2d 1099 (Conn. 1985).

Hull v. *Albrecht*, 950 P.2d 1141 (Ariz. 1997); 960 P.2d 634 (Ariz. 1998).

Idaho Schools for Equal Educ. Opportunity v. *Evans*, 850 P.2d 724 (Idaho 1993).

Idaho Schools for Equal Educ. Opportunity v. *State*, 976 P.2d 913 (Idaho 1998).

King, R. A., & Mathers, J. (1997, Fall). Improving schools through performance-based accountability and financial rewards. *Journal of Education Finance, 23*, 147–176.

Koski, W. S., & Levin, H. M. (2000). Twenty-five years after Rodriguez: What have we learned? *Teachers College Record, 102*, 480–513.

Kukor v. *Grover*, 436 N.W.2d 568 (Wis. 1989).

Lau v. *Nichols*, 414 U.S. 563 (1974).

Leandro v. *State*, 488 S.E.2d 249 (N.C. 1997).

Lehne, R. (1978). *The quest for justice: The politics of school finance reform.* New York: Longman.

Levittown Union Free School District v. *Nyquist*, 408 N.Y.S.2d 606 (Sup. 1978); Affirmed, 443 N.Y.S.2d 843 (App.Div. 1981); Reversed, 453 N.Y.S.2d 643 (Ct.App. 1982); cert. denied, 459 U.S. 1139 (1983).

Lujan v. *Colorado State Board of Education*, 649 P.2d 1005 (Colo. 1982).

Marrero v. *Commonwealth of Pennsylvania*, 709 A.2d 956 (Pa.Cmwlth. 1998).

Matanuska-Susitna Borough School District v. *State*, 931 P.2d 391 (Alaska, 1997).

McCarthy, M. M. (1981). Adequacy in educational programs: A legal perspective. In K. F. Jordan & N. H. Cambron-McCabe (Eds.), *Perspectives in state school support programs* (pp. 315–351). Cambridge, MA: Ballinger.

McDaniel v. *Thomas*, 285 S.E.2d 156 (Ga. 1981).

McDuffy v. *Secretary of the Executive Office of Education*, 615 N.E.2d 516 (Mass. 1993).

McInnis v. *Shapiro*, 293 F.Supp. 327 (1968); Affirmed, *McInnis* v. *Ogilvie*, 394 U.S. 322 (1969).

McUsic, M. (1991, Summer). The use of education clauses in school finance reform litigation. *Harvard Journal on Legislation, 28*, 307–340.

Mills v. *Board of Education of the District of Columbia*, 348 F.Supp. 866 (1972).

Minorini, P. A., & Sugarman, S. D. (1999). Educational adequacy and the courts: The promise and problems of moving to a new paradigm. In H. F. Ladd, R. Chalk, and J. S. Hansen (Eds.), *Equity and adequacy in education finance: Issues and perspectives* (pp. 175–208). Washington, DC: National Academy Press.

Moran, M. (1999). Standards and assessments: The new measure of adequacy in school finance litigation. *Journal of Education Finance, 25*, 33–80.

Northshore School District No. 417 v. *Kinnear*, 530 P.2d 178 (Wash. 1974).

Olsen v. *State*, 554 P.2d 139 (Or. 1976).

Opinion of the Justices, consolidation of *Alabama Coalition for Equity* v. *Hunt* and *Harper* v. *Hunt*, 624 So.2d 107 (Ala. 1993); affirmed, 713 So.2d 869 (Ala. 1997).

Papasan v. *Allain*, 478 U.S. 265 (1986).

Pauley v. *Bailey*, 324 S.E. 2d 128 (W.Va. 1984).

Pauley v. *Kelly*, 255 S.E. 2d 859 (W.Va. 1979).

Pawtucket v. *Sundlun*, 662 A.2d 40 (R.I. 1995).

Plyler v. *Doe*, 457 U.S. 202 (1982).

Powell v. *Ridge*, 189 F.3d 387 (3rd Cir. 1999).

Reform Educational Financing Inequities Today (R.E.F.I.T.) v. *Cuomo*, 578 N.Y.S.2d 969 (Sup. 1991); 655 N.E.2d 647 (NY 1995).

Richland County v. *Campbell*, 364 S.E.2d 470 (S.C. 1988).

Robinson v. *Cahill*, 303 A.2d 273 (N.J. 1973); 306 A.2d 65 (N.J. 1973); cert. denied, 414 U.S. 976 (1973); 335 A.2d 6 (N.J. 1975); 335 A.2d 129 (N.J. 1976).

Roosevelt Elementary School District v. *Bishop*, 877 P.2d 806 (Ariz. 1994).

Rose v. *Council for Better Education*, 790 S.W.2d 186 (Ky. 1989).

San Antonio Independent School District v. *Rodriguez*, 411 U.S. 1 (1973).

Scott v. *Commonwealth*, 443 S.E.2d 138 (Va. 1994).

School Administrative District No. 1 v. *Commissioner*, 659 A.2d 854 (Me. 1995).

School Board of the Parish of Livingston v. *Louisiana State Board of Education*, 830 F.2d 563 (5th Cir. 1987).

Seattle School District No. 1 of King County v. *State*, 585 P.2d 71 (Wash. 1978).

Serrano v. *Priest*, 487 P.2d 1241 (1971); 557 P.2d 929 (1976); 226 Cal.Rptr. 584 (Cal.App. 1986).

Sheff v. *O'Neill*, 678 A.2d 1267 (Conn. 1996).

Shofstall v. *Hollins*, 515 P.2d 590 (Ariz. 1973).

Skeen v. *State*, 505 N.W.2d 299 (Minn. 1993).

Sparkman, W. E. (1983). School finance litigation in the 1980s. In S. B. Thomas, N. H. Cambron-McCabe, & M. M. McCarthy (Eds.), *Educators and the law: Current trends and issues* (pp. 96–108). Elmont, NY: Institute for School Law and Finance.

Sparkman, W. E. (1994, May). The legal foundations of public school finance. *Boston College Law Review, 35*, 569–595.

Sweetland, S. R. (2000). School finance reform: Factors that mitigate legal initiatives. *Journal of Education Finance, 26*, 87–101.

Tennessee Small School Systems v. *McWherter*, 851 S.W.2d 139 (Tenn. 1993); 894 S.W.2d 734 (Tenn. 1995).

Thompson v. *Engelking*, 537 P.2d 635 (Idaho 1975).

Tucker v. *Lake View School District*, 917 S.W.2d 530 (Ark. 1996).

Underwood, J. K. (1989, Winter). Changing equal protection analyses in finance equity litigation. *Journal of Education Finance, 14*, 413–425.

Underwood, J. K. (1994, Fall). School finance litigation: Legal theories, judicial activism, and social neglect. *Journal of Education Finance, 20*, 143–162.

Underwood, J. K., & Sparkman, W. E. (1991, Spring). School finance litigation: A new wave of reform. *Harvard Journal of Law & Public Policy, 14*, 517–544.

Unified School District No. 229 v. *Kansas*, 885 P.2d 1170 (Kan. 1994); cert. denied, 515 U.S. 1144 (1995).

VanDusartz v. *Hatfield*, 334 F.Supp. 870 (D.Minn. 1971).

Vincent v. *Voight*, 614 N.W.2d 388 (Wis. 2000).

Ward, J. G. (1990). Implementation and monitoring of judicial mandates: An interpretive analysis. In J. K. Underwood & D. A. Verstegen (Eds.), *The impacts of litigation and legislation on public school finance: Adequacy, equity, and excellence* (pp. 225–248). New York: Harper & Row.

Washakie County School District No. 1 v. *Herschler*, 606 P.2d 310 (Wyo. 1980); cert. denied, 449 U.S. 824 (1980).

Wood, R. C. (1995). Adequacy issues in recent education finance litigation. In W. J. Fowler (Ed.), *Developments in school finance* (pp. 29–37). Washington, DC: U.S. Government Printing Office.

Woodahl v. *Straub*, 520 P.2d 776 (Mont. 1974).

chapter **11**

VIEWING EQUITY FROM THE PERSPECTIVE OF ADEQUACY

Issues and Questions

- *Achieving High Standards with Equity and Efficiency*: What changes in school governance and finance are needed to facilitate greater equity and adequacy in the distribution of resources to schools and the outcomes of schools?
- *Definitions of Equity*: What is the meaning of equity today? How have its meanings evolved to include the concept of adequacy as well?
- *Analysis of Equity and Adequacy*: On what groups do equity studies focus? What objects should be included in equity studies? What principles should guide equity studies? How is equity measured? How is the measurement of equity changed when adequacy is a consideration?
- *Studies of School Finance Equity and Adequacy*: How equitable and adequate is the distribution of resources committed to elementary and secondary education among states, districts, and schools within districts? How equitable and adequate is the distribution of outputs from elementary and secondary schools among states, districts, and schools within districts?

Courts are the formal mechanisms created by society for evaluating social policy within parameters established by constitutional and statutory authority. The previous chapter examined the assessments made by courts of school finance policy in the United States: in these settings equity and (more recently) adequacy are primary, but not exclusive, concerns. In this chapter, we view these closely related concepts from the perspectives of policy makers and policy analysts, who are not constrained by the same parameters and procedures as those that pertain to judicial reviews. (The findings of these studies are used as evidence in judicial proceedings, however.)

Equality, along with liberty and fraternity, is described in Chapter 1 as an ethical value that influences decisions about school finance. *Equality* was defined as the state, ideal, or quality of being equal, as in enjoying equal social, political, and economic rights. The operational definition of equality within the sociopolitical context also includes factors of condition, placing emphasis on the appropriateness of treatment. Accordingly, equality has taken on the broader connotations of *equity*, defined in Morris (1969) as "the state, ideal, or quality of being just, impartial and fair" (p. 443). In this chapter, the term *equity* is used instead of *equality* as more accurately reflecting modern usage in reference to public policy.

Since the publication of *A Nation at Risk* in 1983 (National Commission on Excellence in Education, 1983), there has been a growing recognition by policy analysts, policy makers, and the courts that an equal distribution of resources will not close the achievement (or outcomes) gaps among ethnic and socioeconomic groups if the amount of resources distributed equitably is not sufficient to provide the instructional resources required to eliminate those gaps. Thus, consideration of equity issues has increasingly been approached from the perspective of adequacy. In Chapter 10, we defined *adequacy* as the state of being *sufficient* for a particular purpose. Guthrie and Rothstein

(2001) elaborate by blending sufficiency with adequacy: "sufficient resources to ensure students an effective opportunity to acquire appropriately specified levels of knowledge and skills" (p. 103).

We begin our discussion of equity by examining the structural causes leading to inequitable distributions of resources and outcomes within the public schools of the United States. We then develop a theoretical construct for approaching the study of equity within the schooling enterprise, and we present tools that are commonly used in empirical studies of equity. We then review a sampling of studies of equity that have made use of these tools and others. The chapter concludes with consideration of adequacy, which is treated as the ideal state of equity. The discussion traces the evolution of the concept of adequacy from its early role in the foundation program that a large majority of states still use to distribute general aid to school districts.

THE ROOTS OF INEQUALITY

Most nations have organized their school systems at the national level. In the United States, we chose to place the responsibility for educating our citizens with the states, and all the states except Hawaii chose to assume only a limited supervisory role and created school districts (some 12,000) to run and to partially finance public schools.

In a critical analysis of public education in the United States, Morrison (1943) referred to its structure disdainfully as "late New England colonial" (p. 258) and described the school district as "a little republic at every crossroads" (p. 75). Morrison was focusing on a characteristic of the system of American public education—its extreme decentralization—that makes it unique among the school systems of the world. Herein lay both its strengths and its weaknesses.

Decentralized systems seem to be more adept than highly centralized and bureaucratic systems at mobilizing the energies of their constituents and adapting curricula and instructional systems to the diversity of their constituents. Yet decentralized systems have a tendency to become inequitable, providing services that are uneven in quality . The good schools in a decentralized system tend to be very, very good; but such a system also generates—and tolerates—very poor schools. To bring about a greater degree of equity and set minimally acceptable social standards requires intervention by higher levels of government, state and/or federal. This intervention has been happening with increasing frequency over the fifty years since Morrison made his observation.

Originally, "common" schools were financed primarily through locally levied property taxes, supplemented with voluntary contributions and some state subsidies. In 1920, 83 percent of elementary and secondary school revenue was generated at the local level; less than 1 percent was provided by the federal government, and the remaining 16.5 percent came from state governments (NCES, 1999, p. 50).

State-generated revenues now account for about 50.7 percent of all school expenditures, and the federal share is nearly 6.9 percent, leaving about 42.4 percent to be generated at the local level, still primarily through the property tax.

As we saw in previous chapters, federal funds are provided largely through categorical aid programs. This form of assistance directs monies and programs toward meeting the needs of children who are identified as being "at risk," including those who qualify for compensatory reading and mathematics instruction as well as those with disabilities. The states make some use of categorical type aids. However, most monies are channeled to local school districts as *equalized* general aid (aid distributed inversely to the taxing capacities of districts to compensate in part for the great differences in taxable wealth among districts).

Despite the efforts to equalize the resources available to school districts, great disparities remain. Table 11.1 shows the average per-pupil current expenditures of school districts by

TABLE 11.1.

Average Current Pupil Expenditure by Quartile by State, 1995

State	Number of Districts	Low	1st Quartile	Median	3rd Quartile	High	Mean	Range
Alabama	127	2,680	3,031	3,262	3,557	5,618	3,347	3,138
Alaska	51	5,750	5,924	6,319	7,057	23,571	7,516	17,821
Arizona	207	2,861	3,579	3,700	4,061	10,826	3,933	7,965
Arkansas	310	2,727	3,142	3,372	3,632	7,253	3,471	4,526
California	976	2,808	4,062	4,403	4,845	17,933	4,488	15,125
Colorado	174	3,556	4,197	4,528	4,743	12,184	4,609	8,628
Connecticut	166	5,412	6,655	7,121	7,747	10,851	7,340	5,439
Delaware	16	4,909	5,285	5,543	5,786	6,002	5,556	1,093
Florida	67	3,868	4,359	4,584	5,035	5,943	4,688	2,075
Georgia	180	2,859	3,691	4,012	4,266	6,194	4,150	3,335
Idaho	109	2,652	2,984	3,236	3,686	10,250	3,349	7,598
Illinois	902	2,342	3,652	4,434	5,025	11,740	4,635	9,398
Indiana	28	3,430	4,553	4,773	5,104	5,785	4,836	2,355
Iowa	380	3,441	4,132	4,393	4,623	8,891	4,440	5,450
Kansas	304	2,901	4,080	4,573	4,823	11,054	4,544	8,153
Kentucky	NA	NA	NA	NA	NA	NA	NA	NA

(continued)

TABLE 11.1.

(Continued)

State	Number of Districts	Low	1st Quartile	Median	3rd Quartile	High	Mean	Range
Louisiana	66	2,976	3,738	4,112	4,379	6,332	4,107	3,356
Maine	223	2,524	4,439	4,779	5,154	9,968	4,880	7,444
Maryland	24	4,931	5,155	5,603	5,996	7,419	5,822	2,488
Massachusetts	295	3,078	4,537	5,063	5,938	12,669	5,362	9,591
Michigan	554	1,759	4,038	4,735	5,478	10,600	4,896	8,841
Minnesota	341	2,810	4,507	4,894	5,423	12,233	5,050	9,423
Mississippi	152	2,049	2,816	2,985	3,281	4,954	3,056	2,905
Missouri	527	2,331	3,271	3,769	4,329	10,300	4,152	7,969
Montana	455	2,286	3,500	3,926	4,784	21,774	4,473	19,488
Nebraska	641	1,909	4,129	4,761	5,208	15,844	4,762	13,935
Nevada	NA	NA	NA	NA	NA	NA	NA	NA
New Hampshire	160	3,398	4,482	5,052	5,870	10,711	5,228	7,313
New Jersey	551	3,976	6,431	7,059	8,001	14,691	7,254	10,715
New Mexico	89	3,007	3,378	3,803	3,842	9,984	3,788	6,977
New York	685	5,066	6,923	6,923	7,959	32,792	7,625	27,726
North Carolina	116	3,453	3,870	4,135	4,293	5,537	4,151	2,084
North Dakota	228	2,616	3,448	3,791	4,179	19,930	3,929	17,314
Ohio	610	2,543	3,702	4,330	5,266	15,000	4,576	12,457
Oklahoma	542	2,798	3,279	3,493	3,863	12,429	3,615	9,631
Oregon	240	3,296	4,596	4,966	5,547	18,750	5,155	15,454
Pennsylvania	NA	NA	NA	NA	NA	NA	NA	NA
Rhode Island	35	4,816	5,652	5,810	5,997	10,405	5,866	5,589
South Carolina	91	3,351	3,744	3,869	4,179	7,145	4,007	3,794
South Dakota	173	3,135	3,502	3,852	4,205	11,343	4,039	3,208
Tennessee	137	2,173	2,943	3,220	3,788	5,472	3,366	3,299
Texas	1,042	2,733	3,622	3,882	4,089	14,786	3,935	12,053
Utah	40	2,583	2,728	2,868	2,950	7,292	2,967	4,709
Vermont	238	2,991	4,987	5,612	6,439	14,667	5,793	11,676
Virginia	133	3,657	4,070	4,482	5,331	8,660	4,806	5,003
West Virginia	55	3,953	4,191	4,284	4,519	5,830	4,343	1,877
Washington	296	3,500	4,655	4,843	5,113	23,000	4,957	19,500
Wisconsin	425	3,693	5,136	5,540	6,207	10,214	5,667	6,521
Wyoming	49	4,687	4,858	5,043	5,297	19,475	5,395	14,788

Source: National Center for Education Statistics. State Equity Calculator **<http://216.181.15/ecalc/EcalaWeb**

quartile by state for 1995. The range in expenditures from high to low varies from $27,726 in a New York State school district to $1,093 in a Delaware district. Hawaii is not included in the table because it operates as a state system and has no school districts. Except for Delaware and Indiana, the difference between the third-quartile expenditure and the highest expenditure is larger than for any of the interquartile differences. These differences suggest that the greatest disparities are created by a relatively few, very-high-spending districts with relatively large tax bases. State equalization policies are targeted primarily toward middle- and low-wealth districts.

Table 11.1 also illustrates that some states have done a better job than others of equalizing expenditures among middle- and low-spending districts. The differences in expenditures per pupil between the first-quartile and third-quartile districts amount to less than $500 in Arkansas and Utah. In contrast, the differences are over $1,500 in New Jersey and Oklahoma.

To illustrate the disparities among school districts, Table 11.2 provides information on the demographic and financial characteristics of selected school districts in the metropolitan New York City area. The data show the inequity created by the proliferation of small school districts in one of the most densely populated regions of the United States. Enrollments in these districts range from over one million pupils in New York City (NYC) to 1,879 in Cold Spring. Cold Spring had no students classified as limited-English-proficient (LEP), and only 0.1 percent qualified for free or reduced lunches. Neighboring Hempstead had 16.4 percent LEP students and 88.5 percent qualifying for free and reduced lunches; the figures for New York City were 16.7 and 74.8, respectively. Suspension rates ranged from 11.2 percent in Mt. Vernon to 0.3 percent in Garden City.

The Roosevelt school district contained a population that was 78 percent African American and 18 percent Hispanic or Latino. Nearby Garden City was 95 percent white, 0.5 percent African American, and 3.2 percent Hispanic or Latino. The population of New York City (NYC) is 77 percent minority, with 32 percent African American and 34 percent Hispanic or Latino; 8.8 percent are Asian. The public school population of NYC (not shown in the table) is even more heavily minority, with 18 percent classified as white, non-Hispanic, 37 percent as African American, 36 percent as Hispanic, and 9 percent as other. Only Sewanhaka had a population distribution that reflected the distribution of the region as a whole. Under these circumstances, the ideal of the common school as a socially integrated institution is difficult to realize.

Differences among school districts in demographic characteristics are reflected in their financial provision for instruction. NYC's per-

pupil expenditure was the lowest in the metropolitan area at $9,034; affluent Great Neck spent nearly twice as much at $17,119 per pupil. Chappaqua and Cold Spring spent at least 50% more per pupil than New York City. Higher state aid to the impoverished districts was not sufficient to bring them to spending levels comparable to their affluent neighbors. NYC's pupil/teacher ratio was the highest in the region at 16.8, compared with 11.4 in Great Neck. The most affluent districts were able to allocate two-thirds of their expenditures to wages and salaries, compared to only 53.1 percent in NYC.

DIMENSIONS OF EQUITY

In this section we build a basis for examining equity issues. We present a theoretical model that classifies philosophical and political considerations. This is followed by a model that classifies methodological considerations in developing an analytical framework.

Philosophical and Political Dimensions

Figure 11.1 represents an adaptation of Alexander's (1982) reconciliation of the philosophical and legal dimensions of equity with the practice of school finance and the relative extent of government involvement required for policy implementation. The continuum of equity definitions ranges from the politically conservative to the politically liberal. The dimensions include commutative equity, equal distribution equity, restitution equity, and outcome equity. School finance policy and practices are associated with each dimension.

Commutative equity entitles a person to something on the basis of property rights alone and leaves the distribution produced by the market place unaltered. Such a philosophy would not support any public intervention in school finance. Given that some intervention is inevitable, however, subscribers to commutative

TABLE 11.2.

Pupil and District Characteristics for Selected School Districts in the New York City Metropolitan Area

Item		Districts										
	New York City	Chappaqua	Cold Spring	Garden City	Great Neck	Hempstead	Malverne	Mt. Vernon	Roosevelt	Scarsdale	Sewanhaka	Yonkers
Enrollment[a]	1,075,710	3,783	1,879	3,701	6,049	6,760	1,839	10,488	3,052	4,278	7,603	25,889
Per-pupil expenditure ($)[b]	9,034	14,193	13,596	12,735	17,119	11,229	12,400	10,547	11,949	13,104	10,904	10,868
Student/teacher ratio[a]	16.8	13.2	13.6	13.2	11.4	16.3	12.6	16.2	14.5	13.1	16.1	14.6
Percentage district revenue from federal sources[b]	11.0	0.4	0.7	0.6	0.9	4.5	1.7	4.8	5.1	0.4	1.5	6.2
Percentage district revenue from state sources[b]	42.1	7.8	7.7	6.6	6.2	40.2	18.9	42.5	60.0	6.9	16.6	34.8
Percentage district revenue from local resources[b]	46.9	91.8	91.6	92.8	92.9	55.3	79.3	52.7	34.9	92.7	81.9	59.1
Percentage district expenditure on salaries and wages[b]	53.1	59.8	63.6	66.3	66.3	59.4	62.9	60.0	59.3	66.2	65.3	60.8
Percentage white alone[c]	34.0	92.0	95.2	94.9	82.2	19.0	50.8	18.4	8.0	83.3	62.0	44.8

Percentage black or African American alone[c]	32.0	1	0.4	0.5	2.3	55.6	38.5	68.5	78.1	1.3	20.1	23.4
Percentage Asian alone[c]	8.8	5.5	2.9	3.0	10.5	0.8	2.4	1.8	0.3	12.5	9.5	5.2
Percentage all other races alone	18.7	0.5	0.3	0.6	2.2	19.5	4.6	6.3	9.3	0.4	4.7	20.6
Percentage Hispanic or Latino[d]	34.0	2	2.6	3.2	6.2	38.1	10.3	12.9	18.3	2.5	11.9	37.0
Total percentage of minority under 18[d]	77.0	10	7.0	7.7	21.6	95.7	53.9	86.4	98.2	18.9	44.5	67.7
Attendance rate[e]	86.5	96	95.0	96.0	95.0	90.0	95.0	92.0	93.0	97.0	95.0	89.0
Suspension rate[e]	3.2	1	1.4	0.3	1.7	7.1	10.2	11.2	8.5	0.5	7.1	9.1
Dropout rate[e]	5.8	0	0.5	0.2	0.2	4.5	0.7	1.8	4.1	0.4	0.4	3.2
Percentage limited English proficiency[e]	16.7	1.6	0.0	0.9	4.7	16.4	3.4	7.8	6.0	4.1	2.2	16.4
Percentage free and reduced lunch[e]	74.8	0.6	0.1	0.2	7.2	88.5	17.5	43.8	52.4	0.0	7.5	62.5

[a] 1999–2000 school year

[b] 1995–1996 school year

[c] Total population under 18, population of one-race adolescents, 2000 U.S. Census data

[d] Percentage of total population under 18, 2000 U.S. Census data

[e] 1997–1998 District Report Card

[f] 1996–1997 school year

[a,c,d] Source: National Center for Education Statistics, School District Demographics System, 2001

[b,f,g] Source: National Center for Education Statistics Common Core of Data (CCD), School Years 1993–1994 through 1997–1998.

[e] Source: New York State District Report Card

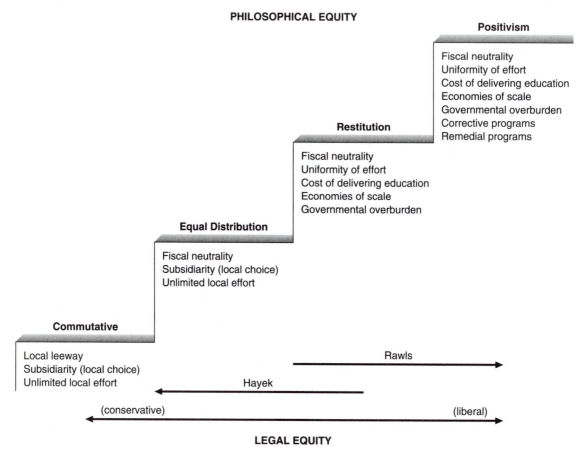

PHILOSOPHICAL EQUITY

Positivism

Fiscal neutrality
Uniformity of effort
Cost of delivering education
Economies of scale
Governmental overburden
Corrective programs
Remedial programs

Restitution

Fiscal neutrality
Uniformity of effort
Cost of delivering education
Economies of scale
Governmental overburden

Equal Distribution

Fiscal neutrality
Subsidiarity (local choice)
Unlimited local effort

Commutative

Local leeway
Subsidiarity (local choice)
Unlimited local effort

Rawls

Hayek

(conservative)   (liberal)

LEGAL EQUITY

FIGURE 11.1. Perspectives of Equity

Source: Adapted from K. Alexander. (1982). "Concepts of Equity." In W. W. McMahon and T. G. Geske (Eds.), *Financing Education: Overcoming Inefficiency and Inequity* (pp. 193–214). Urbana: University of Illinois Press, p. 211.) Reprinted by permission.

equity would endorse the greatest possible local discretion in using local tax bases. This policy moves us on the continuum toward distributive equity.

Distributive equity is concerned with correcting inequitable conditions created by design of government. This approach has direct relevance to school finance because a primary source of inequity—the variation in the capacity of school district tax bases to produce revenue—lies in the school district structure that was created by the state. Those who take this position would endorse the concept of fiscal

neutrality, particularly as it is embodied in tax base equalization formulas that place no restraints on local effort.

Restitution equity endorses the correction of inequitable conditions arising out of social and economic circumstances, as well as those created through government action. Restitution focuses on weaknesses of the system only and not on the personal educational needs of children. In addition to fiscal neutrality, persons accepting this view would endorse public policies of uniform tax effort and adjustments for regional cost variations, economies of scale, and municipal overburden. From this perspective, full state funding would be an acceptable means of financing public schools.

Positivism equity introduces the concept of educational needs of children. Those who take this position justify intervention designed to assist the least advantaged. This approach demands that unique and high-cost corrective, remedial, and compensatory programs be fully financed by government. Alexander (1982) identified several features that would need to be included in an ideal model of education finance in order to satisfy this level of equity: *adequate* financing of basic education programs, complete fiscal equalization of each district's tax-paying ability, uniform tax effort, and supplemental standards for corrective and remedial education programs. The latter may also include programs that link schools and social services in ways that strengthen families' abilities to cope with social and environmental factors outside the school (Adler & Gardner, 1994; Dryfoos, 1994; Howe, 1993; Kirst, 1994; Zigler & Finn-Stevenson, 1994).

Over time, the interest of policy makers and analysts has gradually shifted from commutative equity to, most recently, positivism equity. Prior to the beginning of the current educational reform movement in the 1980s, the focus was on equal distribution and restitution equity. In the early phases of the current movement, little attention was paid to equity considerations, other than to lament the possibility that the emphasis on excellence, high achievement standards, and efficiency might have inequitable consequences. Early reformers wondered whether we can simultaneously satisfy the social objectives of both equity and efficiency.

There was a decided shift in this posture in the 1990s, encouraged in part by court decisions in New Jersey, Texas, Kentucky, and West Virginia (Hirth, 1994; Ladd & Hansen, 1999; Guthrie & Rothstein, 2001). In many instances, court decisions (described fully in Chapter 10) declared state school finance

schemes in violation of their respective state constitutions on the grounds of both inequity *and* inadequacy. In the case of Kentucky, the whole governance structure for education, not just the finance scheme, was nullified. A new social consensus now seems to be building around the common goal of high minimum achievement for all children (Clune, 1994). The emphasis is clearly on positivism equity, which brings with it greater involvement of state and federal governments.

Technical Dimensions

Berne and Stiefel (1984, 1992, 1994) have produced the seminal works on school finance equity from the perspective of policy analysts. They organized their analyses around four questions:

1. What is the makeup of the *groups* for which school finance systems should be equitable?
2. What services, resources, or, more generally, *objects* should be distributed fairly among members of the groups?
3. What *principles* should be used to determine whether a particular distribution is equitable?
4. What quantitative *measures* should be used to assess the degree of equity? (Berne and Stiefel, 1984)

In reference to the first question, two *groups* have been the primary subjects of studies of school finance equity: schoolchildren and taxpayers. Alternative concepts identified by Berne and Stiefel (1984) as involved in the analysis of equity for children are shown in Figure 11.2. A representation of concepts related to taxpayer equity would look similar to those in Figure 11.2 except for the *objects* of analysis. In evaluating taxpayer equity, the primary objects of interests are tax rates and revenue generated.

The *objects* to be distributed equitably among schoolchildren (the second of the foregoing questions) are divided into inputs, outputs, and

Component of Equity Concept	*Alternative for Each Component*		
Who? The Group	*Children*		
What? The Object	*Inputs* Dollars Price-adjusted dollars Physical resources	*Outputs* Student achievement Behavioral output measures	*Outcomes* Earning potential Income Satisfaction

How?
The Principle
	Horizontal Equity
	Equal treatment of equals
	Minimize spread in
	  distribution
		Vertical Equity
		Unequal treatment of unequals
		More of the object to the needier
			Equal Opportunity
			No discrimination on the basis of
			  property wealth in school
			  district or other categories
			Minimize undesirable systematic
			  relationships

How much? The Summary Statistic	*Univariate Dispersion* Range Restricted range Federal range ratio Relative mean deviation The McLoone index Variance The coefficient of variation Standard deviation of logarithm Gini coefficient Atkinson's index The Theil coefficient	*Relationship* Simple correlation Simple slope Quadratic slope Cubic slope Simple elasticity Quadratic elasticity Cubic elasticity Constant elasticity Adjusted relationship measure from simple regression Adjusted relationahip measure from quadratic regression Adjusted relationship measure from cubic regression Implicit weight Average implicit weight	

FIGURE 11.2. Berne's and Stiefel's Alternative Concepts Model of School Finance Equity for Children.

Source: R. Berne and L. Stiefel. (1984). *The Measurement of Equity in School Finance: Conceptual, Methodological, and Experimental Dimensions.* Baltimore, MD: The Johns Hopkins University Press, p. 9.) Reprinted by permission.

outcomes. Inputs, the human and material resources used in the schooling process, were traditionally the focus of equity analyses. Inputs may be measured in terms of dollars or actual amounts of physical resource employed. Dollar inputs are the most commonly used, and they may be analyzed as revenues and/or expenditures. Revenues may be subdivided according to source; expenditures may be subdivided according to purpose (for example, operating expenditure and instructional expenditure). Some categories of revenues and expenditures are of greater interest than others from a policy standpoint, and the selection

needs to be made with care. Berne and Stiefel (1984, 1992) recommended the use of price-adjusted dollars to correct for regional variations that exist within many states and among states.

Inputs can also be measured in terms of the actual amount of resources available: pupil/adult ratios, average class sizes, characteristics of teachers (such as verbal ability and experience), and number of library books. The advantage of using measures of actual resources is that such measurements are not affected by regional price variations or inflation over time. The major disadvantage is that there is no satisfactory way of aggregating quantities of different resources—for example, the combined teacher experience in years and class size. In any consideration of the adequacy dimension of equity, inputs come into play not as the equity criteria of interest but, rather, as *opportunity standards* or *delivery standards* (Guthrie & Rothstein, 1999). This conception of inputs rests on the assumption that there is a minimum provision of physical inputs necessary if the desired equity criteria expressed as outputs and outcomes are to be realized.

Outputs and *outcomes* are related to the goals and objectives of schooling. Outputs represent the immediate products of the schools, often measured in terms of pupil achievement and behavioral changes. Outcomes include such long-range effects of schooling as lifetime earnings and quality of life. These have always been the *implied* equity criteria, but data for analysis based on outputs have become readily available only in recent years; data on outcomes are still not widely available. Further, there has been a growing realization of the tenuousness of the link between resources applied and achievement gained. Now, with the emphasis on adequacy, courts and policy makers alike are focusing directly on the outputs of schooling and are pressuring educators to produce equitable results given adequate resources. Of course, defining what *adequate* resources are is a complex problem, as we will discuss later in this chapter and in subsequent chapters.

The list of possible objects of analysis is almost infinite, and there is no general agreement on what inputs, outputs, and outcomes should be equitably distributed. Objects selected for analysis need to be closely related to the stated or implied purposes of the policy being analyzed. Analyses of distribution equity and restitution equity have tended to focus on inputs. Outputs and outcomes have been used little in equity studies until very recently. They are related to positivism equity as depicted in Figure 11.1.

Berne and Stiefel (1984) proposed three principles that can be used to determine whether a particular distribution is equitable (their third question): horizontal equity, vertical equity, and equal opportunity. The concepts of horizontal and vertical equity were introduced in Chapter 3 with respect to taxation policy. *Horizontal equity* refers to the equal treatment of equals—the traditional meaning of "equality." *Vertical equity* recognizes that equal treatment is not always "fair and just" for pupils (or taxpayers) experiencing extraordinary conditions such as poverty or physical, psychological, or mental disabilities (or high costs of living, dispersed populations, and municipal overburden). Thus vertical equity allows for justifiable unequal treatment of unequals. Underwood (1995) interprets adequacy as a form of vertical equity, the position we take in this presentation, nicely linking the two concepts. We also take this position in interpreting adequacy as *the ideal state of vertical equity*.

Berne and Stiefel (1984, p. 17) defined equal opportunity in negative terms as the condition in which there are no differences in treatment according to characteristics such as race, gender, national origin, or other classifications considered illegitimate. Other analysts treat equal opportunity as a condition of horizontal equity, the position we favor. Until recently, virtually all studies of school finance equity have dealt only with the horizontal and equal opportunity dimensions. Vertical equity has become a critical concept within the adequacy context.

In response to Berne and Stiefel's fourth question, Figure 11.2 lists various statistics that policy analysts use to assess the degree to which distributions of objects satisfy equity principles. In the next section, we describe those measures that are most commonly used. Until recently, the unit of analysis for equity studies has been the school district, and studies continue to be conducted at that level. Now, studies are likewise being conducted at the school level. This focus on the school responds to (1) the growing understanding that the most critical teaching/learning activities are those that involve the child and (2) the increasing interest in outcome equity. School-level analyses have been made feasible by rapid advancements in computer technology that facilitate the collection and analysis of data at a level of detail that was not possible in the past (Berne & Stiefel, 1994).

MEASURING EQUITY

Two categories of statistics used for assessing equity are discussed in this section. The most commonly used measures of dispersion of a single object are the range, coefficient of variation, McLoone index, Thiel coefficient, and Gini coefficient. Measures of relationships among two or more objects include the correlation coefficient, slope, and regression coefficient.

To illustrate the concepts behind each statistic, Table 11.3 presents a set of values for two hypothetical states with twenty hypothetical school districts in each. The districts are arranged in ascending order according to the object of interest—in this case, expenditure per pupil. Each district has 100 pupils and each state has 2,000 pupils. The mean expenditure and the median expenditure per pupil for both states are $5,175. The range is also the same, from $3,750 to $6,600; distributions within that range vary considerably, however. Data are also presented for property values per pupil and percent minority students. The computer simulations accompanying this chapter permit further exploration of these measures of equity.

Dispersion of a Single Object

Restricted Range

The spread between the highest- and lowest-expenditure districts in both states is $2,850 (see Table 11.3). On the surface, this would suggest comparable equity. On closer examination, however, one can see that the states differ considerably in the distribution of expenditures among districts. Districts in state A

are evenly distributed across the range, whereas districts in state B cluster more closely around the median ($5,175).

One way of eliminating the distortion of outlying cases is to use a restricted range—say, between the 10th and 90th student percentiles. The restricted range for state A is $2,250 (from $4,050 in district 3 to $6,300 in district 18). The smaller restricted range for state B ($1,050) reflects the greater equity we observed by inspection.

The restricted range provides a simple, easily understood way for comparing equity in two or more states at a given time. However, because of the historical effects of inflation, restricted range does not provide accurate comparisons over time. To illustrate, if five-year comparisons are to be made, and costs double every five years, then districts would have to double their expenditures to provide the same level of services. This would increase the range for both states to $5,700, and the restricted range would increase for state A to $4,500 and for state B to $2,100. Both sets of statistics suggest that equity has suffered in the two states, and especially within state A, despite the fact that the actual distribution of services has not changed.

Federal Range Ratio

To correct for the effects of inflation, the federal range ratio was developed. It divides the restricted range for the middle 90 percent of students (eliminating from consideration the top and bottom 5 percent) by the value of the object (in the case of our illustration, expenditure per pupil) for the pupil at the 5th percentile. Because both of our states have 2,000 students, we remove from consideration 100 students at the top and at the bottom of the expenditure range in each state—that is, districts 1 and 20. For state A, the restricted range becomes $2,550. When this is divided by the expenditure experienced by the student at the 5th percentile ($3,900), the federal range ratio is 0.65. For state B, the federal range ratio is

TABLE 11.3.
Equity-Related Data for Two Hypothetical States, Each with 20 Districts and 2,000 Students

District Number	Pupils			State A			State B		
	Number	Accumulative Number	Percentile	Expenditure per Pupil	Full Property Value per Pupil	Percentage Minority	Expenditure per Pupil	Full Property Value per Pupil	Percentage Minority
1	100	100	5	$3,750	$75,000	10	$3,750	$67,500	41
2	100	200	10	3,900	67,500	48	4,575	90,000	64
3	100	300	15	4,050	90,000	1	4,650	82,500	29
4	100	400	20	4,200	93,000	50	4,725	105,000	50
5	100	500	25	4,350	82,500	11	4,800	93,000	19
6	100	600	30	4,500	105,000	1	4,875	127,500	20
7	100	700	35	4,650	112,500	20	4,950	120,000	48
8	100	800	40	4,800	102,000	11	5,025	150,000	1
9	100	900	45	4,950	120,000	16	5,100	135,000	10
10	100	1,000	50	5,100	135,000	17	5,175	157,500	20
11	100	1,100	55	5,250	127,500	41	5,175	180,000	11
12	100	1,200	60	5,400	150,000	64	5,250	165,000	22
13	100	1,300	65	5,550	143,500	3	5,325	195,000	11
14	100	1,400	70	5,700	165,000	7	5,400	172,500	7
15	100	1,500	75	5,850	180,000	20	5,475	225,000	16
16	100	1,600	80	6,000	172,500	29	5,550	195,000	17
17	100	1,700	85	6,150	195,000	19	5,625	210,000	7
18	100	1,800	90	6,300	210,000	7	5,700	270,000	0
19	100	1,900	95	6,450	202,500	0	5,775	262,500	1
20	100	2,000	100	6,600	225,000	22	6,600	300,000	3

0.26, calculated as ($5,775 − $4,575)/$4,575. The smaller the ratio, the greater the equity. Perfect equity (all districts with the same expenditure) results in a federal range ratio of zero. When the impact of inflation is equal for all districts, the ratio remains unchanged even though the monetary values of the objects of analysis increase over time. The formula is

$$\frac{(X - Y)}{Y}$$

where: X = 95th percentile of per-pupil expenditure within the state

         Y = 5th percentile of per-pupil expenditure within the state.

Coefficient of Variation

Although it is easy to compute and to understand, the range statistic is determined by only two cases in a distribution. A statistic such as the standard deviation, which encompasses all cases, is preferable. The *standard deviation* measures the extent of dispersion of the cases in a distribution about its mean. In a normal distribution, about one-third of the cases fall between the mean and one standard deviation above the mean. Another one-third fall between the mean and one standard deviation below the mean. Ninety-five percent of the cases fall within two standard deviations above and below the mean. The formula for the standard deviation is

$$\text{Standard deviation} = \left(\frac{\sum P_i (M - x_i)^2}{\sum P_i} \right)^{\frac{1}{2}}$$

where: P_i = student enrollment in school district i

         x_i = expenditures per pupil in school district i

         M = mean expenditures per pupil for all pupils

The standard deviations of the expenditure per pupil for states A and B are $888 and $587,

respectively. The smaller statistic for state B indicates greater equity. Perfect equity is indicated by zero.

The standard deviation suffers from the same problem as the range in that it is sensitive to changes in scale. The solution is similar to that used in correcting the range to get the federal range ratio. The standard deviation divided by the mean of the distribution produces the *coefficient of variation*.

$$\text{Coefficient of variation} = \frac{\left(\dfrac{\sum P_i (M - x_i)^2}{\sum P_i} \right)^{\frac{1}{2}}}{M}$$

where: P_i = student enrollment in school district i

         x_i = expenditures per pupil in school district i

         M = mean expenditures per pupil for all pupils

The coefficients of variation for states A and B are 0.17 and 0.11, respectively. The smaller statistic for state B indicates greater equity. If all districts in a state spent exactly the same, the coefficient of variation would be zero.

The Gini Coefficient

Economists use the *Lorenz curve* to illustrate inequalities in income. This measure is similarly useful in illustrating inequities related to educational resources. The Lorenz curves for states A and B are shown in Figure 11.3. To produce a Lorenz curve, school district data are sorted by the object of analysis—in this case by expenditure per pupil—in ascending order. Then the cumulative expenditures and enrollments (or their percentages) are graphed. The horizontal axis in the figure represents the cumulative percent of pupils, and the vertical axis represents the cumulative percent of expenditures. Perfect equity is represented by the diagonal that bisects the quadrant. That is, 25 percent of the pupils would have access to 25

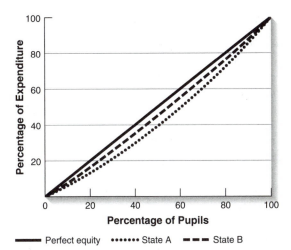

Perfect equity •••••• **State A** − − **State B**

FIGURE 11.3. Lorenz Curve for Expenditures and Pupils for States A and B

percent of the total expenditures, 50 percent of the pupils would have access to 50 percent of the total expenditures, and so on. In reality, for state A, the first 25 percent of the pupils have access to only 19.6 percent of the total expenditures. Thus the Lorenz curve, representing the actual distribution, sags below the diagonal. The greater the area between the ideal (the diagonal line that represents perfect equity) and the actual distribution (the Lorenz curve), the greater the inequity.

The extent of inequity is measured quantitatively by dividing the area between the Lorenz curve and the diagonal by the area of the triangle formed by the diagonal, the x-axis and the right side of the graph. The resulting ratio is known as the Gini coefficient. The formula for computing the Gini coefficient is

$$\text{Gini coefficient} = \frac{G}{(G + A)}$$

where: G = the area between the Lorenz curve and the diagonal

A = the area of the triangle formed by the diagonal and the horizontal and vertical axes.

An alternative formula for computing the Gini coefficient is

$$\text{Gini coefficient} = \frac{\left(\dfrac{\sum\sum \left| x_i - x_j \right| P_i P_j}{\left(\sum P_i \right)^2} \right)}{2M}$$

where: P_i = student enrollment in school district i

P_j = student enrollment in school district j

x_i = expenditure per pupil in school district i

x_j = expenditure per pupil in school district j

M = mean expenditure per pupil for all pupils

In the case of perfect equity, the actual distribution line would coincide with the diagonal. The area between the two lines would be zero, as would the Gini coefficient. In our example, the Gini coefficients for states A and B are 0.10 and 0.05, respectively. The smaller coefficient for state B represents greater equity. A great advantage of the Gini coefficient is that it weights all *students* equally, not all *districts*, which may vary greatly in the number of students served.

The McLoone Index

The statistics we have discussed to this point measure attributes of the total distribution. Such statistics are appropriate in evaluating policies when the intent is to treat all individuals in the group alike. But few state finance plans are intended to accomplish this. More typically, states attempt to ensure a basic level of support above which districts are free to spend to the extent that local resources permit; the foundation and flat grant plans described in Chapter 7 function in this manner. The McLoone index is designed to assess equity under these latter assumptions (Harrison & McLoone, 1960).

The McLoone index is the ratio of the sum of the actual expenditures of all districts at or below the median expenditure for the state to what the sum of those expenditures would be if all such districts actually spent at the median level. In contrast to previous statistics, perfect equity is represented by 1.00, and the greatest amount of inequity is represented by zero. For states A and B, the McLoone indices are 0.855 and 0.992, respectively. The *higher* index for state B represents *greater* equity.

$$\text{McCloone index} = \frac{\sum P_i x_i}{\sum P_i \left(med \right)}$$

where: P_i = student enrollment in school district i

x_i = expenditure per pupil in school district i

med = median expenditure per pupil for all pupils

The Thiel Coefficient

The great advantage of the Thiel coefficient is that, unlike the coefficient of variation and the Gini coefficient, it has a normal (i.e., bell-shaped) distribution when the dependent variable (the object being studied) is expressed as natural logarithms. The formula for the Thiel coefficient is

$$\text{Thiel coefficient} = \frac{\left(\left(\sum P_i x_i \ln x_i \right) - \left(\sum P_i x_i \ln M \right) \right)}{\sum P_i x_i}$$

where: P_i = student enrollment in school district i

x_i = expenditures per pupil in school district i

M = mean expenditures per pupil for all pupils

The Thiel coefficient has a minimum value of zero (perfect equity) with increasing values indicating increasing disparity—that is, decreasing equity.

Measures of Relationships

All of the statistics in the previous section address equity in terms of a single object. There are times, however, when we are interested in relationships, or the lack thereof, between two or more objects (variables). Berne and Stiefel's (1984) equal opportunity dimension represents a class of such instances. Here we are interested in the relationship between an object of distribution, such as pupil achievement or class size, and a characteristic of children, such as race or family income.

To determine the extent of fiscal neutrality, it is also necessary to resort to relationship analyses as we do when studying the impact of percentage equalizing, guaranteed-yield, and guaranteed-tax-base-programs on revenue produced and district tax rates. These finance programs are not intended to eliminate differences in expenditures among pupils but, rather, to uncouple the linkage between expenditures and the wealth of districts and/or tax rates. Several statistics, such as bivariate and multiple correlation and regression coefficients, are useful in understanding these relationships.

Correlation Coefficient

The strength of the relationship between two variables is commonly described by the Pearson product moment correlation coefficient. The coefficient ranges in size from −1.00 to +1.00. A zero coefficient indicates no relationship between the two variables—the desired state in analyses of horizontal equity, equal opportunity, and fiscal neutrality. A coefficient of 1.00 (either positive or negative) indicates a perfect correspondence between two variables; there is no unexplained variation. A positive coefficient indicates that the two variables increase in size together; a negative coefficient indicates that as one variable increases in size, the other variable decreases.

Figure 11.4 shows the scattergrams and regression lines of expenditures against percent minority for states A and B. For state A, the

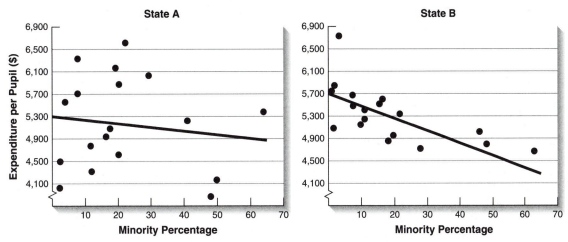

FIGURE 11.4. Scattergram and Regression Line of Expenditure per Pupil with Percentage Minority for States A and B

plots are widely scattered, suggesting little relationship between the two variables. This is confirmed by a low correlation coefficient (–0.12) and a nearly horizontal regression line. There is a very definite pattern for state B, however. As percent minority increases, expenditure per pupil decreases. This is reflected in a high and negative correlation coefficient of –0.68 and a downward-sloping regression line.

In terms of horizontal equity and equal opportunity with respect to percent minority, state A is more equitable than state B.

Slope

Figure 11.5 shows, for states A and B, the scattergrams of expenditure per pupil against property value per pupil and their respective regression lines. The correlation in both states

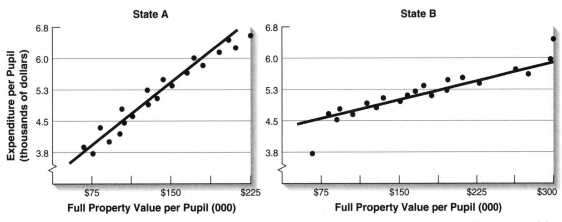

FIGURE 11.5. Scattergram and Regression Line of Expenditure per Pupil with Property Value per Pupil for States A and B

is high and positive, 0.98 and 0.93, respectively. But from an equity perspective, the situation is more serious in state A than in state B, because an increase in property value per pupil is associated with a much larger increase in expenditure per pupil in state A. In other words, the slope of the regression line for state A is steeper than that for state B, indicating that the equalization effect of state policy is greater in state B. The slope of a distribution measures the increase in the dependent variable (*y*-axis), on average, that is associated with a 1-unit increase in the independent variable (*x*-axis). The slope is measured by the regression coefficient, and the larger the slope, the greater the inequity. The regression coefficients for states A and B are 0.02 and 0.01, respectively.

Multivariate methods

Despite a variety of conflicting equity goals, virtually all analyses of school finance equity have until recently used univariate or bivariate methods as described in previous sections. One exception was a study by Garms (1979) that pioneered the use of multivariate techniques to permit the comparison of different states or of one state with itself over time. Garms pointed out that "any attempt to separately analyze the effects of multiple goals must have a way of separating the allocations for those goals" (p. 416). Because this is impossible in an accounting sense (a single allocation may be directed toward several ends), Garms employed multivariate statistics that made possible "the separation of provisions for differences in district wealth from differences in tax rate, and both of these from differences in provision for needs and costs" (p. 435). While acknowledging some problems that may limit its applicability, Garms promoted the method as providing a more comprehensive view of school finance systems than any method previously proposed.

Twenty years later, multivariate procedures are commonly used in equity studies. Parrish, Matsumoto, and Fowler (1995) applied such techniques in analyzing the disparities in public school district spending. They justified the use of multivariate analysis as follows:

> Because the various factors on which school districts differ are correlated with each other (some, like enrollment size and urbanicity, highly correlated), it is impossible to discern from marginal averages which of several correlated variables are most responsible for a difference. By simultaneously allowing all of the descriptive factors under study to account for variation in the dependent variable (e.g., in per pupil expenditures), it is possible to identify which are the "real" factors and which only appear to be factors because of their correlation with the "real" factors. (p. D-19)

Data envelopment analysis (DEA) is a relatively new statistical tool that permits the use of multiple inputs and outputs in analyzing the efficiency of decision units. Walters and Freeman (1993) used this approach in examining equity issues in Utah. Duncombe and Yinger (1997, 1999) and Reschovsky and Imazeki (2001) have used DEA in adequacy studies. DEA accommodates the use of a richer set of variables in the assessment of comparative wealth, tax effort, and spending equity than most other methods reviewed above (Charnes, Cooper, & Rhodes, 1978). DEA is discussed more fully in Chapter 12.

The United States General Accounting Office (GAO) (1997) developed an *implicit foundation level* (IFL) approach to study state efforts to reduce funding gaps between poor and wealthy districts. The IFL is an estimate of the minimum amount of funding that districts within a state could spend per pupil if they were to make an equal minimum tax effort as in a foundation state aid program. This technique produces measures of equity within states and between states. In addition, IFL sheds light on the structural forces that drive inequities, including state equalization policies (overall state percentage of funding and the extent to which aid is targeted to specific types of students) and the extent to which it is due to local policies such as relative differences in local tax rates.

Adjusting for Differences in Costs and Student Needs

Fowler and Monk (2001) were critical of equity studies that do not make cost adjustments to recognize the influence on school costs that arises from such factors as regional differences in the cost of living and interdistrict differences in educational costs related to student characteristics such as disabilities and poverty backgrounds. Their criticism would apply to virtually all such studies done prior to the mid-1990s. Treating data for such cost differences gives equity analyses greater accuracy by shifting the focus from how many dollars are distributed to what goods and services the dollars distributed can actually purchase. Treating differences in student characteristics is one approach to addressing the concept of vertical equity and, thus, adequacy.

When contemplating cost differentials, Fowler and Monk (2001) list three conditions that might be sources of variation: cost differentials from one region to another, change of costs over time (inflation), and differences in the quality and quantity of what is being purchased.

> A cost index, therefore, must simultaneously take into account those discretionary factors that a school district might manipulate, such as quality and quantity of staff, and those nondiscretionary factors that the school district cannot control, such as the cost of living, the competitiveness of the labor market, and amenities, such as climate, absence of crime, and geographic location. (p. 48)

The study by Parrish, Matsumoto, and Fowler (1995), cited above, was also among the first to adjust financial indicators for differences among states and within states for general cost differences (e.g., differences in cost of living) and differences in program cost that arise from variations in student characteristics. For general costs, they used cost-of-living adjustments designed to distinguish between metropolitan and rural areas within each state. McMahon and Chang (1991) developed the adjustments. On the basis of national studies, special educa-

tion students were weighted 2.3, compensatory education students 1.2, and students with limited proficiency in English 1.2.

Parrish, Hikido, and Fowler (1998) extended the 1995 study to address the issue of how general, categorical, and total revenues available for public education vary according to school district and community characteristics. To adjust for differences in buying power of dollars in different communities, they used the Teacher Cost Index developed by Chambers and Fowler (1995). They used the same weightings as did the 1995 study to adjust for variations in student needs. The importance and magnitude of the effect of these adjustments on estimates of revenues per student are shown in Table 11.4.

The 1998 GAO study cited above adjusted fiscal data with a modified Chambers and Fowler Teacher Cost Index. The index was applied to the 84.8 percent of current expenditures that was estimated to be related to personnel costs, including salaries, fringe benefits, and some purchased services. It was assumed that other costs vary little within a state. The index was then rescaled to create district-level indices unique to each state. Adjusting for the cost implications of student need indicators was done by including the indicators as independent variables in regression analyses. Such indicators included district personal income per pupil, percentage of children living in poverty, percentage of students classified as special education students, percentage of district students who are high school students, and the square of district enrollment (to reduce the influence of low-enrollment districts on the statistical analysis).

Selecting Equity Measures and Benchmarks

With respect to federal policy, Berne and Stiefel (1992) recommended the use of the coefficient of variation or the McLoone index in measuring vertical equity. They also recommended that investigators computing these ratios use

TABLE 11.4.

General, Categorical, and Total Revenues per Student by Percentage of School-Age Children in Poverty: 1991–1992

Revenues by School-Age Children in Poverty Category	Percentage of All Students Enrolled (1)	Revenue Type as a Percentage of Total Revenue (2)	Revenues per Student			
			Actual (3)	Cost-Adjusted (4)	Need-Adjusted (5)	Cost- and Need-Adjusted (6)
General Revenues						
School-Age Children in Poverty						
Less than 8%	22.2%	88.7%	$5,555	$5,196	$4,814	$4,505
8%–<15%	23.6	84.5	4,458	4,471	3,811	3,823
15%–<25%	27.7	79.0	4,079	4,274	3,430	3,595
25% or more	26.6	74.9	4,193	4,150	3,440	3,407
Categorical Revenues						
School-Age Children in Poverty						
Less than 8%	22.2	11.3	711	667	613	576
8%–<15%	23.6	15.5	816	819	695	697
15%–<25%	27.7	21.0	1,084	1,135	909	952
25% or more	26.6	25.1	1,406	1,406	1,147	1,147
Total Revenues						
School-Age Children in Poverty						
Less than 8%	22.2	100.0	6,266	5,863	5,427	5,080
8%–<15%	23.6	100.0	5,273	5,289	4,506	4,521
15%–<25%	27.7	100.0	5,162	5,409	4,339	4,547
25% or more	26.6	100.0	5,600	5,557	4,587	4,554

Note: All results are weighted by district enrollment. Percentages may not add to 100 because of rounding. Data are from Bureau of the Census, 1990 Census of Governments, Survey of Local Government Finances; U.S. Department of Education, National Center for Education Statistics, 1991–92 Common Core of Data, 1990 Census School District Special Tabulation (summary file set I).

Source: T. B. Parrish, C. S. Hikido, & W. J. Fowler. (1998). *Inequalities in Public School District Revenues* (NCES 98-210). Washington, DC: Office of Educational Research and Improvement, U.S. Department of Education, p. xvi.

weighted student counts and all operating revenues or expenditures, both general and categorical. They believed that the McLoone index is the most consistent with the federal interest in vertical equity, because it emphasizes the weighted students who receive the fewest dollars. The coefficient of variation was favored as an alternative, because it is commonly used and understood and it performs consistently with other, more esoteric measures of disparity. They recommended the same measures for analyses of horizontal equity, except that student counts should be unweighted and definitions of expenditures and revenues may differ. For equal opportunity equity, they recommended use of a quadratic regression procedure (not described here).

There are no generally accepted benchmarks of equity for the statistics we have described. Evaluations must depend largely on relative comparisons. Odden and Picus (2000) recommended the following values as a desirable level of equity: 0.10 or less for the coefficient of variation, 0.95 or higher for the McLoone index, and 0.05 or less for the Gini coefficient. They discouraged use of the federal range ratio because of the limitations we noted previously.

In using measures of equity in policy analyses, it is important to recognize that each examines a somewhat different aspect of the concept. The measure(s) selected for evaluating the effectiveness of a particular policy should correspond closely to the intended effect of that policy.

FINDINGS FROM STUDIES OF SCHOOL FINANCE EQUITY

Interest in school finance equity peaked during the decade of the 1970s and then waned until the 1990s. Beginning in the 1960s with the civil rights movement and the related compensatory education programs of President Lyndon Johnson's Great Society, concerns over equality of educational opportunities dominated the educational agenda. In the 1970s,

attention focused on equity, and litigation was brought in over half the states to challenge the school finance system's constitutionality (discussed in Chapter 10). The 1970s were dubbed the decade of school finance reform as state after state restructured their finance systems to improve their equity—either under court order or on their own initiative. Researchers from several disciplines joined with jurists, policy makers, interest groups, task forces, and national foundations during this period to sharpen our understanding of equity problems and to evaluate the effectiveness of remedies attempted. During this time, equity was treated as a uni-dimensional concept—that is, as horizontal equity.

In the 1980s, national attention shifted to excellence and efficiency; interest in equity declined but did not disappear entirely. In reviewing approximately 140 pieces of equity research between 1980 and 1987, Barro (1987) referred to them as a "holding operation" (p. 3). He found no newly developed concepts or methods of analysis. The decline in research on school finance equity paralleled a decline in the demand and funding for such studies over that which was available in the prior decade.

Since the mid-1990s and into the new century, there has been renewed interest in equity, but this time the focus is on vertical equity (two-dimensional), the ultimate goal being to define adequacy. New methods of analysis are being developed to handle the greater complexity of the problem as it is now defined. Regional cost differences are being recognized and appropriate adjustments sought. Serious attention is being given to defining program costs (e.g., what the justifiable expenditure levels are for children diagnosed with differing levels of educational need). The challenge of separating higher costs due to justifiable reasons from those due to inefficiency is also being tackled. Thus progress is being made toward identifying vertical equity and adequacy in ways that would inform policy development, but there remains a long way to go.

In this section we review some of the equity research, devoting the most attention to studies of the past decade. We begin with national studies—those that involve all, or most, of the states. These tend to focus on the distribution of resources among school districts. To give the reader a longitudinal sense of the development of equity research, we review research conducted in three states that have been frequently studied over three decades: Michigan, New York, and Texas. We close the section by looking at the latest development in equity research: studies that address the issue at the school or pupil level.

National Studies

Equity with Respect to Economic Inputs

For most states, and for all regions, equity in the distribution of instructional expenditures per pupil among school districts improved over the period 1980 through 1994. At the same time, equity measures were seen to have declined when the nation was treated as a single unit; this was due to differential increases in expenditures among the regions of the country. These are the conclusions of Hussar and Sonnenberg (2000). The focus of the study was horizontal equity; the object of analysis was instructional expenditures per pupil. They made no adjustments of wealth and expenditure data for variations among school districts in program cost differentials due to variations in student characteristics or prices among localities.

The national study of the disparities in public school district spending by Parrish, Matsumoto, and Fowler (1995) involved all school districts in the United States. The study analyzed revenue and expenditure data from the 1990 Survey of Local Government Finances and nonfiscal data from the Common Core of Data of the National Center for Education Statistics. It addressed questions related to who pays, how much, and for whom. To the extent

that these questions pertain to the allocation of education resources to students with comparable education need, they are considered to be horizontal equity issues. Vertical equity issues were addressed by relating expenditure differences with differing educational needs of students. Adjustments were also made for variations among localities in costs due to non-program factors. Bivariate, multivariate, and dispersion analyses were used as noted in the foregoing section on measuring equity.

The critical predictors of variation in school district expenditures identified by Parrish, Matsumoto, and Fowler (1995) were region (highest in the Northeast and lowest in the West), size (inverse relationship), socioeconomic status and education attainment (direct relationships); percentage of minorities (direct relationship), extent of poverty (inverse relationship), and percentage of students in special education programs (inverse relationship). The authors concluded that

> Students in districts enrolling the lowest percentages of students in poverty and the lowest percentages of students in need of special education services received the highest expenditures. While these trends are matters of concern from a student equity perspective, they should be considered in the context of no clear patterns of expenditure differentials for limited English proficiency and at-risk students, and a positive relationship between percentage of minority students and expenditures. (p. 11)

The distribution of public resources for education revealed a degree of equalization. Resource distribution was substantially more equal than wealth measured by housing values and somewhat less varied than wealth measured by household income. Funds allocated by states were the primary equalizing factors for resources directed to education, with some additional equalization resulting from the various federal funding programs.

Parrish, Matsumoto, and Fowler (1995) focused primarily on equity in terms of expenditures. Parrish, Hikido, and Fowler (1998) built on that study but focused on equity of revenues derived from local, state, and federal sources and how they are distributed among different types of students, districts, and communities. Many of these funding sources are categorical, providing supplemental services to special populations of students. All states provide general aid to school districts, and all, in varying degrees, provide some forms of categorical aid. Nearly all federal funding sources for public education are aligned with a special purpose. Local funds can be applied at the discretion of local authorities and thus can be treated as general aid. Unlike this study, traditional equity analyses have usually focused only on expenditures for general education (as did Hussar and Sonnenberg, 2000) to the exclusion of programs made possible by categorical aid.

The revenue measures of Parrish, Hikido, and Fowler's study (1998) were analyzed against such important district characteristics as percentage of children in poverty, percentage of minority children, and wealth. Revenue measures are reported in actual, resource-cost-adjusted, pupil-need-adjusted, and cost-and-need-adjusted forms. The pupil-need adjustments reflect the varying costs of programs appropriate for children of differing characteristics. The cost adjustments reflect variations in cost of resources among localities and regions.

Tables 11.5 and 11.6 report, for forty-nine states (Hawaii is omitted because it functions as a unified district), five common equity statistics resulting from calculations for total revenue per pupil unadjusted (Table 11.5) and adjusted (Table 11.6) for sources of cost differences. For each equity measure, each state is given a quartile rank to facilitate comparisons. To obtain a global measure of the equity of distribution of revenue, the mean rank of all five of the equity indicators is shown in the rightmost column. A quartile rank of 1 indicates relatively high equity, whereas a quartile rank of 4 indicates relatively low equity. The authors

conclude that the most equitable states are Nevada, West Virginia, Delaware, North Carolina, and Florida. The least equitable are New Hampshire, Missouri, Nebraska, Ohio, Illinois, New York, Montana, and Vermont.

Comparing the statistics reported in Tables 11.5 and 11.6 shows how important these adjustments are in determining the relative ranks of states on equity measures. It can be argued that Table 11.5 is an illustration of horizontal equity analysis, because no adjustments are made for special education needs of students, nor are there adjustments for differences in costs arising from other sources. The statistics reported in Table 11.6 are adjusted for the special education needs of students, as well as for other sources of cost differences, so it can be argued that it is an illustration of vertical equity analysis.

Parrish, Hikido, and Fowler (1998) arrived at a number of other important conclusions. The lowest-poverty and the lowest-percent-minority districts had substantially more actual (no adjustments) general revenues than did districts with larger proportions of poor and minority students. However, the reverse was true for categorical revenues. The policy intent of federal Title I monies is to target children in poverty, but the actual funds ended up in the lowest-poverty as well as the highest-poverty districts. The situation is even worse for state funds targeted to students in poverty. State compensatory programs allocate nearly twice as much funding per targeted student to districts with the lowest percentage of students in poverty than to all other districts.

The study also presented compelling evidence that addressing equity considerations alone, without concern over adequacy of provision, is a mockery of the justice sought. It is reported that the highest levels of revenue per student in Mississippi ($4,089 at the 95th percentile) were less than the revenue levels for the 5th percentile students in twenty-nine states. In New York, which ranks among the most inequitable states in distribution of rev-

TABLE 11.5.

Actual Revenues: Equity Measures, Quartile Rankings, and Overall Mean Equity Rankings by State, 1991–1992

State	Restricted Range	Quartile Rank	Federal Range Ratio	Quartile Rank	McLoone Index	Quartile Rank	Coefficient of Variation	Quartile Rank	Gini Coefficient	Quartile Rank	MEAN RANK
Alabama	$1,757	2	0.57	2	0.92	2	12.92	2	0.07	2	2.00
Alaska	$8,545	4	1.24	4	0.95	1	36.46	4	0.16	4	3.40
Arizona	$3,536	3	0.91	4	0.93	2	19.80	4	0.09	3	3.20
Arkansas	$2,298	3	0.64	3	0.95	1	13.24	2	0.06	1	2.00
California	$1,866	2	0.47	2	0.92	2	13.64	2	0.08	3	2.20
Colorado	$1,957	2	0.44	2	0.95	1	13.54	2	0.07	2	1.80
Connecticut	$3,828	4	0.53	2	0.92	2	13.69	2	0.07	2	2.40
Delaware	$1,538	1	0.29	1	0.94	1	8.67	1	0.05	1	1.00
Florida	$1,927	2	0.38	1	0.92	2	9.38	1	0.05	1	1.40
Georgia	$3,050	3	0.80	4	0.91	3	18.03	3	0.10	3	3.20
Idaho	$1,554	1	0.48	2	0.93	2	12.73	2	0.07	2	1.80
Illinois	$5,449	4	1.51	4	0.82	4	31.18	4	0.16	4	4.00
Indiana	$2,177	2	0.50	2	0.92	3	12.98	2	0.07	2	2.20
Iowa	$1,465	1	0.33	1	0.94	1	9.18	1	0.05	1	1.00
Kansas	$2,525	3	0.61	3	0.91	3	13.87	2	0.07	2	2.60
Kentucky	$1,264	1	0.35	1	0.94	1	10.00	1	0.06	1	1.00
Louisiana	$1,506	1	0.42	1	0.92	3	11.33	3	0.06	1	1.40
Maine	$2,664	3	0.54	2	0.92	3	15.13	3	0.08	3	2.80
Maryland	$2,690	3	0.50	2	0.94	1	13.41	2	0.07	2	2.00
Massachusetts	$3,881	4	0.76	4	0.90	4	19.66	4	0.10	4	4.00
Michigan	$4,096	4	0.93	4	0.84	4	21.32	4	0.12	4	4.00
Minnesota	$2,939	3	0.61	3	0.93	2	15.91	3	0.09	3	2.80
Mississippi	$1,253	1	0.44	2	0.92	3	11.78	2	0.07	2	2.00
Missouri	$4,920	4	1.54	4	0.88	4	39.38	4	0.18	4	4.00
Montana	$4,752	4	1.20	4	0.91	3	32.58	4	0.16	4	3.80
Nebraska	$2,845	3	0.67	3	0.85	4	15.62	3	0.09	3	3.20

Nevada	$1,283	1	0.27	1	0.94	1	7.70	1	0.03	1	1.00
New Hampshire	$3,980	4	0.85	4	0.91	4	20.05	4	0.11	4	4.00
New Jersey	$5,138	4	0.70	3	0.90	3	16.01	3	0.09	3	3.40
New Mexico	$2,105	2	0.57	3	0.94	1	15.25	3	0.07	2	2.20
New York	$5,123	4	0.76	4	0.98	1	20.66	4	0.10	4	3.40
North Carolina	$1,698	2	0.42	1	0.93	2	11.26	1	0.06	1	1.40
North Dakota	$2,344	3	0.66	3	0.90	4	18.47	3	0.09	3	3.20
Ohio	$4,498	4	1.22	4	0.87	4	28.92	4	0.14	4	4.00
Oklahoma	$1,556	1	0.46	2	0.92	3	13.06	2	0.07	2	2.00
Oregon	$2,501	3	0.59	3	0.90	4	14.96	3	0.08	3	3.20
Pennsylvania	$3,749	3	0.71	3	0.91	4	16.64	3	0.09	3	3.20
Rhode Island	$1,951	2	0.36	1	0.92	3	9.74	1	0.05	1	1.60
South Carolina	$1,523	1	0.39	1	0.93	2	10.43	1	0.06	1	1.20
South Dakota	$2,262	2	0.68	3	0.92	3	18.75	3	0.09	3	2.80
Tennessee	$1,955	2	0.71	3	0.87	4	18.20	3	0.10	4	3.20
Texas	$1,566	1	0.36	1	0.93	2	10.69	1	0.06	1	1.20
Utah	$1,277	1	0.42	2	0.98	1	15.81	3	0.07	3	2.00
Vermont	$5,908	4	1.10	4	0.84	4	23.73	4	0.13	4	4.00
Virginia	$2,912	3	0.68	3	0.92	3	20.19	4	0.11	4	3.40
Washington	$1,984	2	0.41	1	0.92	3	10.99	1	0.06	2	1.80
West Virginia	$1,028	1	0.21	1	0.95	1	7.16	1	0.04	1	1.00
Wisconsin	$2,108	2	0.42	2	0.93	2	11.55	2	0.06	2	2.00
Wyoming	$3,909	4	0.78	4	0.93	2	21.21	4	0.10	4	3.60

Note: All results are weighted by district enrollment. Data are from Bureau of the Census, 1990 Census of Governments, Survey of Local Government Finances.

Source: T. B. Parrish, C. S. Hikido, & W. J. Fowler, Jr. (1998). *Inequalities in Public School District Revenues*. Washington, DC: U.S. Department of Education, National Center for Education Statistics, p. 112.

TABLE 11.6.

Cost- and Need-Adjusted Revenues: Equity Measures, Quartile Rankings, and Overall Mean Equity Rankings by State, 1991–1992

State	Restricted Range	Quartile Rank	Federal Range Ratio	Quartile Rank	McLoone Index	Quartile Rank	Coefficient of Variation	Quartile Rank	Gini Coefficient	Quartile Rank	MEAN RANK
Alabama	$1,433	1	0.49	2	0.93	2	12.66	2	0.07	2	1.80
Alaska	$4,612	4	0.88	4	0.96	1	32.63	4	0.13	4	3.40
Arizona	$2,940	4	0.84	4	0.92	2	18.30	3	0.09	3	3.20
Arkansas	$2,187	3	0.63	3	0.94	1	13.03	2	0.07	2	2.20
California	$1,783	2	0.58	3	0.90	4	14.10	2	0.07	2	2.60
Colorado	$1,391	1	0.35	1	0.95	1	14.04	2	0.07	2	1.40
Connecticut	$2,737	3	0.52	2	0.92	2	14.42	3	0.07	2	2.40
Delaware	$1,215	1	0.27	1	0.95	1	7.10	1	0.04	1	1.00
Florida	$1,290	1	0.27	1	0.95	1	8.85	1	0.05	1	1.00
Georgia	$1,914	2	0.53	2	0.93	2	13.94	2	0.08	3	2.20
Idaho	$1,431	1	0.49	2	0.94	1	13.61	2	0.07	2	1.60
Illinois	$3,598	4	1.18	4	0.87	4	26.51	4	0.12	4	4.00
Indiana	$1,693	2	0.46	2	0.92	3	11.27	2	0.06	1	2.00
Iowa	$1,670	2	0.41	1	0.94	2	10.86	1	0.06	1	1.40
Kansas	$3,007	4	0.74	3	0.91	3	18.47	3	0.09	3	3.40
Kentucky	$893	1	0.27	1	0.94	2	7.45	2	0.04	1	1.20
Louisiana	$1,481	2	0.44	2	0.92	3	11.03	3	0.06	1	1.80
Maine	$1,950	2	0.49	2	0.91	3	14.02	2	0.08	3	2.40
Maryland	$2,701	3	0.68	3	0.91	3	15.41	3	0.08	3	3.00
Massachusetts	$2,738	3	0.74	4	0.91	3	18.44	3	0.10	4	3.40
Michigan	$2,774	3	0.71	3	0.91	3	17.43	3	0.09	3	3.00
Minnesota	$1,967	2	0.47	2	0.92	2	12.73	2	0.07	2	2.20
Mississippi	$1,427	1	0.52	2	0.93	2	12.98	2	0.07	2	1.80
Missouri	$3,174	4	1.07	4	0.89	4	33.20	4	0.15	4	4.00

State										
Montana	$4,960	4	1.55	4	0.90	4	35.13	4	0.17	4	4.00
Nebraska	$3,284	4	0.81	4	0.87	4	19.70	4	0.10	4	4.00
Nevada	$907	1	0.20	1	0.97	1	5.87	1	0.02	1	1.00
New Hampshire	$3,027	4	0.84	4	0.90	4	19.98	4	0.11	4	4.00
New Jersey	$3,776	4	0.71	3	0.90	3	15.90	3	0.09	3	3.40
New Mexico	$1,995	3	0.56	2	0.96	1	16.21	3	0.07	2	2.20
New York	$4,568	4	1.01	4	0.80	4	25.10	4	0.14	4	4.00
North Carolina	$1,240	1	0.34	1	0.95	1	9.81	1	0.05	1	1.00
North Dakota	$2,687	3	0.80	4	0.91	3	20.07	4	0.10	4	3.60
Ohio	$3,288	4	1.02	4	0.90	4	23.12	4	0.12	4	4.00
Oklahoma	$2,007	3	0.60	3	0.91	3	17.83	3	0.09	3	3.00
Oregon	$2,253	3	0.63	3	0.91	3	15.16	3	0.08	3	3.00
Pennsylvania	$2,525	3	0.57	3	0.94	2	13.69	2	0.07	2	2.40
Rhode Island	$1,620	2	0.43	2	0.93	2	11.16	1	0.06	1	1.60
South Carolina	$1,225	1	0.34	1	0.93	2	9.89	1	0.06	1	1.20
South Dakota	$2,320	3	0.69	3	0.91	3	18.56	4	0.09	3	3.20
Tennessee	$1,680	2	0.64	3	0.89	4	16.50	3	0.09	4	3.20
Texas	$1,881	2	0.49	2	0.91	4	13.91	2	0.07	2	2.40
Utah	$942	1	0.36	1	0.95	1	14.83	3	0.07	3	1.80
Vermont	$5,188	4	1.14	4	0.86	4	24.65	4	0.14	4	4.00
Virginia	$2,268	3	0.59	3	0.90	4	14.40	3	0.08	3	3.20
Washington	$1,493	2	0.39	1	0.93	2	10.97	1	0.06	2	1.60
West Virginia	$954	1	0.21	1	0.97	1	6.88	1	0.04	1	1.00
Wisconsin	$1,728	2	0.38	2	0.95	1	10.20	1	0.05	1	1.20
Wyoming	$3,751	4	0.81	4	0.93	2	19.82	4	0.10	4	3.60

Note: All results are weighted by district enrollment. Data are from Bureau of the Census, 1990 Census of Governments, Survey of Local Government Finances; U.S. Department of Education, National Center for Education Statistics, 1991–92 Common Core of Data, 1990 Census School District Special Tabulation (summary file set 1).

Source: T. B. Parrish, C. S. Hikido, & W. J. Fowler, Jr. (1998). *Inequalities in Public School District Revenues*. Washington, DC: U.S. Department of Education, National Center for Education Statistics, p. 113.

enues and expenditures, students at the 5th percentile receive more revenue per pupil than the majority of students in other states where revenue and expenditures are distributed more equitably. Most New York students receive more revenues than the median student in forty-five of the fifty states. Guthrie and Rothstein (2001, p. 103) argue that "The more modern and still evolving concept of adequacy suggests that something beyond equity is at issue. The 'something else' is a notion of sufficiency, a per pupil resource amount sufficient to achieve some performance objective." Mississippi and New York provide contrasting evidence in support of this statement.

As a rule, greater equity in expenditure and revenue distribution in states results from increasing the proportion of revenue in support of public education provided by states, yet this practice may, in the long term, be associated with a reduction in the adequacy of a state's aid program. In a national study seeking to explain the differences in growth in education revenue among states, Alexander (1997) found that states with high and moderate growth tended to rely more on local sources than on state sources, whereas states experiencing small increases in revenue per pupil relied primarily on the state for those increases.

The study by the United States General Accounting Office (GAO) (1997), described in the foregoing section on measurement, produced a new measure of equity within states—the implicit foundation level—to assist them in their quest to discover structural explanations of inequities. Personal income, rather than the value of real property (which is the basis typically used), was taken as the basis for wealth measures, and total revenue was the object of analysis. Both were adjusted for variations among districts caused by price differences and differences in program costs due to student characteristics. It could be argued that because of the program cost adjustments, the study was one of vertical equity; however, it did not consider issues of adequacy. That adequacy was

not a consideration is apparent from the fact that the national average adjusted implicit foundation level was $3,134 in 1992 dollars, ranging among the states from $4,648 in New York to $721 in New Hampshire.

The GAO found that total funding per weighted pupil in thirty-seven states favored wealthy districts. In only three states (Wyoming, Alaska, and Nevada) did the funding structure favor poor districts. The remaining states had fiscally neutral structures. On average, wealthy districts had about 24 percent more total funding per weighted pupil than did poor districts.

Three strategies reduced the funding gap between a state's poor and wealthy districts: targeting aid to poor districts, increasing the state's relative share of total funding, and increasing local tax effort in poor districts. These factors accounted for 61 percent of the variation among the states in the sizes of their revenue gaps among districts. The most potent strategy for closing gaps was increasing tax efforts among poor districts, even though they were already putting forth higher efforts in thirty-five states. A study of student and taxpayer equity in the six New England states (Fastrup, 1997) drew a similar conclusion. Fastrup pointed out that student equity is a function of local tax policy as well as state policy. The poor districts of New Hampshire and Rhode Island, for example, make substantially greater tax efforts than do the wealthy districts in those states; as a result, student equity is enhanced, but at the expense of taxpayer equity.

The second most effective strategy for reducing gaps, according to the GAO study, was to increase the proportion of revenue provided by the state. Although targeting funding to poor districts typically reduced the gaps, it did not eliminate them and was the least effective of the three strategies. The GAO study concluded that to maximize a state's equalization effort without any increases in state funding, forty-eight states would have to reduce their funding of wealthy districts to increase funding in poor and middle-income districts. In twenty-nine states, the magnitude of the targeted change would have to be substantial to enable all districts to spend at the state average with an average local tax effort.

In an analysis of the distribution of state aid earmarked for educational reform initiatives between 1980 and 1990, Verstegen (1993, 1994) concluded that the new funds benefited children unequally, "advantaging the advantaged but failing the less fortunate" (1993, p. 33). She found that the states were using a new strategy in distributing aid to school districts that linked all new dollars to state reform strategies, 70 percent of which aid was distributed as *unequalized* aid. Among the states, nearly 80 percent of the variation in per-pupil revenue for schools was explained by state wealth as measured by gross state product per pupil, and greater increases in funding were found in states with greater wealth and taxing capacity, growing economic activity, and lower percentages of children in poverty. Wyoming, Vermont, Georgia, and Connecticut more than doubled their state aid (adjusted for inflation). Verstegen's studies provide evidence that over the decade of the 1980s, when new funds for education were targeted toward state reform strategies, mostly in an unequalized manner, variations in spending across the states widened and were significantly related to a state's ability to pay for education (1994, p. 130). This may help to explain the growing horizontal inequity among states found by Hussar and Sonnenberg (2000) that we discussed earlier in this chapter.

A number of studies, most of which are limited to a single state, have been conducted to evaluate the impact of litigation (reviewed in Chapter 10) as a vehicle for improving equity within states. Murray, Evans, and Schwab (1998) reported one such study of national dimension. They used a fixed-effects model with an omnibus measure of inequality (including, among others, the Theil index, the Gini coefficient, and the coefficient of variation) as the dependent variable. The independent variable was the status of litigation. The model controlled for demographic influences and included fixed-state and fixed-year variables and an error term. The fixed-state term enables the model to account for all factors that are constant across time but vary across states; the fixed-year variable enables the model to hold constant those factors that affect all states equally but vary over time. The model was estimated using data from the *Census of Governments: School System Finance* for the years 1972, 1977, 1982, 1987, and 1992. The data base consisted of information on more than 16,000 school districts from 50 states over a 20-year period.

Murray, Evans, and Schwab (1998) found that there was a reduction in spending inequality within states experiencing court-mandated education finance reform. This reduction ranged from 19 to 34 percent, depending on the way inequality was measured. According to these investigators' analysis, the improvement was accomplished by raising spending at the bottom of the distribution while spending at the top remained unchanged. The analysis suggested that the reforms in school finance policy were funded by increases to the education sections of state budgets of reform states without affecting other sections of the budget. By implication, reform states funded the additional spending through higher taxes.

Upon reviewing studies conducted since the landmark U.S. Supreme Court decision in *San Antonio Independent School District* v. *Rodriguez* (1973), Koski and Levin (2000) also concluded that "the reformers' and litigators' time has not been wasted in court" (p. 506). The studies they reviewed suggested that litigation had resulted in greater equity in per-pupil spending among districts and students. Accompanying this greater equity was a larger proportional participation by the state in the financing of the public schools that permitted concomitant tax relief at the local level. The impact on overall level of school funding was not clear.

Equity with Respect to Noneconomic Inputs and Outputs

There is some encouraging evidence that the higher academic standards set by states as part of the education reform movement, and their corresponding assessment strategies, are serving to reduce the inequities in outputs experienced by at-risk children, although achievement gaps remain large. These initiatives have been relatively inexpensive to implement. Between 1973 and 1990, the percentage of all students taking academic courses jumped from 59 percent to over two-thirds, and the national dropout rate declined from 14 percent to 12 percent (Mirel & Angus, 1994). These numbers were even more impressive for minority students.

Minority students are taking more and tougher academic courses than in the past *and* are performing better on national standardized examinations. Between 1976 and 1993, scores for African American students rose 21 points for the verbal section of the SAT and 34 points for the math section; similar progress was shown by Hispanic students. Also, growing numbers of minority students are taking advanced placement examinations. For African American students, the number grew from 10,000 in 1988 to more than 15,000 in 1993. For Hispanic students, the number increased from 10,000 to nearly 30,000. Mirel and Angus (1994) commented on these overall gains:

> [F]or more than half a century, educational policy makers have made decisions based on the presumption that tougher course requirements automatically increase the dropout rate, especially among poor and minority students. Moreover, these policy makers assumed that the only way to keep the dropout rate from soaring was to make the high school curriculum less challenging and more entertaining . . . [P]oor and minority students have been the most frequent casualties of such standard-lowering policies as allowing less rigorous courses to meet academic requirements for graduation or diluting course content in academic courses while keeping course titles the same . . . Much of the failure of American K–12

education lies in our avoiding the formidable task of discovering how to teach difficult subjects in ways that are both accessible to young people and yet still true to the complexity and richness of the material. (pp. 40–42)

Stark disparities remain, however. Although the gap in reading achievement between black and white students, as measured by the National Assessment of Educational Progress (NAEP), had narrowed between 1971 and 1996 (with most of the closure taking place prior to 1988), there remained a 30-point difference at all ages tested (nine, thirteen, and seventeen years) (National Center for Education Statistics, 2001). For the NAEP writing assessment administered in 1998, 16 percent of white seventeen-year-olds failed to meet the basic level of achievement. The percentages were 36 percent for blacks and 35 percent for Hispanics. About half of the teachers in schools with low minority enrollments held master's degrees in 1998, compared to 38 percent in schools with more than half minority enrollment. Over 95 percent of teachers in elementary schools with low enrollments of students in poverty held standard state certification, compared to 88 percent in schools with more than half minority enrollment. The patterns for these teacher characteristics were similar for high schools and for both high schools and elementary schools for the range of students qualifying for free and reduced lunches.

The net result of these disparities is that 32 percent of white high school graduates were considered highly or very highly qualified for college, compared with 16.2 percent of black graduates and 18.7 percent of Hispanic graduates (National Center for Education Statistics, 2001). The percentage of African American students eighteen to twenty-four years of age enrolling in college actually declined since the mid-1970s from 22.6 percent to 21.1 percent, while enrollment of white students increased from 27.1 percent to 31.3 percent (Mirel & Angus, 1994).

Single-State Studies

Numerous studies have examined the equity of resource distribution to school districts within a single state. To illustrate this type of research, we have selected three of the most intensively studied states: Michigan, New York, and Texas.

Michigan

Berne and Stiefel (1984) analyzed data for the state of Michigan for the years 1970 through 1978. They found that measures of horizontal equity started and ended at about the same point but worsened during the middle of the period. With respect to equal opportunity, they found that children in wealthier districts enjoyed better educational opportunities. They also found inequities by region of the state and with respect to race.

Kearney and Chen (1989) continued the study of Michigan from the point where Berne and Stiefel left off, extending the analysis to 1985. Although 1984 and 1985 had brought about some improvements in most criteria for horizontal equity, they concluded that the goal was much further from attainment in 1985 than it had been in 1979. Equal opportunity continued to worsen over the period of the analysis.

The Michigan analysis was extended through 1989 by Kearney and Anderson (1992). They concluded that school finance equity in Michigan, in terms of almost any equity object, any equity principle, and any equity measure, worsened over the period 1976–1989 for both pupils and taxpayers. Frustration over the immutability of these conditions may have contributed to the radical reform adopted by Michigan in 1993, virtually eliminating the property tax as a means of local support of public education (see Chapters 5 and 7). The next year, Michigan voters approved a 2 percent increase in the state sales tax rate, to be dedicated to schools. The combined effect of these and other revenue reforms led to an increase in Michigan School Aid Fund revenues from $2.6 billion in the year before reform (1994) to $7.0 billion the first year of the reform (1995) and to a drop in property tax for school operations from $6.2 billion to $3.1 billion (including a state levy of $1.1 billion). The net effect of the reforms was to increase state funding of the School Aid Fund from 29.4 percent to 77.3 percent and to reduce local funding from 70.6 percent to 22.7 percent.

Prince (1997) studied the impact of the reforms on horizontal equity three years after they were initiated. Given the focus on horizontal equity, the analysis was limited to foundation allowance revenue (the state's general funding program, which includes revenue generated at both the state and local levels). Categorical state aid was excluded from analysis, as were local "enhancement" millage and federal aid. The lowest foundation allowance for a school district under the first year of reform increased by $1,122 (+30 percent) over the prior year, while the highest allowance was reduced by $427 (–4 percent). The mean district expenditure per pupil increased by only $144 while the median increased by $681. All equity indicators studied (the federal range ratio, coefficient of variation, Gini coefficient, and McLoone index) improved. Because some equalization aspects of the reform were still being phased in at the time of the study, further improvement of equity was expected.

Although it was not an equity study, it is instructive to look at Addonizio's (1997) analysis of what the political reaction to these sweeping equity reforms is likely to be in Michigan. In bringing about a greater degree of equity in the distribution of education funding, the Michigan legislature removed—or seriously constrained—the ability of the local electorate to determine its preferred foundation allowance revenue. Over time, the discrepancies between locally preferred and actual expenditures will grow in many districts of the state. Addonizio sought to develop some understanding of the school spending preferences of school districts in terms of income levels, marginal tax prices, and taste preferences in assessing the long-term political prospects for this reform. He predicts that the greatest dissatisfaction will be among high-income districts, followed by urban districts where large nonresidential assessments could allow for relatively high-cost schools at a relatively low tax levy. This situation suggests the possibility of an urban–suburban coalition forming in the future and urging the state legislature to provide greater flexibility for increasing spending at the margin. At the same time, poor and rural districts and some middle-income districts may wish to spend less on schools to lower taxes and increase after-tax income. Addonizio (1997) concludes,

> States may succeed, at least for a time, in constraining public school expenditures, but cannot limit education spending. In the long run, educational spending will tend to conform to local demand and any state legislation designed to prevent that conformity will likely be amended or circumvented. (p. 38)

The Michigan school finance reforms did not address the issue of paying for facilities. These continued to be fully financed by school districts from property tax revenue with no state assistance. Voter approval rates for borrowing to finance capital improvements are very low in Michigan. It had been hoped that, given the tax leeway provided through the reforms to the general aid program, the approval rate would improve; but this did not happen to any great extent. Sielke (1998) studied the equity of the situation and looked for predictors of a favorable vote. She concluded that because the funding mechanism for capital expenditures is tied only and directly to the property tax, the situation was clearly inequitable. She found only two attributes that were favorable to an affirmative vote on a bond issue: low portions of homestead property in a district tax base and districts already paying debt mills or high amounts of debt mills. Both of these rather curious findings could be explained in terms of

Addonizio's (1997) analysis. Those districts already levying debt mills are likely to be the high-income districts with high cost-preferences for schools. Likewise, those districts with relatively low portions of homestead property are likely to be urban districts, also identified by Addonizio as having high-cost preferences for schools while enjoying relatively low tax rates on residential property (because of the large presence of nonresidential property).

New York

Berne and Stiefel (1984) studied equity in New York State for a fourteen year period beginning in 1965 and ending in 1978. On most criteria for horizontal equity, they found improvements up until about 1969; conditions then worsened for five years and remained level or improved slightly during the remainder of the period. As a result, there was greater inequity in educational opportunities in the latter part of the 1970s than in the 1960s. There were consistently positive correlations between indicators of levels of educational services and equalized property wealth per pupil in all of the fourteen years the study covered.

Berne and Stiefel updated their New York State study in 1990. Despite an increase in expenditures per pupil of 40 percent from 1977 through 1988 in inflation-adjusted dollars, a time-series analysis of expenditure per pupil showed that equity had not improved markedly over the period. In 1991–1992, expenditures per pupil at the 90th percentile of spending ($9,586) were nearly twice the level at the 10th percentile ($5,034). They concluded that New York's public primary and secondary education system suffers from serious input and output inequities.

Berne (1994) reassessed the equity of New York schools in 1994, using additional measures of input and introducing measures of output. Children in districts with high percentages of minority and poor children consistently experienced larger classes, less accessibility to instructional technology, and teachers with fewer qualifications. The analysis clearly established that the input inequities extended to outputs as well. Children in the highest-poverty schools were consistently among the lowest achievers on state examinations, and the differences in average scores between high-poverty and low-poverty schools were substantial.

Duncombe and Yinger (1999, 1997; also Duncombe, Ruggiero, & Yinger, 1996) analyzed the spending of school districts in New York state for relationships with student characteristics that might require more intensive application of school resources. They found that to achieve equity of outcomes, New York City would need to spend nearly 3 times as much per pupil as its affluent suburbs. The ratio between major cities upstate and their suburbs was about 2 to 1. Their study is described more fully in a later section of this chapter.

Reformers in New York State have tried to address these inequities for decades. The state pioneered the foundation program in 1924, and the system has been continually under study since, both internally by specially appointed commissions and externally by consultants. The state's school finance system was unsuccessfully challenged in the state courts twice (*Levittown* v. *Nyquist,* 1982; *Reform Education Financing Inequities Today* v. *Cuomo,* 1991). In 2001 a lower state court ruled the state's school finance scheme unconstitutional using adequacy reasoning (*Campaign for Fiscal Equality* v. *State of New York*). An appellate court reversed this decision in 2002, and the case is currently under review by the state's highest court. Over the years, many of the numerous changes made to the school aid formulas by the state legislature were intended to improve equity.

New York traditionally ranks among the top three states in spending per pupil; yet the distribution of resources remains among the most inequitable in the country, as noted in the study by Parrish, Hikido, and Fowler (1998) that we cited earlier. Parrish et al. also observed that even the lowest-spending districts in New York were spending at a level higher than that

provided for most children in the United States. The inequity in New York is created by the expenditures of districts at the top of the distribution, not at the bottom (Verstegen, 1996; Odden & Busch, 1998); its McLoone index (with no adjustments for pupil needs or costs) is the only equity measure on which it scores in an acceptable range. Some might argue that schools in the state are operating at a defensible level of adequacy relative to schools in most other states, even though the inequity of its resource distribution pattern is not defensible.

We have become accustomed to thinking of poor school districts taxing themselves heavily and rich districts carrying a relatively low tax burden, which appears to be the case for most states. This is not the case in New York, however, where the rich districts have higher (often *much* higher) tax rates than the poor districts. In keeping with Addonizio's (1997) Michigan analysis, the citizens of the wealthy districts in New York have very strong preferences for expensive school programs. New York also further illustrates one of Fastrup's (1997) observations in studying the New England states: that state school fiscal policy is not a function of state action alone, as we too often think. Rather, it is a joint product of the state and the local electorate. The difficulty in finding a satisfying and equitable solution to inequity in resource distribution is greatly compounded in a state like New York, which has a history of strong local control and where wealthy school districts have strong preferences for expensive school programs (and are willing to tax themselves to realize those preferences). Odden and Picus (2000) refer to New York as a prime example of this "new" type of school finance problem. Although not new to New York, it is evolving in other states such as Illinois, Missouri, and Wisconsin.

Texas

Verstegen (1987) analyzed data from the Texas school finance system for the period 1976 through 1986 to determine whether legislative action had improved financial equity in the wake of the Supreme Court decision (*San Antonio Independent School District* v. *Rodriguez*, 1973). She found that all measures studied (coefficient of variation, federal range ratio, restricted range, McLoone index, simple correlation, and elasticity) showed improvement, indicating greater equity over time. The improvement was even greater when the upper 5 percent of students, ranked by revenue per pupil, were excluded from the analysis.

The improvement was not sufficient to satisfy school districts having low property wealth, however, and the Edgewood Independent School District led a new series of legal challenges to the Texas school finance system. Toenjes and Clark (1994) conducted an equity analysis of the probable impact of school finance arrangements enacted by the Texas legislature in 1993 to meet the court's equity concerns coming out of the *Edgewood* (1989, 1991) decisions. The simulations they conducted revealed that the new arrangements would increase the equity of the system substantially as measured by statistics that describe the relationship between wealth and revenue. Because of the phase-in provisions of the legislation, the full effect wasn't realized until 1996–1997.

Reschovsky and Imazeki (2001) estimated the resource level (adequacy) required for each district in the state to reach a desired level of achievement, taking into account student and district characteristics that might affect the cost. They followed an econometric approach to the problem: the statistical estimation of a cost function. The district resource levels produced by the estimated cost function were converted into a cost index for each district. School district output was measured by a composite score on the Texas Assessment of Academic Skills (TAAS) for all students in grades 4 through 8. The researchers generated this composite to reflect gain in achievement, or *value added*. Output also included student performance as measured by the ACT. Other variables included

in the cost function were percent of children eligible for free and reduced lunch, teacher salary index, students with disabilities, students with limited English proficiency, percent of students enrolled in high school, and district enrollment. Two cost functions were estimated; one included an efficiency index. Cost indices ranged from 21 to 400, with 100 representing the state average; the range with an efficiency adjustment was from 52 to 177. Five school districts had cost indices greater than 300. That is, to reach the desired outcome (achievement) level would require 3 times the amount of resources that the average district required. The districts with the highest cost-needs, San Antonio and Edgewood, were both previously involved in litigation against the state.

Intradistrict Equity Studies

Equity returned to the political agenda during the 1990s, but the focus of analyses shifted. Output equity and equal opportunity are the center of attention of several studies examining the equity of the distribution of resources and outcomes to schools and pupils *within* districts, even as research continues at the district, state, and national levels. All analyses have become more complicated, because federal and state governments have increased their use of categorical aids targeted to at-risk students as an instrument of public policy to promote vertical equity. In the past, categorical aids were small enough to be ignored or included with other revenue or expenditures in the evaluation of horizontal equity; such a procedure is no longer appropriate. General education funding continues to be used in the evaluation of horizontal equity.

Berne and Stiefel (1994) set the pattern for the study of equity within districts, just as they had for the analysis of equity within states a decade earlier (Berne & Stiefel, 1984). Their 1994 analysis of equity among schools within New York City was made possible by the publication (for the first time) of detailed budgets for the more than eight hundred elementary and middle/junior high schools operated by the city's thirty-two community school districts. The study explored the usefulness of a variety of strategies, statistics, and measures for conducting this type of analysis. These investigators found that the glaring inequities in vertical equity with respect to poverty that were commonplace at the state level did not exist among schools within New York City. Even though elementary schools budgeted and spent more per pupil from general education funds in lower-poverty than in higher-poverty schools, categorical aids were sufficient to bring expenditures of high-poverty schools above those of low-poverty schools, but not nearly to the level suggested by the cost studies reviewed earlier (Duncombe & Yinger, 1999, 1997; Duncombe, Ruggiero, & Yinger, 1996; Reschovsky & Imazeki, 2001). Middle and junior high schools directed greater amounts of general education funds per pupil to higher-poverty schools. High-poverty schools, regardless of grade level, had greater access than low-poverty schools to most other resources (for example, categorical aid).

Berne and Stiefel's (1994) analysis revealed that an alarmingly low proportion of the general education budget for elementary and middle schools was reaching the schools: $2,550 per pupil, compared to the almost $7,000 total per-pupil budgeted for the district as a whole. Poorer subdistricts received more funds per pupil in nonallocated, district office, and indirect categories, but not usually in allocated and direct categories. They concluded that this finding was consistent with the claims of many school districts serving large numbers of poor children that the nonclassroom management and oversight burdens associated with programs targeted at such children are substantial. They questioned whether this practice is productive and asked whether there might be ways of getting more resources to poor children directly with less being used to meet overhead expenses. An analysis by Speakman et al.

(1996) yielded similar results. Of the $7,918-per-pupil expenditure at the district level, only $2,308 (29 percent) was available for a student with no special education classifications in the classroom. For a student with such classifications $4,843 was available, but about half of this amount was spent outside the classroom.

Berne and Stiefel (1994) also found average teacher salaries in high-poverty subdistricts of New York City to be $4,536 less than in low-poverty subdistricts. This difference resulted from the seniority provisions in the contract with the teachers union. Teachers with greater longevity in the district had first choice in selecting school assignments, a common practice in large urban districts. Students from families with low socioeconomic status were taught by less experienced, less educated, and lower salaried teachers. It should be noted that research to be discussed in Chapter 12 on efficiency suggests that more experienced teachers with higher levels of preparation tend to be more successful than less experienced teachers in working with at-risk students. Berne and Stiefel observed that "This raises the critical policy question of how to better allocate teacher resources within urban districts" (p. 419). These findings also suggested the methodological conclusion that "measures of dollars alone are not sufficient in an equity analysis and that to some degree the education process must be examined" (p. 419).

An intradistrict study of New York City, Chicago, Fort Worth, and Rochester, New York by Stiefel, Rubenstein, and Berne (1998) concluded that spending in schools in these cities is in an acceptable range in terms of horizontal equity. For New York City and Chicago, there was evidence of vertical equity in the distribution of categorical funds among schools, but for general education and total funds, the evidence was mixed for all four districts. For the most part, schools with high proportions of minority students received more total funding than schools with low proportions. In all four cities, average teacher salaries tended to be lower in schools with high proportions of poor students than in schools serving a more affluent clientele. However, the pupil/teacher ratio was more favorable in schools with high proportions of students living in poverty.

In a different study of resource distribution among Chicago schools, Rubenstein (1998) found strong evidence of vertical equity among elementary schools in the distribution of categorical funds. This relationship was largely offset, however, by the distribution of general fund monies, which favored schools serving relatively affluent students. This result was due, again, to the higher salaries paid to teachers within higher-wealth neighborhoods.

Hyary (1994) studied the intradistrict distribution of education resources among 1,246 New York State elementary schools in 300 school districts, excluding New York City. The specific school-level resources that she examined were average annual teacher salaries, percent of first-year teachers, percent of teachers teaching outside their certification area, average number of students per class, number of microcomputers per 100 pupils, and number of library books per pupil. She concluded that there was considerable variation within the 300 districts in patterns of intradistrict resource distribution. Districts with high levels of intradistrict inequality tended to have relatively large enrollments, numbers of schools, and percents of minority and/or poor children. There was no evidence that minority and/or poor children were being denied equal access to resources, however. A deliberate district policy of targeting compensatory resources to minority and/or poor children (i.e., vertical equity) could have caused the intradistrict inequities, but the study design (a horizontal equity format) did not permit the investigator to test for such a possibility.

Hertert (1996) analyzed the degree of disparity in per-pupil expenditures at two levels, district and school, within California. The study focused on unified school districts (having all grades K–12) with at least 2,500 students in average daily attendance (ADA). This population included 66 percent of the state's pupils. From that population, 25 school districts were selected to be studied in detail. These districts contained 1,042 schools and 926,740 students. Federal and state categorical funds were not included in the analysis, and no attempt was made to prorate costs of central administration to schools because the focus of the study was on those fiscal resources distributed to schools on behalf of all children (horizontal equity).

Hertert concluded that judgments on the fairness of the distributions found are a matter of perspective. California has a fairly equitable system of financing schools across districts. As anticipated, the coefficient of variation for districts in the sample (.740) was well within the range of acceptability. In contrast, the same statistic for all schools across districts (.226) was well outside the range of acceptability. Similarly, the average coefficient of variation for schools within districts (.184) was outside the range of acceptability. At the extremes, schools in the highest-spending districts spent about twice as much per pupil ($3,184) as schools in the lowest-spending districts ($1,627). In a few of the districts studied, the variation among schools was substantial and could not be explained by school size or ethnicity. Noting that a great deal of attention has been paid to creating equity across districts over the past several decades, she concluded that these efforts might be more productive in California if attention were focused across schools.

Owens (1994) studied the equity of resource allocation among elementary schools in Dade County, Florida, which is the nation's third-largest school district and contains the city of Miami. The purpose of the study was to determine whether variations in allocations were linked to racial/ethnic composition or household income levels of the students. Expenditures were measured in four ways: instructional expenditures for the basic program including and excluding compensatory programs, using per-pupil units without weights and weighted to reflect aggregate student need. Instructional expenditures were composed primarily of teachers' salaries and benefits but also included purchased services and classroom materials.

Owens found that instructional expenditures in some elementary schools within Dade County were much higher than in others. In contrast to the New York City and California studies, he found that these differences were related to racial/ethnic and family income factors. High percentages of African American and low-income students and large schools had lower instructional expenditures per pupil than did schools without those characteristics for all methods of computing expenditures. As in the Chicago and New York City school-level studies, Owens attributed this inequity largely to the practice of permitting senior teachers to control where they will teach; less experienced teachers and teachers with less education were more likely to be found in traditionally minority and high-poverty schools.

Raudenbush, Fotiu, and Cheong (1998) took quite a different approach in studying the equity of the distribution of instructional resources to students of varying ethnic and socioeconomic groups. They used data gathered through the 1992 Trial State Assessment in Mathematics of the National Assessment of Educational Progress (NAEP) from nearly 100,000 eighth-graders attending 3,537 schools in 41 states. Acknowledging the well-established differences in mathematical achievement according to ethnic membership, they sought to discover whether there were corresponding differences in the availability of instructional resources for students according to their ethnicity and socioeconomic status as measured by parents' education. The four resources studied were school disciplinary climate, access to high school algebra, teacher with a major in mathematics, and an instructional emphasis on reasoning. In sum, they found evidence of ethnic and social inequity in access to the four resources across ethnic groups and education levels of parents. The authors concluded that

just as high parental education predicts favorable outcomes, it also predicts access to schools with favorable climates, schools [middle and jr. high] that offer algebra, teachers with training in mathematics, and classrooms that emphasize reasoning. Similarly, ethnic groups disadvantaged in outcomes (African Americans, Hispanic Americans, and Native Americans) also encounter less access to these resources for learning. (p. 261)

Some degree of inequity was found in all states, but the magnitude of inequality varied markedly. States that exhibited a high degree of social inequity also tended to exhibit a high degree of ethnic inequity. The authors also pointed out, as have a number of fiscally based studies, that "Equality is not a good thing if environments are equally bad" (p. 263).

In still another nontraditional approach to looking at the equity of distribution patterns of resources, Wenglinsky (1998) found that instructional and capital expenditures were not related to mean achievement in mathematics but that they were related to *differences* in achievement among socioeconomic groups. Lower spending levels were associated with greater achievement gaps within schools among students of different socioeconomic levels. The study was done using a nationally representative database of twelfth-graders. Only one-fifth of the variation in mathematics achievement for the entire sample was explained by between-school differences, the remainder being attributed to differences among students irrespective of their schools. Higher levels of instructional and capital expenditures were strongly associated with reduced relationships between social background and achievement. "When schools have sufficient funds, they can educate all children based on their needs to help them all reach a common yardstick of proficiency. When funds become scarce, however, schools are not able to intervene as strongly; it becomes easier for the less affluent, less prepared students to 'fall between the cracks' while the more affluent, more prepared students continue to excel" (p. 270). Instructional and capital expenditures can be targeted to students of particular needs. For example, if a choice has to be made, instructional funds could be used for an advanced placement program to help more gifted students or for a remedial program for those of low achievement. Capital funds could build a state-of-the-art biology lab for honor students or a computer lab designed to support multimedia literacy programs.

Doing equity studies at the school level allows researchers to move beyond district averages and brings the analysis closer to the classroom and student levels where learning and teaching actually take place. Analyses at the school level also make it possible to take into account geographic location and characteristics of students in examining the distribution of resources. The major disadvantage is the lack of financial data at the school level, but this situation is improving as more districts budget and orient their accounting practices to schools.

Summary

Horizontal equity of resource input is less among school districts nationally than it is among individual states. Horizontal equity is usually less within states than within districts. Within-district studies have shown a pattern of inequity in the distribution of general funds in favor of the more affluent. This is compensated for in part by the inequity in the distribution of categorical aids in favor of the poor, but no satisfaction should be taken when categorical and general funds combined are distributed equitably among schools. This, in itself, is a violation of the intent of most categorical programs, especially at the federal level, which contain maintenance-of-effort provisions; in other words, categorical funding is to be *in addition to* equitably distributed general funds.

The most informative studies of the past decade are the cost studies that have attempted to put a price on the effort to bring low-performance children up to an acceptably high level. They have shown how formidable the task is in monetary terms and how inadequate are *equitably* distributed funds to inner-city schools. The concept of horizontal equity has become obsolete as our public attention has shifted to obtaining adequacy through vertical equity. Equity studies of the future must take into account variations among children in need for educational resources as well as variation in prices among regions. Greater emphasis should be placed on equity analyses at the school, classroom, and even student levels, because these levels are closest to where teaching and learning take place.

In the next section, we examine the transition from the old studies of horizontal equity to the new studies of vertical equity in search of its ideal, adequacy.

DEFINING AND MEASURING ADEQUACY

Setting the national educational goal at educating *all* children to high standards has transformed the orientation of school finance policy. The challenge directly links finance to the purposes of education (Ladd & Hansen, 1999). Thus, although equity remains a primary goal of public policy, the object of analyzing equity has shifted from inputs to schooling outputs. Because public policy cannot affect these outputs directly, but only indirectly through the amount of resources provided and the practices of schools and related institutions, the *adequacy* of equitably distributed inputs has moved to the forefront of policy debates under the assumption that there are positive relationships between inputs and outputs.

Although the assumption makes intuitive sense, the empirical evidence is weak, and this makes the problem of achieving equity of outputs exceedingly difficult. The evidence of positive relationships is growing, but there is stronger evidence that an equal application of resources under similar conditions yields widely disparate results. Some schools are more adept (dare we say more efficient?) than others in transforming applied resources into desired educational objectives. Efficiency in the use of resources is the focus of Chapter 12.

In the absence of full understanding of these relationships, the best that we can do at the moment from a policy standpoint is to identify resource levels that *can,* with a reasonable degree of probability, produce the results we want to achieve with children of differing characteristics. While providing resources at such levels of *sufficiency,* we must continue to study the mechanisms by which those resources are transformed into desirable changes in student behavior and accomplishments so that children in all schools can be successful.

Because of our meager understanding of the relationships between resource inputs and educational outputs and outcomes, it is important that adequacy be defined in the broadest of terms, such as operational expenditures per pupil, rather than by specific prescriptions, such as class size or particular curricula, for example, which are sometimes called "opportunity-to-learn standards" (Clune, 1995; Guthrie & Rothstein, 2001). At some time in the future, our understanding may justify specific standards; nevertheless, we will always need to guard against bureaucratic inclinations toward policies of "one size fits all."

Early Foundation-Level Studies

The concept of *adequacy* is implicit in the design of the foundation program that is currently used, in one form or another, by a large majority of states to distribute financial assistance to school districts. In their original statement, George Strayer and Robert Haig (1924) described the foundation level as one sufficient to enable schools to "furnish the children in every locality within the state with equal educational opportunities up to some prescribed minimum" (p. 173). Paul Mort, perhaps the most successful purveyor of the foundation concept among the states, described what needed to be taken into account in defining a foundation level:

> Every program must be assessed in terms of how far it gets us along the road to the adequate equalization of a defensible educational opportunity, whatever other tests are pertinent. The essential problem of equalization becomes then the problem of making arrangements to provide the kind of education men of goodwill can honestly support as the minimum necessary for the achievement of our national ends—our welfare as a people and our fullest life as persons. It requires a more realistic assessment of what schools are doing in the individual states and in the nation as a whole. It requires a comparison of the poorest with the best. It requires judgments on the part of individuals and groups interested in the problem and their endorsement of what they consider to be a defensible stand to be taken by agencies to which the responsibility for determination of policy has been delegated. (Mort & Reusser, 1951, p. 385)

Mort pointed out that what Strayer and Haig had given us was the *concept* of a minimum program to be used as a benchmark but that they provided no guidance about what the height of the benchmark should be. Writing in 1957, Mort lamented that in the thirty-three years since Strayer and Haig made their proposal,

> surprising little attention has been given to what would seem to be the most critical aspect of their proposal 'that there be an adequate program offered everywhere, the expense of which would be considered a prior claim on the State's economic resources.' . . . The nut of the matter seems to be [that] the mechanism of the equalization formula, adaptable as it is to the distribution of aid for general assistance for all districts, has got far too much credit for achieving the central purpose for which it was originally designed—the assurance of an adequate foundation program. (Mort, 1957, p. 41)

Rather, from the beginning, the foundation level was defined using political and economic rather than pedagogical criteria. This practice continues today. Without analysis, state average expenditure per pupil quickly became the surrogate for an adequate minimum program, although even that goal was never reached in practice. Indeed, the foundation level for the first application of the Strayer and Haig Foundation Program in New York State in 1925 was set at about two-thirds of the state average expenditure. A national analysis by the American Council on Education (1933) found state foundation levels ranging from 40% to 86% of a "defensible" level, defined as average practice of districts of average wealth for each state.

Although they were not official state studies, during the 1930s through the 1950s a number of attempts were made by academics and educational interest groups to define an adequate minimum program. Four general approaches were taken: (1) estimations of the fiscal implications of state mandatory legislation and education department regulations; (2) average expenditure of satisfactorily organized school districts of average wealth; (3) level of expenditure required to meet a professionally defined basic quality program; and (4) more broadly, the level of expenditure that reasonably ensured an educational program acceptable in terms of socially and individually defined needs (Mort & Reusser, 1951). It should be noted that these early studies were conducted under the assumption that money does matter in the provision of educational opportunities. With the publication of the highly influential study authorized by Congress, *Equality of Educational Opportunity* (Coleman et al., 1966), and its finding that schools were relatively ineffective in improving educational opportunities for disadvantaged children, efforts to define adequacy ceased. Now, in view of new evidence that money *can* matter and given the festering of longstanding inequities in the distribution of educational inputs and outputs (to say nothing of recent court interventions), defining adequacy has become imperative in order to ensure adequate levels of resources for all children.

Contemporary Studies

The data resources for analyses are much richer now than they were in the 1930s, 1940s, and 1950s, and the available hardware and software are infinitely more sophisticated, but the nature of the problem has changed little, and the techniques for finding solutions are similar. Some of the approaches used by contemporary analysts are (1) statistical analysis of statewide databases that include schooling input measures, student achievement, and other measures of output, as well as demographic information; (2) analyzing costs of districts that seem to be achieving adequate outcomes; and (3) costing out whole-school reform designs and other designs originating from professional judgment.

Econometric Approaches

In essence, *adequacy* is the cost of an instructional program that produces the range of results desired. When the adequacy criterion is met, costs are likely to vary among districts according to the characteristics of students served and according to the characteristics of the districts themselves, but the results should be the same regardless of these considerations. The costs of adequacy under varying circumstances (vertical equity) can be estimated statistically when a sufficiently large database is available by estimating cost functions via a variation of multiple regression such as two-stage least-squares regression. A measure of the instructional cost per unit (pupil or classroom) serves as the dependent variable, and the independent variables are measures of pupil performance, pupil characteristics, and district characteristics. Built on the set of basic relationships among variables in the sample, this treatment produces a regression equation that yields a unique cost for each district for producing the desired level of achievement, given the district's characteristics and those of its pupils. This approach has the advantage that it bypasses the necessity to specify an instructional delivery system and eliminates the need to determine costs of instructional components.

Duncombe and Yinger (1999, 1997; also Duncombe, Ruggiero, & Yinger, 1996), whose study was cited in an earlier section, used a two-stage least-squares approach to estimate a cost function as described above, employing a sample of 631 school districts in New York State. These costs were then converted into cost indices showing the relative costs of providing comparable instruction among classifications of school districts. The dependent variable was a measure of per-pupil operating expenditures. The exogenous independent variables (variables over which the district has no policy control) were enrollment, poverty indicators, percent of students with severe handicaps, and percent of students with limited English proficiency. The endogenous independent variables (variables over which the district has some policy control) were measures of pupil achievement, teacher salaries, percent of nondropouts, and percent of graduates receiving a state diploma (requires passing a number of rigorous criterion-referenced subject matter examinations) rather than diplomas granted by school districts, which have less challenging requirements. Duncombe and Yinger also included among their endogenous variables a measure of school district efficiency derived from a process known as data envelopment analysis (DEA), that is described more fully in Chapter 12. With this *best practice* technique, a district is considered inefficient to the degree that it spends more than other districts realizing the same level of performance and with similar characteristics.

Duncombe and Yinger (1999, 1997) found great variation among types of districts in the cost of producing comparable student achievement. With 100 serving as average cost for New York State school districts obtaining average achievement, they found that bringing the achievement levels of New York City students to the state average would require resources costing nearly 4 times as much as the state average (an index of 396). The cost index for New York City suburbs was 108; for large cities upstate, 190; for rural areas, 99; for upstate small cities, 109; and for upstate suburbs, 91.

Reschovsky and Imazeki (2001), whose work we also discussed in a previous section, produced similar results in a comparative study of Texas and Wisconsin. They likewise used statistical estimation of a cost function and corrected for differences in district efficiency via data envelopment analysis (DEA). With the top 10 percent and the bottom 10 percent of districts omitted, the range in cost indices for Texas districts, with no adjustment made for differences in efficiency, was from 51 (i.e., 51 percent of the state average cost) to 168. The same range for Wisconsin was from 74 to 149. When adjustments were made for efficiency of school districts, the ranges dropped to 78–126 in Texas and to 89–117 in Wisconsin. The authors acknowledge the imprecision of their findings and "suspect that the 'true' costs lie between the levels indicated by the cost indices calculated with and without our efficiency adjustment" (p. 390). The high-cost districts included the large cities in both states. The implication is that substantial infusions of new monies would be necessary to raise the performance levels of children in those districts to levels defined as adequate.

> The pattern of aid indicated by our simulations should be interpreted as long-run targets for the distribution of state grants. Even if it were politically possible to implement large grant increases to, for example, urban school districts, it is unlikely that sudden infusions of additional resources would be used effectively to increase student performance. Providing new money to schools and school districts with above-average costs is likely to be most effective in increasing student performance if it is phased in over a period of years. (p. 396)

Empirical Approaches

In an empirical approach, those districts that have successfully achieved a defined level of acceptable student performance are identified and studied as to pedagogy and resource application under the assumption that such practice *can* yield the results desired.

In essence, this is the implicit theory supporting the New Jersey Supreme Court's decision in *Abbott v. Burke* (1997). In a series of eleven decisions resulting from litigation beginning in 1970 (described more fully in Chapter 10), the courts, responding to continuing pressure by tenacious plaintiffs and their attorneys, sought a practical definition of the state constitution's provision that the legislature shall provide for a "thorough and efficient" system of free and public schools. In responding to these court decisions, the legislature and the governor shaped legislation addressing the inequities in funding between affluent suburban districts and twenty-eight poor urban communities (known as the Abbott districts) under the guidance of the court decisions. Early decisions sought equity of inputs, but later decisions sought a level of inputs that would be adequate to enable the poor districts to narrow the achievement gap with the wealthy districts. This evolution signifies a shift in concern from horizontal to vertical equity.

In a 1990 decision, the court acknowledged that New Jersey had established general standards that could be used to test for conformity with the state constitution's requirement of a thorough and efficient system. However, the court found that these standards had not been applied in practice (Goertz & Edwards, 1999). Because of the absence of clear measures of substantive educational opportunity, the court adopted a default remedy: practices in the state's wealthiest districts. "Average spending on the regular education program in the state's 108 wealthiest suburban districts thus became the presumptive standard of thorough and efficient for the state's 28 poorest urban communities" (Goertz & Edwards, 1999, p. 16). This position was affirmed in the court's 1997 decision, and it ordered parity in regular education funding between the poorest and wealthiest districts.

Attention was then directed to the scope and cost of supplemental programs for the poorest districts. These were defined in the 1998 decision, thereby confirming the shift in the court's purview from horizontal equity to vertical equity—and adequacy.

> Spending on regular education programs in the state's 28 poorest urban districts, which educate 22 percent of the state's students and about 75 percent of its students of color, is on par with the average expenditures of the state's wealthiest communities. In addition, students in poor urban communities are guaranteed access to pre-school programs, health and social services, and better educational facilities. All urban elementary schools must undertake some form of "whole school reform" as a way of delivering more effective educational services. (Goertz & Edwards, 1999, pp. 5–6)

That is the practical definition of adequacy as worked out by the powers that be in New Jersey.

A different approach to defining adequacy was taken by the Ohio Department of Education in what turned out to be a two-stage process. Unlike New Jersey, where adequacy was defined on the basis of the experience of high-wealth and high-spending districts, Ohio followed a procedure similar to that followed in the early studies during the 1930s, 1940s, and 1950s. In the initial stage, a representative pool of Ohio school districts included all school districts except those that were at the extremes (high and low) in property wealth and spending per pupil (Augenblick, Alexander, and Guthrie, 1995).

The districts remaining in the pool were ranked by a composite measure of student performance in reading, mathematics, writing, and science. A minimum level of adequacy at the district level was defined as average student performance at the 70th percentile or higher on most measures. Instructional arrangements in the districts that met the adequacy criteria were then examined in terms of school size, class size, pupil/professional ratio, and course offerings. The average practice of these schools was treated as a model of exemplary practice for districts whose students were not achieving at a similar level of performance. An adequate program cost could also be developed by totaling the costs of the components of the model.

Upon review, the 1995 study was criticized for the criterion of adequacy used and for developing a detailed model of implied exemplary practice. In the revised study (Augenblick, 1997), a criterion-referenced measure of percent of students in a district meeting or exceeding minimum competency levels replaced the norm-referenced outcome measure of the original study. The definition of an exemplary instructional model was criticized as potentially restricting school district discretion and initiative. Prevailing sentiment was that although the approach used may be appropriate for state purposes in identifying an appropriate level of adequacy for educational funding, districts should feel free to organize resources available to them as they deem appropriate, given the great variety in local circumstances. The revised report eliminated detailed reference to resource inputs, disclosing only the average per-pupil expenditure level that was associated with the performance criteria.

From 607 Ohio school districts, the revised study identified 102 for the reference pool that met the performance requirements and that were not outliers with respect to property wealth and per-pupil spending. On the basis of 1996 spending levels in Ohio, Augenblick (1997) used data from this pool to compute a weighted per-pupil revenue amount, $3,930, that became the definition of adequacy. Additional resources would be added to this amount for students with special needs and other factors.

Using Whole-School Reform Models and Professional Expertise

A number of organizational strategies intended to make schools more effective have been developed over the past two decades. None of the models has been firmly established by research as being better than the rest, but several have been carefully evaluated with promising results. It could be argued that at least those that have a documented record of success can serve as models of adequacy. Costing out the implementation of such models (King, 1994) would provide a financial measure of adequacy. Odden and Picus (2000) have shown that by reallocating resources already committed, "the average elementary, middle and high school in America has sufficient resources to finance all these school designs, even after providing planning and preparation time" (p. 336). In New Jersey, although the court used the empirical approach to establish a level of adequacy for nonclassified students, it took the whole-school reform model approach in establishing an adequacy level for children at risk. Indeed, with the resources provided to the Abbott schools, the most expensive of the whole-school reform models ("Success for All" and "Roots and Wings") could be implemented with a substantial amount of discretionary money remaining (Odden & Picus, 2000, p. 350).

The whole-school reform models have been designed by practicing educators, or at least in consultation with them, and in tune with national research. It could well be, however, that in defining adequacy, a state might find that none of the models fits its peculiar circumstances precisely. In such cases, it would be advisable for the state to appoint its own panel of experts and consultants to custom-make an adequate model tailored to the state's specific conditions. In building the model, the panel can draw from the knowledge base of existing research, from the experiences of schools around the country in implementing reform models, and from the wisdom and experience of the state's own practitioners. Once an eclectic model is formulated, its components can be costed out and totaled for a measure of financial adequacy. Such a procedure was followed by Guthrie et al. (1997; summarized in

Guthrie & Rothstein, 1999) for the state of Wyoming.

Measuring Adequacy

Although considerable attention has been given in recent years to defining adequacy, little if any attention has been devoted to measuring the distribution of adequacy among school districts, as has been done for other measures of equity. From a legal standpoint, if adequacy were officially defined, it would be untenable to fund districts at less than that level. In the absence of an official definition of adequacy, policy analysts are likely to make "what if" analyses defined at various levels of adequacy. Indeed, a state developing an adequacy policy might wish to undertake such analyses.

So far as we know, the only adequacy measure developed to date is the Odden–Picus Adequacy Index (OPAI) (Odden & Picus, 2000). The procedure is similar to calculating the McLoone index, except that the defined adequacy level is used instead of the median expenditure. The OPAI is calculated as follows:

1. Specify an "adequate" spending level.
2. Identify the percent of students in districts of a state that are spending above this level.
3. Calculate a McLoone-type ratio, substituting the defined adequacy spending level for the median per-pupil expenditure (see the formula presented earlier in this chapter).
4. Multiply the ratio obtained in step 3 by the percent of students in districts spending less than the adequacy level.
5. Add steps 2 and 4 to obtain the OPAI, perfect adequacy being 1.0.

Vertical equity can be taken into account by weighting student units according to educational need or by adjusting expenditures using a cost function index. The total amount of additional money needed by districts in the state that are spending below the adequacy level to bring them up to that level can be calculated by (1) multiplying the difference between the OPAI and 1.0 by the adequacy level, and (2) multiplying that product by the number of students in districts spending less than the adequacy level.

Using the data for hypothetical states A and B reported in Table 11.3, and assuming an adequacy level of $5,700, we can compute the OPAI for each state. In state A, districts 14–20 are spending at or above the adequacy level. These seven districts represent 35 percent of the students in the state. For state B, only districts 18, 19, and 20 are spending above the adequacy level. These three districts include 15 percent of the students in the state. Substituting the adequacy level for the median expenditure level, the McLoone-type calculations produce a ratio of 0.816 for state A and 0.824 for state B. Multiplying these ratios by the percent of students in districts spending below the adequacy level (65 percent and 85 percent, respectively) yields ratios of 0.530 for state A and 0.700 for state B. Adding to these ratios the ratio of students in districts spending at or above the adequacy level (0.350 for state A and 0.150 for state B) produces an OPAI for state A of 0.880 and for state B of 0.850. Because the OPAI for state A is closer to a ratio of 1.000, this state has achieved a higher degree of adequacy than has state B, even though state A was found to be less equitable by most other measures.

SUMMARY

Equality was one of the fundamental principles on which Horace Mann's Common School was built. This concept was a guiding light in the spread of public schooling during the nineteenth century. Early in the twentieth century, it was recognized that equal mediocrity was inadequate for providing the results the nation desired from its public schools (though these results were not clearly defined). Equity had to be provided at a level of resource allocation sufficient to enable public schools to produce the results the public expected of them. The vehicle for doing this was the foundation program, the instrument still used in the vast majority of states for distributing state general aid to school districts. In theory, the foundation level was to be that "adequate minimum amount" capable of supporting an educational program people of goodwill could justify in good conscience for all children. The reality was that agreeing on a specific set of outcomes and identifying the elements of programs proved to be exceedingly difficult. Political expediency stepped in, and the foundation level was (and still is) set according to political and economic parameters. Horizontal equity has improved, but not to a level where all children can reach national, state, and local goals.

During the last two decades of the twentieth century, a distinction was drawn between horizontal equity and vertical equity, but only during the last decade of that century was any serious attempt made to define the level of resources required to provide vertical equity. The results of these studies suggested that massive amounts of new money would be needed, especially in our large urban school districts. At the same time, evidence mounted that monies entrusted to public schools were not being used efficiently. This led some analysts and policy makers to wonder whether the vertical-equity studies didn't overstate the magnitude of the resource shortage, because their treatment of the efficiency issue were crude, if they considered it at all. There was (and is) genuine concern that the failing public schools might be incapable of converting massive influxes of new resources into desired outcomes and thus closing the achievement gaps among ethnic groups and among children of different socioeconomic origins. Not all public schools are failing, however; indeed, most are not. The level of support of schools that are succeeding is not too different from the level of support for those that are failing. In fact, many of the failing schools have access to more resources.

It's clearly a matter of vertical equity. There is general agreement that schools working pri-

marily with poor and non-English-speaking children have a more difficult task than schools working with middle-class children whose native tongue is English. There is also general agreement, as shown by the billions of dollars allocated annually to disadvantaged children through categorical aids, that closing achievement gaps will cost more than educating advantaged children. But how much more money is required? Given the current organization of urban schools and school districts, can society entrust to them significant new infusions of resources in confidence that these resources will be used effectively and efficiently to produce the results desired?

Adequacy is the ultimate definition of vertical equity. In defining adequacy, however, we must be careful not to reward inefficiency. In the next chapter, we examine the principle of efficiency as it is related to the operation of public schools. There can be no equity in education where even some schools function ineffectively and inefficiently.

ACTIVITIES

1. Using data from a state or region (or the hypothetical state database at this book's web page), calculate several of the equity and adequacy measures described in this chapter. Which are the most relevant measures for evaluating school finance policy in that state or region? What are the implications for policy initiatives?

2. Selecting the equity measure that most closely reflects the policy objectives of the state you studied in Activity 1, calculate the measure for each year over a period of a decade or more. Examine the trends in relation to changes in state policy. Have the policies been effective? What changes in state policy, if any, would you propose to improve school finance equity and/or adequacy?

3. Analyze distributions of physical resources among schools *within* a given school dis-

trict, such as class size and the per-pupil numbers of teachers and other professional and support staff, supplies, books, and computers. Discuss your findings with a central office administrator to inquire about the rationale for differences, if any, in resource allocations among buildings. What conclusions and recommendations do you draw from this analysis?

4. Study a whole-school reform model for possible adoption by your school. What new resources, including personnel, would be needed? Can the new resource needs be met by reallocating existing resources? What is your strategy for handling discrepancies between available resources and needed resources?

COMPUTER SIMULATIONS: MEASURES OF EQUITY

Computer simulations related to the content of this chapter are available on the Allyn & Bacon website **<http://www.ablongman.com/edleadership.com**. They focus on calculating the federal range ratio, calculating the coefficient of variation and the McLoone index, estimating the Lorenz curve and the Gini coefficient, and estimating the correlation coefficient and scattergram. Objectives for the exercise are

- To provide experience in computing various measures of equity.
- To compare equity measures for the hypothetical state with measures for actual states as presented in the chapter.

REFERENCES

Abbott v. *Burke*, 693 A.2d 417 (N. J. 1997), 575 A.2d 359 (N.J. 1990), 710 A.2d 450 (N.J. 1998).

Addonizio, M. F. (1997). Equality or choice? School finance reform and the income–expenditure relationship. *Journal of Education Finance, 23,* 22–42.

Adler, L., & Gardner, S. (1994). *The politics of linking schools and social services.* Washington, DC: Falmer.

Alexander, K. (1982). Concepts of equity. In W. W. McMahon & T. G. Geske (Eds.), *Financing education: Overcoming inefficiency and inequity* (pp. 193–214). Urbana: University of Illinois Press.

Alexander, N. A. (1997). The growth of education revenues from 1982–83 to 1991–92: What accounts for differences among states? *Journal of Education Finance, 22,* 435–463.

American Council on Education. (1933). *Report of the National Survey of School Finance: State support for public education.* Washington, DC: Author.

Augenblick, J. (1997). *Recommendations for a base figure and pupil-weighted adjustments to the base figure for use in a new school finance system in Ohio.* Columbus, OH: School Funding Task Force, Ohio Department of Education.

Augenblick, J., Alexander, K., & Guthrie, J. W. (1995). *Report of the panel of experts: Proposals for the elimination of wealth-based disparities in education.* Columbus: Ohio State Education Department.

Barro, S. M. (1987). *School finance equity: Research in the 1980s and the current state of the art.* Washington, DC: Decision Resources Corporation.

Berne, R. (1994). Educational input and outcome inequities in New York State. In R. Berne & L. O. Picus (Eds.), *Outcome equity in education* (pp. 1–23). Thousand Oaks, CA: Corwin.

Berne, R., & Stiefel, L. (1984). *The measurement of equity in school finance: Conceptual, methodological, and empirical dimensions.* Baltimore, MD: The Johns Hopkins University Press.

Berne, R., & Stiefel, L. (1992). Equity standards for state school finance programs: Philosophies and standards relevant to Section 5(d)(2) of the Federal Impact Aid Program. *Journal of Education Finance, 18,* 89–112.

Berne, R,. & Stiefel, L. (1994). Measuring equity at the school level: The finance perspective. *Educational Evaluation and Policy Analysis, 16,* 405–421.

Campaign for Fiscal Equity v. *State of New York.* 719 N.Y.S. 2d 475 (N.Y. Sup. Ct. 2001).

Chambers, J., & Fowler, Jr., W. (1995). *Public school teacher cost differences across the United States,* Analysis/Methodology Report No. 95-758. Washington, DC: U.S. Department of Education, National Center for Education Statistics.

Charnes, A., Cooper, W. W., & Rhodes, E. (1978). Measuring the efficiency of decision making units. *European Journal of Operational Research, 2,* 429–444.

Clune, W. H., (1994). The shift from equity to adequacy in school finance. *Educational Policy, 8,* 376–394.

Clune, W. H. (1995). Accelerated education as a remedy for high-poverty schools. *University of Michigan Journal of Law Reform, 28,* 655–680.

Coleman, J. S., Campbell, E. Q., Hobson, C. J., McPartland, J., Mood, A. M., Weinfeld, F. D., & York, R. L. (1966). *Equality of educational opportunity.* Washington, DC: U.S. Office of Education.

Dryfoos, J. G. (1994). *Full service schools: A revolution in health and social services for children, youth and families.* San Francisco: Jossey-Bass.

Duncombe, W., Ruggerio, J., & Yinger, J. (1996). Alternative approaches to measuring the cost of education. In H. F. Ladd, Ed., *Holding schools accountable: Performance-based reform in education.* Washington, DC: The Brookings Institution.

Duncombe, W. D., & Yinger, J. M. (1999). Performance standards and educational cost indexes: You can't have one without the other. In H. F. Ladd, R. Chalk, & J. S. Hansen (Eds.), *Equity and adequacy in education finance: Issues and perspectives* (pp. 260–297). Washington, DC: National Academy Press.

Duncombe, W. D., & Yinger, J. M. (1997). Why is it so hard to help central city schools? *Journal of Policy Analysis and Management, 16, 1,* 85–113.

Edgewood Independent School District v. *Kirby,* 777 S.W. 2d 391 (1989), 804 S.W. 2d 491 (Tex. 1991).

Fastrup, J. C. (1997). Taxpayer and pupil equity: Linking policy tools with policy goals. *Journal of Education Finance, 23,* 69–100.

Fowler, Jr., W. J., & Monk, D. H. (2001). A primer for making cost adjustments in education: An overview. In W. J. Fowler, Jr. (Ed.), *Selected papers in school finance, 2000–01* (NCES 2001-378). Washington, DC: National Center for Education Statistics.

Garms, W. I. (1979). Measuring the equity of school finance systems. *Journal of Education Finance, 4,* 415–435.

Goertz, M., & Edwards, M. (1999). The search for excellence for all: The courts and New Jersey school finance reform. *Journal of Education Finance, 25,* 5–31.

Guthrie, J. W., Hayward, G. C., Smith, J. R., Rothstein, R., Bennett, R. W., Koppich, J. E., Bowman, E., DeLapp, L., Brandes, B., & Clark, S. (1997). *A proposed cost-based block grant model for Wyoming school finance.* Sacramento, CA: Management Analyst & Planning Associates.

Guthrie, J. W., & Rothstein, R. (1999). Enabling "adequacy" to achieve reality: Translating adequacy into state school finance distribution arrangements. In H. F. Ladd, R. Chalk, & J. S. Hansen (Eds.). *Equity and adequacy in education finance: Issues and perspectives* (pp. 209–259). Washington, DC: National Academy Press.

Guthrie, J. W., & Rothstein, R. (2001). A new millennium and a likely new era of education finance. In S. Chaikind & W. J. Fowler, Jr. (Eds.). *Education finance in the new millennium* (pp. 99–119), Larchmont, NY: Eye on Education.

Harrison, F. W., & McLoone, E. P. (1960). *Profiles in school support 1959–60.* Washington, DC: U.S. Department of Health, Education and Welfare [Misc. 32].

Hertert, L. (1996). Does equal funding for districts mean equal funding for classroom students? Evidence from California. In L. O. Picus & J. L. Wattenbarger (Eds.). *Where does the money go? Resource allocation in elementary and secondary schools* (pp. 71–84). Thousand Oaks, CA: Corwin.

Hirth, M. A. (1994). A multi-state analysis of school finance issues and equity trends in Indiana, Illinois, and Michigan, 1982–1992: The implications for 21st century school finance policies. *Journal of Education Finance, 20,* 163–190.

Howe II, H. (1993). Thinking about kids and education. *Phi Delta Kappan, 75,* 226–228.

Hussar, W., & Sonnenberg, W. (2000). *Trends in disparities in school district level expenditures per pupil,* NCES 2000-020. Washington, DC: U.S. Department of Education, National Center for Education Statistics.

Hyary, A. (1994). *Intra-district distribution of educational resources in New York State elementary schools.* Paper delivered at the American Education Finance Association Annual Meeting, Nashville, TN.

Kearney, C. P., & Anderson, D. M. (1992). Equity measurement in school finance. In K. C. Westbrook (Ed.), *State of the states '92: Bridging troubled finance waters.* Proceedings of the Fiscal Issues, Policy, and Education Finance Special Interest Group. Annual Meeting of the American Educational Research Association, San Francisco, CA.

Kearney, C. P., & Chen, L. (1989). Measuring equity in Michigan school finance: A further look. *Journal of Education Finance, 14,* 319–367.

King, J. A. (1994). Meeting the educational needs of at-risk students: A cost analysis of three models. *Educational Evaluation and Policy Analysis, 16*, 1–19.

Kirst, M. W. (1994). Equity for children: Linking education and children's services. *Educational Policy, 8*, 583–590.

Koski, W. S., & Levin, H. M. (2000). Twenty-five years after *Rodriguez*: What have we learned? *Teachers College Record, 102*, 480–513.

Ladd, H. F., & Hansen, J. S. (Eds.). (1999). *Making money matter: Financing America's schools*. Washington, DC: National Academy Press.

Levittown Union Free School District v. *Nyquist*, 453 N.Y.S. 2d 643 (1982).

McMahon, W. W., & Chang, S. (1990). *Geographical cost of living differences: Interstate and intrastate, update 1991*. MacArthur/Spencer Series Number 20. Normal, IL: Center for the Study of Education Finance, Illinois State University.

Mirel, J., & Angus, D. (1994). High standards for all? The struggle for equality in the American high school curriculum, 1890–1990. *American Educator, 18*, No. 2, 4–9:40–42.

Morris, W. (Ed.). (1969). *The American heritage dictionary of the English language*. Boston, MA: Houghton Mifflin.

Morrison, H. C. (1943). *American schools: A critical study of our school system*. Chicago: University of Chicago Press.

Mort, P. R. (1957). *The foundation program in state educational policy*. Albany, NY: New York State Education Department.

Mort, P. R., & Reusser, W. C. (1951). *Public school finance: Its background, structure, and operation*. New York: McGraw-Hill.

Murray, S. E., Evans, W. N., & Schwab, R. M. (1998). Education-finance reform and the distribution of education resources. *The American Economic Review, 88*, 789–812.

National Center for Education Statistics (various years). *Digest of education statistics*. Washington, DC: U.S. Department of Education.

National Commission on Excellence in Education. *A nation at risk: The imperative for educational reform*. Washington, DC: U.S. Government Printing Office.

Odden, A., & Busch, C. (1998). *Financing schools for high performance: Strategies for improving the use of educational resources*. San Francisco: Jossey-Bass.

Odden, A. R., & Picus, L. O. (2000). *School finance: A policy perspective* (2nd ed.). New York: McGraw-Hill.

Owens, Jr., J. T. (1994). *Intradistrict resource allocation in Dade County, Florida: An analysis of equality of educational opportunity*. Paper delivered at the American Education Finance Association Annual Meeting, Nashville, TN.

Parrish, T. B., Hikido, C. S., & Fowler, Jr., W. J. (1998). *Inequalities in public school district revenues*. Washington, DC: U.S. Department of Education, National Center for Education Statistics.

Parrish, T. B., Matsumoto, C. S., & Fowler, Jr., W. J. (1995). *Disparities in public school district spending 1989–90: A multivariate, student-weighted analysis, adjusted for differences in geographic cost of living and student need*. Washington, DC: National Center for Education Statistics.

Prince, H.(1997). Michigan's school finance reform: Initial pupil-equity results. *Journal of Education Finance, 22*, 394–409.

Raudenbush, S. W., Fotiu, R. P., & Cheong, Y. F. (1998). Inequality of access to educational resources: A national report card for eighth-grade math. *Educational Evaluation and Policy Analysis, 20*, 253–267.

Reform Education Financing Inequities Today v. *Cuomo*, 578 N.Y.S. 2d 969 (Superior Court for Nassau County, 1991).

Reschovsky, A., & Imazeki, J. (2001). Achieving educational adequacy through school finance reform. *Journal of Education Finance, 26*, 373–396.

Rubenstein, R. (1998). Resource equity in the Chicago public schools: A school-level approach. *Journal of Education Finance, 23*, 468–489.

San Antonio Independent School District v. *Rodriguez*, 411 U.S. 1 (1973).

Sielke, C. C. (1998). Michigan school facilities, equity issues, and voter response to bond issues following finance reform. *Journal of Education Finance, 23*, 309–322.

Speakman, S. T., Cooper, B. S., Holsomback, H. C., May, J. F., Sampieri, R. A., & Maloney, L. (1997). The three Rs of education finance reform: Rethinking, re-tooling, and re-evaluating. *Journal of Education Finance, 22*, 337–367.

Stiefel, L., Rubenstein, R., & Berne, R. (1998). Intradistrict equity in four large cities: Data, methods, and results. *Journal of Education Finance, 23*, 447–467.

Strayer, G. D., & Haig, R. M. (1924). *Report of the Educational Finance Inquiry Commission: The financing of education in the State of New York*. New York: Macmillan.

Toenjes, L., & Clark, C. (1994). *Reducing school district wealth to create equity in Texas*. Paper delivered at the American Education Finance Association Annual Meeting, Nashville, TN.

U.S. General Accounting Office (GAO). (1997). *School finance: State efforts to reduce funding gaps between poor and wealthy districts*. Washington, DC: GAO.

Underwood, J. (1995). School finance adequacy as vertical equity. *University of Michigan Journal of Law Reform, 28*, 493–519.

Verstegen, D. A. (1987). Equity in state education finance: A response to *Rodriguez. Journal of Education Finance, 12*, 315–330.

Verstegen, D. A. (1993). Financing education reform: Where did all the money go? *Journal of Education Finance, 19*, 1–35.

Verstegen, D. A. (1994). Efficiency and equity in the provision and reform of American schooling. *Journal of Education Finance, 20*, 107–131.

Verstegen, D. A. (1996). Concepts and measures of fiscal inequality: A new approach and effects for five states. *Journal of Education Finance, 22*, 145–160.

Walters, L. C., & Freeman, M. A. (1993). An assessment of educational spending equity in Utah using data envelopment analysis. *Journal of Education Finance, 19*, 122–156.

Wenglinsky, H. (1998). Finance equalization and within-school equity: The relationship between education spending and the social distribution of achievement. *Educational Evaluation and Policy Analysis, 20*, 269–283.

Zigler, E. F., & Finn-Stevenson, M. (1994). Schools' role in the provision of support services for children and families: A critical aspect of program equity. *Educational Policy, 8*, 591–606.

chapter 12

PROMOTING HIGH STUDENT ACHIEVEMENT EFFICIENTLY

Issues and Questions

- *Achieving High Standards with Equity and Efficiency*: In realizing their goal of all children achieving high academic standards, are American schools hampered by insufficient resources, by poor management of available resources, or by some combination of the two?
- *External Efficiency*: Does the United States allocate a sufficient amount of resources in support of elementary and secondary education? How does it compare in this regard to other postindustrial economies?
- *Internal Efficiency*: Are schools and school districts efficiently using the resources entrusted to them for facilitating pupil learning?
- *Technical Efficiency*: How might the influence of schools on students be increased using only the resources already allocated to them?
- *Scale Effects*: How are school and district size related to pupil achievement and cost?
- *Policy Implications*: What changes in school organization and finance policies are needed to facilitate greater efficiency in the operations of schools?

The term *efficiency* is not commonly used in the parlance of educators. They rarely concern themselves with the connections between the inputs supplied to them by the community; how those resources are used in the classroom; how students fare, as a result of their instructional experiences, in subsequent grades and in other classes; and the quality of life experienced by graduates as a result of their school preparation. This may explain, at least in part, the counterintuitive fact that statistical analyses find small or no relationships between and among these events. In other words, if we think of inputs in terms of dollars, there is, at best, only a weak connection between the amount of dollars spent on public schools and the quality of the schools' impact on children. When confronted with evidence of failing schools, it is unusual for educators to look at their own behaviors and decisions as possible causes; rather, they are likely to respond that they have been given insufficient resources to do an adequate job. Having increased expenditures on public schools at a rate of about 3 percent a year in inflation-adjusted dollars for over four decades, the public at large no longer accepts this response unquestioningly. A great deal of skepticism has developed about how well resources are being used by school officials for the education of children. The question of productivity has been pushed to the forefront of the education policy agenda and has highlighted the importance of learning how to spend education dollars wisely (Ladd & Hansen, 1999).

We focused on the concepts of equality, adequacy, and efficiency from the perspective of the courts in Chapter 10, and on equity and adequacy from the view of policy analysts in Chapter 11. We found a growing recognition that many schools are not effective in guiding children toward the goals society has set for them, and we saw that this is particularly true for school serving primarily educationally at-risk children. And it is not only the children who are being harmed by this ineffectiveness;

when the schools are not doing their jobs properly, taxpayers are not receiving a just return on the investments they make through taxes. Although the concepts of equity and efficiency are quite different, we concluded in Chapters 10 and 11 that schooling cannot be truly equitable without also being efficient. In this chapter, we turn to studies that have applied paradigms drawn from economics to seek ways of using more efficiently the public resources *already* entrusted to schools.

Chapter 1 referred to the concepts of efficiency and economic growth as "derived values" that enhance realization of the ethical values of liberty, equality, and fraternity. Efficiency and economic growth became primary objectives of public policy only during the twentieth century. *Efficiency*, the ratio of outputs to inputs, is improved by increasing desired outputs produced from available resources or by maintaining a given level of output while using fewer resource inputs. Improving efficiency also improves *productivity*, a similar concept.

Hanushek (1986, p. 1166) defined economic efficiency as "the correct share of input mix given the prices of inputs and the production function." *Production function* is defined as the causal relationship between inputs and outcomes—what goes on in schools, classrooms, and the minds of students. He cautioned against confusing *economic efficiency* and *technical efficiency*. The latter considers only the process of combining inputs to produce outcomes and does not take into account the cost of inputs. Both concepts are important considerations in designing educational systems, and both will be considered in this chapter.

There are two aspects of economic efficiency. *External efficiency* considers the contributions to national economic growth that are made by the scarce resources allocated by society to various sectors of production. With respect to education, we are interested in how well the economic returns we receive from investments in education compare to returns from other investment opportunities. *Internal efficiency* concerns the allocation of resources *within* educational enterprises in order to maximize output (for example, academic achievement, skill development, and the behavior and attitudes of students) from the resources committed.

The decision matrix presented in Chapter 1 (Figure 1.3) posed a series of questions to be resolved by policy makers. Analyses of external efficiency aid policy makers in arriving at decisions about the amount of resources to be committed to various educational services and in determining what level of societal investment in "population quality" (an educated citizenry) will best promote economic growth and the general welfare. In other words, studying external efficiencies addresses the issues of how much to spend for educational services and which kinds of services to provide in order to create the greatest amount of aggregate economic benefit. Internal efficiency involves the means by which educational services are produced. The goal of studying internal efficiency is to gain the maximum benefit from the resources committed to an institution or operation such as a school or classroom. Whereas internal efficiency is studied through education production functions and cost–benefit and cost–effectiveness analyses, external efficiency is studied through rate-of-return analysis.

We begin this chapter by looking at external efficiencies. We review studies that have applied the theory of human capital, introduced in Chapter 2, to estimating the contribution of investments in education to national economic growth. The discussion of external efficiency ends with an assessment of the adequacy of expenditures for education in the United States. The second section of this chapter focuses on internal efficiency. In reviewing evidence from studies of both the technical and the economic efficiency of schools, we conclude that there are significant opportunities for redirecting resources already committed to education in such a way as to improve the outcomes of schools.

EXTERNAL EFFICIENCY

In Parts II and III of this book, we discussed the processes by which public revenues are raised for the support of educational services and how they are distributed to school districts. The discussion assumed that we know how much we need to spend on education. As we saw in Part I, deciding how much to spend for educational services is largely a political process, and the decisions made may not be optimal from an economic perspective. Economic analysis can estimate the efficiency with which we are using scarce resources for educational services. In the political process, however, economic efficiency is only one of many, often conflicting objectives of social policy. Concerns for improving economic efficiency must be balanced against other social concerns, and when other concerns take precedence, the policies adopted may, for good reasons, be inefficient from an economic perspective. Too often, however, decision makers adopt public policy without fully understanding its economic ramifications.

Rate-of-Return Approach

Rate-of-return analysis is one of the tools in the economist's arsenal for evaluating alternative investment policies. As we saw in Chapter 2, rate-of-return analysis is intended to help policy makers decide how much to spend on each economic sector and on specific programs within each sector (Benson, 1978, p. 91). With respect to education, rate-of-return analysis compares the increased earnings made possible by additional education to the expense of acquiring that education, including earnings forgone in the process (opportunity costs). The rate of return on investments in education has been studied at two levels, the individual and society.

Correspondingly, two rates of returns are determined: a private rate for consideration by individuals and a social rate for consideration by policy analysts. In determining the private rate, one includes only costs incurred by individuals. But in determining social policy, one must consider all costs, including those that supplement the private costs paid directly by individuals. The price of an education in both public and private institutions is subsidized by public funds and/or private endowments. Hence, to calculate the social rate of return, one must also include the amount of subsidization to individuals (e.g., the difference between tuition charged the student and actual cost, scholarships, and fellowships). As a general rule, social rates of return to education are lower than private rates of return—an argument for having some costs of education, especially for higher education, paid in part by students' tuition and not totally subsidized by government. Social rate of return is the appropriate statistic of reference in studying alternative public policy options.

In our discussion of human-capital theory in Chapter 2, we referred to some of the studies done that include United States data (Schultz, 1963; Becker, 1964; Dennison, 1962; Kuznets, 1966; Pierce & Welch, 1996; Hanushek & Kim, 1995). Psacharopoulos (1981) surveyed such studies across 61 nations, analyzing the average private and social rates of return for primary, secondary, and higher education. The countries were grouped according to stage of development and region. All results, except for the social rate of return for higher education for countries at the advanced and intermediate stages of development, were at or above the 10 percent benchmark commonly expected from capital investment. Returns of 8 percent and 9 percent for higher education may indicate that advanced and intermediate countries are spending at or slightly above the optimal level, given the current organization of education.

The highest returns were for primary education in developing countries. This high rate of return is a function of the interaction between low cost of primary education (including opportunity costs) relative to other levels and the substantial productivity differential (based on market pricing) between primary school graduates and those who are illiterate. (In the advanced countries, illiteracy has been virtually eliminated, which makes the calculations at the primary level in that group of countries meaningless.) Rates of return at all levels of education tend to decline with development, which indicates the relative scarcity of educated personnel in countries with low levels of economic development. For all developmental groups, private returns exceeded social returns. In a subsequent study, Psacharopoulos (1985) found that expenditures on education of women were at least as beneficial as those on men and that expenditures on the general curriculum produced higher yields than those on vocational education. Education was shown to be a worthy investment for all countries at all stages of development. The best investment strategy for countries, however, appears to vary according to level of economic development and other demographic characteristics.

Spending Levels for Education

Making international comparisons of education spending is as much an art as a science. Verstegen (1992) analyzed several studies (conducted by the Economic Policy Institute, the U.S. Department of Education, the Congressional Research Service, and the American Federation of Teachers) that compared education expenditures between the United States and other developed nations. She found that among the factors that affect rankings are the measures used, such as aggregate expenditure, expenditure per pupil, or percent of gross domestic product (GDP[1]); what is included in the definition of expenditure (or revenue); the monetary conversion procedure (for example, using purchasing power parities or market exchange rates); comparisons of expenditures made from public funds only with those made from public and private sources combined; countries included; and education levels included (elementary and secondary, tertiary, or combined).

Verstegen concluded that the United States, in general, leads other developed nations in total spending for education when all levels are combined. When only expenditures for elementary and secondary education are considered, and when expenditures are compared to GDP, the United States loses its preeminent position. For expenditures per pupil at the elementary and secondary levels, the United States ranks relatively high. When rankings are made on the basis of percent of GDP or GDP per capita, the United States ranks relatively low.

Expenditure per pupil is an indicator of the availability of resources for each student's education on average. Expenditures for education as a percent of GDP can be viewed as a measure of effort (similar to a tax rate).

Investment in education in the United States for the period 1959 through 1998 is reported in Table 12.1, along with the percentage of the total population enrolled in precollegiate and

higher education. The percentage of GDP spent for all educational institutions rose steadily from 4.8 percent in 1959 to 7.5 percent in 1970 and 1975. It then declined to 6.7 percent in 1985 and rose to 7.8 percent in 1992. The earlier peak allocation of GDP to education (1970) corresponds to the peak in the percentage of the population enrolled in educational institutions. The 1992 peak allocation of GNP (7.8 percent) to education is for a smaller population cohort than was the case in 1970.

For elementary and secondary school expenditures, the percentage of GDP rose from 3.4 percent in 1959 to 4.8 percent in 1970. Although expenditure per pupil continued to increase in current and inflation-adjusted dollars, the percentage of GDP declined to 4.0 percent in 1985. It then increased to 4.6 percent in 1994 and stood at 4.4 percent in 1995 and 1998. The increase in the percentage of GDP allocated to precollegiate education corresponded to increasing enrollments and to a growing commitment to equalize educational opportunities through desegregation of schools,

TABLE 12.1.

Percentage of Gross Domestic Product (GDP) Spent on Education and Percentage of Total Population Enrolled in Educational Institutions by Level, 1959–1998

Year	Elementary and Secondary Schools		Higher Education		Total	
	Percentage of GDP	Percentage Enrollment of Population	Percentage of GDP	Percentage Enrollment of Population	Percentage of GDP	Percentage Enrollment of Population
1959	3.4	23.0	1.4	2.0	4.8	25.0
1965	4.0	24.9	2.2	3.0	6.2	28.0
1970	4.8	25.0	2.7	4.2	7.5	29.2
1975	4.7	23.1	2.7	5.2	7.5	28.2
1980	4.1	20.3	2.6	5.3	6.8	25.6
1985	4.0	18.8	2.7	5.1	6.7	24.0
1990	4.5	18.4	3.0	5.4	7.5	24.0
1995	4.4	19.2	2.9	5.4	7.3	24.7
1998	4.4	18.8	2.9	5.2	7.3	23.9

Source: National Center for Education Statistics. (2000). *Digest of Education Statistics*. Washington, DC: U.S. Government Printing Office.

compensatory education (e.g., enactment of ESEA), and educating children with disabilities. The decline in the percentage can be attributed at least in part to the dramatic drop in the proportion of the total population attending elementary and secondary schools. Elementary and secondary school enrollment peaked in 1970 at 25.0 percent of the total population, subsequently declining to 18.4 percent in 1990. It then increased to 19.2 percent in 1995 but declined to 18.8 percent in 1998.

The percentage of GDP spent on colleges and universities rose steadily from 1.4 percent in 1959 to 3.0 percent in 1990. In 1998 it stood at 2.9 percent. Actual enrollments in postsecondary education rose from 3,640,000 in 1959 to 8,581,000 in 1970 and continued to increase to over 14,000,000 by 1998. The percentage of the total population enrolled in higher education in 1959 was 2.0 percent. It steadily increased to 1990, when it reached 5.4 percent, and then dropped back to 5.2 percent in 1998.

In reviewing the amount spent on education at all levels and the proportion of gross domestic product invested, Smith and Phelps (1995) concluded that the United States ranks among the highest in comparison with other large postindustrial countries. A smaller portion of the U.S. investment in education is directed to the elementary and secondary sector, however, when compared with other advanced nations. For higher education, the United States spends more per student than any other country (NCES, 2001). Its expenditure at the secondary level is exceeded only by Switzerland and Austria. At the primary level, its expenditure is exceeded only by Switzerland, Austria, Norway, and Denmark. It is only when U.S. expenditures are viewed as a percentage of GDP that the United States falls more to the middle of the pack of advanced nations. In assessing adequacy, though, the level of resources available per child is the critical indicator, and the United States ranks very well on this measure, particularly when compared with its chief economic rivals, Germany and Japan.

On average, the United States appears to be committing a responsible amount of resources to elementary and secondary education. As noted in the previous chapter, however, the distribution of resources among children within the country is highly inequitable. In the next section on internal efficiency, we look at how wisely these resources are being distributed to effect the education of individual children and how well they are being used in the instructional process.

INTERNAL EFFICIENCY

In this section, we begin by setting the context for the current debate over the efficiency with which schools and school districts are using resources entrusted to them to enable students to achieve high academic standards. This is followed by an explanation of education production functions, a principal tool for studying school and district efficiency. Several production function studies are reviewed as examples of this technique, and critiques of these studies are considered. We then examine a new avenue of research dealing specifically with economic efficiency: data envelopment analysis (DEA). We then consider research and applications related to technical efficiency as done by program evaluators and advocates of effective schools, along with whole-school reform models. We next present research on economies and diseconomies of scale in schools and school districts, and we conclude with a discussion of policy implications for improving the internal efficiency of schools.

Context

Figure 12.1 shows the increase in current expenditures per pupil in average daily attendance between 1970–71 and 1999–2000 in constant 1999–2000 dollars and in current dollars. The amount spent in 1970–71, in inflation-adjusted

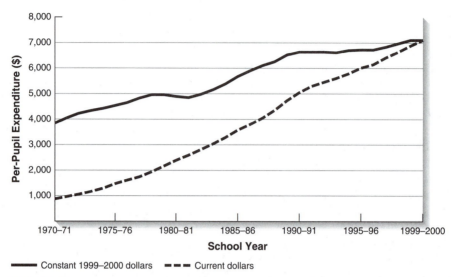

FIGURE 12.1. Current Expenditure per Pupil in Average Daily Attendance in Public Elementary and Secondary Schools: 1970–1971 to 1999–2000

Source: U.S. Department of Education, National Center for Education Statistics: *Statistics of State School Systems; Revenues and Expenditures for Public Elementary and Secondary Education*; and *Common Core of Data* surveys.

dollars, was $3,883. It grew to $7,086 in 1999–2000, an average increase of nearly 3 percent per year. Figure 12.1 shows that the rise has not been steady, however. Increases are shown for the periods 1970–71 through 1977–78 and 1981–82 through 1989–90, with plateaus between 1977–78 and 1981–82 and since 1989–90. The rise beginning in 1981–82 corresponds with the beginning of the current reform movement; growth averaged about 4 percent per year above inflation for the next eight years. For the subsequent 10-year period, growth in inflation-adjusted dollars averaged less than 1 percent per year.

The gradual increase in inflation-adjusted expenditures since the mid-twentieth century has sparked much interest and a number of investigations into the question, "Where has the money gone?" Rothstein and Miles' (1995) study found that the bulk of the increase went into special-education programs. Special-education spending's share of all spending increased from 4 percent in 1967 to 17 percent by 1991. The share of expenditures for regular education actually declined from 80 percent in 1967 to 59 percent in 1991.

Another study of the distribution of new resources allocated to public schools over a 5-year period ending in the early 1990s was conducted by Odden, Monk, Nakib, and Picus (1995). They concluded that the funds had been distributed unfairly and used ineffectively and that the public education system needed to be restructured so that new resources could be strategically linked to improving student achievement. They found that the largest portion of increased spending had been used to hire more teachers to reduce class size and to provide more out-of-classroom services, primarily "pull-out" instruction for disabled and low-achieving students. Funds were also used to increase teacher salaries, but not in a way that would enhance teacher expertise. Large portions of increased revenues were also used to expand special-education services. On the basis of their analysis, the authors contended that the long-term task of reform is to get schools to act more like producers of high levels of student achievement than like consumers of educational resources.

Guthrie (1997) came to similar conclusions. Whether in special education, general education, or elsewhere in the schools, he identified the principal factor contributing to higher expenditures as more people working in the schools and being paid at higher levels. He noted that in 1950, there was one school employee for every 19.3 pupils; this ratio has now dropped to one employee for every 9.1 pupils. Some of these additional people work in expanded special-education programs, and others are required because of fewer dropouts at the secondary level, full-day kindergarten, preschool programs, and compensatory education. Also contributing to higher costs is an increase in the salaries of teachers; more teachers hold advanced degrees, and teachers are generally more experienced than a few years back. The relative number of administrators has not grown over the years and may actually have shrunk slightly.

In Chapter 11 we noted that equity of educational opportunity in the United States has traditionally been measured in terms of distribution of inputs, especially expenditures per pupil, under the assumption that resources would be used at a common level of productivity. This assumption has been strongly challenged over the past decade by Hanushek (1986, 1991, 1996a), who claims that research has shown no consistent relationship between schooling inputs and student achievement, and just as strongly defended by Hedges, Laine, and Greenwald (1994a, 1994b) and Greenwald, Hedges, and Laine (1994), who claim the opposite. But even the most passionate defenders have acknowledged that relationships between inputs and student achievement are not robust across the board. Grissmer (2001) noted that with respect to recent nonexperimental studies, analytical models that were thought to have superior specifications provided no more

consistent results than those previously reviewed. Some studies using better and more current data (we consider them below) did show positive effects from resources (Ferguson, 1991; Ferguson & Ladd, 1996), but on balance, results are still inconsistent (Hanushek, 1996a; Ladd, 1996; Burtless, 1996). Grissmer concluded, however, that "evidence . . . appears to be converging on the hypothesis that certain kinds of targeted expenditures can raise achievement, particularly for disadvantaged students, but additional resources above current levels may not matter much for more advantaged students" (p. 139).

Levin (1994) has included, as necessary conditions for equity, access by all children to a full range of appropriate educational programs and access to the funding and other resources that will enable them to benefit fully from those programs. In citing several studies that have shown large variations in outcomes of schools with apparently similar resource and student characteristics, Levin placed as a sufficient condition that schools be maximally effective with all children so that resources are used optimally to meet their students' educational needs. In coming to these conclusions, he noted that inefficiencies seem to be greatest among schools serving populations that are at greatest risk educationally.

The focus on higher achievement standards has not necessarily been accompanied by a call for substantially more financial resources. There is a prevailing assumption among policy analysts (though not among educational practitioners) that current allocations for education are sufficient, or nearly sufficient, for reaching higher standards if existing resources are distributed more wisely and used more effectively. For example, the plan of the Consortium on Renewing Education (1998) to double the nation's academic achievement by the year 2020 calls for no more total resources than those currently provided, beyond what will be allocated for precollegiate education if the trend of financial increases continues. "Incremental dollars for increased student enroll-ments and cost of living increases should be sufficient to meet this goal, if the nation's sys-tems of schools were concentrating intensively on academic achievement" (The Consortium, p. 12). Under current conditions, the relation-ships between schooling inputs and outcomes are, at best, tenuous. If equity of outcomes is to be realized, the issues of productivity, effec-tiveness and internal efficiency must be satis-fied first.

Summarizing the deliberations of a panel of economists working in the field of education—the Panel on the Economics of Education Re-form (PEER)—Hanushek (1996b), the panel's chair, wrote,

> Reform—in education as in other areas—is often thought of as the process of securing more re-sources. Here our panel breaks with tradition. Analysis of the history of schools in the twentieth century does not suggest that American society has been stingy in its support of schools. Quite the contrary, funding for schools has grown more or less continuously for 100 years. The fundamental problem is not a lack of resources but poor appli-cation of available resources. Indeed, there is a good case for holding overall spending constant in school reform. Not only is there considerable in-efficiency in schools that, if eliminated, would re-lease substantial funds for genuine improvements in the operation of schools, but there also is a case for holding down funding increases to force schools to adopt a more disciplined approach to decision making. Schools must evaluate their pro-grams and make decisions with student perfor-mance in mind and with an awareness that trade-offs among different uses of resources are important. (p. 30)

Fuller and Clarke (1994) divided educators and researchers into two camps when it comes to defining and studying school effectiveness and efficiency: policy mechanics and classroom culturalists. Policy mechanics, working from a production function metaphor, attempt to identify instructional inputs and uniform teaching practices that yield higher achieve-ment—that is, their focus is on economic effi-ciency. They search for universal determinants of effective schools that can be manipulated by central agencies (for example, state education departments) and assume that the same in-structional materials and practices will produce similar results across diverse settings. The class-room culturalists reject this orientation and "focus on the normative socialization that oc-curs within classrooms: the value children come to place on individualistic versus coop-erative work, legitimated forms of adult au-thority and power, and acquired attitudes toward achievement and modern forms of sta-tus" (p.120). The classroom culturalists tend to ignore narrower forms of cognitive achieve-ment and have not been particularly interested in antecedent inputs and classroom rules that are manipulable by central authority. Although they do not normally use the term, their focus is on what economists refer to as technical ef-ficiency. Fuller and Clarke concluded,

> The classroom culturalists have advanced re-searchers' understanding of how motivated learn-ing occurs within particular social contexts, like classrooms. The production function gurus con-tinue to hold comparative advantage in empiri-cally linking classroom tools to achievement. But this advantage will only be retained if these inputs and teaching practices are awarded real cultural meaning—within a particular context which is energized by variable forms of teacher authority, social participation, and classroom tasks. (p. 143)

In this section, we review the findings of both camps. We begin by examining produc-tion function and efficiency studies done by "policy mechanics." Then we consider research and applications related to technical efficiency as revealed by research on effective schools, program evaluations, and evaluations of whole-school reform models. We continue by re-viewing studies of economies of scale in the context of schools and school districts. Finally, we consider the policy implications of improv-ing the internal efficiency of schools.

Education Production Functions

Studies that relate schooling outcomes to inputs have been referred to as research on education production functions, as input–output analyses, and as cost–quality studies. Such research has been pursued from a variety of disciplinary perspectives in an effort to improve educational productivity. In this section, we will refer to such studies in terms of the economic classification *production function*. We begin by providing a general explanation of the education production concept and descriptions of some of the more influential individual studies. Meta-analyses of large numbers of studies will be reviewed, along with the debate over conflicting findings that these analyses have yielded. The section concludes with a discussion of criticisms of the appropriateness of applying the production function concept to education, criticisms of the studies themselves, and implications of the findings for educational policy.

Production Functions Explained

A production function is a set of relations among possible inputs and a corresponding set of outputs for a firm or industry—in this case, schools and education (Burkhead, 1967, p. 18). According to Hanushek (1987), "A firm's production possibilities are assumed to be governed by certain technical relationships, and the production function describes the maximum feasible output that can be obtained from a set of inputs" (p. 33). Monk (1989) states that a production function tells what is currently possible: "It provides a standard against which practice can be evaluated on productivity grounds" (p. 31). Monk goes on to identify two traditions with respect to the study of the production of education services. The first attempts to estimate the parameters of the education production function. The second uses the production function as a metaphor, allowing for the application of broader economic theories and reasoning that can be used to guide inquiry.

An education production function may be expressed simply as output (O) being a function of inputs consisting of student characteristics (S), schooling inputs (I), and instructional processes (P):

$$O = f(S, I, P).$$

Outputs (O) include behavioral and attitudinal changes in pupils induced through school activities. Outputs are usually measured by scores on standardized tests, but they occasionally include other measures such as high school graduation rate, attendance rate, and rate of graduates continuing on to postsecondary education. Student characteristics (S) range from socioeconomic status of family and student IQ to previous achievement. Schooling inputs (I) include peer group characteristics, expenditures, teacher characteristics, class size, characteristics of buildings, and the like. Instructional processes (P) include student time on task, teaching methods, student-teacher interactions, and so on.

If there is an education production function, there must also be a common underlying technology of education—an assumption that may come as a surprise to many educators because production technologies in education are inexact. Nevertheless, the sameness of American schools (and of schools around the world for that matter, both public and private) lends credibility to an assumption of an implicit technology. School buildings are typically arranged with classrooms and certain ancillary spaces such as libraries, auditoriums, and gymnasiums. Each classroom is usually presided over by one teacher only, and there is much similarity in the ways teachers organize and manage classrooms.

Klitgaard and Hall (1975) first tested the assumption of a common technology. They examined the distributions of residual student achievement once the effects of socioeconomic status had been statistically controlled for. They hypothesized that if there were schools functioning under different pedagogical assumptions (that is, different production functions), the distribution of residuals would be multimodal. Although their findings were not definitive, they concluded that it is reasonable to assume that all schools, including highly effective ones, function under the same pedagogical technology.

Illustrative Production Function Studies

The report by James Coleman and colleagues (1966), *Equality of Educational Opportunity* (EEO), was one of the first, and remains one of the largest, production function studies ever attempted for education. It involved over a half-million students in 4,000 schools and thousands of teachers; the unit of analysis was the school. It is perhaps the best known and most controversial of all the input–output studies. The controversy extended not only to its conclusion (that schooling had little potential for closing the achievement gap between white and minority students) but also to the methodology used. Benson (1988) summarized the shortcomings of the early education production function studies:

> They used achievement scores at one point in time. The unit of analysis was the school, or even the school district, and the consequent averaging of results weakened the power of the findings. Each variable on the right-hand side of the regression (independent and control variables) was treated as wholly independent of the other variables. In considering the effects of teacher characteristics on achievement, no account was taken of the fact that the child's progress in school is not determined by his or her current teacher alone but is the result of the cumulative actions of all the teachers in the child's school career. (p. 365)

A number of attempts have been made to overcome the weaknesses of early production function studies. Ferguson (1991) did a most promising study of a large and particularly rich data source that he assembled for the state of Texas. The data included information on nearly 900 school districts serving over 2.4 million students and employing 150,000 teachers. The database included the scores achieved by all teachers on the Texas Examination of Current Administrators and Teachers (TECAT); other measures of school quality, such as teacher characteristics and pupil/teacher ratios; measures of school spending; student reading and math scores from the Texas Educational Assessment of Minimum Skills (TEAMS); characteristics of the region surrounding a school district; and census data and other socioeconomic background and context measures.

Ferguson used multiple regression analysis, just as other production function studies have, but what set this study apart, besides the richness of the data, was the systematic preparation of data that preceded the final analysis. For example, threshold analysis revealed that some factors are important up to a point, but not beyond. This was taken into account in scoring such factors. Also, the flow of influences was traced. As a result of these refinements, Ferguson found a much larger school effect than similar studies had revealed. Between one-quarter and one-third of the variation among Texas school districts in students' scores on the TEAMS reading examination were explained by school effects—primarily teachers' scores on the TECAT. A major weakness of the Ferguson study is that data were aggregated at the district level.

The power of teachers' TECAT scores to predict student achievement is of particular interest and is in keeping with the findings of other studies beginning with the EEO study, which found that the strongest school effect on pupil achievement was teachers' verbal ability. Using threshold analysis, Ferguson (1991) found that class size also matters. Reducing the ratio of the number of students to the number of teachers in the district to 18 to 1—which approximates an average class size of twenty-three—is very important for performance in the primary grades. Dropping the ratio below the threshold of 18 had no effect on test scores. Ferguson also found a threshold effect for teacher experience; up to five years of experience at the primary level and up to nine years at the secondary level have a positive influence on student performance; additional experience was not related to student performance. He found no upper limit for the positive effect of teachers' TECAT scores, however. He concluded,

> The teacher supply results, when combined with the results for student test scores, demonstrate that hiring teachers with stronger literacy skills, hiring more teachers (when students-per-teacher exceeds eighteen), retaining experienced teachers, and attracting more teachers with advanced training are all measures that produce higher test scores in exchange for more money. (Ferguson, 1991, p. 485)

On the basis of his findings, Ferguson makes the policy recommendation that, apart from the common focus by states on equalizing spending per pupil, a serious equalization policy should also equalize the most important of all schooling inputs, teacher quality. Similar recommendations were made in the equity studies of New York City (Berne and Stiefel, 1994), Chicago (Stiefel, Rubenstein, & Berne, 1998) and Dade County, Florida (Owens, 1994) reviewed in Chapter 11. To do this would require state-enforced salary differentials that would result in the highest salaries being paid to teachers working in communities characterized by lower socioeconomic populations.

The Consortium on Renewing Education (1998) identified Texas as the most persuasive example that reform can be productive. In 1993 Texas introduced a high-stakes testing and accountability system that includes a comprehensive database facilitating analyses at the building and grade levels, overcoming one of the limitations of the Ferguson (1991) database. Among those taking advantage of this new and rich data resource were Hanushek, Kain, and Rivkin (1998). In their study, they found large differences in the quality of schooling in a way that ruled out the possibility that the differences were driven by nonschool factors. However, these researchers concluded

that "resource differences explain at most a small part of the difference in school quality, raising serious doubts that additional expenditures would substantially raise achievement under current institutional structure" (p. 31). Like Ferguson (1991), they found the most significant factor explaining variation in student achievement to be variation in teacher characteristics. Most of the specific attributes related to student achievement remained unidentified, but Hanushek, Kain, and Rivkin (1998) were able to draw some conclusions with policy implications. For example, they found no evidence that number of master's degrees among teachers was related to pupil achievement. They did find a relationship between achievement and up to two years of teaching experience, but not thereafter. They noted that "The estimated relationship between achievement and graduate degrees and experience opens questions about the prevalence of teacher pay scales that reward these characteristics" (p. 34). They also found some advantage to small class size for children from low-income families in grades 4 and 5, but the effect declined with grade level.

Ferguson and Ladd (1996) used a value-added model specification at two levels (school and district) in their production function study of Alabama schools and districts. For the school-level specification, students were treated as the units of observation. School input variables were measured for the fourth-grade cohort for 1990–1991 for each specific school. The achievement data for reading and mathematics (the dependent variables) were for 1990–1991, and the corresponding achievement data for 1989–1990 (the control) were matched student for student. Family and school background data were obtained from administrative data at the school level or from the census at the level of the zip code area or the school district. The school-level sample that was studied included 29,544 students in 690 schools. The district-level analysis used achievement data for students in the ninth grade as the dependent variable. Control achievement data were test scores of third- and fourth-graders of the same year. Analysis at this level included 127 public school districts. The authors acknowledge that the district-level specification is less precise than the school-level specification.

School input data included four measures provided by the teachers in each school: class size, percent of teachers with more than five years of experience, percent of teachers with a master's degree, and average teachers' ACT test scores, taken when applying for college. In addition to test scores, student-specific variables included age, race, and gender. Background characteristics included percentage of adults with sixteen or more years of schooling, with twelve to fifteen years, with nine to eleven years, and with fewer than nine years. Family income was proxied by the log of per capita income at the zip code level and by the percentage of children in each school approved for free or reduced-cost lunches. The percentage of students not in the school the previous year was used as a measure of the mobility of students in the school. Four district-characteristic measures were included: total enrollment, percentage of students in public schools, the percentage of the district that is urban, and whether the district is a city or a county district. The production function equation was estimated using a hierarchical linear model.

Teacher test scores had a positive and statistically significant relationship to reading achievement. All other things being equal, a difference between two schools of 1 standard deviation in average teacher ACT score would be associated with a .10 standard deviation in average performance on the students' reading test. To achieve a comparable achievement gain would require a 25 percent increase in the percent of college-educated adults, about a 2 standard deviation increase. The proportion of teachers holding master's degrees had little or no effect on reading scores, but it did have a slight positive effect on math scores. Teachers' experience exerted no effect on either reading or mathematics achievement.

With respect to class size, average mathematics scores in classes of under nineteen pupils exceeded those in classes of over twenty-nine by .14 standard deviation. The effect was greater for girls than for boys. For reading, the gains were smaller and leveled off at class sizes in the mid-twenties.

The district-level analysis yielded similar results. At this level, the production function equations were estimated using weighted least squares. A difference in teacher test scores of 1 standard deviation was associated with increases in student test scores of about .25 standard deviation, the equivalent of about .05 standard deviation per year because the study at this level covered a five-year period. A reduction of three in average class size was associated with an increase of .26 standard deviation in student test scores, approximately the same effect as increasing teacher ACT test scores by 1 standard deviation. The only input variable not associated with higher student achievement was teacher experience.

The district-level analysis also enabled Ferguson and Ladd (1996) to estimate the effect of expenditure increases on student test scores. They found that the effect of increased spending was concentrated among the districts whose spending levels were below the median. For these districts, a 10 percent increase in expenditures per pupil (about 1.5 standard deviations) was associated with a .881 standard deviation increase in student test scores (compared with a .356 standard deviation increase across all districts). This large effect approximates the difference between the tenth percentile and the median of student test scores. For districts above the median in expenditures, the effect of higher expenditures was not statistically different from zero.

Woessmann (2000) conducted a production function analysis using data gathered from the Third International Mathematics and Science Study (TIMSS). This particularly important study was the first to investigate quantitatively the impact of systemic structural reforms. Quantitative studies conducted within a single country or state cannot examine systemic issues because all schools and districts are operating within the same framework. International studies offer investigators such an opportunity, and the TIMSS database is particularly well suited for this purpose. The analysis uses data collected for middle grades for 260,000 students in thirty-nine countries. Analyses were made at the student level and at the country level.

For the microeconometric student–level investigation, Woessmann estimated an education production function of the influence of student background, resources, and institutions on students' educational performance. Achievement and background were measured at the student level, while resources and institutional characteristics were measured at the classroom, school, and country levels. After controlling for family background effects, measures of differences in the ways in which educational systems are structured contributed substantially to differences in student performance in mathematics and science. Both centralized examinations and the size of the private schooling sector (i.e., providing competition to the public schools; see also Hoxby, 1994, and Armor & Peiser, 1997) had significantly positive effects on student performance. School autonomy with respect to the purchasing of supplies, the hiring and rewarding of teachers, and the organization of instruction were positively and significantly related to student performance. On the other hand, decisions about determining the curriculum syllabus, textbook lists, and the size of the school budget were found to be best left with central authority. Although teachers acting independently in making decisions at the school level had (as noted) a positive effect, when they acted collectively through teacher unions, the effect on student performance was negative (with respect to the United States specifically, see Walberg, 1998).

The extent to which institutional differences can account for the cross-country differences in student performance was assessed by estimating country-level production functions. Institutional variables were aggregated to reflect the percentage of students in a country for whom an institutional feature is given and were combined with country-level data on average test scores, family background, and resource endowment for each country. These data were used to devise what the author calls a "rough and ready" method for estimating institutional effects at the country level. Analysis at this level indicated that structural differences matter a lot in explaining cross-country differences in pupil performance but that resource inputs matter little. Three indicators of structural features had strong and statistically significant effects on student performance. Increased school autonomy in supply choice and increased central scrutiny of performance assessments were associated with superior performance levels. Large influence by teachers unions on the education process was associated with inferior performance levels. Together, these three factors explained three-quarters of the cross-country variation in mathematics test scores and 60 percent of the variation in science scores.

Woessmann (2000) concluded,

> For education policy, this means that the crucial question is not one of more resources but one of improving the institutional environment of education to ensure an efficient use of resources. Student performance is influenced by the productivity of resource use in schools. This productivity is determined by the behavior of people who act in the educational process. These people respond to incentives. And their incentives are set by the institutional structure of the system. In short, by setting proper institutions, education policy can favorably affect student performance. By contrast, spending more money within an institutional system that sets adverse incentives will not improve student performance. The only policy that promises positive effects is to create an institutional system where all the people involved have an incentive to improve student performance. (p. 79)

The specific institutional features revealed by Woessmann's research to affect student performance favorably were

- Central examinations
- Centralized control of curricular and budgetary matters
- School autonomy in process and personnel decisions
- An intermediate level of administration performing administrative tasks and educational funding
- Competition from private educational institutions
- Individual teachers having both incentives and powers to select appropriate teaching methods
- Limited influence of teacher unions
- Scrutiny of students' educational performance
- Encouragement of parents to take an interest in teaching matters

Meta-analysis of Education Production Function Studies

Hanushek (1986, 1991, 1996a) compiled a series of meta-analyses of production function studies. His conclusion that *"There is no systematic relationship between school expenditures and student performance"* (1991, p. 425) has proved to be highly controversial and sparked a debate that continues today. The first to challenge his methodology and conclusion were Hedges, Laine, and Greenwald (1994a and 1994b; see also Greenwald, Hedges, and Laine, 1994). They claimed that although the methods that Hanushek used were accepted as adequate when he began his research, they "are now regarded as inadequate synthesis procedures. When examined using more adequate methods, the data upon which his finding is based support exactly the opposite inference: the amount of resources are positively related to the accomplishments of students" (Greenwald, Hedges, and Laine, 1994, p. 2). Because of more stringent standards for including studies

in this reanalysis, it involved fewer cases than Hanushek's original study. Also, Hanushek employed an analytical method known as vote counting, whereas Greenwald and colleagues used combined significance tests and combined estimation methods.

In a rebuttal to this challenge, Hanushek (1994) retorted that the challengers had made the larger error in asking the wrong question. According to Hanushek, the challengers posed the fundamental issue as one of using the right statistical method, whereas he saw it as one of identifying correct policies: "It is important that the policy significance not be lost in the technical details. . . . Most importantly, the policy interpretations do not depend really on the statistical issues" (p. 5). Some credence is given to Hanushek's rebuttal in Greenwald, Hedges, and Laine's (1994) conclusion:

> Even if the conclusions drawn from the studies analyzed in this paper are correct, we would not argue that "throwing money at schools" is the most efficient method of increasing educational achievement. It certainly is not. Greater emphasis must be placed on the manner in which resources are utilized, not simply [on] the provision of those resources. (p. 20)

Another review of the literature on educational production functions by King and MacPhail-Wilcox (1994) summarized the prevailing thinking about the relationships between school inputs and outputs: "A safe conclusion is that the way in which schools, teachers, and students take advantage of whatever materials are available matters as much or more than the actual human, physical and fiscal resources present in schools" (p. 47). According to Hanushek (1991), most economists would readily accept that differences in spending would be directly related to the quality of education *if* schools were operating efficiently. Although some schools are operating close to the efficiency frontier (Engert, 1995), most are not.

Criticisms of Production Function Studies

Monk (1989) criticized the direction that school effectiveness research has taken. According to him, the estimation approach to education production functions is, with a few exceptions, void of economic content because analysts have been forced to make so many simplifying assumptions. Instead of becoming further involved in increasingly sophisticated applications of econometrics that hold very limited value for education policy makers, Monk encouraged the use of the production function as an analogy in the application of economic reasoning to education problems.

Rice (2001) argued that education production function analysis is a useful, but incomplete, tool for informing education policy. She points to four conceptual issues that need to be addressed in an effort to enhance the utilitarian value of production function research. Investigators need to recognize that the education production function involves (1) a complex configuration of resources, (2) multilevel phenomena, (3) multiple forms, and (4) the cumulative effect of a variety of inputs. Not all inputs need to be studied at once; indeed, this would be impossible. But in conceptualizing the problem, analysts must take into account the fact that the productivity of one input can be affected by the amount and quality of another. For example, the impact of small class size may depend on the approach to instruction.

Recognizing multilevel phenomena means acknowledging that the education process is affected by student and family characteristics as well as by policies and practices at many organizational levels, all operating simultaneously. This creates a *nesting* problem that was not dealt with adequately in early studies. A statistical technique known as hierarchical linear modeling (HLM), now commonly used in education production function studies, is designed to solve the nesting difficulty. HLM avoids problems of aggregation and desegregation and provides information on the relations and variance within each level and across levels.

Rice also notes that there are multiple forms of education production functions and cautions that one size may not fit all. In other words, a single production function may not hold true for all groups of students, grade levels, and subjects. The cumulative-effects issue that Rice points out recognizes that education is a process of continuous development and that measures of effectiveness should take into account growth or change over time, not at only one point in time. Further, inputs of one level of education yield outputs that become inputs at the next level of the education process. For example, well-developed reading comprehension skills in the primary grades will lead to better ability in solving word problems in mathematics later on.

Rice (2001) points out that although the conceptual specification of the education production function is quite broad, it has data and methodological limitations; that is, it can deal only with factors that can be readily specified and measured, and it provides no insight into normative matters. To compensate for these weaknesses, analysts need to draw upon a number of other research methods, including case studies and experimental designs. Grissmer (2001) addresses the complementary roles of experimental and empirical (e.g., estimating production functions) research. The main value of experimental data is to provide benchmark measurements for effects of given variables. It is also useful in testing assumptions, bias, and specifications employed with nonexperimental data.

A most significant and consistent finding of the production function studies, beginning with the EEO study, is the very strong relationship between family background and pupil achievement. The relationship is so strong that findings of these studies have frequently been misinterpreted to mean that schools have relatively little impact on pupil achievement. It is well documented that schools have not been very effective in closing achievement gaps among racial and ethnic groups and among socioeconomic classes. Nevertheless, schools do have enormous impacts on the intellectual development of all children.

Even the most gifted of children learn—or at least develop—their basic academic skills in schools. Most children come into schools as nonreaders and leave with varying levels of literacy. Similar statements could be made about mathematics, writing, and other academic skills, as well as about knowledge and attitudinal development. Mayeski et al. (1972) stated it very well in a reanalysis of the EEO data: "Schools are indeed important. It is equally clear, however, that their influence is bound up with that of the student's background" (p. ix). Very little of the influence of schools can be separated from the social backgrounds of their students, and very little of the influence of social background on learning can be separated from the influence of the schools. Dealing with the colinearity of variables is a major challenge to researchers making production function analyses in education.

We are growing in our understanding of the relationships between educational inputs and outputs, but the causal relationships between school inputs and processes and pupil achievement are largely unknown. This high degree of ignorance has serious policy implications for deploying strategies to improve student equity, and it calls into question the efficacy of the provision in the 1994 Improving American's School Act that encouraged states to develop "opportunity-to-learn" standards. At this point, the posture of the classroom culturalists looks quite wise—focusing on the normative socialization that occurs within classrooms. There is not sufficient knowledge to specify a one-best-way for the organization, management, and operation of schools from the center, be it the state or the federal government.

Economic Efficiency

In Chapter 11 we described studies by Duncombe and Yinger (1999, 1997; Duncombe, Ruggerio, & Yinger, 1996) and Reschovsky and Imazeki (2001) as examples of econometric approaches to measuring adequacy of provision. We refer to these studies again in this chapter, because they included in their cost functions a variable that was a measure of school district efficiency derived from a statistical process known as data envelopment analysis (DEA).

Duncombe and Yinger (1999) noted that inefficient practices may contribute to higher costs of some schools and districts. In separate calculations, using New York State data, they treated the efficiency measure as an endogenous variable and as an exogenous variable. The rationale for treating efficiency as an endogenous variable is that it could be influenced by unobserved school district characteristics that also influence spending. This was their preferred treatment. For the rationale for treating it as an exogenous variable, they refer to the large literature on the determinants of governmental efficiency (for example, Osborne & Plastrik, 1997; Hollings, 1996; and Osborne & Gaebler, 1992). Treated either way, efficiency corrections reduce cost indices of districts with high costs and raise them for districts with low costs. The effect was greater when efficiency was treated as an exogenous variable, especially for New York City.

In the Reschovsky and Imazeki (2001) study, the range of cost indices was reduced for the state of Texas from 21–400 to 52–177 when an efficiency adjustment was included. With the adjustment, it meant that the district with lowest costs could enable its students to reach average achievement for the state with 52 percent of the state average expenditure per pupil; the district with the highest cost would require 77 percent above average state expenditures to enable its students to reach average achievement. For the state of Wisconsin, the range was reduced from 50–424 to 77–181.

Swanson and Engert (1999) examined three approaches to measuring school and school district efficiency. Because the efficiency analysis at the school level was considered tentative, only the results of the district analysis will be reported here. At the district level, quadriform analysis, ratio analysis, and data envelopment analysis (DEA) were used to measure efficiency. DEA examined both economic efficiency and technical efficiency. The sample that was studied consisted of the 101 school districts and their 398 schools in the western region of New York State. The region contains the two-county Buffalo–Niagara metropolitan area and six rural counties, three of which contain small cities. The region is geographically about the size of Connecticut and contains about 1.5 million people. Achievement and demographic data were obtained from the 1997 *New York State School Report Card* database. Erie County No. One Board of Cooperative Educational Services prepared the financial data for the 1995–1996 school year.

Two types of outcomes measures were developed: average student achievement and average school and school district effect. Average student achievement was measured by four factor scores, derived from the results of state examinations in reading, writing, mathematics, science, and social studies given at grades 3, 4, 5, 6, and 8 and for fifteen State Regents subject matter examinations given in high school. School district effect was estimated from residual scores derived from a multiple regression process to remove statistically the covariance of family and environmental characteristics from student achievement scores. Input measures consisted of expenditures (adjusted for within-region variations in teacher costs) per pupil unit (adjusted for variations in pupil need characteristics).

Modified "Quadriform" Analysis

The quadriform type of analysis was originated by Hickrod et al. (1989) and slightly modified

by Anderson (1996). In this type of analysis, an adjustment for unalterable school characteristics, mostly related to socioeconomic status, is made for both student achievement and expenditure (similar to those noted in the previous paragraph).

The first level of analysis was merely to plot the 101 districts in the region according to average district school effect (*y*- or vertical axis) and approved operating expenditure per education-need unit (*x*- or horizontal axis) using standard scores for each measure. The measure of school effect was determined by averaging the standard scores of the four district-level measures of school effect (grade 3, grades 4 and 5, grade 6, and high school). The resulting distribution of the districts is shown in Figure 12.2. Districts in Quadrant I (upper left) are above average in school effect and below average in expenditure; school districts in this quadrant are the most efficient in the region, according to this analysis. Quadrant II (upper right) represents districts that are above average in school effect and are also above average in expenditures. Quadrant III (lower left) represents districts that are below average in school effect and in expenditure. Quadrant IV represents districts that are below average school in effect and above average in spending; these districts are the least efficient in the region, according to this analysis.

As in most studies of relationships between student outcomes and expenditures, there was no statistically significant correlation between school district effect and expenditure ($r = .15$; level of significance, .15). The top 17 percent of the districts in school effect (more than 1 standard deviation above the mean) ranged in expenditure from \$3,849 per pupil unit to \$7,987. The lowest 17 percent of the districts in school effect ranged in expenditure from \$3,631 per pupil unit to \$5,892. An illustration of extreme disparity in efficiency is provided by two rural districts in the same county where the difference in expenditure per pupil unit was less than \$200, yet one district's effect on student

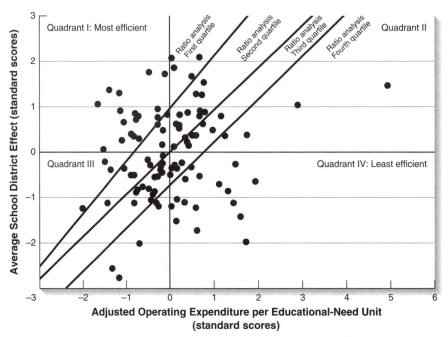

FIGURE 12.2. Bivariate Distribution of Average School District Effect and Adjusted Operating Expenditure per Educational-Need Unit (both measures are represented in standard scores)

Source: Swanson & Engert (1999).

achievement was more than 2 standard deviations higher than the other's.

Looking at school effect from the standpoint of expenditures, school districts spending more than 1 standard deviation below the mean ranged in school effect from 1.36 standard deviations above the mean to 2.76 standard deviations below the mean. Districts spending more than 1 standard deviation above the mean ranged in school effect from 1.94 standard deviations below the mean to 1.46 standard deviations above the mean.

Ratio Analysis

The ratio analysis adheres more closely than the quadriform approach to the classical definition of efficiency as the ratio of outputs to inputs. In this application, the standard score of the school effect measure is divided by the standard score of the expenditure measure.

Both measures are the same as those used in the modified quadriform analysis. Like the modified quadriform analysis, ratio analysis is a measure of economic efficiency. The diagonal lines superimposed on the modified quadriform analysis (see Figure 12.2) represent the boundaries of the quartiles of efficiency of this analysis. The most efficient quartile of schools (the farthest to the left) includes a few very high-performing school districts with expenditures slightly above average for the sample. It also includes a few school districts that are below average in school effect but much below average in expenditure per pupil. The least efficient quartile (the farthest to the right) includes some districts above average in effectiveness but much above average in expenditure. This quartile also includes some districts that have very low school effects but are only slightly below average in expenditure.

Data Envelopment Analysis

The third procedure used to measure school district efficiency was a process known as data envelopment analysis (DEA). DEA uses linear programming concepts to determine the efficiency of an organization in using its resources in terms of outcomes achieved. Charnes, Cooper, and Rhodes (1978) described DEA as "a method for adjusting data to prescribed theoretical requirements such as optimal production surfaces, etc., prior to undertaking various statistical tests for public policy analysis." Figure 12.3 illustrates a hypothetical production possibilities curve for third- and sixth-grade achievement. Efficient districts, such as A, B, C, and D, lie on the curve. District U is inefficient because it is inside the curve and not on its surface. To become efficient, district U would have to modify its use of resources to reflect more closely the practices found in the efficient districts.

DEA has certain advantages over quadriform analysis, ratio analysis, and regression analysis in determining the efficiency of organizations that produce multiple outputs. A number of advantages of the DEA approach are particularly relevant to education:

- DEA can simultaneously handle multiple inputs and outputs.
- DEA does not require parametric specification of the relationships between inputs and outcomes.
- Managerial strategies for improvement of inefficient decision-making units can be determined. Returns-to-scale information may also be available.
- DEA can be used to determine either technical or economic efficiency, if appropriate information is available.

The primary limitation of DEA is that it is an extremal technique and thus is sensitive to inaccurate data. It is also unable to provide measures of statistical association between inputs and outputs, and this makes it more difficult to choose among different model specifications.

It should be noted that DEA determines strict inefficiency. In some cases, good performance in some areas may result in a relatively high efficiency rating even when performance in other areas is mediocre. Given the input and output combinations of *all* the organizations, DEA attempts to optimize the relative efficiency rating of an organization. In determining relative efficiency, the DEA approach compares the district to all other districts in order to assess whether some weighted combination of those districts (subject to appropriate constraints) can outperform the district under consideration. If such a weighted combination *can* be determined, the district is deemed to be inefficient; if not, the district is regarded as efficient. Thus, if it is possible for an organization to be evaluated as efficient, the analysis will identify it as such. A district will be regarded as inefficient only if it truly is inefficient in relation to other districts. Accordingly, this technique errs toward efficiency; that is, low efficiency ratings are the most reliable, and high scores are more likely to be subject to error.

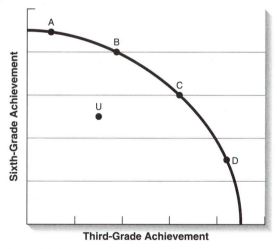

FIGURE 12.3. A Hypothetical Production Possibilities Curve for Third- and Sixth-Grade Achievement

Source: Swanson & Engert (1999).

Two DEA analyses were done in the Swanson and Engert's study (1999), one looking at technical efficiency (DEA technical efficiency model) and the other looking at economic efficiency (DEA economic efficiency model). For the technical efficiency model, the outputs are the four school effect scores; the input measures are the number of teachers, the number of other professionals, and the number of para-professionals per pupil unit. The outputs for the economic efficiency model are the same as for the technical efficiency model, but the inputs are measured solely by the amount of the operating expenditure per pupil unit. The DEA economic efficiency model is most similar to the modified qaudriform and ratio analyses in concept and in results. The DEA technical efficiency model is the only model investigated that attempts to measure technical efficiency.

Table 12.2 reports the Pearson correlation coefficients among the four efficiency models. All are positively correlated with one another, and all relationships are highly significant. The quadriform and ratio models are the most closely correlated, followed by the DEA efficiency and ratio models. As expected because of its different conceptualization, the DEA technical model has the lowest correlations with the three economic efficiency models. School districts in the Buffalo–Niagara metropolitan area were overrepresented in the most-efficient quartile according to the technical efficiency model. However, they were underrepresented in the most-efficient quartiles according to all three economic efficiency models. Rural districts tend to have lower pupil/teacher ratios than urban and suburban districts, so they rank lower on technical efficiency. On the other hand, rural districts pay less for their teachers and other staff, which gives them an advantage on economic efficiency measures. Corrections for differences in salary costs had been made, but apparently the adjustments were not sufficient.

Studies that directly analyze the economic efficiency of schools and of school districts are in their infancy. Much work remains to be done in refining the theoretical conceptualization and the methodologies used before this line of research can be of practical value to policy makers and educational practitioners. But a good start has been made. In the next section, we shift our perspective from that of policy mechanics to that of classroom culturalists as we discuss aspects of technical efficiency.

Technical Efficiency

Technical efficiency is a term used by economists, not educators, but most of the evaluation studies done by educators are of this nature. Technical efficiency is concerned with discovering

TABLE 12.2.

Pearson Correlation Coefficient Matrix for the Four Efficiency Models

Correlations	*Quadriform*	*Ratio*	*DEA Efficiency*	*DEA Technical*
Quadriform	1.000	.737	.535	.275
		P = .000	P = .000	P = .005
Ratio	.737	1.000	.721	.361
	P = .000		P = .000	P = .000
DEA Efficiency	.535	.721	1.000	.433
	P = .000	P = .000		P = .000
DEA Technical	.275	.361	.433	1.000
	P = .005	P = .000	P = .000	

Source: Swanson and Engert (1999).

what combination of inputs has the most favorable effect on outcomes (pupil performance). Unlike in economic efficiency studies, however, the cost of inputs is not a consideration. In this section, we have grouped technical efficiency studies into three categories for discussion purposes: effective-schools research, evaluation studies, and whole-school reform models.

Effective-Schools Research

Effective-schools research constituted another reaction to the conclusions of the EEO study and of other production function studies that schools had little impact on closing the gap between minority and majority pupils in academic achievement. Whereas education production function research takes a normative approach in studying school efficiency, effective-schools research focuses on exceptions to the norm. It consists largely of performing case studies of schools and classrooms that have unusually positive effects on pupil achievement in order to identify practices that might cause or contribute to that effectiveness (Brookover & Lezotte, 1979; Edmonds, 1979; Jackson, Logsdon & Taylor, 1983; Reed, 1985; Sammons, 1999; Venezsky & Winfield, 1980; and, Weber, 1971). Effective-schools research usually ignores cost considerations; thus its findings are more closely related to technical efficiency than to economic efficiency and are especially relevant to the philosophy of the classroom culturalists.

Effective schools have been found to be characterized by effective classroom teaching practices that include high teacher expectations, good classroom management techniques, and greater "time on task" than one would find in most schools. These schools are also characterized by strong leadership, usually in the person of the principal, who coordinates the instructional program at the building level in a manner that is tightly coupled, but not bureaucratic. The principal appears to be a key factor in establishing a common school culture and a sense of community consisting of "shared goals; high expectations for student performance; mechanisms to sustain motivation and commitment; collegiality among teachers, students, and the principal; and a school-wide focus on continuous improvement" (Odden & Webb, 1983, p. xiv). Given current assumptions about schooling, effective-schools research has identified some ways for schools to make more efficient use of the resources they already have.

Monk (1989) referred to effective-schools research as "backwards-looking." He called effective schools, "sites of excellence . . . making exemplary use of traditional, labor intensive instructional technologies" (p. 38). According to him, effective schools accept all the parameters of the present system, and the methodology condemns them to refine the current system's very labor-intensive and expensive organization and practice rather than permitting them to break through into the discovery and use of new technologies.

Evaluation Studies

Evaluation studies of schooling also have important implications for the technical efficiency of schools. For the most part, like effective-schools research, evaluation studies do not take into account the price of inputs. Evaluation studies have produced results that provide a basis for greater optimism about the impact of schools on pupil achievement than those conducted by economists and sociologists. Some examples follow.

Class size reduction. An excellent example of evaluation research is the Tennessee Project Star study of the relationship between class size and pupil achievement (Finn & Achilles, 1999). This study was a controlled scientific experiment involving over 6,000 students in 329 classrooms in 79 schools in 46 districts the first year and nearly 12,000 students during the 4-year intervention. Students entering kindergarten within each participating school were assigned randomly to a small class (13–17 students), to a regular class (22–26 students), or to a regular class with a full-time teacher aide. Children were kept in the same experimental arrangement for four years. All pupils returned to regular classes in grade 4, but the researchers were able to follow the participants in ensuing years. Teachers were assigned to classrooms at random. A new teacher was assigned each year. There were no interventions other than class size and teacher aide. Students took both norm-referenced and criterion-referenced examinations at the end of each school year. Teachers and aides completed questionnaires and time logs to document their perceptions and experiences. The study design permitted analysis of effects on groups of students by race, gender, and socioeconomic status.

On average, students in small classes displayed higher academic achievement than students in other arrangements. Small class size helped boys and girls alike, but the positive impact was substantially greater for minority students and for students attending inner-city schools. The small class achievement advantage in all subjects carried forward to grade 4 and beyond after all students had returned to a regular classroom environment. There were no statistical differences found for most teacher activities, subject emphasis, classroom atmosphere, or quality measures. This led the researchers to conclude that "Small classes are academically superior not because they encourage new approaches to instruction but because teachers can engage in more (perhaps even *enough*) of the basic strategies they have been using all along" (p. 103). A study by Stasz and Stecher (2000) suggested what these strategies might be. Although teaching practices in reduced-size and non-reduced-size classes were quite similar, teachers in reduced-size classes spent more individual time with students identified as poor readers and more time discussing students' personal concerns; they spent less time on student discipline.

In all cases in the Tennessee study, students in small classes outperformed those in regular classes with teacher aides (Gerber, Finn, Achilles, & Boyd-Zaharias, 2001). The researchers concluded that "teacher aides do not offer the academic benefits of small classes and would not constitute an effective alternative" (p. 133).

Levin and McEwan (2001) attribute much of the recent support for small class size in the primary grades to the Tennessee study. At least nineteen states have considered class size reduction plans, and federal resources have been made available as well. Levin, Glass, and Meister (1987) compared the cost-effectiveness of four educational reforms, including class size reduction. They concluded that class size reduction was one of the more costly options for obtaining a fixed gain in student achievement. Peer tutoring was found to be among the most cost-effective in terms of achievement gain per unit of cost.

One of the states that adopted a class size reduction policy was California. Picus (2001) notes that this policy made a severe teacher shortage even worse and threatened to dilute the quality of teaching staff, especially in schools serving the greatest numbers of at-risk children. He pointed out that research also indicates that attention to teacher training and expertise may have a bigger payoff per dollar spent than class size reduction. The National Commission on Teaching and America's Future (1996) proposed new designs for organizing schools that would enable specialized teachers to be used in ways that would make it possible to reduce class size without hiring more teachers.

Extended school year. A study conducted on a randomly selected panel of 790 children in the Baltimore Public Schools provides impressive evidence of the value of preschool and summer school programs (Alexander, Entwisle, & Olson, 2001). The students, selected at random, began first grade in 1982 in twenty Baltimore schools, selected through a stratified random process. Six schools were predominantly African American in enrollment, six were predominantly white, and eight were integrated. Fourteen of the schools were classified as serving a working-class clientele and six as serving middle-class communities. Testing was done in the fall and spring each year, beginning with the fall of 1982 and continuing through the spring of 1987, and thus covering five school years and four summers. The achievement data were obtained from school records, as were demographic information and family socioeconomic standing. The latter was supplemented by parent interviews. Data were analyzed using descriptive procedures and hierarchical linear modeling.

The researchers found that school year gains in achievement were about the same across SES levels. The summer pattern was quite different, however. Lower-SES children stayed at about the same level in reading ability over the summer but lost in quantitative ability. Upper-SES children showed substantial gains in both reading and quantitative abilities over the summer and hence well ahead of their lower-SES peers when school resumed in the fall. The researchers concluded that schools do matter and that they matter most when support for academic learning outside the school is weak. Disadvantaged children "are capable learners. They keep up during the school year, but before they start first grade and in summers between grades the out-of-school resources available to them are not sufficient to support their achievement" (p. 183). On the basis of their findings, the researchers recommend preschool and full-day kindergarten experiences for all low-SES children, as well as summer school or extended-year programs.

Special education. Reynolds and Wolfe (1999) studied the effect on children's achievement of placement in special education during the elementary grades. They also examined the effects of grade retention and mobility from school to school. The sample, which was representative of Chicago children at-risk who participated in government-funded early-childhood programs, included 1,234 children who were in the sixth grade in 1992 and were involved in the Chicago Longitudinal Study (Reynolds, Bezruczko, Mavrogenes, & Hagemann, 1996). Performance was measured by scores on standardized achievement tests taken by each child in each grade from kindergarten through grade 6. The database included extensive information on the twenty-five schools in which the children were enrolled, as well as limited information on the children's families. Children in special-education programs were divided into two categories: those with learning disabilities and all others.

Data were analyzed using multiple regression analysis for each grade level, with achievement test scores for either reading or mathematics serving as the dependent variable. The core independent variable of interest was participation in special education. Achievement test scores for the previous year were included as a pretest control variable. Other control variables were included for demographic and background factors, school characteristics, and school experiences.

Reynolds and Wolfe (1999) concluded that "Only in the earlier grades, and only for children with disabilities other than learning disabilities (such as hearing, sight, or physical handicaps) does the [special-education] program seem to add in a significant way to achievement in reading and math" (p. 263). Children with learning disabilities assigned to special-education programs actually did worse than would be expected on the basis of their scores from the previous year. Except for kindergarten retention (suggesting that some children enter school too immature to advance immediately), children who were retained tended to do worse after repeating a grade. Children who moved from school to school showed reduced achievement, and in schools where there was extensive mobility, the achievement of all children was negatively affected. In discussing their findings, Reynolds and Wolfe noted the $10,000 (or more) per-pupil cost of special-education programs and suggest that the money might better be spent making improvements in the schools generally, or for early-childhood interventions, peer tutoring, or cooperative learning. Alternatively, special-education programs could be integrated with or used in combination with other educational and family services.

School Reform Networks

A number of organizational strategies intended to make schools more effective have been developed over the past decade and a half. Eight of these were developed through the initiative of New American Schools (NAS). NAS, a private, not-for-profit organization, was formed in 1991 by a group of corporate executives at the urging of President George H. W. Bush, who challenged them "to harness the nation's special genius for invention to create the next generation of American schools" (NAS, 2000a, p. 15). Toward that end, in 1992 NAS awarded start-up grants to 11 design teams selected from 686 proposals. The teams developed eight model school designs, "a plan for reorganizing an entire school around a common vision of higher student achievement, replacing the traditional approach of piecemeal programs" (p. 15). The RAND Corporation has served as a third-party evaluator of the process from the beginning. By 2001 approximately 3,000 schools nationwide were attempting to implement one of the NAS designs. All told, some 6,000 schools have engaged in comprehensive school reform using NAS or other models. It is estimated that there are nearly 300 comprehensive school reform consultants available to assist them.

Fashola and Slavin (1998) pointed out that classroom-level change cannot be dictated from above; however, not every school must reinvent the wheel. School staffs and commu-nity representatives can select among a variety of existing, well-designed methods and materials that have been shown to be effective with children. Schools subscribing to a given set of organizing principles have formed networks, usually under the direction of the model designer.

Fashola and Slavin (1998) point out the advantages to schools and school districts of adopting these "off the shelf" instructional models.

> Organizations behind each of the school-wide models provide professional development, materials, and networks of fellow users. These reform organizations bring to a school broad experience working with high-poverty schools in many contexts. Unlike district or state staff development offices, external reform networks are invited in only if they are felt to meet a need, and they can be invited back out again if they fail to deliver. Their services can be expensive, but the costs are typically within the Title I resources available to high-poverty school-wide projects. (p. 371)

These reform models assumed new importance with the passage by Congress of the 1994 Title I of the Elementary and Secondary Education Act (ESEA). This reauthorization of ESEA made it easier for high-poverty schools to be designated school-wide Title I projects (see Chapter 10). This designation, which can be obtained by any school with at least 50 percent of its students in poverty, allows a school to use Title I funds for school-wide change, not just for changes that serve individual students who are having difficulties. The release of a national evaluation of Chapter I of ESEA (subsequently renamed Title I) (Puma et al., 1997) called into question the effectiveness of the entire program, and Congress responded by passing the Comprehensive School Reform Demonstration Program (CSRD) bill in 1997. This bill authorized $150 million in federal grants to schools to undertake "whole-school" reform; seventeen models were listed in the bill as examples of the types of reforms that could be considered for funding.

Fashola and Slavin (1998; 1997) evaluated thirteen schoolwide models for elementary and middle schools that they considered "promising, ambitious, comprehensive, and widely available." Subsequently, the American Institutes for Research (AIR) (1999) released *An Educators' Guide to School-wide Reform* rating twenty-four designs of whole-school reform. The development of the guide was commissioned by the National Education Association, the American Association of School Administrators, the American Federation of Teachers, the American Association of Elementary School Principals, and the American Association of Secondary School Principals. The guide was intended to provide school officials with reliable information as they sought proven solutions for low-performing schools. The guide rated the reform models according to whether they improved achievement in such measurable ways as boosting test scores and attendance rates. It also evaluated the level of assistance provided by model developers to schools that implemented the models, and it compared the first-year costs of the programs.

As a consequence of the CSRD, the U.S. Department of Education contracted with Northwest Regional Educational Laboratory (NWREL) to develop a *Catalog of School Reform Models*, first published in 1998.[2] The 2001 edition contained detailed descriptions of thirty-two whole-school reform models, eleven reading/language arts models, six mathematics models, four science models, and ten models identified as "other." Each entry analyzes (among other elements) the model's general approach, results with students, implementation assistance, and costs. Demographic data and contact information are also provided. Among the criteria for selecting models for inclusion were evidence of improving student academic achievement, extent of replication, implementation assistance provided to schools, and comprehensiveness.

NAS (2000b) produced guidelines to help schools and school districts choose models appropriate to their purposes and circumstances. The guide offers frameworks for selecting a model and for evaluating assistance providers. Experience has shown that the real challenge, however, is in implementing a model once it has been chosen (Viadero, 2001). In tracking 163 schools that had implemented one of the NAS designs over a 5-year period, RAND evaluators found that only about half had shown greater improvement in student achievement than students in their overall districts (Kirby, Berends, & Naftel, 2001). They observed that programs were adopted more fully in smaller schools and in elementary schools. Schools where teachers tended to blame students and their families for poor achievement were less likely to embrace the models fully. Having a stable team of consultants who could provide staff development for the entire faculty, rather than just for a selected few, greatly enhanced the possibility of success. Finally, active support from the principal was essential, as was district-level support. As noted in Chapter 11, an analysis by Odden and Picus (2000) showed that even after allowing for planning and preparation time, the average elementary, middle, and high school in the United States has sufficient resources to finance all these school designs by reallocating resources already committed.

Studies of technical efficiency provide clear evidence that some educational practices are better than others. This means there is great hope for improving effectiveness of schooling. But public policy should not be built on the findings of these studies alone, because they do not take into account cost—that is, the price of inputs. Effective practices must be costed out, and we need studies that compare the costs and effectiveness of alternative policy options. The next section addresses economies of scale, which is an area where we find both policy mechanics and classroom culturalists busily at work. Clearly, *economies of scale* is an economic term with strong economic implications. But the recent triumphs of the "small is beautiful" advocates are due largely to the research of the classroom culturalists.

Economies and Diseconomies of Scale

If we assume a universal education production function, economies of scale are realized when average production costs decline as more units are produced or serviced. Conversely, there are diseconomies of scale when average production costs increase as more units are produced or serviced. Traditionally, the cost curve of educational institutions has been assumed to be continually falling, supporting policies of district consolidation and large schools. Now, however, there is strong evidence that the cost curves for schools (and school districts), as for most other enterprises, decline to a point and then rise. Finding the point of inflection is now an important target of scale research in education. These are key concepts that need to be taken into account in designing efficient educational enterprises.

School district consolidation attempts to realize economies of scale, whereas decentralizing large city school districts entails an effort to avoid diseconomies of scale. Likewise, during periods of declining enrollments, closing underutilized buildings is a strategy for minimizing operating costs. Reorganizing very large schools into "houses" or "schools within schools," is a strategy for realizing the benefits of both large and small units, while minimizing their disadvantages. Interest in scale economies derives from concern over both economic and technical efficiency.

Policy implications drawn from studies of relationships among school and district size, pupil achievement, and cost have taken a dramatic turn in the last two decades. From the beginning of this century through the 1960s, the overwhelming evidence seemed to support large schools and school districts in terms of both economics and the higher number, diversity, and caliber of professional and administrative personnel that large schools could attract. These early studies were concerned primarily with inputs (costs) and gave little if any attention to outputs and ratios of outputs to inputs. As researchers began to take into account total cost and socioeconomic status of pupils, and to include measures of output such as achievement, pupil self-image, and success in college, economies of scale evaporated at relatively low numbers of pupils. The disadvantages of large size became readily apparent. A recent review of the literature on the impact of size on school effectiveness (Raywid, 1999) found consistent evidence that in small schools, students learn more, are more satisfied and drop out less often, and behave better. This is particularly true for at-risk students. Raywid concluded that these things have been confirmed "with a clarity and at a level of confidence rare in the annals of education research."

The new emphasis in research on the relationships between size and quality of schooling may have been a by-product of disenchantment with large city schools. City educational systems had served through the 1950s as the standard of quality education to which rural and suburban schools aspired. Beginning in the 1960s and continuing through the present, evidence has surfaced of low cognitive achievement, low attendance rates, and high dropout rates in urban school systems. This, coupled with the large urban schools' inability to use substantial federal and state funds to raise the achievement levels of most disadvantaged children, severely marred their image as exemplary educational institutions.

It now appears that, given present assumptions about how schools (and school districts) should organize, the relationships between size and quality of schooling are curvilinear. The benefits brought by larger enrollments increase to an optimal point and then decline, following an inverted U-shaped curve (Riew, 1981 & 1986; Fox, 1981; Engert, 1995). Ballou (1998) concluded that the evidence strongly suggests that urban districts exceed the size that is optimal for realizing economies of scale. "It would appear that scale economies at the district level are exhausted somewhere between the typical suburban size (about 5,000 students) and the average urban enrollment of 15,000" (pp. 69–70).

Scale research has two foci: the district and the school. For very small districts, these are the same thing. Large districts have choices, however, and can operate schools over a wide range of sizes. Thus a large district may operate small schools as a matter of district policy, although most do not. Large districts also may formulate most policy centrally, or they may empower schools to make policy within general parameters established at the center. Large schools can operate as a single unit or can organize "schools within schools" to secure the advantages inherent in both large and small size.

What size should a school be? Barker and Gump (1964) presented a contrarian view for that period. Although they were not specific, they provided a guide that remains helpful today as they concluded their classical work with these words:

> The data of this research and our own educational values tell us that a school should be sufficiently small that all of its students are needed for its enterprises. A school should be small enough that students are not redundant. (p. 202)

Barker and Gump (1964) found that large school size has an undesirable influence on the development of certain personal attributes of students. Specifically, they found that in most large schools, just a few students dominate the leadership roles, whereas in small schools, proportionately more students take an active part in school programs. The actual proportion of students who participated in extracurricular activities, as well as the satisfaction of students with their schooling, clearly supported small local schools over large centralized ones.

Although more varieties of subjects are available to students in large schools, Baker and Gump observed that a given pupil participates in proportionately fewer of these electives in large schools than in small schools. They concluded that " . . . if versatility of experience is preferred over opportunity for specialization, a smaller school is better than a larger one; if specialization is sought, the larger school is the better" (p. 201).

A 1986 study by the U.S. Department of Education updated Barker and Gump's analysis (1964) and concluded that their findings still held. The 1986 study reported that participation rates in extracurricular activities were consistently greater for small high schools (200 or fewer seniors) than for larger ones. Small schools also compared favorably with larger schools with respect to course credits taken by students, hours of homework, test scores and grade average, and involvement in extracurricular activities (Sweet, 1986). Lindsay (1982), replicating the Barker and Gump study by using a representative national sample of 328 elementary schools, found higher participation in extracurricular activities, greater student satisfaction, and better attendance in small schools (fewer than 100 in each grade level). Studies conducted in the decade of the 1990s continued to produce similar findings (Lee & Smith, 1995; Howley, 1994; McMullan, Sipe, & Wolf, 1994; Stockard & Mayberry, 1992).

Newman (1981) reported the optimal size of secondary schools to fall in the range of 500 to 1,200 pupils. Student participation in school activities and general interaction were greatest, and vandalism and delinquency were lowest, in that range.

> The opportunity that small schools provide for sustained contact among all members is a significant safeguard against alienation. The larger the school, the more difficult it is to achieve clear, consensual goals, to promote student participation in school management, and to create positive personal relations among students and staff. (p. 552)

In a similar vein, Rogers (1992) pointed to the disaffectedness and disconnectedness of many of today's youth of all types.

When kids belong, they are engaged, they are "available" to learn and be taught. However, behind the pedagogical justification which argues for small schools where kids can be easily known, there is a psychological advantage as well. Adolescence is a time of craving acceptance, ways to fit in, a sense of *belonging*. In a large school where anonymity is the rule, kids go to what we might consider foolish lengths in order to gain attention and acceptance. . . . The lack of connection that leads some kids to join gangs is frighteningly pervasive, invading even those communities we think of as "safe." (pp. 103–105)

Goodlad (1984), in his comprehensive national study of *A Place Called School*, observed,

Most of the schools clustering in the top group of our sample on major characteristics were small, compared with the schools clustering near the bottom. It is not impossible to have a good large school; it is simply more difficult. What are the defensible reasons for operating an elementary school of more than a dozen teachers and 300 boys and girls? I can think of none. (p. 309)

With respect to secondary school size, Goodlad wrote,

Clearly we need sustained, creative efforts designed to show the curricular deficits incurred in very small high schools, the curricular possibilities of larger schools, and the point where increased size suggests no curricular gain. . . . The burden of proof, it appears to me, is on large size. Indeed, I would not want to face the challenge of justifying a senior, let alone a junior, high of more than 500 to 600 students (unless I were willing to place arguments for a strong football team ahead of arguments for a good school, which I am not). (p. 310)

Berlin and Cienkus (1989), after co-editing an issue of *Education and Urban Society* devoted to the subject of size of school districts, schools, and classrooms, concluded that "smaller seems to be better."

Why does smaller seem to work better? . . . The literature on educational change repeats the answer. That is, people seem to learn, to change, and to grow in situations in which they feel that they have some control, some personal influence, some efficacy. Those situations in which parents, teachers and students are bonded together in pursuit of learning are likely to be the most productive. Small size by itself can only aid the complex process. (p. 231)

In reporting on a Carnegie Foundation study, Boyer (1983) noted that research over the past several decades has suggested that small schools provide greater opportunity for student participation and greater emotional support than larger ones. Acknowledging the difficulty of knowing at exactly what point a high school becomes too large, he proposed that schools enrolling 1,500 to 2,000 students were good candidates for reorganizing into smaller units (using a schools-within-a-school concept). Turning to the issue of the small high school, Boyer raised another key question:

Can a small school provide the education opportunities to match the social and emotional advantages that may accompany smallness? We believe the preferred arrangement is to have bigness *and* smallness—a broad education program with supportive social arrangements. (p. 235)

There is evidence, however, that it is more difficult to gain the advantages of smallness in the schools-within-a-school environment than when small schools stand alone (Raywid, 1996a, 1996b; Viadero, 2001). When a unit becomes more successful than others in the host unit, staff in the successful unit are likely to be called upon to coach and consult with sister units, which may distract them from their instructional purpose. Other units may also become resentful and work to undermine the successful unit.

New York City discovered the value of small schools combined with parental choice and community involvement in its Central Park East Project in East Harlem, one of the poorest sections of the city (Bensman, 2000; Meier, 1995a and 1995b, 1998; Fliegel & MacGuire, 1993). Over thirty small schools of choice were created. Rather than trying to fit all students into a standard school, planners designed a variety of schools so that there is a school to fit every student. The concept is now being replicated throughout the city (Bradley, 1995).

Meier (1995b) stressed the importance of smallness to the success of the pedagogical innovations implemented in the schools she founded in Central Park East. She recommended a maximum size for elementary schools of 300 pupils, and for high schools of 400. She contended that small and focused educational communities enhance the climate of trust between families and schools and facilitate deep ongoing discussions in ways that produce change and involve the entire faculty. Small schools enable the faculty to know students and their work individually, and they permit adults to play a significant role in the development of a positive school culture. Small schools more easily provide for the physical safety of all and are more readily made accountable to parents and to the public.

There also appears to be no cost disadvantage to smaller schools. Stiefel, Berne, Iatarola, and Fruchter (2000) studied the effect of size of high school on cost per graduate in New York City. Their sample included 121 high schools ranging in size from 185 to 4,957. When viewed on a cost-per-student-enrolled basis, small academic high schools (fewer than 600 students) were somewhat more expensive. But when viewed according to the number of students they graduate, small high schools, because of their lower dropout rates, were less expensive than medium-sized ones (600–2,000 students) and about the same in cost as large high schools (over 2,000 students).

Through her work in Philadelphia, Fine (1993) saw large schools as promoting a general, rather than a particularistic, perspective on students. "They encourage passivity rather than participation, and they stress, by definition, the need to control students rather than to engage them critically" (p. 273). To address the concerns of Philadelphia school officials over low student achievement and high dropout rates, the city followed a strategy similar to that being pursued in New York. Big secondary schools are being broken up into charter schools of 200–400 students with ten to twelve core faculty working with students from ninth grade through graduation. This restructuring aims to address the emotional and social needs of students and to engage the intellects and passions of educators and scholars. According to Fine, accomplishing these goals is much more difficult in large settings.

Research in Chicago also supports the value of small schools in the inner-city environment. Lee and Loeb (2000) studied 264 schools there with a K–8 grade configuration. The schools ranged in size from 150 to nearly 2,000 students. These investigators concluded that school size influences student achievement directly and indirectly through its effect on teacher attitudes. They found that teachers in smaller schools assumed more responsibility for student learning than teachers in middle-size and large schools. This resulted in more intimate and personal social relations among teachers and students—an atmosphere that facilitated a wholesome learning environment and led to higher student achievement.

Citing supporting research, Darling-Hammond (1996) identified small size as one of the important characteristics of high-performing schools. All else being equal, small schools in the range of 300 to 500 students are associated with higher achievement, better attendance rates, fewer dropouts, and lower levels of misbehavior. Because they are less fragmented, are more personalized, and facilitate frequent and purposeful interaction among and between students and staff, "they are more effective in allowing students to become bonded to important adults in a learning community that can play the roles that families and communities find harder and harder to play" (p. 148).

A number of other studies have produced recommendations of optimal size. Chicago's Cross City Campaign for Urban School Reform set the limits at 350 students for elementary schools and 500 students for high schools (Fine & Somerville, 1998). Williams (1990) recommended up to 800 students for high schools. Lee and Smith (1997) found the optimal range for high schools to be 600 to 900 students. Raywid (1999) concluded that studies emphasizing the importance of the school as a community tend to set lower limits than studies emphasizing academic effectiveness as measured by test scores. Nevertheless, most schools in urban and suburban areas (and even some rural schools) are larger than the size supported by research conducted in the last fifteen years.

Economist Ronald Coase (1988) developed a theory of "transaction costs" to explain such phenomena in organizations in general (for this work, he received the Nobel Prize in economics in 1991). Transaction costs are costs of communication, coordination, and deciding. Eventually, expansion of an organization (for example, a school or district) can lead to diseconomies and higher unit costs because of managerial problems that are characteristic of large operations. Conventional estimates of economies of scale have vastly underestimated transaction costs.

Tainter (1988), an archaeologist, came to similar conclusions. He observed that sociopolitical organizations constantly encounter problems that require increased investment merely to preserve the status quo. This investment comes in such forms as increasing size of bureaucracies, increasing specialization of bureaucracies, cumulative organizational solutions, increasing costs of legitimizing activities, and increasing costs of internal control and external defense. The reason why complex organizations must allocate ever larger portions of their personnel and other resources to administration is that increased complexity requires greater quantities of information processing and greater integration of disparate parts. All of these increased costs are borne by the support population, often to no increased advantage. Educational organizations are no exception; as complexity and specialization increase, so does

the cost of education, and at the same time the marginal product declines.

Like other organizations, large school districts and schools have experienced the dysfunctional forces of bureaucratization. But through restructuring, public school organizations appear to be able to compensate at least partially for these natural tendencies through practices such as those being tried in New York City, Philadelphia, and Chicago, among other places. In the past, providing diversity in curriculum and support services at an affordable cost was the primary justification for large urban schools and rural school consolidation. Now, the disadvantages of bigness and the virtues of smallness have been well documented. Furthermore, technological advances characteristic of the "Information Age" have made it possible for any individual in almost any place to access curricular diversity easily. These developments compel reassessment of the large-school policies of central cities and of states' school consolidation policies for rural areas. Although it is clear that there are disadvantages in being very small and in being very large, there is little agreement on optimal size. The challenge before us is to provide the stimulating learning environments and broad educational programs that are characteristic of large schools *and* the supportive social structure that characterizes small schools, within the oversight of a responsive, coordinating centralized framework.

Aligning Economic and Technical Efficiency

Analyses of economic and technical efficiency have presented us with conflicting results. Economic efficiency studies suggest that schools are using the resources allocated to them inefficiently and that there are, at best, tenuous links between financial inputs and student outcomes. Analyses of the technical efficiency of programs and even of whole-school reform models, however, show that some approaches work much better than others and that students can experience significant educational gains from some program innovations. The disparity between the findings of these two approaches suggests at least two possible explanations. Schools, in general, are not using what has been shown to be best practice. Or, because evaluations of technical efficiency do not consider the *cost* of resources as do studies of economic efficiency, the problem may lie with the pricing and distribution of resources commonly used in the instructional process. Both explanations are probably correct, but in this section we will consider the latter. We will focus on paying for and distributing professional staff because they represent over half of all school expenditures. With respect to the former, much of the literature reviewed in Chapters 11–15 points out many areas where demonstrated best practice is not commonly used by the public schools of the United States.

Current Practice

With few exceptions, teachers are paid according to a single salary schedule that has two dimensions: length of service and amount of formal education beyond the bachelor's degree. Thus a teacher with twenty years of experience and thirty graduate credit hours beyond the master's degree is likely to earn about twice as much as a beginning teacher with a bachelor's degree. Yet research, some of which was cited in the previous section on production functions, has shown that there is little evidence of any relationship between the number of graduate hours that a teacher has accumulated and student achievement. Furthermore, even though length of teaching service has been found to be generally unrelated to academic achievement of most students after the first three to five years, it is common practice for school districts to provide salary increments for length of service up to fifteen years—and sometimes more. (There is some evidence that experienced teachers are more effective in working with educationally at-risk children, but not with advantaged children.)

In assigning teaching duties, school districts recognize the lack of relationship between student performance and teacher education level and longevity; beginning teachers with a bachelor's degree are assigned responsibilities nearly identical to those assigned to teachers with long tenure and much graduate education. Thus, one first-grade teacher may be earning $30,000 per year while the first-grade teacher in the adjoining classroom may be earning $60,000, even though their responsibilities are nearly identical. To make matters even more bizarre, it is not unusual for teachers to have gained, through collective bargaining, the right to transfer to open teaching positions on the basis of their seniority in service. This frequently results in the schools with the best working conditions (schools that enroll high-achieving and well-disciplined children) having the most senior and expensive staffs, while the schools with large portions of educationally "at-risk" children have the least experienced and least expensive teachers. In effect, because of the higher salaries paid to teachers in the more attractive schools, proportionately more economic resources are placed in those schools than in schools with greater need, although physical resources (such as the numbers of teachers) may be the same in all schools (Guthrie, 1997). Illustrations of this phenomenon were given in the discussion of intradistrict equity in Chapter 11 for New York City, Chicago, and Dade County, Florida.

Another practice that contributes to the disparity in results between analyses of economic and technical efficiency is the growing use of specialists and support staff. Some research has indicated the importance of small class size and the continuity of relationship between teacher and student, but school districts have added relatively fewer regular classroom teachers than they have professional specialists who supervise and consult with classroom teachers and operate "pull-out" programs. This practice has been shown to weaken teacher-student relationships and the influence of classroom teachers on their students, while adding greatly to the cost of public schooling and doing little to enhance student achievement.

From 1960 to 1998, the number of pupils per teacher (classroom and special teachers in grades K–12) dropped from 25.8 to 17.2 (down 33 percent), and average class size at the elementary level dropped from 29 to 24 (down 17 percent). At the secondary level, average class size actually increased from 28 to 31 (up 11 percent), although the mean number of students taught per day dropped from 138 to 97 (down 30 percent) (NCES, 1999). From 1960 to 1996, the number of pupils per staff member (including classroom and special teachers, administrators, and support staff) declined from 16.8 to 8.9 (down 47 percent), indicating that support staff have been added at a greater rate than professional staff.

Looking at the trends from a different perspective, the National Commission on Teaching and America's Future (NCTAF) (1996) reported that the proportion of professional staff classified as teachers declined from more than 70 percent in 1950 to 52 percent in 1993. Of this 52 percent, more than 10 percent were specialists not engaged in classroom teaching. For every four classroom teachers, there are nearly six other school employees. By contrast, NCTAF reports that in other developed countries, teaching staffs represent from 60 to 80 percent of public education employees. In defense of school districts that have added specialists and support staff to their rosters, it is in response to state and federal categorical aid programs and mandates that are only now beginning to allow greater discretion at the local level.

Miles (1995) identified four managerial and educational practices behind these staffing trends:

1. Large numbers of specialized teachers working outside regular classrooms with specifically defined classifications of students

2. The practice of providing teachers with planning time in short, fragmented periods during the school day and using other classroom teachers to cover instruction at these times

3. A formula-driven approach to grouping students for instruction that is guided by formal student classification and contract guidelines rather than by school-level decisions

4. The fragmented daily schedule at the secondary school level in which teachers instruct five completely different groups of students for less than an hour each day (pp. 477–478)

NCTAF has soundly criticized the resulting bureaucracy:

> Far too many people sit in offices at the sidelines of the core work, managing routines rather than promoting innovation aimed at improving quality. A bureaucratic school spends substantial resources on controlling its staff; a thoughtful school invests in knowledge and supports that liberate staff members to do their jobs well. A traditional school administers rules and procedures; a learning organization develops shared goals and talents. Our inherited school anticipates the worst from students and teachers; the school of the future expects and enables the best. (p. 101)

NCTAF has expressed well the case for "whole-school" and, indeed, systemic reform.

Rethinking the Allocation of Teacher Resources

This situation has led a number of analysts to call for a reallocation of teaching resources. Miles and Darling-Hammond (1998) have observed six resource reallocation strategies used by high-performing schools to improve achievement within general constraints of existing resources. These are reduction of specialized programs, more flexible student grouping by school-level professionals, structures that create more personalized environments, longer and varied blocks of instructional time, more common planning time for staff, and creative definition of staff roles and work schedules.

NCTAF (1996) has developed a five-pronged strategy for ensuring that all communities have teachers with the knowledge and skills they need so that all children can learn and so that all school systems are organized to support teachers in this work. Two are particularly relevant to the concerns of this section: encourage and reward teacher knowledge and skill, and create schools that are organized for student and teacher success.

Figure 12.4 illustrates how a typical elementary school of six hundred pupils can be reorganized following NCTAF's guidelines. The plan reduces average class size from twenty-five students to sixteen or seventeen and increases teachers' planning time from less than four hours per week to at least ten hours. *All of this is accomplished using only the personnel normally assigned to such a school.* This is done by creating teams of teachers who share students. Nearly all adults in these teaching teams are engaged in such a way that they can share expertise directly with one another, thereby reducing pullouts and nonteaching jobs. "The school's resources are pushed into the core classroom structure where they can be used in the context of extended relationships with students rather than sitting around the periphery of the school to be applied in brief encounters with students or in coordinative rather than teaching roles" (p. 105).

The school is divided into two divisions: one for primary grades and one for intermediate grades. Each division has three instructional teams consisting of seven teachers, including one with counseling expertise, one with special-education expertise and one with arts expertise. Each team serves one hundred students representative of all ages within a given division, permitting the team and students to remain together for at least three years

(Veenman, 1995; Osin & Lesgold, 1996). The teams in each division share a media/computer specialist and a lead teacher who is released half-time from teaching to facilitate planning and to cover classes while other teachers visit and observe one another. The support staff for the school consists of a principal, a secretary/bookkeeper, and a social worker. NCTAF also urges that the investment in teachers be accompanied with investments in technology that extend the capacity of every teacher and child to connect with an infinite variety of resources and tools for learning. NCTAF proposes that principals come from the ranks of highly skilled teachers and that they continue to have some teaching responsibilities.

Odden (1996) notes that compensation theory counsels policy makers on the importance of matching pay practices to the strategic needs of organizations. NCTAF does this by linking teacher salaries to a progressive demonstration of growing knowledge and skills that mark a career continuum. NCTAF starts with the presumption that teachers will be hired only after completing a high-quality preparation program accredited by the NCATE (National Council for Accreditation of Teacher Education) and passing tests of subject matter knowledge and teaching knowledge to receive an initial license. In 1995 NCATE established new standards reflecting the evolution of a much stronger knowledge base for teaching and requiring schools of education to demonstrate how they are incorporating these higher expectations into their preparation programs. NCTAF recommends that licensing examinations be based on the standards set by the Interstate New Teacher Assessment and Support Consortium (INTASC), a consortium of more than thirty states that has tackled the question of what beginning teachers must know and must be able to do to teach in the ways the new student standards demand. INTASC standards are aligned with NCATE standards. NCTAF proposed that, once hired, a new teacher go through a 1- or 2-year induction period during

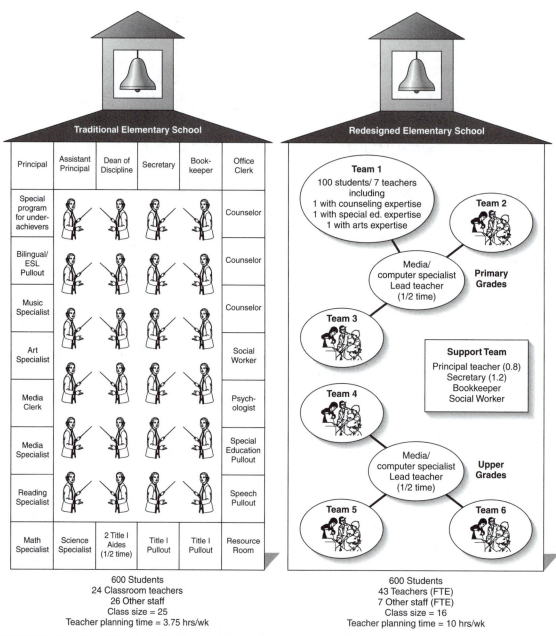

FIGURE 12.4. Traditional and Redesigned Elementary Schools as Developed by the National Commission on Teaching and America's Future

Source: National Commission on Teaching and America's Future. *What Matters Most: Teaching for America's Future* (p. 106). New York: NCTAF. Reprinted by permission.

which the teacher receives mentoring and is closely evaluated. After the new teacher then passes an assessment of teaching skills, recognition of *professional teacher* status is granted, along with a substantial salary increment.

NCTAF recommends that teachers be encouraged, through additional salary increments, to become certified in more than one subject area. This would acknowledge the value to the school of teachers being able to teach expertly in two or more subject areas or to bring counseling or special-education expertise to a teaching team. Having teachers certified in more than one area gives schools greater flexibility in organizing instructional teams.

For experienced teachers to gain the highest level of recognition, advanced certification from the National Board for Professional Teaching Standards would be recognized through additional salary increments. The National Board's standards are aligned with those of NCATE and INTASC. National Board certification would also be a prerequisite for qualification as lead teacher and principal.

There are numerous barriers to implementing reallocation of resources as proposed by NCTAF and others. Most teacher-district labor agreements would have to be changed with respect to definitions of teacher workday and seniority transfers. Some state and federal policies might need to be relaxed in order for barriers between programs, subjects, and age groupings to be broken down. Teacher, parent, and student attitudes and expectations might also have to change (Miles, 1995; Miles & Darling-Hammond, 1998). Tradition dies hard and it has many allies.

SUMMARY

In this chapter, we have looked at evidence concerning the efficiency of elementary and secondary schools. We concluded that as a nation, the United States is spending more per pupil than most other advanced nations, especially its chief economic rivals. Most other na-

tions, however, finance and administer their educational systems at the national level, and the resources committed are more evenly distributed throughout the school population than in the United States, where fifty states and thousands of school districts are involved. Strong evidence presented in this chapter and in the discussion of equity in Chapter 11 shows that the internal distribution of these resources to school districts and to schools is seriously flawed. Although horizontal equity in the distribution of resources has improved over the years, there is still a tendency for schools and districts serving advantaged children (whose achievement appears to be unaffected by resource allocation policies) to receive more resources than schools and districts serving primarily educationally at-risk children (whose academic achievement is highly dependent on the level and quality of educational services provided).

Further, state policies are only beginning to grapple with the issue of vertical equity. Cost function studies (reported in Chapter 11) show that we have grossly underestimated the amount of resources required to eliminate achievement gaps between ethnic and socio-economic groups. Federal policy since 1965 has focused on vertical equity, but the amount of resources allocated have been relatively small and have carried constraints that sometimes impair the ability of local officials to use the resources in cost-effective ways. Thus we have a problem in the internal allocation of the total resources committed by the nation collectively to education.

At the same time, we have an efficiency problem. The evidence provides little reason for confidence that, given additional resources, schools and districts serving primarily at-risk children would use them in a manner that would improve student achievement. Studies of the use of resources by public schools and school districts indicate with great consistency that many—probably most—are not using their resources to full advantage. If there are to be improvements in educational outcomes, those improvements will depend not only on additional resources for the educationally at-risk population but also on significant improvements in the internal efficiency of schools and districts (Consortium on Renewing Education, 1998).

Elmore (1994) argued that educators and those who influence them must think differently about resources and how they are applied to student learning:

> So at the core of the problem of adequacy, I would argue, is a problem of productivity and incentives. And behind the problem of productivity and incentives is a problem of knowledge and practice. There is virtually nothing in the background and preparation of educators that prepares them to confront the difficult and messy problems involved with using existing resources, or new resources, to cause dramatic shifts in student performance. Furthermore, there are many factors in the environment of schools that encourages educators not to think systematically about resources: categorical policies that "solve" the resource allocation problem for schools by mandating staffing patterns and ratios; collective bargaining contracts that set limits on the ability of schools to use resources flexibly; line-item budgeting practices; and the like. Most of the factors that limit the capacity of educators to pay attention to resource and output problems are either deeply ingrained in their background and prior experience or hard-wired in the organizational and policy context in which they work. (p. 457)

Some production function studies, evaluation and scale studies, whole-school reform networks, and effective-schools research have identified instructional and organizational interventions that do affect student achievement in cost-effective ways. Most, if not all, of these interventions require few new resources but, rather, a redirection of existing resources. As an example of the radical changes required to make schooling more effective and more efficient, we presented in some detail the recommendations of the National Commission on Teaching and America's Future for restructuring the use and compensation of personnel in schools.

There is much that we do not know about how to close the achievement gaps between children of varying ethnic and socioeconomic groups. But there is much that we do know that we are not using. The barriers to fundamental school reform are related more closely to politics and changing school structures and cultures than to economics. Political, structural, and sociological barriers are far more difficult to overcome than economic barriers. The nature of the task of educational reform must not be misdiagnosed, nor the difficulty in bringing it about underestimated.

In Part V, we analyze the financial implications of proposals for the fundamental restructuring of the organization and delivery of educational services. In Chapter 13 we examine how changing the incentives provided by financial rewards and teacher compensation might improve school and student performance. Chapters 14 and 15 consider the financial implications of policies directed toward injecting marketlike incentives into the provision of educational services through school-based decision making and by permitting parents to choose the schools their children attend through arrangements such as charter schools, vouchers, and choice among public schools.

ENDNOTES

1. Gross domestic product (GDP) is an aggregate measure of the value of the goods and services produced in a country.
2. The *Catalog of School Reform Models* is updated on a regular basis and is available on the Internet at **http://www.nwrel.org/scpd/natspec/catalog/**.

ACTIVITIES

1. Has the investment in your own education "paid off"? Estimate in current dollars the cost of your education beyond high

school, including the income forgone in acquiring your education. Find the present values of your investments by compounding annually each cost, from the time it was incurred, at a 10 percent rate of interest. Now estimate, in current-dollar values, the earning differentials between the positions you have held (and are likely to hold over your lifetime) and the positions you would probably have held if you had terminated your education at high school graduation. Estimate the present value by discounting the differentials from the times they were incurred at a 10 percent rate of interest. Is the present value of the sum of the earnings differentials as large as, or larger than, the present value of the sum of the costs? If so, you have at least broken even; if not, from an economic standpoint, it would have made more sense to have entered the workforce directly after high school or to have pursued another career.

2. List and discuss arguments for and against using the educational production function as a paradigm for analyzing resource allocations within public schools.

3. In this chapter, we concluded that the barriers to fundamental school reform are more closely related to politics and changing school structures and cultures than to economics. Do you agree with this position? List and discuss arguments that support it and arguments that oppose it.

4. Using the information provided in the "Internal Efficiency" section of this chapter, devise a configuration for using public school resources that is likely to be more efficient than configurations typically employed at the present time.

5. Visit a large school and a small school serving the same grade levels and try to answer the questions that follow. Alternatively, form a study group made up of persons with experience in schools of different sizes and compare experiences as you discuss the questions.

   a. Do you find any differences between schools that can be attributed to their differences in size?

   b. What are the advantages and disadvantages of being large? Of being small?

   c. What strategies might enhance the good effects of large schools and reduce their harmful effects? Answer the same question for small schools.

6. In the summary of this chapter, Elmore (1994) is quoted to the effect that there is little likelihood that professional educators are capable of designing new methods of delivering instruction that would result in dramatic positive shifts in student performance in a cost-effective manner. Furthermore, the schooling bureaucracy is characterized as being hamstrung with organizational limitations that make fundamental reform unlikely. These limiting factors include mandated staffing patterns and ratios, collective bargaining contracts that limit flexibility in the use of resources, and incremental budgeting.

   a. Do you agree with Elmore's observations? Why or why not?

   b. What, if anything, can be done to correct the situation?

   c. If educators cannot reform schooling, are there any other possible sources of reform?

COMPUTER SIMULATIONS: EDUCATION PRODUCTION FUNCTION

Computer simulations related to the content of this chapter are available on the Allyn & Bacon website **http://ablongman.com/edleadership**. They focus on manipulating education production functions. Objectives for the exercises are

- To further understanding of the statistical concepts behind education production functions
- To introduce multiple regression analysis

REFERENCES

Alexander, K. L., Entwisle, D. R., & Olson, L. S. (2001). Schools, achievement, and inequality: A seasonal perspective. *Educational Evaluation and Policy Analysis*, 23, 171–191.

American Institutes for Research. (1999). *An educators' guide to schoolwide reform*. Arlington, VA: Educational Research Service.

Armor, D. J., & Peiser, B. M. (1997). *Competition in education: A case study of interdistrict choice*. Boston, MA: Pioneer Institute for Public Policy Research.

Anderson, D. M. (1996). Stretching the dollar: Increasing efficiency in urban and rural schools. In L. O. Picus & J. L. Wattenbarger (Eds.), *Where does the money go? Resource allocation in elementary and secondary schools*. Thousand Oaks, CA: Corwin.

Ballou, D. (1998). The condition of urban school finance: Efficient resource allocation in urban schools. In W. J. Fowler, Jr. (Ed.), *Selected papers in school finance, 1996* (NCES 98-217). Washington, DC: U.S. Department of Education, National Center for Education Statistics, pp. 65–83.

Barker, R. G., & Gump, P. V. (1964). *Big school, small school*. Stanford, CA: Stanford University Press.

Bensman, D. (2000). *Central Park East and its graduates: "Learning by heart."* New York: Teachers College Press.

Benson, C. S. (1978). *The economics of public education* (3rd ed.). Boston: Houghton Mifflin.

Benson, C. S. (1988). Economics of education: The U.S. experience. In N. J. Boyan (Ed.), *Handbook of research on educational administration* (pp. 355–372). New York: Longman.

Berlin, B., & Cienkus, R. (1989). Size: The ultimate educational issue? *Education and Urban Society*, 21, 228–231.

Berne, R., & Stiefel, L. (1994). Measuring equity at the school level: The finance perspective. *Educational Evaluation and Policy Analysis*, 16, 405–421.

Boyer, E. L. (1983). *High school: A report on secondary education in America*. New York: Harper & Row.

Bradley, A. (1995). Thinking small. *Education Week*, 14, 37–41.

Brookover, W., & Lezotte, L. (1979). *Changes in school characteristics coincident with changes in student achievement*. East Lansing MI: State University, College of Urban Development.

Burkhead, J. (1967). *Input and output in large-city high schools*. Syracuse, NY: Syracuse University Press.

Burtless, G. (1996). *Does money matter? The effect of school resources on student achievement and adult success*. Washington, DC: The Brookings Institution.

Charnes, A., Cooper, W. W., and Rhodes, E. (1978). Measuring the efficiency of decision making units. *European Journal of Operational Research*, 2, 429–444.

Coase, R. H. (1988). *The firm, the market, and the law*. Chicago: University of Chicago Press.

Coleman, J. S. (1966). *Equality of educational opportunity*. Washington, DC: U.S. Government Printing Office.

Consortium on Renewing Education. (1998). *20/20 vision: A strategy for doubling America's academic achievement by the year 2020*. Nashville, TN: Peabody Center for Education Policy, Vanderbilt University.

Darling-Hammond, L. (1996). Restructuring schools for high performance. In S. H. Fuhrman & J. A. O'Day (Eds.), *Rewards and reform: Creating educational incentives that work*. San Francisco: Jossey-Bass, pp. 144–192.

Duncombe, W., Ruggerio, J., & Yinger, J. (1996). Alternative approaches to measuring the cost of education. In H. F. Ladd (Ed.), *Holding schools accountable: Performance-based reform in education*. Washington, DC: The Brookings Institution.

Duncombe, W. D., & Yinger, J. M. (1999). Performance standards and educational cost indexes: You can't have one without the other. In H. F. Ladd, R. Chalk, & J. S. Hansen (Eds.), *Equity and adequacy in education finance: Issues and perspectives* (pp. 260–297). Washington, DC: National Academy Press.

Duncombe, W. D., & Yinger, J. M. (1997). Why is it so hard to help central city schools? *Journal of Policy Analysis and Management*, 16, 85–113.

Edmonds, R. (1979). Effective schools for the urban poor. *Educational Leadership*, 37, 15–24.

Elmore, R. F. (1994). Thoughts on program equity: Productivity and incentives for performance in education. *Educational Policy*, 8, 453–459.

Engert, F. (1995). *Efficiency analysis of school districts using multiple inputs and outputs: An application of data envelopment analysis*. Buffalo, NY: Unpublished Ph. D. dissertation, State University at Buffalo.

Fashola, O. S., & Slavin, R. F. (1998). Promising programs for elementary and middle schools: Evidence of effectiveness and replicability. *Journal of Education for Students Placed at Risk*, 2, 251–307.

Fashola, O. S., & Slavin, R. F. (1998). Schoolwide reform models: What works? *Phi Delta Kappan, 79,* 370–379.

Ferguson, R. F. (1991). Paying for public education: New evidence on how and why money matters. *Harvard Journal on Legislation, 28,* 465–498.

Ferguson, R. F., & Ladd, H. F. (1996). How and why money matters: An analysis of Alabama schools. In H. F. Ladd (Ed.), *Holding schools accountable: Performance-based reform in education* (pp. 265–298). Washington, DC: The Brookings Institution.

Fine, M. (1993). Democratizing choice: Reinventing, not retreating from, public education. In E. Rasell & R. Rothstein (Eds.), *School choice: Examining the evidence* (pp. 269–300). Washington, DC: Economic Policy Institute.

Fine, M., & Somerville, J. I. (1998). *Small schools, big imaginations: A creative look at urban public schools.* Chicago: Cross City Campaign for Urban School Reform.

Finn, J. D., & Achilles, C. M. (1999). Tennessee's class size study: Findings, implications, misconceptions. *Education Evaluation and Policy Analysis, 21,* 97–110.

Fliegel, S., & MacGuire, J. (1993). *Miracle in East Harlem: The fight for choice in public education.* New York: Random House.

Fox, W. F. (1981). Reviewing economies of size in education. *Journal of Education Finance, 6,* 273–296.

Fuller, B., & Clarke, P. (1994). Raising school effects while ignoring culture? Local conditions and the influence of classroom tools, rules, and pedagogy. *Review of Educational Research, 64,* 119–157.

Gerber, S. B., Finn, J. D., Achilles, C. M., & Boyd-Zaharias, J. (2001). Teacher aides and students' academic achievement. *Educational Evaluation and Policy Analysis, 23,* 123–143.

Goodlad, J. I. (1984). *A place called school: prospects for the future.* New York: McGraw-Hill.

Greenwald, R., Hedges, L. V., & Laine, R. D. (1994). When reinventing the wheel is not necessary: A case study in the use of meta-analysis in education finance. *Journal of Education Finance, 20,* 1–20.

Grissmer, D. (2001). Research directions for understanding the relationship of educational resources to educational outcomes. In S. Chaikind & W. J. Fowler, Jr. (Eds.), *Education finance in the new millennium: AEFA 2001 Yearbook* (pp. 139–155). Larchmont, NY: Eye on Education.

Guthrie, J. W. (1997). School finance: Fifty years of expansion. *The Future of Children, 7,* 24–38.

Hanushek, E. A. (1986). The economics of schooling: Production and efficiency in public schools. *Journal of Economic Literature, 24,* 1141–1177.

Hanushek, E. A. (1987). Education production functions. In G. Psacharopoulos (Ed.), *Economics of education: Research and studies* (pp. 33–42). Oxford, England: Pergamon.

Hanushek, E. A. (1991). When school finance "reform" may not be good policy. *Harvard Journal on Education, 28,* 423–456.

Hanushek, E. A. (1994). Money might matter somewhere: A response to Hedges, Laine, and Greenwald. *Educational Researcher, 23,* 5–8.

Hanushek, E. A. (1996a). School resources and student performance. In G. Burtless (Ed.), *Does money matter? The effect of school resources on student achievement and adult success.* Washington, DC: The Brookings Institution.

Hanushek, E. A. (1996b). Outcomes, costs, and incentives in schools. In E. A. Hanushek & D. W. Jorgenson (Eds.), *Improving America's schools: The role of incentives* (pp. 29–52). Washington, DC: National Academy Press.

Hanushek, E. A., Kain, J. F., & Rivkin, S. G. (1998). *Teachers, schools, and academic achievement* (Working Paper 6691). Cambridge, MA: National Bureau of Economic Research.

Hedges, L. V., Laine, R. D., & Greenwald, R. (1994a). Does money matter? A meta-analysis of studies of the effects of differential school inputs on student outcomes. *Educational Researcher, 23,* 5–14.

Hedges, L. V., Laine, R. D., & Greenwald, R. (1994b). Money does matter somewhere: A reply to Hanushek. *Educational Researcher, 23,* 9–10.

Hickrod, G. A., et al. (1989). *The biggest bang for the buck: An initial report on technical economic efficiency in Illinois K–12 schools with a comment on Rose v. The Council.* Normal, IL: Center for the Study of Educational Finance (ERIC No. ED329013).

Hollings, R. L. (1996). *Reinventing government: An analysis and an annotated bibliography.* Commack, NY: Nova Science Publishers.

Howley, C. B. (1994). The academic effectiveness of small-scale schooling (an update). *ERIC Digest.* Charleston, WV: ERIC Clearinghouse on Rural Education and Small Schools. (ED 372 897)

Hoxby, C. M. (1994). *Does competition among public schools benefit students and taxpayers? Evidence from natural variation and school districting.* (Working Paper No. 4979) Cambridge, MA: Harvard University, National Bureau of Economic Research.

Jackson, S., Logsdon, D., & Taylor, N. (1983). Instructional leadership behaviors: Differentiating effective from ineffective low-income urban schools. *Urban Education, 18,* 59–70.

King, R. A., & MacPhail-Wilcox, B. (1994). Unraveling the production equation: The continuing quest for resources that make a difference. *Journal of Education Finance, 20,* 47–65.

Kirby, S. N., Berends, M., & Naftel, S. (2001). *Implementation in a longitudinal sample of New American Schools: Four years into scale-up.* Santa Monica, CA: RAND.

Klitgaard, R. E., & Hall, G. R. (1975). Are there unusually effective schools? *Journal of Human Resources, 10,* 90–106.

Ladd, H. F. (Ed.). (1996). *Holding schools accountable: Performance-based reform in education.* Washington, DC: The Brookings Institution.

Ladd, H. F., & Hansen, J. S. (Eds.). (1999). *Making money matter: Financing America's schools.* Washington, DC: National Academy Press.

Lee, V. E., & Loeb, S. (2000). School size in Chicago elementary schools: Effects on teachers' attitudes and students' achievement. *American Educational Research Journal, 37,* 3–31.

Lee, V. E., & Smith, J. B. (1995). Effects of high school restructuring and size on early gains in achievement and engagement. *Sociology of Education, 68,* 241–270.

Lee, V. E., & Smith, J. B. (1997). High school size: Which works best, and for whom? *Educational Evaluation and Policy Analysis, 19,* 205–227.

Levin, H. M. (1994). The necessary and sufficient conditions for achieving educational equity. In R. Berne & L. O. Picus (Eds.), *Outcome equity in education.* Thousand Oaks, CA: Corwin.

Levin, H. M., Glass, G. V., & Meister, G. R. (1987). Cost effectiveness of computer-assisted instruction. *Evaluation Review, 11,* 50–72.

Levin, H. M., & McEwan, P. J. (2001). *Cost-effectiveness analysis* (2nd ed.). Thousand Oaks, CA: Sage.

Lindsay, P. (1982). The effect of high school size on student participation, satisfaction, and attendance. *Educational Evaluation and Policy Analysis, 4,* 57–65.

Mayeski, G. W., et al. (1972). *A study of our nation's schools.* Washington, DC: U.S. Government Printing Office.

McMullan, B. J., Sipe, C. L., & Wolf, W. C. (1994). *Charters and student achievement: Early evidence from school restructuring in Philadelphia.* Bala Cynwyd, PA: Center for Assessment and Policy Development.

Meier, D. (1995a). How our schools could be. *Phi Delta Kappan, 76,* 369–373.

Meier, D. (1995b). *The power of their ideas: Lessons for America from a small school in Harlem.* Boston: Beacon.

Meier, D. H. (1998). Can the odds be changed? *Phi Delta Kappan, 79,* 358–362.

Miles, K. H. (1995). Freeing resources for improving schools: A case study of teacher allocation in Boston public schools. *Educational Evaluation and Policy Analysis, 17,* 476–493.

Miles, K. H., & Darling-Hammond, L. (1998). Rethinking the allocation of teaching resources: Some lessons from high performing schools. In W. J. Fowler, Jr. (Ed.), *Developments in school finance, 1997.* Washington, DC: U.S. Department of Education, National Center for Education Statistics.

Monk, D. H. (1989). The education production function: Its evolving role in policy analysis. *Educational Evaluation and Policy Analysis, 11,* 31–45.

National Center for Education Statistics. (Various years). *Digest of education statistics.* Washington, DC: U.S. Government Printing Office.

National Commission on Teaching and America's Future. (1996). *What matters most: Teaching for America's future.* New York: Author.

New American Schools. (2000a). *Every child a star.* Arlington, VA: Author.

New American Schools. (2000b). *Guidelines for ensuring the quality of national design-based assistance providers.* Arlington, VA: Author.

Newman, F. M. (1981). Reducing student alienation in high schools: Implications of theory. *Harvard Education Review, 51,* 546–564.

Northwest Regional Educational Laboratory. (1998). *Catalog of school reform models: First edition.* Portland, OR: The Laboratory.

Odden A. R., & Picus, L. O. (2000). *School finance: A policy perspective* (2nd ed.). New York: McGraw-Hill.

Odden, A. (1996). Incentives, school organization, and teacher compensation. In S. H. Fuhrman & J. A. O'Day (Eds.), *Rewards and reform: Creating educational incentives that work* (pp. 226–256). San Francisco: Jossey-Bass.

Odden, A., Monk, D., Nakib, Y., & Picus, L. (1995). The story of the education dollar: No academy awards and no fiscal smoking guns. *Phi Delta Kappan, 77*, 161–168.

Odden, A., & Webb, L. D. (1983). Introduction: The linkages between school finance and school improvement. In A. Odden & L. D. Webb (Eds.), *School finance and school improvement: Linkages for the 1980s* (pp. xiii–xxi). Cambridge, MA: Ballinger.

Osborne, D., & Gaebler, T. (1992). *Reinventing government: How the entrepreneurial spirit is transforming the public sector.* Reading, MA: Addison-Wesley.

Osborne, D., & Plastrik, P. (1997). *Banishing bureaucracy: The five strategies for reinventing government.* Reading, MA: Addison-Wesley.

Osin, L., and Lesgold, A. (1996). A proposal for re-engineering of the educational system. *Review of Educational Research, 66*, 621–656.

Owens, Jr., J. T. (1994). *Interdistrict resource allocation in Dade County, Florida: An analysis of equity of educational opportunity.* Paper delivered at the annual meeting of the American Educational Finance Association, Nashville, TN.

Picus, L. O. (2001). *In search of more productive schools: A guide to resource allocation in education.* Eugene, OR: ERIC Clearinghouse on Educational Management.

Psacharopoulos, G. (1981). Returns to education: An updated international comparison. *Comparative Education, 17*, 321–341.

Psacharopoulos, G. (1985). Returns to education: A further international update and implementations. *Journal of Human Resources, 20*, 583–604.

Puma, M. J., et al. (1997). *Prospects: Final report on student outcomes.* Cambridge MA: Abt Associates.

Raywid, M. A. (1999). Current literature on small schools. *ERIC Digest.* Charleston, WV: ERIC Clearinghouse on Rural Education and Small Schools. (ED425049)

Raywid, M. A. (1996a). Taking stock: The movement to create mini-schools, schools-within-schools, and separate small schools, Urban Diversity Series No. 108. New York: ERIC Clearinghouse on Urban Education, Teachers College, Columbia University. (ED 396 045)

Raywid, M. A. (1996b). The Wadleigh Complex: A dream that soured. In B. Boyd, B. Crowson, & H. Mawhinney (Eds.), *The politics of education and the New Institutionalism: Reinventing the American school.* Philadelphia: Falmer.

Reed, L. (1985). *An inquiry into the specific school-based practices involving principals that distinguish unusually effective elementary schools from effective elementary schools.* Unpublished doctoral dissertation, State University of New York at Buffalo.

Reynolds, A. J., Bezruczko, N., Mavrogenes, N. A., & Hagemann, M. (1996). *Chicago longitudinal study of children in Chicago public schools: User Guide (version 4).* Madison/Chicago: University of Wisconsin and Chicago Public Schools.

Reynolds, A. J., & Wolfe, B. (1999). Special education and school achievement: An exploratory analysis with a central-city sample. *Educational Evaluation and Policy Analysis, 21*, 249–269.

Reschovsky, A., & Imazeki, J. (2001). Achieving educational adequacy through school finance reform. *Journal of Education Finance, 26*, 373–396.

Rice, J. K. (2001). Illuminating the black box: The evolving role of education production function research. In S. Chaikind & W. J. Fowler (Eds.), *Education finance in the new millennium: AEFA 2001 Yearbook* (pp. 121–138). Larchmont, NY: Eye on Education.

Riew, J. (1981). Enrollment decline and school reorganization: A cost efficiency analysis. *Economics of Education Review, 1*, 53–73.

Riew, J. (1986). Scale economies, capacity utilization, and school costs: A comparative analysis of secondary and elementary schools. *Journal of Education Finance, 11*, 433–446.

Rogers, B. (1992). Small is beautiful. In D. Durrett & J. Nathan (Eds.), *Source book on school and district size, cost, and quality.* Minneapolis, MN: North Central Regional Educational Laboratory.

Rothstein, R., & Miles, K. H. (1995). *Where's the money gone? Changes in the level and composition of education spending, 1967–1991.* Washington, DC: Economic Policy Institute.

Sammons, P. (1999). *School effectiveness: Coming of age in the twenty-first century.* Lisse, The Netherlands: Swets & Zeitlinger.

Schultz, T. W. (1963). *The economic value of education.* New York: Columbia University Press.

Smith, T. M., & Phelps, R. P. (1995). Education finance indicators: What can we learn from comparing states and nations. In W. J. Fowler, Jr. (Ed.), *Developments in school finance* (pp. 99–107). Washington DC: National Center for Educational Statistics.

Stasz, C., & Stecher, B. M. (2000). Teaching mathematics and language arts in reduced size and non-reduced size classrooms. *Educational Evaluation and Policy Analysis, 22,* 313–329.

Steifel, L., Berne, R., Iatarola, P., & Fruchter, N. (2000). High school size: Effects on budgets and performance in New York City. *Educational Evaluation and Policy Analysis, 22,* 27–39.

Stiefel, L., Rubenstein, R., & Berne, R. (1998). Intra-district equity in four large cities: Data, methods, and results. *Journal of Education Finance, 23,* 447–467.

Stockyard, J., & Mayberry, M. (1992). *Effective educational environments.* Newbury Park, CA: Corwin. (ED 350 674)

Swanson, A. D., & Engert, F. (1999). *Benchmarking: A study of school and school district effect and efficiency.* Buffalo, NY: State University of New York, Graduate School of Education Publications.

Sweet, D. A. (1986, September). Extracurricular activity participants outperform other students. *Office of Educational Research and Improvement Bulletin* (CS 85-2136).

Tainter, J. A. (1988). *The collapse of complex societies.* Cambridge: Cambridge University Press.

Veenman, S. (1995). Cognitive and noncognitive effects of multigrade and multi-age classes: A best-evidence synthesis. *Review of Educational Research, 65,* 319–381.

Venezsky, R., & Winfield, L. (1980). *Schools that exceed beyond expectations in the teaching of reading: Studies on education, technical report 1.* Newark, DE: University of Delaware.

Verstegen, D. (1992). International comparisons of education spending: A review and analysis of reports. *Journal of Education Finance, 17,* 257–276.

Viadero, D. (2001). Whole-school reform projects show mixed results: Reform models suffer string of setbacks. *Education Week, 21,* 1, 24–25.

Walberg, H. J. (1998). Uncompetitive American schools: Causes and cures. In D. Ravitch (Ed.), *Brookings papers on education policy 1998* (pp. 173–226). Washington, DC: The Brookings Institution.

Weber, G. (1971). *Inner city children can be taught to read: Four successful schools.* Washington, DC: Council for Basic Education.

Williams, D. T. (1990). *The dimensions of education: Recent research on school size* (Working paper series). Clemson, SC: Strom Thurmond Institute of Government and Public Affairs. (ED 347 006)

Woessmann, L. (2000). *Schooling resources, educational institutions, and student performance: The international evidence* (Kiel working paper No. 983). Kiel, Germany: Kiel Institute of World Economics.

V

Creating Incentives to Foster High Performance

In Part III we presented strategies for improving equity in the allocation of resources for elementary and secondary education. However, the evidence discussed in Part IV showed that many of these well-intended strategies have failed. Inequities in the distribution of resources within and among school districts remained, despite the many attempts to remove them. Furthermore, the evidence strongly suggested that bringing about equity in the distribution of funding would not produce equity in student achievement unless the efficiency of the school system was improved. Many critics of the educational system place the blame for these inefficiencies and poor student performance on the structure and governance of public schools.

In Part V we examine some of the major reforms that have been proposed to improve the functioning of the education system and their implications for school finance policy. In Chapter 13 we examine ways in which performance measures can be used to direct state funds to districts and to compensate teachers. We discuss state accountability systems, the potential role of financial rewards as incentives to improve school productivity and teacher quality, and emerging compensation systems that link teacher pay with performance measures. Chapters 14 and 15 examine the financial implications of policies directed toward injecting marketlike incentives into the provision of educational services. These chapters focus on school-based decision making and parental choice of the schools their children attend.

chapter 13

LINKING FINANCIAL REWARDS AND TEACHER COMPENSATION TO PERFORMANCE INDICATORS

Issues and Questions

- *Achieving High Standards with Equity and Efficiency*: In what ways do financial rewards for gains in pupil performance and restructured compensation policies promise to improve schools?
- *Performance-based Accountability Systems*: Do state accountability systems that include standards, assessments, multiple indicators, rewards, and sanctions offer potential for school improvement?
- *Linking Financial Rewards to Performance Measures*: Are policies that relate allocations of funds from states to districts or schools with student achievement and other performance indicators likely to have an incentive effect?
- *Supply of and Demand for High-quality Teachers*: In what ways is the teacher labor market becoming more similar to the private-sector labor market as demands for quality intensify?
- *Strengthening Teacher Quality and Compensation*: Do some approaches to compensating teachers offer greater promise for attracting and retaining high-quality teachers? Are there ways to strengthen the relationship between remuneration and teachers' responsibilities, skills, and performance? Are these restructured compensation strategies likely to have an incentive effect in improving schools and student learning?

Discussions of efficiency and accountability in education raise questions about the ways in which states allocate funds to districts and, in turn, how districts pay teachers. Mechanisms for the allocation of funds have not traditionally considered pupil achievement or teacher performance to a great extent. However, neither of these structures can be ignored in conversations about systemic reform. If performance-based allocations and compensation structures can induce changes in the productivity of schools or classrooms, then these policies may be powerful levers in educational reform.

Efficiency and accountability goals mean that the public and their elected representatives desire improvements in student performance at the same or a lower cost of schooling. In this context, schools or districts would not receive additional allocations per pupil, nor would teachers receive additional compensation without demonstrable improvements in school programs, teacher skills, student achievement, and other performance indicators. Linking these inputs and outputs of schooling was the focus of our discussion of the efficiency of school systems in Chapter 12. This chapter offers a more detailed examination of potential strategies for bringing performance measures in line with state allocations, as well as with the largest expenditure of school systems, teacher salaries.

We first distinguish between rewards and incentives and discuss theories of motivation. This theoretical framework lays a foundation for understanding the probable effects of state-level allocation and compensation systems that take performance measures into account. We examine accountability systems in which financial rewards, including salary bonuses, depend on improvements in selected measures of school productivity. We then revisit the discussion of salary schedules that we initiated in the previous chapter, concluding that the way in which most school systems pay teachers is a major source of inefficiency. Finally, we examine state- and district-level strategies that

link salaries with teachers' responsibilities, skills, and performance in order to improve school efficiency.

FINANCIAL REWARDS AS MOTIVATORS

Performance-based allocations and salary bonuses are strategies that policy makers advance in efforts to improve the productivity of schools and teachers. Understanding conditions under which financial rewards might motivate school personnel to improve teaching and learning in ways that yield improved student achievement is important in analyzing these policies.

Rewards and Incentive Effects

Cibulka (1989) advanced rational-choice theory as a framework for understanding financial rewards:

> Incentives are a case of voluntary contractual exchange in which the donor sets forth the terms. Both the donor and the recipient are assumed to be utility-maximizing; they strive to maximize benefits and to minimize costs to themselves. Incentives work to the extent that both the donor (in this case, state officials) and the recipients (here, the school, school district, teachers or administrators) perceive that their gains sufficiently exceed their costs so as to justify the voluntary arrangement. (p. 419)

Benefits (such as improved pupil achievement, workforce skills, and citizenship) accrue to society, and incentives are offered to motivate recipient schools or teachers to achieve such goals. Interestingly, this perspective suggests that district and school personnel design programs and learning activities that attain rewards at the least possible cost in order to maximize gains. Similarly, the size of the state's incentive or the district's salary bonus is gauged to the perceived value of benefits to be realized in order to minimize the burden on state or local resources.

The terms *incentive* and *reward* are often used interchangeably in the literature. We adopt Boe's (1992) view that rewards differ from incentives. What is intended to be an incentive may not always motivate people to change behaviors. For example, when teachers receive a salary bonus (a reward) for past increases in student achievement, the bonus may or may not have been a factor in encouraging some action that resulted in the performance. Similarly, the promise of future rewards may or may not have the intended effect of changing behavior. Thus, in describing allocations related to performance, the term *reward* is a better descriptor of the financial benefit received than the term *incentive*. An *incentive effect* (Boe, 1992) occurs only when there is a link between the reward and the intended outcome. We present theories of motivation to understand better which forms of financial rewards are likely to have incentive effects.

Theoretical Perspectives

There are several theoretical bases for analyzing policies that link allocations for districts or salary bonuses for teachers to their performance. Offering rewards to alter workers' behavior follows Skinner's (1974) view that people are basically passive and must be motivated by carrots and other incentives in the environment. These incentives direct behavior toward outcomes and rewards that provide pleasure and away from consequences and sanctions that produce pain (Atkinson, 1964).

Several theories address workers' perceptions about the value and attainability of rewards and about the relationship between goals and potential rewards. Vroom's (1964) *expectancy theory* suggests that a person's motivation to exert effort depends on personally held expectations (i.e., expectancies) and the value placed on the outcomes anticipated from achieving goals. The expectancies include a person's beliefs that (1) the effort exerted will bring success in attaining the goal, and (2)

achieving that goal will lead to valued outcomes (rewards). Thus, in order for a financial reward to have an incentive effect in inducing meritorious performance, the goals to be achieved must be seen as both attainable and valuable. Mohrman and Lawler (1996) describe factors, including aspects of organizations, that are related to expectancies and motivation for high performance:

> Some of the factors that influence the effort-to-performance expectancy are whether the individual believes that he or she has the skills and knowledge required, whether there is clear understanding about the nature of the performance that is to be attained and it is viewed as attainable, and whether the individual believes that there is situational support for the performance (resources such as time, information, and supporting performances by other people). (p. 121)

Providing clear performance expectations and support structures improves people's expectancies that their efforts contribute to organizational goals.

Goal-setting theory posits that specific and challenging goals are motivating when workers view them as achievable (Locke, 1968; Locke & Latham, 1990). In this context, rewards have an incentive effect in improving workers' commitments to those goals (Wright, 1989). There must also be a direct *line of sight* (Lawler, 1990) between the anticipated reward and the actions taken to achieve both the goal and the reward. Otherwise, the reward may not have the intended effect.

The nature of the rewards offered may make a difference in job satisfaction and in teachers' motivations to improve individual or group performance. Some people perceive *extrinsic* rewards such as salary bonuses to be valuable and attainable—and thus motivating. Lawler (1994) argued that these extrinsic rewards "help to define which behaviors are valued, motivate particular kinds of performance . . . and ultimately play a key role in determining how satisfied individuals are with their work experiences" (p. xviii). A merit pay policy, for example, assumes that external and material rewards motivate teachers or administrators to be more productive. Financial rewards may include salary increases or travel funds for professional conferences. There may also be nonmonetary rewards for individuals, such as relief from close supervision or from undesired responsibilities, and for schools, such as presentations of plaques or banners for outstanding performance.

Extrinsic rewards may not, however, be sufficient motivators. Herzberg, Mausner, and Snyderman (1959) suggested that extrinsic rewards, including monetary bonuses, can play an important role in inducing dissatisfaction among workers. Furthermore, individual performance-based rewards have been shown to have severe unintended consequences. Resulting competition may work against organizational goals that depend on teamwork (Deming, 1986). Rewards can hurt relationships among workers and between workers and supervisors, discourage risk taking and setting high standards, and even encourage illegal or unethical behavior (Kohn, 1993).

By contrast, there is general agreement in the literature that *intrinsic* aspects of work contribute positively to people's motivation. The pleasure of performing tasks provides intrinsic motivation (Herzberg, 1966). These internal and intangible rewards may include recognition, greater variety in work responsibilities, and a sense of achievement. Lawler (1994) noted that people work harder because of internal feelings of satisfaction: "For work to be motivating, individuals must feel personally responsible for the outcomes of the work, need to do something that they feel is meaningful, and need to receive feedback about what is accomplished" (p. xix). Intrinsic rewards are of greater importance to educators than extrinsic motivators (Lortie, 1975; Jacobson 1988). School-based management that involves teachers in the decision-making process is intended, in part, to enhance intrinsic rewards (see Chapter 14).

A blend of intrinsic and extrinsic rewards may provide the most effective motivation. Intrinsic rewards may not motivate all the behaviors that make organizations successful, and they sometimes motivate the wrong behaviors (Lawler, 2000). There is a role for extrinsic rewards in motivating workers and ensuring organizational effectiveness. These rewards are most effective when they are linked strategically with desired outcomes (Odden & Kelley, 2001). In school organizations, performance-based salary bonuses and other extrinsic rewards can motivate school improvement:

> Performance incentives . . . do not attempt to dictate which teaching methods will work, although providing good information on what has worked in the past is an important element of any well-functioning system of incentives. Incentives encourage individuals to decide for themselves which route toward improved performance is most appropriate in specific circumstances. Thus incentives can be viewed as a way to expand the methods for delivering a good education. (Hanushek, 2001, p. 301)

In the search for policies that provide effective incentives for school improvement, group performance rewards have emerged from the failure of individual merit pay plans to motivate teachers (Murnane & Cohen, 1986; Ballou & Podgursky, 1993). The competition for individual performance bonuses results in divisiveness that undermines the collective efforts demanded of work groups (Hackman, 1987). In contrast, rewards for groups of workers foster norms that favor good performance and encourage cooperation. They often lead to demonstrable gains in organizational performance and worker satisfaction (Galbraith, E. E. Lawler, & Associates, 1993; Mohrman, Cohen, & Mohrman, 1995; Lawler, 2000). Group synergy and productivity are maximized when tasks are motivationally engaging, when reward systems provide challenging performance objectives and reinforce their achievement, and when interactions promote the members' commitment to the team and its work (Hackman, 1987). Rewards for all school personnel based on schoolwide performance may bring a blend of intrinsic and extrinsic benefits as these group rewards encourage collaboration in efforts that are clearly connected to desired outcomes.

In summary, financial rewards in school settings are most likely to have an incentive effect when several conditions are satisfied. School personnel must

- View the goals to be achieved to earn potential rewards as *valuable* and *attainable*.
- Have a direct *line of sight*—that is, be able to see the connections among the actions necessary to achieve desired goals and outcomes, performance measures, and rewards.
- Receive *intrinsic benefits* from achieving goals, *along with any extrinsic rewards*.
- *Collaborate* in achieving school improvement goals that school faculty agree to be important.

With these theoretical underpinnings in mind, we next examine financial rewards in state performance-based accountability systems and in teacher compensation plans.

FINANCIAL REWARDS IN PERFORMANCE-BASED ACCOUNTABILITY SYSTEMS

As the accountability movement began in the 1980s, some states' policies encouraged the adoption of performance-based pay or career ladders that would reward individual teachers for improving instruction or assuming greater responsibilities (see the discussion later in this chapter). Other states gravitated toward making a portion of state funds (typically a small amount outside of formula aid) conditional on demonstrated school performance. Rewarding schoolwide efforts would overcome objections that rewards paid to individuals work against other reforms designed to build effective teamwork. This money flows directly to schools rather than to district offices. School-level gov-

ernance groups typically help principals decide how to use this discretionary money for various schoolwide improvements. In some states, rewards may be allocated as salary bonuses for all school personnel.

We examine both the concept of accountability and the nature of rewards within state accountability systems. We then discuss whether these structures offer the potential to motivate school personnel to improve schools and student achievement.

Performance-Based Accountability Systems

Accountability systems reflect the importance of holding school personnel responsible for results. Peterson (1992) delineated four questions to be addressed by a well-functioning assessment and accountability system:

- Which goals, outcomes, or performance objectives are critical?
- What measurements, indicators, or data will tell us whether we are making progress toward those goals or objectives over time?
- How do we know whether we are successful, given that circumstances differ among schools, districts, and states?
- How can information from the assessments be used by policy makers to improve decision making in general, reward success, and intervene in situations of poor performance? (p. 110)

These questions are evident in the policy strategies identified as "entrepreneurial restructuring" (Boe & Boruch, 1993) and the "new educational accountability" (Elmore, Abelmann & Fuhrman, 1996). Financial rewards are one of five components of performance-based accountability systems:

- *Standards* are statements of what students should know and/or be able to do.
- *Assessments* are designed to be aligned with the standards and to measure how successful students are in meeting them.

- Multiple *indicators* measure various dimensions of school performance and may activate rewards and sanctions.
- *Rewards* are granted to districts, schools, or teachers when performance exceeds either an established performance level or previously reported results.
- *Sanctions* apply to districts or individual schools when performance falls below expectations.

The primary goals of these accountability systems are to establish clear expectations for student performance and to measure school success in closing the gap between actual and desired performance. Indicators of student performance are either criterion-referenced (i.e., assessment that is aligned with state curriculum standards) or norm-referenced (i.e., assessment in which achievement is measured relative to students in state or national samples). States may identify a target performance level and compare school or district scores against this state performance standard. Alternatively, they may establish threshold levels that differ among districts or schools. This approach compares improvements in students' scores from prior performance levels in one of two ways. A longitudinal analysis traces changes in the scores of individual students from one year to the next, whereas a cross-sectional approach compares average achievement scores of students at a given grade level with the performance of students at that grade level in a prior year.

Statistical models may be adopted to observe the contributions of individual teachers or of all school personnel to efforts made in closing performance gaps. For example, the Tennessee Value-Added Assessment System (TVAAS) determines annual estimates of teacher and school effects on student performance as measured by the state's Comprehensive Assessment Program (Sanders & Horn, 1994). TVAAS presumes that schools and teachers have important influences on student achievement and

that the gains made are valid measures of their effects. These value-added assessments enable states and districts to identify the schools that bring about the most academic progress in their students, regardless of whether the test is criterion- or norm-referenced. Sanders and Horn state that the focus is academic progress of all students rather than the particular assessment:

> TVAAS was developed on the premise that society has a right to expect that schools will provide students with the opportunity for academic gains regardless of the level at which the students enter the educational venue. In other words, all students can and should learn commensurate with their abilities. (p. 301)

In addition to assessments of student achievement, the most commonly used indicators in state accountability systems are dropout rates, graduation rates, student attendance, student behavior (e.g., truancy, suspension), student transition to postsecondary education or work, and expenditures and uses of resources (Education Commission of the States, 2001). Other important but less easily measured factors that influence school performance, such as school climate and parent involvement, are not generally included. In order to make assessment systems fairer and more comprehensive, Reville (2001) urged states to rely on multiple measures that meet six criteria:

- Validity: Do the additional tools accurately measure learning embodied in the standards?
- Reliability: Will the additional measure repeatedly and accurately generate consistent results in a variety of circumstances?
- Transparency: Would its use be understandable and clear to the public, parents, and educators?
- Practicality: Is it relatively easy to compile or administer? Is it feasible for teachers and students?
- Affordability: Are the costs reasonable and affordable?

- Political feasibility: Could any self-respecting politician support the use of this measure in public?

State accountability systems may assign weights to selected indicators in forming a composite rating for each school's performance. Notable improvements in school performance may bring public recognition, financial rewards to encourage principals and teachers to continue successful practices, mechanisms to diffuse ideas to other settings, and relaxed or waived state regulations that often inhibit local innovation (U.S. Department of Education, 1988; Fuhrman & Elmore, 1992). Deficiencies in school performance may also trigger local and state responses in the form of assistance or sanctions. Progressively stronger interventions in low-performing schools may include technical assistance and targeted funding, changes in personnel and curricula, and consolidation with more effective schools.

A recent review of accountability and assessment policies across the nation (Goertz and Duffy, 2001) focused on several questions:

- How are states measuring and reporting student performance?
- How are states holding students, schools, and districts accountable for student outcomes?
- How are states assisting low-performing schools?
- How aligned are accountability policies for Title I and non–Title I schools?

In responding to the first question, the researchers found that all but two states (Iowa and Nebraska) used state-developed assessments as the primary indicator of school performance. These two states required districts to test students in specified grades, but the state left the choice of instrument to the locality. A majority of states assessed student performance in a single grade per subject in elementary, middle, and high schools. Twelve states tested students in consecutive grades, typically between grades 2 or 3 and 8, in the same subject

areas using the same assessment. Three states tested consecutive grades between these same grade spans in different subjects and/or made use of multiple assessments.

Goertz and Duffy (2001) observed that states faced technical and political challenges in including students with disabilities and students with limited English proficiency in assessments. States offered a range of test accommodations and modifications, but they faced challenges in developing and implementing alternative assessments for students with disabilities. Some states exempted English-language learners on the basis of length of residency in the country, time in a bilingual or English as a second language (ESL) program, or level of English proficiency as determined by a different assessment.

All fifty states published, or required districts to prepare, school or district reports of assessments. The majority of states also included additional performance indicators (including student attendance, dropout rates, and graduation rates) in reports to the public. Some reports included indicators of school climate, discipline, teacher qualifications and experience, class size, and such fiscal resources as per-pupil expenditures. Of those with state assessment systems, thirty-nine states disaggregated test results by race/ethnicity and gender, as is required by the federal Title I program. Although Title I requirements specified three levels of student performance (advanced, proficient, and partially proficient), states typically added one or more levels of partial proficiency to indicate how well students have mastered content related to state standards.

In response to the second question, Goertz and Duffy (2001) noted that thirty-three states set performance goals for schools and districts. In holding school personnel accountable, many of these states established rewards for meeting or exceeding goals as well as sanctions for not meeting targets. Public reporting of school or district performance was the primary accountability mechanism in thirteen states. Only a few states permitted districts to define performance criteria and make use of school or district improvement plans as the means for holding them accountable.

There was wide variation in school performance goals in the thirty-three states that Goertz and Duffy (2001) identified as having state-defined accountability systems. States differed in the measures of proficiency, the percentage of students expected to meet proficiency standards, and the measures used to determine annual progress. Fourteen states defined an absolute target or performance threshold that all schools must attain to have made satisfactory progress. Another five required schools to meet an annual growth target that reflects past performance and the distance from the state's goals. Eight states gave an option of one or the other of these measures, and another four required schools to reduce the number or percentage of students scoring in the lowest performance levels. Two others required districts to meet all three goals: attain an absolute target, make relative growth, and narrow the achievement gap. Only a few states took into account the performance of specific groups, such as racial/ethnic or economically disadvantaged students.

The third question posed by Goertz and Duffy (2001) concerned the consequences for poor performance. These policies varied across states, depending on the locus of authority (local or state) and the state's willingness to intervene. The thirty-three states with state-defined accountability systems provided assistance and applied sanctions to low-performing schools that failed to improve after a period of time. A majority of states required school improvement plans to address areas of weakness. Only seventeen states held districts accountable for student or school performance. Even fewer emphasized *student* accountability, making advancement to the next grade level contingent on meeting performance standards. By 2008 students will have to pass a state examination to graduate from high schools in twenty-eight states.

In their final question, Goertz and Duffy (2001) inquired about the alignment of state accountability systems between Title I and non–Title I schools (see Figure 9.3 for a description of Title I). Goertz and Duffy (2001) found twenty-two states to have a "seamless" accountability system, as is desired by this federal program. In such a system, all schools/districts are held for the same performance standards regardless of status as a Title I school. The other twenty-eight states either held Title I and non-Title I schools accountable using different sets of indicators or they held only Title I schools accountable.

Another report of the status of state financial assistance for low-performing schools and rewards for successful schools appears in Table 13.1. This listing, which was compiled by Education Week (2001), notes that twenty-six

TABLE 13.1.

Status of Financial Assistance and Rewards, 2001

| State | Assistance for Low-Performing Schools | | Rewards for Successful Schools Based on | | Option to Spend on Teacher Bonuses |
	On-site Team	Extra Funds	Targets	Improvement	
Alabama	X		X	X	
Alaska[a]					
Arizona					
Arkansas[a,b]					
California	X	X		X	X
Colorado		X	X	X	X

TABLE 13.1.

(Continued)

| State | Assistance for Low-Performing Schools | | Rewards for Successful Schools Based on | | Option to Spend on Teacher Bonuses |
	On-site Team	Extra Funds	Targets	Improvement	
Connecticut	X	X		X	
Delaware	X		X	X	X
Florida	X	X	X	X	X
Georgia[a]			X	X	X
Hawaii					
Idaho					
Illinois[a,b]					
Indiana	X	X		X	
Iowa					
Kansas	X				
Kentucky	X	X		X	
Louisiana	X	X			
Maine					
Maryland	X	X		X	
Massachusetts[b]	X	X			
Michigan	X		X	X	
Minnesota					
Mississippi[a,b]					
Missouri	X	X			
Montana					
Nevada	X	X			
New Hampshire					
New Jersey			X	X	
New Mexico[a]	X			X	
New York	X	X			
North Carolina	X		X	X	X
North Dakota					
Ohio				X	X
Oklahoma	X				
Oregon	X	X			
Pennsylvania			X		X
Rhode Island[a]					
South Carolina	X	X	X	X	
South Dakota					
Tennessee	X	X	X	X	X
Texas	X		X	X	X
Utah[a]				X	X
Virginia	X				
Washington[a]					
West Virginia	X	X			
Wisconsin	X				
Wyoming					
Total	25	16	12	19	11

[a]States reporting that low-performing schools will receive assistance in the future.

[b]States reporting that successful schools will receive rewards in the future.

Source: Education Week. (2001). Assistance and rewards. *Quality Counts 2001: A Better Balance: Standards, Tests, and the Tools to Succeed*. Bethesda, MD: Author, pp. 82–83. Reprinted with permission from *Education Week*.

states offer some form of assistance for low-performing schools. All but one of these states assign teams to assist school personnel with designing and implementing improvement plans. Although somewhat fewer (sixteen) direct financial assistance to low-performing schools, another eight intend to do so in the future. Overall, there are financial rewards based on school performance in twenty states. All but one of these states make the rewards contingent on a measure of improvement in school performance. Eleven states' rewards depend on schools meeting specified targets or improvement goals. Another four states reported that their accountability systems will include monetary rewards in the future. Of the states that have rewards, eleven permit schools to pay salary bonuses to teachers and other personnel.

Performance-Based Rewards as Incentives

Systemic educational reforms that link allocations of state funds to performance measures are likely to grow in the future. The challenge is to design a system of financial rewards that has an incentive effect. Achieving this goal requires showing that rewards are related to efforts of school personnel to improve their own and students' performance.

King and Mathers (1997) examined performance-based rewards as motivators in Indiana, Kentucky, South Carolina, and Texas. Findings from their interviews indicated that rewards offer the potential to motivate school improvement in several ways:

- There were reported effects of accountability systems that include rewards and sanctions, but intrinsic aspects of teaching and non-monetary recognition had greater incentive effects than financial rewards.
- Accountability systems stimulated school improvement efforts and team building, particularly in elementary schools and low-performing schools.

- School-level personnel focused on the needs of low-performing students when ratings and rewards considered the performance of student groups.
- The avoidance of negative publicity and sanctions was a more powerful motivator than the promise of rewards.

However, King and Mathers (1997) also discussed reports that accountability systems in these states had several unintended, and potentially negative, consequences:

- Curriculum narrowed and instructional practices altered as school personnel responded to priorities within accountability systems.
- The purposes of testing changed as public purposes displaced classroom purposes.
- Unethical or illegal practices became more prevalent.
- Accountability systems created morale problems and divisions among personnel.

Ladd (1996) also commented on the possible consequences of linking money to narrow indicators of performance:

> Although economists typically endorse greater use of incentive programs, a well-known theorem in organizational economics demonstrates that when only one of the multiple goals of an organization can be measured, and hence rewarded, incentive programs are undesirable because they will encourage people to focus all their attention on the measurable and rewarded goal to the exclusion of other goals. (p. 12)

Rewards and sanctions that reflect narrow performance indicators, for example, may exert pressure to teach *the* test or alter students' responses to assessments. These consequences are quite different from teaching *to* the test. In fact, teachers in many states are expected to align curricula to standards to be assessed on criterion-referenced assessments.

Although teaching to the standards may be an intended effect of state accountability systems, Stronge and Tucker (2000) noted the dangers of distorting the curriculum to meet the demands of assessment:

> Ideally, curriculum and instruction drive assessment, but if assessment is fixed and determines high stakes decisions such as teacher evaluation, then it can drive the curriculum and instruction. . . . No one intends this to happen, but evidence abounds that it is occurring, and it is one of the reasons many teachers object to testing programs. This concern seems justified based on a standard of fairness. (p. 58)

Ladd and Hansen (1999) found mixed evidence from studies of rewards: "empirical evidence from the private sector is neither solid enough to conclude that financial incentives generate large increases in productivity nor detailed enough to provide such guidance for the design of incentive programs in the education sector" (pp. 182–183). Similarly, studies of accountability systems in several urban school districts yielded either mixed effects on pupil achievement or "few or no gains from the incentive system" (p. 183). Ladd and Hansen speculated that these findings reflected the failure of programs to embed incentives within a broader program of educational reform.

Milanowski (2000) reported findings from surveys and interviews with teachers and principals who experienced reward programs in Kentucky, Maryland, and the Charlotte–Mecklenburg county schools of North Carolina. Although conclusions of this study parallel those of King and Mathers (1997), there are subtle differences:

- There were not strong motivational effects, but teachers valued the rewards about as much as many of the intrinsic and recognition rewards received.
- Rewards had positive effects on some motivational variables, including understanding of the performance goals, commitment to them, and choice of performance level to try to attain.
- Negative consequences of trying to achieve goals (including stress and more work hours)

and concerns about the fairness of the programs offset some of the motivational potential of the rewards.
- Negative publicity, loss of professional pride, and the threat of sanctions were strong motivators in some settings.

Adopting a performance-based accountability system, including results-based rewards and sanctions, sends a clear message to educators and to the public that school personnel are accountable for school performance. However, performance-based school finance policies may not themselves be sufficient to motivate school personnel to achieve the state's educational reform goals. King and Mathers (1997) observed that educators and local school boards often see performance-based accountability systems as heavy-handed reform strategies. The number of state assessments and the resulting effects on curriculum and instruction make accountability systems appear to be top-down, intrusive, and overly directive. These investigators concluded that there must be an appropriate balance between state and local control over setting the direction of reform, and that there must be local commitment to reforms and local involvement in the design of school improvements.

In addition, the effectiveness of accountability systems and rewards may be tied to schools' will (desire) and capacity (human and material resources) to change (Firestone & Corbett, 1988). When schools perform below expectations and lack the desire to change, the promise of monetary rewards does little to move reform agenda. Similarly, when educators desire to make improvements but lack the necessary skills and resources, neither rewards nor mandates have an incentive effect. A more effective strategy is *capacity building* (O'Day, Goertz, & Floden, 1995; Lashway, 2001), particularly to help low-performing schools meet expectations.

Massell (2000) noted four major capacity-building strategies that were observed in twenty-two districts in eight states over a 2-year period. These strategies included interpreting and using data in school improvement plans, building teacher knowledge and skills, aligning curriculum and instruction, and targeting interventions on low-performing students and/or schools. In particular, she discussed the use of performance data to focus and drive decision making: "Districts and schools are using performance and other data to plan professional development activities, to identify achievement gaps, to align curriculum and instruction, to assign and evaluate personnel, and to identify students for remedial or gifted and talented programs" (p. 2). If these strategies and targeted assistance do not result in performance improvements, then stronger sanctions, including changes in leadership when there is no desire or ability to lead change, are appropriate. In this case, the best strategy may be to follow the logic of accountability by dismissing underperforming teachers and principals and reconstituting the school (Lashway, 2001).

Cohen (1996) noted the importance of building capacity as rewards are instituted: "The success of such schemes depends heavily on whether state or local school systems could enhance the capacity of the worst schools to respond constructively to more powerful incentives, for those would be the schools least likely to be able to respond well on their own. But precisely because of the educational weaknesses that reformers wish to correct, state and local systems have at best only modest professional capacity to solve this problem" (p. 124). Milanowski (2000) included capacity building among the strategies needed to maximize the motivational impacts of performance-based award programs: provide support, professional development and knowledge and skills to increase teacher expectancy; make stronger connections between rewards and goal achievement; promote the active support and commitment of principals; and design the program and communicate about it to ensure that teachers view it as fair. Lashway (2001) argued

the importance of leadership in school improvement, stating that results are becoming the universal yardstick of leadership. Building the capacity of principals to devise motivational systems is important in the successful integration of new external standards with existing internal initiatives.

Schools that have already attained standards may not need technical assistance or rewards (they already have both the will and the capacity). Public recognition and banners may be sufficient motivators to maintain performance in these high-achieving schools. There are often issues of equity and adequacy to be considered in expecting all schools to make performance improvements. Focusing technical assistance and other resources on low-performing schools that have the desire to improve but lack necessary financial or human capacity may more quickly advance the reform agenda. Targeted capacity building to improve instructional skills, school leadership, and resources may be a more effective use of limited state funds than directing a large proportion of revenue through a performance-based reward. Once all schools have the capacity to make improvements, then a reward may have the desired incentive effect.

The findings from research on rewards and the importance of building schools' capacities to achieve expectations suggest that financial rewards alone are not likely to have desired incentive effects. In order to maximize their potential, policy makers should carefully consider the following questions as they design reward programs within state accountability systems (see also Richards & Shujaa, 1990; Picus, 1992; King & Mathers, 1997; Goertz & Duffy, 2001).

- What *cognitive indicators* of student performance are best linked to rewards? Should schools be held accountable for performance on criterion-referenced assessments that are aligned with state standards or for performance on norm-referenced assessments that give an indication of student achievement relative to a larger national population? Which students are to be included in assessments for accountability purposes? What testing conditions will enable those with legitimate needs for accommodations or alternative assessments to demonstrate their knowledge?

- What *noncognitive indicators* of student, teacher, or school performance should be included? Should schools be held accountable for attendance or dropout rates, enrollments in advanced placement classes, teachers' skills and performance, school climate, parent involvement, or other factors related to learning? Does a mix of cognitive and noncognitive indicators offer the best opportunity to motivate school improvement via an incentive effect?

- Which cognitive and noncognitive indicators are least likely to have *unintended consequences*? Which factors might result in such unethical or illegal actions as teaching the test, altering test results, classifying students who leave school as intending to pursue home schooling or other alternatives rather than as dropouts, and inflating reports of parent involvement?

- Is a *structure* that rewards schools for performance at predetermined target levels more effective than one that considers improvements and the value added (Sanders & Horn, 1994) by schools in approaching those goals? What targets or annual growth expectations are appropriate so that school personnel will see the goals as attainable? Is a mix of absolute standards and gains better able to communicate to schools the expectations to be achieved, while also stimulating improvement for even the lowest-performing schools?

- What *amount of money*, in relation to the overall school finance program, should be allocated to an incentive program? How large a reward is necessary for teachers to view the reward as valuable? How large a proportion of state funds should be diverted to rewards versus programs to reach other state goals, including equalization and capacity building?

- What *organizational unit* should be the recipient of funds? What advantages and what disadvantages are associated with the use of rewards for the performance of entire districts, for schools, for grade levels or departments, and for individual teachers? Which level offers the best opportunity for satisfying the conditions identified previously for rewards to have an incentive effect?

- Should all schools or districts that meet targets or growth expectations be *eligible for financial rewards*? Is the additional money likely to have an incentive effect in high-performing schools, or is nonmonetary recognition (such as a banner displayed in the school) a sufficient motivator for maintaining this status? Are the available funds more effectively used to build capacity and then reward lower-performing schools where incentive effects are most likely to be realized?

- What should be the *permissible uses* of rewards? Are salary bonuses, funds for national conferences, or additional instructional supplies and equipment likely to have desired incentive effects?

- Do performance-based rewards affect *equity and adequacy* goals? What is likely to be their effect on a state goal of closing the achievement gap between high- and low-performing groups of students that are identified in terms of race, ethnicity, gender, disability, or family income? Do these accountability systems and rewards reduce relationships among district financial wealth, family socioeconomic status, and pupil achievement? Do all students have access to teachers with a strong content knowledge and to the academic programs needed to meet high standards? Do rewards offer a viable means for low-performing schools, which often serve students from low-income families, to acquire needed funds for programs to enhance learning?

• What is the *political reality* surrounding financial rewards? Do policy makers offer these strategies primarily because they give the impression that the state is allocating funds in ways that improve public education? Are rewards useful in gaining educators' acceptance of state-established reforms and standards by offering an opportunity to acquire additional funds to raise salaries or enhance local school improvement efforts? Do performance-based rewards truly motivate school improvement?

We opened this chapter with an exploration of theoretical perspectives on rewards and motivation. Policies that promise rewards for performance may satisfy several of the conditions identified as essential for an incentive effect. The strength of these rewards is that they encourage teachers and administrators to cooperate in achieving school goals and in attaining intrinsic benefits as well as financial rewards. They may view the performance expectations and school improvement goals as important and attainable. However, even when there is agreement on these goals, teachers and principals may not have a direct line of sight. That is, they may not see the connection between the rewards offered and the actions necessary to achieve desired outcomes.

These group rewards in state accountability systems differ from financial gains that are realized by an individual teacher for his or her teaching skills and performance. We examine both of these policy strategies in this chapter, because both are meant to have an incentive effect in improving the productivity of schools.

PERFORMANCE-BASED REWARDS IN TEACHER COMPENSATION

Achieving the goal of improved student performance depends in large part on improvements in the knowledge and skills of teachers. Ladd and Hansen (1999) discussed the factors

to be addressed when strengthening the capacity of teachers to improve student outcomes. They must have knowledge of the subject matter, of how students learn, and of methods for teaching. They must have the ability to select appropriate teaching materials, make wise instructional decisions, and monitor student progress. They must be able to teach the kinds of knowledge and skills demanded by twenty-first-century jobs and citizenship. Finally, teachers must have the skills to teach highly diverse groups of students, including those with disabilities and those whose language and culture differ from their own. These authors observed that the challenge is to develop the best policies to enhance these forms of knowledge and skills.

School finance policies can contribute to the goal of strengthening the knowledge and skills of current and prospective teachers. Additional investments in personnel in the form of fair compensation that is in line with that of other professions may help attract and retain excellent classroom teachers. In addition, strategies to target funds to strengthen teachers' knowledge and skills may enhance the effectiveness of efforts to restructure other aspects of schools as organizations (Firestone, 1994).

We first examine the supply of and demand for teachers' services in the context of the larger labor market. We observe that differences between the public and private sectors are disappearing as state policies encourage competition among education providers and as schools face shortages of teachers. These pressures and the goal of improving teacher quality and student outcomes urge the adoption of compensation systems that link pay to teachers' performance and skills.

Teacher Compensation and the Labor Market

We introduced the concepts of supply and demand (see Chapter 2) in the context of the flow of resources between households and producers in a market-oriented society. Households purchase products and offer labor. Businesses hire workers for production processes. These transactions create the supply and demand sides of product and labor markets. In this section, we differentiate the teacher labor market from the operation of the larger economy. We discuss factors, including compensation, that affect the decisions people make to seek and remain in teaching positions.

The Private-Sector Labor Market

Conditions of supply and demand in a free-market economy influence the level at which equilibrium is reached for prices of goods and services (see Figure 2.2). The prevailing wage for labor is the amount of money necessary to ensure that there are enough qualified applicants (supply) for the available jobs (demand). Wage differentials move workers to occupations (and positions) in which the demand for labor is the greatest and away from those occupations (and positions) where the demand is the least. Differentials exist among job assignments within a given enterprise, among different business firms within a given industry, and among the many industries that employ people of the same occupation.

The setting of wages in the private sector assumes that consumers exercise free choice among available products and that employers exercise choice among similarly skilled laborers. Workers are presumed to be free and willing to move among jobs and geographic locations in response to conditions of labor surplus and shortages. In reality, such a perfect free-market economy does not exist. Workers are not uniform in motivation, attitudes, ability, and mobility. Nor do they have information about all the alternatives available to them. In our mixed economy, the government intervenes in the marketplace by setting minimum wages and specifying such benefits as social security and unemployment insurance. The public sector also influences wages in the private sector through its ability to attract labor into public employment. The private sector similarly influences the wages that must be paid to attract and retain public-sector workers.

Personal and economic considerations influence the supply of labor that households are willing to provide employers. The desire for income is balanced with individual and family decisions about alternative uses of their talents. Alternatives may include working within the household itself, obtaining additional education, and volunteering time and effort in any number of pursuits. Employers decide how much compensation to offer and structure the working conditions. They use these monetary and nonmonetary benefits to entice people to enter the workforce and to prepare for particular occupations. Not all individuals who are willing and able to perform a given job, however, find satisfactory employment. A ready supply of willing workers does not elicit a demand for their services on the part of employers. Rather, the demand for workers with particular skills depends on the public's consumption of goods and services and on opportunities to alter the mix of labor and capital required in production processes. The goal of maximizing profits encourages private-sector businesses to increase workers' productivity and to substitute capital for labor in production processes.

Many of these statements about setting wages and influencing people's decisions to move among occupations or employers apply just as well to the public sector. However, some characteristics of the private-sector labor market do not apply to the market for teachers' services or the basis for their remuneration.

The Labor Market for Teachers

Teachers and other certified personnel constitute a labor market that has operated somewhat differently, but not independently, from the larger economy. Public schools produce a service that is not marketed at a price to their clients. It is difficult to determine how much an individual teacher or administrator contributes to the product (which may be, for example, a graduate who meets knowledge and performance expectations). Legislatures and school boards typically determine compensation levels and working conditions via political compromise. In most states and districts, teachers unions influence salary models and working conditions through collective bargaining.

State policies often restrict teachers' mobility and the supply of potential school employees. Licensing or certification requirements define the minimum qualifications needed to enter the profession. There may be alternative routes to licensure, and emergency certificates may be readily granted to ease shortages of qualified teachers. In addition, state-determined minimum salary schedules may influence both the structure of salary schedules and the amounts offered to teacher applicants. These salary and benefit packages may deter some candidates from seeking positions, especially when suitable employment opportunities in other fields offer relatively higher wages and more extensive benefits. Tenure statutes, state retirement systems, and policies that limit the years of prior out-of-district experience that may be applied toward salaries often impede teachers' mobility to respond to changes in labor markets.

Societal factors and school environments influence the applicant pool. During the past several decades, there has been an exodus of women and minorities from teacher preparation and from teaching careers into other professions. The number of teachers seeking employment varies greatly among subject fields and geographic areas. Working conditions, poor pupil discipline, and threats of violence in some districts lessen the attractiveness of the profession. The age of school facilities, lack of appropriate computer technologies, and minimal budgets for teaching materials in many districts may discourage candidates. Furthermore, social and economic factors influence the quality of the teacher candidate pool in that higher-ability teachers are more re-

sponsive to changes in wages paid in various occupations.

The demand for teachers has also differed from free-market assumptions. In many states and labor markets within states, there is not a large number of buyers (public and private school systems) demanding teachers' services. Stable or declining enrollments and limited competition among public and private schools may restrict the demand for new teachers or the ability of teachers to move among employers. Newly certified or newly licensed teachers may postpone their entry into the profession, and those who do are likely to leave before retirement. For these reasons, teacher supply and demand are difficult to predict (Fox, 1988), and salaries are less responsive to market conditions than are wages paid to other workers. The teacher labor market has traditionally resembled a *monopsony* (Fleisher & Kniesner, 1980). In this type of a labor market, there is effectively one demander of workers with given skills. In the restricted labor market of a monopsony, wages tend to be lower than they might be in competitive marketplaces.

At the dawn of the new millennium, conditions in the teacher labor market changed rapidly from this traditional view. Enrollment growth and competition for teachers in selected subject fields induced many districts to increase or differentiate salaries. Districts offered bonuses or housing supplements and paid moving expenses to attract teachers generally or those in certain subject fields. Urban or rural districts offered salary bonuses to teachers who were willing to work in low-performing or remote schools. Changes in state policies enabled retirees to return to teaching without losing benefits. Policies to lower class size, to expand offerings for preschool children and for those with disabilities, and to increase advanced placement opportunities stimulated demand and raised salaries. Policies that encouraged student choice and mobility among charter schools and other public schools, and vouchers that permitted families to spend public money in private schools (see Chapter 15), induced wage differentials within and among sectors. Schools in competitive markets found it necessary to improve compensation packages to attract and retain high-quality teachers. For example, districts provided salary bonuses for teachers who earned certificates from the National Board for Professional Teaching Standards (see later discussion). These options for families to choose schools—and for teachers to move among schools—exerted pressure on districts to enhance salaries and improve working conditions.

These supply-and-demand conditions mirror those described above for the private sector. There is greater competition for teachers within and between the two sectors of the economy. The supply curve in Figure 2.2 suggests that as salaries increase, more individuals prepare for careers in teaching, and more people in the reserve pool of certified teachers reenter the profession. Once this larger supply meets the demand, salaries stabilize at a new equilibrium level. The demand curve in this figure suggests that as society requires additional teachers to serve more children, reduce class size, or expand offerings, the equilibrium price rises until it attracts people to enter the teaching profession from other occupations or to move among schools. The converse is also true. Lower salaries are possible when demand and mobility are lower.

When the supply of teachers differs from the demand for teachers, instabilities in the marketplace result in shortages and surpluses. The labor market is slow to respond to these changes. This is because it takes a long time for the demand for teachers in particular subject fields to increase, for individuals to select different college majors, and for new entrants into the profession to graduate. Periods of high teacher demand, such as the 1950s, 1960s, 1990s, and early 2000s, lead to aggressive recruitment and relatively higher salaries. Eventually there is an oversupply, such as that experienced in the 1970s. At that time, en-

rollments rapidly declined and an economic recession in the nation diminished job opportunities in both public and private sectors. When the applicant pool exceeds the demand for teachers, salaries stabilize or decrease in terms of purchasing power.

This trend is apparent in the elementary and secondary teachers' salaries depicted in Figure 13.1. The average salary paid to teachers in 1969–1970 was $37,574 ($36,641 for elementary and $38,782 for secondary teachers) in equivalent 1998–99 dollars. There was a slight increase in the early 1970s to an average inflation-adjusted salary of $39,106. Salaries declined through the 1970s during a period characterized by diminished enrollments, an oversupply of teachers, and a high rate of inflation. The low in purchasing power of salaries occurred 1980–1981, when teachers earned an average adjusted salary of $33,514 ($32,728, elementary; $34,460, secondary). The increase through the 1980s brought salaries to a high of $40,650 ($39,920, elementary; $41,648, secondary) in 1990–1991. Salaries rose again in relative terms at the end of the twentieth century, the average reaching $40,582 in 1998–1999. This period was characterized by lower unemployment, increasing enrollments, and a growing shortage of teachers. As this text went to press, the nation had entered a recession and a period of higher unemployment. As a result, the shortages of applicants that occurred early in the 2000s may end, and districts may be able to fill positions without having to raise salaries relative to inflation.

Ladd and Hansen (1999) analyzed data from 1940 to 1990 and concluded, "Overall these trends based on average salaries suggest that teaching is becoming less financially attractive for college graduates compared with other occupations" (p. 172). Nelson, Drown, and Gould (2000) reported that teachers' salaries were less than those paid in other white-collar occupations, including accountants, attorneys, computer systems analysts, engineers, and professors. They concluded that many graduates

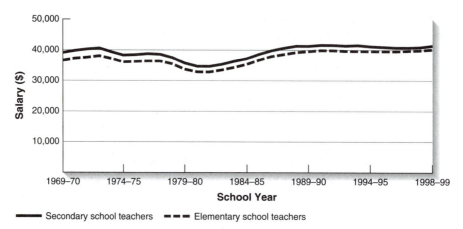

FIGURE 13.1. Average Salaries for Elementary and Secondary School Teachers, 1969–1970 to 1998–1999 (constant 1998–1999 dollars)

Source: National Education Association. *Estimates of School Statistics, 1998–99*. As published in NCES. (2001). *Digest of Education Statistics, 2000*. Figure 10, Report 2001-034. **http:nces.ed.gov/pubs2001/digest/ch2.html** (accessed October 5, 2001). Reprinted with permission of the National Education Association.

who might otherwise have chosen a teaching career turned to other professions:

> During the past six years, salary offers for college graduates in all fields have grown faster than offers for new teachers. In several fields, salary offers grew at twice the rate for new teachers. In 2000, new college graduates received average salary offers reaching almost $40,000 compared to an average beginning teacher salary of $27,989. (p. 33)

School boards may increase salaries for beginning teachers in an effort to increase the supply of high-quality teachers. Nelson, Drown, and Gould (2000) compared average of all teachers' salaries with those paid new entrants into the profession. Beginning teachers' salaries rose more quickly in recent years than the average for all teachers. They reported that this difference reflected in part the retirement of many experienced teachers who were at the top of salary schedules (thus their departure lowered the average salary). The difference may also have been due in part to decisions of school boards to increase beginning salaries to

attract higher-quality applicants. Although Ballou and Podgursky (1997) found some improvement in selected measures of teacher quality during the 1980s as states increased allocations for education, they found no evidence that increases in salaries had the intended effect of improving the quality of applicants: "Certainly it would be unwise simply to assume that raising pay will improve teacher quality" (p. 41). They noted that senior teachers chose to remain in the profession longer because of the salary increases, thus limiting districts' ability to replace them with recent college graduates.

An indicator of the supply of high-quality teachers is the percentage assigned to teach classes outside their areas of expertise (Monk & Rice, 1994; Goldhaber, 2001). Darling-Hammond (2000) presented data showing a wide distribution in this characteristic among states and districts in recent years. Overall, 28 percent of mathematics teachers did not have a college major or minor in that subject area (the range was from 9 to 45 percent). Furthermore, schools and districts with large percentages of minority and low-income students experienced greater shortages of qualified teachers. A prior report noted that 23 percent of teachers throughout the nation taught in fields other than their majors (Bobbitt & McMillen, 1990). Over 40 percent of teachers in bilingual education, computer science, and mathematics did not have these college majors.

Teacher quality is likely to improve with stronger teacher preparation programs, more rigorous licensing standards, national board certification, and improved induction and professional development (Ladd & Hansen, 1999; Darling-Hammond, 2000). Ballou and Podgursky (1997), among other researchers, concluded that increasing salaries alone is not an effective policy strategy to improve quality: "In our judgment, further increases in teacher salaries should be conditional on the removal of structural impediments in the market, requiring significant changes in the way teachers are licensed, recruited and compensated" (p. 106).

These reforms, including the redesign of compensation policies, hold greater promise for improving the quality of teachers than merely increasing the average salary. In the next sections, we explore limitations of the traditional salary schedule and the promise that linking teacher salaries to performance measures can effectively motivate, reward, and retain teachers who have the ability to improve student learning.

Strategies to Link Salaries to Responsibilities and Performance

Among the most important aspects of personnel policies is the relationship of people's skills, responsibilities, and job performance to their remuneration. The presumptions that these factors affect the internal efficiencies of schools, and that the salaries that are offered influence the future supplies of capable teachers, make them the subject of educational reform proposals.

In this section we discuss various structures of teacher compensation systems. We begin with the single salary schedule and the presumed relationship between teachers' experience and training and teachers' skills. We then examine merit pay, career ladders, and other strategies that relate compensation to skills, responsibilities, and performance.

Assumptions and Limitations of the Single Salary Schedule

A uniform salary schedule for all teachers in a school district emerged early in the twentieth century in response to prevalent inequities. At that time, wages differed according to such factors as grade levels and subjects taught, gender, number of dependents, political affiliations, and bargaining between individual teachers and school boards. The principle of equal pay for equal qualifications urged districts to pay the same salary for teachers of equal training and experience. Minimal differentiations in pay resulted from such extra services as coaching athletic teams and sponsoring extracurricular activities. The base pay for nearly all teachers in the United States and many other countries today is determined by two objective criteria.

The two-dimensional structure of the single salary schedule typically differentiates teachers' pay in accordance with years of experience (longevity) and advanced preparation (training). The first dimension brings annual step increases that raise salaries annually until a stated maximum number of years of teaching experience is reached. Teachers who move among districts or states may be placed on the schedule in accordance with their prior years of experience. However, districts generally restrict to between 5 and 10 years the number of years of out-of-district experience that can be applied to determining salaries. Once teachers reach the top of the schedule, they receive across-the-board increases in salary without movement on the schedule for additional longevity.

The average number of step increases in schedules in the United States is sixteen. Nelson (1995) and Lawton (1988) compared this practice with policies in other nations. Nelson observed that primary-level teachers in thirteen of the nineteen nations that were studied received longevity increases for more years than in the United States. On schedules in other countries, the time it took for teachers to achieve the maximum salary ranged from ten to forty-three years. Lawton commented that pay scales with fifteen or fewer steps were limited to countries with historical connections to Great Britain. Other countries used scales with twenty or more steps, including forty years in Italy and forty-three years in Spain.

The second dimension included in salary schedules is advanced preparation. This training factor rewards and encourages continued preparation in pedagogy and in fields related to the subjects taught. Four to six training categories in a salary schedule typically range from having no college degree to having earned a doctoral degree. Teachers advance along this continuum upon completion of advanced degrees or specified numbers of hours of graduate course work. In some districts, teachers may receive continuing-education units and salary increments for district-sponsored professional development. Salary increases for this advanced preparation may influence teachers' decisions to complete graduate degrees.

The effect of these experience and training dimensions is generally to double salaries from the initial cell of the matrix (e.g., first-year teacher with a bachelor's degree) to the final step increase (e.g., teacher with sixteen years of experience and a doctoral degree). In addition to these increments, actual annual increases in salaries, including those of experienced teachers who are frozen on the top step, depend on legislative or school board actions. All cells of the matrix change to reflect increases in the cost of living, state legislative appropriations, negotiations between boards of education and teachers' associations, and other factors.

This two-dimensional structure survived through the twentieth century. The American Federation of Teachers argued that the only fair procedure for paying teachers was "by the use of an adequate single salary schedule based upon training and experience," which would "permit the experienced teachers to perform their services in an atmosphere of dignity and personal satisfaction." (Magel, 1961) When this structure was criticized, the National Education Association (1985) responded that a single salary schedule

- Promotes positive working relationships among teachers and between teachers and administrators
- Is a relatively inexpensive and unburdened system for allocating pay when compared with other systems
- Avoids racial, ethnic, and gender discrimination among teachers

In contrast, critics of the single salary schedule contend that there is little opportunity for teachers to be given monetary recognition for their performance. The structure of the schedule rewards the number of years teachers have taught rather than their skills or performance. It rewards the number of graduate courses or continuing-education units completed, rather than their usefulness or relevance to the subjects taught. These traditional dimensions permit little or no recognition of initiative, enthusiasm, efficiency, innovation, cooperation, ability, or improvements in performance. These factors may affect teachers' decisions to leave the profession voluntarily or school boards' decisions to dismiss teachers for poor classroom teaching. However, they are not direct determinants of the amount of salaries paid to individual teachers, nor do they offer incentives to improve teaching skills (Hanushek, 1997). Odden and Kelley (2001) concluded that the single salary schedule is not strategically aligned with needed knowledge and skills, with current educational goals, or with the expertise needed to improve student achievement.

Determining salaries by criteria of training and experience would be defensible if these characteristics were related to instructional skills or pupil performance. We challenged these assumed relationships when we discussed input–output relationships in Chapter 12. We conclude that the salary model in place in most school systems is a major source of inefficiencies in schools. For this reason, policy makers are giving greater consideration to alternative compensation plans that link remuneration to measures of skills, performance, job responsibilities, or cooperative efforts to improve schools. In the third National Education Summit in 1999, the governors and business leaders resolved to create systems of rewards and consequences for teachers (Miner, 1999/2000). They urged competitive salary structures that would link salaries with student achievement and provide salary advances for professional development only when it is standards-based.

Compensation plans based on merit pay, on a career ladder, or on group performance are visible initiatives that demonstrate to the public an emphasis on accountability. These strategies may increase the supply of teachers who seek careers in which their efforts can be recognized. They offer opportunities and incentives for professional growth, improved teaching skills, and increased productivity in upgrading student performance (Poston & Frase, 1991; Odden & Kelley, 2001). We discuss their potential and limitations, describe state and district initiatives for relating teachers' compensation to skills and performance, and discuss their potential incentive effects.

Merit Pay

In this form of a salary incentive plan, individual teachers receive financial rewards, or merit pay, when they demonstrate particular effectiveness through some form of performance assessment. This plan generally directs a one-time salary bonus to those teachers who are deemed to be at or above a given performance expectation. A merit award typically does not advance these teachers on the salary matrix beyond what is warranted for longevity and advanced degrees. (Such advancement for merit bonuses would effectively raise salaries into the future for past performance.)

The adoption of merit pay for teachers is cyclical. Murnane and Cohen (1986) observed that "while interest in paying teachers according to merit endures, attempts to use merit pay do not" (p. 2). This strategy became popular in the early 1960s after *Sputnik* raised concerns about the productivity of schools. It reappeared in the last decades of the twentieth century in the context of educational reform. The National Commission on Excellence (1983) recommended that "Salaries for the teaching profession should be increased and should be professionally competitive, market-sensitive, and performance-based" (p. 30).

Advocates of merit pay for teachers argue that

- The amount of merit pay earned reflects the skills and performance of an individual teacher.
- Performance-based pay provides a competitive environment with higher pay for effective teachers.
- Teachers are held accountable, bringing public support to schools that pay teachers in accordance with performance.
- Evaluation processes improve, and more individuals become involved in the appraisal and improvement of instruction.
- Merit compensation helps to attract and retain effective teachers, while discouraging ineffective ones from continuing in the profession (National Education Association, 1984; Herndon, 1985; Frohreich, 1988; Odden & Kelley, 2001).

In contrast to arguments that merit pay can be effective in school settings, critics note the serious shortcomings of this strategy. Rewards for individual teacher performance do not have the desired incentive effect in terms of improving teaching and learning:

- There is no clear agreement on what constitutes effective teaching or on which teacher qualities influence pupil achievement.
- Most evaluation systems do not provide valid or comprehensive indicators of teaching ability that are related to professional standards of good practice.
- Teachers resist evaluation systems that are linked to compensation.
- There is no evidence that individual rewards contribute to student achievement. It is difficult to separate an individual teacher's contributions to pupils' successes from other school (e.g., previous teachers') and non-school (e.g., families') influences.
- Competition for bonuses may be counterproductive, lowering morale and decreasing cooperation among colleagues.
- A fixed amount of money available for merit increases pits teachers against one another.
- Like abuses in the operation of many local governments, the selection of deserving teachers can be driven more by political forces (including nepotism, racism, sexism, and cronyism) than by professional considerations.
- Plans may punish average teachers while only minimally motivating those deemed to be productive.
- Plans are expensive to initiate and maintain. The cost and time necessary to develop and implement an effective evaluation and compensation plan detract from more critical responsibilities (Astuto, 1985; Johnson, 1986; Ballou & Podgursky, 1993; Kohn, 1993; Hatry, Greiner, & Ashford, 1994; Odden & Kelley, 2001).

These criticisms focus on the structure and cost of merit pay plans, as well as on the difficulty of developing valid and objective criteria to measure performance. The failure of merit pay to motivate teachers may be rooted in the theoretical assumptions underlying this incentive system. Kohn (1993) challenged the premise that financial rewards can effectively change people's behavior and motivate them to improve their performance. He argued that people focus on the reward and become less interested in the quality of the task, that improvements occur for only a short period of time, that extrinsic motivators erode intrinsic motivation, that rewards harm relationships among workers, and that rewards are instruments of control that reinforce hierarchy. Because there is not a clear line of sight between the potential reward and people's performance, merit pay is not an effective motivator. These criticisms suggest that individual performance-based rewards do not have much potential for improving teacher quality or school productivity.

Although few districts have adopted performance as a determinant of salaries, some reports attest that merit pay can be successfully implemented. Murnane and Cohen (1986) characterized successful merit plans as those that supplemented already high salaries and good working conditions and that compensated teachers for extra responsibilities outside classrooms, rather than determining relative abilities of teachers within classrooms. Ballou and Podgursky (1993) analyzed data from the 1987–1988 Schools and Staffing Survey of 56,000 public school teachers and concluded that teachers in districts with merit pay were not demoralized or hostile toward the compensation plan and that teachers of disadvantaged and low-achieving pupils supported merit pay. Farnsworth, Debenham, and Smith (1991) described a successful plan in one district. They concluded that "merit pay, when properly administered and funded, can increase teaching effectiveness" (p. 321).

A career ladder approach changes the nature of teacher work along with differentiating compensation. However, like merit pay, career ladders have limitations in school improvement efforts because the focus of rewards is the individual teacher.

Career Ladder

A career ladder differentiates levels of responsibility, status, and salary. Unlike merit pay, which does not assign formal status distinctions, career ladders and other differentiated staffing approaches restructure salary schedules along with a hierarchy of job classifications. This approach evolved to blend intrinsic and extrinsic rewards. Making responsibilities more varied and challenging would provide greater motivation for teachers to advance on the ladder, as well as resulting in greater organizational productivity.

The National Commission on Excellence (1983) advocated the development of career ladders that would distinguish among beginning, experienced, and master teachers. The Holmes Group (1986) called for three levels within a staged career that would make and reward formal distinctions on the basis of responsibilities and degrees of autonomy. The first-level instructor would teach for several years under the supervision of experienced teachers. The majority of autonomous classroom teachers would hold the title of professional teacher. The highest level, career professional, would include teachers who are capable of using their pedagogical expertise to improve other teachers' work. A four-step model advanced by the Association of Teacher Educators (1985) included teacher, associate teacher, senior teacher, and master teacher. The Carnegie Forum (1986) called for more responsibilities to be given to board-certified teachers who would serve in the role of lead teacher. Wise (2001) urged a staffing structure consisting of national-board-certified teachers, fully licensed teachers, beginning interns, teacher candidates, and those with little formal preparation.

The Tennessee and Utah plans are the oldest continually operating career ladders. Since enactment of the Comprehensive Education Reform Act in 1984, Tennessee teachers have been eligible to participate in a three-step ladder. This plan has been fully funded by the state. Peevely and Dunbar (2001) reported that 47,500 educators participated in the program, with about $104.5 million in funding, in 1998–1999. The Utah program offered several options to districts. These included a performance bonus that rewarded excellence by individuals or groups of teachers, a job enlargement plan to provide additional pay for extra work, extended contract days that enabled teachers to earn more for nonteaching days beyond the school year, and the career ladder. When school boards, administrators, teachers, and parents in Utah were given latitude to develop programs cooperatively around these incentives, the career ladders that included job expansion or redesign were found to be superior to those based on merit pay (Malen, Murphy & Hart, 1988). Astuto (1985) also concluded that career ladders are more effective than traditional merit pay. She encouraged states to support local districts' experiments with diverse approaches.

Schlechty (1987) urged states and districts to adopt career ladders because of their potential for encouraging and developing high-quality teaching performance. He argued that an effective compensation system must provide increased rewards, including money, status, and responsibility, over a long period of time. A career ladder inspires high-quality performance and encourages long-term commitment from teachers who perform at high levels. The strength of career ladders is in their potential for

- Recognizing, rewarding, and encouraging increased responsibilities, as well as improved performance, as teachers grow in the profession
- Making possible the advancement of teachers, who no longer need to leave the classroom to gain intrinsic and extrinsic rewards
- Increasing teacher efficacy and self-fulfillment, as colleagues and the public recognize the honor of a promotion

- Improving instructional conditions school-wide, by encouraging students to learn and by mentoring beginning or struggling teachers

Several limitations of this compensation strategy contrast with these advantages. Like merit pay, career ladders are expensive to initiate and maintain. They presume to recognize excellence within teaching roles, but often the added responsibilities remove teachers from classrooms into quasi-administrative positions. Responsibilities may be difficult to distinguish at different levels of career status. Pay and status differentials create divisions and low morale among teachers. Limited funds may restrict the number of teachers who are paid for added responsibilities, which may be assumed by others who do not receive recognition and salary increases. Quotas and poor morale may result from the public's perception that there are unwarranted advancements on the ladder solely for salary gains. As in merit awards, decisions about career advancement may rest on subjective evaluations and thus may breed similar concerns about unfairness (MacPhail-Wilcox & King, 1988; Firestone & Bader, 1992; Hatry, Greiner, & Ashford, 1994).

States and school systems incur many monetary and nonmonetary costs under career ladder programs (Smith, 1987; Weeks & Cornett, 1985). Developing the plan itself is costly in teacher and administrator time. A new evaluation system may be required, along with instruments for testing basic skills, content knowledge of the subject field, professional knowledge, and classroom performance. Performance assessment itself is costly, because multiple observers (including teaching colleagues) and conferences mean released time and evaluator training. The incentives must be sufficiently large to encourage teachers to achieve the standards for advancement. Many nonsalary costs must also be recognized in planning and implementing an effective career ladder. These potential consequences may include the fears and concerns of teachers and administrators about the fairness of the system. Even public recognition of career advancement and performance awards can inflict pain on those not advancing and embarrassment on those who receive them (Hatry, Greiner & Ashford, 1994).

Poston and Frase (1991) identified five factors that characterized successful career ladders: no legislative involvement or restrictive outside funding; teacher cooperation in planning; clear and attainable objectives that are creatively designed to meet local needs; freedom to determine the form of rewards, including both extrinsic and intrinsic incentives to improve skills; and sound and valid performance measures. Hawley (1985) and Hatry, Greiner, and Ashford (1994) recognized the importance of involving teachers in the development and implementation of plans. Firestone and Pennell (1993) concluded that increased participation, collaboration, and feedback contributed to teachers' commitment to this compensation strategy.

Career ladders improve on merit pay policies by recognizing the importance of blending extrinsic and intrinsic rewards. This approach is limited, however, in focusing attention primarily on the responsibilities assumed by those teachers who choose to assume different roles. This job-based compensation strategy differs from approaches that link salary increases to the knowledge and skills that teachers bring to their work.

Knowledge- and Skills-Based Compensation

Lawler (2000) urged businesses and other organizations to focus on rewarding excellence and to treat employees as human-capital investors. This approach would alter reward structures in several ways.

First, it suggests basing rewards on the value of the human capital that people bring to the organization. What their job is at a particular moment is much less important than the value of their knowledge and skills. Second, it suggests rewarding people according to how effectively they use their human capital—their knowledge, skills, and competencies—to help the organization improve its business performance. (pp. 10–11)

The focus shifts from the responsibilities a job entails to the knowledge and skills an employee brings to and applies within the position. There is still a concern for an individual's performance. However, the ability to apply one's knowledge and skill to the organization's goals makes this approach more strategic.

In Chapter 12, we discussed the National Commission on Teaching and America's Future (NCTAF) (1996) report's recommendations for improving teachers' knowledge and skills. This report also urges school districts to link teacher salary increases to a progressive demonstration of growing knowledge and skills over a career. Odden and Kelley (2001) also recommended approaches to link salaries with each teacher's knowledge and skills. This approach would encourage teachers to develop their competencies in several areas: effective forms of pedagogy, the deeper and more conceptual subject matter knowledge needed to help children acquire advanced cognitive expertise, and leadership and management skills to engage in effective school-site management and decision making. Unlike merit pay plans, which often pit teachers against one another for bonuses from a limited pool of money, this approach rewards all who demonstrate knowledge and skills deemed to be important in school improvement efforts. The knowledge and skills to be rewarded reflect standards and competencies desired by the school and district. For example, annual increases in salary might be based on skills essential in aligning curriculum to state or district standards in respective subject areas (Darling-Hammond, 2000).

Odden and Kelley (2001) note the following as being essential in a knowledge- and skills-based compensation strategy:

- Teaching standards that describe what teachers need to know and be able to teach so that students attain high performance
- A performance assessment system that identifies performance levels of teachers in relation to the teaching standards
- A salary structure that links pay levels to teachers' performance levels

The teacher compensation system recently enacted by the Iowa legislature emphasizes professional development (Iowa Department of Education, 2001). The goal is to improve student learning through "the most effective professional support for beginning teachers and the strongest professional development and continued learning for experienced teachers" (p. 1). The eight Iowa Teaching Standards create a framework for local educators to define high-quality teaching. This framework guides mentoring and induction, professional development, and teacher evaluation. Formal induction and mentoring programs for first-year teachers must meet the teaching standards to receive state funds. Professional development opportunities for all teachers are meant to foster the skills that reinforce the eight standards and that respond to the student achievement goals of the school improvement plan. Eventually, all Iowa teachers will fall within four career levels in terms of teaching skills in relation to the standards: Beginning, Career I, Career II, and Advanced. During a two-year pilot of the new system, the state will finance team-based variable pay. This reward program provides building-level cash awards to teachers and others in participating schools that meet student achievement goals.

The Cincinnati, Ohio, public school's evaluation and compensation system relates performance expectations with teachers' advancement through five career levels (Ware & Beck, 2001). Sixteen standards within four domains define good teaching in the evaluation system. Portfolios demonstrate teachers' understandings and skills for both Domain 1, "Planning and Preparing for Student Learning," and Domain 4, "Professionalism." Classroom observations by trained evaluators determine whether teachers satisfy Domain 2, "Creating an Environment for Learning," and Domain 3, "Teaching and Learning." Performance ratings for each standard follow a four-part rubric that is based on Charlotte Danielson's Framework for Teaching: 1, unsatisfactory; 2, basic; 3, proficient; and 4, distinguished. Teachers advance along the five career levels displayed in Table 13.2 according to comprehensive evaluations of teaching performance on the domains. In addition to the salary ranges listed for teachers with a bachelor's degree are additional salary amounts for having a master's degree in the content area, having a doctorate in education or the content area, earning National Board certification, or having dual certification in any two of eight content specializations. Teachers

may advance as a consequence of one comprehensive evaluation, and they may move down a career level and lose salary as a result of two evaluations. Teachers who earn "2" on any domain are placed on intervention status and work with a mentor. Those who earn a "1" on any domain may be nonrenewed.

As in the Cincinnati structure, teachers in other states and districts may qualify for salary bonuses when they demonstrate excellent teaching skills and earn recognition from the National Board of Professional Teaching Standards. Table 13.3 indicates that as of December 2000, the National Board had issued 9,524 certificates to teachers who provide evidence of skills through portfolios and reports of peer coaching. About three-quarters of the states award financial bonuses for this designation, including those offered to teachers in the states listed in Table 13.3. A number of states, in-

TABLE 13.2.

Career Levels and Salary Ranges in Cincinnati Public Schools

Career Level	Description	Salary Range (with bachelor's degree)
Apprentice	Beginning teachers; nonrenewal if no advancement to novice level in two years	$30,000
Novice	Teachers learning about profession; must score "3" (proficient) in all domains; may advance after two years and must exit level or be nonrenewed within five years	$32,000–35,750
Career	Good, solid performing teachers; must have "3" or better on all domains; may remain at this level and receive cost-of-living increases for the duration of career	$38,750–49,250
Advanced	Veteran teachers who may be eligible for lead teacher credentials; must have "4" (distinguished) in domain 3, Teaching and Learning, "4" in at least one other domain, and "3" in others; may remain at this level for career	$52,500–56,250
Accomplished	Teachers at highest levels of practice who are eligible for lead teacher credentials; must have "4" in all domains; may remain at this level for career	$60,000–62,250

Source: K. Ware & R. Beck (2001). *Teacher Evaluation System.* Presented at the Annual Conference of the American Education Finance Association. Cincinnati, Ohio. p. 17. Reprinted with permission.

TABLE 13.3.

National Board Certificates and Rewards in Selected States

State	Certificates Issued as of December 2000	States Rewards for Teachers with National Certification
United States total	9,524	
Delaware	66	Annual 12 percent bonus for the life of the certificate
Georgia	112	Annual payment for the life of the certificate, calculated as 10 percent of salary at the time of certification
Maryland	70	State matches the annual bonus (up to $2,000) provided by local boards
Mississippi	755	$6,000 annually for the life of the certificate
North Carolina	2,407	Annual 12 percent bonus for the life of the certificate
Oklahoma	273	$5,000 annually for the life of the certificate; increases to $7,000 when per-pupil spending reaches 90 percent of the regional average
South Carolina	361	$2,000 upon certification; annual bonus of $7,500
Virginia	142	$5,000 the first year; $2,500 annually for the life of the certificate

Source: Southern Regional Education Board (2000). *Teacher Salaries and State Priorities for Education Quality— A Vital Link*. Atlanta: Author. **http://www.sreb.org/scripts/focus/reports/BoardCertificationTeachers .pdf** (accessed September 9, 2001). Reprinted with permission of the Southern Regional Education Board.

cluding Mississippi, Oklahoma, South Carolina, and Virginia, pay a flat dollar amount annually as a salary bonus. Delaware, Georgia, North Carolina, and other states increase salaries by a specified percentage each year. Maryland encourages school districts to provide financial rewards by matching the amount paid locally. Odden and Kelley (2001) describe the bonuses paid by several districts. For example, Los Angeles provides a 15 percent salary increase, Cincinnati pays $1,000 in addition to that provided by the state, and Broward County (Florida) promises a flat $2,000.

Ladd (1996) raised a number of questions and issues about knowledge- and skills-based compensation strategies. One question inquires about the degree to which the knowledge and skills identified in a competency pay plan correlate with teacher effectiveness in improving student learning. Another asks whether the package of skills would be uniform across a district or whether the skills would vary according to the types of students present in a given class or school. There is also concern that teachers might secure the necessary skill training without actually applying the new techniques in the classroom. In addition to these potential limitations are the high costs of designing and implementing systems that effectively align desired student performance goals with teaching standards and performance assessments. The development of portfolios and videos requires such a large time commitment that deserving teachers may not seek performance reviews to advance in salary. Training assessors who then conduct classroom observations and follow-up conferences with teachers places a large burden on school districts.

In the absence of financial commitments to adopt an effective program, districts may choose to adopt less costly—and potentially less effective—means for assessing teachers' performance.

The primary limitation of merit pay, career ladders, and knowledge- or skill-based pay is their practice of rewarding individual teacher responsibilities and performance. These approaches may foster divisiveness when school improvement rests on teamwork. Other strategies, in contrast, encourage and reward group accomplishments.

Group Performance Incentives

Rewarding successful *schools* promises to encourage schoolwide improvement efforts. In the second section of this chapter, we discussed these collective or group performance rewards in the context of state accountability systems. Group-based rewards address many of the limitations of merit and career ladder plans that focus attention on individual teachers.

When teamwork is important to an organization, there must be alignment between rewards and desired group performance. Drucker (1995) recognized the importance of rewarding people for their performance as a member of a team: "And their rewards, their compensation, their appraisals, and their promotions must be totally dependent on their performance in their new roles on their new teams" (p. 101). Lawler (2000) argued that group rewards are most appropriate in organizations that rely on integration and teamwork: "If people feel they can benefit from others' good performance, they are likely to encourage and help others perform well" (p. 45). Zingheim and Schuster (2000) discussed the role of rewards when an organization desires results from work groups:

> Because pay is such a strong communicator, the message it delivers makes the company attractive to the type of people with the talent it wants. Team pay attracts people who can, and want to, work effectively on teams. Also, because pay gets everyone's attention, pay based on team results is particularly likely to get the attention of people who are reticent to accept team membership. . . . If the business wants team results, a decision to implement team pay makes practical business sense. (pp. 205–206)

Rosenholtz (1987) noted that in school settings, the competition evident in merit pay and career ladders does not foster teamwork and collegiality. Hawley (1985) identified this deficiency in performance-based pay (PBP) plans that reward individual achievements: "Indeed, some types of PBP systems are likely to reduce the collegial and supervisory support that research has shown to be related to teacher effectiveness" (p. 6). In contrast, schoolwide performance incentives use intrinsic and extrinsic rewards to motivate teachers to reach common goals. Because the teachers' fortunes are linked, the competitiveness and divisiveness of individual incentive plans are avoided. Moreover, when teachers collaborate and participate in decision making, the intrinsic incentives boost their motivation and commitment (Firestone, 1994).

The comprehensive performance pay system developed in a rapidly growing suburb of Denver, Colorado, illustrates how group performance efforts can be rewarded along with individual teacher salary increases (Douglas County, 2001). In addition to base pay, which represents the starting salary for a beginning teacher, are several adjustments. First, teachers earn increases by acquiring additional knowledge through approved in-service programs, as well as via graduate degrees and credits from colleges and universities. Second, they earn evaluation credits if they are deemed to be outstanding or proficient through formal evaluation processes. Those whose performance is unsatisfactory, or who fail to complete professional-growth plans in a satisfactory manner, receive no salary increase. Third, teachers earn salary bonuses during a given year for demonstrating outstanding skills through several options. They may develop portfolios to give evidence of content knowledge, pedagogy, assessment, collaboration, standards-based instruction, and student growth. Alternatively, they may submit portfolios created for the National Board for Professional Teaching Standards. Fourth, they may earn additional salary for assuming greater responsibilities, including serving as a master teacher. Finally, they may earn group incentive pay.

Kelley (2000) noted that the group incentive pay plan gives pay bonuses to all teachers in a school or to groups who undertake planned efforts to improve specific student performance objectives. Groups submit proposals that detail goals, identify responsibilities and timelines, describe the value of the proposal to the school and to students, and include assessment mechanisms to measure performance goals. Teachers who participate in successful improvement processes receive equal shares of the amount designated for group incentive pay. Kelley concluded that the performance pay plan "created a web of incentives for teachers, principals, and entire schools to clarify goals and expectations, and focus individual and collective energies on improving organizational effectiveness" (p. 14).

In an evaluation of the Douglas County performance pay plan, Hall and Caffarella (1998) found the group incentive pay plan to be the "most powerful and widely accepted" component. Teachers reported that this incentive not only brought teachers together but also enhanced professional collaboration: "Students gain by being targets of the efforts, and teachers gain by working together on a whole school project that focuses on student achievement. The development and execution of the plan bring together and encourage communication among teachers from various disciplines and grade levels." Among the positive results were increased awareness of and involvement in schoolwide goals, improved linkages between what teachers do and school improvement plans, improved student performance, and increased collegiality across department levels.

School-based group performance rewards may be a preferred strategy in the future, particularly as restructured schools come to rely increasingly on collaborative efforts. Basing a portion of salary increases on shared efforts to achieve state, district, or school goals addresses many of the conditions identified at the beginning of this chapter. We discussed previously the potential of performance-based rewards for successful schools to have desired incentive effects. This strategy, especially when used strategically with performance- and skills-based rewards for individual teachers, may be the policy lever that states and school districts seek to accomplish educational reform.

Compensation Plans and Incentive Effects

We have examined several ways in which states and districts have attempted to use compensation systems to motivate improvements in teachers' skills and performance. We have noted the strengths and shortcomings of the traditional salary schedule, merit pay, career ladders, and performance- and skills-based compensation. And we have cited group performance rewards as a strategy that may characterize compensation of teaching professionals in the future. We now examine the question of whether these approaches to redesigning compensation systems have an incentive effect in motivating school improvement.

After tracking incentive plans for a decade, Cornett and Gaines (1994) made the following observations about their potential:

- Comprehensive incentive programs that alter fundamentally the ways in which teachers work and are paid can produce fundamental change and show promise for improving results for students.
- Teachers who participate in incentive programs are positive about the programs; those who do not are negative.
- Most teachers, when given a chance, choose to receive additional pay for more work, rather than for demonstrating high performance.

- Teacher evaluation has changed, becoming more comprehensive and using teachers to evaluate teachers.

These authors also described frustrations in gaining support for successful implementation of incentive programs:

- Changes in leadership at local and state levels have meant that programs move away from the original intent, never become implemented as intended, or are not given enough time to work.
- Individual pilot incentive programs designed at the district level, without a guiding vision or support from the state, have resulted in few fundamental changes and few programs that last.
- Incentive programs have brought about fundamental change in structures in very few schools across the nation.
- Decisions to fund, not to fund, or to disband programs are rarely based on real knowledge of programs and their effects on students.

These limitations make it hard to determine whether incentive programs have brought about meaningful improvements in teachers' skills and performance or in students' learning. Plans may have been poorly designed, poorly executed, or poorly researched. Political agendas on the part of policy makers at state and local levels, and those of school administrators and teachers, may have influenced the direction of policies and affected results.

Although we recognize these limitations, our assessment of the incentive effects of the strategies presented in this chapter is as follows:

- Rewarding longevity, advanced preparation, and changes in the cost of living through a single salary schedule has little or no incentive effect in motivating teachers to accomplish school improvement goals.
- Focusing salary increases on an individual's performance, as with merit pay, has some incentive effect. This effect is greatest when there are valid and objective criteria to mea-

sure skills and performance, when the reward is perceived as valuable, and when teachers see the link between their performance and the reward.

- Differentiating salaries along with levels of responsibilities, as with a career ladder, has an incentive effect in motivating individuals who receive or aspire to career advancements. This effect is greatest when there are valid performance measures, when others within and external to the school recognize the honor, and when lead teachers work effectively with beginning and poorly performing teachers to develop their skills.
- Rewarding teachers' abilities to apply their knowledge and skills to specific school improvement goals and to students' learning needs has an incentive effect on individual teacher's professional growth. This effect is greatest when there is alignment among potential rewards, clearly identified teaching standards, and assessments of knowledge, skills, and performance.
- Sharing group-performance-based rewards among all school personnel has an incentive effect on schoolwide improvement efforts. This effect is greatest when there are valid performance measures, a clear line of sight between the improvement efforts and rewards, resources available in all schools to meet goals, and public recognition of school improvements.
- Blending career ladders, performance- and skill-based compensation for individual teachers, and group performance rewards offers great potential for maximizing the incentive effects of these strategies while minimizing the limitations of each.

SUMMARY

In this chapter we focused on financial rewards and their potential incentive effects in improving schools. We explored motivation theories and the probable effects of linking state allocations and teacher compensation systems to performance measures. We discussed state accountability systems that include rewards for teachers and other school personnel when there are gains in pupil performance. We then examined compensation systems in which teachers' salary increases depend in part on individual merit, responsibilities, knowledge, and skills and on group performance.

These state and district policies rest on theoretical assumptions about human behavior. Performance-based rewards for groups and salary bonuses for individuals are most likely to motivate school personnel when they see the rewards as valuable and attainable, when there are clear links between promised rewards and actions to improve schools, when both intrinsic and extrinsic rewards are forthcoming, and when educators collaborate to achieve important school improvement goals.

State allocations of financial rewards publicly recognize schools that achieve certain levels of performance or demonstrate gains on specified indicators. There is evidence that performance-based accountability systems advance states' reform agendas, and thus rewards and sanctions can exhibit desired incentive effects. There may also be unintended negative consequences, particularly when accountability systems rest on limited performance indicators. An accountability system and financial rewards by themselves—without targeted capacity building to ensure adequate professional development, leadership, and resources—may do little to advance reforms and foster achievement gains in low-performing schools.

Differences between the teacher labor market and that of the private sector are disappearing as schools compete for teachers and as they resolve to improve teacher quality. A host of social and political considerations influence the availability of teachers (supply), schools' needs for teachers generally and in specific subject areas (demand), and teachers' salaries. These supply-and-demand conditions affect districts' decisions to increase salaries. However, it is not clear that increases in salaries

contribute to improvements in the quality of those who are hired or choose to remain in the profession. Instead, efforts to improve the quality of teachers—and thus the efficiency of schools—depend in large part on reforming compensation systems.

Restructured compensation plans are designed to improve education by motivating teachers to improve their skills in relation to teaching standards, assume greater responsibilities including mentoring beginning teachers, and ultimately raise student achievement. Unlike the single salary schedule, which rewards limited but easily measured characteristics, these compensation systems strive to link remuneration to teaching standards, skills and performance, and responsibilities. We concluded that the greatest incentive effect would result from a blended compensation system. This approach would realize the benefits of differentiated staffing that reflects skills and responsibilities, salaries that reflect demonstrated skills and performance, and rewards for collaborative efforts on the part of faculty to improve school performance.

Basing a portion of state allocations on school performance and restructuring compensation systems to reward teacher skills and performance promise to enhance the efficiency of schools. The next chapters continue this discussion of school improvement and efficiency by examining the potential of empowering school personnel and parents.

ACTIVITIES

1. Discuss with a teacher, a school administrator, and a school board member the conditions identified early in the chapter that seem to be necessary for rewards to have an incentive effect. What recommendations do they (and you) have for improving state policies and district compensation systems to maximize their effects on student achievement and other school improvement goals?

2. Discuss the questions and issues presented in the section on accountability systems and financial rewards. What might be a feasible approach for modifying your state's finance plan to direct additional resources to schools that prove themselves to be effective in raising levels of pupil achievement or on other performance measures? How can the state or district best guard against unintended consequences as schools seek rewards or avoid negative publicity and sanctions for low performance?

3. Examine teacher supply and demand in a given state, region, or school district. Construct a chart or spreadsheet that compares the numbers of applicants for teaching positions with the numbers of personnel hired for different grade levels and subject areas over a 10-year period. Interview state and local officials about the trends that emerge and about any steps that have been or might be taken to stimulate supply, particularly in high-demand subject areas.

4. Interview principals and teachers, including (if possible) one who has earned certification through the National Board for Professional Teaching Standards, to learn about the potential benefits and costs of encouraging teachers to seek national recognition. Should states or school districts provide incentives for teachers to participate in assessments? Should there be pay differentials, such as those illustrated in Table 13.3, to attract and retain board-certified teachers?

5. Contrast the advantages and limitations of these compensations systems: merit pay for an individual teacher's performance, career ladders for differentiating salaries in accordance with the responsibilities of redefined positions, skills- and performance-based plans that align expectations for teachers with standards for student learning, and group performance rewards for schoolwide improvements. How might you

research whether any one of these approaches has an incentive effect in improving teachers' skills or pupil achievement?

COMPUTER SIMULATIONS: SALARY MODELS

Computer simulations related to the content of this chapter are available on the Allyn & Bacon website **<http://www.ablongman.com/edleadership**. They focus on using single salary schedules and performance-based salary models. Objectives for the exercises are

- To develop an understanding of the structures of traditional and performance-based teacher salary models
- To conduct "what if" analyses on teacher salary models using spreadsheets

REFERENCES

Association of Teacher Educators (1985). *Developing career ladders in teaching.* Reston, VA: Author.

Astuto, T. A. (1985). *Merit pay for teachers: An analysis of state policy options.* Educational Policy Studies Series. Bloomington, IN: Indiana University.

Atkinson, J. W. (1964). *An introduction to motivation.* Princeton, NJ: Van Nostrand.

Ballou, D., & Podgursky, M. (1993). Teachers' attitudes toward merit pay: Examining conventional wisdom. *Industrial and Labor Relations Review, 47,* 50–61.

Ballou, D., & Podgursky, M. (1997). *Teacher pay and teacher quality.* Kalamazoo, MI: Upjohn Institute for Employment Research.

Bobbitt, S. A., & McMillen, M. M. (1990). *Teacher training, certification, and assignment.* Paper presented at the Annual Meeting of the American Educational Research Association, Boston. ERIC Document, ED 322 138.

Boe, E. E. (1992). *Incentive and disincentive phenomena in education: Definitions and illustrations.* Report No. 1992-ER2. Philadelphia, PA: Center for Research and Evaluation in Social Policy.

Boe, E. E., & Boruch, R. (1993). *Performance-based accreditation of public schools.* Philadelphia, PA: Center for Research and Evaluation in Social Policy.

Carnegie Forum. (1986). *A nation prepared: Teachers for the twenty-first century.* New York: Carnegie Forum on Education and the Economy.

Cibulka, J. G. (1989, August). State performance incentives for restructuring: Can they work? *Education and Urban Society, 21*, 417–435.

Cohen, D. K. (1996). Standards-based school reform: Policy, practice, and performance. In H. F. Ladd (Ed.), *Holding schools accountable: Performance-based reform in education* (pp. 99–127). Washington, DC: The Brookings Institution.

Cornett, L. M. (1985). Trends and emerging issues in career ladder plans. *Educational Leadership, 43*, 6–10.

Cornett, L. M., & Gaines, G. F. (1994). Reflecting on ten years of incentive programs: The 1993 SREB career ladder clearinghouse survey. *Career ladder clearinghouse.* Atlanta, GA: Southern Regional Education Board.

Darling-Hammond, L. (2000). *Solving the dilemma of teacher supply, demand, and standards: How can we ensure a competent, caring, and qualified teacher for every child?* New York: National Commission on Teaching and America's Future.

Deming, W. E. (1986). *Out of the crisis.* Cambridge, MA: Massachusetts Institute of Technology Press.

Douglas County School District Re. 1. (2001). *Douglas County pay for performance.* Douglas County, CO: Author. **http://www.dcsd.k12.co.us/district** (accessed September 9, 2001).

Drucker, P. F. (1995). *Managing in a time of great change.* New York: Truman Talley/Dutton.

Education Commission of the States. (2001). *Rewards and sanctions for school districts and schools.* Denver, CO: Author. **http://www.eds.org/clearinghouse/18/24/1824.htm** (accessed December 12, 2001).

Education Week (2001). *Quality counts 2001: A better balance: Standards, tests, and the tools to succeed.* Bethesda, MD: Author

Elmore, R. F., Abelmann, C. H., & Fuhrman, S. H. (1996). The new accountability in state education reform: From process to performance. In H. F. Ladd (Ed.), *Holding schools accountable: Performance-based reform in education* (pp. 65–98). Washington, DC: The Brookings Institution.

Farnsworth, B., Debenham, J., & Smith, G. (1991). Designing and implementing a successful merit pay program for teachers. *Phi Delta Kappan, 73*, 320–325.

Firestone, W. A. (1994). Redesigning teacher salary systems for educational reform. *American Educational Research Journal, 31*, 549–574.

Firestone, W. A., & Bader, B. D. (1992). *Redesigning teaching: Professionalization or bureaucracy?* Albany: State University of New York Press.

Firestone, W. A., & Corbett, H. D. (1988). Planned organizational change. In N. Boyan (Ed.), *Handbook of Research on Educational Administration* (pp. 321–340). White Plains, NY: Longman, 1988).

Firestone, W. A., & Pennell, J. R. (1993). Teacher commitment, working conditions, and differential incentive policies. *Review of Educational Research, 63*, 489–525.

Fleisher, B. M., & Kniesner, T. J. (1980). *Labor economics: Theory, evidence, and policy.* Englewood Cliffs, NJ: Prentice-Hall.

Fox, J. M. (1988). The supply of U.S. teachers: Quality for the twenty-first century. In K. Alexander & D. H. Monk (Eds.), *Attracting and compensating America's teachers* (pp. 49–68). Cambridge, MA: Ballinger.

Frohreich, L. E. (1988). Merit pay: Issues and solutions. In K. Alexander & D. H. Monk (Eds.). *Attracting and compensating America's teachers* (pp. 143–160). Cambridge, MA: Ballinger.

Fuhrman, S. H., & Elmore, R. F. (1992). *Takeover and deregulation: Working models of new state and local regulatory relationships.* Rutgers, NJ: Consortium for Policy Research in Education.

Galbraith, J. R., Lawler, E. E., & Associates. (1993). *Organizing for the future: The new logic for managing complex organizations.* San Francisco, CA: Jossey-Bass.

Garris, J. M., & Cohn, E. (1996). Combining efficiency and equity: A new funding approach for public education. *Journal of Education Finance, 22*, 114–134.

Goertz, M. E., & Duffy, M. C. (2001). Assessment and accountability across the 50 states. *CPRE Policy Briefs*, RB-33. Philadelphia, PA: CPRE.

Goldhaber, D. D. (2001). How has teacher compensation changed? In W. J. Fowler, Jr. (Ed.), *Selected papers in school finance, 2000–01* (pp. 15–35). Office of Education Research and Improvement, NCES 2001-378. Washington, DC: U.S. Department of Education. **http://nces.ed.gov/pubs2001/2001378_2.pdf** (accessed October 1, 2001).

Hackman, J. R. (1987). The design of work teams. In J. W. Lorsch (Ed.), *Handbook of organizational behavior* (pp. 315–334). Englewood Cliffs, NJ: Prentice-Hall.

Hall, G., & Caffarella, E. (1998). *Third year implementation assessment of the performance pay plan for teachers (1996–97)*. **http://www.dcsd.k12.co.us/district/hr/Third.year.assess.98.html** (accessed October 1, 2001).

Hanushek, E. A. (1997). Assessing the effects of school resources on student performance: An update. *Educational Evaluation and Policy Analysis, 19,* 141–164.

Hanushek, E. A. (2001). Incentives: Linking resources, performance, and accountability. In Jossey-Bass, *The Jossey-Bass reader on school reform* (pp. 299–334). San Francisco, CA: Jossey-Bass.

Hatry, H. P., Greiner, J. M., & Ashford, B. G. (1994). *Issues and case studies in teacher incentive plans* (2nd ed.). Washington, DC: Urban Institute.

Hawley, W. D. (1985). The limits and potential of performance-based pay as a source of school improvement. In Johnson, H. C. (Ed.), *Merit, money and teachers' careers: Studies on merit pay and career ladders for teachers* (pp. 3–22). Lanham, MD: University Press of America.

Herndon, T. (1985). Merit pay and the concerns of the teaching profession. In H. C. Johnson (Ed.), *Merit, money and teachers' careers: Studies on merit pay and career ladders for teachers* (pp. 93–98). Lanham, MD: University Press of America.

Herzberg, F. (1966). *Work and the nature of man.* Orlando, FL: Harcourt.

Herzberg, F., Mausner, B., & Snyderman, B. (1959). *The motivation to work.* New York: Wiley.

Holmes Group. (1986). *Tomorrow's teachers: A report of the Holmes Group.* East Lansing, MI: Holmes Group.

Iowa Department of Education. (2001). *Teacher compensation.* Des Moines, IA: Author. **http://www.state.ia.us/educate/programs/tc/summary.html** (accessed October 5, 2001).

Jacobson, S. L. (1988). Merit pay and teaching as a career. In K. Alexander & D. H. Monk (Eds.), *Attracting and compensating America's teachers* (pp. 161–177). Cambridge, MA: Ballinger.

Johnson, S. M. (1986). Incentives for teachers: What motivates, what matters? *Educational Administration Quarterly, 22,* 54–79.

Kelley, C. (2000). *Douglas County Colorado performance pay plan.* Madison, WI: Consortium for Policy Research in Education (CPRE).

King, R. A., & Mathers, J. K. (1997). Improving schools through performance-based accountability and financial rewards. *Journal of Education Finance, 23,* 147–176.

Kohn, A. (1993). *Punished by rewards: The trouble with gold stars, incentive plans, A's, praise, and other bribes.* Boston: Houghton Mifflin.

Ladd, H. F. (1996). Introduction. In H. F. Ladd (Ed.), *Holding schools accountable: Performance-based reform in education* (pp. 1–19). Washington, DC: The Brookings Institution.

Ladd, H. F., & Hansen, J. S. (Eds.). (1999). *Making money matter: Financing America's schools.* Commission on Behavioral and Social Sciences and Education. Washington, DC: National Academy Press.

Lashway, L. (2001). *The new standards and accountability: Will rewards and sanctions motivate America's schools to peak performance?* Eugene, OR: Clearinghouse on Educational Management, Educational Resources Information Center (ERIC).

Lawler, E. E. (1990). *Strategic pay: Aligning organizational strategies and pay systems.* San Francisco, CA: Jossey-Bass.

Lawler, E. E. (1994). From job-based to competency-based organizations, *Journal of Organizational Behavior, 15,* 3–15.

Lawler, E. E. (2000). *Rewarding excellence: Pay strategies for the new economy.* San Francisco, CA: Jossey-Bass.

Lawton, S. B. (1988). Teachers' salaries: An international perspective. In K. Alexander & D. H. Monk (Eds.), *Attracting and compensating America's teachers* (pp. 69–89). Cambridge, MA: Ballinger.

Locke, E. A. (1968). Toward a theory of task motivation and incentives. *Organizational Behavior and Human Performance, 3,* 157–189.

Locke, E. A., & Latham, G. P. (1990). *A theory of goal setting and task performance.* Englewood Cliffs, NJ: Prentice-Hall.

Lortie, D. C. (1975). *Schoolteacher: A sociological study.* Chicago: The University of Chicago Press.

MacPhail-Wilcox, B., & King, R. A. (1988). Personnel reforms in education: Intents, consequences, and fiscal implications. *Journal of Education Finance, 14,* 100–134.

Magel, C. J. (1961). Merit rating is unsound. *Phi Delta Kappan, 42,* 154–156.

Malen, B., Murphy, M. J., & Hart, A. W. (1988). Restructuring teacher compensation systems: An analysis of three incentive strategies. In K. Alexander & D. H. Monk (Eds.), *Attracting and compensating America's teachers* (pp. 91–142). Cambridge, MA: Ballinger.

Massell, D. (2000). The district role in building capacity: Four strategies. *CPRE Policy Briefs*, RB-32. Philadelphia, PA: Consortium for Policy Research in Education.

Milanowski, A. (2000). School-based performance award programs and teacher motivation. *Journal of Education Finance, 25*, 517–544.

Miner, B. (1999/2000, Winter). 1999 National Education Summit. *Rethinking Schools*, 3–10.

Mohrman, S. A., Cohen, S. G., & Mohrman, A. M. (1995). *Designing team-based organizations: New forms for knowledge work.* San Francisco, CA: Jossey-Bass.

Mohrman, S. A., & Lawler, E. E. (1996). Motivation for school reform. In S. H Fuhrman and J. A. O'Day (Eds.), *Rewards and reform: Creating educational incentives that work* (pp. 115–143). San Francisco, CA: Jossey-Bass.

Monk, D., & Rice, J. K. (1994). Multi-level teacher resource effects on pupil performance in secondary mathematics and science: The role of teacher subject matter preparation. In R. G. Ehrenberg (Ed.), *Contemporary policy issues: Choices and consequences in education.* Ithaca, NY: ILR Press.

Murnane, R. J., & Cohen, D. K. (1986). Merit pay and the evaluation problem: Why most merit pay plans fail and a few survive. *Harvard Educational Review, 56*, 1–17.

National Center for Education Statistics (NCES). (2001). *Digest of Education Statistics 2000.* NCES 2001-034. Washington, DC: U.S. Department of Education. **http://nces.ed.gov/pubs2001/digest/ch2.html** (accessed October 5, 2001).

National Commission on Excellence in Education. (1983). *A nation at risk: The imperative for educational reform.* Washington, DC: U.S. Department of Education.

National Education Association. (1984). *Merit pay: promises and facts.* Washington, DC: NEA.

National Education Association. (1985). *The single salary schedule.* Washington, DC: NEA.

Nelson, F. H. (1995). International comparison of teacher salaries and conditions of employment. In W. J. Fowler, Jr. (Ed.), *Developments in school finance* (pp. 109–127). Washington, DC: U.S. Government Printing Office.

Nelson, F. H., Drown, R., & Gould, J. C. (2000). *Survey and analysis of teacher salary trends 2000.* Washington, DC: American Federation of Teachers, AFL-CIO. **http://www.aft.org/research/survey00/salarysurvey00.pdf** (accessed September 27, 2001)

O'Day, J., Goertz, M. E., & Floden, R. E. (1995). Building capacity for education reform. *CPRE Policy Briefs.* New Brunswick, NJ: Consortium for Policy Research in Education, Eagleton Institute of Politics, Rutgers University.

Odden, A., & Kelley, C. (2001). *Paying teachers for what they know and do: New and smarter compensation strategies to improve schools* (2nd ed.). Thousand Oaks, CA: Corwin.

Peevely, G., & Dunbar, D. K. (2001). Tennessee. In National Center for Education Statistics. (2001). *Public school finance programs of the United States and Canada, 1998–99.* NCES 2001-309. Washington, DC: U.S. Department of Education, Office of Educational Research and Improvement. Available on CD-ROM or at **http://nces.ed.gov/pubsearch/pubsinfo.asp?pubid=2001309**.

Peterson, T. K. (1992). Designing accountability to help reform. In C. E. Finn & T. Rebarber (eds.), *Education reform in the '90s* (pp. 109–132). New York: Macmillan.

Picus, L. O. (1992). Using incentives to promote school improvement. In A. R. Odden (Ed.), *Rethinking school finance: An agenda for the 1990s* (pp. 166–200). San Francisco: Jossey-Bass.

Poston, W. K., & Frase, L. E. (1991). Alternative compensation programs for teachers: Rolling boulders up the mountain of reform. *Phi Delta Kappan, 73*, 317–320.

Reville, S. P. (2001, November 14). Multiple measures? Why adding more tools to a state's assessment process may be easier said than done. *Education Week, 21*, 52.

Richards, C., & Shujaa, M. (1990). State-sponsored school performance incentive plans: A policy review. *Educational Considerations, 17*, 42–52.

Rosenholtz, S. J. (1987). Education reform strategies: Will they increase teacher commitment? *American Journal of Education, 92*, 352–389.

Sanders, W. L., & Horn, S. P. (1994). The Tennessee value-added assessment system (TVAAS): Mixed-model methodology in educational assessment.

Journal of Personnel Evaluation in Education, 8, 299–311.

Schlechty, P C. (1987). The concept of career ladders. In Burden, P. R. (Ed.), *Establishing career ladders in teaching: A guide for policy makers* (pp. 4–16). Springfield, IL: Charles C Thomas.

Skinner, B. F. (1974). *About behaviorism.* New York: Knopf.

Smith, G. N. (1987). Costs for a career ladder. In Burden, P. R. (Ed.), *Establishing career ladders in teaching: A guide for policy makers* (pp. 216–225). Springfield, IL: Charles C Thomas.

Southern Regional Education Board (2000). *Teacher salaries and state priorities for education quality—A vital link.* Atlanta, GA: Author.

Stronge, J. H., & Tucker, P. D. (2000). *Teacher evaluation and student achievement.* Washington, DC: National Education Association.

U.S. Department of Education. (1988). *Measuring up: Questions and answers about state roles in educational accountability.* Washington, DC: Office of Educational Research and Improvement.

Vroom, V. H. (1964). *Work and motivation.* New York: Wiley.

Ware, K., & Beck, R. (2001). *Teacher evaluation system.* Paper presented at the Annual Conference of the American Education Finance Association. Cincinnati, Ohio

Weeks, K., & Cornett, L. M. (1985). Planning career ladders: Lessons from the states. *Career Ladder Clearinghouse.* Atlanta, GA: Southern Regional Education Board.

Wise, A. E. (2001). Differentiated staffing. *The school administrator, 58,* 34–37.

Wright, P. M. (1989). Testing the mediating role of goals in the incentive–performance relationship. *Journal of Applied Psychology, 74,* 699–705.

Zingheim, P. K., & Schuster, J. R. (2000). *Pay people right! Break through reward strategies to create great companies.* San Francisco: Jossey-Bass.

chapter 14

SCHOOL-BASED DECISION MAKING

Provider Sovereignty

Issues and Questions

- *Achieving High Standards with Equity and Efficiency*: How can changing the governance structure of public schools by devolving to schools more authority over curriculum, budget, personnel, and strategic planning facilitate achieving high standards with equity and efficiency?
- *Definition of School-based Decision Making (SBDM)*: What is school-based decision making? Why is SBDM being seriously considered as a possible reform of education governance?
- *Privatization*: Can SBDM contribute to the stimulation of marketlike forces in the public provision of education services?
- *Experience with SBDM*: What have been the results in places that have implemented SBDM? What has been the impact on students, educators, and the quality of service?
- *School-based Budgeting:* What kind of financial infrastructure is needed to support SBDM?

A growing number of critics of public education believe that the school governance structure itself causes the inequities and inefficiencies in the education system. They view the education policy-making process from the perspective of "institutionalism" as presented in Chapter 2. Those who share this view initiated the second wave of education reforms that began in the mid-1980s. Some were advocates of administrative decentralization (school-based decision making), and some were advocates of market solutions involving parental choice of schools. Devolution of authority to schools continues as a central theme of the third wave of systemic reform, which involves greater centralization of some functions (especially finance and setting curricular and achievement standards) and decentralization of other functions (notably the organization and operations of schools).

Two fundamental questions are associated with radically reforming the governance of education. The first is to what extent parents and students should be empowered to choose among schools or among programs within schools. Elmore (1988) called this the "demand side" question. "It poses the question of whether the consumers of education should be given the central role in deciding what kind of education is appropriate for them" (p.79). Chapter 15 focuses on this issue through the lens of market concepts.

The second question is to what extent educators should be empowered to organize and manage schools, to design educational programs, and to receive public funds for providing education to students. Elmore referred to this as the "supply side" question. "It poses the issue of whether the providers of education should be given the autonomy and flexibility to respond to differences in judgments of consumers about appropriate education" (p.79). In this chapter we address the supply side issue by considering proposals for school-based decision making (SBDM) and budgeting (SBB) as strategies for stimulating alternative means of combining schooling inputs to obtain de-

sired outputs. We examine arguments for, and experiences with, the devolution of educational governance to the school level. Actual experiences implementing SBDM in the United States and elsewhere are reviewed. The chapter closes with discussions of school-based planning and budgeting.

SCHOOL-BASED DECISION MAKING

The concept of school-based decision making (SBDM) involves a *system* of schools within which a significant amount of authority to make decisions about curriculum and allocation of human and fiscal resources has been vested in each school. This takes place within a centrally determined framework of goals, policies, standards, and accountabilities (Caldwell & Spinks 1998). Actually, there is little evidence that SBDM per se leads directly to improved pupil achievement (Summers & Johnson, 1996; Wohlstetter, Smyer, & Mohrman, 1994; Malen, Ogawa, & Kranz, 1990; Conway, 1984; Smylie, 1994). Therefore, SBDM must be viewed as just one element of systemic reform if a connection with improved pupil achievement is to be made. Other elements need to involve higher performance expectations, more directed pedagogical demands, and clear accountability systems. These elements may include such reforms as national and state curricula, performance standards, and assessment; national teacher certification; and family choice of schools (Guthrie, 1998; The Consortium on Renewing Education, 1998; Hannaway, 1996; Hannaway & Carnoy, 1993). Although not linked directly to improvement in student outcomes, SBDM is credited with being an efficacious means of addressing conflicts over the distribution of scarce resources and enhancing the legitimacy of institutions authorized to make those decisions.

The bottom line is that school-based management is not an end in itself, although research indicates that it can help foster an improved school culture and higher-quality decisions. School-based management is, however, a potentially valuable tool for engaging the talents and enthusiasm of far more of a school's stakeholders than traditional, top-down governance systems. Moreover, once in place, school-based management holds the promise of enabling schools to address students' needs better (Wohlstetter & Mohrman, 1994, p. 1).

School-based decision making as a strategy of reform is founded on the premise that the school is the fundamental decision-making unit within the educational system. The school's administrators, teachers and other professional staff, who constitute the "technical core" of the educational system, are a natural decision-making and management team. This core has knowledge about teaching methods and learning processes, as well as information about the diverse learning styles and needs of the children for whom they are responsible. Thus the school staff is equipped to make better decisions about appropriate educational programs than are those at some remove from the specific teaching and learning process. Shifting decision-making responsibilities from central administrative offices to schools means a redistribution of power among principals, teachers, parents, and community that enables these key stakeholders to make schools more responsive to unique local conditions, while effectively harnessing the knowledge, creativity, and energy of all these parties. Furthermore, if the professional staff is to be held responsible for student progress, that staff should have flexibility in designing the learning environment (Drury, 1999).

Structures for making policy at the school level vary (Kirst, 1990). Authority may rest with the principal alone (administrative decentralization), or the responsibility may be shared in some combination among administrators, teachers, parents, community representatives, and upper-grade students. Some versions of SBDM place authority with a school-based governing board dominated by lay persons; examples include Chicago, England, and New Zealand. This governance structure is a form of political decentralization. When power is placed with lay boards, specific provision is usually made for formal professional involvement in the decision-making process. In *administrative decentralization*, authority devolves from the district to members of the professional staffs in the schools. *Political decentralization* empowers those outside the traditional school structure, such as parents and other community members (Ross, 1997).

Under SBDM, school authorities may develop the budget, select staff, and refine the school's curriculum to meet specific needs of pupils within legal constraints set by the school district or higher levels of government (Cawelti, 1989; United States General Accounting Office, 1994). The school district, state, and federal government continue to set general priorities and guidelines within which all schools must function; they also develop overarching educational objectives and the basic curriculum for meeting those objectives. School districts continue to allocate resources to schools on the basis of student numbers and needs, to negotiate labor contracts, and to provide facilities and other support services such as transportation, payroll, and accounting.

Arguments for Administrative Decentralization

Organizational analysts have found that high-involvement decision-making structures are particularly appropriate in settings where the work is not routine, where employees have to deal with great variation in inputs, and where there is uncertainty about the relationships between means and outcomes (Lawler, 1986). It is also appropriate where the work and decisions of employees are interrelated in their impact and need to be coordinated in a manner that cannot be fully anticipated in advance. These conditions accurately characterize the school setting (Mohrman & Lawler, 1996).

Sizer (1985) claimed that hierarchical bureaucracy is paralyzing American education. "The structure is getting in the way of children's learning" (p. 206). Sizer's first imperative for better schools was to give teachers and students room to work and learn in their own, appropriate ways. He saw decentralized authority as allowing teachers and principals to adapt their schools to the needs, learning styles, and learning rates of students individually. Although he did not deny the need to upgrade the overall quality of the educating profession, Sizer believed that there were enough fine teachers and administrators to lead a renaissance of American schools, if only they could be empowered.

Goodlad (1984) identified the school as *the* unit for improvement. The approach to educational reform that Goodlad viewed as most promising was the one "that will seek to cultivate the capacity of schools to deal with their own problems, to become largely self-renewing" (p. 31). He did not see the schools as being "cut loose" but, rather, as being linked to the hub (district office) and to each other in a network. State officials should be responsible for developing "a common framework for schools within which there is room for some differences in interpretation at the district level and for some variations in schools resulting from differences in size, location, and perspective" (p. 275). According to Goodlad, the district should concern itself with the balance in curricula presented, the processes employed in planning, and the equitable distribution of funds. "What I am proposing is genuine decentralization of authority and responsibility to the local school within a framework designed to assure school-to-school equity and a measure of accountability" (Goodlad, 1984, p. 275).

Boyer (1983) also saw heavy doses of bureaucracy "stifling creativity in too many schools, and preventing principals and their staffs from exercising their best professional judgment on decisions that properly should be made at the local level" (p. 227). For Boyer,

"Rebuilding excellence in education means reaffirming the importance of the local school and freeing leadership to lead" (p. 316). Among his recommendations for accomplishing this was granting more authority to school personnel:

> Principals and staff at the local school should have more control over their own budgets, operating within the guidelines set by the district office. Further, every principal should have a School Improvement Fund, discretionary money to provide time and materials for program development and for special seminars and staff retreats. Principals should also have more control over the selection and rewarding of teachers. Acting in consultation with their staffs, they should be given responsibility for the final choice of teachers for their schools. (p. 316)

Cuban (1988) argued that the bureaucratic organization of schooling is responsible for the lack of professional leadership. Autonomy is necessary in order for leadership to arise.

> Without choice, there is no autonomy. Without autonomy, there is no leadership. . . . Schools as they are presently organized press teachers, principals, and superintendents toward managing rather than leading, toward maintaining what is rather than moving to what can be. The structures of schooling and the incentives buried within them produce a managerial imperative. (pp. xx–xxi)

Cuban also recognized the need for federal, state, and district regulations and their accompanying forms of accountability. He called for balanced procedures that grant sufficient discretion to those delivering a service, while allowing prudent monitoring by higher levels of authority. Such procedures would focus "less on control through regulation and more on vesting individual schools and educators with the independence to alter basic organizational arrangements (if necessary) to reach explicit goals and standards" (p. 248).

After an extensive review of the research on decentralization (SBDM) and on performance-based incentives such as holding schools accountable for meeting state standards, Hannaway (1996) concluded that incentives alone, like decentralization alone, may do more harm than good but that in tandem, they hold great promise of raising achievement levels among elementary and secondary students. She pointed out that a major drawback of decentralization is that many schools, especially those serving disadvantaged students, may not have the capacity to guide school behavior effectively. Performance-based incentives can counter this weakness by directing a significant amount of school activity toward meeting societally defined academic achievement objectives, even if those objectives are narrowly focused. Thus schools with low capacity would not be left totally on their own to flounder aimlessly. The major drawback of performance-based incentives is curricular distortion, but this can be countered by SBDM, which provides a way to balance the system relatively easily when it becomes distorted, because it leaves the school largely unencumbered by bureaucratic red tape, procedures, and hierarchy.

Key elements in the strategy of the Consortium on Renewing Education (CORE) (1998) for doubling America's academic achievement scores by the year 2020 are focusing on student achievement and shifting the primary locus of control from districts to individual school sites. CORE argued that school control places decision-making authority for day-to-day instructional operations at the school site, empowering schools to make all legally permissible decisions that are professionally appropriate to meet specific state academic performance objectives. CORE proposed that about 75 percent of the dollars spent on education be allocated directly to schools and that schools be allowed to use these monies in ways they deem most productive in improving achievement. However, CORE did not rely solely on SBDM to meet its strategic objective. As recommended by Hannaway (1996), it couples SBDM with an accountability scheme that involves high-stakes proficiency examinations for students graduating. Third-graders would need to demonstrate their proficiency in reading before they could be promoted into fourth grade. Likewise, students would need to demonstrate proficiency in mathematics and algebra before they could enter high school.

Guthrie (1998) reminded us that the American educational crisis lies primarily in the large, urban school districts where, because of their size, governance reforms such as SBDM are critical. He pointed out that 90 percent of school districts in the United States have fewer than 5,000 pupils and that 80 percent have fewer than 2,500 pupils, making them small enough to avoid the most devastating effects of bureaucratic impairment. The problem lies with the 5 percent of the districts that educate 50 percent of the nation's public school population. In these large, urban districts, decision making has become remote, diffuse, and divorced from the operating authority of the school. The enormous web of district, state, federal, and judicial rules affecting urban schools has undermined their operational integrity, making it more difficult for principals and staffs to forge a unified vision of the way a school should operate or of how a strategy should be implemented.

Guthrie saw SBDM as an idea that makes logical sense when coupled with other, compatible reforms such as a statewide or districtwide achievement accountability system. He feared, however, that genuine school-based management and related reforms are unlikely to happen because of the political controversy that they would be likely to provoke. The ability of school boards to micro-manage would be diminished. Many school principals fear the spotlight of accountability. Teachers union officials fear the erosion of their districtwide base of influence. And potential proponents of the reforms who would benefit most from them—students, parents, and other citizens—are ill informed regarding the idea and are not organized for political action.

In summary, despite the political obstacles pointed out by Guthrie, analysts see SBDM as an integral part of systemic school reform and as especially needed in large school systems.

Experiences with School-Based Decision Making

The concept of SBDM has been applied in almost as many ways as there are school systems. There are three general areas over which authority may be devolved: curriculum, budget, and personnel. In all cases, devolved authority is constrained, but the degree of constraint varies markedly. At first, SBDM was limited primarily to decisions related to delivery of curriculum. Experience indicated, however, that schools could not make significant decisions about curriculum delivery without at least some discretion over resource allocation, including the deployment of personnel (Odden, 1999; Odden & Busch, 1998; David, 1994). This realization has increased interest in school-based budgeting (SBB) as part of SBDM. For example, some schemes extend to schools authority over 90 percent of the budget, including personnel, whereas others permit school discretion over less than 2 percent. Granting schools control over 90 percent of their operating budget enables them to design their staffing patterns and to determine the allocation of funds between personnel and other purposes.

The possibility of giving schools extensive authority over developing and managing their own resources is a relatively new concept in the United States. Much attention has been paid to formulas for distributing state and federal aid to school districts, but not to schools, except possibly a per-student discretionary grant for instructional supplies. Traditionally, the district has made resource allocation decisions for the schools. This began to change in the late 1980s when a few states adopted school choice plans that allowed parents to enroll their children in schools outside their district of residence. With a policy of the money following the child, it became necessary to reimburse the receiving district and to charge the sending district. Rather than determining the amount by a straightforward cost analysis, most states developed obtuse and cumbersome transfer procedures (Odden, 1999).

The authorization of charter schools and the contracting out of school operations to private vendors are more recent examples of the need to trace the flow of funds to schools. The spread of SBDM, however, has given the greatest impetus to costing out school operations and developing formulas for distributing funds from the district to schools.

At this writing, no state has developed a formula to disburse funds directly to schools, but a number are studying options, and several large districts are already doing so. American school districts that are delegating to schools budgetary authority over half of the total cost per pupil include Cincinnati, Pittsburgh, Seattle, and Broward County, Florida (Odden, 1999). In Dade County, schools are allocated staff units, but these units may be exchanged for a monetary amount to be used for other purposes. Chicago schools do not have control over the resources assigned to the basic program, but they do have authority over funds provided by categorical aids in support of students; these funds may be used to purchase human and/or physical resources at the discretion of the school's council. In Kentucky, districts allocate monies to schools to hire certified and classified staff and to purchase instructional supplies and equipment (Dunn, James-Gross, & Trampe, 1998), but state and district constraints on how the monies can be spent severely limit school discretion (David, 1994). Goertz and Stiefel (1998) also noted limits on school discretion over school-based budgets in a study of four large, urban school districts (Chicago, Fort Worth, New York, and Rochester) that had implemented SBB to some degree. They found truly discretionary funds to represent less than 20 percent of total school resources.

In this section, we examine some of the variety in SBDM plans currently in operation. Because the United States has been quite cautious in embracing the idea, applications abroad are included to illustrate its full potential. In the descriptions, emphasis is given to resource allocation and budgeting. The SBDM schemes we focus on are those of Edmonton, in Canada (the first school district to adopt such a plan), Chicago, Kentucky, England, and the state of Victoria in Australia.

Edmonton

Edmonton, Alberta, Canada, has been functioning under a SBDM configuration since 1976. It is an urban district serving 80,000 students in 205 schools. Decisions related to the allocation of resources have been decentralized to schools for approximately 92 percent of district revenues (Ozembloski & Brown, 1999). This allows schools to make decisions about teaching and nonteaching staff, maintenance, utilities, equipment, and supplies. But accountability has been clearly placed with the principal. School administrators and teachers develop their budgets on the basis of priorities established in an annual school plan. The budget is submitted to the superintendent and school board for review and approval. Schools contract with district providers or outside vendors for consultant and other services, as needed. The district also operates a professional-development program that derives its funds by charging the budgets of schools that purchase those services. All of the associate superintendent positions have been removed and replaced by principal teams. Principals are now considered to be the senior staff of the district (Ozembloski & Brown, 1999).

Funds are allocated to schools on the basis of a per-full-time equivalent (FTE) child amount, weighted according to student characteristics plus supplements. Children in grades K–8 serve as the basic unit and are weighted 1.0; secondary students (grades 9–12) are weighted 1.03. Students with limited English proficiency are given additional weightings of .27 in the elementary grades and .24 in the secondary grades. Students with disabilities receive additional weightings that range from 1.27 to 5.93, depending on the severity of the disability. Special funding is provided for several small programs such as reading, foreign language instruction, high incidence of special needs, and enrollment growth. An allocation is also provided for routine maintenance of the building, 75 percent of which is based on square footage and 25 percent on weighted enrollment (Odden, 1999; U.S. General Accounting Office, 1994).

A survey of Edmonton principals and teachers conducted after the system had been in operation for over a decade revealed that principals saw flexibility, efficiency, and staff involvement in decision making as strongly positive attributes of SBDM (Brown, 1990). Resource allocation was a problem for some, but time demands and the stress accompanying decentralization were viewed as its major disadvantages. Seventy-nine percent of the principals recommended that other districts consider SBDM.

Teachers in Edmonton identified flexibility and staff involvement in decision making as being the major advantages of SBDM. Like the principals, teachers saw the primary weakness of SBDM as the time it demands. This was followed by problems with the allocation of resources, heightened stress, and the increased authority of the principal. Teacher involvement appeared to be primarily consultative.

The Edmonton school district has formal procedures for monitoring SBDM. In addition to standardized tests administered to students on a regular basis, parents, students, and staff are surveyed to measure their level of satisfaction with matters affecting them. Results are reported by school, with district averages indicated. Satisfaction among the three groups has steadily improved under SBDM; the growth in satisfaction has been particularly strong among parents and students at the secondary level

(Brown, 1990). The monitoring system revealed that student achievement was falling behind district expectations in the late 1990s, and a 4-year plan was put in place to correct the situation (Ozembloski & Brown, 1999).

The Edmonton program was implemented gradually. It began in 1976 as a pilot project involving seven volunteer schools that represented the variety in the district. Community support for the concept grew, and in 1979 the Board of Education voted to implement the idea districtwide. Alberta is now encouraging the use of SBDM throughout the province with Edmonton, serving as a model for consideration.

Chicago

One of the most ambitious attempts at school-based governance in the United States is taking place in the city of Chicago. The Illinois legislature adopted the plan in December 1988, in a desperate attempt to reform a school system that had been characterized as the "worst in America." The primary strategy was to realign its incentives and power structure by creating school councils controlled by parents and authorizing them to make decisions that had been made previously by the district's education bureaucracy (Hess 1990). Complementing SBDM was an open-enrollment plan that allowed parents to enroll their children in any school in the district that had space available. The reforms, phased in over a 5-year period, had ten goals, but priority was given to raising student achievement, attendance rates, and graduation rates to national norms for *all* schools. A 1995 amendment to the plan reorganized the district-level structure by reducing the size of the school board from fifteen to five members and empowering the mayor to appoint the board members, its president, and the district's superintendent of schools. The new board was charged with establishing "system-wide curriculum objectives and standards which reflect the multi-cultural diversity of the city." School councils were continued, but the central board's power of oversight was enhanced. The 1995

legislation also authorized a new position to improve the financial efficiency of the district and to oversee privatization of district services (Wong, 2001). Together, these two acts have produced a balanced system of school empowerment *within* district oversight (Hess, 1999a).

The 1988 Chicago reform, perhaps more than any other in the United States, was based mainly on the theory that schools can be improved by strengthening democratic control at the school–community level (Hess, 1993). The key to achieving the goals of the 1988 act was Local School Councils (LSCs) composed of six parents, two community representatives, two teachers, and the principal. For high schools, councils also include one nonvoting student. Except for teacher representatives and the principal, employees of the system may not serve as members of LSCs. District employees are also barred from voting in elections of parent and community representatives. This configuration was designed to give parents a major voice in the education decisions affecting their children and to avoid the problems encountered in New York City, where employees were able to dominate elections to the thirty-two Community Boards of Education that govern elementary and middle schools (Hess 1990).

Each council has the responsibility for adopting a School Improvement Plan, developing a budget for spending its discretionary funds, and selecting and evaluating the school's principal. In recognition of the authority of these new semiautonomous LSCs, the powers of the city board of education were redefined in the 1988 legislation from *management of* to *jurisdiction over* the public education and the public school system of the city (Hess, 1990).

Granting LSCs the power to hire and fire principals brought about a significant change in the characteristics of principals. Within two years, about half were new to the job, although they were not new employees of the district. Ninety-four percent of the newly appointed principals had had no previous experience as a principal. Over half were African American and nearly 60 percent were women. Their average age dropped to forty-six (it was fifty-two prior to reform). New principals were most likely to be found in racially isolated schools, and they were likely to be matched racially or ethnically with the majority of their school's population.

Unlike most other school-based plans, the Chicago plan places greater responsibility with parents and community representatives than with teachers. The importance of staff participation in decision making was recognized in the legislation, however, by the establishment of a Professional Personnel Advisory Committee (PPAC) in each school for the purpose of advising the principal and the LSC on the educational program. The PPAC is composed of teachers and other professional personnel in the school.

Although this was never stated explicitly, the Chicago School Reform Act is built on the assumption that the principal is the chief instructional leader in each school (Hess, 1990). Principals were given the right to select teachers, aids, counselors, clerks, hall guards, and any other instructional program staff for vacant or newly created positions. Principals are responsible for initiating a needs assessment and a School Improvement Plan in consultation with the LSC and the PPAC. They are also responsible for drafting a budget for amendment and approval by the LSC. Principals hold no tenure rights in the position other than those they hold as teachers.

In addition to restructuring the governance of Chicago schools, the 1988 legislation was intended to correct inequities in the allocation of resources among school and district administration. The Chicago Panel (1988) revealed that prior to reform, one-third of targeted funds (state and federal categorical aids) were being misappropriated into supporting central-office bureaucratic positions. Furthermore, compensatory funds were being used to provide basic services in schools with high proportions of children from low-income families, yielding to schools that served children from middle-

income families greater access to financial support for basic programs. Implementation of the reforms has corrected these inequities. Categorical funds are now directed to schools, which determine how they are to be spent through the LSC. The average elementary school has approximately $490,000 in discretionary funds, the average high school $850,000 (Hess, 1999b). Unlike the authority distribution in Edmonton, LSCs in Chicago do not have discretion over personnel allocations, other than for the principal and for personnel that may be employed with discretionary funds.

By the fourth year of the reforms, 1,755 district- and subdistrict-level administrative positions had been eliminated, and 4,594 new positions had been created in schools. When the reform began, 88.5 percent of the system's staff were budgeted to schools. The proportion had grown to 93.1 percent by 1992–1993 (Rosenkranz, 1994). Initially, schools used their discretionary funds to take care of support needs by adding clerks and aides in greater numbers than teachers, but by the fourth year of the reforms, schools began focusing their discretionary resources on direct student services through the addition of teaching positions.

The overall fiscal situation of the district was precarious during the mid-1990s, and this contributed to the need for the 1995 reform legislation. Following the 1988 reform legislation, the central school board entered into contracts with employee unions that included wage increases that the board could not fund. By 1995, the board had accumulated a $150,000,000 deficit. Responding to the district's on-going financial crises and to disappointment over the slow improvement in academic achievement, the Illinois legislature passed the 1995 reforms.

The 1995 law retained local school councils but placed them under the purview of the central board. Principals were granted much desired authority over custodial and food service workers and over work schedules (Harp, 1995). The law limited the items that may be negotiated with employee unions and placed a moratorium on strikes for eighteen months. Managerial employees were barred from union membership.

There is considerable evidence of substantially improved achievement among Chicago's elementary students; however, the reform goals are far from having been realized. The percent of students at or above national achievement norms increased between 1990 and 1998 from 23.5 percent to 34.7 in reading, and from 27.1 percent to 39.6 percent in mathematics (Hess, 1999b). The evidence at the secondary level is not so impressive, however. At that level, the percentages above national norms in reading actually dropped over the period, from 30.6 percent to 28.6 percent. Mathematics achievement improved, however, from 21.6 percent to 31.1 percent.

Analyzing achievement data for the period 1987–1988 through 1995–1996, Bryk (1999) categorized elementary schools into three groups of about equal size: improving, struggling, and unaffected by the reforms. Bryk found that the improving group had been able to assemble and integrate the resources required for progress despite a poorly functioning central support structure. Whether they could sustain their progress in the absence of external support was doubtful. Bryk concluded that the prognosis for the struggling group was even less hopeful: "[A] more organized and sustained form of external assistance would probably be needed to move these school communities forward" (p. 83). For the unaffected group, none of the school sites of power—not the LSC, the principal, or the faculty—had been able to overcome the dysfunctional inertia of the schools. Bryk determined that "Left to their own devices, these schools seemed unlikely to improve" (p. 83). This situation is similar to that found in New Zealand as described in Chapter 1, especially in the inner city of Auckland.

The needed central structure was provided by the 1995 reform act. The new regime adopted a business management model and

acted quickly to demonstrate a commitment to efficient management (Wong, 2001). The board adopted curricular frameworks and achievement standards. In 1996, 109 of the district's 550 schools (38 high schools and 71 elementary schools) were placed on probation because 15 percent or less of their students scored at grade level on nationally normed tests. The following year, 9 schools were removed from probation and 15 were added. Seven high schools were reconstituted. The principals of 5 of these reconstituted schools were replaced. All teacher and staff positions were vacated, but former staff were permitted to apply to be retained. Seventy percent were retained. Of those not retained, about 30 percent were unable to find employment elsewhere in the district and faced dismissal (Hess, 1999a).

In 1997 the central board adopted a high school design that was mandated for schools on probation and strongly recommended for all others. The purpose of the design was to enable large, anonymous schools to become more personalized for inner-city students, while increasing the academic press on school personnel. (See the discussion of economies of scale in Chapter 12.) The design divides high schools into junior and senior academies. Freshmen entering junior academies, which serve grades 9 and 10, are organized into cohorts with five teachers who remain with the cohort for two years. Curriculum is limited to core courses required for graduation. Promotion gates are placed at the entrance to ninth grade to ensure that students are prepared to do high school work. Students need to show proficiency in reading in ninth grade in order to advance further. Senior academies are organized in a similar fashion, although some electives are permitted. The designs are intended to enable students to come to know some adults and their classmates well and to enable teachers to come to know the students well.

In 1998, the minimum-achievement benchmark for schools to avoid being placed on probation was raised from 15 to 20 percent of students scoring at or above the national average; it is expected to be raised further in subsequent years. Another 7 high schools were reconstituted, and 108 schools remained on probation. Along with the sanctions came support for improvement (Wong, 2001). The central office provided to schools on probation funds (averaging $100,000 each) to hire "external partners" from a board-approved list to assist them in improving their instructional performance. A "probation manager" is provided to oversee the school improvement plan and to assist the principal in all areas of school operations. Finally, "business managers" are provided to oversee school budget and financial operations.

The central board also put an end to social promotion. First-, second-, third-, sixth-, eighth-, and ninth-grade students who do not meet set levels on nationally normed tests are required to participate in a district-sponsored Summer Bridge program. Students who participate in the program are promoted to the next grade level if they bring their grades up to the established cut-off point; if they are not successful, they are retained.

The district also initiated an aggressive teacher recruitment program. New teachers are paired with mentors during an introductory period. Mentors and new teachers meet regularly for district in-service programs and collaborative learning. All teachers are offered in-service opportunities through the Teachers Academy. Principals are still selected by LSCs, but the district has developed new, rigorous standards for them. The district provides in-service training for all principals through two leadership programs created by the district in cooperation with the Chicago Principals' and Administrators' Association and local universities (Wong, 2001).

The 1995 reform legislation gave the system direction and coordination and created tension for excellence that had been assumed would be provided by the LSCs, principals, and staff in the 1988 reform legislation but that wasn't, at least for two-thirds of the schools. Bryk (1999) summed it up this way:

> [T]he division of responsibilities under decentralization gives local schools the authority to act and the resources and assistance to use that authority productively in advancing children's learning. Schools in turn are held accountable to assure that serious efforts are advanced in this regard. The educational work of the system center focuses on policy-making to support decentralization, maintaining an external assistance capacity for local schools, engaging rigorous external accountability for improvement, and stimulating innovation. (p. 89)

Kentucky

In 1990 the state of Kentucky enacted sweeping legislation transforming its entire educational governance structure. This action was precipitated by a decision of the Kentucky Supreme Court, which ruled that the entire school governance and school finance systems of the state were in violation of the state's constitutional requirement of an "efficient system of common schools" (see Chapter 10). The Kentucky reforms are considered by some to be a blueprint for change nationally (Danzberger, Kirst & Usdan, 1992). The reforms involve both centralizing and decentralizing features. Over the decade since the reform system was put into place, adjustments have been made, but the only aspect that has received a major overhaul is the accountability system.

Student achievement is the centerpiece of the new system in Kentucky, which focuses on outcomes, not inputs. The expectation is that every child will learn and that the educational system will become performance-driven and results-oriented. A state Council on School Performance Standards was established to set learning goals and definitions of expected student learning outcomes. Marking the tenth anniversary of the reform act's passage, the state education department (SED) found that students from every ethnic group were scoring higher on the state's tests than a decade earlier.

The state's third-, sixth-, and ninth-graders scored at or slightly above the national average on the Comprehensive Tests of Basic Skills (CTBS). Progress was also made on other national tests, including the NAEP. Improvement has been mostly at the lower cognitive levels, however; relatively few students have reached the top levels. The achievement gap between white and minority students remains, and the state's dropout rate hasn't been reduced (but it isn't any higher either, despite the higher achievement expectations). The per-pupil spending gap between rich and poor districts has been reduced from $1,199 to $757 (Hoff, 2001a). The gap in the availability of computer technology and Internet access has been virtually wiped out (Hoff, 2001b).

A school council made up of three teachers, two parents, and the principal governs each school. Councils are empowered to adopt curriculum, select instructional materials, set policies for discipline and classroom management, oversee extracurricular activities, and assign students and staff. A council can select staff, including the principal, from a list of candidates recommended by its district's superintendent of schools. Under the 1998 revisions of the accountability system, councils were granted authority to determine how cash rewards for schoolwide improvements in student achievement are to be distributed. Previously, the teachers of the school held this power.

The Kentucky Instructional Results Information System (KIRIS) was established to provide evidence on attainment of the six broad learning goals set forth in the reform act. There were three components to the original accountability strand of assessment: performance measurements (heavily weighted in terms of cognitive achievement), portfolio tasks, and transitional items and tasks. Schools that showed significant improvements in KIRIS results received financial awards to be distributed as determined by a majority of teachers in each school receiving awards (Kannapel et al., 2000). Schools that failed to improve or de-

clined were subject to sanctions.

Managerial and technical problems associated with the accountability system have been widespread since it was first used in 1992 (Keller, 1999). A new system, the Commonwealth Accountability Testing System (CATS), was adopted in 1998 and was fully implemented in 2000-2001. The new assessment procedure is a mixture of multiple-choice questions from national standardized tests and open-ended essays geared to the state's academic standards. The academic progress of schools is measured using these tests, and cash awards continue to be given to schools that make substantial progress. Schools that are not making satisfactory progress continue to be subject to intervention by the SED. Intervention includes audits, staff support, and (if necessary) money. Students in the lowest-performing schools are given the option of transferring to better-performing schools.

The SED has designed a school report card that must be disseminated by each school. The four-page report includes information on student achievement, school climate, and teacher qualifications. Opportunities for parent involvement are also identified. Individual students' test results are analyzed by the SED and mailed to the student's home.

Critics argue that making teachers rather than students accountable for student test scores assumes that teachers are fully in control of students' learning. "Kentucky's approach to accountability is undermining the very changes in teaching and learning that it was intended to promote, thereby calling into question the use of performance assessment for high stakes accountability" (Jones & Whitford, 1997, p. 280). The original intent of KIRIS was to build the accountability system in conjunction with moving teachers and principals toward performance-based instruction and assessment. Instead, test designers and legislators determined that the reliability of the test was the most important determinant in test construction. As a result, open-ended performance assessments have been reduced in importance in favor of objective formats (Wasley, 2000). This, along with linking objective test scores to high-stakes accountability, has led teachers to narrow their focus to teaching to the test.

> Accountability that reduces school quality to a numeric formula is oversimplified and ill-suited to evaluating many important aspects of schooling. In fact, it contradicts the very premise behind systemic reform that school improvement is complex and requires multiple, interlocking components. What is true about systemic reform in general is also true about accountability systems in particular. A simple scoring mechanism just will not do. What is needed is a "next generation" of thinking about what school accountability means. (Whitford & Jones, 2000, pp. 21–22)

The American examples that these investigators give of "next generation" thinking about accountability are roughly modeled after the British inspectorate, which is described in the next section and in Chapter 1. We view the Victorian accountability structure as an equally appropriate prototype (it is also described in a following section and in Chapter 1).

Two years into a 5-year study of SBDM in Kentucky, David (1994) found that it has been a major force in communicating the importance and seriousness of the reform effort and in forging a critical link between schools and their communities. Teachers especially welcomed the opportunity to select their principals, and parents have appreciated having an official voice in making school policy. Typically, school districts have not given school councils discretion over the staffing portions of their school budgets. Councils are permitted to carry over unspent funds to subsequent years. The biggest problem with the allocation process is that districts have inadequate accounting systems to track all expenditures to the school level and to permit schools on-line access to the status of their accounts (David, 1994).

England

No country has had more experience with school-based decision making than England. In Chapter 1, we described the nature of the English reforms in general, and you may wish to refer to that description for context as we now focus specifically on English reforms related to SBDM—or, as the English call it, local management of schools (LMS).

Prior to the 1980s, approximately 95 percent of English children were educated in a national system of state schools administered by local education authorities (LEAs). These authorities were part of the local governance structure much as are fiscally dependent school districts in the United States. The LEAs exercised considerable political and bureaucratic control over schools within their jurisdictions and provided them with significant professional and ancillary support. There was (and continues to be) much greater equity in the distribution of human and fiscal resources among schools in the English system than is characteristic of the U.S. system.

Reforms related to SBDM. Reforms of a "privatizing" nature that were enacted by the Conservative government when it was in power from 1979 to 1997 are given in the following list. Modifications made by the succeeding Labour government are indicated in the descriptions.

- *Reformed Governing Bodies.* Prior to the reforms of the Conservative party, all schools had governing bodies with limited powers and with the majority of the membership of each body appointed by the LEA. The 1986 Education Act removed majority control by LEA-designated membership and increased representation of parents and local business interests. The Education Reform Act of 1988 gave to school governing bodies control over their own budgets (over 80 percent of total school costs) and day-to-day management of operations.

- *Local Management of Schools (LMS).* Schools remaining under LEA jurisdiction receive funds according to a formula, developed by the LEA under national guidelines, that ensures that 80 percent of a school's allocation is determined directly by the number and ages of its pupils. Thus the money follows the child in a system where parents have considerable influence in determining which schools their children attend. The amount allocated to schools includes teachers' salaries. Previously, LEAs set the budgets for each school. Between 80 and 85 percent of the funding for schools is provided to the general local governing agency by the national government, and the balance is provided by the local agency.

- *City Technology Colleges (CTC).* These are secondary inner-city schools chartered by the national government beginning in 1986 and run by independent trusts with business sponsors that provide some capital funding. Recurrent funding and net capital costs are provided by the national government directly to the schools' boards of trustees. Their curricula emphasize science and technology. CTCs are totally outside the control of any LEA and are similar to charter schools in the United States.

- *Grant-Maintained Schools (GMS).* The 1988 Education Reform Act established a procedure whereby state schools could opt out of their LEAs and run themselves with direct funding from the national government. Parameters governing a school are set forth in a charter negotiated by school authorities and the national government. By 1997 there were 1,139 GM schools, 17 percent of the secondary schools and 2 percent of the primary schools, educating 18 percent of the secondary population and 3 percent of the primary population. Under the new Labour government, no additional schools are being chartered. The existing ones have been returned to the purview of their LEAs as foundation schools and are funded by their LEAs

as LMS schools, but the governing structure is little changed.

Under these reforms, parents gained in representation on school governing bodies and have freedom of choice among schools that are not oversubscribed. In the case of oversubscribed schools, each school determines criteria for selection with the approval of the LEA or the Department for Education. Schools have gained control over their own budgets and are able to decide matters previously decided by LEAs, such as staff deployment, personnel selection, and employee remuneration within national guidelines. Schools are also permitted to contract directly for building maintenance, accounting, purchasing, payroll, insurance, and auditing. The reforms shifted authority from LEAs to schools and parents on the one hand, and to the national government on the other. The new Labour government has returned some authority to the LEAs.

Formula funding of schools. The national government does not specify how much LEAs must spend on schools, but it does provide clear guidelines on how the Aggregate Schools Budget (ASB) is calculated. The ASB equals the total LEA General Schools Budget, less mandatory and discretionary exceptions. Mandatory exceptions include educational psychology and welfare services, European Community and national government grants, and capital expenditures. Discretionary exceptions include insurance, LEA initiatives, student grants, LEA support teams, school meals, transportation, repair and maintenance, special staff, and special measures for failing schools. In 1997–1998, the ASB represented 77 percent of total primary school budgets and 81 percent of total secondary school budgets (Levacic, 1999).

Pay scales are set nationally for teachers and support personnel, but governing bodies have some discretion in awarding additional scale points and in determining job descriptions of support staff. Schools are funded according to the LEA average cost of teachers but are charged the actual salary of teachers employed. Schools have the right to a bank account for their delegated budgets, or they may have these funds held in account with their LEA. Schools carry forward surpluses (which are common) or deficits (which are discouraged) into the next fiscal year. Schools may retain all income earned from such activities as renting out premises, sponsorships, and parent–teacher associations (which are accounted for separately). School-generated income typically ranges from 1 to 3 percent of the school budget (Levacic, 1999).

The Aggregate Schools Budget has to be allocated to schools by a formula developed by the LEA and approved by the national government. Seventy-five percent of the ASB has to be distributed on the basis of school enrollment and grade-level configuration. Another 5 percent may take into account other student characteristics, such as special educational needs. The remaining 20 percent may take into account other student needs (such as family background and English proficiency) to supplement the funding provided under the basic student allocation (about 7 percent on average) and school site needs (about 13 percent on average). The average student weighted funding in 1997–1998 was as follows: ages 4–6, 1.0; ages 7–11, .94; ages 11–14, 1.34; ages 14–16, 1.61; and ages 16–18, 1.94. These ratios reflect historical budgeting patterns, but there is growing interest in replacing them with activity-led funding to improve the effectiveness and efficiency of the resource allocation system (Levacic, 1999).

Evaluations. There is little doubt that LMS is the most popular of the English reforms. The support is so broad that it withstood the change in government in 1997. Even people who were highly critical of Tory policy generally have become supporters of LMS. A survey conducted by Fitz and Halpin (1994) found no head teacher in a GMS or LMS school who wished to return to the former system of LEA control.

A study sponsored by the National Association of Head Teachers was broadly positive but conceded that direct evidence of the influence of self-management on learning was elusive (Bullock & Thomas, 1994). The initial survey revealed that school heads felt that LMS enabled them to make more effective use of a school's resources. However, they also felt that too much of their own time was spent on administrative matters, diverting their attention from matters related to student learning (Arnott et al., 1992).

It should be noted that the relatively few classroom teachers who were interviewed in the Bullock and Thomas study were more cautious in their assessment of its benefits for pupil learning and overall standards. A study by Marren and Levacic (1994) also found teachers to be less positive in their assessment of self-management than were school governors or heads.

The debate in England centers on collective (societal) rights and responsibilities versus private rights and responsibilities. LMS and other reforms were initially proposed and implemented by the political right. The reforms have been heavily criticized by the political left because there is evidence that they are re-creating a selective school system that is highly inequitable in its effects on lower socioeconomic classes and immigrant groups. But a new Labour government has made only marginal changes. The political right argues that the reforms encourage the growth of different types of schools responsive to the needs of particular communities and interest groups. The right's arguments appeal to those subscribing to concepts of multiple identities and radical pluralism. Whitty (1994), in a study of educational reforms in the United Kingdom, Australia, New Zealand, and the United States, recommended striking a balance between these views by creating new forms of association to counterbalance the prerogative of the state and to act as a generator of new ideas. "[P]art of the challenge must be to move away from atomized decision making to the reassertion of collective responsibility without re-creating the very bureaucratic systems whose shortcomings have helped to legitimate the current tendency to treat education as a private good rather than a public responsibility" (p.18).

State of Victoria, Australia

We present the Victorian model in greater detail than the previous examples of SBDM, because we believe it to have great relevance for the largest school districts in the United States—the ones in greatest need of reform. The state of Victoria operates its school system as a singletary unit—that is, there are no school districts. The state has a population of five million persons, two-thirds of whom live in Melbourne and environs. The 1,700 schools in the state system enroll over 500,000 students and employ 35,000 professional staff. Twenty-five percent of the students are from non-English-speaking backgrounds, and 34 percent come from low-income families receiving financial support from the government. The system is administered from the Department of Education (ED) in Melbourne. The ED organized regional offices for purposes of administering the system, but these offices have no policy-making capacity.

Until the "Schools of the Future" legislation in 1993, Victoria, like other Australian states, operated its schools in a highly centralized fashion. In 1955 an American scholar, Freeman Butts, challenged the efficacy of these centralized arrangements. He questioned the prevailing thinking of the time in Australia that a system required uniformity to achieve equality of educational opportunity, and he pointed out that strong governmental controls operated at the expense of community empowerment. Nevertheless, all states remained firm in their commitment to central control until the report of the Interim Committee for the Australian Schools Commission (1973) was issued. Then, supported by federal and state grants, several approaches to devolving decision-making

responsibilities were initiated. These included dezoning school attendance and the establishment of school councils in all states and territories (Caldwell & Hill, 1999). The Commission study was motivated by the fact that the public schools were exhibiting many of the characteristics that cause concern in the highly bureaucratized and unionized big-city school systems of the United States. The centralized state systems in Australia were perceived as impersonal, uncaring, and institutional (Anderson, 1993). Teachers and principals tended to identify with the state bureau for employing teachers (which was also responsible for the venues of their assignments) rather than with the schools and communities to which they were assigned. Instructional quality was deteriorating and public dissatisfaction was growing, along with client defections to private schools heavily subsidized by the federal government.

An overview of the "Schools of the Future" reforms in Victoria. The decentralization movement began in Victoria with the creation of school councils in 1975. Initially, their role was largely advisory to school principals, but over the years, their responsibilities and authority have grown significantly. In the early 1980s, program budgeting was introduced, and the school councils were given the authority to determine the educational policies of their schools and to approve school budgets that amounted to about 5 percent of recurrent expenditures (Caldwell & Hill, 1999).

In 1993, Victoria embarked on a systemic reform of its school governance through an initiative known as "Schools of the Future." School councils play a key role in the reforms and have received important increases in authority. Today, council responsibilities include

- Managing school funds, which includes approving the budget representing 90 percent of recurrent expenditures
- Developing the education policy of the school
- Participating, with veto power, in selection of the school principal

- Employing nonteaching staff
- Contracting for financial and student services, school cleaning, minor repairs, and maintenance work
- Managing capital grants for major capital work after ED approval
- Developing the school charter
- Reporting to the community and to the ED (Gurr, 1999).

Councils range in size from six to fourteen persons drawn from parents of children in the school and teachers. The principal is an ex officio member, and councils have the option of including students and non-school-related community persons as co-opted members. ED employees (including teachers and administrators in any school) cannot constitute more than one-third of council membership. Terms are for two years and are staggered. Councillors do not formally represent any group requiring its mandate before voting.

The Schools of the Future reforms created a system of self-managing schools with authority vested in principals and school councils within a curriculum and standards framework

established by the state. The reforms have four dimensions, as illustrated in Figure 14.1. The Curriculum Framework specifies outcomes that all students are expected to achieve in eight key learning areas (KLA): arts, English, health and physical education, languages other than English, mathematics, science, technology, and society and environment studies. It provides a comprehensive and rigorous curriculum with established performance levels for all KLAs across all years, as well as assessing and reporting mechanisms.

The People Framework provides for full staffing flexibility and for the local selection of staff. Although most full-time professional personnel remain employees of the state, the school can determine the mix of professional, paraprofessional, and support arrangements and select people to fill positions when vacancies occur. At the beginning of the reform, schools were obliged to retain staff who had previously been assigned, but as vacancies occur, schools gain greater control over achieving their preferred staffing profile. To this end, each school is required to develop and file with the ED a 3-year workforce plan that indicates

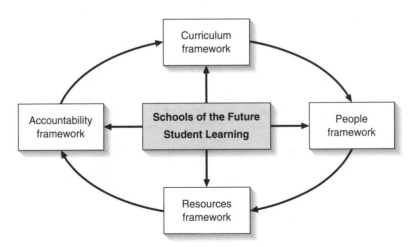

FIGURE 14.1. The Four Dimensions of Victoria's Schools of the Future

Source: Cooperative Research Project. (1998). *Assessing the Impact: The Final Report of the Cooperative Research Project, Leading Victoria's Schools of the Future*. Melbourne, Victoria, Australia: Victoria Department of Education, p. 19.

known and anticipated staff movements and how the resources freed up by those movements will be used to implement the preferred staffing profile within the constraints of the school's allotted resources. Schools can hire non-tenure-track staff to fill in for people on extended leave. The People Framework also introduced a Professional Recognition Program to provide a new career structure for teachers that includes two levels of lead teachers in addition to the principal and assistant principal levels. A performance management procedure was developed for principals, assistant principals, and lead teachers. An annual review of level-one teachers is required, although the actual procedure is left to each school to determine. The People Framework makes substantial provision for professional development.

Under the Resources Framework, 90 percent of recurrent expenditure for education is distributed directly to schools through a *school global budget*. Although the basic allocation is determined on the basis of the characteristics of the school and its students, each school has wide latitude in the use of allocated funds (except for designated state priority programs).

The Accountability Framework is the main mechanism through which the performance of schools is monitored. Illustrated in Figure 14.2, it consists of each school's charter, three annual reports, and an external triennial review that leads to the development of a new school charter. The purposes of the framework are to satisfy the expectations of the state in terms of student achievement and to help schools and teachers improve the standards of student learning (Office of Review, 1998)

The school charter is the key accountability document and sets a school's strategic direction for a 3-year period and serves as a guide to resource allocation and staff evaluation. The charter is developed by the school council and approved by the Secretary of Education (the CEO of the ED). The annual reports are prepared in accordance with ED guidelines and specifically address (1) the progress made by the school toward meeting the goals set forth in the charter and (2) student achievement within the curricular framework. The reports

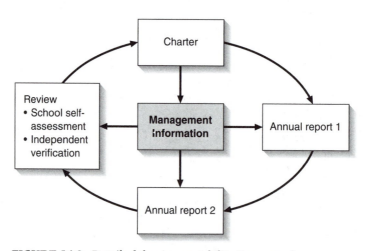

FIGURE 14.2. Detail of the Accountability Framework

Source: Source: Gurr, D. (1999). *From Supervision to Quality Assurance: The Case of the State of Victoria (Australia)*. Paris: International Institute for Educational Planning/UNESCO, p. 33. Reprinted by permission.

also include a financial analysis. The reports are approved by the school council, submitted to the ED, and made available to the school's local constituencies.

Every third year, a school must undergo a triennial review. This begins with a self-assessment that summarizes the school's performance over the 3-year life of the charter and suggests the continuation of goals not realized and the establishment of new goals for the next three years. External reviewers are contracted by the ED to verify the self-study. In addition to establishing the accuracy of the self-study, the external reviewers suggest new goals, improvement priorities, and foci for the next three years. This process leads to a new charter to guide the school's operations for the next three years. Although the accountability system emphasizes formative evaluation, the ED places a school that does not meet accepted standards under continuing scrutiny. If conditions do not improve over a reasonable period of time, the school will be reconstituted.

School-based budgeting. The allocation from the state to a school is determined through the school global budget (GB). The GB consists of two parts: cash and credit. The credit portion consists of monies allocated for salaries, which remain with the ED. School personnel, with a few exceptions, have continued as employees of the ED. Other monies are deposited quarterly in the schools' checking accounts, which was the practice for about twenty years prior to the Schools of the Future reforms. Credit can be converted to cash (less 10 percent to cover benefit costs that are not eligible for conversion), thereby reducing the workforce and making it possible to use the freed-up funds for other purposes. Likewise, cash can be converted to credit to enable the school to employ additional personnel. Except for a small portion set aside for state priority funding (such as categorical aids), the schools are free to spend the money as they see fit, although most follow rather closely the categories in the GB.

Using data describing a school's enrollment by grade level, site characteristics of the school (such as size, rurality, and isolation) and the characteristics of children enrolled, the ED determines the school's GB. Authorized staffing is based on one professional for every twenty-one students, with students in the primary grades weighted 1.00 and those in the secondary grades weighted 1.43. Supplementary cash and credit allowances are provided for curriculum enrichment, special educational needs of students, and school site needs through a variety of formulas. An average-cost approach to budget and charge-out is used for costing Level 1 teachers. Budget and charge-out rates for Level 2 and Level 3 teachers are based on appointment salaries. Principal-class personnel are treated on a notional-cost basis using the bottom of the relevant salary range. Funding is provided as though 15 percent of the school's staffing allocation were at the Leading Teacher 2 level and 15 percent at the Leading Teacher 3 level or the Principal-Class level (Victoria Department of Education, 1999).

Salary scales are determined at the state level. The ED can make recommendations to the government about school funding levels, but the final decisions rest with the government. The credit portion of the GB is monitored closely by the School Personnel and Resources division of the ED and updated every two weeks when payrolls are processed. A school's surplus is carried over from year to year. If a school should overspend its budget in one year (a serious offense), the deficit is deducted from the GB for the next year.

To facilitate planning, a GB Ready Reckoner is available on the ED website for use by school officials to estimate their GB in advance of official notification, which comes in the form of an Indicative GB issued in Term 3 of the preceding year using enrollment projections provided by the schools. A Confirmed GB is issued early in the budget year following the collection of enrollment census information. A Revised GB may be issued for specific updates or changes arising from such events as a census audit or student mobility.

The school program budget. Each school develops a *school program budget* for spending the cash portion of the GB plus revenues generated at the school level. This budget reports the source and amount of anticipated cash receipts and the allocation of resources to each school program by accounting category. Along with each program allocation is a description of the program, its goals and objectives, its implementation plan, and the way performance will be evaluated. Programs are likely to be organized around the key learning areas of the state Curricular Framework, along with charter priorities and special state initiatives. In addition to cash generated through the GB, a school may realize revenue from carry over of funds from the previous year, conversion of GB credit to cash, rental of facilities, school enterprises such as bookstores and food service, admission fees, fund raising, donations, sale of equipment, interest, voluntary student fees, and assessments on students enrolled in courses that require expensive equipment and materials.

The program budget must be approved by the school council, but the key players in its development are usually the principal and the school's business manager (in the case of larger schools). Coordinators of the key learning areas are typically consulted during the process, and charter priorities are given first attention. A draft budget is submitted to the finance committee of the school council for refinement. Subsequently, the proposed budget is submitted to the full council for approval. The principal and the school business administrator monitor the program budget on a daily basis. The only monitoring of the cash budget by the ED is through the annual audit.

Information systems. Critical to the success of the Schools of the Future reforms—and to the GB in particular—has been the development of a supporting information system. *There are no paper forms in the financial transactions between the state and the schools.* All data are transferred via computer networks. The most important information system for financial transactions is CASES (Computerized Administrative Systems Environment for Schools). CASES is the strategic information system designed as the standard administrative platform for the Schools of the Future reforms. It is through this vehicle that communication between the schools and the ED is maintained. CASES stores and processes a range of data, including student records and financial, physical, and human resource information. CASES has the capacity to be tailored to the information needs of a specific school, but few schools have exercised this option. CMIS (CASES Management Information System) is an add-on to CASES. It is a valuable tool for principals, in particular, to generate reports and otherwise enhance the worth of the data recorded and maintained in CASES (Gurr, 1999).

CASES is user-friendly. Coupled with an extensive program of staff development, CASES has enabled people without an accounting background, including school secretaries and clerks, to perform all of the financial operations required at the school level. The ED provides telephone back-up support.

KIDMAP is an information system designed for teachers. It is able to monitor individual and aggregate student progress on the standards related to the state curriculum. It also has the capability of assisting teachers in making individualized lesson plans around those standards. The early versions of KIDMAP were seriously flawed, discouraging many teachers and schools from using it. The most recent version comes close to realizing its potential. KIDMAP can be fully integrated with CASES.

Financial auditing procedures. All financial reporting is done through CASES. When a school completes its end-of-year procedures, the data are automatically downloaded to the ED.

The financial status of schools is reviewed annually through an internal and an external audit. The external audit, done by the state's auditor general, is a macro-audit focusing primarily on procedures. The internal audit is supervised by the ED but is conducted by independent auditing firms contracted and assigned by the ED. ED has established a standard, computerized audit procedure with standard reporting formats the contracting auditors must use. The auditors are trained by ED in the use of the software. The performance of the auditing firms is carefully evaluated each year, and they are notified of any shortcomings. Continuing unsatisfactory performance leads to removal from the department's approved list of auditing firms.

Evaluations. To advise the Minister of Education on matters related to the new funding mechanisms for schools, especially the matching of resources to student learning needs, an Education Committee was established at the beginning of the Schools of the Future policy initiative. This committee issued three reports (August 1994, June 1995, and December 1996) monitoring progress of the implementation and making suggestions for overcoming difficulties where they arose. Recognizing that advice on the policy framework for the GB needed to be firmly established in best practice at the school level, the committee used data from a sample of eighty-three schools that were representative of the different types of schools across the state. A principals' reference group also guided the committee. This group acted as a sounding board to react to the committee's ideas. The primary challenge to the committee was to develop a formula for allocating resources to schools on the basis of educational rationales. The issues addressed included the disparity in per capita funding between primary and secondary schools, and reducing this where no educational rationale was evident; establishing or improving indices of school and student need; making the GB simpler and more readily understandable; ensuring that schools have flexibility in the use of

funds; minimizing requirements for submission of written reports and unnecessary central control; and ensuring appropriate accountability (Education Committee, June 1995).

Another formal vehicle for evaluating the processes and outcomes of the Schools of the Future reforms was The Cooperative Research Project, Leading Victoria's Schools of the Future, which was organized in 1993 at the beginning of the policy initiative. This was a joint venture of the ED, the primary and secondary principals associations, and the University of Melbourne. The project was a 5-year longitudinal study with several components, including seven broadly framed surveys of principals' opinions about the benefits gained from the reforms and several highly focused investigations (Cooperative Research Project, 1998).

The Cooperative Research Project was not able to monitor progress in student achievement directly, because baseline data were not available prior to the reforms. Further, the teachers unions discouraged teachers from furnishing the project with information on student achievement.

The 1997 survey of principals' opinions (the last survey conducted by the project) revealed overwhelming support for the reforms, with 81 percent of the principals indicating a preference for the current arrangements over those previously existing. Noting curricular and student achievement gains, the principals nevertheless considered the greatest benefits to have come from the area of planning and resource allocation. Principals saw the GB as enhancing a school's capacity in planning and resource allocation. High ratings were given for establishing links between resources and curriculum programs, allocating resources to educational needs of students, and achieving priorities set forth in the school charter. On the negative side, workload and time demands had greatly increased under the reforms, with the average principal working fifty-nine hours per week. Concerns were also expressed over the rapid rate of change and the difficulty in keeping up with it, career uncertainty, and decreased opportunity for staff to transfer among schools (Cooperative Research Project, 1998).

Taken together, the Victorian reform experience represents an extraordinary case of research-driven policy initiatives that have translated into a system of central oversight, SBDM, and parental freedom in the choice of schools.

CHARTER SCHOOLS

The charter school is the innovation in the United States that is most similar to Schools of the Future in Victoria and Local Management of Schools in England. Charter schools are one of the fastest-growing innovations in public policy and enjoy broad bipartisan support from presidents, governors, and state legislators. Although the late Albert Shanker, long-time president of the American Federation of Teachers, was one of the early proponents of charter schools, opposition to them comes largely from teacher unions and local school boards. Thirty-six states and the District of Columbia have enacted charter legislation since 1991, when Minnesota was the first state to do so. As of 2000–2001, more than 2,000 charter schools were operating, serving half a million children (Gill et al., 2001).

Charter schools are public schools that come into existence through a contract with either a state agency or a local school board. The charter—or contract—establishes the framework within which the school operates and how public support for the school will be provided. Charters are for a specific period of time, usually three to five years, at the end of which they may be renewed. A school's charter gives it autonomy over its operation and frees it from many regulations that other schools must follow. In exchange for the flexibility afforded by the charter, a school is held accountable for achieving the goals set out in the charter, including improved student performance (U. S. Department of Education, 2000).

School charter laws vary widely from state to state, but they usually contain the following provisions:

- Who may propose a charter, how they are granted, and the number to be granted
- How the school is legally defined and related to governance, operations, and liability issues
- The levels and type of funding provided and the amount of fiscal independence and autonomy
- How schools are to address admissions, non-discrimination, racial/ethnic balance, discipline, and special education
- Whether the school may act as an employer, which labor relation laws apply, and staff rights and privileges
- The degree of control the school has over the development of its instructional goals and practices
- Whether the charter serves as a performance-based contract, how assessments are made, and charter revocation and renewal issues. (<**http://www.uscharterschols.org/**>, accessed January 9, 2002)

The SRI International study of charter schools (U.S. Department of Education, 2000) revealed that the demand for charter schools is strong: 70 percent report a waiting list of applicants. Since the first charter opened in 1992, fifty-nine have closed—about 4 percent of those ever opened. Most charter schools are small; their median size is 137, compared with 475 for other public schools. Half of the charter schools have a grade configuration that deviates from the standard elementary, middle, and high school. One-quarter spanned grades K–8, spanned grades K–12, or were ungraded, compared with one-tenth for other public schools. Seventy percent of charter schools are newly created, about 20 percent are converted public schools seeking greater flexibility, and the remaining 10 percent are converted private schools seeking funding stability. The median student-to-teacher ratio is 16 to 1, slightly smaller than for other public schools. They are about comparably equipped with computer technology.

Seventy percent of charter schools have a racial/ethnic composition similar to that of their surrounding district. About 17 percent enroll a higher percentage of students of color, and about 14 percent enroll a lower percentage of students of color. Nationally, white students make up 48 percent of charter school enrollment, compared to about 59 percent for other public schools. Charter schools enroll a slightly higher percentage of students eligible for free or reduced-price lunch than do other public schools. Students with limited English proficiency represent 10 percent of charter school enrollments. This percentage is comparable to that in other public schools. Enrollment of special education students in charter schools (8 percent) is lower than for other public schools (11 percent) (U.S. Department of Education, 2000). With respect to achievement of students in charter schools, Gill et al. (2001) concluded, in a review of available research, that, despite some promising evidence on achievement scores, there is as yet no evidence on the long-term academic effects of charter schools.

Manno (2001) points out that the charter school movement is largely an urban phenomenon. Gill and colleagues (2001) agree that charter schools tend to flourish where public schools have been failing. Two-thirds of charter school students are enrolled in schools in large cities or their urban fringes. Manno attributes the attraction of charter schools in urban areas to their serving as a refuge from failing schools and unresponsive systems controlled by bureaucrats and union activists. He characterizes these urban districts and their non-chartered schools as remnants of our industrial past. (See related discussion in Chapter 1.)

> The very system itself is outdated. Its decision making process has evolved from the deliberations of selfless elites into the brokering of competing interests including instructional aides,

textbook and test publishers, social workers, administrators, bus drivers, maintenance staff, and teachers. The system frustrates parents who seek the best for their children and thwarts educators . . . who yearn for autonomy and professionalism. Essentially every group must agree to change before any change can be made. Since many of those interests have been codified into law—teacher certification and tenure, for example—even when agreement is reached, its implementation occurs at glacial speed. . . . The expansive and expensive educational system is reminiscent of the command-and-control economy of the former Soviet Union. It is a big, lethargic, hyper-regulated, all-powerful, one-size-fits-all government bureaucracy that does not have to change because it enjoys a virtual monopoly. (p. 50)

Good and Braden (2000a), while recognizing the potential of the charter school concept, are more cautious in their assessment of the charter school movement. They are critical of some of the enabling legislation that does not adequately oversee these schools' performance. They describe numerous problematic charter schools and their practices. To protect against improper practices and to facilitate the realization of these schools' potential, Good and Braden (2000b) recommend that application for charters be a competitive process, with only the best and most thoroughly prepared proposals being accepted. Every proposal should be accompanied by a financial plan. All charter operators should understand special education laws and paperwork. The supervising agency should have a rigorous monitoring plan in place before awarding charters. A strong program of research and development should be supported to facilitate the understanding and dissemination of successful charter school practices. Good and Braden (2000a) also recommend that no management companies be involved in the chartering process.

Per-pupil-based funding is at the heart of charter school financing. It is based in some cases on state average per-pupil expenditure and in others on average district revenue or expenditure. In still others, it is negotiated between the charter schools and the chartering agency (Nelson, Muir, & Drown, 2000). Typically, funding flows from school districts to charter schools. About half of the states fund elementary and secondary students in charter schools at the same level. Most states provide supplementary funding for at-risk children either directly or through negotiations. Special education is a contentious issue, and six states fund it on the basis of school district average cost rather than according to the specific needs of the students. This may explain, at least in part, the underrepresentation of special education children in charter schools. Other states link special education funding to actual cost through pupil-weighting formulas or negotiations.

Charter schools are eligible for federal and state categorical program funding, such as Title I and special education, and for specific programs such as technology literacy. Transportation is provided by the district or aided by the state. Some funding is provided for facilities in six states and the District of Columbia, but financial assistance for facilities is not provided by most states, which is a source of great concern for charter schools in those states. Charter schools may acquire debt in most states. About half of the states provide some accelerated funding for charter schools to help them weather cash flow difficulties; for schools in other states, this represents a serious problem. Twelve states require charter schools to participate in the state teacher retirement system, and the participation level is high in most states. All states require charter schools to conduct an independent financial audit.

Planning and start-up costs are a major problem for newly created schools. Nine states provide such assistance, but the others do not. Federal assistance has provided some relief in this situation. In 1994, the Public Charter Schools Program (PCSP) was enacted as Title X, Part C, in the reauthorization of the Elementary and Secondary Education Act, with an ini-

tial appropriation of six million dollars. The PCSP is intended to support the planning, development, and/or initial implementation of charter schools, providing relatively unencumbered seed funding for states with charter school laws to distribute to charter school groups during the first three years of a charter school's existence. The statute also makes provision for individual charter schools to apply directly to the secretary of education for a grant if their states choose not to participate or deny a grant. Congress reauthorized the PCSP in 1998 by passing the Charter School Expansion Act. Eligibility for subgrants was expanded to include mature charter schools, which could apply for funds to disseminate promising school practices. For FY 2000, the appropriation was increased to $145 million (U.S. Department of Education, 2000).

With respect to comparability of funding between charter schools and district-controlled schools, Nelson et al. (2000) concluded that it is difficult to assess without an understanding of the specific educational tasks that charter schools undertake, including the types of students they seek to educate. A number of factors support the conclusion that charter schools receive less funding than district-controlled schools, because they sometimes receive less than 100 percent of operating revenue; do not usually receive funds to finance facilities and debt; do not have equal access to all of the funding streams of district-controlled schools; and may be required to pay administrative fees, even when they do not receive offsetting services. Charter schools that focus exclusively on special-needs and at-risk students may be substantially underfunded. On the other hand, there are mitigating circumstances that may balance this possible underfunding, such as receiving "in kind" services (e. g., transportation) at no charge. Also, the average district expenditure includes many services that charter schools do not provide. Furthermore, the flexibility of charter schools enables them to configure their grade level structure and enrollment in order to generate optimal funding (or to match available funding).

The 1998 study of charter schools sponsored by the U.S. Department of Education (Berman et al., 1998) found that

> Charters start from the inspiration of individual educators, groups of parents, community leaders, or teachers with a dream. They gather support, overcome skeptics and political resistance if they need to—and they often do—and create a proposal that says why they want to start their charter school, what students they want to serve, and what they plan to do. Once a charter is founded, parents and students make deeply personal decisions, exercise their choice and take a chance on enrolling in this new opportunity. Their reasons vary greatly. (p. 75)

The study found that parents and students choose charter schools partly because of dissatisfaction with their former public schools, expressing concerns about low academic standards, a dehumanizing culture, student safety, and unresponsiveness to parental involvement. The chief characteristics that attract them to their charter school are a nurturing and safe environment, its value system, the quality of its academic program, high standards for achievement, small school and class size, clear goals for each student, and a central role for parents. Gill et al. (2001) found strong evidence that parents are satisfied with their choices.

Newly created charter schools tend to be established to realize an alternative vision for public education or to serve a special target population of students. Public schools that convert to charter status also seek to realize an educational vision, but they frequently start from an established—and often highly regarded—educational program. The primary reason why they convert is to gain autonomy from their districts or to bypass various regulations. Private schools that convert to charter status seek public funds so that they can stabilize their finances and, often, attract students whose families could not afford private school tuition (U.S. Department of Education, 1998).

STRATEGY FORMATION AND BUDGETING AT THE SCHOOL LEVEL

Given the growing interest in school-based decision making and school-based budgeting in the United States, we now direct our attention to the managerial practices required by such innovations. First we focus on strategy formation and planning. Then we address issues specifically related to school-based budgeting.

School-Level Strategy Formation and Planning

Within a district planning scheme, the school is likely to be viewed as a program—one of the quasi-independent units within the system. The growing practice of school-based management has led to schools themselves becoming the primary planning unit. This is already true of charter schools. SBDM is relatively new in the United States and very limited in its application. But it is used extensively elsewhere, as the foregoing descriptions of practice in England and Australia indicate, and in such places a valuable experience base has developed. One of the school-based management models that is built upon the collective experiences of schools in those two countries and New Zealand is Caldwell and Spink's (1992, 1998) Model for Self-Management (MSM). We feel that it offers an appropriate guide for American schools and will describe it in some detail.

The Model for Self-Management (MSM) is illustrated in Figure 14.3. It integrates the annual management functions of design, budgeting, implementing, and evaluating with the strategic governance functions of setting direction and priorities and policy making. MSM focuses on the essence of schools—learning and teaching—and is intended to involve administrators, teachers and other staff, students, parents, and other members of the community. The management of the school is organized around "programs" that correspond to the preferred patterns of work in the school.

MSM attempts to dispel confusion created by the simultaneous shifts in authority toward centralization of some decisions (e.g., state curricular mandates, standards, and assessment) and decentralization of others (e.g., school-based management and teacher and community empowerment). This model acknowledges the influence of central authority (shown above the dark broken line in Figure 14.3), be it national or state government or local school district, through the "Central Framework" and the "Charter." The presence of "Policies" and the creation of a "Development Plan" are the points where the laws and regulations of the central authority are integrated with the school's unique characteristics, philosophy, and mission.

A school charter is a document to which both government and the school policy group assent (Caldwell & Spinks, 1992, p. 40). Charters within the context of schools in England and in the state of Victoria in Australia are the rule rather than the exception, just as in the United States. But, even within the United States, charter schools are by definition empowered by charters; private schools are chartered (or incorporated), and any school district could adopt a policy of "chartering" its component schools. A charter summarizes the centrally determined framework of priorities and standards and also outlines the means by which the school will address this framework. It provides an account of the school's unique mission, vision, priorities, needs, and programs, and it specifies how decisions will be made and how evaluation will be handled.

The coordinating body for MSM is the policy group, operating between the two broken lines in Figure 14.3. The implementing bodies are the program teams operating below the light broken line in the figure. The composition of the policy group varies according to the setting. In the Australian state of Victoria, it would be the legally established school council. In England, it would be a school's board of governors. In the United States, where there is no universally established pattern of school governing boards, the nature of the policy group could be established by the state, as in the cases of Chicago and Kentucky; established by the district, as in the case of Dade County, Florida; or left to the discretion of the school. The policy group is solely responsible for goal setting, need identification, and policy making, although it is likely to seek advice broadly in carrying out these responsibilities. It must approve budgets prepared by program teams and ensure that the proposals reflect established policy and are supportable by the resources allocated to the school. The policy group is responsible for summative evaluation of programs, making judgments on the effectiveness of each program and of the policy that supports program efforts.

Caldwell and Spinks (1988) defined a policy as a statement of purpose accompanied by one or more guidelines on how that purpose is to be achieved. A policy provides a framework for the operation of the school or of a program, and it may allow discretion in its implementation. A policy's statement of purpose should be derived from the school's statement of philosophy as expressed in the school's charter or from a goal statement or statements. The guidelines should clearly state the intent of the policy and the desired pattern of action, without becoming so specific as to leave no room for professional judgment by those concerned with implementing the policy.

The policy group adopts the development plan as a strategic plan for improvement, specifying in general terms the priorities to be addressed in the next three to five years and the strategies to be employed. This is similar to the concept of school improvement plans in Chicago and Kentucky. The development plan includes a careful assessment of where the school is in relation to where it should be. A "need" exists when there is a significant gap. Schools typically have far more needs than their resources permit them to address, so it

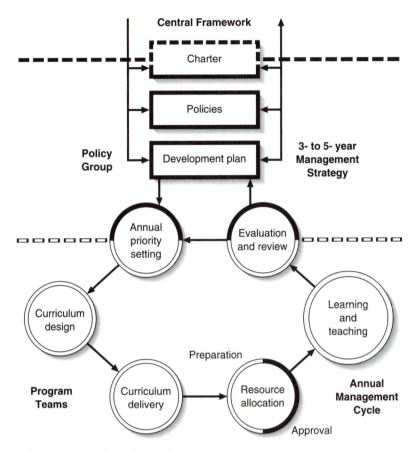

FIGURE 14.3. Model for Self-Management

Source: B. J. Caldwell & J. M. Spinks (1992). *Leading the Self-Managing School*. London: Falmer, p. 33. Reprinted with permission from Falmer Press.

must be decided which are the most pressing. Caldwell and Spinks (1988) suggest that one consideration in setting priorities is the extent of identifiable harm caused by each gap or need.

A program is defined as an area of learning and teaching, such as English, mathematics, art, and music, or a support service, such as administration, audiovisual media, and maintenance of buildings and grounds. A program team is usually composed of everyone involved in the delivery of the program service. Each team should have a designated leader—usually a person with formal authority related to the

program, such as a subject coordinator or department head. The teams prepare plans for their areas of responsibility within the parameters of the development plan and specify the resources needed to support those plans. The teams are responsible for the implementation of their plans as approved by the policy group. They are also responsible for formative evaluation of their respective programs and for submitting information to the policy group as required for their summative reviews. Although the division of responsibility is clear, some individuals are likely to serve on both the policy group and one or more program teams, an arrangement that facilitates a high level of formal and informal communication.

On the surface, MSM resembles the largely discredited Planning, Programming, Budgeting System (PPBS) model that was experimented with in the United States during the 1960s and 1970s. But although they are similar in concept, they are very different in design. The creators of MSM learned much from the pitfalls of using PPBS and have largely succeeded in avoiding them. PPBS was very rigid, devoted too much attention to the formal technology and minutia of planning and budgeting, and required excessive paperwork.

> To these shortcomings may be added an inappropriate emphasis on the specification of performance requirements or criteria for evaluation. PPBS assumed a greater degree or capacity for rational or analytical planning than existed or was possible. In short, PPBS suffered from the "paralysis through analysis" which is to be avoided if effectiveness along the lines studied by Peters and Waterman (1982) is to be attained. (Caldwell & Spinks, 1988, p. 68)

MSM keeps paperwork to a minimum. Each goal statement is a single sentence; policies are limited to one page, program plans and budgets to two pages, and evaluation reports to one or two pages. Criteria for evaluation are kept simple and are clearly related to learning and teaching. Priorities can be reordered quickly and simply as new needs emerge. All written material should be free of technical jargon so that it can be easily read and understood by all members of the school community.

MSM recognizes three levels of planning: program, curricular, and instructional. Program planning is determining, in general terms, how a program is to be implemented. It entails specifying the manner in which students will be grouped vertically (among grade or year levels) and horizontally (within a grade or year level); the number and nature of teachers and support staff associated with the program; the supplies, equipment, and services required; and initiatives (additions or deletions) that are noteworthy. Curriculum planning provides a relatively detailed specification of what will be taught, how it will be taught, and when it will be taught. Instructional planning is planning undertaken by individual teachers when implementing a curriculum plan in their own classrooms. (Caldwell & Spinks, 1988, pp. 43–44)

The costs of personnel allocated to specific tasks are included in program and school budgets, even though the district may pay the actual salaries. The salary rate used is the average salary for the district (plus the costs of fringe benefits), rather than the actual salaries paid to personnel assigned to a program. Caldwell and Spinks (1988) noted that "the inclusion of such [salary] estimates is an acknowledgment that the major resource in a school is the staff" (pp. 46–48).

A program budget is a comprehensive plan for a program. It contains a statement of the program's purpose, a list of broad guidelines on how the purpose is to be achieved, a plan for implementation with elements listed in order of priority, an estimate of resources required to support the plan, and a plan for evaluation. All must be summarized and reported to the policy group in two pages or less.

The program budgets for all programs in the school are brought together in a single document for submission to the policy group for review, possible revision, and eventual approval. During the process of reconciliation, expenditure requests are adjusted, if necessary, so that combined approved expenditures fall within the school's estimated income.

With the adoption of the program budget by the policy group, program teams are authorized to proceed with implementation of their plans in the forthcoming year. There is no need for further reference to the policy group during the course of the year, unless a program team desires to make a major change in its plan.

The final phase of the MSM cycle is evaluation and review, defined by Caldwell and Spinks (1988) as

> the gathering of information for the purpose of making a judgment and then making that judgment. Two kinds of evaluation should occur during or following the implementation of program plans. One is evaluation of learning, where information is gathered to form judgments about the progress or achievement of students. Another is evaluation of programs, when information is gathered to form judgments about the extent to which progress toward goals has been made, needs have been satisfied and policies have been implemented. (p. 49)

The policy group holds the major responsibility for program summative evaluation and may call in external authorities to help in the process. Planning teams have a similar, but more detailed, interest and gather much of the information needed for program evaluation for their own purposes as formative evaluation. The school evaluation scheme may be coordinated with district and state evaluation schemes. Minor evaluations are carried out annually, and their reports to the policy group are limited to a one-page summary. Major evaluations are scheduled to occur every three–five years, and their reports are limited to two-page summaries. "The emphasis is on a manageable and usable approach to program evaluation, in contrast to the frequently exhausting approach to school review and evaluation which has been encountered in many schools in recent years" (Caldwell & Spinks, 1988, p. 50).

The MSM cycle is completed when judgments in program evaluation result in the setting of new goals, the identification of new needs, the formulation of new policies, or the introduction of new programs by the policy group. The model provides a comprehensive portrayal of all that eventually must be accomplished; but fortuitously, there seems to be no best point of entry to the model. A school may enter the cycle at any phase, completing the other phases in a manner appropriate for

each setting. In a more recent volume, Caldwell and Spinks (1998) provide strategic guidelines for creating schools for the "knowledge society," focusing on learning outcomes, and building systems of self-managing schools.

The mere existence of decentralization mechanisms does not guarantee positive results, however. The nature of the culture, or attitudes/beliefs permeating the organization, is also influential. Ross (1997) concluded that schemes resulting in effective participation by teachers "require new forms of collaborative and collegial involvement that shift the traditional isolated decision making environment to a team-based, power sharing one" (p. 317). A balanced approach of centralization-decentralization supports a combined top-down, bottom-up planning process to meet the competing needs of the organization. "A co-existing loose-tight coupling between horizontal and vertical levels of the organization underlies a framework focused on systemic, rather than piecemeal, reform" (p. 319).

Ross (1997) found the most successful SBDM in schools where teachers were offered a high-involvement form of participation, the power to influence decisions, and a context that fostered the effective engagement of teachers. The pervading culture needs to be one of mutual respect and trust throughout all levels of the organization, nurtured by effective leadership and top-down commitment and support. It is critical that principal–teacher relationships be based on mutual influence in the decision-making process and that professional learning and staff development be focused on creating an ongoing capacity for school improvement, remaining responsive to student needs, and meeting changes in the school community over time.

School-Based Budgeting

School personnel cannot make meaningful curricular decisions without the authority also to make the related resource commitment decisions (Drury, 1999; Guthrie, 1998; Odden & Busch, 1998; Consortium on Renewing Education, 1998). School-based decision making must include school-based budgeting as an integral component. The degree of empowerment of school staff is directly related to the proportion of the school budget that is under the control of school authorities. In this section we focus on issues related to school-based budgeting (SBB).

Wohlstetter and Buffett (1992) described the differences between traditional centralized budgeting at the district level and school-based budgeting. At whatever level it takes place, the budgeting process involves formulation, adoption, and monitoring. Under the traditional centralized mode, all three are accomplished at the district level with minimal involvement of school personnel. Human and physical resources are then assigned to schools for use in district-specified areas. Schools are usually given discretionary control over a small allocation, primarily for purchasing instructional supplies and providing student enrichment experiences.

Where budgetary authority has been decentralized, the district still forecasts the resources that will be available at the district level. But from that point on, the procedures become quite different. Decentralized districts must first determine the extent of budgetary authority to be extended to schools. The primary issue is what degree of control to give the schools over personnel expenditures, which account for between 60 and 80 percent of school and district budgets. Schools in Edmonton, Alberta, Canada, and in England are granted a lump-sum allocation, as described in previous sections, covering virtually all costs encountered by schools, with no specific amount designated for personnel or for any other expenditure category. American school districts have been very cautious in delegating budgetary authority to schools, as noted in several studies already cited (Odden, 1999; Dunn, James-Gross, & Trampe, 1998; David, 1994; Goertz & Stiefel,

1998).

The second district-level decision is how much to allocate to schools and in terms of what unit. Some districts make their allocations by pupil units and others by staff units. In either case, the number of students in a school, their characteristics, their previous performance, and the nature of the school (for example, grade levels served and the presence of special programs) are primary determinants of the size of the school's allocation (Gurr, 1999; Wohlstetter & Van Kirk, 1996). We described the procedures followed in Edmonton, England, and Victoria in previous sections.

Once the district arrives at an estimate of a school's allocation, school authorities must devise a detailed plan for using the funds in accordance with the school's curricular plan and within the constraints established by higher authority (Wohlstetter & Buffett, 1992). Whatever procedure is followed, budget building should be done within the context of the school's curricular plan.

Budget adoption is much the same as in centralized districts. Final approval is by the board of education in either case. Wohlstetter and Buffett (1992) pointed out that the main difference is in the flow. Whereas centralized districts may consult with school authorities, in the decentralized mode the school develops the budget and recommends its adoption to district officials. District review of school budgets should be in terms of compliance with district and other strategic and legal constraints, not in terms of educational substance or philosophy, which should be allowed to vary freely among schools.

Expenditures need to be monitored by both district and school personnel. The district role in the decentralized mode is primarily to give the schools information and to ensure that schools do not exceed their spending authorizations. In Chicago, Dade County, Victoria, and Edmonton, the district provides budgetary information to school personnel on a regular basis. Edmonton school officials have the option of being "on-line" to access financial information held in computer memory at any time, and they have the flexibility of establishing their own accounting codes within the constraints of the district code structure. In Victoria, this involvement is required.

In her study of the implementation of education reforms in Kentucky, David (1994) found that the biggest problem with the process of making allocations to schools was the lack of appropriate accounting systems and technological support by school districts. England and the state of Victoria in Australia faced a similar problem in moving to their systems of local management of schools. Before financial allocations can be made to schools, it is necessary to know the total resource requirements of schools, and most current school accounting procedures are incapable of providing such information. Except for minor portions of the budget such as instructional supplies, most accounting systems do not link expenditures to buildings, programs, or classrooms. Computer and accounting technology have the capacity to provide such linkages, and our ability to trace all expenditures to the school level will improve as the practice of SBB spreads.

Most accounting systems can be adapted to SBB, and software is also available that enables states and school districts to disaggregate their financial data to schools and programs with relative ease, using current accounting configurations. One such software is In$ite™, created by the K–12 Education Team of Coopers & Lybrand, L.L.P., on the basis of the Finance Analysis Model for Education developed by Cooper and Sarrel (1993).

In$ite™ is a technology-based management information tool that can operate on a standard personal computer. The Finance Analysis Model for Education (1995) on which In$ite™ is based consists of a series of multidimensional spreadsheets that compile information on district and school expenditures. The three basic dimensions of the model are functional, program, and site-level (Speakman, et al., 1996).

The functional dimension is divided into five components: instruction, instructional support, operations, other commitments, and leadership. The program dimension is flexible and may include such programs as special education, bilingual education, gifted and talented, Title I, and summer school. The site-level dimension of the model requires that the time of people working in more than one site be prorated according to the amount of time spent at each site. Salaries and fringe benefits are then prorated to the respective sites accordingly. Utility bills and other expenditures that are not normally distributed to cost centers are likewise prorated under this model.

In$ite™ has been used by numerous school districts and by the states of Hawaii and South Carolina to trace expenditures to the school, program, and grade levels (Cooper & Randall, 1998; Cooper, 1998). Other states with the ability to trace school expenditures to the school level include Florida, Ohio, and Texas (Busch & Odden, 1997).

Resource allocation and expenditure information is critical to the successful functioning of SBDM. Tracing resource demands to the school and classroom level is essential for informed decision making in SBDM and SBB environments. It also has the potential, with appropriate analysis, to enhance our understanding of how inputs affect educational outcomes and equity in the allocation of resources.

SUMMARY

In this chapter, we have addressed the "supply side" question of education provision: To what extent should providers of education be given the autonomy and flexibility to respond to differences in the judgments of consumers about appropriate education? School-based decision making is a strategy for granting education professionals greater autonomy in this regard. School-based budgeting is an integral support system. We defined SBDM and SBB and reviewed the rationales for their adoption. Several examples of the implementation of SBDM and SBB were described.

In the next chapter, we address the "demand side" question of education provision: To what extent should consumers of education be given a central role in deciding what kind of education is appropriate for them? In that chapter, we examine the implications that family choice proposals have for school finance policy and the continuing need for some governmental regulation.

ACTIVITIES

1. Imagine a policy board for each public school, composed of the principal (serving as the chief executive officer) and representatives of teachers, parents, and students.
   - What are the advantages and disadvantages of such an arrangement?
   - Would you add representation of any other group?
   - Would you eliminate representation of any group?
   - Assuming that each representative has one vote, how many representatives should there be from each group?
   - What constraints, if any, would you place on the decision-making powers of the board?
   - Provide your rationale for each response.
2. Within the context of the decision matrix presented in Figure 1.3, what educational decisions are best made by professional educators at the school level? What safeguards need to be implemented to protect societal and family interests? Give your rationale for each response.
3. In what ways can the public interest be protected in a system of SBDM without the bureaucratization of schools? Explain the rationale supporting your answer.
4. To what extent, if any, should public control and regulation follow public finance? Give examples of alternative ways of providing publicly financed support of educa-

tional services, and indicate the levels of control and regulation that accompany each.
5. Under a school-based budgeting scheme, what factors should be taken into account in determining the amount of a school's lump-sum distribution?

COMPUTER SIMULATIONS: SITE BASED BUDGET

Computer simulations related to the content of this chapter are available on the Allyn & Bacon website, **<http://www.ablongman.com/edleadership**. They focus on using site-based budgets and implementing budget recissions and additions. Objectives for the exercises are

- To understand the construction and management of a site-based budget
- To contemplate opportunities and challenges in making budget adjustments

REFERENCES

Anderson, D. S. (1993). Public schools in decline: Implications of the privitization of schools in Australia. In H. Beare, & W. L. Boyd (Eds.), *Restructuring schools: An international perspective on the movement to transform the control and performance of schools* (pp. 184–199). Washington, DC: Falmer.

Arnott, M., Bullock, A., & Thomas, H. (1992). Consequences of local management: An assessment by head teachers. Paper presented to the ERA Research Network, February 12.

Berman, P., Nelson, B., Ericson, J., Perry, R., & Silverman, D. (1998). *A national study of charter schools: Second year report*. Washington, DC: Office of Educational Research and Improvement, U.S. Department of Education.

Boyer, E. L. (1983). *High school: A report on secondary education in America*. New York: Harper & Row.

Brown, D. J. (1990). *Decentralization and school-based management*. London: Falmer.

Bryk, A. S. (1999). Policy lessons from Chicago's experience with decentralization. In D. Ravitch (Ed.), *Brookings papers on education policy, 1999*. Washington, DC: The Brookings Institution.

Bullock, A., & Thomas, H. (1994). *The impact of local*

management of schools: Final report. Birmingham, England: University of Birmingham.

Busch, C., & Odden, A. (1997). Introduction to the special issue: Improving educational policy and results with school level data—A multiplicity of perspectives. *Journal of Education Finance. 22*, 225–245.

Butts, R. F. (1955). *Assumptions underlying Australian education: opportunities for reform in the middle years of schooling*. Melbourne, Victoria, Australia: Australian Council for Educational Research.

Caldwell, B. & Hill, P. (1999). Formula funding of schools in Australia. In K. N. Ross & R. Levacic (Eds.), *Needs-based resource allocation in education via formula funding of schools* (pp. 139–160). Paris: UNESCO.

Caldwell, B. J., & Spinks, J. M. (1988). *The self-managing school*. London: Falmer.

Caldwell, B. J., & Spinks, J. M. (1992). *Leading the self-managing school*. London: Falmer.

Caldwell, B. J., & Spinks, J. M. (1998). *Beyond the self-managing school*. London: Falmer.

Cawelti, G. (1989). Key elements of site-based management. *Educational Leadership, 46*, 46.

Chicago Panel on Public School Policy and Finance. (1988*). Illegal use of State Chapter I funds*. Chicago: Author.

Consortium on Renewing Education (CORE). (1998). *20/20 vision: A strategy for doubling America's academic achievement by the year 2020*. Nashville, TN: Peabody Center for Education Policy, Vanderbilt University.

Conway, J. A. (1984). The myth, mystery, and mastery of participative decision making in education. *Educational Administration Quarterly, 20*, 11–40.

Cooperative Research Project. (1998). *Assessing the outcomes*. Report of the Cooperative Research Project on "Leading Victoria's *Schools of the Future,*" Department of Education, Victorian Association of State Secondary Principals, Victorian Primary Principals Association, the University of Melbourne (Fay Thomas, Chair). Melbourne, Australia: Victoria Department of Education.

Cooper, B. S. (1998). Using school-site budgeting to improve management and shared decision-making. *NJASA Perspective, 15*, 10–17.

Cooper, B. S., & Randall, E. V. (1998). From transactional to transformational accounting. *School Business Affairs*, October, 4–16.

Cooper, B. S., & Sarrel, R. (1993). Managing for school efficiency and effectiveness. *National Forum of Educational Administration and Supervision Journal, 8*, 3–38.

Cuban, L. (1988). *The managerial imperative and the practice of leadership in schools*. Albany, NY: State University of New York Press.

Danzberger, J. P., Kirst, M. W., & Usdan, M. D. (1992). *Governing public schools: New times, new requirements*. Washington, DC: The Institute for Educational Leadership.

David, J. L. (1994). School-based decision making: Kentucky's test of decentralization. *Phi Delta Kappan, 75*, 706–712.

Drury, D. W. (1999). *Reinventing school-based management: A school board guide to school-based management*. Alexandria, VA: National School Boards Association.

Dunn, R. J., James-Gross, L., & Trampe, C. (1998). Decentralized budgeting: A study in implementation and implications. *Journal of School Business Management, 10*, 22–28.

Education Committee. (1995). *The school global budget in Victoria: Matching resources to student learning needs, Interim Report*. Melbourne, Victoria, Australia: Victoria Department of Education.

Elmore, R. F. (1988). Choice in public schools. In W. L. Boyd & C. T. Kerchner (Eds.), *The politics of excellence and choice in education* (pp. 79–98). New York: Falmer.

Fitz, J., & Halpin, D. (1994). Grant-maintained schools: Problems and prospects of school autonomy. Philadelphia, PA: Paper presented at the annual meeting of the Politics of Education Association, October 27–28.

The Finance Analysis Model: Linking resources for education. (1995). Chicago, IL: Coopers & Lybrand, L.L.P. and Center for Workforce Preparation.

Gill, B. P., Timpane, P. M., Ross, K. E., & Brewer, D. J. (2001). *Rhetoric versus reality: What we know and what we need to know about vouchers and charter schools*. Santa Monica, CA: RAND Education.

Goertz, M. E., & Stiefel, L. (1998). School-level resource allocation in urban schools. *Journal of Education Finance, 23*, 435–446.

Good, T. L., & Braden, J. S. (2000a). *The great school debate: Choice, vouchers, and charters*. Mahwah, NJ: Erlbaum.

Good, T. L., & Braden, J. S. (2000b). Charter schools: Another reform failure or a worthwhile investment? *Phi Delta Kappan, 81*, 745–750.

Goodlad, J. I. (1984). *A place called school: Prospects for the future.* New York: McGraw-Hill.

Gurr, D. (1999). *From supervision to quality assurance: The case of the State of Victoria (Australia).* Paris: International Institute for Educational Planning/UNESCO.

Guthrie, J. W. (1998). Reinventing education finance: Alternatives for allocating resources to individual schools. In W. J. Fowler, Jr. (Ed.), *Selected papers in school finance 1996* (pp. 85–107). (NCES98-217). Washington, DC: U.S. Department of Education, National Center for Education Statistics.

Hannaway, J. (1996). Management decentralization and performance-based incentives: Theoretical consideration for schools. In E. A. Hanushek & D. W. Jorgenson. *Improving America's schools: The role of incentives* (pp. 97–109). Washington, DC: National Academy Press.

Hannaway, J., & Carnoy, M. (1993). Preface. In J. Hannaway & M. Carnoy (Eds.), *Decentralization and school improvement: Can we fulfill the promise?* San Francisco, CA: Jossey-Bass.

Harp, L. (1995). Governor signs bill putting mayor in control of Chicago schools. *Education Week, 14,* 11.

Hess, Jr., G. A. (1990). *Chicago school reform: What is it and how it came to be.* Chicago: Chicago Panel on Public School Policy and Finance.

Hess, G. A. (1993). Decentralization and community control. In S. L. Jacobson & R. Berne, *Reforming education: The emerging systemic approach* (pp. 66–86). Thousand Oaks, CA: Corwin.

Hess, G. A. (1999a). Comment on A. S. Bryk's "Policy lessons from Chicago's experience with decentralization." In D. Ravitch (Ed.), *Brookings papers on education policy 1999* (pp. 99–109). Washington, DC: The Brookings Institution.

Hess, G. A. (1999b). Understanding achievement (and other) changes under Chicago school reform. *Educational Evaluation and Policy Analysis, 21,* 67–83.

Hoff, D. J. (2001a). Kentucky. *Education Week, 20,* 139.

Hoff, D. J. (2001b). Kentucky. *Education Week, 20,* 86–87.

Interim Committee for the Australian Schools Commission. (1973). *Schools in Australia, Report of the Interim Committee for the Australian Schools Commission.* Canberra, Australia: Australian Government Publishing Service.

Jones, K., & Whitford, B. L. (1997). Kentucky's conflicting reform principles: High-stakes school accountability and student performance assessment. *Phi Delta Kappan, 79,* 276–281.

Kannapel, P. J., Coe, P., Aagaard, L., Moore, B. D., & Reeves, C. A. (2000). Teacher responses to rewards and sanctions: Effects of and reactions to Kentucky's high-stakes accountability program. In B. L. Whitford & K. Jones, *Accountability, assessment, and teacher commitment: Lessons from Kentucky's reform efforts* (pp. 127–146). Albany, NY: State University of New York Press.

Keller, B. (1999). To a different drum: Kentucky adopts a new testing system. *Education Week, 18,* 147, 193.

Kirst, M. (1990). *Accountability: Implications for state and local policymakers* (Report 1590-982). Washington, DC: U.S. Department of Education.

Lawler, III, E. E. (1986). *High involvement management.* San Francisco: Jossey-Bass.

Levacic, R. (1999). Formula funding of schools in England and Wales. In K. N. Ross & R. Levacic (Eds.), *Needs-based resource allocation in education via formula funding of schools* (pp. 161–197). Paris: UNESCO.

Malen, B., Ogawa, R. T., & Kranz, J. (1990). What do we know about school-based management? A case study of the literature—A call for research. In W. H. Clune & J. F. Witte (Eds.), *Choice and control in American education,* Vol. 2: *The practice of choice, decentralization and school restructuring* (pp. 289–342). New York: Falmer.

Manno, B. V. (2001). Chartered governance of urban public schools. In M. C. Wang & H. J. Walberg, *School choice or best systems: What improves education?* Mahwah, NJ: Erlbaum.

Marren, E., & Levacic, R. (1994). Senior management, classroom teacher, and governor responses to local management of schools. *Educational Management and Administration, 22,* 39–53.

Mohrman, S. A., & Lawler, III, E. E. (1996). Motivation for school reform. In S. H. Fuhrman, & J. A. O'Day, *Rewards and reform: Creating educational incentives that work* (pp. 115–143). San Francisco: Jossey-Bass.

Nelson, F. H., Muir, E., & Drown, R. (2000). *Venturesome capital: State charter school finance systems.* Washington, DC: Office of Educational Research and Improvement, U.S. Department of Education.

Odden, A. (1999). Formula funding of schools in the United States and Canada. In K. N. Ross & R.

Levacic (Eds.), *Needs-based resource allocation in education via formula funding of schools*. Paris: International Institute for Educational Planning.

Odden, A., & Busch, C. (1998). *Financing schools for high performance: Strategies for improving the use of educational resources.* San Francisco: Jossey-Bass.

Office of Review. 1998. *Building high-performance schools: An approach to school improvement.* Paper presented at the national seminar on School Review and Accountability, Hobart, Tasmania, Australia, April.

Ozembloski, L. W. & Brown, D. J. (1999). The institution of school-based management in Edmonton. In M. E. Goertz & A. Odden (Eds.), *School-based financing* (pp. 129–152). Thousand Oaks, CA: Corwin.

Peters, T. J., & Waterman, R. H. (1982). *In search of excellence: Lessons from America's best-run companies.* New York: Warner Books.

Rosenkranz, T. (1994). Reallocating resources: Discretionary funds provide engine for change. *Education and Urban Society, 26*, 264–284.

Ross, M. L. (1997). *A comparative case study of teacher participation in planning in three types of decentralized schools.* (Unpublished doctoral dissertation, State University of New York, Buffalo).

Sizer, T. R. (1985). *Horace's compromise: The dilemma of the American high school.* Boston: Houghton Mifflin.

Smylie, M. A. (1994). Redesigning teachers' work: Connections to the classroom. *Review of Research in Education, 20*, 129–177.

Speakman, S. T., Cooper, B. S., Sampieri, R., May, J., Holsomback, H., & Glass, B. (1996). Bringing money to the classroom: A systemic resource allocations model applied to the New York City public schools. In L. O. Picus & J. L. Wattenbarger (Eds.), *Where does the money go? Resource allocation in elementary and secondary schools* (pp. 106–131). Thousand Oaks, CA: Corwin.

Summers, A. A., & Johnson, A. W. (1996). The effects of school-based management plans. In E. A. Hanushek & D. W. Jorgenson. *Improving America's schools: The role of incentives* (pp. 75–96). Washington, DC: National Academy Press.

U.S. Department of Education, Office of Education Research and Improvement. (1998). *A national study of charter schools.* Washington, DC: U.S. Government Printing Office.

U.S. Department of Education, Office of the Under Secretary, Planning and Evaluation Service, Elementary and Secondary Division. (2000). *Evaluation of the public charter schools program: Year one evaluation report.* Washington, DC: U.S. Department of Education.

U.S. General Accounting Office (GAO). (1994). *Education reform: School-based management results in changes in instruction and budgeting.* Washington, DC: GAO.

Victoria Department of Education. (July 1999). *Principal class handbook.* Melbourne, Victoria, Australia: Author.

Wasley, P. A. (2000). Foreword. In B. L. Whitford & K. Jones, *Accountability, assessment, and teacher commitment: Lessons from Kentucky's reform efforts* (pp. xi–xiii). Albany: State University of New York Press.

Whitford, B. L., & Jones, K. (2000). *Accountability, assessment, and teacher commitment: Lessons from Kentucky's reform efforts.* Albany: State University of New York Press.

Whitty, G. (1994). Consumer rights versus citizen rights in contemporary education policy. Paper presented to a conference on "Education, Democracy and Reform," at the University of Auckland, Auckland, New Zealand, August 13–14.

Wohlstetter, P., & Buffett, T. M. (1992). Promoting school-based management: Are dollars decentralized too? In A. R. Odden (Ed.), *Rethinking school finance: An agenda for the 1990s* (pp. 128–165). San Francisco, CA: Jossey-Bass.

Wohlstetter, P., & Mohrman, S. A. (1994). School-based management: Promise and process. *CPRE Finance Briefs*, December.

Wohlstetter, P., & Van Kirk, A. (1996). Redefining school-based budgeting for high involvement. In L. O. Picus & J. L. Wattenbarger, (Eds.), *Where does the money go? Resource allocation in elementary and secondary schools* (pp. 212–235). Thousand Oaks, CA: Corwin.

Wohlstetter, P., Smyer, R., & Mohrman, S. A. (1994). New boundaries for school-based management: The high-involvement model. *Educational Evaluation and Policy Analysis, 16*, 268–286.

Wong, K. K. (2001). Integrated governance in Chicago and Birmingham (UK). In M. C. Wang & H. J. Walberg, *School choice or best systems: What improves education?* (pp. 161–212). Mahwah, NJ: Erlbaum.

chapter **15**

PRIVATIZATION AND FAMILY CHOICE OF SCHOOLING

Consumer Sovereignty

Issues and Questions

- *Achieving High Standards with Equity and Efficiency*: How likely is it that a policy of choice would lead to general improvement in school quality? How would it improve efficiency?

- *Definition of Family Choice of Schooling*: What is meant by the term *family choice of schooling*? Why is it being considered as a possible reform of education governance? How are school choice plans related to other proposals for systemic education reform?

- *Relationships Between Choice and Student Achievement*: How do the effectiveness and efficiency of schools in the private and public sectors compare?

- *Criteria Parents Use in Choosing Schools*: What criteria do parents use in choosing schools? Are there any relationships between *these* criteria used and socio-economic status and/or ethnicity? Would a policy of choice lead to greater social stratification among schools?

- *Alternative Policies for Implementing Choice*: How well have policies of open enrollment worked in the United States and elsewhere? In what ways might education voucher plans be designed to protect equity considerations? How might schools with religious affiliation be included in a publicly funded choice plan? Should such schools be included if they could be?

School choice is the last, and potentially the most radical, of the reforms we examine that are designed to change the incentives that shape public school fiscal policy and performance. Whereas school-based decision making (SBDM) empowers the profession (and possibly parents and other community members) to design and operate schools according to their best judgment, school choice empowers parents to select those schools that most closely match their family values and expectations. SBDM, by itself, still leaves the traditional institutions of democratic control intact. School choice challenges even these.

For no issue do the values of liberty, efficiency, and economic growth on the one hand, and equity and fraternity on the other, come into sharper conflict than for the issue of family choice of schooling. Arguments raised in the debate over policies of choice can be divided into three major groups: political, economic, and educational contexts directed toward school improvement; an important philosophical and moral subtext about values, identity, and freedom; and the sociocultural impact on schools exerted by the voluntary association of parents and others through school choice.

School choice is seen as a means of increasing the influence of the "consumers" of educational services over what goes on in schools and reducing the control of government, professional administrators, and educators. The major objectives of school choice include

- Providing affordable options among desirable schools to those who do not currently enjoy such options
- Enhancing the efficiency of the education enterprise by improving student achievement at little or no increase in expense
- Accommodating cultural pluralism and diversity in values and philosophies

Referring to the schools she founded in New York City's District Four, Deborah Meier (1995) wrote, "It would have been impossible to create these successful experiments without choice. Choice was a necessary prerequisite—not an end in itself, but a tool for effecting change" (p. 93). She also noted that choice may be the only way to create schools that can experiment with radically new pedagogical practices. The most efficient strategy for rapid change is undercutting the natural layers of resistance—going with the willing and the able and not trying to bludgeon people into accepting changes for which they may not be ready.

Critics of choice fear that it will weaken the social cohesion of communities and increase ethnic and class polarization. When choice options include private schools, there is concern that support of public schools will be reduced and their quality harmed. When those private schools have religious associations, constitutional concerns are raised. Critics claim that choices will be made mostly by privileged persons and that popular schools will begin to choose students, leading to greater stratification of students according to socioeconomic characteristics and academic ability. Rather than promoting innovation, critics believe that choice will make school leaders more conservative and tempt them to tailor their curriculum to ensuring a dependable clientele.

About 12 percent of American children are being educated outside the public sector, at the choice of their parents and at the parents' expense. The middle class and more affluent people frequently consider the quality of the public schools in selecting a place of residence. Within a school district, however, public officials typically assign children to schools. For growing numbers, a degree of discretion is being allowed within the public sector. Where they exist, choice structures are of three basic types: choice among public schools within district of residence, choice among public schools within the state (including charter schools), and choice among public and private schools.

In this chapter, we begin by examining the different political and organizational environments found in the public and private sectors and how these environments have differential effects in shaping school organizations and their effectiveness. We then describe the nature of existing choice policies and review studies of possible links between student achievement and choice. We assess whether criteria used by parents in selecting schools are likely to enhance efficiency in the schooling system and/or encourage greater inequities. The implications of extending public funding to private and religious schools via vouchers are studied through the experiences of other nations and of some cities in the United States. Finally, we bring together the arguments and evidence concerning decentralized administration of schools and choice and show the need for systemic reform that combines school-based decision making and choice with social controls such as a required core curriculum, standards, and assessments.

REDEFINING PUBLIC EDUCATION

Reaching a new settlement on the nature of public education is one of the defining projects for education in the early years of the twenty-first century. The central issue is the role of government and the concept of "public good." For more than a century, public education has been synonymous with public control, public funding, public ownership and public delivery, with *public* represented by *government* in this prescription. This view is now being actively challenged.

The conceptual model of the political–economic system of education policy development presented in Chapter 1 (Figure 1.3) places the initiative for making decisions about education with three broad groups: individuals, families, and communities; the educating profession; and society at large. Venues of decision making are government, the market, and the family. Natural tensions arise among these three groups. To the extent that families make school choice decisions through the market, individuals can maximize their personal aspi-

rations according to value preferences within the limits of their economic resources. However, personal resources are not evenly distributed, and this creates a problem of equity. Professionals are free to provide or withhold services and to determine the nature of those services in a free-market setting, which compounds the equity problem. But when decisions are made through the political process (i.e., government) individuals and groups of varying value orientations must negotiate a single solution, and their value preferences are likely to be compromised in the process.

In this section, we examine arguments for allowing parents greater choice in selecting schooling options for their children, and greater involvement in the schooling process. These arguments are presented in three subsections, wherein we consider sociocultural effects, democratic versus market control effects, and the effects of competition on the overall quality of schooling.

Sociocultural Considerations

Several authors have written about the bifurcation of social space between the personal and the collective. Tonnies (1940) referred to Gemeinschaft and Gesellschaft; Litwak, and Szelenyi (1969) to primary and secondary groups, and Coleman (1990) to primordial institutions and corporate actors. The personal is characterized by simple relationships between individuals within families and friendships. Actions are governed by love, understanding, and custom. The relationships between individuals are self-sustaining and become building blocks in forming a natural social environment of community (Brown, 1998). The collective space involves calculated relationships in which all things, including people, are seen as means to ends; thus contracts are based on results alone. Collective institutions are wholly instrumental and do not require binary personal obligations and expectations as mechanisms for social success. The traditional public school falls into this latter classification.

Brown (1998) identified two themes that writers stress about these two spaces. The first theme is the extreme tension between the two realms of social interaction and their outright incompatibility. The other is that over the past 500 years, modern corporate actors have gained near supremacy over primordial institutions. According to Hewitt (1989, p. 119), "modern society has disrupted, transformed, and in many cases simply destroyed the organic communities of the past, but it has not eliminated those human tendencies that were satisfied within those communities."

A reaction to the domination of corporate actors—and of government in particular—has set in. Some analysts perceive that government is one of the greatest barriers to systemic reform of education (see, for example, Danzberger, 1992). There is a growing appreciation of the importance of primordial relationships in the education of children.

The Kettering Foundation's study "Is There a Public for Public Schools?" (Mathews, 1996) warned that public schools in the United States are becoming dangerously disconnected from the public to the point where the public school system as we have known it may not survive. In a commentary on that report, Mathews (1997) wrote,

> What do site-based management programs, vouchers, charter schools, home schools, private schools, and state takeovers of "bankrupt" systems have in common? They all have to do with control of education. There are evidently a great many people who don't believe that the public schools are responsive to their concerns. So they are creating their own schools, trying to take back the schools, or putting someone in charge who will make schools respond to their priorities. (p. 741)

Mathews argued that restoring legitimacy to the public school system will require educators to see the public in a new light.

Enhancing the power of primordial actors in the control and operation of schools is expected to transform their nature. Brown (1998) found that extensive use of primordial actors ultimately affects the climate and organization of the school itself. Being dependent directly on parental and community contributions causes schools to become a collectivity with a shared ethos, informal and enduring social relationships, and diffuse roles. Or, in the words of Coleman and Hoffer (1987, p. 3), such a school is "an extension of the family, reinforcing the family's values. . . . The school is, in this orientation, an efficient means for transmitting the culture of the community from the older generation to the younger."

On the other hand, Brown (1998) characterized the typical public school as a bureaucratic environment where there is

> a distinct division of adult labour, governance by rules, and affectively neutral treatment of students. The bureaucratic school has a relatively clear hierarchy of control, and boundaries that are not difficult to define. Teachers are seen to have universalistic expectations of children; achievement and growth are valued highly. (p. 92)

Hence, public schools in the absence of primordial influence have been organized as state agents to be standardized and impartial and to have special knowledge to impart to students. As social instruments, they serve the interests of the larger society, not necessarily those of the parent. When parents (and other potential lay participants) are kept at a distance, teachers and parents may become natural adversaries as a consequence of their divergent interests regarding the child (Waller, 1932; Lortie, 1975).

Coleman (1990) noted that the shift from primordial institutions to corporate structures has led to a change in incentives as well:

> [P]rimordial social organization [generates] the incentive structure that brings into being actions on behalf of another, norms, trustworthiness, and

other components of social capital. The constructed social organization purposively created by governments and other modern corporate actors undermines that existing incentive structure (by encouraging free riding) and does not generate a comparable replacement. . . . Incentives (for example, the incentive to care for particular others) are supplied through extrinsic means, ordinarily a wage payment for professional services (for example, those of a teacher, nurse, or day care attendant). The knowledge of how to use these intrinsic rewards to bring about interest in, attention to, and care for others is weak. (Coleman, 1990, pp. 653–654)

Coleman suggested that the interests of children may be better served by primordial institutions than by modern corporate actors because of their differences in social structure. One consequence of the dominance of space by modern corporate actors has been the depletion of social capital for children in schools.

Sarason (1994) invoked the "political principle" in justifying the broadened participation of primordial groups in education decision making: "[W]hen you are going to be affected, directly or indirectly, by a decision, you should be in *some* relationship to the decision making process" (p. 7). Coons and Sugarman (1978) justified the involvement of primordial groups in schools by using the principle of *subsidiarity*. This principle holds that responsibility for dependent individuals is best placed with the smaller and more intimate community to which the individual belongs rather than with larger and more anonymous ones.

> [A] small community is more likely to listen to and respect constituent voices, to know individual interests, and to be motivated to serve them—particularly when it is so structured that all members are affected by its decisions about any member. Subsidiarity represents the impulse to preserve individualistic values within a collective. (Coons and Sugarman, 1978, p. 50)

Deciding for a child should always involve the voice of the child expressed within a community that is knowledgeable and caring about the child. The caring concern can stem from personal concern or mutual self-interest. The combination of the two is normally the ideal.

Adjusting the balance of power over education between cooperate and primordial actors requires the redesign of the governance structure for schooling. Society, through government, has basic interests in the quality and content of the education of its citizens. But so do parents and the educating profession. The competing concerns of society, parents, and educators must be recognized and accommodated. Further, meeting societal interests in education can be accomplished in less intrusive ways—and probably in more effective and efficient ways—than having government own and operate schools.

Democratic Control Versus Market Control

McAdams (1999), writing as a Houston school board member, observed that "Urban school reform is almost impossible because urban schools are under direct democratic control. Schools are in the middle of the political arena. In urban America, schools are battlegrounds for competing values, political power, contracts, and jobs" (p. 129). A decade earlier, Chubb and Moe (1990) also blamed "direct democratic control" (p. 2) for the poor performance of public schools. In their study of politics, markets, and American schools, they contrast the differences between the institutional environments in which public and private schools function and the differences those environments make in the schools' organizational cultures and effectiveness.

The public school environment is characterized by politics, hierarchy, and authority, whereas the private school environment is characterized by markets, competition, and volunteerism (Chubb and Moe, 1990, 1985). These authors described public schools as bureaucratic and political and pointed out that democracy (or any form of government) is essentially coercive, giving those in public authority power to impose their policies on all and to extract resources from all to finance these policies. In the market, or choice, setting, individuals are free to enter into voluntary exchanges as they see fit. Effective authority within market settings is radically decentralized.

Chubb and Moe (1985) concluded that the external environment in which public school principals work placed complex and conflicting expectations on them:

> Public schools relative to private, live in environments that are complex, demanding, powerful, constraining, and uncooperative. As a result, their policies, procedures, and personnel are more likely to be imposed from the outside. Public principals make the best of this environment by blending two roles, the middle manager and the politician. Like the middle manager, he consolidates whatever power is given him and guards the school's few prerogatives against the influence of a staff over which he has inadequate control. In the same role he emphasizes efficient administration as a safe way to please the administrative hierarchy of which he is a part. But the principal must also deal with a more complex and less friendly environment than the private principal—an environment that is politicized by school boards, state politicians, superintendents, local communities, and last but not least, parents. To do so, he plays the role of a politician, campaigning for the support of his school from a host of sometimes hostile constituencies. (p. 41)

The sources of signals to which private school principals must respond are clear; they are the school clients and the school trustees. The sources of signals to which public school principals must respond are varied, and the messages are frequently conflicting and ambiguous, which makes coherent response difficult.

These differences in organizational environments are reflected in the attitudes and behaviors of those working in public and private schools and, ultimately, in the effectiveness of their organizations. Because of the stronger influences of outside authority on public schools

than on private schools, public school personnel have less freedom in choosing how to respond to their more difficult environments; they are more constrained by formal rules and regulations and by informal norms than are private school personnel. Chubb and Moe (1985) were surprised, however, that within the private school sector, the external influence on Catholic schools was even less than that experienced by independent private schools. This was surprising because unlike other private schools, Catholic schools are part of a rather substantial hierarchy. This last finding supported their conclusion that bureaucracy need not be the stultifying force it often becomes in the public sector.

Among their other findings, teachers in private schools rated their principals as better all-around leaders than did teachers in public schools. Private school principals were also rated by their teachers as being more helpful than were their counterparts in the public sector. Further, private school teachers indicated that the goals of their schools were clearer and more effectively communicated by the principal than did public school teachers. Teachers in private schools were also more likely to rate their principals as encouraging, supportive, and reinforcing. "Private school principals are likely to be in a position to lead their organizations. They may not succeed, but they should have the tools and the flexibility to do what leaders need to do. Public school principals, on the other hand, are systematically denied much of what it takes to lead" (Chubb & Moe, 1990, p. 56).

These investigators also found that private schools delegate significantly more discretion to their teachers and are more likely to involve them in school-level policy decisions than are public schools. Private schools seemed to do a better job of relieving teachers of routine tasks and paperwork. There was a higher level of collegiality among private school staff; teachers were more likely to know what their colleagues were teaching and to coordinate the content of their courses. Private school teachers spent more time meeting to discuss curriculum and students and observing each other's classes. Private school teachers felt that they had more influence over school policies governing student behavior, pupil assignment to classes, curriculum, and in-service programs. Within their classrooms, private school teachers felt that they had more control over text selection, course content, teaching techniques, and student discipline. Private school teachers even felt that they had more influence over hiring and firing practices than did public school teachers.

Of all the potential barriers to hiring excellent teachers, not one barrier was rated higher by private school principals than by their public school counterparts. Public school principals regarded "central office control" and "excessive transfers from other schools" as particularly onerous. They also faced substantially greater obstacles in dismissing teachers for poor performance than did private school principals. The complexity of formal dismissal procedures was the highest barrier to firing cited by public school principals. For private school principals, it was "a personal reluctance to fire."

Public school pupils were less likely than students in private schools to be familiar with school policy. Public school students also regarded their school policies as less fair and effective. Parents were found to be much more involved and cooperative in private schools. In public schools, parents were more likely to be required to communicate with school officials through formal channels, and school officials had less flexibility in addressing reasonable grievances of parents.

Chubb and Moe (1990) hypothesized, however, that the differences these environments make for school organization may not be due entirely, or even primarily, to qualities that are inherently public or private. Rather, they suggested that organizational differences may derive from environmental characteristics such as control, constraint, and complexity that vary among school environments regardless of sector. Thus they concluded that, through organizational redesign, the strengths characteristic of schools in one sector may be incorporated into schools in the other sector. They proposed a radical choice system that would free public schools from the disabling constraints imposed by an unyielding bureaucracy and democratic control.

Chubb and Moe's findings about Catholic schools are of particular interest and worthy of further treatment. Coleman and Hoffer (1987) conducted a study of the impact of communities on public and private high schools. (Chubb and Moe's study was partially based on the Coleman/Hoffer database.) Like Chubb and Moe, they found that student achievement was higher in private schools than in public schools, even when statistical controls were imposed for differences in student backgrounds. This aspect of both studies was hotly debated, and the correctness of the methodologies used was challenged. Nevertheless, none of the challengers found public school achievement to be superior to that in private schools. The argument was over the magnitude of the private school advantage and whether it was significant from a policy perspective (Haertel, 1987). This is particularly meaningful with respect to Catholic schools because they succeeded in obtaining performance levels at least comparable to those of their public school counterparts, despite the fact that their classes were larger, their teachers held fewer advanced degrees and were less likely to be state-certified, resources were more limited, and per-pupil costs were far smaller than those characteristic of public high schools. As a result, Catholic high schools could be said to be functioning, on average, at greater economic efficiency than public high schools (Hoffer, Greeley, & Coleman, 1987).

Hoffer, Greeley, and Coleman (1987) attributed the success of Catholic schools to their higher demands on students. These schools placed larger proportions of their students in the academic track, including many who would be relegated to general or vocational tracks in public high schools. Catholic high schools also demanded more course work, more advanced course work, and better discipline. The researchers found that at-risk pupils did especially well in Catholic schools and that the productive characteristics of this school climate could be successfully replicated in public schools:

> Catholic schools are especially beneficial to the least advantaged students: minorities, poor, and those whose initial achievement is low. For these students, the lack of structure, demands, and expectations found in many public schools is especially harmful. *Our analyses show that those public schools which make the same demands as found in the average Catholic school produce comparable achievement.* (p. 87, emphasis added)

The description of the average Catholic high school culture (verified for all private schools by Chubb and Moe, 1990) sounds very much like that characteristic of "effective" public schools and many of the whole-school reform models.

Coleman and Hoffer (1987) attributed the ability of Catholic high schools to make greater demands on their students to their greater "social capital." Social capital, which we discussed in Chapter 6 in the context of partnerships and volunteerism and earlier in this chapter in the context of primordial social organization, consists of the relationships between people. Social capital provides norms and sanctions that in turn "depend both on social relations and [on] the closure of networks created by these relations" (p. 222). The religious communities surrounding Catholic schools provide the social capital that is not found in most public and independent private schools today.

In a simpler time, according to Coleman and Hoffer, public schools were part of a functioning community. This is still the case in many rural areas where achievement tends to be unexpectedly high, given the relatively low average socioeconomic status of rural communities and the relatively low investment of economic resources in rural schools. But functioning communities in metropolitan areas, where most Americans live, are no longer based on residence as are most public school attendance boundaries; functioning communities have been replaced by value communities. Residential proximity is no longer the source of dense interaction in metropolitan areas, so the reference groups of public schools still organized around residential proximity are incapable of providing them with norms, sanctions, and networks in support of the schools' educational missions. To bring significant amounts of social capital to public schools, Coleman and Hoffer urged choice among schools built around value communities: "Policies which would bring about expansion of choice should contain provisions that encourage the growth of social structures that can provide the social capital important to a school" (p. 243).

In a similar vein, Bryk, Lee, and Smith (1990) pointed out that the voluntary nature of Catholic schools and their shared communal theology and values were central to their success—especially with at-risk children.

> In the case of Catholic schools, field research describes strong institutional norms directly linked to basic religious beliefs about the dignity of each person and a shared responsibility for advancing a just, caring society. Not surprisingly, the educational philosophy that derives from these ideals is well aligned with social equity aims. When such understandings meld to a coherent organizational structure, desirable academic and social consequences appear to result. (p. 191)

Bryk, Lee, and Smith observed that much of what happens in schools involves discretionary action. In the bureaucratic structure of public schooling, great effort is required to secure agreement on issues that are intrinsically judgmental. Under a choice system, the effort expended on fostering such agreements can be redirected to the actual work of the school. They also observed that the effectiveness of parochial schools, especially with respect to at-risk children, is not always realized in other private schools. Therefore, they doubt that market-driven schools would excel in the way that Catholic schools have. Walberg (1993), however, argued that self-interest can compel caring for others, as it has in psychiatry, nursing, and other serving professions and that there is little reason to believe that competition for pupils would not encourage a posture of caring when this is a characteristic sought by potential clients.

Effect of Competition on School Quality

The most important effect of a school choice policy may be not on the quality of the schools chosen (whether private, charter, magnet, or neighborhood), but, rather, on the quality of the schools not chosen and on the satisfaction of the client. When coupled with SBDM, a school choice policy opens up the possibility of better matches between schools and students. Schools would be free to tailor their programs toward particular learning styles and interests of students. Students could then select a school on the basis of their unique needs and preferences. This could happen within the public sector itself, without extending the policy to include private schools.

Proponents of choice argue that market competition will induce improvement in public schools and that innovation will induce replication. Opponents worry that choice will drain public schools of their best students, thereby reducing the positive influence of high-achieving peers. They are also concerned that parental pressure for improving the public schools will be reduced as the most motivated parents leave the system.

All 25,000 publicly funded schools in England and Wales, serving over eight million students, have been choice schools since 1988, and on a more limited basis, since World War II. A study by Gorard, Fitz, and Taylor (2001) on the impact of the 1988 reforms led them to conclude that the academic qualifications of students have improved and that socioeconomic stratification has declined since adoption of the policy. The percent of students receiving at least five "good" passes on the General Certificate of Secondary Education (GCSE), a form of mastery-level evaluation, increased from 26.9 percent in 1985, before the reforms, to 46.4 percent in 1998. It is not possible to attribute this rise in performance to the choice reform alone, because a number of other reforms were put into effect at the same time (see Chapters 1 and 14). However, the fact that comparable improvement did not occur in the elite private-sector schools, which administer the same examinations, strongly suggests that at least part of the increase can be attributed to market forces. "It is clear that state-funded schools have been catching up with fee paying schools at all levels of attainment" (p. 20). Recent figures confirm this trend (Howson, 2000). Gorard et al. (2001) concluded that the whole system is becoming more equitable in that improvements in attainment have resulted for highest and lowest achievers, ethnic groups, boys and girls, socioeconomic regions, and school sectors.

With respect to social stratification, Gorard et al. (2001) found that the national proportion of children officially designated as being "in poverty" who would need to change schools for there to be an equivalent number in each school declined steadily from 1989 through 1996. They offer, as a possible explanation of the slight increase since 1996, the enactment in 1998 of legislation that weakened the market forces in education by allowing local authorities to revert to establishing attendance boundaries for schools. They conclude that market reforms have worked in that they have allowed children of poor families to attend schools in areas where their families cannot afford to live. "What we have shown is not that choice is SES-free, but that it certainly is no worse, and probably a great deal better, than simply assigning children to their nearest school to be educated with similar children living in similar housing conditions" (p. 22).

Hoxby (1996) uses the Tiebout effect to postulate similar results for the United States should vouchers come to be widely used. Tiebout (1956) presented a theory for the existence of local governments. This theory argues that local governments permit people with similar tastes for public services to cluster together within jurisdictions. Variety in local government offers households arrays of public services that are significantly different in type and quality. Although there is generally little choice among schools within a district, in most metropolitan areas there is a substantial choice among school districts for those who can afford to exercise a choice. The Tiebout effect explains the capitalization of tax rates and quality of services in housing costs. People tend to move to another school district if, in their district, the school tax exceeds the value they perceive educational services to have. Thus the Tiebout process links marginal costs and marginal benefits of schooling so that, over time, the households within each school district have similar demands for schooling and all households consume the amount of schooling they desire.

[I]t is worth emphasizing that discussion of vouchers has been badly confused in the past because people often analyze them relative to a theoretical world in which the public schools are perfectly integrated with respect to income and human capital. Instead, they should be analyzed relative to our real world, where many people already live in quite homogeneous school districts and school finance cannot prevent people from sorting on the basis of their demand for human capital spillovers. Essentially, vouchers bring the forces of the Tiebout process to areas where it does not provide much discipline, such as in central cities. . . . Where the Tiebout process already functions strongly [as in most suburbs], vouchers could be almost irrelevant. (Hoxby, 1996, p. 69)

The Woessmann (2001) international study, which we reviewed in Chapter 12, found that student achievement was higher in the state schools of countries where there was strong competition from schools in the private sector. Most studies using United States data have found existing competition to have little if any effect on the performance of other schools (Goldhaber, 2001; Gill et al., 2001; Carnoy, 2000). There are a few exceptions, however. Minnesota has allowed statewide choice among public schools since 1987, subject to availability of space and desegregation regulations. About 2 percent of students have exercised their right to attend schools outside their district of residence. Funkhouser, Colopy, and Kelly (1994) interviewed school district administrators of districts losing large numbers of students and found that many were implementing innovative programs designed to attract students into the district. Massachusetts has an interdistrict choice policy similar to that of Minnesota. Armor and Peiser (1998) studied the Massachusetts policy and found that districts that lost students in the early years of the policy tended to stem the loss and become net receivers. The choice policy had little impact on the ethnic and racial distributions among school districts that were net senders or receivers of students. Goldhaber (2001) inferred from a review of these and other studies that districts appear to respond to the competitive threat of losing students and funding by initiating changes that make them more attractive to parents. He concluded further that relatively few students need to move before responses are forthcoming.

CURRENT CHOICE POLICIES AND PRACTICE

Whereas public schools are financed through taxation and are tuition-free, private schools depend primarily on tuition, donations, and volunteer or low-priced labor. Some public assistance is provided to students enrolled in private schools, which, to a small degree, facilitates the possibility for family choice in that sector. Many states provide public support of transportation, health services, testing and remedial services, and textbooks to children enrolled in private schools. Some services provided by federal aid to education, such as Title I, are available to private schools. In addition, governments provide assistance to not-for-profit private schools, sectarian and independent alike, through exemption from property taxation (see the discussion in Chapter 5). And as an incentive to private contributors, donations to not-for-profit private schools may be deducted from the contributor's taxable income. Students in school districts in Maine and Vermont that do not operate high schools have been able to choose among public and nonsectarian private schools at public expense since the middle of the nineteenth century.

Traditionally, parents have been able to choose between free public and tuition-supported private schools, but even this option was seriously challenged during the 1920s. In 1925 the U.S. Supreme Court, in its landmark decision in *Pierce* v. *Society of Sisters* (1925), ruled that the Constitution protected the right of private schools to exist as an alternative to public schools. In so doing, the Court recognized parents' right to direct the education and upbringing of their own children, foreclosing the possibility of a public monopoly. On the other hand, *Pierce* and other decisions permit reasonable regulation of private schooling by government, without requiring public subsidization of the choice of private schooling.

Without subsidization, schooling can become very expensive, forcing most parents out of the private school market. In the absence of public support, it is primarily religious groups that both have the financial capacity and are organized and motivated to sponsor non-government schooling that is a feasible option for sizable numbers of families. About 12 percent of elementary and secondary pupils have chosen private school options, and another 1 percent are schooled at home. About 80 percent of those enrolled in private schools are enrolled in schools with a religious affiliation

and about half of those attend Roman Catholic schools. The percentages in private schools and the percentages in schools with a religious affiliation have remained fairly stable over the years, but the nature of religious affiliation is rapidly changing from almost exclusively Catholic to a heterogeneous mixture of denominations.

At the federal level, until 1965, the issue of aid to private schools—or the lack of it—often led to the defeat of aid proposals for public schools. The Elementary and Secondary Education Act (ESEA) was the first federal program that required federally funded services be provided to elementary and secondary private school children (see Chapter 9). Contending interest groups reached a compromise over a child-benefit approach to federal aid. The resulting policy focused on educationally disadvantaged children wherever they were enrolled. Services that were provided on-site to children who were enrolled in private schools remained under public control and supervision. Subsequently, assurances were extended to make services purchased through federal funds equitably available to private school students for vocational education, bilingual education, education of children with disabilities, and instructional and library materials. Enactment of the Education Consolidation and Improvement Act in 1981 brought substantially greater support for programs serving private school children.

Within the public sector, there is also a degree of choice. The most widespread choice is selection of courses at the high school level. Large cities have traditionally offered specialty schools to the entire city school population. Magnet schools have often been instituted in school districts under order to end racial segregation. Other districts have permitted choice of schools within schools. A small number of districts allow choice among all public schools within the district. An extralegal means of exercising choice is selecting a public school in the process of selecting a place of residence.

Henig and Sugarman (1999) estimated that nearly 60 percent of parents have exercised some form of choice in placing their children in a school. In addition to those in private schools and home-schooled, another 1 percent are in charter schools. Choice within public schools is exercised by about 11 percent. An estimated 36 percent exercise residential choice. For many of these families who are already choosing, further choice options such as vouchers may not have any political appeal. Advocates of greater choice options, however, are particularly concerned about the estimated 41 percent who have not exercised a choice option. Many of these are poor and minority students served by inner-city schools of questionable quality.

Choice through Selecting Place of Residence

The most common vehicle of school choice in the public sector is choice through the selection of a residence. Through the Tiebout effect, described above, choice of residence becomes a middle ground between a free market and centralized governmental control. In metropolitan areas, this has meant that people with high demands for educational services have often clustered in specific—usually affluent—suburbs and that people with low demand and those who are unable to afford the cost of high levels of service, have clustered in central cities and other—usually blue-collar—suburbs.

In a random survey of the attitudes of Minnesota residents about educational choice, Darling-Hammond and Kirby (1988) found impressive evidence of the Tiebout effect. Households that had considered the quality of public schools in making residential decisions had a lower propensity for expressing interest in private schools, even with governmental subsidies. They felt that their educational needs were already well served by the public schools of the communities they had selected. Murnane (1986) also pointed to compelling evidence that families pay premiums for housing

in school districts with reputations for good schools.

Kutner, Sherman, and Williams (1986) reported on a survey of a national random sample of approximately 1,200 households with school-age children. About half of the parents indicated that the public schools their children would attend influenced their choice of a place to live. Eighteen percent said that it was the most important factor in their choice of residence.

The Balkanization of local government, and of school districts in particular, does advance libertarian objectives to a limited extent. But it also creates serious inequities and impedes realization of fraternal objectives. This phenomenon was illustrated in Table 11.2, which reflects data drawn from the New York City metropolitan area. Balkanization works to the advantage of rich and upper-middle-class households, because they have sufficient resources to choose a community whose array of services includes those that they most desire. Other affluent households with high educational demands may choose to live in a jurisdiction with low-quality public schools and send their children to high-quality private schools. Poor households do not have the wherewithal to exercise such options. Those among them with very strong desires for high-quality educational services might be able to afford to meet the cost of tuition for high-quality private schools by sacrificing in other areas such as housing and transportation and by taking on additional employment. However, attending a high-quality public school is out of their fiscal reach where the quality of educational services and their costs have been capitalized into housing prices.

Other Forms of Public School Choice

Choice Among Public Schools

More than half the states have passed laws permitting other forms of public school choice, and other states are considering such laws (Elam & Rose, 1995). In 1987 Minnesota established the first statewide plan permitting parents to enroll their children in virtually any public school district of their choice in the state (Nathan, 1989; OECD, 1994; Pearson, 1989). Since then, numerous other state legislatures have adopted some form of public school choice as statewide policy (Rothstein, 1993). For over a quarter of a century, Massachusetts has encouraged and financed interdistrict transfer of pupils to improve racial balance. In 1991 the state broadened its choice policy by enacting open-enrollment legislation permitting all schoolchildren to attend public schools outside their home districts. Similarly, St. Louis city and county school districts voluntarily exchange students to improve racial balance as part of a court-ordered desegregation plan. Voluntary integration plans also operate in the Rochester, New York; Hartford, Connecticut; Milwaukee; and Boston metropolitan areas, among others.

A number of large cities have developed open-enrollment plans within their districts, frequently for the purpose of improving racial and ethnic balance in schools. For generations, New York City has operated a variety of specialty schools (including the prestigious Bronx High School of Science) that draw their students from throughout the city. The Boston Latin School dates to colonial times. Boston also operates a universal form of public school enrollment choice (OECD, 1994) as an alternative to the forced busing imposed by the courts to remedy racial imbalances in the district. The Boston plan includes decentralized decision making and school-based management. At least a dozen other large cities have used a variety of choice plans to end racial segregation. One of the most successful is the magnet school program in Buffalo, New York.

District Four in New York City's East Harlem has received much attention for the academic success of its students and its open-enrollment policies (Fliegel & MacGuire, 1993; Meier, 1995; Bensman, 2000). The district serves a generally poor population with 80 percent of its 14,000 students eligible for free or reduced-cost lunch. Ninety-five percent of its students are from minority populations: Hispanics constitute the majority of the enrollment. Meier (1995) observed that choice was enacted as a means of attracting pupils to educational innovations generated by teachers and that it was the innovations that were directly responsible for the gains in achievement. The practice is spreading throughout the city and to other cities, such as Philadelphia and Chicago.

Tuition Tax Credits and Deductions

One approach to helping people pay private school tuition, rather than subsidizing the schools directly, is through tax credits and deductions. A tax credit reduces the amount of the tax (usually an income tax) owed, up to a specified sum. Tuition payments (or a percentage of them, depending on how the law is written) can be subtracted from the computed tax amount owed.

Tax deductions apply to income taxes exclusively and are not as favorable for qualifying taxpayers as are tax credits. Tax deductions, similar to those that allow homeowners to deduct property taxes on their place of residence, reduce the amount of taxable income on which the tax is computed. Thus the reduction in tax liability is only a percentage (the marginal tax rate) of tuition payments. Such deductions are allowed in Minnesota. In computing their state income tax liability, the Minnesota law allows parents with children in public and private schools to deduct, from their taxable income, educational expenses of up to $650 per elementary school child and of up to $1,000 per secondary school child. The expenses eligible for deduction include tuition, the cost of secular textbooks, transportation, and school supplies, and fees. With marginal tax rates in Minnesota ranging from 1.6 percent to 16 percent, the maximum reduction in tax liability per secondary school child ranges from nothing for nontaxpayers to $160. The Minnesota law has been reviewed at all levels of the court system and was upheld by the United States Supreme Court (*Mueller* v. *Allen*, 1983).

At the turn of the twenty-first century, tax credits or deductions for private school tuition were allowed in Arizona, Illinois, Iowa, and Minnesota. Since 1997, Arizona has also allowed a tax credit of up to $500 annually for donations to organizations that provide scholarships to private schools. Since 2001, Pennsylvania has allowed up to $20 million aggregate per year in tax credits for businesses that contribute to private voucher programs. The credits are limited to 90 percent of the amount contributed, up to $100,000 per business. The vouchers are limited to students whose families have annual incomes below $50,000 plus $10,000 per child. The 2001 federal tax cuts expanded education savings accounts (ESAs), which were originally limited to higher-education tuition, to include K–12 tuition. The law permits parents to place up to $2,000 per year in ESAs that earn interest tax-free as long as these accounts are used for the intended purpose.

Opponents of tax credits and deductions argue that the benefits flow disproportionately to high-income persons and to religious organizations. To qualify for either a credit or a deduction, a person has to incur a tax liability and file a return. Thus the very poorest do not benefit. Poor parents could be brought into a tax credit scheme through refundability provisions—that is, the government would pay the individual the amount of the credit. This would still require the filing of a tax return, however. Proposals usually contain civil rights guarantees based on school eligibility requirements. Credits and deductions would be allowed only for expenditures incurred in schools that had received governmental approval.

EDUCATION VOUCHERS

An education voucher is an entitlement extended to an individual by a government permitting that individual to receive educational services up to the maximum dollar amount specified. The voucher can normally be redeemed according to the preference of the holder at any institution or enterprise approved by the granting agency. According to Guthrie, Garms, and Pierce (1988),

> Regardless of operating details, voucher plans possess a common fundamental principle. Their intent is to enfranchise households as the basic decision-making unit. Vouchers do not eliminate government interest in education. Rather, voucher plans retain the prospect of government responsibility for financing and otherwise maintaining a marketplace of education providers, which would require regulation. (p. 356)

The differences between the public and private sectors in making decisions about resource allocation were described in Chapter 2. In the private sector, each household can maximize its satisfaction within the amount of purchasing power it has, because multiple decisions are allowed among consumers. In the public sector, however, a single decision is generally required. This decision tends to reflect the opinion of the average voter, making it difficult for households that deviate substantially from the average to match their tastes optimally with their resources.

> At an abstract level, educational vouchers represent an approach to the provision of a collective good that challenges the dominant public goods approach to American education. The market model on which vouchers are based assumes a set of private choices by families and providers, which in the extreme would be unfettered by government interference or regulation. As such, it deviates considerably from the public provision of education—controlled democratically and heavily regulated by local, state, and federal rules, statutes, and constitutional provisions. It also as-

sumes a very different approach to accountability, with public schools held accountable through external promulgation and review of results, while the market model bases accountability on consumer (family) satisfaction. (Witte, 1998)

Education vouchers dramatically enhance the power of parents relative to society and the educating profession as portrayed in the sociopolitical model in Figure 1.3. The government's (or society's) point of contact in schooling is shifted from the school to the family (Loveless, 1998). In a money-follows-the-child environment, public revenues enter the educational system via decisions made by parents instead of bureaucrats. Customer satisfaction becomes the ultimate criterion.

The Political History of the Vouchers Movement

Vouchers have initiated what Moe (2001) calls *the new politics of education*: "an ongoing political realignment in which the urban poor, joined by conservatives, do battle against their traditional allies, who are bound to defend the existing system" (p. 68). Poor and minority people are among the strongest supporters of educational vouchers and choice. More generally, support of vouchers is negatively related to income and education. School choice has become a political movement that crosses racial, religious, economic, moral, and ideological lines (Morken & Formicola, 1999)—and vouchers are its most hotly contested aspect. Advocates of education vouchers include pro-market libertarians, business, the Christian right, and the Catholic Church (Kennedy, 2001). Opposing vouchers are the education establishment, civil libertarians, church–state separationists, and African American organizations (although there is substantial support of school choice among individual African Americans (Reid, 2001)).

Milwaukee became the first site for K–12 vouchers in the United States in 1991 after a bruising battle led by a coalition headed by Polly Williams, a Democratic state legislator and former welfare recipient, and Republican Governor Tommy Thompson. Williams's initial voucher efforts were staunchly opposed by her traditional allies: Democratic politicians, the National Association for the Advancement of Colored People, and the educational establishment. Therefore, she turned instead to Republicans, conservatives, and business groups. Similarly, in Cleveland in 1995, Fanny Lewis, a black Democrat, led the fight in the Ohio legislature in coalition with Governor George Voinovich and other Republicans.

The struggle that preceded these two voucher victories made their proponents realize that getting coherent plans through the political process would be extraordinarily difficult because of the intensity of opposition to choice and vouchers among the poor's traditional allies. Thus they have sought resources from the private sector through philanthropy. This has enabled them to bring about immediate change on their own terms. Also, the private voucher plans offer prototypes that analysts can study and the public can observe (Moe, 2001). The political conflicts over vouchers are classic examples of coalition building as described by group theory (Chapter 2) as well as elite theory.

The first private voucher initiative was backed by J. Patrick Rooney, CEO of the Golden Rule Life Insurance Company in Indianapolis, in 1991 following the defeat of a voucher proposal in the Indiana legislature. The Golden Rule program was built around five elements: (1) Vouchers would be half the receiving school's tuition (to a ceiling amount) with parents responsible for the rest. (2) Only low-income children would be eligible, including those already attending private schools. (3) Vouchers could be used in religious as well as independent private schools. (4) Vouchers would be granted on a first-come-first-served basis. (5) There would be no academic or other qualifications beyond those set by the school to which application was being made. These elements were used for several of the voucher plans to follow in other cities, although the first-come-first-served element yielded to lottery procedures as the number of vouchers desired came to exceed the number of vouchers available many times over. A few of the later plans also dropped the requirement that matching funds by provided by the parent.

The San Antonio voucher program was the second to be instituted. It was funded by grants from prominent businesspeople of the city who established the Children's Educational Opportunity Foundation (CEO). With a $2 million grant in 1994 from the Walton Family Foundation, the San Antonio group set up a national coordinating agency, CEO America, to provide institutional leadership for the voucher movement. It serves as an umbrella and clearinghouse for existing voucher programs. It also assists in creating new programs and expanding existing ones through $50,000 challenge grants (Moe, 2001).

In the summer of 1998, the Children's Scholarship Fund (CSF) was established by Theodore Forstmann and John Walton with a contribution of $100 million and was supplemented almost immediately with matching local contributions of $70 million (Archer, 1998). In 1999, CSF carried out a lottery in which 40,000 low-income children were selected to be recipients of scholarships to be used in cities across the country. There were over one million applicants for the available awards (Hartocollis, 1999).

By the year 2000, private voucher plans were operating in 41 cities, involving over 50,000 children. Although most media attention has focused on the public voucher programs in Milwaukee and Cleveland, the major action has been quietly growing in the private sector. There, a variety of models have been piloted, and much has been learned from the accompanying evaluations. Nevertheless, publicly funded vouchers are the ultimate goal of the private voucher strategy. In the next section we look at the public voucher programs.

Public Voucher Programs

At the time of this book's publication, there were three publicly funded voucher programs in the United States: Milwaukee, Cleveland, and the state of Florida. Let's look at each of these in turn.

Milwaukee

Milwaukee launched the first publicly financed private school voucher program in the country. Under the program enacted by the Wisconsin legislature in 1990, up to 950 (raised to 1,500 in 1993) low-income Milwaukee families were eligible for state tuition grants equivalent to the per-pupil aid for the Milwaukee Public Schools (MPS) (about $5,550 in 2001) to send their children to any private, nonreligious school. *Low-income* was defined as not exceeding 1.75 times the nationally defined poverty line. Poor children already enrolled in private schools or in districts other than MPS were not eligible. Participating schools could not receive the subsidy for more than 49 percent (raised to 65 percent in 1993) of their students and were required to use random selection to admit students if requests for admission exceeded available space. A 1990 court ruling exempted the private schools from having to admit children with disabilities.

In 1995, legislation was passed that greatly opened up the program and expanded participation. Religious schools were allowed to participate. Children in grades K–3 in private schools became eligible for vouchers. The maximum number of children allowed to take part in the program was increased tenfold to 15,000. All children (up from 65 percent) in a receiving school could be voucher children, a provision that greatly facilitated the establishment of start-up schools. Data collection and evaluations were dropped; however, the Wisconsin

Legislative Audit Bureau was required to file a report in the year 2000. In 2001, approximately 10,000 students participated in the program, 70 percent of whom were enrolled in religious schools.

Having lost in the legislature, voucher opponents challenged the constitutionality of the 1995 law in state court, arguing, among other things, that it violated the separation of church and state. Implementation was delayed until a decision could be rendered. The plaintiffs were successful in the lower courts, but in 1998, the Wisconsin Supreme Court ruled that the law did not violate the establishment issue, largely because the pivotal decisions about which schools get public support are made by parents, not government, and because the program takes a neutral stance between religious and secular schools, as well as among schools of different religions (Moe, 2001). The plaintiffs appealed the decision to the U.S. Supreme Court, which declined to hear the case, allowing the Wisconsin court decision to stand.

Cleveland

The Cleveland voucher program began operating in 1996 for children in grades K–8. The scholarship covers a maximum of 90 percent of private secular and sectarian school tuition, up to $2,250. Parents are required to make up the difference in tuition. Smaller scholarships are available for higher-income families. Scholarship recipients are selected by lottery, with priority given to low-income families. In 2001 approximately 96 percent of the more than 4,000 children receiving vouchers were enrolled in schools with a religious affiliation (Walsh, 2001).

The law was challenged in Ohio state courts in 1996 by a coalition of teachers unions and civil liberties groups. In 1999 the Ohio Supreme Court invalidated the law on technical grounds but held that the inclusion of religious schools did not violate the federal constitutional prohibition against a government establishment of religion. The state leg-islature quickly corrected the technical flaws in the law, and its implementation continued unabated. The plaintiffs then challenged the law in federal district court, where the judge ruled in late 1999 that the program was in violation of the establishment clause because the vast majority of participating private schools were religious. The federal judge refused to allow new students to enter the program in the fall of 1999 (although school was about to begin when the decision was rendered). The U.S. Supreme Court intervened and blocked the judge's injunction, thereby permitting the program to continue through the appeal process. In September 2001, the U.S. Supreme Court agreed to hear the case (Walsh, 2001).

Florida

Florida's Opportunity Scholarship Program, enacted in 1999, is the first statewide voucher program. It is an integral part of the state's accountability act, which grades all schools each year on students' academic progress. Any student attending a public school that receives failing grades for any two years out of four is eligible for a voucher of approximately $4,000 to attend other public or private schools, including religious schools. Receiving schools cannot charge tuition in addition to the voucher amount. Two schools have met the failure criteria since enactment, enabling 136 students to exercise the voucher option. Private schools were selected by 58 of those students, and 78 transferred to other public schools.

Florida has another voucher program, also enacted in 1999. This program provides vouchers for children with disabilities to attend private schools or out-of-district public schools. Approximately 4,000 students were expected to participate in this program in 2001–2002.

These voucher programs have also faced court challenges to block their implementation. A lower court has found them to be in violation of the Florida state constitution's education clause requiring a public education system for Florida citizens. In 1998, Florida voters had adopted new wording for that clause, which contains some of the strongest and unambiguous language of any state constitution, declaring that it is "a paramount duty of the state to make adequate provision for the education of all children. . . . this provision shall be made by law for a uniform, efficient, safe, secure, and high quality system of free public schools that allows students to obtain a high quality education. . . ." Although religious schools are involved, the programs were not held unconstitutional on the establishment issue. The case is being appealed.

Evaluations of Voucher Programs

Most of the evidence on the effect of vouchers comes from evaluations of the privately funded programs. The Milwaukee voucher program has been studied the most among the publicly financed schemes, but those studies are limited in number and highly contested.

Private Voucher Programs

Findings about the impact of voucher programs on student achievement, relative to the achievement of children attending public schools, are not robust. There is some support of a modest benefit for African American students from low-income families after one or two years in voucher schools (Myers et al., 2000; Howell et al., 2000; Greene, 2000). There is little evidence of any effect on academic achievement for children of other racial or ethnic groups, however.

The demand for participation in voucher programs that target low-income families is generally strong, exceeding the supply of scholarships in most instances (Gill et al., 2001; Moe, 2001). The best evidence of the ability for the private sector to respond to this demand comes from Milwaukee; in the 1998–1999 school year, nearly one-third of the private schools participating in that program had been founded since its beginning in 1991 (Wisconsin Legislative Audit Bureau, 2000). There is strong evidence that once they are in a program, parents are happy with their schools of choice (Howell & Peterson, 2000; Wolf, Howell & Peterson, 2000; Weinschrott & Kilgore, 1998).

Programs designed with low-income qualifications have succeeded in placing low-income, low-achieving, and minority children in voucher schools, although children with disabilities tend to be underrepresented (Metcalf, 1999; Peterson, 1998; Peterson, Myers & Howell, 2000; Wisconsin Legislative Audit Bureau, 2000). There is little information on the numbers of children with disabilities participating in private voucher programs. Voucher schools in Milwaukee and Cleveland are not required to serve such children. Gill et al. (2001) conclude that ensuring participation by children with disabilities is a real challenge for voucher programs.

In general, there is little evidence that targeted voucher plans "cream" better students from public schools. The only contrary evidence is that although they are poor, voucher parents tend to have somewhat higher levels of education than others at comparable income levels. In highly segregated communities, targeted voucher programs appear modestly to increase racial integration in that minority children are placed in voucher schools without reducing integration in public schools (Gill et al, 2001).

Families whose children are currently in low-performing public schools and are most in need of educational alternatives are the strongest advocates of vouchers (Gill et al., 2001). The 1999 *Phi Delta Kappan* poll found that their strongest support was among minorities and from parents whose children were not doing well in public schools (Rose & Gallop, 1999). Similar results were obtained in a poll conducted by the Joint Center for Political and Economic Studies, in which 71 percent of African American parents supported vouchers (Bositis, 1999). The overwhelming defeats of voucher initiatives in California and Michigan, however, suggest that the minorities are in the minority on this issue also.

Milwaukee

The Wisconsin legislature commissioned a five-year evaluation of the Milwaukee program that was conducted by John Witte, a professor of political science at the University of Wisconsin, who had sole access to the data from 1991 to 1994. As of this printing, all published analyses of the MPS data have been based on the limited program prior to its expansion in 1995. Because of the constraints then in place, very few private schools participated in the program, and the majority of the voucher students were in only three schools. Moe (2001) criticizes the database as being inadequate for evaluating the effects of vouchers. Nevertheless, much attention has been given to the analyses of Witte and to those of Peterson, a professor of political science at Harvard who subsequently gained access to the data.

Witte (1998) found that despite the limited number of participating schools (six in 1990 and eleven in 1992, out of twenty-three secular private schools in the city), the supply of spaces always exceeded demand. He also points to a competing private voucher program, Partners Advancing Values in Education (PAVE) (Moe, 2001), that reduced demand for public vouchers and participation by private schools by making scholarships available to all private schools, including religious ones. Applicant students and enrollees were clearly from very low-income families and were primarily black or Hispanic. Their achievement was lower than that of other low-income MPS students and well below national averages. However, "choice mothers" reported considerably more education than did the control group of "MPS mothers" and were more likely to be engaged in school and community activities; choice families tended to be smaller. "Choice parents" rated their previous public school much less favorably than did the MPS control. Their dis-

satisfaction lay, primarily, with the quality of education and discipline. The reasons given for participating in the choice program were educational quality (89 percent), teaching approach and style (86 percent), discipline (75 percent), general educational atmosphere (74 percent), and classroom size (72 percent).

Witte (1998) identified strong parental satisfaction with the voucher school (especially in contrast to the prior public school) as one of the beneficial outcomes. Other benefits identified were increased parental participation and some benefits to the private schools. With respect to achievement, however, Witte found no substantial difference between voucher and control MPS students over the five-year period. After they gained access to the data following legal and informal moves (Moe, 2001), Peterson and others (Peterson, Greene & Noyes, 1996; Greene, Peterson, & Du, 1998) challenged Witte's conclusions about achievement by questioning the appropriateness of his statistical procedures. Using what the challengers believed to be a more appropriate statistical model, Witte found growth in reading and mathematics achievement by voucher students to be significantly higher that the MPS reference group. Witte (1998) staunchly defended his research procedures.

Alternative Voucher Plan Designs

All voucher programs are not the same. Some proposals facilitate free-market competition and are likely to further segregation of students along racial, ethnic, achievement, and socioeconomic lines. Others are heavily regulated to guard against segregating proclivities; the Milwaukee and Cleveland plans are of this nature. In this section, we describe three proposals: the Friedman unregulated voucher plan; Coons and Sugarman's Family Power Equalizing Plan; and the Regulated Compensatory Model developed by the Center for the Study of Public Policy.

The Friedman Unregulated Voucher Plan

Noting that the quality of public schooling is the worst where parents have the fewest, or no, options, Friedman (1962) argued that equity and fraternal, as well as libertarian and efficiency, goals would be better served through governmentally financed vouchers. Vouchers would sever the nexus linking public support of education, place of residence, and public ownership of educational enterprises. Under the Friedman scheme, parents sending their children to private schools would be paid a sum equal to the estimated cost of educating a child in a public school, provided that at least that amount was spent on education in an approved school. If the cost of the private school were greater, the parent would have to make up the difference. Such a plan, Friedman argued, would greatly expand educational options available to poor families.

> One way to achieve a major improvement, to bring learning back into the classroom, especially for the currently most disadvantaged, is to give all parents greater control over their children's schooling, similar to that which those of us in the upper-income classes now have. Parents generally have both greater interest in their children's schooling and more intimate knowledge of their capacities and needs than anyone else. Social reformers, and educational reformers in particular, often self-righteously take for granted that parents, especially those who are poor and have little education themselves, have little interest in their children's education and no competence to choose for them. This is a gratuitous insult. (Friedman & Friedman, 1980, p. 150)

Critics of the Friedman plan argue that unregulated vouchers would merely enable private schools to raise their tuitions, still keeping them out of reach of low income families. At the same time, unregulated vouchers would make private schools more accessible to higher-income families, encouraging them to abandon the public schools, which would become enclaves of the poor. This, they claim, would further stratify society. Some critics do see merit in the general concept of vouchers, however, and propose modifications to the Friedman plan that they believe would overcome perceived inequities while retaining what they consider its more attractive features.

Family Power Equalizing

Coons and Sugarman (1978) approached family choice through a plan designed to promote variety in the quality of schools rather than uniformity. Their plan has been called both Family Power Equalizing (FPE) and the Quality Choice Model (QCM). Under their plan, all schools, public and private, would charge whatever tuition they wanted within a very broad, but specified, range. Tuition would be paid partly by the parents and partly by the state. State subsidies would be based on tuition charged and family income so that poorer parents could, in some meaningful sense, afford high-priced schools as easily as the rich. The actual formula would work in a fashion similar to the district power equalization formula discussed in Chapter 7, families rather than school districts being the focus of wealth equalization. Even the poorest family would be required to pay something to establish a personal stake in the choice. No additional charge would be imposed on families with more than one child in school. After the first child, tuition would be fully subsidized by the state. The financial obligation of families sending their children to differently priced schools would be based on the average of tuition amounts charged. Open access to participating schools would be ensured by having oversubscribed schools make selections of students on a random basis.

Coons and Sugarman acknowledged social science research that questions the relationship between cost and quality in schooling. They projected that FPE "would encourage families to exercise their own judgment about the efficacy of extra school purchases compared to other goods and services" (p. 200). Enactment of this plan would constitute a marked departure from the current financing of public schools in that, for the first time since the nineteenth century, tuition would be charged by public schools.

Regulated Compensatory Voucher

One of the most comprehensive studies of vouchers ever done in the United States was conducted by the Center for the Study of Public Policy (CSPP, 1970); it analyzed the potential impact of seven voucher models, including Friedman's unregulated marketlike model. The report concluded that regulations were necessary to ensure more equitable distribution of resources over the system of neighborhood schools. Only their Regulated Compensatory Model, described below, was judged likely to give the poor a larger share of the nation's educational resources.

The Regulated Compensatory Voucher Model is described here in some detail as one that provides most of the benefits of education vouchers while addressing societal concerns over equity and fraternity. According to this model, every child would receive a voucher roughly equivalent to the cost of the public schools in the area. A supplement would be paid for children who were in some way disadvantaged because of poverty or physical, psychological, or other learning disabilities. The receiving school would not necessarily have to spend the supplement exclusively on the child for which it was given; for example, it could be used to reduce class size throughout a school. No school could charge tuition beyond the voucher amount awarded for a given student. Schools wishing to increase their revenue beyond the voucher amount could seek subventions from such sponsors as churches and businesses or from special-purpose grants from federal and state governments and foundations. Income could also be

enhanced by increasing the proportion of disadvantaged students enrolled. Schools would have considerable latitude in developing their curricula and in setting their expenditure levels (by admitting larger numbers of students qualifying for supplements). Parents desiring high-expenditure programs would be able to find them only in schools accommodating significant numbers of disadvantaged children. Thus the basic choice for parents under the plan would be between schools with high financial resources and schools with more able classmates; parents could continue to finance their children's education fully, with their own resources, at schools not participating in the voucher plan.

The CSPP (1970) study concluded that equal access to schools for disadvantaged students could not be ensured by financial incentives alone; regulations governing application, admission, and transfer procedures would also be required. The Regulated Compensatory Voucher Model provides for such regulations designed to facilitate social equity.

Any marketlike plan for distributing educational services depends on parents making informed choices in selecting schools for their children. Parents must be able to obtain accurate, relevant, and comprehensive information about the advantages and disadvantages of *all* available alternatives. In the absence of a public initiative, private information sources would probably develop, as has been the case with higher education, but such sources are likely to charge fees for services and would therefore not be readily available to the poor. Hence, providing a public information system must become a responsibility of a coordinating public agency. The CSPP proposed that such an agency's responsibilities should include

- Collecting information about each school on matters of social and parental concern
- Compiling information in clear and comprehensible printed formats

- Providing counselors who can explain the printed information to those who do not understand it
- Monitoring information provided to parents, protecting them against misleading advertising claims
- Investigating claims of fraud, discrimination, and deception, and taking appropriate remedial action when these abuses occur. (pp. 62–63)

CSPP recommended a procedure whereby parents would have to appear personally at an office of the coordinating agency to fill out the necessary voucher application forms. At that time, a voucher counselor would provide information on available options and review procedures for making application. Individual schools would probably establish their own recruiting procedures.

The CSPP found the most promising device for preventing discrimination in admissions by oversubscribed schools to be a lottery for at least half of their admissions. In recognition that there needs to be some correlation between the curriculum of a school and the characteristics of its students, a case was built for allowing schools some discretionary admissions so long as their criteria do not reinforce patterns of invidious discrimination.

> The idea of favoring cellists over pianists, for example, seems harmless because it does not aggravate any of the more general problems of the educational system. The idea of favoring Spanish-speaking or black applicants seems acceptable to us for the same reason. The idea of discriminating against children against whom everyone else also discriminates is less acceptable. (p. 77)

There are other reasons justifying discretionary admissions. For a number of very good reasons, families with one child already in a school would probably want to enroll any younger brothers and sisters in the same school. To encourage new schools that would enhance variety, parents who established

schools would need to be guaranteed a place for their children in recognition of their efforts. So long as the roster of founders was limited to a reasonable number, and so long as all founders were listed when the school was incorporated, the CSPP saw no serious objections to this procedure.

According to the model, either the school or the parent initiates transfers. A parent may become dissatisfied with a school or may find, with experience, that the school has not lived up to expectations. In either case, parents should have the option to withdraw their children from a school at any time, as long as they can continue to meet compulsory-attendance laws by enrolling them in other schools. Admissions counselors should be available to them.

Schools also sometimes enroll students whom they would rather not have. Private schools may persuade such children to withdraw; public schools are constrained by compulsory-attendance laws but may deal with the situation by placing problem children in "special" schools or programs, by removing them through suspension or expulsion, or by encouraging them to "drop out." Private schools have a great deal of flexibility in eliminating misfits, but public schools must follow formal bureaucratic procedures. The CSPP could see no justification for providing publicly and privately managed schools with the same amount of money as public schools and then allowing the private schools to shirk the responsibilities that are placed on public schools. They recommended that the constraints placed on public schools in these matters be extended to private schools receiving vouchers. Normally it should be assumed that once a child is admitted to a school and surrenders a voucher, the school is obliged to educate that child until he or she has completed the course of study or elects to transfer. If a school finds it necessary to expel a child, evidence supporting such action should be submitted to an impartial arbitrator. Both the school and the parents of the child should have access to professional consultation. Parents should also have access to the services of an educational ombudsman to ensure the protection of their rights.

The Boston public schools use procedures similar to those proposed in the CSPP model in administering their universal program of choice among the city's public schools (OECD, 1994). All parents are required to list their school preferences prior to their children's entering grades 1, 6, and 9. Selections are made to satisfy as many choices as possible in a manner, however, that must be consistent with racial integration. Parent information centers help parents make informed choices. Approximately 94 percent of children are placed in the school of their first or second choice. The phenomenon of best-informed parents selecting a handful of socially favored schools has been avoided by forcing everyone to choose, spreading information as evenly as possible to all parents, and making it virtually impossible for the most privileged to manipulate the system. Most parents do not select the school closest to their residence, and it appears that "white flight" from the system has been stemmed. Similar plans are functioning in Cambridge, Massachusetts, and White Plains, New York (Yanofsky & Young, 1992).

CRITERIA PARENTS USE IN CHOOSING SCHOOLS

Advocates argue that policies of school choice as a means of school improvement will succeed because parents value high achievement. Critics say that parents choose schools for many reasons that are unrelated to school effectiveness. Further, critics fear that the choosers would come disproportionately from the higher-income and better-educated classes if a voucher or other publicly financed plan were instituted. In this section, we examine the reasons people give for choosing a particular

school and the relationship, if any, of those reasons to people's background characteristics.

Bauch and Small (1986) developed a topology with four dimensions for categorizing the reasons parents give for choosing private schools: academic/curriculum, discipline/safety, religion, and values. Among these, academic reasons are overwhelmingly the most commonly listed responses (Bauch & Goldring, 1995; Martinez, Thomas, & Kemerer, 1994; Slaughter & Schneider, 1986; Witte, 1993).

In a national study, Kutner, Sherman, and Williams (1986) found that the reasons most commonly given by public school parents for choosing the schools they did were as follows: it was the school assigned (28 percent), transportation (24 percent), and academic quality (17 percent). The reasons most commonly given by private school parents for exercising choice included academic quality (42 percent), religious instruction (30 percent), and discipline (12 percent). Nearly half of the children in the study who were attending private schools had once attended public schools, and 17 percent of those who were attending public schools had once attended private schools. The reasons given for switching from private to public schools included cost (24 percent), change of residence (21 percent), and availability of public alternatives (17 percent). The reasons for switching from public to private schools included academics (27 percent), discipline (25 percent), religious instruction or values orientation (25 percent), and quality of teachers (12 percent). Respondents with a child in a private school tended to be better educated, to earn a higher income, to be Catholic, to have attended private schools themselves, and to live in large or medium-size cities. Parents sending their children to public schools were more likely to live in nonmetropolitan environs and to have attended only public schools themselves. Kutner et al. concluded that for any given level of funding, "access and choice would be expanded most for low-income and minority families by increasing the proportion of tuition eligible" (p. 80).

Zhang (1995) studied the attitudes of parents who had switched their children among public neighborhood schools, public magnet schools, and parochial schools. He solicited information on attitudes about curriculum, school–parent relationships, and values in schooling. Significant differences in opinion were found only with respect to the latter classification. Parents transferring their children from public to parochial schools placed greater importance on curricula stressing moral values and religion. Parents transferring their children from parochial to public schools placed greater importance on cultural diversity.

Similar findings on preferential differences among public and private school parents were evident in surveys by Darling-Hammond and Kirby (1988) in Minnesota and by Erickson (1986) in British Columbia. Erickson also found that among parents with children in private schools,

> the preferential differences were much more pronounced among school types [i.e., Catholic, Calvinistic, and high-tuition] than among social class strata. The data suggest that private school types, rather than being mere vehicles of social stratification, attracted parents with different preferences, with limited regard to social class. The schools were products, as it were, of different preference structures. (pp. 95–96)

Bauch and Goldring (1995), in a study of metropolitan high schools of choice in Chicago, Washington, DC, and Chattanooga, Tennessee, found that parents usually had multiple reasons for selecting a particular school. Catholics placed high priority on a school's academic reputation, but they were also concerned about moral development and discipline. The value profile of parents choosing single-focus magnet schools was similar to that of parents choosing Catholic schools, except that they didn't give as high a priority to moral development. Multifo-

cus magnet schools were chosen most frequently by minority families. Their primary motivation for choice was academic considerations, but they also transferred for career and transportation/proximity reasons.

Lee, Croninger, and Smith (1994) studied the attitudes of parents in the Detroit metropolitan area. They found some support for the contention that choice would reduce socioeconomic stratification in that socially disadvantaged adults were the strongest supporters of the policy. Favorable attitudes toward choice were inversely related to the quality rating that respondents gave to their local schools. This latter finding produced a paradox, however, in that persons in districts that they perceived to be high in quality were less interested in choice and less likely to give persons seeking choice an opportunity to choose their districts. The researchers raised the question "Are those who favor choice likely to actually gain access to better schools?" They concluded, "Although disadvantaged families see choice (in theory) as a vehicle for better education for their children, and although the exercise of such choice could benefit a few children and their families, . . . the overall effect of implementation of a choice plan would be to increase, rather than decrease, social stratification in education" (p. 450).

The Massachusetts legislature passed in 1991 a law permitting children to attend schools outside their home districts. The law provided that the state would pay the cost of tuition to the districts that enrolled nonresident students and deduct the amount from allocations to districts that lost students. The law did not require a school district to accept students from another district, but the incentives to do so were high. Fossey (1994) studied the nature of student flow after the first year. He found that parents switched their children to schools with higher expenditure levels and student achievement in communities with higher-SES populations. His findings also lend credence to the conclusion of Lee, Croninger, and Smith (1994) reported above. Only about 15 percent of the state's school districts accepted school choice students. No suburban district within convenient commuting distance of Boston participated; consequently, only 15 Boston students out of 60,000 transferred under this program. Only 4 percent of the 3,000 school choice students were African American or Hispanic. Even in districts with large minority populations, most of the students who transferred were white. Fossey concluded that families seemed to be making rational decisions when transferring their children out of their home communities, not making decisions for reasons of mere convenience. The Massachusetts choice plan was improving the schooling options of a few students, but it was not effective in improving the mixing of ethnic groups.

Martinez, Thomas, and Kemerer (1994) studied the characteristics of choosing families and their rationales for exercising choice in Minnesota, San Antonio, Milwaukee, and Indianapolis. They found that parents overwhelmingly cited educational quality or learning climate as their number 1 reason for choosing a school for their children. Discipline and general atmosphere in the schools were also highly rated criteria. Choosing families were quite different from nonchoosing families in that both education level of parents and parents' educational expectations for their children were higher. They also found that lack of awareness about the availability of school choice programs was a formidable obstacle to participation among some low-income minority families.

In weighing the evidence of numerous studies, Levin (1990) concluded that empirical evidence supported the interpretation that choice schemes, whether market or public, will tend to favor more advantaged families. Cohen (1990) put it this way:

> [P]art of the appeal of choice and decentralization is their promise to improve schooling by opening

it to greater influence from parents. But both reforms would thus only be effective to the extent that parents mobilized to take advantage of the opportunities that new market or political organization offered. Some parents would make good use of these opportunities, but many others would not. And those parents with the greatest need for improved education would have the greatest difficulty taking advantage of the reforms. (p. 378)

Cohen's conclusion is supported by the findings of Ambler (1994) in an analysis of school choice plans in Britain, France, and the Netherlands. He found that school choice increased the educational gap between the privileged and the underprivileged, primarily because students from higher socioeconomic backgrounds were more likely to exercise the prerogative of choice. When subsidies are provided to private education, the benefits derived by higher-income families is even greater.

In a study of the exercise of choice in Scotland, Adler, Petch, and Tweedie (1989) found that transfer requests had been made by parents across the social class spectrum and not predominantly by a middle class minority. Ball, Bode, and Gars (1992), however, detected two distinct discourses of school choice in England that were related to class. The working-class discourse was dominated by practical and immediate considerations, such as convenience in location of the school. The middle class used the school strategically for the furtherance of social mobility. If this is true, the belief that choice will serve significantly to reduce disparities in the delivery of educational services is seriously challenged; although the evidence to the contrary presented by Gorard, Fitz, and Taylor (2001), described in an earlier section, is quite compelling.

Adler and colleagues' (1989) study of Scotland, which has had a relatively long experience with choice, found that the policy had a greater impact on secondary schools than on primary schools. The arrangement clearly led to the widening of educational inequalities and to the reemergence of a selective system of schooling in the big cities. Most of the schools that lost large numbers of pupils were situated in the least prosperous housing neighborhoods, whereas most of the schools that gained were located in mixed inner-city areas. Pupils transferred from schools with poor examination results and higher dropout rates to schools with better examination results and lower dropout rates. Choice exaggerated the problems of schools that lost pupils. Willms and Echols (1993) arrived at similar conclusions in a later study based in Scotland.

Adler (1993) did not recommend abandoning the choice scheme altogether, however. Rather, he called for "a better balance between the rights of parents to choose schools for their children and the duties of education authorities to promote the education of all children." He called for procedures whereby all parents, with the assistance of teachers, would be able to make more informed choices in the selection of schools that would best promote their children's learning while addressing legitimate equity concerns that have been eclipsed by the construction of a "quasi-market." Similar recommendations were made by an OECD (1994) study of choice policies in England, Australia, the Netherlands, New Zealand, Sweden, and the United States.

In summary, American studies of the criteria used by parents in selecting schools for their children clearly show that academic, moral, and religious concerns dominate. When given a choice, parents tend to select schools that are better than the ones their children attended previously. These findings support the claims by market advocates that a policy of school choice will be a force for improving the quality of schools generally.

Parents (usually low-income) living in areas served by poor schools are more desirous of the opportunity for choice than are parents (generally high-income) living in areas served by good schools, and the latter are not particularly willing to open their good schools to others.

This raises concern among market opponents that a choice policy would maintain an already inequitable system. This fear is supported by international studies where choice of schools has been the norm for generations. In applying international studies to the United States, however, one needs to keep in mind that any publicly supported system in the United States must function under the equal-protection provisions of the Fifth and Fourteenth Amendments to the U.S. Constitution. Such protection is generally not available in other countries where school choice is national policy. OECD (1994) has observed that the United States, unlike most other nations, has made explicit attempts to design choice policies that are socially just. As Goldhaber (2001) notes, "the devil is in the details" (p. 69).

INCLUDING PRIVATE AND RELIGIOUS SCHOOLS IN FAMILY CHOICE SCHEMES

About 80 percent of private schools have religious affiliations. Gill et al. (2001) recommend that in order to avoid further social and achievement stratification, existing private and parochial schools be included in any choice program targeted to low-income families. Enrollment of low-income choice children in existing private schools would reduce stratification because these schools' enrollments currently consist largely of white middle-class children. Further, newly created schools under a targeted choice scheme would probably cater to children from low-income families because the demand from high-income families has already been met, and this would increase stratification. Thus including religious schools in choice programs becomes an important issue.

Coleman (1990) contended that excluding public funds from religious schools sacrifices an opportunity to strengthen the strongest asset a child has: a parent's interest, involvement in, and attention to the child's growth.

Religious involvement is and has been stronger on average for those who are less advantaged, white and black, than for those who are more advantaged. And it is the children of the less advantaged who are most at risk of being harmed by drugs, crime, alcohol, delinquency. The possibility of having their children under the care of a church-related school offers a far greater benefit to these parents than to those whose children are less at risk. And it does so because the church constitutes a basis for community that builds upon, reinforces, and extends the most worthy of the values the parent holds and would transmit to the child. (p. xx)

Cibulka (1989) noted that in many nations, it would not be necessary to fashion a philosophical defense of private schooling, because the distinction between public and private is not so sharply drawn. Outside the United States, it is not common to think of the government-run schools as public and of all others as private. Private schools are assumed to serve a public purpose and are frequently aided by public funds.

Doyle (1992) argued that providing vouchers for at-risk children in the United States is a known policy remedy for the shortcomings of inner-city schools and that failure to implement such policies is due not to constitutional restrictions but to "the intransigence of public school advocates" (p. 518). Viteritti (1999) recast the establishment issue from a legal one to one of ethnicity and class. He contended that the church is the most significant force available to poor people for social change and that the issue of separation of church and state is a white middle-class legal and social construct that is out of step with the ethos of the black community.

Constitutional Constraints

There appear to be no constitutional restrictions on family choice among public schools, as long as the civil rights of children (for example, nondiscrimination) are not violated in the process. Direct government aid to private schools with a religious affiliation, however, is a different matter. Here, there is potential conflict with the First Amendment to the U.S. Constitution, which bars governmental actions "respecting the establishment of religion." Several state constitutions have even more restrictive terminology that bars any form of public assistance to religious institutions. We noted earlier that state income tax deductions for tuition and other educational expenses for both public and private school children have been determined to be constitutional (*Mueller* v. *Allen*, 1983). We also noted the U.S. Supreme Court's holding in support of tuition assistance for low-income families whose children attend religious or secular schools participating in the Cleveland voucher program (*Zelman* v. *Simmons-Harris*, 2002).

In *Lemon* v. *Kurtzman* (1971), the Supreme Court established a three-part test to determine whether statutes violate the establishment clause: (1) The statute must have a secular legislative purpose. (2) Its principal or primary effect must be one that neither advances nor hinders religion. And (3) the statute must not foster an excessive government entanglement with religion. Applications of this test to various forms of governmental aid preclude direct subsidy of religion-affiliated private schools. Thus the constitutional amendment that, under the free exercise clause, protects the right of parents to select a private school for their children virtually prohibits, under the establishment clause, direct aid to the largest class of private schools.

Aid to parents is another matter, however. Anthony (1987) detected a change in position by the U.S. Supreme Court on this issue. Ten years prior to their *Mueller* decision, the Court had found deductions unconstitutional in a New York case (*Levitt* v. *Committee for Public Education and Religious Liberty*, 1973). According to the Court, a critical difference in the two cases is that in the Minnesota statute, all parents could take advantage of the deduction, whereas, in the New York case, only parents paying tuition to private schools could benefit.

Anthony related the change in this and other interpretations to the shift in the composition of the Supreme Court from liberal domination to conservative domination during the Reagan administration. She saw a softening in the Court's position on parochial aid as a result, drawing on the *Mueller* decision in particular to support her position. First, she noted the majority's unsolicited endorsement of Minnesota's efforts to defray costs for parents of parochial school children. Because of the heavy burden born by parents in educating their children in parochial schools, the majority found that "whatever unequal effect may be attributed to the statutory classification can fairly be regarded as a rough return for the benefits . . . provided to the state and all taxpayers by parents sending their children to parochial schools" (at 3070). As further evidence of the Court's softening position, Anthony referred to the majority's opinion concerning the founding fathers' interpretation of the establishment clause.

> Here, again, Rehenquist [writing for the majority] suggests that the Court no longer needs to be concerned about the separation of church and state. Thus he writes, "At this point in the 20th century we are quite far removed from the dangers that prompted the Framers to include the Establishment Clause in the Bill of Rights. . . . The risk of significant religious or denominational control over our democratic processes—or even of deep political division along religious lines—is remote" (at 3069). (p. 599)

Anthony concluded that the application of the "original intent" doctrine to future parochial school aid is likely to result in decisions that hold public funding of parochial schools constitutional. "However, due to the tendency of conservative jurists to uphold precedent, one can expect a gradual chipping away at previous parochial aid decisions rather than a total renunciation of those rulings" (p. 604).

McCarthy (2000) noted mixed messages coming from the Supreme Court during the 1980s. For example, *Aguilar* v. *Felton* (1985) put an end to a 20-year practice of providing remedial services funded under Title I by public school personnel in sectarian schools. Doyle (1992), however, interpreted statements made by Justice Lewis Powell in his concurring opinion to the *Aguilar* decision as inviting Congress to devise a voucher program for poor children. Powell's statement to which Doyle referred reads as follows:

> [T]he court has never foreclosed the possibility that some types of aid to parochial schools could be valid under the Establishment Clause. . . . If, for example, the Congress should fashion a program of evenhanded financial assistance to both public and private schools that could be administered, with government supervision in the private schools, so as to prevent the diversion of the aid for secular purposes, we would be presented with a different question. (Cited in Doyle, 1992, p. 516)

The Reagan administration unsuccessfully attempted to overcome the restrictions that the *Aguilar* decision imposed on aid to poor children attending religious schools. He proposed to Congress that the then more than $3 billion provided annually through Chapter I (now Title I) of the Education Consolidation and Improvement Act for supplementary educational services for educationally disadvantaged children be distributed through "mini-vouchers." Under the Reagan proposal, states and local school districts would give low-income parents vouchers to spend on their children's education at public schools within or outside their home district or at private schools. Successor presidents were similarly unsuccessful in getting Congress to accept vouchers in any form.

McCarthy (2000) found that since 1985, Supreme Court decisions have been back on the trajectory of a relaxing judicial posture toward government aid to sectarian schools. Among the cases she cited as evidence was *Agostini* v. *Felton* (1997), which overruled the separationist decision the Court had rendered twelve years earlier in *Aguilar*. This restored the ability of public school personnel to provide remedial services in sectarian schools. The U.S. Supreme Court further eased the constitutional restriction on using public funds as vouchers to assist families when choosing among religious and secular schools. The majority concluded that, "The Ohio program is entirely neutral with respect to religion." Because the tuition assistance is for families rather than schools, the program is one of "true private choice" (*Zelman* v. *Simmons-Harris*, 2002).

Impact on Diversity of Schools

Although the intent of vouchers and tax credits is to provide parents with more educational options for their children, some evidence suggests that there is actually a narrowing in range of choice when governmental assistance becomes available—but that more people may participate in this narrower range. Currently, with no governmental aid and with only a small percentage of the population attending private schools, there is very little governmental regulation or oversight of private schools in the United States. Adoption of increased fiscal support of private schools can come only as a result of extensive political compromises that recognize other objectives, such as equality and fraternity. Greater aid and greater participation would thus, undoubtedly, be accompanied by greater governmental control and regulation over private schools to address equity and fraternal considerations (as we have already seen in Milwaukee and Cleveland and in the Regulated Compensatory Voucher Model). This restricts the flexibility of private schools, making them more acceptable to the "average voter," but not necessarily to their original clientele.

Policies on the support of public, private, and religious schools in Canada vary markedly from province to province, and hence provide an excellent setting for the empirical study of the impact of alternative policies. Erickson

(1986) reported on such a series of studies beginning in 1975. These studies involved interviews of persons associated with Catholic school systems in Alberta, Saskatchewan, and Ontario, where Catholic schools were fully supported with public funds, and in Manitoba and British Columbia, where they were not. Evidence from the interviews convinced Erickson that "the lengthy period of total support has significantly 'deprivatized' Catholic schools in Alberta, Saskatchewan, and Ontario, attenuating or obliterating numerous characteristics which elsewhere distinguished Catholic schools from public schools" (pp. 99–100).

In 1978 British Columbia embarked on a new policy of partial support of private schools, in which most private schools were provided with a grant per pupil equal to 30 percent of the per-pupil public school operating cost. Regulations that would protect the public interest were held to a minimum to avoid homogenizing the private schools. Erickson subsequently launched a follow-up to his 1975 study in British Columbia. He found that in Catholic elementary schools, dramatic declines were detected in teacher commitment as perceived by parents and in parent commitment as perceived by teachers. The most pronounced negative consequences of increased public assistance were in the Catholic secondary schools. At this level,

> there was a notable decline in the sense among parents that their schools needed their help, in the extent to which parents viewed their schools as responsive, in teacher commitment as perceived by both parents and students, in parent commitment as perceived by teachers, in student affection toward teachers and classes, and in the perception by students that their schools, rather than being just like public schools, were doing something special. (p.102)

Erickson concluded that the Canadian examples do not lend much credence to efforts to encourage educational diversity by extending public funds to private schools.

In one important sense, what the British Columbia government is attempting to do is far from unusual. Faced with the evidence of what they have done to bias the marketplace, governments have often attempted to rectify the situation by returning to the citizens, for their unbiased use, some of the funds previously extracted from them through taxation. It soon turns out, unfortunately, that the money has been transformed by passing through the public pipeline. It cannot be freely used. It has become a political instrument, laden with constraints produced by the anxieties, pressures, and concerns of public officials. (p. 106)

Erickson suspected that the negative effects would not have been nearly so great if the aid had been provided directly through parents in the form of vouchers, tax credits, or tax deductions. Such strategies would encourage less centralization and less erosion of parental influence.

James (1986) came to remarkably similar conclusions in a study of school finance and control in the Netherlands, where private schools have been almost wholly supported by public funds since early in the twentieth century. At the primary level, 31 percent of the children are enrolled in public schools, 28 percent in Protestant schools, 38 percent in Catholic schools, and 3 percent in other schools. At the secondary level, the corresponding percentages are 28 percent, 27 percent, 39 percent and 6 percent.

Families in the Netherlands are free to choose the school or schools that their children attend. Teachers are prorated to schools on the basis of school enrollments. The central government fully pays teachers' salaries in all schools. Private schools may supplement neither the staffing levels nor teachers' salaries. Municipal governments provide buildings for both public and private schools. A small fund for operating expenses is allocated to each school, public or private, and it may be used at the school's discretion for such items as maintenance, cleaning, heating, libraries, and instructional supplies. Private schools have severely limited rights to supplement the fund with student fees; public schools do not have such rights. James comments, "Both society in choosing its system, and private schools, in choosing where they fit into the system, would then face a trade-off between autonomy and more funds" (p. 122). James (1986) concluded that private schools sacrifice their individuality when they accept public support:

> Cultural heterogeneity often generates a demand for private education and for government subsidies to help cover the associated costs. The subsidies facilitate private sector growth, but they also allow government to impose regulations, particularly over inputs and other behavioral characteristics. Thus, the initial demand for differentiation, if successful, sets in motion forces which make the private sector quasi-governmental; subsidized private sectors are very much like public sectors. If we [in the United States] institute a voucher scheme or other privatization policies, we may end up with a private sector which is larger but less distinctive than the one we have now. (p. 135)

Hill (1993) contended that you cannot have an unregulated system that uses public money. The reason why public money is spent on education is to satisfy a public interest in ensuring a minimum school experience for all children. That public interest will drive legislatures to regulate schools that accept public funds—even private schools accepting vouchers. Hill, an advocate of Catholic schools, warned Catholic audiences that if they want to have Catholic schools, they shouldn't take public money. "In the long run, schools in a publicly funded choice system will be public because they'll be regulated" (p. 248).

Hirschoff (1986), after a thorough review of the legal structure of schooling in the United States, found that a significant degree of choice already exists. She cautioned that the expansion of family choice brought about by increased public funding of private schools has to be weighed against the increased governmental regulation that is sure to follow and the resultant loss of flexibility. She closed her analysis with the following observation: "Particularly with regard to fiscal change, then, one might conclude that the present legal structure of the mixed system—with perhaps minor adjustments—maximizes parental choice more than would the major changes on which public discussion usually focuses" (p. 52).

THE NEED FOR SYSTEMIC REFORM

The evidence makes it clear that neither school-based decision making (SBDM) nor family choice is a panacea and that neither, by itself, would enable schools to educate upcoming generations more effectively than the current system. Neither policy is directly linked to significant improvement in scholastic achievement, although both facilitate implementation of practices that *are* so linked. Both policies, however, can be part of a multifaceted solution. The basic question remains: How can society provide good schools universally?

At the heart of the debate over choice and SBDM is the need to satisfy societal interests in education, while at the same time allowing individuals to satisfy their educational interests in those areas that confer private benefits and are of particular interest to them. Meier (1995) observed that Americans have long supported two levels of schooling:

> Whether schools are public or private, the social class of the students has been and continues to be the single most significant factor in determining how a school works and the intellectual values it promotes. The higher the student body's economic status, the meatier the curriculum, the more open-ended the discussion, the less rote and rigid the pedagogy, the more respectful the tone, the more rigorous the expectation, the greater the staff autonomy. . . . What we need are strategies for giving to everyone what the rich always valued. The rich, after all, have had both good public schools and good private schools. The good public ones looked a lot like the good private ones.

Bureaucratization of public schools and balkanization of communities seem to be the greatest barriers to high student achievement and school reform. SBDM holds the potential for diminishing the power of the center by placing authority over the design and implementation of learning systems in the hands of practicing professionals. This frees practicing professionals to tailor programs to the needs and interests of their student clients, *if* they so desire, and *if* parents wish to have their children exposed to the innovations designed by teachers. This second "if" introduces the need for parental choice of schools to balance parental interest against professional expertise.

> Once you create good schools, choice is inevitable. A good school has a definite purpose. Staff has the opportunity to collaborate on that purpose. A good school can sustain itself by the way it selects and socializes staff. It can make demands on students, telling them what they have to do in order to stay in school. A school can't be good if it has to satisfy all demands. It can say from the beginning what demands it will satisfy. A public school system as a whole can satisfy all demands, but no one school can do so.
>
> Likewise, good schools can't be constrained by staff members who say, "I'm not doing it your way. I'm a senior teacher. You can't boot me out, and I'll be dammed if I'll change the way I teach." Where you have good schools, questions of fit, not just competence, have to be considered in the assignment of staff. (Hill, 1993, p. 249)

A good school has a coherent and sharply defined curriculum, although the focus may differ among schools. When schools are different, choice becomes a necessity because both teachers and students in a given school must fit and subscribe to its focus. Choice and SBDM policies, individually, do not create good schools. However, good schools are more likely to be developed in a climate of SBDM and choice.

However, the reality of the situation is that under policies of SBDM and choice, most schools are likely to remain as they are because of professional inertia and parental disinterest.

Choice will work only if parents take full advantage of their new freedoms. Some parents will make good use of these new opportunities, but many others will not. Unfortunately, those parents of children with the greatest need for improved education may experience the greatest difficulty in taking advantage of a choice policy. This would do little to improve the inequalities of the current system and could lead to even worse inequalities. To provide equity in a choice system, government intervention is required to provide mechanisms for informing and guiding parents who desire or need assistance in making their choices. Regulation of school admissions would also be necessary to ensure that oversubscribed schools do not use socially discriminatory criteria in selecting students. The CSPP's Regulated Compensatory Voucher Model presented in a previous section describes one way for doing this.

Likewise, SBDM will work only if teachers and administrators take full advantage of their new freedoms. Some will, but many won't. To protect against professional inertia or incompetence, external standards are also needed in the form of curricular guides and uniform assessments (Bauch, 1989; Cookson, 1992; Elmore, 1990; Glenn, 1990; Lee, Croninger & Smith, 1994; Levin, 1990; OECD, 1994). Taken together, these constitute the elements of systemic reform.

SUMMARY

One of the most controversial issues on the school reform agenda is family choice of schooling. In this chapter, we looked at the implications for school finance policy of possible mechanisms for enhancing choice. Considered were choice within the public sector, education vouchers, tax credits, and tax deductions. The latter three strategies extend public funding to private schools. Mechanisms for choice within the public sector include magnet schools and open-enrollment plans. International studies focused our attention on the reduction in flex-

ibility and diversity in the private school sector that would probably result from public subsidization of that sector because of the public regulation that would follow. Potential constitutional barriers to the use of tax monies in support of religion-affiliated schools have been eased considerably following the 2002 U.S. Supreme Court decision permitting vouchers for low-income families. In this chapter, we concluded that policies of SBDM and school choice are not sufficient by themselves to bring about the degree of educational reform needed, especially in our worst schools. They can be highly important elements in an overall strategy of systemic reform, however.

This chapter concludes our presentation of possible reforms to the incentive structure within which schools function—reforms intended to make it more likely for all children to reach high academic standards, while assuring taxpayers that public resources are being used efficiently. In the next chapter, the last in the book, we return to the decision model presented in Figure 1.3 to consider the alternatives before us for use in organizing school governance and finance in the years ahead.

ACTIVITIES

1. Within the context of the decision matrix presented in Figure 1.3, what educational decisions might best be placed with parents? What safeguards need to be implemented to protect legitimate social and professional interests? Provide the rationales for your responses.

2. If parents have freedom to choose the schools their children attend, how might their interests best be represented in the designing of educational programs (assume school-based decision making)?

3. Interview public, private and parochial school administrators or board members about the likely impact of the U.S. Supreme Court's decision that education vouchers do not violate the First Amendment of the

United States Constitution against the establishment of religion even if some parents choose to enroll their children in schools with a religious affiliation.

4. Examine the provisions of a state's or of another nation's laws governing church–state relationships. Compare them with the provisions in the United States Constitution. In what ways are this state's provisions more or less restrictive with respect to making public monies available in support of children attending religion-affiliated schools?

5. Discuss the advantages and disadvantages of each of the following approaches for efforts to expand diversity:

   • Free publicly financed and operated schools with direct aid to private schools prohibited, but allowing supporting services that benefit children attending private schools

   • Education vouchers, with options among public and private schools

   • Tax deductions for tuition and other expenses incurred in public and private education

   • Tax credits that rebate the cost of tuition up to a specified amount

   • Direct aid to private schools, such as the plan used in the Netherlands

   • Open enrollment among public schools without public aid for private schools

6. Design a voucher scheme that would enhance family choice of schools while protecting equity.

REFERENCES

Adler, M. (1993). An alternative approach to parental choice. *NCE Briefing No. 13*. London: National Commission on Education.

Adler, M., Petch, A., & Tweedie, J. (1989). *Parental choice and educational policy*. Edinburgh, Scotland: Edinburgh University Press.

Agostini v. *Felton*, 521 U.S. 203 (1997).

Aguilar v. *Felton*, 473 U.S. 402 (1985).

Ambler, J. S. (1994). Who benefits from educational choice? Some evidence from Europe. *Journal of Policy Analysis and Management, 13*, 454–476.

Anthony, P. (1987). Public monies for private schools: The Supreme Court's changing approach. *Journal of Education Finance, 12*, 592–605.

Archer, J. (1998). Millionaires to back national voucher project. *Education Week, 17*, 39, 3.

Armor, D., & Peiser, B. (1998). Interdistrict choice in Massachusetts. In P. E. Peterson & B. C. Hassel (Eds.), *Learning from school choice*. Washington, DC: The Brookings Institution.

Ball, S. J., Bode, R., & Gars, S. (1992). *Circuits of schooling: A sociological exploration of parental choice of school in social class contexts*. London: Centre for Educational Studies, King's College.

Bauch, P. A. (1989). Can poor parents make wise educational choices? In W. L. Boyd & J. G. Cibulka (Eds.), *Private schools and public policy: International perspectives* (pp. 285–314). Philadelphia: Falmer.

Bauch, P. A., & Goldring, E. B. (1995). Parent involvement and school responsiveness: Facilitating the home–school connection in schools of choice. *Educational Evaluation and Policy Analysis, 17*, 1–21.

Bauch, P. A., & Small, T. W. (1986). *Parents' reasons for school choice in four inner-city Catholic high schools: Their relationship to education, income, and ethnicity*. Paper presented at the Annual Meeting of the American Educational Research Association.

Bensman, D. (2000). *Central Park East and its graduates*. New York: Teachers College Press.

Bositis, D. A. (1999). *1999 national opinion poll*. Washington, DC: Joint Center for Political and Economic Studies.

Brown, D. J. (1998). *Schools with heart: Voluntarism and public education*. Boulder, CO: Westview.

Bryk, A. S., Lee, V. E., & Smith, J. L. (1990). High school organization and its effects on teachers and students: An interpretive summary of the research. In W. H. Clune and J. F. Witte (Eds.), *Choice and control in American education*, Vol. 1, *The theory of choice and control in education* (pp. 135–226). Philadelphia: Falmer.

Carnoy, M. (2000). School choice? Or is it privatization? *Educational Researcher, 29*, 7, 15–20.

Center for the Study of Public Policy. (1970). *Education vouchers: A report on financing education by grants to parents*. Cambridge, MA: Author.

Chubb, J. E., & Moe, T. M. (1985). *Politics, markets, and the organization of schools*. Stanford, CA: Institute for Research on Educational Finance and Governance, School of Education, Stanford University.

Chubb, J. E., & Moe, T. M. (1990). *Politics, markets, and America's schools*. Washington, DC: The Brookings Institution.

Cibulka, J. G. (1989). Rationales for private schools: A commentary. In W. L. Boyd and J. G. Cibulka (Eds.), *Private schools and public policy: International perspectives*. Philadelphia: Falmer.

Cohen, D. K. (1990). Governance and instruction: The promise of decentralization and choice. In W. H. Clune & J. F. Witte (Eds.), *Choice and control in American education*, Vol. 1, *The theory of choice and control in education* (pp. 337–386). Philadelphia: Falmer.

Coleman, J. S. (1990). Choice, community and future schools. In W. H. Clune & J. F. Witte (Eds.), *Choice and control in American education*, Vol. 1, *The theory of choice and control in education* (pp. ix–xxii). Philadelphia: Falmer.

Coleman, J. S., & Hoffer, T. (1987). *Public and private high schools: The impact of communities*. New York: Basic Books.

Cookson, Jr., P. W. (1992). Introduction. *Educational Policy*, 6, 99–104.

Coons, J. E., & Sugarman, S. D. (1978). *Education by choice: The case for family control*. Berkeley: University of California Press.

Danzberger, J. P., Kirst, M. W., & Usdan, M. D. (1992). *Governing public schools: New times, new requirements*. Washington, DC: Institute for Educational Leadership.

Darling-Hammond, L., & Kirby, S. N. (1988). Public policy and private choice: The case of Minnesota. In T. James and H. M. Levin (Eds.), *Comparing public and private schools*, Vol. 1, *Institutions and organizations* (pp. 243–267). New York: Falmer.

Doyle, D. P. (1992). The challenge, the opportunity. *Phi Delta Kappan*, 73, 512–520.

Elam, S. M., & Rose, L. C. (1995). The 27th annual Phi Delta Kappa Gallup poll of the public's attitude toward the public schools. *Phi Delta Kappan*, 77, 41–56.

Elmore, R. F. (1990). Choice as an instrument of public policy: Evidence from education and health care. In W. H. Clune & J. F. Witte (Eds.), *Choice and control in American education*, Vol. 1, *The theory of choice and control in education* (pp. ix–xxii). Philadelphia: Falmer.

Erickson, D. A. (1986). Choice and private schools. In D. C. Levy (Ed.), *Private education: Studies in choice and public policy* (pp. 57–81). New York: Oxford University Press.

Fliegel, S., & MacGuire, J. (1993). *Miracle in East Harlem: The fight for choice in public education*. New York: Random House.

Fossey, R. (1994). Open enrollment in Massachusetts: Why families choose. *Educational Evaluation and Policy Analysis*, 16, 320–334.

Friedman, M. (1962). *Capitalism and freedom*. Chicago: University of Chicago Press.

Friedman, M., & Friedman, R. (1980). *Free to choose: A personal statement*. New York: Avon.

Funkhouser, J. E., Colopy, J. E., & Kelly, W. (1994). *Minnesota's open enrollment option: Impacts on school districts*. Washington, DC: U.S. Department of Education/Policy Studies Associates.

Gill, B. P., Timpane, P. M., Ross, K. E., & Brewer, D. J. (2001). *Rhetoric versus reality: What we know and what we need to know about vouchers and charter schools*. Santa Monica, CA: RAND.

Glenn, C. L. (1990). Parent choice: A state perspective. In W. H. Clune & J. F. Witte (Eds.), *Choice and control in American education*, Vol. 1, *The theory of choice and control in education* (pp. ix–xxii). Philadelphia: Falmer.

Goldhaber, D. (2001). The interface between public and private schooling: Market pressure and the impact on performance. In Monk, D. H., Walberg, H. J., and Wang, M. C. (Eds.), *Improving educational productivity* (pp. 47–75). Greenwich, CT: Information Age Publishing.

Gorard, S., Fitz, J., & Taylor, C. (2001). School choice impacts: What do we know? *Educational Researcher*, 30, 7, 18–23.

Greene, J. P. (2000). *The effect of school choice: An evaluation of the Charlotte Children's Scholarship Fund*. New York: Center for Civic Innovation at the Manhattan Institute.

Greene, J. P., Peterson, P. E., & Du, J. (1998). School choice in Milwaukee: A randomized experiment. In P. E. Peterson & B. C. Hassel (Eds.), *Learning from school choice* (pp. 335–356). Washington, DC: The Brookings Institution.

Guthrie, J. W., Garms, W. I., & Pierce, L. C. (1988). *School finance and education policy: Expanding educational efficiency, equity and choice*. Englewood Cliffs, NJ: Prentice-Hall.

Haertel, E. H. (1987). Comparing public and private

schools using longitudinal data from the HSB study. In E. H. Haertel, T. James, and H. M. Levin (Eds.), *Comparing public and private schools,* Vol. 2, *School achievement* (pp. 9–32). New York: Falmer.

Hartocollis, A. (1999). Private school choice plan draws a million aid-seekers. *New York Times*, April 21, A1, A25.

Henig, J. R., & Sugarman, S. D. (1999). The nature and extent of school choice. In S. D. Sugarman, & F. R. Kemerer (Eds.), *School choice and social controversy: Policy, politics, and law* (pp. 13–35). Washington, DC: The Brookings Institution.

Hewitt, J. P. (1989). *Dilemmas of the American self.* Philadelphia: Temple University Press.

Hill, P. (1993). Comments and general discussion. In E. Rasell & R. Rothstein (Eds.), *School choice: Examining the evidence* (pp. 247–249). Washington, DC: Economic Policy Institute.

Hirschoff, M. U. (1986). Public policy toward private schools: A focus on parental choice. In D. C. Levy (Ed.), *Private education: Studies in choice and public policy* (pp. 33–56). New York: Oxford University Press.

Hoffer, T., Greeley, A. M., & Coleman, J. S. (1987). Catholic high school effects on achievement growth. In E. H. Haertel, T. James, and H. M. Levin (Eds.), *Comparing public and private schools,* Vol. 2, *School achievement* (pp. 67–88). New York: Falmer.

Howell, W. G., & Peterson, P. E. (2000). *School choice in Dayton, Ohio: An evaluation after one year.* Cambridge, MA: Program on Education Policy and Governance, Harvard University.

Howell, W. G., Wolf, P. J., Peterson, P. E., & Campbell, D. E. (2000). *The effect of school vouchers on student achievement: A response to critics.* Cambridge, MA: Program on Education Policy and Governance, Harvard University. Available at **http://hdc-www.harvard.edu/pepg**.

Howson, J. (2000). Solid state. *Times Educational Supplement*, July 14, 24.

Hoxby, C. M. (1996). Are efficiency and equity in school finance substitutes or complements? *Journal of Economic Perspectives, 10*, 51–72.

James, E. (1986). Public subsidies for private and public education: The Dutch case. In D. C. Levy (Ed.), *Private education: Studies in choice and public policy* (pp. 113–137). New York: Oxford University Press.

Kennedy, S. S. (2001). Privatizing education: The politics of vouchers. *Phi Delta Kappan, 82,* 450–456.

Kutner, M. A., Sherman, J. D., & Williams, M. F. (1986). Federal policies for public schools. In D. C. Levy (Ed.), *Private education: Studies in choice and public policy* (pp. 57–81). New York: Oxford University Press.

Lee, V. E., Croninger, R. G., & Smith, J. B. (1994). Parental choice of schools and social stratification in education: The paradox of Detroit. *Educational Evaluation and Policy Analysis, 16,* 434–457.

Lemon v. *Kurtzman,* 403 U.S. 602 (1971).

Levitt v. *Committee for Public Education and Religious Liberty,* 413 U.S. 472 (1973).

Levin, H. M. (1990). The theory of choice applied to education. In W. H. Clune & J. F. Witte (Eds.), *Choice and control in American education,* Vol. 1, *The theory of choice and control in education* (pp. ix–xxii). Philadelphia: Falmer.

Litwak, E., & Szelenyi, I. (1969). Primary group structures and their functions: Kin, neighbors and friends. *American Sociological Review, 34,* 465–81.

Lortie, D. C. (1975). *School teacher: A sociological study.* Chicago: University of Chicago Press.

Loveless, T. (1998). Uneasy allies: The evolving relationship of school and state. *Educational evaluation and policy analysis, 20,* 1–8.

Martinez, V., Thomas, K., & Kemerer, F.R. (1994). Who chooses and why: A look at five school choice plans. *Phi Delta Kappan, 75,* 678–681.

Mathews, D. (1996). *Is there a public for public schools?* Dayton, OH: Kettering Foundation Press.

Mathews, D. (1997). The lack of a public for public schools. *Phi Delta Kappan, 78,* 740–743.

McAdams, D. R. (1999). Lessons from Houston. In D. Ravitch (Ed.), *Brookings papers on education policy, 1999* (pp. 129–183). Washington, DC: The Brookings Institution.

McCarthy, M. M. (2000). School voucher plans: Are they legal? *Journal of Education Finance, 26,* 1–21.

Meier, D. (1995). *The power of their ideas: Lessons for America from a small school in Harlem.* Boston: Beacon Press.

Metcalf, K. K. (1999). *Evaluation of the Cleveland Scholarship and Tuition Grant Program: 1996–1999.* Bloomington: Indiana Center for Evaluation.

Moe, T. M. (2001). Private vouchers: Politics and evidence. In M. C. Wang & H. J. Walberg, *School* choice or best systems: What improves education? (pp. 67–126). Mahwah, NJ: Erlbaum.

Morken, H., & Formicola, J. R. (1999). *The politics of school choice*. Lanham, MD: Rowman & Littlefield.

Mueller v. *Allen*, 463 U.S. 388 (1983).

Murnane, R. J. (1986). Comparisons of private and public schools: The critical role of regulations. In D. C. Levy (Ed.), *Private education: Studies in choice and public policy* (pp. 138–152). New York: Oxford University Press.

Myers, D., Peterson, P., Mayer, D., Chou, J., & Howell, W. G. (2000). *School choice in New York City after two years: An evaluation of the School Choice Scholarships Program*. Washington, DC: Mathematica Policy Research.

Nathan, J. (1989). Helping all children, empowering all educators: Another view of school choice. *Phi Delta Kappan, 71*, 304–307.

Organization for Economic Co-operation and Development (OECD). (1994). *School: A matter of choice*. Paris: OECD.

Pearson, J. (1989). Myths of choice: The governor's new clothes? *Phi Delta Kappan, 70*, 821–823.

Peterson, P. E. (1998). *An evaluation of the New York City School Choice Scholarships Program: The first year*. Cambridge, MA: Program on Education Policy and Governance, Harvard University.

Peterson, P. E., Green, J., & Noyes, C. (1996, Fall). School choice in Milwaukee. *Public Interest, 125*, 38–56.

Peterson, P. E., Myers, D., & Howell, W. G. (1999). *An evaluation of the Horizon Scholarship Program in the Edgewood Independent School District, San Antonio, Texas: The first year*. Cambridge, MA: Program on Education Policy and Governance, Harvard University.

Pierce v. *Society of Sisters*, 268 U.S. 510 (1925).

Reid, K. S. (2001). Minority parents quietly embrace vouchers. *Education Week, 21*, 1, 20–21.

Rose, L. C., & Gallup, A. M. (1999). The 31st annual Phi Delta Kappa/Gallup poll of the public's attitudes toward the public schools. *Phi Delta Kappan, 81*, 41–58.

Rothstein, R. (1993). Introduction. In E. Rasell & R. Rothstein (Eds.), *School choice: Examining the evidence* (pp. 1–25). Washington, DC: Economic Policy Institute.

Sarason, S. B. (1994). *Parental involvement and the political principle: Why the existing governance structure of schools should be abolished*. San Francisco: Jossey-Bass.

Slaughter, D., & Schneider, B. (1986). *Newcomers: Blacks in private schools. Final report to the National Institute of Education*. Vols. I and II. (Contract No. NIE-G-82-0040). Northwestern University, ERIC Documents ED 274 768 & ED274 769.

Tiebout, C. M. (1956). A pure theory of local expenditures. *Journal of Political Economy, 64*, 416–424.

Tonnies, F. (1940). *Fundamental concepts of sociology*. New York: American Book Co.

Viteritti, J. (1999). *Choosing equality: School choice, the Constitution, and civil society*. Washington, DC: The Brookings Institution.

Walberg, H. J. (1993). Comments and general discussion. In E. Rasell and R. Rothstein (Eds.), *School choice: Examining the evidence* (pp. 301–303). Washington, DC: Economic Policy Institute.

Waller, W. (1932). *The sociology of teaching*. New York: Wiley.

Weinschrott, D. J., & Kilgore, S. B. (1998). Evidence from the Indianapolis Voucher Program. In P. E. Peterson & B. C. Hassel (Eds.). *Learning from school choice*. Washington, DC: The Brookings Institution.

Willms, J. D., & Echols, F. H. (1993). The Scottish experience of parental school choice. In E. Rasell & R. Rothstein (Eds.), *School choice: Examining the evidence* (pp. 49–68). Washington, DC: Economic Policy Institute.

Wisconsin Legislative Audit Bureau. (2000). *Milwaukee parental choice program: An evaluation*. Madison, WI: Author.

Witte, J. F. (1998). The Milwaukee voucher experiment. *Educational Evaluation and Policy Analysis, 20*, 229–251.

Witte, J. F. (1993). The Milwaukee parental choice program. In E. Rasell & R. Rothstein (Eds.), *School choice: Examining the evidence* (pp. 49–68). Washington, DC: Economic Policy Institute.

Woessmann, L. (2001). *Schooling resources, educational institutions, and student performance: The international evidence* (Kiel working paper No. 983). Kiel, Germany: Kiel Institute of World Economics.

Wolf, P., Howell, W. G., & Peterson, P. (2000). *School choice in Washington, DC: An evaluation after one year*. Cambridge, MA: Program on Education Policy and Governance, Harvard University.

Yanofsky, S. M., & Young, L. (1992). A successful parents' choice program. *Phi Delta Kappan, 73,* 476–479.

Zelman v. *Simmons-Harris,* ___U.S.___2002.

Zhang, Z. (1995). *A comparative study of parental attitudes towards public and parochial schools.* Unpublished doctoral dissertation, State University of New York, Buffalo.

Charting New Directions in School Finance Policy

We hope that this journey through the concepts and issues that make up the field of school finance has been an enlightening one for you. Our purpose in Part VI is to bring together the themes of this book in an integrated discussion of the problems that must be addressed in the years immediately ahead and to identify some of the more promising alternatives before us.

We discuss the concept of systemic reform and explore the promise of coordinating governance, curriculum, and finance policy for improving schools. In Chapter 1 we presented five educational policy issues within a model of the political–economic system. We now examine each of these societal decisions about the nature and extent of education with regard to the systemic reform of the school system. We conclude the text with a discussion of ways in which states, school districts, and schools can reach the goal of attaining high standards with equity and efficiency.

16

IMPLICATIONS OF SYSTEMIC REFORM FOR SCHOOL FINANCE POLICY

Issues and Questions

- *Achieving High Standards with Equity and Efficiency*: How might the systemic reform of governance, curricula, and finance bring about this goal?
- *Setting Goals and Objectives for Education*: What is the optimal allocation of authority for deciding appropriate education goals and objectives under current circumstances?
- *Distributing Educational Services*: To what extent should services be available to help people of varying characteristics meet high expectations?
- *Investing in Education*: What proportion of society's resources should be invested in education to enable all students to achieve high standards?
- *Organizing for Schooling*: How can society ensure that schools use resources efficiently?
- *Allocating Resources for Public Education*: How should states distribute resources in a way that achieves, with equity and efficiency, the societal goal of all students meeting high performance expectations and yet recognizes the importance of promoting the goal of liberty?

For many years, school finance policy debates centered on inputs and their distribution. This concern for ensuring that state finance policies would bring about a fully accessible and fair educational system continues today. However, a dramatic shift occurred in the mid-1990s from a focus on equity with regard to inputs to a concern for schooling outcomes in relation to curricular standards. In this context, reforms of policies affecting governance, curriculum, and finance are systemically related to each other and to the outcomes of the schooling process.

We open this final chapter with a discussion of the systemic reform movement. We then present five educational policy issues that frame societal decisions about the nature and extent of education. We conclude with recommendations for restructuring school finance structures to enable districts and schools to reach the goal of meeting high standards with equity and efficiency.

THE SYSTEMIC APPROACH TO REFORMING EDUCATIONAL POLICIES

Smith and O'Day (1991) wrote cogently about systemic school reform. They argued for coherent state leadership that is grounded in clear and challenging standards for student learning. Within this structure, school personnel would have the flexibility they need to develop appropriate instructional strategies. Centralized coordination and decentralized implementation are key elements of systemic reform:

> We argue, however, that if states can overcome the fragmentation in the system by providing coordination of long-range instructional goals, materials development, professional training, and assessment, they can set the conditions under which teacher empowerment and professionalization, school site management, and even parental choice can be both effective and broad-based. Indeed, what we propose is an interactive and dynamic relationship between increasing coherence in the system through centralized coordina-

tion and increasing professional discretion at the school site. (p. 254)

The Consortium for Policy Research (CPRE) elaborated on these concepts in developing a framework for thinking about systemic reform and capacity building. In a CPRE report that presented studies of education reform, Goertz, Floden, and O'Day (1995) discussed three components of systemic reform: the promotion of ambitious student outcomes for all students, the alignment of policy approaches and the actions of various policy institutions to promote such outcomes, and restructuring the governance system to support improved achievement. They concluded that there are five potential avenues for capacity building within the broader systemic reform strategies: articulating a vision for reform, providing instructional guidance toward the realization of that vision, restructuring governance and organizational structures to facilitate learning and more effective delivery of services, providing needed resources, and establishing evaluation and accountability mechanisms that provide incentives for improvement while addressing problems and barriers.

The systemic reform movement that is evolving early in the third millennium calls for a coordinated set of policy initiatives. These policy directions include

- *Centralized* goal setting and accountability via standards, curricula, and assessments
- *Decentralized* reforms via school site decision making involving teachers, administrators, staff, parents, and community members
- *Family choice* of schooling within the public sector through charter schools, and across public and private sectors through vouchers for low-income families.

Systemic reform attempts to coordinate state policies, including school finance policies, with restructured district and school governance. The goal is to improve the performance of the whole school, treating all students as though they can meet high expectations and increasing the coherence of teachers' and students' engagement in learning by closely coordinating various elements of the policy infrastructure around outcome expectations. In addition to systemic reforms within states, the federal government's reauthorization of the Elementary and Secondary Education Act in 2001 (see Chapter 9) reflects these themes. The No Child Left Behind Act of 2001 promises to centralize accountability through required annual state assessments and report cards and national assessments of a sample of students every other year. In addition, this act promotes giving districts and schools greater flexibility in using federal funds, and it encourages parental choice of public schools for students in continually low-performing schools.

The challenge for policy makers and educators in this context is to rethink the most effective ways of integrating policies and structuring organizations in support of core teaching–learning activities. State policy makers should alter government structures and oversight and change allocation mechanisms in ways that reduce "turf protection" among public agencies. School finance policy can encourage systemic reform by

- Financing high-quality instructional programs and technologies that successfully help students achieve challenging outcomes
- Redesigning compensation systems to reward the acquisition and application of knowledge and skills related to school improvement plans and to school and student performance
- Financing professional development at a level that is adequate to enable teachers to gain the knowledge and skills necessary to design better instructional systems that reflect pupil learning expectations
- Directly funding community-based groups to better focus public programs on the needs of children and families and to support school-level decisions

The multiple waves of reform that shaped the current movement for systemic changes, and the increasing competition for state and local resources, mean greater political pressure from policy makers for evidence of positive results from education spending. National goals and parallel state policies urge schools to evaluate organizational structures and educational practices in terms of their relationship to student learning. It is anticipated that state finance reform in the coming decade will emphasize incentives for school improvement and financial links among state standards and goals, spending for programs and personnel, and pupil outcomes. We anticipate that school-based decision making and family choice of schools will play facilitating roles in these changes.

The apparent emphasis on efficiency, accountability, and economic growth that drives many of these reforms does not diminish the importance of the goals of equality, fraternity, and liberty. Systemic reform efforts will need to embrace these values; otherwise, policy changes will not receive the broad political support necessary to ensure their success. Systemic reform will need to demonstrate concern for improving education for children of all backgrounds and learning abilities, for drawing together diverse groups within caring communities, and for enabling parents and students to choose among school structures and philosophies that achieve expected outcomes despite their differences. The various values that frame the issues and the debate must be seen not as antagonistic but as challenges to policy makers and educators as they strive to construct finance policies and practices that support school improvements in education for a continually changing society.

School finance reforms are linked to school improvement efforts in a quest for equity along with efficiency and adequacy. Critics believe there is little benefit in changing financial policies if the performance of students does not also improve. A primary challenge of the standards-based reform movement is adequacy. School finance policies must ensure that there are sufficient resources to enable all students to acquire appropriately specified levels of knowledge and skills (Guthrie & Rothstein, 2001). Policy analysts must strive to improve our understanding of the links between fiscal inputs and student outcomes so that these resources are used effectively.

Linking student performance to inputs makes enormous sense conceptually. It is very difficult, however, to develop school finance policies for allocating resources in relation to measures of student and school performance. Research has found little evidence of strong and dependable causal relationships between schooling inputs and outcomes. The lack of such identifiable relationships has supported the conclusion of many that schools are functioning inefficiently. Consequently, we see improving our understanding of these relationships as one of the most important educational issues before us. Incorporating this understanding into decisions about the allocation of resources would greatly improve the internal efficiency of schools.

Lack of vertical equity in the distribution of resources for schooling is a continuing problem related to achieving efficiency. The concern for equity has traditionally been expressed in terms of inputs, such as the ability of communities to raise revenue and the distributions of state funds among districts (see Chapters 5 and 7). In the context of adequacy, this concept is also concerned with inequities in the distribution of desired schooling outcomes among districts and schools. For this reason, we referred in Chapter 11 to adequacy as the ideal state of vertical equity.

The adequacy—or sufficiency—of the resources provided to schools is a critical concern in systemic reform. Reaching the goal of having all students meet high academic standards depends in part on their having access to equitable *and adequate* resources. As we strive to know more about the relationship between inputs and schooling outcomes, we must also address questions about the amount of resources essential for reaching the expected ends. Guthrie and Rothstein (2001) state that the determination of adequate funding levels rests upon a twofold policy judgment about

- Learning or performance levels to be attained (the outcomes)
- Resource levels needed for schools to enable students to achieve these learning levels (the educational technology)

Fuhrman (2001) observed that districts and schools vary widely in their ability to interpret and implement policies and in the resources essential to improving schools in the ways demanded by standards-based reforms:

> Districts also have design and support functions, creating policy systems and providing personnel and materials that help schools improve instruction. Importantly, districts also mediate between state policy and schools; their capacity to interpret and tailor state policies to their own settings is vital. And, of course, capacity at the school and classroom levels is most essential; principals and teachers must believe in their own ability and that of their students to reach high standards, and they must have the knowledge and skills, as well as sufficient material resources, to achieve such goals. (p. 269)

In order to improve schools in the context of systemic reform, we must direct school finance policy toward improving (1) the *efficiency* of the school system through acquiring a better understanding of the relationships between financial resources and the expected (and actual) outcomes, (2) the *equity* of the distribution of opportunities to learn and outcomes in terms of student achievement and other performance measures, and (3) the *adequacy* of resources available to build the capacity of low-performing schools to enable all students to reach performance expectations.

We place the concerns of equity and adequacy second to that of efficiency because the evidence is very strong that the persons most affected by the inefficiencies of the education system are children and youth who are at risk of academic failure. Simply providing more resources for them will not improve their achievements *unless* we make their instructional systems more effective. Students from middle- and upper-income families in general appear to be achieving at a competitive level by both national and international standards. The school system seems to be working reasonably well for them, and their schools seem to receive an appropriate level of fiscal resources. It is the inefficiencies of low-performing schools and classrooms and the inadequate level of resources invested in them that need to be the focus of policy reform over the next decade.

We must clearly understand, however, that developing school finance policy is largely a *political* process. Decisions about the provision of elementary and secondary education are made primarily in the public sector. But the public sector functions within a market economy in which two-thirds of the nation's GNP is allocated through decisions made by individuals. Thus we must study the impact of political decisions about financing education by using economic paradigms. We assume here that school finance policy is made within a political–economic context.

In Figure 1.3 (see Chapter 1), we presented a model of the political–economic system of education policy development. In this conceptualization, we divided education policies into five groups that followed Benson's (1978) conceptualization: setting goals and objectives, identifying recipients of services, determining levels of investment, producing and distributing services, and allocating resources. In the next sections, we discuss each of these educational policy issues in terms of the policy alternatives we considered in earlier chapters. We give particular attention to systemic reforms that coordinate policies related to governance, curriculum, and finance.

SETTING GOALS AND OBJECTIVES FOR THE EDUCATIONAL ENTERPRISE

The history of the governance of public education in the United States has been largely one of centralization of authority. Compulsory-school-attendance legislation in the nineteenth century was one of the first acts of centralization. The movement to compel formal education denied parents the right to decide *not* to educate their children. The establishment of the common school with the use of public funds relegated the setting of educational goals and objectives to school districts. For the most part, these school units were very small and were easily controlled by family constituents.

At the same time, parents continued to have the privilege of home-schooling their children or enrolling them in private schools, at the family's *own* expense, if they so desired. This was an important accommodation for those whose value orientations were not satisfied by the philosophy and orientation of the public schools or who were dissatisfied with the quality of the public schools. The compulsory-attendance laws and publicly financed and operated schools were intended to improve the fraternity and equality of educational opportunity within, but not among, school districts. The intention of permitting families to choose among delivery systems, including home schooling and privately financed private schools, was to minimize the diminution of liberty. This political compromise, struck by the courts and legislatures, balanced the interests of society with those of parents.

During the first half of the twentieth century, the growth of cities and the policy of consolidating rural and suburban school districts weakened the control of family clients over the direction of public schools. Within many larger schools and districts, there was a strengthening of the authority of the teaching profession. Teachers and administrators received much better professional preparation during that period than they had had before. Educating more students and broadening the curriculum enhanced the efficiency of schools at the expense of liberty for the 90 percent of parents who sent their children to public schools.

Immediately following World War II, the state and federal governments began to play a larger role in shaping public schooling through legislation and litigation. Increasing numbers of young people found it necessary to complete secondary school in order to qualify for satisfactory employment. This increased the cost of education beyond that which most communities could support through the property tax alone. The heavy reliance on local revenue magnified the disparities among school districts in their ability to finance educational services and in the quality of their services. Most states responded by gradually assuming a greater proportion of the financial support of public schools. In the process, states assumed more control over curriculum and teacher qualifications. States sought equality, efficiency, and economic growth at the expense of the liberty interests of family clients, local communities, and the profession.

In the pursuit of equality and fraternal objectives, litigants successfully challenged through federal courts, in the 1950s and 1960s, the practices of segregating schools by race, and in the 1970s of discriminating by gender, English-language ability, and disabilities. Court-ordered desegregation, race- and gender-sensitive hiring policies, limits on the disciplinary discretion of educators, and curricular change resulted. Similarly, plaintiffs in many states successfully challenged the policies that permitted large disparities in spending due to reliance on local property taxes within and supplemental to state school aid formulas (see Chapter 10). State and federal legislation often reinforced the holdings of courts, making specific decisions universal. Little discretion was left to family clients within public schools. Bureaucratic rules and regulations severely constrained the discretion of teaching professionals. Collective bargaining agreements further restricted teachers' and administrators' abilities to act independently. The objectives of fraternity and equality came into sharp conflict with those of efficiency and client liberty.

Greater centralization of governance and decision making continued with the first wave of educational reform in the 1980s. The so-called excellence movement responded to national concerns for global economic competitiveness. A key government report (National Commission on Excellence in Education, 1983) declared that "the educational foundations of our society are presently being eroded by a rising tide of mediocrity that threatens our very future as a Nation and a people." The report urged society and schools to raise expectations: "We must demand the best effort and performance from all students, whether they are gifted or less able, affluent or disadvantaged, whether destined for college, the farm, or industry." In an effort to raise expectations and increase student achievement, many states instituted more rigorous curricula, more stringent high school graduation requirements, statewide standardized testing, and higher certification standards for teachers and administrators.

The centralization of authority that resulted from these policies did not always produce the results desired. People quickly realized that it might be necessary to differentiate among those decisions that were appropriate to centralize and those that were not. From the mid-1950s through the early 1980s, efficiency and equity had been pursued through centralizing authority. Policy implementation studies of that period showed that state and federal governments are particularly effective in dealing with issues of equity and access. But those governments appear to be ineffective in dealing with matters of efficiency and "production"—that is, how a school is organized and operated. We have learned from our experience, and there is now a growing systemic reform movement to pursue efficiency through decentralized authority and equity through centralized authority.

School-based decision making (discussed in Chapter 14) and family choice (discussed in Chapter 15) represent important tactics in an overall strategy of decentralization. These strategies return some decision-making authority to professional educators and to parents in order to introduce marketlike forces into the public school sector. The goal is to increase the efficiency of schools. In responding to the issue of who should set goals and objectives for educational enterprises, these chapters concluded that extreme centralization had sapped public schooling of much of its vitality and efficiency and had alienated a significant proportion of its family clients. Notwithstanding, we recognized that society has important interests that have to be protected through intervention by state and federal governments in matters of equity and fraternity. People have legitimate and varying concerns about the goals and objectives of education at all levels of the sociopolitical hierarchy. In considering reforms of governance, our task is to achieve an acceptable *balance* among legitimate interests in setting educational goals. Although state and federal authorities can best make decisions concerning equity and access, teaching professionals hold the technical expertise of schooling. Parents are the guardians of the interests and needs of individual children. It is through the family that the child's voice can best be heard. This voice needs to be empowered by enabling parents to choose which schools their children will attend.

The current systemic reform movement is bringing a better balance among levels of government and families with respect to governance, curriculum, and finance. The pattern emerging in the United States and other industrialized nations (e.g., New Zealand, the United Kingdom, and Victoria in Australia) is that of dividing the responsibility for setting goals and objectives for the educational enterprise among interested parties, as appropriate. At the national level, the federal government is cooperating with state governments and professional associations in setting voluntary achievement standards for students. National policies that require assessments in all states (see Chapter 9) reinforce the relationships between standards and school improvement. In turn, these standards and assessments influence state curricular frameworks and certification (or licensure) standards for teachers. These frameworks and standards serve as *guides* to policy; it is up to each state and school district to determine how these guides are to be incorporated into state and local policy. Teachers and principals determine, with district curriculum coordinators, how these policies will be implemented in schools and classrooms.

In order to increase the pace of implementing standards-based curricular reforms throughout states and districts, policy makers are adopting performance-based accountability systems. States are assuming greater responsibility for setting student achievement standards, are encouraging school personnel to align curricula with these standards, and are monitoring performance via standardized testing. Some states have linked these assessments to allocations of rewards for high performance and to various forms of assistance and sanctions for low-performing schools. In addition, some school districts are tying measures of teachers' knowledge, skills, and performance to their salaries (see Chapter 13).

At the same time that the standards movement centralizes authority over what is included in the curriculum, the focus of implementation is the school. Accountability ratings, rewards, and sanctions focus attention primarily on school-level reforms and performance. In many states and districts, the education profession is getting greater authority to develop policy at the school building level (see Chapter 14). In some cases this authority is shared with parents, community members, and students. More and more parents are enjoying the right to select schools whose philosophies and expectations match their own, as charter schools, magnet schools, inter- and intradistrict choice plans, and vouchers for low-income children become more pervasive (see Chapter 15).

Choice of schools enhances the influence of parents in setting goals and objectives for the education enterprise.

This balance of responsibility in this systemic reform movement offers great promise for improving the quality of schools and student outcomes. State government, local districts, schools, and families have important, though different, roles to play in setting goals and implementing school improvement plans.

DETERMINING WHO SHOULD RECEIVE WHICH EDUCATIONAL SERVICES

Over the years, society has expanded the availability of schooling until virtually all people between the ages of five and eighteen now have access to some form of publicly funded instruction. Horizontal equity has been a long-standing focus of school finance policy, as states have attempted to ensure equal treatment of students with similar needs. There is now emerging a strong concern for vertical equity, as finance structures enable districts and schools to provide different educational services and resources to students with special needs. The goal of enabling all students to meet high standards requires adequate resources to provide appropriate services—the ideal state of vertical equity. Systemic reform of policies related to governance, curriculum, and finance must be directed at achieving each of these equity goals.

Expansion of educational opportunities is frequently the result of intensive lobbying on the part of special-interest groups. For example, the pursuit of equity goals, which greatly expanded public school services for children with disabilities in recent years, is now urging universal preschools. Because society recognizes the differences in the quality of preschool experiences among children and has a stake in ensuring that all children begin school ready to learn (the first of the eight national education goals), growing numbers of publicly financed preschool programs, such as Head Start, are available for at-risk children. Some state funding structures make preschools accessible to low-income families and full-day kindergartens available to all students (see Chapter 8). Systemic reform goals and concerns for the later performance of students who do not avail themselves of preschool opportunities will strengthen arguments for making publicly funded preschools universally available. The private sector is also rapidly developing preschools, nursery schools, and after-school centers to meet the demand of families in which all adults work. Both public- and private-sector forces are striving to expand educational opportunities; as educators and parents seek to provide appropriate learning experiences so that all children will enter schools ready to learn.

Just as higher levels of government address the educational needs of students who have disabilities and of children who are in preschool, society must consider more fully the cost of services for students who are identified as being at risk of academic failure. Since the mid-1960s, compensatory funds have been directed to some schools on the basis of family income. Many state finance structures include adjustments in pupil counts using similar criteria (see Chapter 8). The standards-based reform movement gives evidence that these investments have not sufficiently raised the achievement of at-risk students in low-performing schools. We believe that the costs of educating academically at-risk students have been underestimated and that such strategies as pull-out programs to serve students who qualify for Title I services have not been effective. There must be a reallocation of funds to districts and schools serving low-performing students and whole-school reforms in how instruction is organized for these students (see Chapter 12).

Although people generally recognize the value of education to the individual, they have different opinions about the philosophy, content, and context appropriate for specific individuals. Differences in educational tastes create social tension over the orientation of services to be offered through the public sector. One concern about the centralizing effects of the standards-based movement is that it may increase this tension as schools' goals and curricula narrow to meet performance expectations. However, different organizational patterns will develop as the design and implementation of whole-school reforms, school-based decision making (SBDM), and charter schools spread throughout the public school system. This can serve to ease tensions, particularly as districts permit clients to choose freely among alternative approaches to meeting common standards.

Once the bureaucratic uniformity among schools is broken, it is difficult to justify district assignment of pupils to schools. Family choice of schooling permits the matching of child characteristics and family preferences to school characteristics. It also provides a monitoring mechanism to ensure that each public school is satisfactorily providing a service desired by a sufficiently large clientele. Choice enhances the policy objectives of liberty and efficiency. Unfettered choice, however, could violate the objectives of equality and fraternity. This can be avoided with social controls such as those exercised through magnet schools, charter schools, and the Regulated Compensatory Voucher Model described in Chapter 15.

SBDM and charter schools free the producers of educational services to use their professional knowledge, experience, insights, and imagination to design learning systems to fit specific situations. Family choice of schooling permits clients to select the options that they think are best for their children and family circumstances. When a money-follows-the-child strategy is used for allocating resources to schools, marketlike forces make producers more sensitive to the needs of clients and potential clients. Producers also become more aware of alternative uses of available resources in order to maximize the positive impact of

those resources. A dissatisfied client who leaves takes resources from a school. Likewise, each new client attracted to a school brings additional resources.

In the systemic reform movement, society (through government) will continue to exert the primary influence in determining what range of educational services to provide. Whole-school reforms, school-based decision making, and charter schools will enlarge the role of professional educators and parents in designing those services. School choice within the public sector, and between public and private schools, will enhance the voice of parents in determining what kind of education is appropriate for their own children. Providers and consumers interact in this way to determine which form of schooling—and which services within the schools chosen—will best enable all students to meet high standards.

DETERMINING THE LEVEL OF INVESTMENT

Decisions about the goals for education and the extent of services to be provided within schools influence the levels of investments made by government. Because of the heavy involvement of state and local governments in providing elementary and secondary education, the level of investment in schooling is largely a political decision. In the systemic reform movement, ensuring that the resources provided are adequate to enable all students to acquire appropriately specified levels of knowledge and skills should drive decisions about the level of investment in schools.

In Chapter 12, we reviewed a number of studies of the external efficiency of resources allocated to education. This is an important consideration in determining what amount of a society's resources should be allocated to educational services. We showed that a person's formal education is directly and strongly correlated with expected earnings. Education increases the value of one's labor by increasing the cache of knowledge at one's command and by honing one's occupational skills. The anticipation of higher incomes persuades individuals to invest some of their own resources in further education, especially at the postsecondary level. By the same token, the more sophisticated the technological development of a country, the greater is the demand for highly skilled workers. Thus the percentage of a nation's resources allocated to education increases with the sophistication of its technology.

Rate-of-return studies have shown that the United States, along with most other developed countries, had been investing in education at an appropriate level, given the prevailing goals and organization of elementary and secondary schools in the 1980s. Recent international comparisons of spending have indicated that the United States continues to spend a relatively high amount per pupil for elementary and secondary levels (Verstegen, 1992; Smith & Phelps, 1995). But although the level of investment in education for the United States has been strong on some measures, the internal distribution of investment is very uneven. As a result, the United States has some of the best-financed and some of the worst-financed schools in the developed world. The most poorly financed schools serve the educationally at-risk children who are most dependent on schools for the development of academic skills, even basic language skills. Schools serving the majority of children seem to be financed at an adequate level. It appears, however, that we have grossly underestimated the amount of resources necessary to close the achievement gap among ethnic and socioeconomic groups (see Chapter 11). Thus the internal distribution of resources allocated to education is flawed and needs to be corrected.

Nevertheless, efficiency studies (see Chapter 12) instill little confidence that additional resources allocated to schools serving educationally at-risk children would be used in effective ways. Radical structural reforms are

required—reforms that will revamp the incentive systems shaping policy making and professional behavior in public schools (see Chapters 13, 14, 15).

In addition to making investments and changes in instructional delivery systems in low-performing schools, society must address the adequacy of resources to construct or remodel facilities within which schooling occurs. We noted the wide range in quality of public school buildings that resulted from the nearly exclusive reliance on local revenue sources for capital outlay (see Chapter 6). Judicial decisions in several states reflected jurists' views on whether finance structures met constitutional requirements for uniform, thorough, and efficient systems of education when there were not adequate facilities. These recent holdings required greater investment of state resources in school buildings to ensure adequate levels of support for education (see Chapter 10). We anticipate that in the future there will be greater pressure for states, rather than solely burdening local property taxes, to invest revenue from broader tax bases, in the construction and remodeling of schools.

Improving the ability of all students to perform at high levels will depend on increasing the allocation of resources to educationally at-risk children and improving the efficiency of all school operations. In this context, improving the adequacy of resources for those students who are furthest from meeting high academic standards will require not only commitments of local and state revenue but also commensurate changes in the design of instructional delivery and the use of technology in low-performing schools.

DETERMINING THE MEANS BY WHICH EDUCATIONAL SERVICES ARE PROVIDED

Systemic reform places the responsibility for developing and implementing improvement plans at the school level. Responsibility to determine the best way to deliver educational services should be vested largely in schools and classrooms. Principals and teachers—along with parents—must have latitude to develop appropriate school organizational arrangements, instructional strategies, and uses of technologies.

In Chapters 14 and 15, respectively, we explored the possibility of injecting marketlike incentives into public school organizations through school-based decision making and through family choice of schooling. We observed that the school, rather than the district, is the place where students learn and that the major decisions about school operation should be made at that level. School-based decision making (SBDM) gives teaching professionals the authority to make decisions that require their special expertise. This approach to governance, as well as the development of charter schools in an increasing number of states, enables schools to adapt to unique local and individual circumstances. Given the lack of knowledge about the causal relationships between schooling inputs and outputs, SBDM enables organizations to use a variety of instruction delivery systems, all of which prepare students for the same standards-based assessments. Careful evaluation of the diversity of schools, including magnet schools and charter schools, should contribute to a better understanding of what educational practices work best under specific circumstances. Systematic evaluation would thereby contribute to improved operational efficiency. To ensure equity, SBDM must function within a state and federal framework that permits professional discretion and parental choice among schools within and across district boundaries. At the same time, this structure must allow prudent monitoring by higher levels of authority through performance-based accountability systems.

Increasing the authority of schools at a time when states are assuming greater responsibility for defining curriculum and setting achieve-

ment standards for pupils raises serious questions about the future viability of school districts as they are currently organized. Large city school districts will gradually take on characteristics of regional service units, similar to those of intermediate units serving rural and suburban areas in a number of states. But they will have the added responsibility of acting as a funding conduit for schools. This is already happening in Chicago, Cincinnati, Seattle, and Dade and Broward Counties in Florida.

In rural areas, except for very small districts with graduating classes of under one hundred students, pressures for the consolidation of districts are likely to subside. Rural school districts already embody many of the characteristics of school-based decision making. They consist of one school (or a very few schools) with a self-governing board of education. On the other hand, county or regional intermediate units can more efficiently assume responsibilities currently exercised by rural districts for providing services to schools, such as levying taxes and furnishing financial and personnel support. In considering the most effective governance model, some states may dissolve school districts. The current responsibilities of districts would then be divided between regional or county units and school-level authorities.

Recent studies of economies of scale in schools show that there is a certain beauty in small schools. Small schools provide for sustained contact among all members of the learning community and with the community at large. This serves as a safeguard against the alienation found in many large schools. Compared to large schools, small schools provide greater opportunity for student participation and greater educational and personal support. These influences appear to be especially beneficial for at-risk students. The primary advantage of large schools is their enriched curricular offerings. But advances in electronic and communication technologies are rapidly bringing such variety to small schools also. A challenge of the next decade will be to design arrangements that combine the advantages of big schools and those of small schools in one setting, while eliminating the disadvantages of both. This is taking place in Chicago, New York City, Philadelphia, and other major cities. Large, impersonal, bureaucratic schools are being divided into independent schools of choice with no more than four hundred students each. The reported beneficial effects on students are gratifying (Fliegel, 1993; Meier, 1995; Bensman, 2000).

As we have noted, technological advances can assist in correcting some of the shortcomings of present-day schools. Computers facilitate individualized instruction and provide a mechanism for continuously and patiently monitoring individual progress. Multimedia presentations via CD-ROM, the Internet, and other video technologies provide for instructional enrichment that cannot be matched by words alone—written or spoken. Communication technology makes the world's information resources available to any person in almost any place.

Integrating technology into the instructional process helps reduce the number of professionally trained personnel needed and encourages the more extensive use of lower-cost paraprofessionals. This in turn facilitates the upgrading of the teaching profession, permitting teachers to concentrate on activities in which professional discretion is essential. Differentiated staffing allows for more professional career options, and because fewer professional teachers will remain, their salaries could be made competitive with other professions.

Given all these factors, production decisions are best made at the school building level, with support services provided at district, intermediate, and state levels and through the private sector. Reforming the structure of schools by integrating technology into the teaching and learning processes brings about a redefinition of the role of teaching and its rewards in such ways as to make the profession more attractive to persons with exceptional skills. Available

technology can improve the efficiency of schooling by enabling students, teachers, and support personnel to use their time and talents more productively and by upgrading the competence of those attracted to the teaching profession.

These structural and instructional changes in the delivery system will make possible improvements in school outcomes and thus in the efficiency of schools. We noted previously the importance of improving the efficiency of low-performing schools as society raises its expectations and makes greater investments in education. These improvements in the delivery of educational services are critical as decisions are made about changing the way in which states allocate funds to districts and schools.

ALLOCATING RESOURCES

Two basic policy decisions must be made concerning the allocation of resources to education:

- Should there be governmental intervention?
- If so, what should be the nature and extent of that intervention as allocations are made to support schools?

In Chapters 1 and 2, we developed the case for governmental involvement in the financing of education. Such involvement ensures that societal interests in a literate citizenry are satisfied and promotes equality of educational opportunity within the population. The current practice of public ownership and operation of schools, however, is only one form of intervention. Other public policy options include aid to privately owned and operated schools and direct aid to parents in the form of education vouchers. Nevertheless, we believe that the most likely scenario for the immediate future is a continuation of the near public monopoly of the ownership and operation of elementary and secondary schools. Accommodation of efficiency and liberty concerns is more likely to be made through incremental adjustments to the current system via innovations such as school-based decision making, open enrollment among public schools, and charter schools, than through more radical reforms that would privatize ownership of schools.

Growing state involvement in school finance and in ensuring adequate resources in all districts makes the structuring of mechanisms for distributing state resources an even more important policy consideration than it has been in the past (see Chapters 7 and 8). Flat-grant and foundation programs of state aid to school districts—programs that permit a great deal of local leeway—are inequitable to students and taxpayers. These approaches were designed at a time when states sought to ensure a minimum level of education in all districts. However, they worked to the great disadvantage of property-poor districts that may have desired to spend beyond established aid levels. When the guaranteed base is low, districts may not have sufficient local revenue sources to meet the state's expectations for student learning.

Tax-base-equalizing schemes greatly improved the partnership of states and localities in financing education. In their ideal form, these approaches remove the inequitable effects of variations in the distribution of property wealth. But they do not remove the inequitable effects of variations among school districts in the priority given to education—and therefore in their willingness to tax themselves to provide an adequate level of educational services. Unless a high-minimum floor is created to ensure adequate resources, there may not be sufficient resources in all districts to meet high performance expectations.

Of all financing strategies, full state funding most clearly recognizes that providing for the basic educational needs of citizens is a responsibility of the state as required by state constitutions. This approach is equitable in that it treats all alike, but the cost to liberty is high. Full state funding does not necessarily eliminate the possibility of decentralized decisions about how schools are organized and operated, however. Further, this approach does not preclude the recognition that some children require more expensive sets of educational services than other children. The greatest difficulty with full state funding arises in defining the level of funding—that is, in determining adequacy. It assumes that state legislatures are fully competent to determine unilaterally an adequate standard of finance for education, a role currently played in most states by local school boards and state legislatures jointly. Equally distributed resources that are inadequate are of little value to anyone. They would certainly encourage all who are able to abandon the public schools. On the other hand, no state can afford uniform opulence. Substantial financial support of public schools generated by local communities has enabled most state legislatures to avoid facing fully the issue of funding adequacy.

Full state funding replaces many independent decisions of local districts about funding for schools with a single state-level decision. On the surface, this appears to be the height of equity and efficiency—if only we knew the technical relationships between schooling inputs and outcomes and if only state legislatures were not distracted by concerns other than education. Unfortunately, we do not fully understand those relationships, and state legislatures must compromise among multiple demands. School districts have a singular focus. But they also are drawn in many directions by a variety of special interests. Unwise decisions made by any but major city districts affect only a small portion of a state's population. The law of averages works to dilute the bad decisions. We can learn from both good and bad decisions. This is not to suggest that we condone the resulting inequities. Rather, we accept them, within limits, as political trade-offs among the goals of equity, liberty, and efficiency.

The pattern of finance operating in most states assumes a partnership between state and local authorities. States define the standards for student knowledge and skills, but local districts and schools determine how best to organize and deliver programs to meet these expectations. In addition to an adequate base of funding, local authorities define financial requirements on the basis of constituent demands for schooling, educational program needs, and the availability of resources from locally generated revenue. State aid to education represents a series of political compromises within the economic constraints inherent in a state's tax-collecting capacity. Legislators and governors forge compromises in response to pressures generated by advocates of the public schools, including school district officials, advocates of all other functions of state government, and those who would reduce public services and taxes.

Because in most states the level of state support does not cover total expenditures, the definition of an adequate level of financial support has actually been made by the school districts that have a tax base sufficient to pay for desired programs and facilities. A district does this through its regular planning and budgeting processes, which primarily involve school-related groups and individuals. In seeking funds at the state level, the advocates of high-quality educational services have greatly enhanced the effectiveness of their arguments in the past through their ability to draw on data generated from independent decisions of many school districts. To remove all local discretion in establishing expenditure levels would be to remove a very important experience test in determining the adequacy of state support levels. It would leave resource allocation decisions to be made largely on the basis of state politics and would reduce the impact of input from an educational perspective.

Permitting variation in expenditures also enhances the ability to accommodate local preferences. With no absolute pedagogical principles to guide educational decision makers, valuable empirical evidence is gained through encouraging a variety of educational programs and expenditure levels. From a political stand-

point, such a procedure has the potential to reduce social stress as long as local resource bases are equalized. This is because there are fewer interest groups that must be satisfied for any substate jurisdiction than for the state as a whole. A limited amount of local discretion in setting expenditure levels enables authorities to meet higher costs because of unique local conditions or aspirations without unduly complicating a state aid formula with technical corrections and special categorical aids (see Chapter 8).

Growing out of the foregoing discussion, we recommend the following as guides for structuring a state school finance program.

1. The state has the overall *constitutional responsibility* for establishing and maintaining a system of schools within which all of the children and youth of the state may be educated.

2. The state determines the *standards* for expected student and school performance and a commensurate level of *funding* necessary to build the capacity of school personnel to enable *all* children to meet those standards.

3. The state may establish a range of per-pupil expenditures that defines *minimum* (linked with performance expectations noted in guideline 2) and *maximum* district/school spending in light of state resources. However, it should not set an absolute level of expenditure for all jurisdictions or unnecessarily restrict the use of those resources. There are several aspects of this guideline:

   • Given societal interest in equality of educational opportunities and in having all children meet high academic standards, wide variation in educational expenditures based on local property wealth cannot be justified.

   • Economic, social, and environmental variations within most states preclude the establishment of a single expenditure level for the entire state. Local authorities are in the best position to fine-tune expenditure levels, but they need some leeway to do so and some financial assistance to attain their program goals.

- Because there is no absolute standard of an adequate educational program, limited local discretion provides state authorities with data critical to the establishment of a realistic range of expenditure levels.

4. Within established constraints, the *financial capacity* of each local authority should be the same throughout the state. For example, a given tax rate in any jurisdiction should produce as much revenue per pupil as, but no more than, the same tax rate levied against all the state's property. State revenue should guarantee a defined level of adequacy in each district by supplying the difference between the defined level of adequate spending associated with expected school performance and what can be raised locally with a specified level of effort. The state should recapture amounts raised above this level. (See the discussion of tax-based equalization in Chapter 7.)

5. State governments should gradually *increase the percentage* of educational costs that they provide to about 60 percent of all spending levels combined.

6. Any aid formula should *automatically adjust* to changes in costs of delivering education, pupils' educational needs, and local financial capacity.

7. Categorical aid for meeting *extraordinary* pupil needs should be separate from general state aid. The cost of meeting extraordinary pupil needs in relation to expected outcomes should be financed solely from state and federal funds.

The foregoing guidelines could be made operational with a state finance program that blends concepts from the foundation program and tax base equalization. This state–local part-nership satisfies goals of *equity*, *adequacy*, and *liberty*. Furthermore, the funding available in any district supplies the resources essential to help all students achieve high standards *efficiently*. The finance plan includes the following features for state allocations:

- A first-tier *foundation for adequacy* program that guarantees an adequate revenue base at a high-minimum level. The guaranteed levels of funding in all districts, charter schools, or intermediate units vary with the characteristics of students (e.g., educational needs) and communities (e.g., cost of delivering education) outlined in Chapter 8. In addition, this foundation varies directly with the size of the gap between desired and actual school performance as measured by valid and reliable indicators (see Chapter 13). These indicators include, but are not limited to, an expected level of knowledge and skill acquisition in relation to academic standards.

- *Full state funding* of this first tier. No local authority (for example, no charter school, school district, or intermediate unit) may spend below the respective foundation for adequacy. In order to fund this high-minimum foundation, a state-levied property tax (see Chapter 5) contributes revenue to the state's general fund.

- A second tier that consists of a *fully equalized discretionary range of expenditure* (not to exceed 20 percent of the first-tier foundation program). State and local funds support this variable level of spending according to one of the alternative methods for implementing a tax-base-equalizing concept. This second tier includes a recapture provision (see Chapter 7).

- Special financial assistance for meeting *extraordinary* educational needs. These categorical programs are fully financed by state and federal governments.

The objective of the foundation-for-adequacy program is to make available to every child in a state the educational services that are appropriate to his or her educational needs and that are necessary for him or her to meet high academic expectations. This commitment of state funding is meant to provide an adequate base, but local communities may choose to increase spending above this foundation level. The objective of the second tier of funding is to permit local choice of total spending to reach educational goals beyond those financed by the foundation for adequacy. State revenue equalizes the district property tax ability at chosen levels of effort. The objective of the special categorical aids is to provide adequate educational services for children with extraordinary needs without burdening the resource base provided via the foundation program.

In order to promote efficiency goals for the use of resources provided by the foundation-for-adequacy program, the finance plan provides for the following allocations from the state *directly* to schools or *through* school districts and intermediate units to schools:

- Allocations that reflect characteristics of students and schools as indicated above, including the gap between actual and desired performance
- Allocations for personnel that make salary increases contingent on the acquisition and application of knowledge and skills related to performance expectations
- Allocations that stimulate educators and parents to design whole-school reform of instructional delivery and that encourage parents to choose among alternatives
- Allocations that support preschools, extended day programs, and summer schools for students in low-performing schools
- Accountability for improved performance, including financial rewards and nonmonetary recognition for high performance and sanctions for continued low performance

The objectives of these allocations to schools is to help them become more effective in meeting performance expectations and more effi-
cient in maximizing school outcomes for the funds invested. Students' educational needs, including the nature of disabilities and predictors of educational failure, drive the allocations from the foundation for adequacy described previously. Annual allocations for principals and teachers depend solely on their acquisition and application of knowledge and skills that contribute to improvements in school performance, including (but not limited to) student achievement.

These features also recognize the importance of school-based decision making. Decisions about the appropriate design and delivery of instructional programs to meet students' educational needs are best made at the school level. A critical aspect of gaining the commitment of policy makers to fund a high-minimum foundation-for-adequacy program such as that outlined here is the commitment of educators to improve the effectiveness and efficiency of education delivery systems. There would be a high degree of latitude for principals and teachers to work with parents to improve school performance. However, school personnel would be accountable for results in terms of improvements in school performance. The state, intermediate unit, or district to which the school is accountable should create rewards (monetary and nonmonetary recognition) for improvements in school performance. There should also be sanctions, including changes in leadership and close monitoring of school improvement plans in low-performing schools.

This school finance model casts intermediate units and school districts in new roles. They become conduits of funds rather than direct procurers of human and material resources. In keeping with these new roles, school districts will have to develop formulas for the equitable distribution of adequate resources to schools. They will have to develop data-driven accountability systems appropriate for the new governance and standards-based decision making environment. They will have to develop technical assistance, rewards, and sanctions to encourage and enable all schools to meet performance expectations.

We believe that the foundation-for-adequacy plan addresses a key component of systemic reform. Along with centralized standards and accountability for pupil and school performance, this allocation method directs adequate resources to schools where they are most needed to achieve high standards with equity and efficiency.

SUMMARY

The greatest challenge facing policy makers today in the field of public school finance is designing systems for financing schools that encourage improvement in their efficiency. The second-most-important challenge is improving the equity and adequacy of the distribution of resources to schools so that all children may have access to good facilities, competent instruction, and state-of-the-art learning materials. These challenges must be addressed systemically.

The primary barriers to the implementation of reforms directed toward making the educational system more efficient appear to be the bureaucratic nature of its current organization and the balkanization of school districts. Federal categorical aid and state categorical aid, along with court interventions, state regulation, and negotiated labor contracts, especially in large cities, have contributed significantly to this condition. To counter its bureaucratic nature, governance and decision making about the organization and operation of schools and the allocation of resources within schools need to devolve to persons at the school level. To provide incentives for school personnel to be more sensitive to the demands of family clients and more concerned about the quality of service provided, the ironclad assurance of school funding needs to be removed and funding be linked, instead, to the quality of school performance. One way of accomplishing this is by permitting parents to select the schools their children are to attend, ignoring traditional school and district boundaries, and by linking the flow of resources to the flow of children. The school finance strategies that facilitate such arrangements include school-based decision making, open enrollment among public schools, charter schools, and educational vouchers. The latter are appropriate only if private schools are brought within the purview of the publicly supported system.

To safeguard legitimate societal interests, especially concern for equal educational opportunities, and to overcome inequities created by small and diverse school districts, school-based decision making and family choice among public schools must function within a framework of state and federal finance, coordination, and accountability. Societal controls may well include a required basic curriculum linked with standards, protection of the rights of minorities and children with disabilities to attend their schools of choice, monitoring performance in relation to the standards through formal systems of evaluation, and a system of information and counseling available to parents to assist them in enrolling their children in the most appropriate schools. The percentage of school funding derived from state resources must continue to increase, and it is entirely conceivable that more states will formally take over the taxation of property for school purposes.

Equity and adequacy goals demand that states provide financial support that is commensurate with the cost of an adequate educational program to enable students to acquire appropriately specified levels of knowledge and skills. In addition, there must be local discretion in determining total spending, up to a ceiling that is some reasonable proportion above the defined foundation level of adequacy. These two tiers of funding should be fully equalized by state revenue, which may include a statewide property tax. The current links between per-pupil expenditure levels, the wealth of school districts, and the priority assigned to education by constituents of school districts must be broken. Along with improving the equity and adequacy of funds, models for financing schools must bring greater efficiency by encouraging alternative means of delivering instruction, personnel compensation that considers knowledge and skills, and performance-based rewards and sanctions. With the centralization of some decisions at the state and federal levels, and with the decentralization of many decisions to school personnel and to parents, the future viability of school districts as currently organized is in question.

The new millennium will see dramatic changes in the financing of elementary and secondary schools as part of a series of systemic reforms that will also include governance, standards, curriculum, and assessments. The problems are sufficient to challenge the best and the brightest of policy analysts, policy makers, and educators and the improvements to be achieved are worthy of their expertise and diligence.

ACTIVITIES

1. Develop your own recommendations for school finance policies in your state during the next decade. Present your rationale for those recommendations in terms of equality, liberty, and efficiency goals. Give your recommendations a reality check by discussing them with a local- or state-level policy maker. Revise your recommendations as appropriate.
2. Identify those issues presented in this chapter on which you agree with the authors and those issues on which you disagree. Reflect on the areas of disagreement and possible reasons for them.
3. Develop a model for determining the cost to a state of implementing the foundation-for-adequacy program as a first tier of funding. How might a state project the additional revenue demands of a formula adjustment that considers the gap between desired and actual performance in all schools or districts?

REFERENCES

Bensman, D. (2000). *Central Park East and its graduates: "Learning by heart."* New York: Teachers College Press.

Benson, C. S. (1978). *The economics of public education* (3rd ed.). Boston, MA: Houghton Mifflin.

Fliegel, S. (1993). *Miracle in East Harlem: The fight for choice in public education.* New York: Random House.

Fuhrman, S. H. (2001). Conclusion. In S. H. Fuhrman (Ed.). *From the capital to the classroom: Standards-based reform in the states* (pp. 263–278). Chicago, IL: National Society for the Study of Education.

Goertz, M. E., Floden, R. E., & O'Day, J. (1995). *Studies of education reform: Systemic reform,* Vol. 1, *Findings and conclusions.* Rutgers: The State University of New Jersey, Consortium for Policy Research in Education.

Guthrie, J. W., & Rothstein, R. (2001). A new millennium and a likely new era of education finance. In S. Chaikind & W. J. Fowler, Jr. (Eds.), *Education finance in the new millennium* (pp. 99–119). Larchmont, NY: Eye on Education.

Meier, D. (1995). *The power of their ideas: Lessons from a small school in Harlem.* Boston: Beacon Press.

National Commission on Excellence in Education. (1983). *A nation at risk: The imperative for educational reform.* Washington, DC: U.S. Government Printing Office.

Smith, M. S., & O'Day, J. (1991). Systemic school reform. In S. H. Fuhrman & B. Malen (Eds.), *The politics of curriculum and testing* (pp. 233–267). Bristol, PA: Falmer.

Smith, T. M., & Phelps, R. P. (1995). Education finance indicators: What can we learn from comparing states and nations? In W. J. Fowler, Jr. (Ed.), *Developments in school finance* (pp. 99–107). Washington: National Center for Educational Statistics.

Verstegen, D. (1992). International comparisons of education spending: A review and analysis of reports. *Journal of Education Finance, 17,* 257–276.

NAME INDEX

SUBJECT INDEX